READINGS in the
HISTORY of
AMERICAN
MARKETING
Settlement to Civil War

COMPILED BY

STANLEY J. SHAPIRO
McGill University

AND

ALTON F. DOODY
The Ohio State University

PREPARED UNDER THE SPONSORSHIP OF THE
AMERICAN MARKETING ASSOCIATION

1968
RICHARD D. IRWIN, INC.
Homewood, Illinois

First Printing, January, 1968

PRINTED IN THE UNITED STATES OF AMERICA
Library of Congress Catalog Card No. 66-29977

ACKNOWLEDGMENTS

The editors wish to express their gratitude for the many and varied types of assistance they received. Those who edit books of readings are, first and foremost, beholden to the publishers and authors who allowed material to be reproduced. Although a formal permission credit appears at the beginning of each selection, we again wish to thank those who waived company policy to facilitate inclusion or accompanied their letter of permission with a personal expression of interest and encouragement.

Those who performed the necessary secretarial and typing chores also deserve recognition. These chores were ably performed by Miss Eva Reiff, Mrs. Aileen Cummings, and the late Dolores Moss of the Wharton School; Miss Zenia Kanasawiecz of Canadian Advertising Agency Limited, and Miss Norma Cottom of the Marketing Research Centre Limited.

Many individuals affiliated with the American Marketing Association contributed to the undertaking. Publication of the book was made possible when it received the endorsement of the Publications Policy and Review Board of the A.M.A. The assistance of the board's chairmen during the time of preparation, Dr. Edwin H. Lewis of the University of Minnesota and Dr. Taylor Meloan of the University of Southern California, was especially helpful.

In addition to his administrative efforts, Dr. Lewis reviewed the manuscript, along with Dr. Fred M. Jones of the University of Illinois, Dr. Perry Bliss of the State University of New York at Buffalo, and Dr. Stewart Rewoldt of the University of Michigan. Suggestions made by these four reviewers were gratefully received and carefully considered. Finally, Mr. Earl G. Johnson, executive director of the American Marketing Association and Mrs. Marguerite Kent, his executive assistant, greatly facilitated this project as they do so many other A.M.A. undertakings.

The intellectual interests that resulted in preparation of the volume were nurtured at the Wharton School and The Ohio State University. The editors will always be grateful for the repeated emphasis these institutions place on the fact that a managerial orientation is but one of a number of relevant approaches to the study of marketing. We attribute our interest in marketing history to the intellectual impact of Alderson, Breyer, and Cox at the University of Pennsylvania and to Beckman, Bartels, and Davidson at The Ohio State University. Other colleagues at

Acknowledgments

both these universities also provided information and encouragement. Worthy of special mention is Dr. David D. Monieson, now of Queens University, Kingston, Ontario.

Finally, for a myriad of reasons that could not be adequately cataloged, we dedicate this volume to our wives, Roberta and Sue.

STANLEY J. SHAPIRO
ALTON F. DOODY

January, 1968

TABLE OF CONTENTS

PART II. MARKETING IN AMERICA, 1790–1860

BIBLIOGRAPHY

INTRODUCTION

SOME 30 YEARS AGO, Ralph M. Hower discussed then existing areas of ignorance as to the history of American marketing and the contributions a definitive study of this topic could make. "Despite the importance of the distribution of commodities in modern society, there is a surprising lack of factual data regarding the major historical developments in the field. . . . An adequate history of marketing in America would not only be of general interest but would also be of direct value in solving some of the distribution problems which confront business today.[1]

Hower agreed that information was lacking on both the marketing activities of early firms and the conditions under which various types of marketing agencies developed. Deserving special emphasis, he believed, was the task of explaining the constant rise and fall in middlemen and the perpetual shift between "specialization and the recombination" of marketing functions.[2]

The history of American marketing for which Hower proceeded to solicit business records, letter books, and other primary material was never written. Subsequent to his remarks, however, a number of books and articles on various aspects of marketing history appeared. Although some light was shed on the subject, the material was neither exhaustive nor definitive. Speaking a quarter of a century after Hower, Reavis Cox cited the history of American marketing as one of the "dark continents" of the discipline.

We know very little about the most elemental kinds of events in marketing, even recent events. When someone asks when or where this or that aspect of marketing appeared, how it developed, how it was changed over time, we ordinarily have to plead ignorance, substantial if not complete. Whenever we know, as in a few cases, that something happened at a particular time and place, we have almost no ability to tell why it happened at that particular place, in that particular form.[3]

The comments of Hower and Cox notwithstanding, the present volume of readings on marketing history has been prepared. The editors are convinced that a discipline growing ever more concerned with the

---

[1] Ralph M. Hower, "Wanted: Material on the History of Marketing," *Bulletin of the Business Historical Society*, Vol. IX (October, 1935), p. 79.

[2] *Ibid.*, pp. 79–80.

[3] Reavis Cox, "The Dark Continents of Marketing," in Richard M. Hill (ed.), *Marketing Concepts in Changing Times* (Chicago: American Marketing Association, 1960), p. 237.

development of a theory and/or science of marketing is ready to pay some heed to its own history. Furthermore, we believe the already existing literature deserves more attention than it has as yet received. Marketing theory became an important area of research after the appearance of a seminal article by Reavis Cox and Wroe Alderson less than 20 years ago.[4] We are hopeful that a similar interest in marketing history will be awakened by our editorial efforts.

The quality and usefulness of any book of readings depends primarily on the merits of the material reprinted. Nevertheless, the editors of such volumes must do more than merely provide introductory headnotes. They should also set forth the rationale of the publication and indicate the basis on which choices were made from the available literature. This is especially true when their objective is to awaken interest in a neglected area of intellectual inquiry. Consequently, the following issues are explored in the remainder of this Introduction: the reasons why marketing scholars have failed to investigate the history of marketing, the potential usefulness of marketing history and the possible insights obscured by its neglect, the parallels that can be drawn between contemporary marketing and marketing before 1860, and the criteria used in selecting the material included in the volume.[5]

WHY THE DARK CONTINENT REMAINS UNEXPLORED

Why have the study and even the existing literature of marketing history been neglected? Many reasons could be advanced, with apparent lack of interest on the part of marketing scholars one obvious explanation. Cox has stated the problem simply enough: "No one has been willing to make a scholarly career of going into dusty records and patiently piecing together scattered bits of information so that he can tell us how and when and through whose efforts this fantastically complicated set of activities or institutions we call marketing came into existence."[6]

But what, in turn, accounts for the lack of interest Cox cites? Why has this area of intellectual endeavor been neglected while others have been pursued? Part of the explanation can be found in the academic background and training of marketing scholars. With but few exceptions, nothing in their education acquaints aspiring teachers of marketing with the existence, the nature, or the uses of historical material. Once the doctoral candidate obtains his degree, the need to keep abreast of con-

---

[4] Reavis Cox and Wroe Alderson, "Towards a Theory of Marketing," *Journal of Marketing,* Vol. XIII (October, 1948), pp. 137–52.

[5] For an expanded treatment of similar material but in a different context, see Alton F. Doody, "Historical Emphasis: Its Contribution to Marketing Education," and Stanley J. Shapiro, "Marketing in America: Settlement to Civil War," in L. George Smith (ed.), *Reflections on Progress in Marketing* (Chicago: American Marketing Association, 1965), pp. 559–57.

[6] Cox, *op. cit.,* p. 237.

temporary developments in marketing usually suppresses any embryonic interest in marketing history. Examining directly all the literature relevant to the teaching of marketing and one's major research interests is a staggering task. Little time remains for pursuing a tangential interest requiring exploration of a very different kind of source and reference material.

Has neglect by his peers kept marketing history an area of intellectual "differential advantage" which a young scholar can profitably develop? Unfortunately, this does not appear to be the case. Recognition and financial rewards from the business community require expertise in some aspect of contemporary marketing practice. Since few editors of business journals encourage historical manuscripts, winning the approbation of one's academic peers and superiors by publishing in prestige periodicals is also difficult. The young scholar would thus labor under a variety of pressures encouraging the abandonment of historical pursuits for more fashionable endeavors.

A final factor contributing to the neglect of marketing history is a mistaken belief as to its lack of relevance in a dynamic marketplace. Admittedly, one reference to marketing history is almost invariably made. Students are told that once upon a time, when the United States was industrializing and demand exceeded supply, production-oriented companies existed. These were dinosaur-type creatures appropriate to their era but now required either to adopt the marketing concept or to suffer the dinosaur's fate. This is an apt analogy, but those who draw it have not exhausted the intellectual applications of marketing history.

THE USES OF MARKETING HISTORY

What are the contributions that marketing history and historical analysis can make? The editors consider the subject one of great intellectual promise, with many applications that will emerge only after considerable exploration. One need not fear, however, that the results obtained will not justify the effort expended. It is already clear that reference to historical materials can make the study of marketing a more meaningful and exciting experience. A perceptive examination of the historical record also contributes to the difficult intellectual task of developing a theory of marketing. Finally, historical analysis can provide insight into the factors underlying structural change in the marketing system. Let us consider each of these applications in turn.

THE PRECEPT PERSONIFIED

Much of what is taught about marketing is presented in an unnecessarily abstract fashion. A case in point is the concept of consumer sovereignty and its relationship to product quality and value. Most marketing texts and teachers emphasize that quality and value are relative, customer-determined terms. But many students fail to grasp the true significance of this statement and other marketing precepts.

Reference to the historical literature could be of great assistance to teachers encountering this problem. For example, the meaning and implications of quality being a customer-determined concept are clearly demonstrated by the discussion in *Catalogues and Counters* of Sears' merchandise at the turn of the century:

> Sears offered men's suits at $4.98, when the general market price was often twice that figure. True, they were made of shoddy wool (and frequently contained a high percentage of cotton); they were ill-fitting; and they did not wear long in every case. But where else could the farmer buy a Sunday suit for $4.98? When one talks of the quality of Sears Roebuck's early merchandise—and most of the talk in that period rated Sears' quality pretty low—one must never forget the relationship between quality and price. Sears' bedroom suite, three pieces for $8.50 at one point was of inexpensive, hard birch. Birch has utility; beauty is to be found in oak and mahogany and other woods, but the Sears customers could not afford—and to a great extent probably did not want anything better.
>
> Sears guaranteed his $11.96 cookstove to cook. It cooked. And it cooked for years and years. Sears' plows would plow, and Sears' washing machines would wash. That was what farm families wanted; and that was that they got from Sears Roebuck.[7]

Also overlooked by academicians who slight marketing history is the insight this subject provides into the nature of entrepreneurial effort. Many excellent "company histories" disclose how all manner of individuals operated their businesses. Reference to this literature allows the student to observe in context the personalities, policies, and conditions under which enterprises were able to grow and prosper.[8]

HISTORICAL ANALYSIS AND MARKETING THEORY

Historical material also has its place in the recent trend toward considering marketing as a science. Whether or not marketing is or ever will be a science depends in large part on how one defines "science." Semantics aside, a major effort is underway to make marketing more scientific or at least to utilize the logic of science. This implies the development of marketing theory, an end toward which historical analysis contributes by facilitating the formulation and testing of hypotheses.

---

[7] Boris Emmet and John E. Jeuck, *Catalogues and Counters* (Chicago: University of Chicago Press, 1950), p. 113.

[8] See particularly Bert C. McEmmon, "Alternate Explanations of Institutional Change and Channel Evolution," in Stephen A. Greyser (ed.), *Toward Scientific Marketing* (Chicago: American Marketing Association, 1963), pp. 477–90.

This contribution can be demonstrated by reference to a study of the nature of institutional change in retailing. In his history of Macy's, Ralph M. Hower reports on how every aspect of that firm's operation—including such things as merchandise assortments, promotional strategies, plant and equipment, pricing policies, and services offered to customers —evolved over time.[9] Macy's started out as a "discount type" of operation and ended up a full-fledged department store. One immediately realizes the obvious relevance of Professor McNair's "Wheel of Retailing." Macy's did trade up, add to its merchandise assortment, provide more customer services, and improve the character of its physical plant. The net effect was a price and expense structure significantly higher than that with which it started.

Hower's history of Macy's, however, did more than merely provide some basis for verifying McNair's hypothesis. His analysis affords the opportunity to refine McNair's work and, hopefully, to go beyond it. The "Wheel of Retailing," for example, does not explore *why* firms trade up. Is this fact explained by J. M. Clark's theory of "differential advantage"? If so, why haven't some firms traded down?

Hower's work helps to clarify these issues, for his analysis shows both how and why Macy's changed. His detailed account also demonstrates that there was special significance in the *manner* in which these changes took place. It was found, for example, that the changes were very gradual and that each step was but a slight modification of the existing operation.

This historical record of Macy's development has provided the basis for the following theoretical constructs.[10] During the period of institutional development in retailing (as in the case of the department store, the supermarket, etc.), individual firms exhibit a definite pattern of change. This pattern of change can be described as a gradual or incremental modification of existing operations over time. The changes in operations made by individual firms over time have a tendency to be incremental because:

1. There is a smaller amount of risk inherent in this type of change due to the greater predictability of its effects, the lesser likelihood of loss of customers, or of customer discontent, resulting from change of image, and the ease of reverting back to the previous policy if a change proves to be in error.

2. The pattern or history of competitive actions utilized by the firm conditions the character of its new moves. (A corollary to this is that since new firms have no history, they would be more likely to introduce non-incremental innovations than would maturing firms.)

---

[9] Ralph M. Hower, *History of Macy's of New York, 1858–1919* (Cambridge: Harvard University Press, 1946).

[10] For a more detailed treatment of incrementalism, see Alton F. Doody, "Historical Patterns in Marketing Innovation," in William S. Decker (ed.), *Emerging Concepts in Marketing* (Chicago: American Marketing Association, 1963), pp. 245–53.

EXPLORING THE CAUSES OF STRUCTURAL CHANGE

Since progress in the social sciences is slow and difficult, developing a theory of marketing will be a demanding and intellectually painful task. For some time to come, we shall lack an adequate conceptual framework for explaining certain phenomena. In many of the cases where this is true, an understanding of marketing history can, in and of itself, yield useful insights into the marketing process.

Although no theory or hypothesis has been advanced to explain the emergence of a Macy's, a Sears Roebuck, or a King Cullen, available historical material explains in detail the environmental conditions surrounding their rapid development. Hower, for example, shows why Macy's could locate its original 14th Street store outside the "high rent district," north of the then heavily populated areas of New York. Because of the network of trolley lines, this location was no longer a critical liability. Boris Emmet and John E. Jeuck analyze the conditions present in rural America, circa 1900, which contributed to the enthusiastic reception of Sears Roebuck merchandise at that time. These included the isolation of the farmer, the many inadequacies of country general stores, and—of no minor importance—the emergence of railway express and rural free delivery.

One of the most detailed treatments of the factors contributing to structural change is presented by M. M. Zimmerman in his study of the supermarket.[11] The depression is cited for making economic purchasing a necessity in many households. The automobile, which had become commonplace during the 1920's, was also important. The family shopper could now get to the new stores regardless of location and could transport the groceries home as well. Changing shopping patterns were still another factor, since the trend toward a single weekly shopping trip and a high average sale boosted volume. Once-a-week shopping, in turn, was practical only because the refrigerator had become a common household possession. The widespread acceptance of self-service also contributed to the supermarket's success. But self-service was feasible only because extensive radio and magazine advertising during the 1920's had preconditioned consumers to purchase national brands without any prompting by a sales clerk. To isolate and attempt to measure the impact of all the factors mentioned above on the "supermarket revolution" is probably an impossible task. Nevertheless, an appreciation of their existence and interdependence is necessary if we are to understand the development of the supermarket and the dynamics of change in the marketing system.

---

[11] M. M. Zimmerman, *The Supermarket* (New York: Mass Distribution Publications, Inc., 1955).

MARKETING HISTORY FOR ITS OWN SAKE

The preceding discussion of the uses of marketing history must not obscure the fact that knowledge of this subject is also acceptable as an end in itself. Reading in the area for its own sake can yield interesting and currently relevant intellectual dividends. Awareness of then prevailing practices must come first, however, and meaningful synthesis later. The nature of the intellectual dividends received will depend in large part on the interest, training, and experience one brings to the field of marketing history. These dividends are likely to accrue, however, primarily to those concerned with marketing's role in the economy as well as its performance as a managerial function.

Let us discuss at some length one of these intellectual bonuses—the relationship of continuity and change in the marketing environment. We began our review of the literature on marketing in the United States before 1860 without any preconceived position as to the existence of historical patterns and similarities. We completed our task with the realization that despite centuries of revolutionary change, major influences on our contemporary marketing system were equally important factors in the period under study. These conclusions are based on the evidence presented below.

POLITICS AND PRESSURE GROUPS

"The politics of distribution" may be a recently coined phrase, but it describes a phenomenon characteristic of the American marketing scene for 300 years.[12] Appeals for governmental assistance were frequently made before 1860 by marketing agencies and disadvantaged channels of distribution. As early as the 17th century, there were attempts to establish interprovincial trade barriers that would protect local merchants.[13]

The system introduced after the War of 1812 of auctioning English goods directly to American retailers also produced pleas for protective legislation. So intense did feelings become in New York, the location of most of these auctions, that an antiauction political party contested local elections. Federal and state governments received testimonials, petitions, and appeals from advocates as well as opponents of the system. As is now customary, both sides argued that the growth and prosperity of the

---

[12] Joseph C. Palamountain, Jr., *The Politics of Distribution* (Cambridge: Harvard University Press, 1955).

[13] Carl A. Bridenbaugh, *Cities in the Wilderness* (New York: Ronald Press Co., 1938), p. 33.

nation depended on their position being adopted and that of their opponents being rejected.[14]

Finally, antipeddler legislation of various types and differing degrees of effectiveness was passed by a number of states and counties during the first half of the 19th century. The shrewd and cunning Yankee peddler is a familiar figure in American folklore. Considerable truth must underlie the innumerable anecdotes as to his bargaining ability and the frequency with which he duped his ill-educated and poorly informed customers.[15] But a concern with the consumer interest does not appear to have been the cause of antipeddler legislation. Rather, such laws reflected a mercantilist hostility to nontaxpaying outsiders taking a county's money elsewhere and the efforts of "legitimate" sedentary retailers to eliminate their itinerant rivals.[16]

URBAN AND REGIONAL TRADE RIVALRY

A second central theme of pre–Civil War American marketing was the commercial rivalry existing between cities and regions. Citizens of Chicago and St. Louis soon realized that the two cities were competing for the wholesale trade of the Middle West.[17] On the eastern seaboard, Boston, New York, Philadelphia, and Baltimore competed vigorously after 1800 for the position as America's major port of entry for European goods. Turnpikes, canals, and railroads were financed by local governments and businessmen on the ground that the future growth and prosperity of the community depended on their completion. Otherwise, local promoters warned, trade belonging by history and by right to their fair city would be diverted to competing ports.[18]

On the regional level, southern and western wholesalers attempted to discourage local retailers from purchasing supplies in the East. Despite

---

[14] Roy B. Westerfield, "Early History of American Auctions: A Chapter in Commercial History," *Transactions of the Connecticut Academy of Arts and Sciences,* Vol. XXIII (May, 1920), pp. 159–210; and Fred M. Jones, *Middlemen in the Domestic Trade of the United States, 1800–1860* (Urbana: University of Illinois Press, 1937), pp. 62–63.

[15] Gerald Carson, *The Old Country Store* (New York: Oxford University Press, 1954), pp. 37–63.

[16] Jones, *op. cit.,* pp. 62–63.

[17] George W. Stephens, "Some Aspects of Intersectional Rivalry for Commerce of the Upper Mississippi Valley," *Washington University Studies* (Humanistic Series, Vol. X, No. 2 [April, 1923]), pp. 277–300; and Wyatt W. Belcher, *The Economic Rivalry between St. Louis and Chicago, 1850–1880* (New York: Columbia University Press, 1947).

[18] Robert G. Albion, *The Rise of New York Port* (New York: Charles Scribner's Sons, 1939), pp. 373–86; Robert G. Albion, "New York Port and Its Disappointed Rivals, 1815–1860," *Journal of Economic and Business History,* Vol. IV (August, 1931), pp. 601–29; and James W. Livingood, *The Philadelphia–Baltimore Trade Rivalry, 1780–1860* (Harrisburg: Pennsylvania Historical and Museum Commission, 1947).

these efforts, economics rather than emotional appeals to local patriotism prevailed. Eastern wholesalers retained the bulk of this trade because they offered broader assortments and could provide liberal credit. Ease of financing was an especially important consideration to country store-keepers, who were compelled to finance their customers from one harvesttime to another. Only when nearby wholesalers provided comparable assortments and services did southern and western retailers purchase extensively from local sources.[19]

Regional rivalry was also aroused by the indirect shipment of cotton from southern ports through New York to Europe. If cotton were shipped directly to England and the Continent, militant Southerners argued, the South would no longer be required to pay millions in tribute to New York cotton merchants. The same ships on their return trips could deliver manufactured goods directly to southern ports. Consequently, the assortment and competitive position of southern wholesalers would be strengthened, and more retailers would purchase from them.[20]

TRANSPORTATION AND MARKET OUTREACH

Successive technological advances in transportation affected patterns of interregional trade, freight rates, and wholesale market areas. Between 1815 and 1860, the turnpike system speeded land transportation, while substitution of the steamboat for the flatboat made it feasible to sail up as well as down the Mississippi. A network of canals markedly reduced the costs in money and time of transporting bulk commodities. The patterns of rail transportation developing at the end of the period had the most profound effects of all. Continual reductions in freight rates and the time goods spent in transit extended the number of markets which could be supplied by the plants or farms of any given area.[21]

Successive changes over time in the dominant mode of transportation also had an important political impact. The invention of the steamboat made two-way shipment of freight on the Mississippi River practical and strengthened marketing ties between the South and the West. In subsequent years, however, previously prevailing trade patterns were revolutionized by the construction first of the Erie Canal, and then of

---

[19] Lewis E. Atherton, *The Southern Country Store, 1800–1860* (Baton Rouge: Louisiana State University Press, 1949), pp. 132–44; and Lewis E. Atherton, "The Pioneer Merchant in Mid-America," The *University of Missouri Studies*, Vol. XIV (April, 1939), pp. 47–82.

[20] Herbert Wender, *Southern Commercial Conventions, 1837–1859* (Johns Hopkins University Studies in Historical and Political Science, Series XLVII, No. 4 [Baltimore: Johns Hopkins Press, 1930]); and Robert R. Russel, *Economic Aspects of Southern Sectionalism, 1840–1861* (University of Illinois Studies in the Social Sciences, Vol. XI, Nos. 1 and 2 [Urbana, 1924]).

[21] George Rogers Taylor, *The Transportation Revolution, 1815–1860* (New York: Holt, Rinehart & Winston, Inc., 1951), pp. 132–40, 153–75.

railroads running from eastern centers of population to Chicago. By the time of the Civil War, the economic community of interest between East and West that had developed because of the canal and rail networks was a factor contributing to western support of the Union cause.[22]

Contemporary counterparts of the developments described above can be cited easily enough. Cities now compete for major government installations and organize commissions to solicit new industry. Any proposed change in existing freight rates causes potentially disadvantaged locations to protest violently. The St. Lawrence Seaway project was opposed by East Coast legislators fearful of its impact on the foreign trade of their districts. Indeed, the Seaway has influenced distribution patterns in a manner similar to but not so far-reaching in importance as the streamboat, the Erie Canal, and the railroad. Technological advances such as refrigerated cars and airfreight have revolutionized the physical flow of merchandise and altered the importance of wholesale trading areas. Finally, attempts by marketing agencies to obtain legislative protection seem likely always to be with us. The proposed legislation—whether it be an antiauction law or the Quality Stabilization Act —is invariably advanced as "in the public interest." All that changes is the agency against which protection is sought. Over the last century, chain stores, supermarkets, and discount houses have replaced peddlers and the auction system as the "illegitimate forms of retailing threatening to undermine the very sources of our nation's greatness."

EDITORIAL GUIDELINES EMPLOYED

Hower and Cox were unquestionably correct in arguing that much remains to be learned about the early history of marketing in the United States. Nevertheless, we have provided illustrations in the preceding sections of how what is already known can be of assistance to the teacher, the theorist, and the innovating entrepreneur. The presently existing literature on the history of American marketing deserves more attention than it has as yet received. Let us next consider the extent of that literature and the criteria employed to choose the material included in this collection of readings.

Over 150 books and articles providing useful insights into American marketing before 1860 are noted in the Bibliography accompanying this publication. The excerpts that appear have been selected from 35 different sources. Of course, the existing literature differs in comprehensiveness and quality. Some topics are better covered than others, and most of the emphasis is on description rather than on analysis. But

---

[22] Louis B. Schmidt, "Internal Commerce and the Development of the National Economy before 1860," *Journal of Political Economy*, Vol. XLVII (December, 1939), pp. 798–822.

studies on marketing before the Civil War are neither limited in number nor unworthy of examination.

The editors must admit to being surprised by the quantity of material their search of existing sources unearthed. Original plans called for a single volume of readings on the history of marketing in the United States before World War II. We also believed that the available literature might have to be supplemented by original essays. Investigation revealed, however, that two volumes would be required merely to derive maximum benefit from already existing material. That a wealth of information on marketing before 1860 is available cannot be emphasized strongly enough. Preparation of a two-volume study made it possible almost to triple the previously proposed coverage of marketing prior to the Civil War. Nevertheless, we were still required to exercise great selectivity, to omit significant articles due to space limitations, and to abridge much material more severely than would otherwise be desirable.

How were the readings which appear in this volume chosen? Given a wide range of possibilities, no two editorial teams would select the same items for a readings book on any subject. Variations in choice would reflect basic differences in judgment as to the publication's objectives, the importance of topics, and the relative merit of available materials. This being the case, some discussion of the criteria the editors used in making their selections seems in order. To the extent that they can be made explicit, the guidelines employed are set forth below.

First and foremost, we attempted to fashion from available sources a chronologically ordered, fairly continuous, and reasonably complete history of American marketing before 1860. The objective was a broad treatment of operating practices and regional marketing systems rather than detailed information on specific areas and enterprises. Phrased another way, our concern was with patterns rather than particulars and with the representative rather than the unique. Also, emphasis was placed on marketing within and between provinces or states rather than on foreign commerce. This was done to correct an existing imbalance in previously accessible material. Far more has been written about trade between each of the American colonies and distant parts of the British Empire than on commerce within or between these colonies. Similarly, the readily available literature on foreign trade and tariff controversies between 1790 and 1860 far exceeds that on domestic marketing during the same period.

The material included in this volume was deliberately drawn from secondary sources. In an initial effort to focus attention on marketing history, it seemed best to develop a list of publications and to select readings from that list. Many of the authors whose work appears relied heavily on older sources which could alternately have been included in this publication. The student of history might have been better served had the source materials and not the contemporary treatment been selected. But those most likely to benefit from such material are well aware of its existence and its content. Our objective was to awaken the interest of students of marketing in history and historical analysis. More recent manuscripts and even popularized treatments seemed best suited for this purpose. In keeping with our objective, most footnotes appearing with the material reprinted have been omitted. Deletions in these texts were made so frequently that use of the traditional periods to indicate ellipses became impractical.

A book conceived and executed along the above lines is but a first step toward gaining for marketing history the recognition and importance it deserves. What must follow if historical materials are to be more closely integrated with scholarly research and the teaching of marketing? We believe further progress can be attained in two ways. Some students of marketing may decide that history is a fertile and interesting area in which to specialize once the academic disadvantages now inherent in such a course of action disappear. These individuals will have to familiarize themselves with the scientific method in historical research and, depending on the area under investigation, also acquire some expertise in other disciplines. Professor J. D. Glover, for example, contends that considerable progress can be made through the integration of historical materials and the behavioral sciences.[23]

Even for those choosing to specialize in the subject, however, a knowledge of history and a grounding in historiography are not being proposed as a replacement for a thorough understanding of marketing and business phenomena. As the preceding discussion of incrementalism reveals, historical analysis is advocated as a method of obtaining a better and more complete understanding of marketing practices and the marketing system. Those who would teach marketing history and contribute to its intellectual development must approach these tasks as students of marketing and not as economic or business historians.

Most marketing scholars, however, will not choose to specialize in the history of the discipline. This larger group, in which the authors classify themselves, can proceed along the lines previously indicated to utilize historical materials as a teaching and research aid. This readings book and its companion volume are designed primarily to assist such an endeavor by presenting the relevant literature in convenient form. At the halfway mark in their undertaking, the editors are even more convinced than they were at its inception that historical material can improve our understanding of marketing systems and marketing behavior.

---

[23] J. D. Glover, *Business History Review*, Vol. XXXVI (Spring, 1962), p. 70.

PART I

Marketing in Colonial America, 1607-1790

A. THE ROLE OF MARKETING IN ECONOMIC DEVELOPMENT

1. MARKETING IN COLONIAL VILLAGES, 1625-90*

The emergence of Boston, Newport, Philadelphia, New York, and Charleston as dominant colonial settlements was due in large part to their success in becoming the marketing centers of the New World. The importance of orderly markets in facilitating the exchange of goods was recognized from the beginning. Particular days of the week were set aside as "market days," and semi-annual "fairs" were planned with great care. Designated marketplaces were established, with village squares used for this purpose, and special buildings were erected for trading activities. The success of these five villages in creating a favorable environment for exchange gave them substantial economic power over surrounding communities, enabled them to regulate wholesale and retail trade, and facilitated their political development.

PURSUIT OF TRADE and commerce was the all-embracing activity of the early colonial villages—the very basis for their existence. These little seaports served as the focal points at which immigrants and manufactured articles from the mother country converged for redistribution in the New World, while through them the produce of rural and frontier settlements found its way to distant markets. The colonial town was primarily a commercial community with its daily exchange of goods—a community of marketplaces, warehouses, wharves, and shops. This fact more than any other tended to weld these five widely scattered villages into a uniform type of society, differing radically from that of farming community or wilderness outpost.

The first concern of colonial authorities was to provide their villages with an adequate food supply when provisions brought by sea had become exhausted. Some inhabitants kept cows and pigs, and cultivated little gardens, but a settled community must soon be fed from sources outside itself. William Wood described the problem of Boston in 1634: "Those that live here upon their Cattle, must be constrayned to take Farmes in the Countrey, or else they cannot subsist; they [sic] place being too small to contain many, and fittest for such as can Trade into

---

* Reprinted from Carl A. Bridenbaugh, *Cities in the Wilderness* (New York: the Ronald Press Co., 1938), pp. 26–54.

15

England, for such commodities as the Countrey wants." Medieval towns met this problem by erecting markets and fairs to be held at stated intervals, and their colonial children quite naturally followed their example. Every village had by 1690 made some provision for the holding of regular markets, occurring generally on a stated day each week at a place designated by provincial or village authorities, and in the northern towns the custom of yearly fairs had become well established.

The Dutch West India Company arranged, with indifferent success, for the food supply of its servants during the first years at New Amsterdam. "Food here is scanty and poor," wrote Dominie Michaelius in 1628. "Fresh butter and milk are difficult to obtain, owing to the large number of people and the small number of cattle and farmers. These articles are dear." Not until 1648 was a weekly market opened on the Strand, where "strangers" as well as burghers could set up their booths. Here, on Saturdays, meat, pork, butter, cheese, turnips, carrots, cabbage, and other country produce were brought and exposed for sale "on the beach." In 1662 the court designated Tuesdays and Saturdays as the days on which "country people" might offer their wares to the townsfolk. Market day in New Amsterdam, when farmers from Brooklyn, Gowanus, and Bergen haggled over the sale of their produce to wary Knickerbockers from their boats in the "great Graft," was a reenactment in the New World village of scenes from the life of Old Holland. Transition from Dutch to English rule apparently dislocated existing market arrangements. Governor Andros in 1677 ordered a weekly market to be held on Saturdays, for which there was "a fit house beinge now built" at the waterside. Three years later the mayor and common council provided for an additional market on Wednesdays at the same place. The Dongan charter of 1683 introduced English market custom into New York, and from then on the mayor and aldermen appointed a clerk, or clerks, of the market. In 1684 the corporation published elaborate market regulations which closely resemble those of English market towns.

Although the most complete development of markets occurred at New York, the institution had first appeared at Boston. On March 4, 1633/4, the court of assistants ordered the erection of a "mercate" in the bay town, "to be kept upon Thursday, the fifth day of the week, being lecture day," when the countrypeople all came into town. This market was held in an open space at the head of King Street until 1658, when funds left by Robert Keayne made possible the building of a townhouse, concerning which the general court decreed that "the place underneath shall be free for all inhabitants in this jurisdiction to make use of as a market place forever." Increased trading at the Boston market led the town meeting in 1649 to follow the old English custom of appointing "Clarkes of the market" to supervise its business, a method of regulation that continued in use for nearly 200 years.

The essentially rural character of life in early Newport made it possible for inhabitants to supply themselves with foodstuffs throughout most of the period. By 1672, however, conditions had so greatly changed that George Fox, after a visit to Rhode Island, wrote to the governor earnestly advising "that you have a market once a week in your town and a house built for that purpose." His wise counsel soon bore fruit in the setting apart of Saturday as market day. In 1677 the governor humored the religious scruples of the Sabbatarians by naming Wednesday an additional day for the holding of markets. No market building was erected in Newport until well into the 18th century.

The intentions of William Penn for the development of Philadelphia included a market, inaugurated shortly after the colonists arrived. Two weekly markets were in operation in 1685; and the next year, James Claypoole, in a letter to the proprietor, mentioned that "Provisions [are] very cheap . . . in our market." Alone of the five villages, Charles Town enjoyed no market facilities in this period, although in 1690 the parliament of South Carolina did set aside land for a "market place" in the town.

Like their European fathers, colonial town dwellers instituted annual or semiannual fairs in addition to their regular market days. Governor Kieft of New Amsterdam in 1641 appointed annual cattle and hog fairs to be held in the "open spaces" before the Fort. The cattle fair was a "free market"; that is, strangers as well as burghers might retail goods and enjoy exemption from arrest while there. To encourage trading, proclamations were issued in English as well as Dutch, and farmers with their herds and flocks came from points as distant as Milford, Connecticut, and Southampton, Long Island. In 1659 the burgomasters designated the space before the Fort a "market for fat and lean cattle" to be held continuously for 40 days each autumn, and for this purpose erected a building with a tiled roof, later called the "Broadway Shambles." Governor Andros ordered an annual fair to run for three days in November, 1677, for cattle, grain, and other country produce, "att the market house & Plaine afore the Forte." Boston was granted "two faires in the yeare" in 1648, but here the custom soon fell into disuse.

At Philadelphia a yearly fair seems to have been held from shortly after the beginning of settlement. Not confined to livestock, it more resembled English fairs, where all manner of merchandise changed hands. The handiwork of the Mennonite weavers of Germantown, to the dismay of Francis Daniel Pastorius, brought only 10 thalers at the fair of 1684. Quaker merchants and farmers valued their fair, and the various districts of Philadelphia County contended eagerly for the privilege of holding it. In the year 1688 the provincial council granted the petitions of the residents at "ye Center of Philadelphia," requesting that the fair be kept there. There is no evidence of fairs held in the 17th century in either Newport or Charles Town.

Medieval towns grew in proportion to their success in catering to their own needs and those of nearby villages. They cultivated enough purely local trade to meet their daily requirements and to supply them with commodities for exchange in the world market, where their chief interests lay in the exploitation of the most profitable portions of distant international commerce. They made little effort to realize the rich possibilities in the economic subjugation of a wide hinterland. The colonial villages were modeled after the economic pattern of medieval towns, and colonial commerce became chiefly an "ocean-borne, out-going commerce, rather than a continental, inland traffic." By 1650, however, Boston had begun to extend its control into the backcountry, and to develop a metropolitan form of economy that was essentially modern. Toward the close of the century a similar tendency to become the economic center of its province became noticeable at New York. This process was simultaneous with like developments all over Europe, but was speeded and facilitated in the case of colonial towns by the pioneer nature of the countryside. The frontiers of the New World were far more dependent upon districts of earlier settlement than were corresponding geographic areas in the Old, and there was here no need to break down any prearranged economy of little towns, with their local interests and jealousies, before the larger town could become "the economic centre for a very large number of goods and services."

The only town to extend its economic control beyond nearby hamlets to the hinterland in the 17th century was Boston. By 1680, Newfoundland, Maine, New Hampshire, Massachusetts, Rhode Island, and the river towns of Connecticut all paid tribute to the bay town's commercial leadership. In 1640, cattle began to move overland from the Piscataqua; and after 1660, Hampshire County, Massachusetts, specialized in grass-fed cattle for the Boston market. Newport was throughout the period the commercial satellite of Boston. Thither, Peleg Sanford sent overland his flocks of sheep in 1667, and received in exchange clothing and dry goods by packhorse. The "mart town" assiduously drained Connecticut of its surplus produce, occasionally taking more than that region could spare. From Milford came beaver pelts and grain; peas and pork were shipped from the river towns to Boston, whence they went to feed the fishermen of Salem and Marblehead. An overland route from Windham County was opened after 1686, when people from Muddy River, Massachusetts, settled there. Clement Corbin of Woodstock carried produce by oxcart over the hills into Boston, and returned with dry goods, liquor, ammunition, and "other necessaries" for his general store. Connecticut authorities tried in vain to stem the flow of produce into Massachusetts. Their order of 1650 that "no Foreigners . . . shall retaile any goods, by themselves in any place within this Jurisdiction, nor shall any Inhabitant retayle any goods wch belongs to any foreigner," was fruitlessly directed against the ubiquitous bay traders. With a predominantly agricultural population and inadequate harbors, it was inevitable that Connecticut should be subordinated to Boston, as it later was to New York. In 1683 the governor and council of New Hampshire proposed to forbid lumber ships from Boston to enter the ports of the province without a permit from the governor, in an effort to prevent their more aggressive neighbors from absorbing their entire trade, "drawing all ye Shipps to Boston, & thereby supplying all ye neighboring Colonies." The assembly rejected the bill, because, as Cranford explained, "some interested & ill tempered persons" blocked it.

The coastal towns of Massachusetts also came under the aegis of Boston; and apart from Salem, they did not venture much into distant trade. They suffered the fate of Ipswich, where there were some merchants, "but Boston being the chiefest place of resort of Shipping, carries all the Trade." Randolph reported in 1676 that about 300 small vessels, ranging from 6 to 10 tons burden, were employed in carrying goods between Boston and surrounding towns.

At the same time that Boston was draining produce from the hinterland settlements, she acted as the agent by whom they were in return supplied with the European and West Indian commodities they believed necessary for their existence and comfort. By means of crude but improving roads, the little metropolis maintained a growing trade, not only with the 70-odd coastal and inland settlements of Massachusetts, but also with the neighboring colonies of New Hampshire, Rhode Island, and Connecticut. Boston, Sir Robert Carr summarized tersely, had "engrossed the whole trade of New England."

As the staple for New Netherland, New Amsterdam until 1664 was the port of both entry and departure for all commerce of the province; but after that date, especially with its loss of the fur trade to Albany, the business of the town, like the radius of its economic influence, greatly contracted. It now had to regain by slow penetration the control over its hinterland which once it had enjoyed by statute; and from this time on, though on a much smaller scale, its economy developed similarly to that of Boston. With its admirable location, it found in the Hudson River a ready avenue by which it drew to itself provisions from Esopus and even furs from Fort Orange. A packet service of some regularity for carrying freight and passengers up the Hudson had been begun by Cornelius Van Tienhoven in 1633. By way of Long Island Sound the Dutch and English at Manhattan drew within their orbit the villages of Connecticut as far east as Milford; while on Long Island, they gradually weaned Southold and other eastern towns from their New England connections.

The other villages had perforce to be content to act as marketing and distributing centers for hamlets and rural districts within their immediate vicinity. Newport had almost no inland territory to serve, a fact of no little importance in explaining its slow commercial development. After the destruction of the Indian power in King Philip's War, the Narragansett country and northeastern Connecticut could be tapped, but it was many years before the town's inland trade assumed any large proportions. Carolina Indian traders pushed many hundred of miles into the interior of the Southwest in search of deerskins: supplies for their little posts and caches were served out of Charles Town by means of periaugers and canoes, winding up the numerous rivers to their headwaters, and thence overland by packhorse. But this was a peculiar traffic, and Charles Town in this period developed no staple of trade to support her economic life when the supply of furs should become depleted. Philadelphia in 1690 had not yet exhausted the rich possibilities of the Delaware Valley, and Quaker merchants had only just begun to probe the backcountry of the Schuylkill. They had as yet no opportunity to realize the broad and fertile hinterland that was to enable them in the course of the next century to outstrip their New England rivals.

All this activity, this far-flung trade, these ships which were built, equipped, and kept in repair, and whose holds were filled with commodities for exchange by a small army of laborers, presupposed capital, imagination, and direction. These the little towns were not slow in developing. In each community a small group of men arose, some of them "damnable rich," who gathered into their hands the control of colonial commerce, and with it political power and social prestige. Active, ambitious, and venturesome, these merchants made it possible for the five little villages to grow up into sizable towns. It was their accomplishment from the untouched resources of a new continent to create a traffic that penetrated every corner, and a fleet that found its way into nearly every harbor of the western world.

Village merchants either owned or took shares in the ships that carried their ventures. In addition, they built wharves and erected warehouses in which to store their goods. Frequently, also, they kept shops in their homes for retail trade. Thus the 17th-century merchant conducted a general business which aimed to supply the diverse needs of people in both town and country. Peleg Sanford's dealings were probably those of the average merchant. He imported sugar, molasses, rum, and cotton from Barbados, and dry goods and hardware from England. These he disposed of in Newport at both wholesale and retail. In 1666–67, he sold at his shop 5,000 pins, £20 worth of haberdashery, brass kettles worth £5, a quantity of Barbados brooms, and some English hats and furniture. In exchange, he accepted pork, beef, peas, butter, and cheese, which he marketed in the West Indies.

Bostonians conducted business on a larger scale, frequently acting as agents for merchants of other villages. Sanford made his English purchases through Elisha Hutchinson and Peter Oliver of Boston. Much of the town's business consisted in the transshipment of European goods destined for small coastal villages or for inland shopkeepers. In addition to utilitarian dry goods and hardware, Boston merchants imported considerable quantities of wines and spirits, and luxuries such as spices, chocolate, raisins, figs, and oranges. For the towns especially, butter and cheese had to be imported, as the countryside did not yet produce a sufficient surplus to meet the demand.

Country storekeepers and "petty traders," who purchased goods in quantity, dealt directly with the merchants at their warehouses, but townsfolk who made small individual purchases resorted to the increasing number of little shops in the towns. There were two classes of shops: those conducted by persons "who buy to sell again," and those kept by various artisans for disposal of their handiwork. Of the first class, there were but few in the 17th century, and the absence of evidence circumscribes our knowledge of their activities, but it is certain that a shop trade of this type was flourishing in the villages by 1690.

The first shopkeepers of whom we have any record were John Coggan and Solomon Stoddard of Boston, both merchants, who conducted retail shops as well. Stoddard, a linen draper, was in business for over half a century. Merchants of Newport, Philadelphia, and Charles Town, and the West India Company at New Amsterdam, maintained similar shops and probably transacted the bulk of the retailing in these towns.

Sometime prior to 1645, the Widow Howin kept a tiny shop at Boston, and the following year "Wm Davice, the apothecary," was conducting a small retail business there. Most shops sold dry goods and groceries, occasionally offering other "European" items for sale. "For rayment, our cloth hath not been cut short," wrote Johnson in 1650, "as but of late years the traders that way have encreased to such a number, that their shops have continued full all the year long, all one [the same as] England." "The town is full of good Shopps well furnished with all kinds of Merchandise," reported Maverick in 1660; and by 1675, Bostonians were beginning to complain bitterly of "Shopkeepers and merchants who set excessive prices on their goods." The journal of a Boston shopkeeper for the years 1685 to 1689, recording hundreds of small purchases by a large number of persons, yields unmistakable evidence of the existence of a retail trade. Some sales were very small, as on occasions when "Joseph Wheeler, Taylor," dropped in to buy "6 yds cloth at 1s." Most transactions were by barter; the word "cash" occurs but seldom in the record.

In none of the other towns did the retail shop trade develop so early as at Boston. The director and council of New Amsterdam made regulations in March, 1648, regarding persons who "kept a public or private shop . . . in cellar or garret, or . . . carry on any Trade by the small weight and measure," and in September forbade "Scottish Merchants and small traders" from Holland, who undersold the burghers "in wholesale and retail," to do business in New Amsterdam. In a petition from inhabitants of New Amsterdam to Peter Stuyvesant in 1657, protesting the high prices of necessary commodities and household supplies, distinction is carefully made between "Merchants, . . . Shop-keepers, Tradesmen, Brewers, Bakers, Tapsters and Grocers." At Newport, in 1668, Peleg Sanford did business with Mahershallalhasbaz Dyer, who kept a tobacconist's shop, and probably purchased his medical supplies of Thomas Rodman, to whom the town in 1677 granted a lot "whilst he lived & practiced the (trade of) an Apothecarie." As early as 1685, Cornelius Born opened a notions shop in Philadelphia, and by 1690 the town sheltered "twenty-nine Shop-Keepers, great and small."

Among shopkeepers, only apothecaries and tobacconists approached the specialization of modern retailing. Most little shops resembled the general store of today, and their stocks included such diverse articles as looking glasses, candlesticks, gloves, tin lanterns, rattraps, woodenware, fishing tackle, bottles, and trays. They carried an assortment of dry goods and imported groceries for sailors, laborers, and the "poorer sort of people," who could not afford to buy in bulk, to purchase in small quantities.

The problem of transportation arose early in each settlement. Merchants had goods to send to shops, artisans needed conveyance for their raw materials, and the heavy loads of builders had constantly to be carried from one part of the village to another. In each little seaport, carters or carmen, with their "Draughts & teams & the like," served this need, playing a vital part in the conduct of trade and well aware of their importance. The functions of the carters were much the same in all the villages, and their activities occasioned considerable legislation by town or provincial authorities. As early as 1637/8, the general court of Massachusetts regulated the rates which carmen might charge, because of complaints of their "excessive prizes for . . . work." Bridges had to be made "sufficient for Cart and horse," and wear and tear on the streets led to frequent regulation of the size of cartwheels. The growing traffic of Philadelphia demanded in 1690 the service of "six carters that have Teams daily imployed to carry and fetch Timber and Bricks, Stone and Lime for Building," and about 24 others with four- and six-horse carts to bring merchandise from the wharves through the Arch into the town. New York merchants and shopkeepers could also be served by "porters," available at the Bridge and Weighhouse for carrying parcels and light burdens during specified hours at rates set by the corporation. In Boston, too, porters played an important part in the daily traffic of the town after 1660.

Certain economic ideals of medieval England came with the colonists to America. These included the beliefs that the prime function of merchant, craftsman, artisan, and laborer was the service of the community, and that careful and minute regulation of all phases of commercial life was the proper responsibility of municipal authority. Hence, municipal provision for a "fair customary price" for goods and labor, for wares of a standard quality, for strict supervision of food supply and regulation of weights and measures, for payment of debts when due, and for protection of the community's trade by the exclusion of strangers and interlopers—all these were medieval legacies to America. By 1690, these inherited institutions had become adjusted to their new locale. Some had been discarded as useless in a frontier society; others, though obviously outmoded, were still retained; and many had been successfully transplanted to the new soil.

In the beginning, village inhabitants trafficked gladly enough with any merchant or trader that appeared; but as soon as they had completed the first business of pioneering, the authorities followed the Old World custom of protecting their local businessmen against intruders. In 1648 the director and council of New Netherland ordered "That no person shall henceforward be allowed to keep a public or private Shop on shore, in cellar or garret, or to carry on any Trade by the small weight and measure . . . except our good and dear Inhabitants," while in 1657 the selectmen provided that only admitted inhabitants might keep shop or set up business in Boston. In the latter year the burgomasters of New Amsterdam likewise forbade anyone to do business there before he had receive the "burgher right" of the city. Some time prior to 1680 the village of Newport also prohibited all save inhabitants, who had "liberty," from opening shops there. So far as is known, only New Amsterdam, and later New York, set any fee for the burgher right; here, in 1675, a shopkeeper had to pay six beavers, and a "Handi Craft man," two, for the coveted privilege.

The towns very carefully enforced their regulations against the intrusion of strangers within their precincts. The New Amsterdam ordinance of 1648 was directed against certain "Scottish merchants and small traders," who undersold Dutch burghers in "wholesale and retail," and in 1662 the town of Boston fined Nathaniel Milles and Thomas Alline 20 shillings each for having opened shops in the town before becoming admitted inhabitants. Not always did the towns have the support of provincial authorities in their attempts to protect their infant industries. A petition from craftsmen of Boston to the general court, complaining of the "frequent intruding of strangers from all parts, especially such as are not desirably qualified," who set up as tradesmen when they could not even pay their taxes, and desiring a grant of power to the selectmen for the regulation of this evil, came to nothing in 1677.

Village authorities sought to dominate the economic life of the townsmen. At almost every point, inhabitants found themselves limited in their actions and inspected in their dealings, for prevailing theory held that the individual owed more to the group than did society to him. The measures taken by town fathers thus to circumscribe the activities of the citizen were in all cases adaptations of English or Dutch law and practice. The authorities of Massachusetts Bay made a brave but unsuccessful attempt in 1630 to regulate prices and wages, but after having tried every possible means of securing a "just price" for labor and commodities, repealed their orders in 1635, and placed the burden on the towns, whose freemen were, from time to time, "to agree about the prices, & rates of all workmen, laborers & servants wages." Regulation of wages in a new country where labor was scarce was foredoomed to failure, for many artisans "would remove to other places," or else they would take up farming and "would not be hired at all."

The famous case of Robert Keayne indicates that in spite of this defeat, the people of Boston did not discard the ideal of a fair price. Keayne, a merchant rich by the standards of the day, who kept a shop in Boston, was accused in 1639 of "oppression used . . . in the sale of foreign commodities." Though not alone in the offense, he "notoriously above others" took profits in excess of sixpence in the shilling, occasionally as high as "two for one." Keayne used his influence to secure the halving and then the entire remittance of his fine of £200, and finally escaped with only the censure of the court. The magistrates found Keayne the worst of all offenders, because of his wealth and the fact that he sold "dearer" than most tradesmen. His dealings so outraged community sentiment that some members of the Boston church demanded his excommunication. Aware of his duty as upholder of the social discipline, the Reverend John Cotton took the case as subject for his weekly lecture, and expounded from the pulpit the medieval doctrine of the just price. Winthrop tells us that "although the cry of the country was so great against oppression [profiteering]," and although the deputies voted for Keayne's punishment, the Bostonians, being mostly tradesmen, exerted their influence on the side of leniency.

Fair prices were also a matter of concern to the burghers of New Amsterdam. In 1657, townsmen and strangers petitioned Stuyvesant to remedy the prevailing high prices, especially of "necessary commodities and household supplies." They charged that not only "Merchants, but also, consequently, Shop-keepers, Tradesmen, Brewers, Bakers, Tapsters, and Grocers make a difference of 30, 40 & 50 per cent when they sell their wares." There is no record of any action taken in this case. The West India Company also made strict rules concerning the work of its servants. An ordinance of 1638 decreed that none might leave the village without permission from the director, and another the next year required them to go to work at the ringing of a bell. A "Commissary of the Workmen" supervised their labors. In 1658 the burgomasters laid down regulations for village workmen, dictating the length of the working day and the recess period allowed for meals. At Philadelphia, complaints of "the Great grievance of Tradesmen's Exaction" led the council to issue a trade-regulating ordinance in 1683. Two years later, Penn wrote: "The hours for Work and Meals to Labourers are fixt, and known by Ring of the Bell."

Village authorities maintained a similar surveillance over weights and measures. In 1631 the general court of Massachusetts ordered all weights and measures used by tradesmen to be "sealed" according to standards proclaimed by the colony, and in 1650 the town of Boston began its annual practice of selecting a "Sealer of weights and measures." New Amsterdam in 1649 required all wholesale and retail merchants to have "Old Amsterdam" weights and measures, which had been inspected at the Fort, and in 1675 the court of assistants at New York ordered that henceforth Winchester measures should be standard for city and province. Newport adopted the English peck and half-peck measures in 1643, and in 1675 sent to Boston for a set of Winchester measures. English standards were adopted in Philadelphia in 1683, and were probably also in use at Charles Town.

The medieval assize of bread, insuring a fair price and weight for all products of the bakers' ovens, soon appeared in the villages. At Boston, in 1639, John Stone and his wife were admonished to make "bigger" bread and "to take heed of offending by making too little bread hereafter." The next year the general court of Massachusetts passed a law providing an assize of bread for all towns. In 1646, every baker was required to mark his product in order that they might be identified if found lacking in weight or quality. All bread so found was to be forfeited to "the use of the poore." In each town the clerks of the market enforced the assize. The bakers of Boston petitioned the court in 1681 about the set price of bread in times when wheat was high, seeking permission to choose annually three or more "meete persons" familiar with their trade to set the assize. This was granted; but although the town meeting the next year chose three inhabitants to make the assize, no further regulation appears until 1701. At New Amsterdam the assize of bread was regularly published after 1649. David Provoost, baker, was brought into the mayor's court in 1681 "for having bad breed not fitt for Sale." Leniency ruled, and the offender escaped with an admonition to take greater care in the future.

Save at Charles Town, colonial authorities everywhere exercised great care to insure fairness in all dealings, and their records teem with accounts of "Corders of Wood," "Cullors of Staves," "Packers of flesh and fish," "Searchers of leather," "Measurers of Sale," and so on. To describe the activities of all these officers would result only in wearisome detail. Their duties were all much the same: the examination of products for quality and the supervision of gauging and measuring to insure fair treatment to both inhabitants and strangers. In Boston and Newport, these minor functionaries were generally tradesmen and artisans elected to their offices at town meeting; in New York and Philadelphia, they owed their appointments to the local authorities.

The history of the colonial villages in the 17th century is primarily a tale of commercial expansion. In this period the five towns grew from wilderness settlements to fully developed little seaports challenging comparison with any European centers of the same size. The necessary corollary of this growth was the accumulation of capital, derived not only from the extension of wholesale trade by enterprising merchants but also from the small savings of prosperous tradesmen and artisans. A rise in the standard of living, historically one of the outstanding characteristics of American life, accompanied the increasing prosperity of life in the villages. "The infectious winds of trade, blowing through the colonial settlements, everywhere stirred up the commercial spirit." As early as 1650, Edward Johnson noted that the merchants, traders, and vintners of Boston "would willingly have had the Commonwealth tolerate divers kinds of sinful opinions to intice men to come and sit down with us, that their purses might be filled with coin." "New England was originally a plantation of Religion, not a plantation of Trade," thundered John Higginson in his election sermon of 1663. "Let Merchants, and such as are increasing Cent per Cent remember this." And John Hull, who, though a merchant, was an ardent theocrat, perceived sadly that "Self-interest is too predominant in many." So soon did dwellers in this city of God find profits in the service of Mammon! This same leaven was quietly at work increasing cent percent in the other villages, preparing the breakdown of timeworn medieval practices, and facilitating the transition to modern capitalism that was transforming the western world.

Commercial development in both Boston and New Amsterdam quickly outgrew the system of barter, and these years saw many unsuccessful attempts to provide a sufficient medium of exchange. In early New Amsterdam, beaver skins and wampum circulated in place of money. From time to time, efforts were made to regulate the value of these media, always with small success. In 1657 the burghers petitioned the director and council in regard to the decline in the value of beaver and wampum currency, alleging that profiteering by merchants and tradesmen resulted, and declaring that the supply of silver coin from the fatherland failed to meet the demands of their growing trade. The need for a circulating medium in Massachusetts became acute by the mid-century, and in 1652 the general court set up a mint to coin the gold and silver brought into the colony, "bringing it to the sterling standard of fineness, and for weight every shilling to be three pennyweight." John Hull, merchant and silversmith, was made mintmaster, and struck off the famous pine tree shillings, "flatt and square on the sides." The money question, however, grew increasingly complicated and was farther than ever from an answer when the period ended. The events of the 1680's, the closing of the mint, the enforcement of the navigation acts, and the temporary suppression of piracy effectively dried up the colony's few poor sources of metal coin. "The Labyrinth New-England was in, for want of a Conveniency to mete their Trade with," led to proposals for a medium of exchange based upon real estate, which would eliminate "the mystery of Trucking by sinking Barter." Proposals for a "Bank of Credit Lumbard" were made to the colony council in July, 1686, and two tracts were written to defend the new credit schemes. The coming of the Revolution of 1689 prevented any action in this period.

The expansion of trade made communication among the several villages a necessity. At Boston, as early as 1639, an office was opened to serve as a clearinghouse for the town's mail, and in 1652 a similar arrangement was introduced at New Amsterdam. In 1672, Governor Lovelace of New York inaugurated a monthly postal route between New York and Boston, but the service was discontinued after a few trips. Nine years later, William Penn's post between Maryland and the falls of the Delaware was more successful. Just as the period ended, Andrew Hamilton of New Jersey, royal deputy for the King's post in America, established a line of posts from Portsmouth, New Hampshire, to Philadelphia. The villages remained unconnected by stage routes in this period; land communication was undeveloped, and trade was forced to rely almost entirely upon water transportation.

Of the five villages, Boston in 1690 enjoyed preeminence in respect to her ocean-borne commerce. Her success was the result of a location most favorable for a center of distribution and of her priority in the field of trade. A highly developed shipbuilding industry, which enabled Boston merchants to monopolize most of the colonial carrying trade, the aggressiveness of her mariners and merchants, and the existence of a relatively large population in the New England hinterland also aided this port in her chosen sphere of activity. Rural districts did not always regard her domination of their trade with pleasure. Edward Randolph saw this resentment developing in the political factions of 1686: "There are no small endeavors betwixt the Landed men and the Merchts: how to ease the publick Charges: The Merchts: are for Land Taxes: but . . . others who haue gott very large tracts of Land are for laying all upon the trading party." This divergence of interests was an important factor running through the whole history of the dominion of New England; an incipient antagonism between town and country, based upon economic differences, was already becoming evident.

At the close of this period the five villages exhibited varying degrees of economic development. Boston stood far in advance of the others in every respect, and her economic superiority made her a cause of jealousy to the other towns; merchants of both New York and Newport covertly resented the control exercised by "Bostoners" in their own villages. Philadelphia and New York approached nearest to Boston in economic development, while Newport and Charles Town lagged behind. But in all five, the spirit of economic enterprise created a commercial society definitely contrasted to the agricultural society of the backcountry. The maritime activity of the villagers brought the mercantile groups of each town increasingly in contact with one another and with Europe as the century progressed. The mutual isolation of the villages was far less in 1690 than in 1640; indeed, it is probable that at the close of the period, many townsmen possessed greater familiarity with other villages than with the backcountry of their own provinces. Commercial and economic factors, more than any others, were making for the development of an early village society.

2. COLONIAL PORTS AS MARKETING AND DISTRIBUTING CENTERS, 1690-1720*

By 1690, two distinct types of retailing had emerged: (1) the shops operated by artisans and serving as outlets for the goods they made, and (2) those stores or places of business operated by persons who would buy for resale. The latter would be retailers in the modern sense of the term. The period from 1690 to 1720 saw a number of new marketing institutions arise in response to the needs of a changing environment. In the larger communities of Boston, New York, Newport, Philadelphia, and Charleston, specialty shops flourished as a result of increased urbanization, greater wealth, and marked improvement in the standard of living. By 1700 the itinerant "Yankee peddler" had begun to compete with established merchants, and auctions had grown in popularity as a marketing mechanism. Increased commercial activity involving the exchange of goods gave impetus to demands for a postal system and an adequate supply of money, objectives which were not easily attained.

THE THREE DECADES following 1690, years of great commercial expansion in the New World, constituted a hothouse period in the growth of the five little ports. Nineteen years of war stimulated general trade, both legal and illegal, and gave rise to the sister activities, privateering and piracy. But in some respects, the effects of conflict could not but seriously retard commercial development in the towns, as the inevitable period of depression followed hard on the heels of feverish war prosperity. However, the five years following 1715 saw a gradual recovery from this temporary setback; and by the end of the period, all five towns were facing a long era of peace and thriving trade.

The outstanding feature in the economic life of the towns at this time was the rapid growth of the trade of Philadelphia, New York, Newport, and Charles Town. As later entrants in the field, these towns had originally been hampered in their commercial activities by the economic power of Boston. But now, their merchants sought by every means to

* Reprinted from Carl A. Bridenbaugh, *Cities in the Wilderness* (New York: Ronald Press Co., 1938), pp. 175-205.

carve a niche for themselves in the commercial system of the Empire, and to acquire a money supply sufficient to pay for the great importation of English goods now needed to meet the demands of an ever-rising standard of living. By 1720, these merchants had largely succeeded in establishing the avenues of trade that their successors followed throughout the colonial period.

Bostonians imported the major portion of European goods consumed in America and distributed them by means of their coasting fleet to every colony except South Carolina. Despite their entrance into direct trade with England and Portugal, both Philadelphia and New York still obtained many of their manufactured articles by way of Boston. So keen was the rivalry between Boston and New York for the business of Long Island and the provision trade to the West Indies that during the administrations of Dongan and Hunter the New York Assembly levied a heavy duty on goods imported into New York from other colonies. Similar complaints against bay traders were made at Philadelphia. As Bostonians everywhere took the profits of middleman and carrier, their town maintained a favorable balance of trade against its competitors; gold and silver from other colonies flowed into the coffers of Massachusetts merchants, who in turn used it to redress adverse balances with English creditors. The bay town was by 1720 the "coin center of the continental colonies"; and Philadelphia and New York, despite the unprecedented expansion of their commerce, still remained "tributary" to Boston.

The primary commercial service of Boston was as a marketing and distributing center, which, while it extended throughout the colonies, was particularly important in New England. As earlier, Boston drained coastal and inland towns of their surplus produce, and sent them in return the manufactured goods they needed. Most of the lumber of New Hampshire went to Boston, whence the mast fleet annually departed, while the New Hampshire naval stores industry was financed from King Street. Newport successfully competed with bay merchants in the West India trade, but was completely dependent upon Boston for its English manufactures. The farm produce of Connecticut likewise came to Boston, for that colony had no merchants sufficiently wealthy to import stores of European goods or West India products.

Improved roads greatly facilitated this inland traffic. By about 1700, most of the modern roads out of Boston had been laid out, and carts came into general use. The postrider covered the distance from the "mart town" to New York in one week in summer. The great eastern road, running from Winnisimet Ferry eastward through Salem and Newbury, was improved for the post as far as Portsmouth, and travel over it was made easier by the opening up of more ferries. Highways across the province of Connecticut also were made passable for carts and calashes at this time.

Along these roads passed the carts of "Merchants and Inland Traders," with loads of "Mens wearing Apparel, viz., Coats, Breeches, Shoes, Buckles, Shirts, Neckcloaths, and Gloves, . . . also Salt, Nutmeg, Mace, Olives, Cinamon, and several other sort of Goods," to stock the shelves of country stores like that of James Corbin at Woodstock, Connecticut. The itinerant Yankee peddler or country chapman with his mysterious pack became an institution in these years, and drove a profitable trade throughout the countryside. So large became this inland traffic, conducted by pedlars, petty Chapmen and Hawkers," that Boston merchants and country shopkeepers began by 1713 to complain of competition and the consequent decay of trade. Among other things, they accused hawkers and walkers of selling large quantities of goods stolen during the Great Fire of 1711. The general court, ever sensitive to mercantile demands, promptly passed a law forbidding the traffic, and laying a fine of 20 shillings on violators. But in 1716 the law had to be reenacted, and from all indications the illicit traffic continued to thrive under cover.

During these years, Philadelphia, too, began to develop a hinterland traffic. By 1720 the Pennsylvania frontier line had moved about 40 miles west of the Delaware, and Scotch–Irish and Palatine refugees were rapidly pouring into this backcountry. Philadelphia thus added a new sphere of influence to the southern counties, Maryland, and West New Jersey, which had been under its commercial dominance since about 1700. With these regions, Quaker merchants exchanged European goods for export produce. The whole trade of West Jersey and the lower counties passed through Penn's town, and countrymen frequently resented their loss of "Coyne" to the metropolis. As early as 1694, Marylanders complained that Pennsylvania traders had taken £1,500 in sterling out of the province in the past two years. As a result, the Maryland Assembly enacted discriminatory duties and laws against export of specie to Pennsylvania in 1694, 1695, and 1704.

In 1695 the Pennsylvania Assembly moved to better the "Cartways" leading to the backcountry of the Schuylkill region and to Chester County; and by 1710, Chester County farmers were able to haul their produce regularly to town by cart. "The roads are good here," reported a traveler from Europe in 1716. In 1706, Lord Cornbury granted a monopoly for a stage line between Amboy and Burlington in New Jersey, and another for a ferry from Burlington to Philadelphia, to complete a through line of communication between Philadelphia and New York, for "the transportation of goods and passengers" in "coaches and Waggons," and doubtless for country chapmen as well.

New York's inland traffic did not attain the proportions of that of

Philadelphia, and of course could not compare with the trade centering around Boston. To the territory up the Hudson as far as Albany, the settlements of eastern Long Island, and lower Connecticut, the New Yorkers after 1690 added East New Jersey as a part of their economic sphere. They did not achieve this without a struggle with the Jerseymen, who made Perth Amboy a port of entry in hope of forestalling the draining off of their trade and specie by Manhattan merchants. New York's traffic was carried on largely by water, although some "very bad and stony" roads were extended into Westchester in this period. A large share of upcountry trade fell into the hands of hawkers and peddlers, who were required in 1714 to take out licenses from the governor before they could "trade from town to town" or cry their wares.

Settlement in South Carolina advanced very slowly; and by 1720, only a few scattered hamlets and trading posts could be found more than 30 miles distant from Charles Town. Thus the little southern port did not serve a very large area. On the other hand, it continued to be the center of the southern fur trade, which had by 1700 penetrated nearly a thousand miles into the interior of the continent. By 1720, Charles Town had begun the development of an inland trade which in the next two decades, when roads displaced forest paths, was to grow with great rapidity.

Newport was sadly handicapped in her efforts to create a dependent countryside, for both to north and south of Rhode Island lay the commercial domains of Boston. The only opportunity for inland traffic open to Newport merchants was in the Narragansett country and the region of Windham County, Connecticut. This latter section already enjoyed wagon-road connection with Boston. In 1720, all the produce of the Naragansett plantations was coming over the Jamestown Ferry to Newport, and a small beginning had been made in northeastern Connecticut, but the town remained largely tributary to Boston. Even so, Massachusetts peddlers after 1714 often found it hard going in Rhode Island.

Although in the year 1720 the commercial hegemony of Boston over the North American continent was still virtually complete, it was no longer undisputed, and there were ample signs of incipient competition from the four other towns. Philadelphia's growth promised great things for the future, when its almost limitless backcountry should become settled; and New York, too, was expanding at a rapid rate. In its chosen fields, the slave and West India trades, Newport was a potential rebel within the New England empire; and Charles Town was staking out a claim that would eventually be closed to Yankee traders.

Expanding population, increasing wealth, and a rising standard of living in the towns led naturally to multiplication and elaboration of agencies for the marketing and distribution of goods to town dwellers. More retail shops for those not wealthy enough to buy in bulk became a prime necessity. In addition, retailing, one of the most developed forms of merchandising, began in this period to realize some of the possibilities from numerous small sales and from specialization in one or two lines of goods.

The increase in the number of Boston shops, even during the war years, was remarkable. Probably the majority were small retail groceries from which townsfolk bought their sugar, tea, coffee, spices, and molasses. Another important group carried a general line of dry goods and seamen's clothing. A few shopkeepers conducted specialty shops with a definite line of goods for sale. Numerous booksellers' and stationers' shops clustered about the Town House, and in Sudbury Street was located the musical instrument shop of Lewis Enstone. Mirrors and lanterns might be had at the "Glass-Shop in King Street," which also advertised to silver "old Looking-Glasses." Innkeepers, like Sarah Cross, often maintained small shops in their public rooms; and frequently, some returned mariner who had made a modest venture of his own rented a corner of a taproom for the display of his wares.

There was a good deal of life in and about the Boston shops. Their keepers were shrewd enough to resist invitations to extend doubtful credit. In 1696, when a customer named Lewis tried to defer payment on purchases at the fashionable shop of Mr. Thomas Banister, the owner's reply was: "Pay the old debt first before you run of a new" (Lewis already owed Banister £50). Lewis next tried to run up a bill of £30 for cloth at the shop of Hannah Cowell, but the canny widow informed him that "being a Woman [she] was not able to ride up and down to get in debts."

The 29 retail shops existing in Philadelphia in 1690 multiplied yearly. By 1720, retail trade was flourishing, and observers reported that "Tradesmen's Shops and Streets are well frequented." Business slackened at times, to be sure, when shops became overstocked and prices fell. "Markets . . . wer never worse for dry goods," wrote the dour Colden to Samuel Eveleigh in 1712. "I am obliged in a manner to retail for ye shop-keepers will hardly look at goods." But stable conditions returned after the Peace of Utrecht; and in May and June, 1717, 28 shopkeepers took out freedoms from the corporation. There seems to have been less differentiation of stocks in Philadelphia shops than in those of Boston.

Retail shop trade developed more slowly in other towns. Although the number of shops at New York increased after 1710, far more of Manhattan's retailing remained in the hands of merchants and English factors than at Boston or Philadelphia. Governor Hunter could find none but English clothes for sale, and reported that 100 percent advance over London prices was "reckoned cheap . . . in the shops" of New York. Gotham shopkeepers learned early and well how to take the middleman's profit. New Yorkers willingly paid high for the latest and best of goods, but they steadfastly refused to buy anything save quality merchandise.

There were several retail establishments at Charles Town, among them two milliners' shops, which "shut up for 6 weeks" during the epidemic of 1699, to the inconvenience of townsfolk who had come already to depend on them. The disastrous Indian wars greatly injured retail as well as wholesale business in the town; but by the end of the period, this too had in a measure recovered. In 1720 an official reported most of the people living in and about Charles Town, "planters, merchants, and shopkeepers," to be "in very good circumstances."

Although Newport in 1708 was rumored to have "a greater plenty of European goods" than any place in New England, it probably possessed fewer shops than any other town, most of its retailing being still in the hands of merchants. A favorite device with young tradesmen of the town was to get a small stock laid by and invest it in a voyage. When the goods arrived, they could be retailed in the public room of some tavern like the King's Arms.

Side by side with shops of those who bought to sell again were the establishments of those who offered for sale the results of their own labor or the product of their particular craft. A very large part of the population of each town consisted of artisans and tradesmen, many of whom possessed "Land and Some Estate." This class fell naturally into two groups: tradesmen occupied in the food and provision business, and craftsmen or artisans who worked at all other trades. By the early 18th century, every town was fairly well supplied with purveyors of the first class. Butchers, bakers, confectioners, victualers, brewers, distillers, vintners, and "cookes" in increasing numbers labored daily to feed the townsfolk or to prepare foods for export.

No less important was the increase in both number and variety of artisans. To necessary crafts like those of the tailors, smiths, carpenters, cordwainers, tanners, and bricklayers were now added many new and more specialized skills. These artisans usually maintained little shops in their homes, which could be recognized from the street by some sign characteristic of their craft. As in the 17th century, these shops were generally tended by womenfolk or apprentices. When newspapers appeared, they were among the principal advertisers. In 1707, James Batterson, clockmaker, newly arrived from London, notified the people of Boston that "if any person   .   .   .   hath any occasion for New Clocks, or to have Old Ones turn'd into Pendulums: or any other thing either in making or mending: Let them repair to the Sign of the Clock Dial on the South Side of the Town House." James Allen of Philadelphia, goldsmith, maintained a shop on High Street, where he made "Money Scales and Weights and all sorts of Work in Silver and Gold," and his wife, Margaret, who tended shop, also sold "best Virginia Tobacco, Cutt." This tendency to combine retail shopkeeping with craftsmanship also developed at Boston.

The shops of tradesmen and artisans in this period far outnumbered establishments for retailing dry goods and groceries. The principal features in their development were the diversity of crafts represented and the fact that in a few cases artisans had found it possible to branch out from their own particular trades and venture a little into general retailing. In no town does there appear to have been a serious shortage of skilled craftsmen.

Another form of merchandising popular in the towns in this period was the auction or, as it was then known, the "publick vendue." Prior to 1690, the vendue was known only in New York. Here, as early as 1704, the corporation received a petition from the burghers asking for an ordinance to prevent the holding of "Retaile and wholesale Vendues" by any but freemen, in order to keep outsiders from carrying off the town's cash. At Newport and Charles Town, petitions exhibiting the need for well-regulated auctions led to the appointment of public vendue masters in 1709 and 1710. The governor of Pennsylvania appointed a similar official for Philadelphia about the same time. In 1720, Philadelphia shopkeepers memorialized the provincial council "setting forth the loss they sustain" because the vendue master made a practice of retailing "Shop Goods to the value of One Shilling and under." By the close of this period the public auction in all towns had come to require municipal regulation. At Boston, where the auction became extremely popular, it was apparently so well conducted as to create little need for official supervision. Ships, wines, and "European Goods" constituted favorite articles for disposal in this fashion.

In view of the growing populations of this period, markets became increasingly important as sources of food supply for the citizens. The usually lethargic corporation of New York exhibited rare activity in this department, with the result that during these years the town's market facilities far surpassed those of all other communities. In April, 1691, the authorities opened a "Butcher's Shamble" on the Green, a meat market "under the trees by the Slipp," and a market for fish and vegetables near the City Hall. All markets opened at 7:00 o'clock on Tuesday, Thursday, and Saturday mornings at the ringing of a bell. In keeping with English practice, no produce could be sold elsewhere, and no persons might buy to sell again until after the markets had been open for two hours. In 1707 a market house was built in Heeregraft Street to serve residents of the Coenties Slip neighborhood. Three other market buildings, at Clarke's Slip, Countess Key, and the Burgher's Path on the East River, were opened before 1712. These were not public markets but were constructed by private individuals with the approbation of the corporation.

Pennsylvania authorities merged the two Philadelphia markets into one in 1693, and erected stalls at Second and High streets. In appointing Robert Brett clerk of the market, Governor Markham instructed him to follow "the Custom of new yorke." Wednesday and Saturday were market days, but perishable provisions might be sold there at any time. With the exception that hucksters did not always observe the two-hour rule, High Street market served the town well. As early as 1707, the corporation proposed building a market house; and finally, in 1710, the Court House, with market stalls underneath, was completed. The stalls were let at 9 shillings a year to freemen only; the Shambles at the west side of the market were reserved for selling meat, while vegetables and other provisions could be obtained in the east stalls. By 1720 the town had become so "full of all Country business" on market days as to require the enlarging of the market. Indeed, Philadelphia butchers complained of the large amounts of meat sent into town by Jerseymen.

The act of 1690 establishing a marketplace in Charles Town for two years was in 1692 made permanent by the South Carolina Assembly. Though in 1706 the governor branded the absence of all market regulations "a living Sin," it was not until 1710 that an act of the assembly put into effect the main provisions of English market law and appointed a clerk to enforce them. At Newport the market continued to be open on Wednesdays and Saturdays as earlier, and a clerk was named in 1706 to see that the market was kept in good order and that fair measure was given. Trafficking at this one market had increased tremendously by 1720.

Although a place under the Town House had been made available to the people of Boston, the custom of holding a regular market there had lapsed. In 1696, in pursuance of provincial law, the selectmen ordered a market to be open every Tuesday, Thursday, and Saturday. On these days, no provisions might be sold anywhere else; and to give townsfolk first opportunity to buy, hucksters were forbidden to purchase before noon. The market operated with little trouble for about five years. Then the evils of forestalling by hucksters became so flagrant as to cause the town meeting to vote that no one should go out to buy provisions on the Neck before 2:00 o'clock in the afternoon. For many years the Boston market was well supplied with a great variety of country produce, although the growth of settlement round about the town led to frequent scarcity of game. Trouble with hucksters forestalling the market continued; and in 1711, they and "others" were again forbidden to bargain for any sort of provisions coming into town for sale until midafternoon.

As a result of the fire of 1711, which destroyed the Town House and most of the section about it, the market ceased to be held, and hucksters and retailers came back into their own. Their complete disregard of the regulation about purchasing provisions before 3:00 o'clock led the town meeting to direct the selectmen in 1714 "to take Effectual Care to Prosecute the Town order" against those who sold to hucksters. But as the trouble continued, a committee recommended to the meeting in 1716 that "the best way to prevent that abuse, is for ye Town to come into ye Setting up of a Public Market." Opposition to the project was so stubborn that a consideration of the committee's report was three times deferred; and when it was finally "read & debated" in March, 1718, it was "Voted disallowed." Instead, the town chose 16 clerks of the market to enforce existing orders. At the root of this contest over market arrangements lay the growing feeling among countrypeople against the town of Boston. In 1720, Boston alone, of all the towns, lacked adequate market facilities.

Improvements in communication and in retail marketing in this period led to a decline in the importance of fairs everywhere but at New York. There, in 1692, the assembly ordered the holding of two fairs a year for four days each. They followed English custom, the old cattle fair yielding to that for sale of all kinds of goods. The Massachusetts market law of 1696 provided for two yearly fairs to be held at Boston on the last Tuesday of May and October. Like those of New York, the Boston fairs were "markets overts" of the English type, supervised by the clerks of the market, who were charged to prevent frauds and abuses. For some reason, however, Boston fairs were never popular and seem to have died out long before 1720. Newport seems to have enjoyed only the "Fair" kept by Abraham Anthony at rural Portsmouth for three days each May.

The disorder which attended the holding of Philadelphia fairs from their beginning had by 1697 become so great that the assembly resolved the institution to be "of little Service, but rather of ill Tendency," and requested the governor and council "to put the said Fair down." Governor Markham diplomatically passed the buck by leaving the matter to the justices of the peace. So the fair continued, for the justices, as county officers, naturally listened to the arguments of the countrypeople, who believed they would have lost much by its discontinuance.

Shops, markets, and fairs supplied the towns adequately with foodstuffs and provisions from day to day. But they were designed for normal times, and the intercolonial wars bred extraordinary conditions with which they were not suited to cope. The strains of wartime bore especially heavily on citizens of Boston and Charles Town, where in times of crisis usual means of distribution broke down. Philadelphia, Newport, and New York were located in grain-producing regions and suffered no lack of supply during the wars.

Business expansion in the towns enhanced the importance of carters and draymen, who in both New York and Philadelphia became subject to municipal regulation. The many draymen and carters of the other three towns did not in this period create any considerable problems.

The transferred economic institutions of the Old World became thoroughly adjusted to their new setting in the 30 years following 1690. There was no change in the theory of the just price, or in the belief that it was the function of town governments to regulate all economic life so as to secure the greatest good to their inhabitants. By 1720, most of the machinery set up to control the economic life of the towns was running smoothly, and in much the same manner as similar institutions at Norwich, Bristol, or Exeter in England.

Town authorities everywhere except at Charles Town took continual pains to protect their tradesmen and artisans from outside competition, while at the same time they sought to make their regulations sufficiently flexible to insure infiltration of an adequate supply of craftsmen and laborers. New and more stringent laws appeared concerning the "freedom" to open and conduct business in all the northern towns.

Enforcement of these regulations against "foreigners" was not altogether successful. Especially troublesome were "divers transient persons" who drifted into the towns for a little trading and soon departed, carrying with them a goodly share of the inhabitants' ready cash. New York and Boston resented these interlopers because they paid no taxes, and Newporters complained that they undersold local tradesmen. Intruding Jerseymen and peddlers aroused the ire of Philadelphia tradesmen, who branded them public nuisances. Everywhere the itinerant tradesmen disrupted local business, and strange artisans were unwelcome in towns already well supplied with representatives of the various crafts. But as time went on, the problem became increasingly difficult to handle.

This period was notable for increased activity of both town and provincial authorities in making regulations to insure that artisans and tradesmen charged a "just" price for their goods, gave fair measure, and maintained a high standard of quality in their products. As bread formed the staple of diet among townsfolk, the assize was carefully set by town fathers. By 1700 the bakers of every town except Charles Town had to conform their products in size, weight, and price to officially published standards. Fees for services rendered by carters, porters, and many minor functionaries of the town were also carefully stated. Profiteering continued to be a cardinal sin. At Charles Town, in 1703, the governor, aroused at shoemakers for "exacting upon ye people [a price] of twelve Royall a pair when leather is Sold at a royall a pound," put pressure on profiteers by proposing a bill "Against ye Combination of all Tradesmen."

In the interests of trade and competition with other colonies, the government of each province made laws to regulate the quality, weight, and measure of all commodities. The size of lumber, shingles, and casks, as well as the quality of grain, flour, meat, and leather exported to the West Indies, was carefully scrutinized by town authorities, who chose officials to inspect these articles regularly. At Boston the size of bricks was specified; Newport chose a "Viewer of Cattle and Horses to be transported"; and New York required all butter for export in firkins to be branded with the letters "N.Y." In 1702, English weights and measures became standard at Charles Town; and thereafter, Winchester measures were used to the exclusion of all others in each of the five towns. So widespread was the demand for these weights that Caleb Ray of Boston opened a shop in 1708 and advertised himself as the "Chief Skale-Maker of New England."

Some persons there were, as always, who tried to beat the law and their customers, but vigilant authorities usually detected them. Thus, in September, 1713, a surveyor at Boston found 10,000 shingles to be defective and consigned them to a bonfire at the end of Long Wharf. When in October a countryman was discovered trying to sell a cartload of turnips by a false bushel measure at the Dock, the justices ordered the measure "to be broke into Pieces, and the Turnips that were unsold to be given to the Poor." Many people who kept sheep on Rhode Island complained bitterly to the Newport town meeting in 1715 that town butchers secretly stole and slaughtered their animals at night, with the result that an ordinance was promulgated forbidding anyone to set up a slaughterhouse without a license, and requiring those who engaged in the business to show the ears of all slaughtered beasts to the clerk of the market, so that the marks might be identified. In 1713 the strong moral influence of religion was brought to bear upon sharp trading practices at Philadelphia, when the yearly meeting "Advised that all Friends be very careful in making and vending all provisions and other commodities for transportation, taking care that the same be of good and due fineness, measure and weight."

One of the most important institutions growing out of the towns' commercial needs was the colonial post office. Absence of any regular mails between towns or with Europe had "always been a great hindrance to the Trade of those parts." In 1692 a court favorite, Thomas Neale, received a royal patent giving him authority to institute and operate a post office in the colonies for a period of 21 years. Andrew Hamilton of New Jersey, Neale's deputy in America, opened the first office at New York; and the first route, from New York to Philadelphia, began in 1693. The Boston office also opened at this time. By 1698 a weekly postal route ran from Portsmouth, New Hampshire, through Boston, Newport, New York, and Philadelphia to Newcastle, Delaware. At Charles Town an unofficial post office to receive and send off West India and European mail was established in 1698, and in 1702 an effort was made to unite Charles Town to the system of the northern towns; but traffic apparently did not warrant it, and the postmaster, Edward Bourne, confined his efforts to mails going and coming by sea. It cannot be said that the colonial post office as yet provided either cheap or regular service, but even the erratic mails afforded were a great improvement over anything the towns had known before.

The expanding activities of the period also emphasized the need for a better medium of exchange. Lack of much ready money and the heavy demands made on the colonies during the wars resulted in large issues of paper currency. Massachusetts led the way in 1690; and by 1712, Rhode Island, New York, and South Carolina had fallen into line. Undoubtedly, a more ample medium of exchange was needed, and the use of bills facilitated the conduct of trade, but the "evils of inflation" soon came upon the colonists. The situation at Boston and Charles Town was particularly significant, in that it uncovered violent antagonisms between debtor and creditor classes, and between rural districts and the town.

In 1720, Boston was still the leading seaport, the center of the great shipbuilding industry, and the money capital of the American colonies. Her supremacy was, however, being vigorously contested by her ambitious and somewhat jealous rivals. More remarkable for the period as a whole, and more charged with future import, was the rapid economic development of the other four towns, especially of Philadelphia. These settlements had definitely emerged as the economic centers of their respective provinces and, with their new commercial maturity, were challenging Boston as serious contenders in a field where for nearly a century the bay town had enjoyed unquestioned sway.

3. MARKET OUTREACH AND URBAN TRADE RIVALRY, 1720-42[*]

A common interest in marketing and trade welded the merchant class into a distinct social group eager to influence colonial affairs. The merchants sought legislation protecting their established businesses from new forms of competition such as the peddler, and regulations covering standards, weights and measures, and selling practices. Regulatory legislation was often written to favor those firms occupying entrenched positions. Although restrictive to some extent, such legislation did have its positive effects, as abuses in trade practices were prevalent. Laws and legislatures notwithstanding, a developing economy continued to produce new marketing institutions and practices. This period also saw the continued growth of specialized retailing, the beginnings of the urban dry goods or general store, and the introduction of credit on the consumer level.

THE TWO DECADES of peaceful, though fluctuating, prosperity that followed 1720 brought a tremendous expansion of business to the five colonial towns. The mounting demand for manufactured articles and luxuries, created by growing hinterland and wealthier urban markets, led to large importations from Europe, to pay for which American merchants had to push their West India and South European traffic with renewed vigor. Along commercial routes staked out prior to 1720, the volume of colonial trade continuously increased. The outstanding economic development of the period was the climax of Boston's maritime supremacy and the beginning of that town's decline. Her commerce grew steadily until about 1735, and her merchants waxed rich; but after 1730, competition from rivals cut so heavily into the carrying trade as to render Boston at the close of the period no longer the commercial metropolis of the American colonies. Instead, there were five "mart" towns on the Atlantic seaboard.

Further restriction of the Boston sphere followed the creation of separate economic domains by each of the four smaller ports. Bay mariners lost ground in the southern coastwise trade, and gave way

---

[*] Reprinted from Carl A. Bridenbaugh, *Cities in the Wilderness* (New York: Ronald Press Co., 1938), pp. 330–63.

before competition from New Yorkers in Connecticut and Long Island. On the other hand, the growing populousness of the backcountry and its improving roads increased the volume of goods distributed from Boston to the interior of New England. Shrewd merchants turned to "inland Trade of buying and selling in Towne, which is the best and most Certain profitt, with least of risque or hazard." Jonathan Waldo, shopkeeper, made a specialty of "Country Customers," despite their frequent delinquency "in Paying their Just Debts," and John Lubbock advertised in 1727 to serve rural buyers "at a Days warning." Merrett and Fletcher, "Grocers," carried a large line of domestic and imported foodstuffs, selling by whole-sale or retail to inland buyers, as well as to more distant places like New York. Dependence of Connecticut on the Boston market for cattle and produce was clearly revealed in 1740, when "Drovers and Inhabitants" complained of being "Oppress'd by the hard-money attitude of Boston merchants.

Better roads made travel throughout New England relatively safe and easy by 1720, and connections with the South on through highways were developed during this period. Newport's continuing position as a commercial dependent of Boston made possible and encouraged these excellent facilities for communication between the two towns. Rhode Islanders usurped much of Boston's West India trade and cut into the inland traffic in Connecticut and southern Massachusetts, but they still relied upon their rivals for manufactured and European goods.

Geography aided the other towns to a greater success than Newport in the development of a hinterland trade. The great movement of population into the interior of Pennsylvania, which by 1742 had filled the area as far as Tulpehocken and Bethlehem with Scotch–Irish and German settlers, created a market which enabled Philadelphia to grow as a distributing center. Quaker merchants eagerly drew off the produce of this rich agricultural region, and in return supplied the farmers with the manufactured articles they needed. As early as 1724, Christopher Sauer reported that "the wholesale trade is very brisk on account of the adjoining counties." The Delaware counties, Maryland, and West New Jersey became more than ever attached to Philadelphia in commercial matters at this time. Builders at Chestertown, Maryland, had to send to the Pennsylvania capital in 1730 for carpenters and bricklayers. As at Boston, certain Philadelphia businessmen made a specialty of country trade.

Under guidance from the provincial council, country roads became much better. By 1742, several thousands of four-horse farm wagons "from time to time" brought their produce into town "from 10 to 100 miles distance." The new roads proved a boon to country hawkers, who found business excellent. In 1722, Philadelphia merchants and shopkeepers complained of the "Ill Practices of Pedlars," and secured the passage of a law requiring the licensing of all chapmen. Similar agitation in 1728 resulted in more rigid regulation.

Scotch–Irish and Germans also opened up the Carolina backcountry, and the founding of Georgia provided a buffer province to the southward which aided the building up of intervening districts. Round about Charles Town, plantations were rapidly springing up to form an expanding market for the servants, dry goods, earthenware, and clothing sold by town merchants. The planters developed an insatiable taste for English goods, purchasing from Charles Town merchants everything from a four-wheeled chaise to materials for japanning a tea caddy.

There were passable cart roads for about 20 miles out of Charles Town, but the presence of many rivers and creeks made canoes and periaugers the favorite means of transportation. Coastal packets carried freight north to Cape Fear and as far south as Savannah. So many petty chapmen traveled through the plantation country that in 1738, taxpaying town and country shopkeepers complained of this cutthroat competition and clandestine traffic with servants and slaves. The assembly thereupon passed a law setting high fees for hawking licenses, £50 by land and £100 by water, and requiring the posting of a bond not to trade with servants or slaves.

The trading area dominated by New York expanded little save in lower Connecticut, where Knickerbockers successfully elbowed out the Bostonians. However, increased immigration into the region already served greatly enlarged the market. Firewood, cattle, wheat, and other produce came into New York from country districts to be exchanged for manufactured and West India goods. Unpleasant treatment of countrymen by condescending city merchants frequently bred resentment in the hearts of the farmer. "You have forgot the nature of Trade and Exchange."

Most of Manhattan's trade with rural regions went on by water. In New Jersey, however, good roads were built, making lands near Perth Amboy and the Raritan River available to New York speculators. Regular weekly stage service from Amboy to Trenton, Burlington, and Philadelphia began after 1730, thus making the Jerseys a region of economic contest between traders from the two provincial capitals.

Peddlers and hawkers, especially after their expulsion from the city in 1731, swarmed over the New York backcountry. In 1738 a letter to the *New York Gazette* reported continuance of their activities, "both in City and Country." The writer declared "That many Idle and lazy Stragglers, who have no Families to maintain, who pay neither Lot nor Scot, nor do any Duty in the Service of their King or Country, yet are suffered to wander from House to House, and from Place to Place, to dispose of all manner of Wares and Merchandise, to the ruin of Trade, and is a great hurt to the Traders and Shopkeepers." Despite more repressive legislation in 1739, the peddlers continued to prosper, largely because, here as elsewhere, they performed a real service as distributing agents to remoter countrysides.

Fair trade winds favored these years. In every town, merchants amassed considerable fortunes; and many a shopkeeper, by dint of shrewd management, attained merchant status. Most colonial merchants continued to traffic in general merchandise, importing and exporting any commodities for which a market could be found. Many traded independently; others sold European goods on credit and commission for London and Bristol exporters. At New York, and especially at Charles Town, factors directly represented British houses. In the southern town, also, "country factors" acted as brokers for marketing planters' crops. Yet, despite this catholicity, there was noticeable a drift toward specialization by some merchants.

By means of voluminous correspondence and constant travel, the merchants of the various towns developed intimate connections in these decades. They also linked themselves with members of their class in the West Indies, London, and Bristol. Sea captains, traders, and supercargoes from all towns furthered these commercial relations, and could be found in exchanges or coffeehouses of every port, discussing with one another world markets and the state of trade.

This commercial intercourse led also to social and cultural interchanges of the greatest importance. By 1742 the continued exchange between merchants of each town and their mutual interest in the traffic of the Empire were slowly and surely welding them together into a distinct social group—the only one in the colonies with a common outlook. In each province, they were the leading political interest, exerting a far-reaching influence on legislation; in each town, they managed municipal affairs, whether through corporation or town meeting; and in each community, they constituted the cultured, aristocratic circle whose roots lay deep in the structure of the British Empire. Under their leadership the spirit of commerce pervaded the towns, infecting even the womenfolk and children.

The large number of people living in the towns and the growing populations in surrounding areas provided an expanding market for the goods of retail shops. Well-to-do inhabitants were at the same time bringing more of their patronage to such establishments because of the improvement in both the quality and the variety of their stocks. The bulk of shop trade, however, still came from those classes whose incomes did not permit the purchase of groceries and apparel in large quantities.

Retail shop trade reached its highest development at Boston, where some degree of specialization prevailed. Large and small groceries were to be found all over town, this petty trade apparently constituting the chief means of support for widows.

Since Boston merchants imported "nothing but the Cream of Goods the City of London affords," town shopkeepers could place choice merchandise before their customers. Shops carrying dry and household goods multiplied rapidly. One such emporium advertised in 1725: "Just imported from London, To be sold *up one pair of Stairs*, . . . opposite the Exchange in Cornhill, all sorts of Womans Shoes, and Pattoons, fine Macklins, & English Laces & Edgings, Mantua Silks, Paderina, fine Cambricks, Lawns, Hollands, Muslins, Gold & Silver Stomachers, Ribbons, Gloves, &c." Some shops displayed extensive stocks of the latest English fashions. Richard Waddington, couturier, kept an exclusive ladies' shop in 1737, at which he also made garments after the "neatest and most fashionable Manner, according to the Court of Great Britain." Numerous specialty shops made their appearance in this period, so that by 1742, Boston retail trade was well on its way to specialization in stocks.

"Anything may be had at Philadelphia," wrote Christopher Saur in 1724, "but everything is twice as dear" as in Europe. The number of retail shops, most of them located in Market Street, increased rapidly. Good groceries were to be had at Moses Marranda's or at Thomas Clarke's, where ladies went to buy their sweets. Many shops on Market and Second streets carried stocks of clothing and dry goods. Philadelphia shopkeepers did not confine themselves so much to one line of goods as did Bostonians; but occasionally, a speciality shop appeared.

In the first decade of the period, only eight shopkeepers took out freedoms at New York; but after 1730, their numbers more than trebled, and retail trade began to flourish. General merchants still supplied most of the groceries and provisions consumed at New York. Although the retail provision trade developed slowly, Manhattan taste for European "creations" led to an expansion of general shops, resembling in embryo the modern department store. At the "New Store in Hanover Square," in 1736 the shopping center of Manhattan, one might have bought haberdashery, dry goods, laces, pictures, pipes, snuff, juniper berries, cutlery, hardware, and glass. Some few persons at New York sought a profit in one line of goods. The New York cosmetic industry was inaugurated in 1736, with the announcement by a Mrs. Edwards of "An admirable Beautifying Wash, for Hands Face and Neck, it makes the skin soft, smooth and plump, it likewise takes away Redness, Freckles, Sun-Burnings, or Pimples, and cures Postules, Itchings, Ring-worms, Tetters: Scurf, Morphew, and other like Deformities of the Face and Skin, (Intirely free from any Corroding Quality) and brings to an exquisite Beauty, with Lip Salve and Tooth Powder, all Sold very Cheap." With such potions as these did New York gentlewomen, like their sophisticated sisters in all ages, seek to improve on nature.

At Newport, much of the merchandising remained in the hands of merchants, who kept retail shops at their wharves or sometimes further uptown. So many of the inhabitants were either sailors or connected in some way with the town's shipping, venturing their small savings in some stock or other, that it appears that "everyone in Newport had something to sell."

Most of Charles Town's traffic in general commodities with the plantations fell into the hands of "country factors," who marketed planters' crops. As a consequence, retail shopkeepers in the town confined their stocks to imported groceries, hardware, and dry goods for local consumption, or to specialties such as millinery goods or wines for both local and country custom. Carolinians paid dearly for their goods. "This place is within a trifle as dear as the West Indies," Mark Catesby complained; "few European goods are sold for less than 300 p. cent and oftener for 400 or 500."

By 1742, retail merchandising had made a flourishing beginning in every town; and at Boston and Philadelphia, with their wider and more sophisticated markets, it had reached as high a stage of development as in the second city of England. Only the strictest candor forbids the application of this rhyming description of Temple Street, Bristol, to such New World thoroughfares as Cornhill or Market Street:

> The Spacious Street, where London Wares
> Display the tawdry Pageantry of Fairs,
> Here's the whole Wardrobe of the female Dress
> In wealthy folds a standing Camp possess.
> Temptations offered to the Virgins there
> To choose a Marriage-dress of Modish Air.

As in the previous period, much of the retail trade in each town continued to be conducted by artisans who, while marketing the products of their own manufacture, frequently sold other items as well. The most important development among the skilled crafts was the increasing number of highly specialized arts and luxury industries.

The auction increased in popularity as a form of merchandising. At Philadelphia, nearly every variety of article or property could be disposed of by inch of candle. Whether it were a ship, a house and chattels, or a lot of imported merchandise to be sold, auctions were well attended, and timely passing of the bottle insured brisk bidding. Flagrant abuses, whereby poor people especially suffered loss by enforced sales, led in 1729 to an act of the assembly giving the corporation power of regulation. In 1730, this body appointed Patrick Baird sole vendue master and, to avoid competition with private shopkeepers, forbade him to auction goods under the value of 20 shillings. Yet, in 1742, tradesmen again protested the prejudice to their interests caused by the auctioneer's disposing of "merchandise in Small Quantities," and the corporation had to raise the limit to 40 shillings on all items save clothing and secondhand goods.

In other towns, too, the auction enjoyed considerably popularity. In December, 1732, William Dyer and Nicholas Easton disposed of the estate of Daniel Seblar by auction at the Newport schoolhouse; at this time the town appointed William Thurston under bond to conduct all vendues fairly. New York, too, had official vendue masters; and at Charles Town, regular slave auctions were held after 1733 at the new market house. Boston merchants often auctioned off shipments of merchandise, rather than selling them by usual wholesale or retail channels. Ships and marine equipment were generally disposed of in this fashion. In 1731, Thomas Fleet, printer, announced his newly fitted auction room at the Heart and Crown, as well as his well-known "Tallent" at the business. His principal stock turned out to be books, household goods, and wearing apparel.

The gambling spirit of the townsmen showed itself in the prevalence of lotteries. Nowhere was this method of disposing of goods so frequently employed as at Newport. In 1732, John Coddington "sold by Lottery" a large wharf running off Thomas Street, 12 lots of land, and a parcel of imported goods, and within a space of two months the *Rhode Island Gazette* carried notices of eight different lotteries. The man behind most of them was Augustus Lucas; and at Boston, where lotteries were forbidden, Elias Boutineau managed the sale of his tickets. The institution also found favor at New York and Philadelphia; but in all towns, merchants, shopkeepers, and auctioneers condemned it as prejudicial to legitimate trade and conducive to fraud. Before the period closed, New York, Pennsylvania, and Rhode Island had all joined the bay colony in outlawing private lotteries.

As the towns grew into cities, the problem of feeding swelling populations became ever more pressing, producing as a consequence great activity in the establishment and regulation of markets, fairs, and other agencies for the distribution of foodstuffs. Philadelphia's location in the finest agricultural region of the colonies assured its market ample and varied provisions. Although the corporation had built new stalls for the High Street market in 1720, 30 more had to be erected two years later at a cost of £400. In another eight years, 20 additional stalls were put up between the Court House and the Delaware River "for the accomodation of such as bring provisions from the Jerseys." Further enlargements took place in 1736, when the corporation also spent £200 for the paving of Market Street and the installation of posts to protect the new movable stalls with their coverings of painted canvas. At this time the market booths and shambles extended down the middle of High (Market) Street from Front to Third, a distance of about a quarter of a mile.

The principal problem in the operation of this splendid plant arose over the collection of rents. Stall lessees continually fell behind in their payments, and in 1721 the gentlemen who financed the new buildings demanded security for their investment from the corporation. The butchers, as chief delinquents, pleaded the excessiveness of the rents and succeeded in obtaining a reduction. The next year, however, some of them still failed to remit; and the common council, with its usual energy in matters pertaining to its income, decided to use "all lawful means" to secure its due.

Cleanliness and good order characterized the Philadelphia market. Slaughtering and the "Smoking of Tobacco" were strictly forbidden in the market house, and large fines awaited those who cast refuse of any sort in the stalls. "Persons blowing of Meat, Selling Goods, bringing Empty Carts & lying of Horses in the Market place" met with severe treatment from the market committee. Forestalling by hucksters, who met people coming to market "at the end of the Streets" to buy up their provisions, was stopped in 1728.

The excellence of the Philadelphia market aroused envy and admiration everywhere in the colonies. Robert Parke wrote in 1724 that "all sorts of provisions are Extraordinary Plenty in Philadelphia market, where the Country people bring their commodities." At the close of the period, William Black of Virginia, while visiting the Quaker town, penned a charming description of this institution:

The days of the Market are Tuesday and Friday, where you may be Supply'd with every Necessary for the Supply of Life thro'ut the whole year, both Extraordinary Good and reasonably Cheap, it is allowed by Foreigners to be the best of its bigness in the known World, and undoubtedly the largest in America; I got to this place by 7 [a.m.]; and had no small Satisfaction in seeing the pretty Creatures, the young Ladies, traversing the place from Stall to Stall, where they could make the best Market, some with their Maid behind them with a Basket to carry home the Purchase, Others that were designed to buy trifles, as a fresh Butter, a dish of Green Peas, or the like, had the Good Nature and Humility enough to be their own Porters.

In contrast to the one large market at Philadelphia, New York had many. Ownership of all was vested in the corporation, which until 1741 rented stalls in each directly to tradesmen. After this date, all market houses, with the right to sublet them, were leased at public auction to the highest bidder. The five markets established before 1720 served until 1738, the Countess Key and Clark's Ferry markets undergoing some enlargement and repair. Residents of the South and Dock wards built a new market in Broad Street in 1738, which the corporation generously accepted for the public use. About the same time, expansion created a demand for a market in the West Ward, where citizens erected the Oswego market on Broadway. This structure served as the distributing point for the "great quantities" of provisions frequently brought from Hackensack, Tappan, and "other parts up North River." No meats were sold here until 1741, when countrymen received permission to sell them "by the Joynt or in Pieces."

Save when epidemics ravaged the city, Manhattan markets offered an ample supply of all varieties of meat and produce. In 1731 the prevalence of smallpox frightened "Country People from Supplying this Place," and the market in consequence grew very slim. Markets opened every weekday at sunrise, closing at sunset, and no huckster could buy in them before noon. Efficient clerks maintained the high quality of merchandise by levying fines of 40 shillings on the unscrupulous traders who sold "unwholesome or Stale victuals, . . . Blown meat or Leprous Swine."

Extension of settlement in Newport south along Thames Street made necessary a new market there, and in 1732 the town erected one at the foot of King Street. A year later the town meeting voted to build a "mercat House" at the head of the Dock between the Carr and Tillinghast wharves. Close to the ferry slip, this market received most of the produce from the Narrangansett country. Fish in plenty were to be had in the bay. The new buildings were large and well equipped; town meetings were held in the ferry market house, and both markets appear to have been places of popular resort.

Charles Town citizens erected the town's first market house in 1722, on the bay at Tradd Street, but repeal of the incorporation act deprived the southern community of a planned market system, leaving it to struggle along under the inadequate law of 1710 as rarely enforced by deputies of absentee market clerks who owed their appointments to the Duke of Newcastle. The consumer suffered from the fact that Negroes could "buy and sell, and be Hucksters . . . , whereby they wait Night and Day on the several Wharfs and buy up many Articles necessary for the . . . Inhabitants, and make them pay exorbitant Price." Absence of proper market officials encouraged irresponsible hucksters, forestallers, and regraters, and the perpetration of scandalous frauds in weights and measures. All this the grand jury presented as "intolerable hardship" in 1735, and the inhabitants prodded the assembly into passage of another inadequate market act. Although a fine building was erected at Broad and Meeting streets for the daily sale of provisions and meat, Charles Town did not until 1739 have a really well-regulated market. The authorities now appointed their own clerk of the market to superintend its business, which began at sunrise, and forbade purchases by any huckster until the ringing of the 9:00 o'clock bell. At the old Market Place on the Middle Bridge a structure was built for the sale of all produce save meats. Under the new law, English market practice was closely followed, and Charles Town for the first time enjoyed the benefits of proper regulation of its food supply.

Continued opposition by countryfolk prevented establishment of a market at Boston for many years. Those favoring erection of a market urged the benefit to farmers as well as tradesmen, and pointed to the successful operation of the system at Philadelphia. The town suffered considerably from the buying up of provisions by hucksters, Indians, Negroes, and mulatto servants, who resold them at exorbitant prices; but all efforts to prevent the abuse failed, and the question became a football in local politics for several years. After repeated votes in turbulent sessions the town meeting decided by a very narrow margin in 1734 to open markets at Eliot's Wharf, the Dock, and the Old North Church. Though the *News Letter* hailed the event with enthusiasm, rural opposition soon revived, securing by a close vote in the town meeting of March, 1736, the discontinuance of the clerks of the market. Feeling ran very high, and on the night of March 24, 1737, a "Number of Persons Unknown," disguised as clergymen, demolished the Middle Market House and several adjacent shops, and "sawed asunder" the posts of the North Market. The country faction, with its artisan and laborer allies in the town, meant real business, and the market experiment had soon to be abandoned.

Nevertheless, those in favor of the project did not despair; and in July, 1740, Peter Faneuil came forward with an offer to build the town a market house. On the morning of July 14, so many people attended the town meeting called to discuss Faneuil's proposal that it had to be adjourned to the Brattle Street Church, where, in anticipation of a stormy session, it was first resolved that the town should be responsible for any damage done to pews or building. When, after bitter debate, the vote was called for, the promarket group directed the assessors to bring in their lists; so that "none might be allowed to Vote in the Affair, Excepting . . . such as were Rated in the last Tax Two Shillings and One Penny." Amid "Heat and Vehemence on both Sides," property thus triumphed over numbers, and Boston accepted Faneuil's magnificent gift by a vote of 367 to 360. Work on the building, designed by John Smibert, began immediately; and on September 24, 1742, Faneuil Hall was opened with appropriate ceremonies.

As the century wore on, fairs became less important, tending to move out into the country districts, where they frequently became the object of excursions by town dwellers. The only town fair was that held semi-annually at Philadelphia. "They sell no Cattle nor horses nor living Creatures," wrote Robert Parke, "but altogether Merchants Goods . . . & all Sorts of Necessarys fit for our Wooden Country. & here all young men and women that wants wives or husbands may be Supplyed."

During these years of peace, all towns normally enjoyed an adequate grain supply. Boston authorities, however, continued to keep a public granary ready to open when conditions should call for it. In 1729 the town built a permanent timber structure on the Common near the Alms House, and provided another "Grainery" at the North End four years later. The keeper, appointed by the town in 1737, had instructions not to deliver more than a half bushel of grain to a person at one time. Notwithstanding these commendable precautions, occasional shortages occurred. In contrast to Boston's concern for its food supply stood Charles Town, where, because nearby planters raised only enough grain for their own use, the townsfolk had to depend on shipments from Pennsylvania and New York. This kept prices continually high; and frequently, as in 1741, the community found itself "entirely without Flour or Bread of any Sort."

Carters and porters in all the towns carried goods to and from wharves and shops. In general, they quietly performed their duties and needed no official regulation. At New York, however, the custom of licensing drivers and regulating their charges survived. Hackney coaches stood for hire in Boston and Philadelphia, while livery stables kept teams or saddle horses available in all towns.

The townsmen never seriously questioned the ideals of their mercantilistic age, in accordance with which authorities in each community rigidly continued to order the economic life of the inhabitants. Although no change was made in the policy of restricting the exercise of trade within the towns to freemen or inhabitants, the coming in of foreigners made it extremely difficult to enforce. Charles Town welcomed all white immigrants, but every other town made determined efforts to confine the privileges of trading to persons who paid scot and lot. Peddlers and chapmen were everywhere forbidden to hawk their wares from house to house.

By 1720, all towns had made regulations to insure fair dealing by merchants and tradesmen, and the use of standard weights and measures. After this date, increased business necessitated strict official supervision over the trading practices of inhabitants. Millers, meat-packers, and coopers were constantly in need of surveillance at New York and Philadelphia. Many tended to pack poor-quality flour and meat in casks of false size. The Pennsylvania Assembly regulated the "Gauging of Cask" in 1722, and the next year laid an embargo on exportation of unmerchantable flour. Important additions to this act were made in 1725 and 1734. This action resulted from requests from the corporation and from newspaper publicity given the "disgrace" brought on by unscrupulous packers and bolters, who had secured a bad name for the colony in the West Indies. After 1723 the quality of Pennsylvania products improved so much that inferior New York goods were rapidly driven out of West Indian markets. Manhattan merchants memorialized their assembly in vain for cask and packing regulations. Rhode Island passed acts to insure fair practices in the lumber, cooperage, and meat-packing industries in 1731.

Charges of sharp practice by Bostonians had some foundation in fact. In 1725, "Peter Bolt" complained in the *Courant* of the town being "unmercifully pinch'd by the Bakers, whose Bread very often wants nearly a quarter Part of its due Weight, notwithstanding the extraordinary Diligence of the Bread weighers, who daily seize great Quantities of it." He attributed the evil to the practice of permitting hucksters to sell bread, since the bakers had to give short weight in order to make a profit. Eventually, this agitation led to more frequent judicial visitations at the bakeries. Out of 70,000 shingles coming from Weymouth in 1725, the surveyors burned 60,000 on Copp's Hill, "they not being made according to Law," and on another occasion a shipment from Hingham met a similar end. Within the town, abuses in the sale of firewood were notorious, and carters and sloopmen were frequently guilty of "guessing" the weight of hay in order to evade the weighmaster's fees. In general, however, town officers successfully reduced such unfair practices to a minimum.

The increasing volume of business in the towns and the fact that most available specie went to redress adverse trade balances with the mother country placed a tremendous strain on the feeble financial structure of the colonies. In addition, country districts found all their coin filtering into the towns to pay for imported goods. The only known exit from the dilemma was the issue of paper money. Not even the most conservative of merchants denied the need for a currency, which was acutely felt by all classes. The difficulty lay in controlling the amounts of script to be printed. New York and Pennsylvania issues were well managed and, on the whole, served their purpose. In South Carolina, depreciation was rapid, until by 1730 bills of credit were exchanged at 7 to 1 with sterling.

In New England the currency problem contributed an important chapter in urban history by deepening the conscious antagonisms already existing between town and country dwellers. The agriculturally-minded countryside, denuded of coin and bound in financial dependence to the seaports, demanded a more liberal expansion of the currency than city merchants with their eyes on world markets dared permit. In Rhode Island, after almost unrestricted issue of province bills during the twenties, Newport business interests found their credit impaired and trade with their Boston connections impossible to conduct in depreciated paper. Massachusetts managed its paper currency more conservatively; but its inevitable depreciation, coupled with the business depression of the thirties, produced bitter complaints of the tightness of money from debtor classes in both town and country, intensifying a social cleavage that had been long a-growing. The "Land Bank" of 1739, a proposal to issue bills of credit backed by real estate and by the personal security of

"Artisans and Traders," crystallized antagonisms between agricultural and debtor classes and mercantile and business interests. Steadfast opposition from Boston merchants, governor, and council, and threat of parliamentary intervention, finally quashed the scheme. But the natural divergence between town and country interests, now conscious and vocal, and the latter's resentment of control by the former, were come to stay. In Rhode Island the showdown between inflationary country and mercantile city parties was not resolved for many years, and in Massachusetts the scars from the Land Bank fracas lasted throughout the colonial era.

Philadelphia experienced a lack of small change in the winter of 1740–41, and English halfpence in large quantities had to be imported to relieve the stringency. Trouble arose over the passing of these coins as pennies, and in January the bakers refused to accept them, ceasing their baking till the value should be changed. After two nights of mob activity, during which numerous merchants suffered broken windows, the frightened corporation hastened to adjust the difficulty, and in June issued a proclamation setting the rate at 15 English halfpence to the shilling, and declaring that he who refused to accept them at their legalized value "ought to be deemed a Disturber of the Publick Peace."

Improvements in the postal service in these years greatly facilitated the transaction of interurban business. The route was extended from Philadelphia as far as Annapolis by 1722, and reached Williamsburg, Virginia, in 1732. North Carolina's delinquency created a temporary obstacle to a through route to South Carolina; but Charles Town, too, enjoyed monthly postal connection with the rest of colonial America by 1740. Not only was the colonial post extended, but under the management of Governor Spotswood, service considerably improved; and north of Virginia, regular weekly post were maintained.

Rapid economic development everywhere characterized these years. Fostered by world peace and undeterred by temporary depression, colonial commerce enjoyed unprecedented expansion; and the appearance of surplus capital, specialized business services, and the beginnings of modern credit revealed how complex had become its needs and organization. Profits from trade sought outlets in speculation in land and in manufacturing enterprises sufficiently vigorous to inspire panic among industrial interests in the mother country. As the period advanced, Boston largely lost the great advantage reaped from its priority in the shipbuilding and carrying trades; and the importance of the production of staple crops that could find a place in the economic planning of a mercantile empire or of a populous, fertile, and expanding backcountry became increasingly evident. The doubled population and growing wealth of Charles Town are instances of the former. To the latter, Philadelphia owed the sound commercial prosperity that was soon to make the Quaker town the first city of colonial America, and next only to Bristol and London in the Empire. New York experienced a temporary depression in these years and was at all times overshadowed in the provision export trade by her younger and vigorous southern rival. But Newport, on the strength of a growing merchant marine, climbed upward on the economic ladder and seriously threatened Boston interests in the Caribbean. Attacked from all sides, in the local carrying trade by the smaller ports of New England, and on a wider map by the expanding economic orbits of other colonial capitals, the former "mart town," though still the largest on the continent, began in the 1730's to experience the decline in population and the contraction of business that were to continue until after the Revolution. Boston had for a time to yield its position to Philadelphia.

4. AMERICAN COASTWISE TRADE*

While foreign commerce, particularly with England, overshadowed all else during the entire colonial period, the nature of American coastwise trade serves to illustrate the adaptive and opportunistic character of marketing activities. The commodities native to the South could be processed and exported in large quantities. Production in the northern colonies was on a smaller scale and more diversified, lending itself to exchange and distribution within the various American markets. Conditions eventually encouraged a degree of specialization in the products shipped to and from the ports of Boston, New York, and Philadelphia. The British navigation acts greatly strengthened the shipping industry of the northern colonies by assuring their vessels a virtual monopoly of intercolonial trade. Chaotic conditions prevailed following the Revolutionary War, with the various states vying with one another for competitive advantage. The discriminatory legislation they passed encouraged the subsequent adoption of a federal Constitution assigning Congress the power to regulate interstate commerce.

THE COASTWISE COMMERCE of the continental colonies planted in America had its origin partly in the work of collecting commodities for export and of distributing imported goods, and partly in the interchange of the various colonial products. The Plymouth colonists established trading posts along the New England coast for the collection of furs and other native commodities, from the sale of which they secured the funds to pay their debt to the English investors who had furnished the capital for their colonizing venture. In 1631, Governor Winthrop built the *Blessing of the Bay* for trade with the other plantations, and he records that during the same year a vessel arrived from Virginia laden with corn and tobacco to be exchanged for fish.

To the Dutch who settled at New Amsterdam may be given the credit for being the first to develop an extensive coastwise commerce on a systematic basis. From New Amsterdam, small vessels sailed to the English plantations both to the north and to the south, exchanging gunpowder, salt, clothing, and European manufactures of all kinds for large quantities of tobacco, grain, fish, and furs, part of which was consumed

* Reprinted from E. R. Johnson, T. W. Van Metre, G. G. Huebner, and D. S. Hanchett, *History of Domestic and Foreign Commerce of the United States*, Vol. I (Washington, D.C.: Carnegie Institution, 1915), pp. 162–74.

at the Dutch colony, but most of which was transported to the markets of Holland. In the ubiquitous Dutch trading vessels, England found the greatest obstacle to her own commercial and naval progress, and it was only after a stubborn conflict that the restrictive commercial policy of the Commonwealth prevailed and the formidable rival was crushed. In 1664, New Amsterdam was seized by the English; and though the Dutch continued for a time to share in the American trade, and even recovered their colony for a brief period, their power in the American continent, both political and commercial, was broken; and before the close of the 17th century, Dutch shipping virtually ceased to figure in either the foreign or the domestic trade of the English colonies.

Meanwhile, even before any attempt had been made to exclude the Dutch from the English colonial trade, the shipping of New England had begun to assume a position of no small importance in the intercolonial and oversea commerce of America. During most of the first century of their existence the New England colonies had a surplus of grain for export, which, with fish and other provisions and imported wares from Europe, found a ready market in Virginia and Maryland as well as in the West Indies. From Virginia and Maryland, large quantities of tobacco were taken coastwise to Boston and Salem; and regardless of the admonition of Charles I, this product was then sold in the markets of continental Europe; while from the West Indies, sugar and dyewoods were collected for export, and molasses was imported for the rum manufacture. Aside from the coastwise trade with the southern colonies, the New England people developed a thriving and prosperous trade along their own coasts, collecting at their important seaports the grain, fish, fur, and other products of the smaller settlements, and distributing among them the imports from Europe and the other colonies.

There were several reasons why the colonies of New England, as well as New York—and later, Pennsylvania—should develop a commerce to be carried on by their own people and in their own ships. In the first place, the comparative lack of native commodities which could be sold in England made it almost imperative that the people of these settlements should provide their own vessels to transport their surplus products to whatever markets they could find, and it was inevitable that a portion of the population should engage in trade as a means of securing a livelihood. The development of the fisheries gave a tremendous stimulus to shipbuilding; and both of these industries, as well as the rum manufacture and small-farm agriculture, were conducive to the growth of seaport cities, which became the centers of a thriving and prosperous commerce. With such advantages as cheap ships, little external competition, and well-located markets, the traders of the northern colonies were able almost completely to monopolize the intercolonial trade of the British possessions in America. In the South, exactly opposite conditions prevailed. The two chief products, tobacco and rice, were demanded in England, and English merchants sent out the ships necessary for their transportation. Agriculture, conducted on a large scale, was the chief industry; navigation and shipping remained undeveloped; few cities arose; and the number of merchants and traders was relatively small.

For the development of coastwise trade, conditions in the northern colonies were much more favorable than in the southern. In the former, the population lived near the sea; and while there was a large number of ports to be found along the coast, it was from only a few of them that an important oversea trade was carried on. To these larger ports, numerous small shipments of articles intended for the export trade were carried from the other settlements, and from them were distributed the imported wares which poured in from Europe, Africa, the Western Islands, and the West Indies. To this business of collection and distribution was added the interchange of colonial products intended for domestic consumption, a trade which became increasingly important during the 18th century, when New England was compelled to rely for breadstuffs on the farms of Pennsylvania, New Jersey, and New York. In the South a large part of the oversea trade was carried on directly from the plantation wharves which lined the numerous navigable rivers, a single plantation often being able to give employment to two or more vessels. The work of the collection of exports and the distribution of imports in small vessels was relatively unimportant; and consequently, the local coastwise trade never approached the magnitude of the local trade of the northern colonies, where production was on a smaller scale, industry more diversified, and trading more active. The coastwise trade between the North and the South came to be of some importance, but it was small in comparison either to the local coastwise trade of the northern colonies or to the trade between the continental colonies and the West Indies—the most important branch of the intercolonial trade. Only a small amount of southern products was consumed in the northern colonies, and the demand for the products of the northern settlements among the southern plantations was likewise relatively small.

During most of the colonial period, Virginia and Maryland raised grain in sufficiently large quantities to have a surplus for export, and many of the southern plantations maintained small fishing industries to supply domestic needs. Rum was probably the most important domestic commodity purchased from New England, and even rum could be secured as easily from Jamaica as from Rhode Island. The exportation of the southern surplus to Europe fell for the most part into the hands of British merchants; and though the carriers of New England and New York collected some southern tobacco and rice at northern ports for shipment to Europe, the quantity was very small as compared to that carried directly in the vessels of England. The shipping of England likewise carried to the southern planters most of the European imports they consumed.

BRITISH NAVIGATION ACTS AND THE COLONIAL COASTWISE TRADE

The enactment of the acts of trade of 1660, 1663, and 1673 had a tendency to crystallize the conditions of trade described above. That is, these laws practically gave control of the intercolonial trade to the shipping of the northern colonies, made direct trade with England the most important branch of the commerce of the southern colonies, and greatly limited the possibility of the expansion of the coastwise trade between the two sections. The strict enforcement of this act [of 1660] would have meant, of course, that a vessel sailing from England would not be able to transport any of the enumerated articles from one colony to another, and that for the most part this trade would be left to colonial vessels. There is no printed evidence available to show whether this apparent discrimination in favor of colonial vessels was ever rigorously enforced; but it is true, nevertheless, that the colonial vessels did almost completely monopolize the intercolonial trade, and not until after the Revolution did ships from England engage to any large extent in the carrying trade between the continental colonies and the West Indies.

Under the law of 1660 the colonists had perfect freedom of trade in enumerated commodities and were able to secure them for their own consumption at a smaller price than was charged the English consumers, who were compelled to pay an import duty. This privilege, however, the colonial merchants soon abused, especially in connection with the Virginia tobacco trade. It appears that after the tobacco was landed at a New England port, no effort was made at the time of its reexporation to secure a bond that it would be shipped to some other plantation or to some port in England or Wales. Consequently, the tobacco was carried directly to continental Europe, and not only did the English crown suffer the loss of the revenue it would have obtained had the tobacco been sent to England, but the English merchants were deprived of the commissions they would have received had the trade passed through their hands. It was estimated that in 1663 the English government was losing annually £10,000 on account of the activity of the New England merchants in the Virginia tobacco trade.

To prevent the loss of revenue, and to compel the shipment directly to England of the enumerated commodities beyond the amount actually demanded for colonial consumption, the act of 1673 was passed, levying export duties on enumerated commodities shipped from one colonial port to another, the duties being practically the same as the import duties paid on the goods when taken to England. For a time, this law had but little effect. The New England traders smuggled tobacco out of the southern colonies and exported it to Holland and France as before. Moreover, they interpreted the law to mean that once they had paid the export duties required, they were then at liberty to send the tobacco wherever they chose. After carrying tobacco to ports on the European Continent, they returned with cargoes of manufactures which, contrary to the law of 1663, were not "laden and shipped in England." These open violations of the acts of trade called forth a vigorous protest from British merchants, who, in a petition to the King in 1676, stated that New England was becoming the "great mart and staple" of all the colonies, and that England was being robbed of her trade and the King of his revenue. Notwithstanding the opinion of the attorney general of England that the act of 1673 did not abolish the necessity of giving bond for the shipment of enumerated goods to some English dominion, the direct trade with the Continent of Europe continued. Even after the passage of the act of 1696, which specifically provided that bond should be given whenever the enumerated articles were shipped and that the export duties should be paid just as often as these articles were sent from one colony to another, the illicit trade was carried on to some extent.

However, it is apparent that the act of 1673 had a restrictive effect on the coastwise trade. There is little doubt that but for the acts of trade, Boston, New York, and Philadelphia would have competed actively for the trade of Virginia; and if so, the coastwise commerce between the northern and southern colonies would have attained a much greater magnitude. The largest part of the colonial shipping belonged to merchants who preferred to carry the commodities they themselves bought and sold. The carriage of tobacco and rice directly from the southern colonies to England apparently did not appeal to them as a profitable business, and the field was left to the shipping of England.

CHARACTER AND VOLUME OF INTERCOLONIAL COASTWISE TRADE

While there is no source of information from which one may derive an accurate statement of the development of the coastwise trade during the 18th century, there is abundant evidence that indicates the general character of the trade and shows its relative importance. Next to the West Indian trade, the coastwise trade of the northern colonies was unquestionably the most valuable branch of commerce carried on by American merchants and shippers, though neither the West Indian trade of the colonies as a whole nor the coastwise trade ever attained during the colonial period the value of the total direct commerce between the colonies and Europe. Among the northern colonies, New Hampshire, Connecticut, New Jersey, and Delaware had comparatively little shipping engaged in the transatlantic or the West Indian trade; and their people sold their surplus produce at the important seaports of the neighboring colonies and bought at those cities the salt, clothing, sugar, tea, spices, wines, and manufactured goods which had been brought in from Europe and the West Indies. In 1725 the little colony of New Hampshire reported that its trade with Boston had a value of £5,000 a year. In 1730 the general assembly of Connecticut reported to the Board of Trade: "The Trade of the Colony is but small. Horses and lumber are exported from hence to the West Indies, for which we receive in exchange, sugar, salt, molasses and rum. What provisions we can spare, and some quantity of tar and turpentine, are sent to Boston and New York, and Rhode Island, for which we receive European goods."

Forty-two vessels, the largest of which was of a burden of 60 tons, belonged to the people of the colony. There was no trade with Europe "excepting only a few voyages to Ireland with timber and some few, one or two, that have of late been built here made their voyage to Bristol, there sold ship and cargo and brought their returns hither." All kinds of British manufactures, such as "woolen cloath, silks, glass, nails, scythes, pewter, brass and fire-arms," were imported, but they were nearly all purchased from the merchants of Boston.

In the report of the Board of Trade on the state of the plantations in 1721, New Jersey was said to have no ships but coasting vessels, in which the colonists sent their produce, chiefly grain and cattle, to New York and Philadelphia, to be exchanged for English manufactures. Regular packet service was established between all the more important northern ports, and both travel and trade among these cities grew constantly in volume. During the three years from June 24, 1714, to June 24, 1717, the vessels clearing from Boston to other ports on the continent numbered 390, with a tonnage of 11,589. This was equal to the tonnage cleared from Great Britain and about one third of the tonnage cleared for the West Indies. During the three years from 1715 to 1718 the clearances from New York for other continental colonies amounted to 4,234 tons. In one week in May, 1741, Boston received 6,650 bushels of corn, 200 bushels of peas, 180 bushels of beans, 534 barrels of flour, 291 barrels of beef, 278 barrels of pork, and 79 barrels of rice. Governor George Clinton wrote to the Board of Trade and Plantations in 1749 that New York received from the northern and southern portions of the continent "Fish, Oil, Blubber, Whale Fins, Turpentine Oil, Seal Skins, Hops, Cyder, Flax, Bricks, Cole, Lamp Black, certain Wrought Iron, Tin and Brasiery, Joinery, various Carriages and Chairs"; while to the English districts north and south, New York sent "Provisions, Chocolate, Lumber, European and India Goods with those enumerated in the Plantation Trade Acts and such other Imported here for conveyance home regularly." After 1730, New York refined sugar for sale to the other colonies. Boston was the center of a large domestic trade in beef, butter, timber, fish, and rum, while New York and Philadelphia were centers for the collection and distribution of flour and grain. Boston would unquestionably have been the center of a considerable coastwise trade in domestic woolens had it not been for the repressive policy of England. The hatmaking industry of the northern colonies was also restricted; and as a consequence, there was little trade in colonial manufactures, if one excepts breadstuffs, lumber, and rum.

The trade between the northern and southern colonies gradually expanded. With the increase of population, there was a growing interchange of products, the tobacco, rice, and naval stores of the South being traded for rum, flour, fish, beef, pork, and European manufactured goods. In the report of the Board of Trade above referred to, several statements were made indicating the nature of the state of the trade between North and South during the early 18th century. Maryland sent tobacco, beef, pork, and grain to the other colonies and received in return rum and sugar. Virginia likewise sold tobacco and provisions to the other plantations. North Carolina had but little commerce, and that was carried on by the sloops of New England, which brought clothing and ironware to exchange for pork, corn, pitch, and tar, the two articles last mentioned being carried first to New England and then to Great Britain. Few of the southern colonies possessed any shipping to speak of, the planters depending upon the merchants and carriers of Great Britain and New England.

During the early part of the 18th century an interesting coastwise commerce began between New England and the southern colonies which, as Weeden says, "sheds light both upon the general development of coasting trade and upon the peculiar tendency of early New England enterprise to join capital and labor." During the winter, when there was little fishing carried on, the owners of small fishing sloops would load their craft with salt, rum, sugar, molasses, iron- and woodenware, hats, caps, cloth, handkerchiefs, and stockings, which they carried to the southern colonies and peddled from place to place, returning early in the spring with a valuable lot of pitch and tar, and supplies of corn and pickled pork. These trading expeditions of the fishermen were private ventures entirely, which offered a good opportunity to secure a profit even during the winter season from the investment in fishing craft.

Thus, while the most important portion of the commerce of the southern plantations was with Great Britain, the trade with the colonies of the North formed a regular feature of their economic life. Part of this trade was carried on in connection with the West India trade of the northern colonies, vessels stopping on the voyage each way, once to exchange rum and imported merchandise for staves, headings, and provisions for the sugar islands, and again to leave sugar, molasses, rum, and Negroes. Goods which had been smuggled into New England from Europe were sold regularly in the South, though probably not in large quantities, and manufactures of all kinds from England were also distributed among the southern ports by the northern merchants. Peter Faneuil and Thomas Amory, Boston merchants, traded regularly with the southern colonies, and the merchants of New York and Philadelphia also bought and sold there. The Newport traders had dealings with merchants at practically every port of any importance along the entire coast, selling rum, clothing, manufactures, and slaves, and buying provisions, rice, tobacco, and other native products. That they met with competition is indicated by a letter from Charleston, South Carolina, in 1770, saying that the market there had been supplied with sugar from New York and Philadelphia. That the acts of trade were not enforced with complete effectiveness is indicated by the sailing orders given a Captain Hammond in 1770 to take a cargo of rice, sugar, and ginger to Gothenburg or to Hamburg and lay out the proceeds in Bohea tea and other articles, which were to be consigned to one of the French islands in the West Indies, but carried to Rhode Island and secretly unloaded.

The volume of the coastwise trade of the colonies on the eve of the Revolution is indicated in Table 1, showing the entrances and clearances at the ports of the northern and southern colonies in 1769. The statistics in the fourth column of Table 1 indicate fairly well the volume of the coast-

TABLE 1

GROSS REGISTERED TONNAGE OF THE VESSELS ENTERED AND CLEARED AT THE PORTS OF THE NORTHERN AND SOUTHERN COLONIES IN 1769

	From Great Britain and Ireland	Southern Ports of Europe and Africa	British and Foreign West Indies	Continent of America, Bahamas, Newfound-land, etc.	Total
		ENTERED			
Total for northern colonies	30,353	20,906	60,888	78,198	190,345
Total for southern colonies	60,357	13,245	34,028	34,171	141,801
Total for all colonies	90,710	34,151	94,916	112,369	332,146
		CLEARED			
Total for northern colonies	31,675	21,888	63,651	72,875	190,089
Total for southern colonies	67,466	20,713	32,731	28,323	149,213
Total for all colonies	99,121	42,601	96,382	101,198	339,302
Total entrances and clearances ..	189,831	76,752	191,298	213,567	671,448

wise trade. Part of the entrances and clearances here indicated were for the trade with Newfoundland, Canada, Nova Scotia, Florida, Bermuda, and the Bahamas; and in order to consider only the trade among the Thirteen Colonies, it would be necessary to make some subtraction, though at the most the deduction would not amount to more than 25,000 tons. Even with this deduction, the coastwise trade of the Thirteen Colonies would, from the standpoint of tonnage or shipping engaged, rank among the leading branches of colonial commerce. It may be safely assumed, however, that its value was less than that of the trade with Great Britain or of the West Indian trade. The most important feature Table 1 brings out is the difference in the character of the commerce of the northern colonies. In the North the coastwise business took high rank in all the colonies, employing in Rhode Island and Connecticut practically one half of the tonnage entered and cleared, and more than one third of the tonnage of the entrances and clearances of Massachusetts, the leading commercial colony. Among the southern colonies the coastwise business held a much less important position. Direct trade with Great Britain, as shown in Table 1, employed almost one half of the tonnage of the entrances and clearances of southern ports, and the coastwise trade was represented by little more than one fifth.

Like all the other branches of trade carried on in colonial vessels, the coastwise commerce was almost utterly destroyed during the Revolution. American ships which were not employed as privateers were compelled for the most part to lie rotting at the wharves until the war was ended; and though a small amount of trade was carried on among the colonies, the business was dangerous and therefore small and irregular. It was during these years that the need for home manufactures and better means of inland transportation was effectually demonstrated. It is of interest to note that almost as soon as the war ended, steps were taken to improve the inland navigation of Virginia and other states, in order that a sheltered waterway might be provided for at least a part of the distance along the Atlantic coast.

INTERSTATE TRADE AFTER THE REVOLUTION; PROVISIONS OF THE CONSTITUTION

At the close of the war the coastwise trade was at once resumed. It was, in fact, the only branch of the old colonial trade of the American merchants and carriers which it was possible freely to take up again, the trade to the West Indies being forbidden by the navigation laws of Great Britain and the commerce with southern Europe ruined by the withdrawal of British protection against pirates. Direct trade with Great Britain immediately resumed its former volume; but as before, it was carried on chiefly in British ships. For a time the coastwise trade prospered; but before long, in common with the other branches of trade, it experienced a severe depression. Credit everywhere was impaired; there was little money; and the various states, jealous and fearful of the commercial prosperity of one another, began to erect barriers that crippled the commerce of all. New York attempted to break up the trade of Connecticut and New Jersey by imposing heavy fees on every vessel entering from those states. Delaware and New Jersey tried to attract to their ports the foreign trade of Pennsylvania and New York by a system of legislation offering lower import duties and more favorable trade regulations. When Massachusetts and Rhode Island placed almost prohibitive duties on imports carried in British ships, Connecticut admitted such imports free, hoping to obtain a monopoly of domestic trade in British products. Several of the states imposed heavy duties on goods from all other states, with the twofold object of encouraging domestic production and of conserving the supply of coin. It was due primarily to the extreme need of a system of uniform regulation of interstate and foreign trade that the Annapolis Convention was held in 1786, the convention which called the meeting of the body that framed the federal Constitution at Philadelphia in 1787.

The disputes among the makers of the Constitution over what power of commercial regulation should be given to Congress were exceedingly bitter, and in no other phase of the work of the convention did the opposing economic interests of the sections of the country stand out more clearly. The northern navigating and trading states wanted complete power placed in the hands of the federal government; but the southern delegates feared that Congress might at some time, if dominated by the commercial interests of the North, enact a navigation law excluding foreign carriers. The result of such an act could only be a tremendous increase in freight rates, which would impoverish the southern planter and enrich the northern carrier. Almost unanimously, therefore, the southern delegates insisted that a provision be inserted in the Constitution by which Congress would be prohibited from enacting a navigation law unless by a two-thirds vote of both houses. Furthermore, the South demanded that Congress be forbidden to levy export duties or prohibit the importation of slaves. Out of these conflicting views a compromise was eventually reached. Congress was given general power "to regulate commerce with foreign nations, and among the several states, and with the Indian tribes," and empowered to levy import duties on the condition that they be uniform throughout the United States. However, it was stipulated that "no preference shall be given by any regulation of commerce or revenue to the ports of one State over those of another; nor shall vessels bound to or from one State, be obliged to enter, clear, or pay duties in another"; that "no tax or duty shall be laid on articles exported from any State"; and that "the migration or importation of such persons as any of the

States now existing shall think proper to admit, shall not be prohibited by the Congress prior to the year 1808." Furthermore, it was agreed that "no State shall, without the consent of the Congress, lay any imposts or duties on imports or exports, except what may be absolutely necessary for executing its inspection laws; and the net produce of all duties and imposts, laid by any State on imports or exports, shall be for the use of the Treasury of the United States; and all such laws shall be subject to the revision and control of the Congress." No state shall, without the consent of Congress, lay any duty of tonnage or "enter into any agreement or compact with another State, or with a foreign power."

Before the new Constitution went into operation, economic conditions in the United States began to take a turn for the better. Under the stimulating influence of renewed industrial activity, the trade among the states quickly revived. Not only in the commodities of the colonial period did trade expand; but in the products of the growing manufactures and the imports from the newly opened East India markets, a healthy domestic commerce sprang up. However, at the time the new government was launched, there was as yet no indication that the coastwise trade would ever occupy a more important relative position than during the colonial period, when it was exceeded in value both by the direct trade with Europe and by the West Indian trade. Domestic trade of great volume occurs only when there is a sectional diversity of products for which there is a great intersectional demand. Diversity of production of this kind did not exist to a large extent during colonial days; and even at the time of the adoption of the Constitution, there was no indication that conditions favorable to a large interregional domestic commerce would soon arise. But two events, one occurring within a little more than a year after Washington's inauguration and the other four years after, foreshadowed a fundamental change in the economic organization of the nation. The first was the building of a cotton mill by Samuel Slater at Pawtucket, Rhode Island, and the second was the invention of the cotton gin by Eli Whitney. Out of the change heralded by these two events was to grow a domestic commerce, both coastwise and internal, more valuable than the foreign or domestic trade of any other nation of the world.

5. MARKETS FOR COLONIAL MANUFACTURES*

From the very outset, the availability of markets and transportation facilities helped to shape the economic development of American industry. The relative isolation of the colonies, the great difficulties of overland transportation, and restrictive British trade regulations were among the problems confronting colonial producers. These same conditions, however, had their beneficial effects. The monopoly on coastal shipping meant that American colonists would be well aware of the local manufactures needed to supplement those of Great Britain. The cost and delays of land transportation protected the neighborhood industries of inland settlements from competition. Colonial manufacturing was further stimulated by a rapid growth in population, an increasing standard of living, and the development of natural resources in great demand at home and abroad.

THE ISOLATION of the colonists, both local and international, was greater than can now be realized. Cut off by political regulations from many sources of natural trade with European countries and with other American colonies, and separated by a sea voyage of several weeks from what are today near neighbors, it often was impossible for colonial producers to estimate the demand for their commodities abroad or to insure themselves a profitable exchange. In 1734, Governor Cosby wrote: "In case of Spain and Portugal the sales of flour and bread are hindered because the intelligence of a demand reaches us so late that the markets are supplied before our vessels come over." Similar conditions subjected the nascent industries of the colonies to uneven and often destructive competition. Though they were occasionally helped by high prices caused by a scarcity of competing imports, at other times their small capital was exhausted in a struggle with low prices due to an overstock of European merchandise. Goods sometimes sold in America for less than they cost in England. Equally disadvantageous to the colonial tradesman or manufacturer was his isolation in the home market. If he were at an inland town or one of the less frequented ports, there was no regular service by which he could keep informed as to prices and demands for his wares outside the immediate neighborhood. This lack of commercial information and the ever-present

* Reprinted from Victor S. Clark, *History of Manufactures in the United States, 1697–1860* (Washington, D.C.: Carnegie Institution, 1916), pp. 87–122.

difficulty of getting goods to market caused many colonial industries to stagnate as soon as the volume of their production exceeded the demand of their immediate vicinity. Such conditions checked the growth of centralized industries even in the northern colonies, where township organization and closer settlement afforded at least a community market; and in the plantation colonies, they entirely prevented the rise of manufactures. American markets were so dispersed that they were commercially about as remote from the centers of colonial industry as from the ports of Great Britain. English merchantmen were surer of return cargoes than were the coastal vessels that distributed colonial merchandise from settlement to settlement; and as the goods brought to America were far less in volume than those carried eastward, so that ships often came to the colonies in ballast, they formed back loads burdened with relatively lighter freights.

Nevertheless, there were two influences flowing from transportation which were an advantage to colonial manufacturers. American colonists were the distributors of British merchandise, their coasting vessels carrying goods from the warehouse cities to the villages and plantations of the seaboard. They were thus able to gauge in the first instance the tastes and needs of consumers and to supply with the products of local industry any default in importations. Colonial manufactures thus became supplementary to those of Great Britain in constantly widening circles of distribution. In the second place, the cost and delays of land transportation protected the neighborhood industries of inland settlements from competition and further stimulated such industries by lessening the profit of agriculture. This is instanced by the relative development of Pennsylvania and New York in the 18th century. Both were colonies having similar natural resources—timber, iron ore, and wheat lands. New York was a river settlement, and it was estimated that three days' labor would put the produce of any farm in the colony at a boat landing, whence two or three men could navigate to New York a cargo that could be brought to Philadelphia, from the Pennsylvania backcountry, only by 40 wagons, 160 horses, and 80 men. The average cost of carrying a bushel of wheat 100 miles was estimated in New York at 2 pence and in Pennsylvania at 1 shilling. The profits of farming in New York were said to exceed those in Pennsylvania by 30 percent. Partly—perhaps largely—for this reason, Pennsylvania became a seat of diversified industries and home manufactures, while New York remained chiefly a commercial and agricultural colony until the end of the colonial period. The respective destinies of two American states were determined at this early date and were governed then, as they were later, chiefly by transportation influences.

So long as inland traffic was conducted solely along roads and rivers radiating from the principal ports, it opened a market to British and colonial manufactures on practically equal terms. But when overland routes were established, subsidiary centers of manufacture—small in their way, but not unimportant relative to the population—sprang up along their course, and at some competitive advantage supplied purchasers in their own vicinity and the more remote interior. Particular industries thus rose at Worcester and Springfield between Boston and Albany; at Albany itself on the highway to Canada and the Indian country; at Lancaster, Pennsylvania; in the north Maryland towns; and at Winchester and Salem on the great trail southward into the Carolinas. From Pennsylvania, the colony of the Conestoga wagon and land freighting, two routes left Lancaster, through Chambersburg and Cumberland westward, and through Hagerstown, Winchester, and the valley of the Virginia southward. Along the latter, in the wake of the Scotch–Irish and German settlers, wended pack trains for the frontier laden with salt and with Pennsylvania iron and linen. Wagon travel came slowly. The first team was driven from Connecticut to Rhode Island in 1722, more than a century after the settlement of New England; and it was not until 1789, the year of the adoption of the Constitution, that a freight road was open to the Monongahela. During the Revolution, settlement was driven inland by the incursions of the British along the coast, new interior highways were opened and old ones improved, and capital was diverted from sea trading to internal development.

An increase of inland and ocean freights affected differently manufactures for export and those for home consumption. Generally, a rise in the cost of carriage depressed the former and stimulated the latter, because exports brought a smaller return and imports cost more when freights were high, and people therefore turned their attention from making things to be sold abroad to making things to be used at home. Ocean freights upon tar were so heavy, as compared with those between the Baltic ports and England, that American producers were at a disadvantage in the British market. In 1699, this freight was about £4 sterling a ton in time of peace and £6 in time of war. Insurance with convoy was 9 percent. In 1715, it cost £4 per thousand feet to carry lumber from New England to Great Britain. The freight on iron, on account of its lesser bulk, was considerably lower, or 7s. 6d. a ton from Virginia to Bristol or London in 1732. Rates must have fallen decidedly in times of peace, for in 1736 sugar was carried from Boston to Bordeaux for £2 10s. a ton, though the freight on this commodity normally would be as much as or more than that on tar. We have seen that the volume of traffic westward was less than that eastward. This was so true that it was profitable sometimes even to ship coal and limestone from England and the West Indies to the colonies, and Newcastle coals were not infrequently cheaper than wood at Annapolis, New York, and Boston. Colonial merchants complained that their British competitors had better back loading to the sugar colonies than themselves, though this is to be doubted. But though sugar, rum, and molasses were diverted from the West Indies to North America in part by the cheap freights to the northern colonies, the extent of this commerce, favorable to refining and distilling, was somewhat checked by the higher eastbound freights across the Atlantic. The lack of back loads from Europe stimulated the sale abroad of colonial vessels, because owners taking over a vessel with bulky cargo thereby avoided a profitless voyage on their return.

Ocean charges, however, constituted only a fraction of the freight burden borne by colonial commodities and imports. In 1667 the freight from Long Island and Connecticut to Boston, whence produce was then exported, was £1 10s. a ton. It cost a shilling a bushel to carry wheat from Northampton to Windsor, 2 pence from there to Hartford, and 6 pence from Hartford to Boston, or 1s.8d., in colonial currency, for the entire journey. This was nearly one third the market price. In 1673, grain was carried from Hadley to Hartford for from 4 to 6 pence a bushel, and goods brought back in return for 12 shillings a ton. Meanwhile, to ship a barrel of pork or flour from Hadley to Hartford cost 3s. 6d. to 4 shillings, and from thence the freight to Boston was about 3 shillings. A century later, coastwise freight on iron from Baltimore to Massachusetts was about $4.60 a ton, and it cost $2.60 a hogshead to bring rum by land from Philadelphia to Baltimore. The cost of transporting such commodities was less than one eighth of the market price. This explains why agricultural produce was exported so largely in the form of manufactured provisions, for the average saving of freight amounted to 10 or 20 percent of the proceeds from their sale.

Franklin, in his plea for opening the Ohio lands to settlement, presented figures to show that by combined land and water carriage, even at the high rates then prevailing, such agricultural commodities as flax and hemp could be exported, and British manufactures imported, at a profit; and he maintained that those rates were then less than was "daily paid in London for the carriage of course woolens, cutlery, ironware, etc., from several counties in England." This was not a disinterested plea, as Franklin was seeking land grants in the interior, but it may have accorded with facts. Yet the high cost of land carriage did constantly stimulate and protect the manufacture in America of articles which commonly were imported from Great Britain, and it caused a dispersion throughout the country of manufactures by which bulky raw materials were converted into more valuable commodities for exchange.

MANUFACTURES CLASSIFIED BY MARKETS

The manufactures of the colonies may be classified in relation to their market as homespun, domestic-commercial, and foreign-commercial. These terms are not in all cases mutually exclusive, but they describe the dominant consuming area each class of industries served.

Homespun manufactures did not enter into exchange except more or less accidentally. The chief homespun industries were carding, spinning, and weaving wool, flax, hemp, and cotton for clothing and various household uses. Relative to these, in the opinion of the time, other home manufactures were unimportant, yet the latter supplied many wants that are today served by large and highly organized industries. Hardware, tools and implements, furniture, clothing, shoes, caps, and bedding were made in the family. Many southern plantations conducted, with slave labor, household manufactures sufficiently extensive to supply what under a different labor system would have been a community market; and at no time, unless at the very earliest period, was the consumption of homespun manfactures confined exclusively to the family that made them. As soon as such articles entered neighborhood exchange and became to that extent domestic-commercial, they began to be specialized and localized at points of advantageous production. Though this process was slow, before the end of the colonial period most homespun industries had become domestic-commercial in some parts of the country. On the other hand, however, they retained their primitive character in remote districts long after the Revolution, and even after the Civil War.

Domestic-commercial industries were not developed exclusively from homespun. Brick and pottery, hollow ware, and bar iron were made in the colonies for local consumption at a very early date. Certain agricultural implements, including scythes, were among the first manufactures of Massachusetts. Comestibles, such as bread, beer, cider, rum, chocolate, and refined sugar, were manufactured for domestic markets. Printing was necessarily domestic-commercial; so was the manufacture of glass and paper as soon as these industries were introduced. The same is true of tanning, saddlery, and shoemaking. The manufacture of cottons and woolens at Rowley, of linen at Londonderry and Germantown, and of knit goods at the latter place appears to have been begun with the idea of supplying both the neighborhood and more distant markets. Soap and candles were made by people who followed this occupation exclusively. Provisions were produced for local exchange as well as for foreign trade.

The chief foreign-commercial manufactures were lumber, ships, iron, pitch, tar, turpentine, flour, salt provisions, potash, and rum—the latter, like iron, supplying markets both at home and abroad. Whale oil was refined for export, and soap and candles, as well as hats, brick, and pottery, were sent to the island colonies.

Practically all the markets for colonial manufactures, outside the province within which they were situated, were reached by sea. Products shipped from one colony upon the mainland to another were technically exports, and the political and commercial relations of those colonies to each other were no closer in theory than the relations of any one of them with Jamaica or the Barbados, or with the mother country itself. For convenience, however, in order to avoid a distinction that would apply only to the colonial period, the Thirteen Colonies are considered here a domestic market, and their trade is termed intercolonial, while England and the West Indian colonies are treated as part of the foreign market.

In relation to manufactures, the foreign market fell into two divisions—the transatlantic countries and the islands. Of the two, the islands were the more important. Known at the time as the "Sugar Islands" and the "Wine Islands," respectively, the West Indies and the neighboring mainland settlements supplied the most profitable trade to the colonists, while the Azores, Madeira, and the Canaries supplemented this market with a ready demand for pipe staves and provisions. The foreign market took principally products of extractive and primary rather than of reproductive manufactures, especially lumber and naval stores, flour, and salted meats. But this stream of trade carried with it bread, rum, and some articles of handicraft.

THE TRANSATLANTIC MARKET

Great Britain was the chief transatlantic market of the colonists. In the order of development, this market encouraged in America the manufacture of lumber, ships, naval stores, and iron. The South European countries took all of these things except iron and afforded a market for provisions. Trade statistics are too defective to give much information as to the volume of this demand. England consumed more imported iron and forest products than the colonies supplied, but the competition of home producers and of the Baltic countries caused British prices to fluctuate, and sometimes to fall too low to give a profit to American manufacturers. This condition seems to have affected the lumber trade least of all, partly because the market was wider—extending to the islands—and because labor was relatively a less important item in the cost of sawing boards and timbers by waterpower than in that of making tar, smelting iron, or building ships.

Lumber formed part of the earliest cargoes from Virginia and Plymouth to the mother country. In 1671, when its population hardly exceeded that of a good-sized village, New Hampshire annually shipped, though not entirely to transatlantic countries, 20,000 tons of boards and staves, besides 10 ships laden with masts. That colony and Massachusetts conducted a lucrative timber trade with Spain and Portugal. About 1700, a Salem ship loaded for these countries with "12,000 feet of the noblest plank that ever was seen in America"; and between 1712 and 1718, New Hampshire shipped to Lisbon and Cadiz, in addition to over 135,000 staves and large quantities of dressed timber and rafters, nearly 100,000 oak planks and two thirds that quantity of pine planks and boards. In 1739 a Piscataqua merchant had large contracts for timber with the court of Spain, and the lumber trade with southern Europe continued active until 1765, when it was prohibited by parliament.

Market conditions, reinforced by political regulations, affected the relative profit of exporting timber in a manufactured or in an unwrought state. When, in 1722, Great Britain removed its duty upon colonial lumber and timber, the effect was to increase the exportation of the latter. The premium upon masts and spars was a further incentive for shipping direct from the forest, and a growing demand from Spain and Portugal for the same class of timber helped a movement already under way; therefore, about this time, it was found better to export hewn logs than to saw them into boards. The market for riven timber, being broader, was probably also steadier than that for sawed lumber. Ireland took coopers' stock from the colonies, to use in packing butter and salt provisions. During 1768, over 2 million staves were shipped from the colonies to that island, and about double that number to Great Britain. Pennsylvania supplied most of the former trade and Virginia most of the latter; Ireland, in the same year, took over 300,000 feet of boards and planks, while Great Britain imported about 388,000 feet of oak planks and over 2,275,000 feet of pine planks and boards. Though the central and southern colonies supplied most of the riven timber, Massachusetts alone, including the province of Maine, shipped considerably over one half of the sawed lumber. North Carolina, with 50 sawmills in operation on the Cape Fear River, ranked second of the colonies in this branch of the transatlantic trade.

The English and European market for colonial vessels seems to have determined the prosperity of shipbuilding, although the aggregate home demand, for the fisheries and the coasting trade as well as for oversea traffic, usually must have exceeded the demand from abroad. In 1676, it was considered not remarkable for New England builders to receive orders from Great Britain for 30 ships in one year, though frequently foreign wars greatly reduced these commissions. The English market for colonial shipping was strengthened not only by the fact that vessels could be built cheaply in America but also by favorable conditions of exchange. On account of the regular balance of trade against the northern colonies, English merchants sent cargoes of merchandise to America, with the proceeds of which they built a ship and freighted it with lumber for Great Britain or southern Europe. Colonial undertakers also built on speculation for the foreign market. In 1721, it was estimated officially that the greater part of the tonnage built in the northern colonies was on orders from British merchants. As early as 1697, Bristol merchants built ships in Virginia. About the year of settlement, a shipyard at Philadelphia received large foreign orders; and in 1718, Jonathan Dickinson wrote from Pennsylvania: "Here is a great employ for ship work for England. It increases and will increase."

The manufacture of tar, pitch, turpentine, and similar naval stores began in America before the British bounties were established, but probably such early supplies were consumed mainly by local dockyards. After 1700 the English market, under the influence of government encouragement, became the most important factor governing the production of these commodities. Between 1701 and 1718 the shipments of tar from America to England rose from 177 to 82,084 barrels; at the latter date, colonial tar constituted nearly 90 percent of the British imports. In 1719, Governor Johnson, in a letter to the Board of Trade, reported that South Carolina the previous year had supplied for the use of the British navy 32,000 barrels of tar, 2,643 barrels of pitch, and 473 barrels of turpentine. Five years later, the annual export of pitch, tar, and turpentine from that colony was stated to be 52,000 barrels. Thereafter the increase in these commodities was not so rapid. In 1768 the total importations into Great Britain from the colonies were somewhat over 135,000 barrels. The growth of this branch of manufacture in America was limited directly by foreign demand and by competitive conditions in the transatlantic market.

Iron was the last manufactured commodity to become an important item in the colonial exports to England. This trade differed from that in lumber, ships, and naval stores in that there was a reciprocal movement of this article in its various forms, imports and exports occurring simultaneously. Small quantities of bar iron shipped from Massachusetts to England during the 19th century, but there was no regular eastbound commerce in this article. As yet, the colonists did not manufacture enough for their own consumption, but depended upon bars imported from Spain and England, and hardware from the latter country. During the following century, also, though the colonies became iron exporters, they continued to buy bar iron from Great Britain. These exports, small as they appear in comparison with modern figures, formed a large fraction of the total colonial product. Some of the principal furnaces in America were erected specifically to supply the English market; and though it cannot be said that the prosperity of this industry was based upon a foreign demand to the same extent as the manufacture of lumber and naval stores, that demand greatly assisted its progress.

Toward the close of the colonial period, American manufactures began to reach England and Europe in slightly greater variety. In 1768 the colonies shipped across the Atlantic and to the Azores, in the wake of 4,000 tons of whale oil, 11,000 pounds of soap and a few hundred pounds of sperm candles; also 1,344 tons of potash and 201 tons of pearl ash; and more than 10,500 tons of bread and flour, and 150 tons of salted beef and pork. There also were exported to the same destinations, in round numbers, 281,000 gallons of rum, of which a portion doubtless was distilled in the West Indies. For none of these manufactures, except oil and potash, were the transatlantic countries more than a subsidiary market. The trade in manufactured provisions was supported mainly by the tropical islands, which, during the last century of colonial dependence, had more influence than any other section of the outside world upon the industrial development of the North American settlements.

THE ISLAND MARKET

The sugar islands of the West Indies, not only those belonging to Great Britain but also the colonies of France and Spain—with which the northern settlements conducted an active illegal or tolerated trade—afforded a market practically uniform in character. This influenced colonial manufactures in three ways: by a direct demand for certain commodities, by supplying raw materials for manufacture, and by providing a supply of coin, facilitating exchange and through this the diversification of industry. This market was supplemented by the wine-producing islands of the East Atlantic, and in the chain of commerce thus created was comprehended the slave trade with Africa.

The West Indies took in varying quantities almost every product of colonial industry, and a complete record of this trade might reveal the history of commercial manufactures in America of which all knowledge has been lost. The tropics demanded lumber in its finished forms; and therefore, this market was more favorable to manufactures than that of England, where the call was mainly for unwrought timber. An active demand existed in the sugar countries for containers for sugar, molasses, and rum, which were shipped in the form of staves, hoops, and headings, and sometimes made into barrels on shipboard during the journey southward. This trade began with the Wine Islands during the first decade of Virgina settlement and, except for the vicissitudes of war, continued uninterrupted through the following 150 years; with the West Indies, its origin dates at least from the first new England settlements. Shortly before the Revolution, the annual shipment of staves to the sugar colonies was between 11 million and 12 million. Closely associated with this branch of the lumber trade was the demand for building materials. Ready-framed houses were sometimes shipped from New England and from Louisiana to the English and French islands. The rapid deterioration of such structures in the tropics made the request for new materials almost constant. In 1768 the West Indies took from the northern colonies nearly 39 million shingles and over 35 million feet of boards and planks, besides scantling and other sawed timber. New York built ships for the Barbados and Jamaica merchants. One of the earliest exports from Virginia was a cargo of bricks to the Bermudas, and many New England invoices to the West Indies mention this commodity. In 1768 the total number of bricks shipped from North America to this destination was over 1.5 million.

Equally important with the trade in lumber and building materials was that in manufactured provisions, of which, in the year just mentioned, 135,000 barrels of bread and flour and over 25,000 barrels of beef and pork were shipped to the island colonies. Butter, Rhode Island cheese, lard, and pickled oysters contributed somewhat to this branch of traffic. Merchant milling, next to lumbering the most important and profitable export manufacture of the colonies, was therefore mainly dependent on this market; but its influence extended farther, for a current of trade thus started bears with it commodities that of their own momentum might not reach distant consumers. In 1768, there were shipped to these islands nearly 6,000 barrels of naval stores, 220 tons of oil, between 150 and 200 tons of bar and wrought iron, and 3,548 boxes of soap. Possibly the last was not solely of colonial manufacture. The West Indies also took annually from the colonies over 500,000 pounds of sperm and tallow candles. New England cider, Phildelphia beer, New Jersey pottery, New York and Carolina hats, Virginia leather, Massachusetts shoes, colonial furniture and vehicles, all found their way southward in the wake of the lumber and provision traffic. The progress of the latter manufactures in America was not dependent upon the West Indian market; but though that market was quite subsidiary to local demands in causing their development, it promoted the differentiation of colonial industry already occurring in response to other conditions.

The principal returns from the West Indian trade were sugar, molasses, rum, cotton, dyewoods and cabinet woods, and coin. At the northern ports, molasses was converted into rum, and sugar was refined. Most of the cotton and some part of the dyewoods and cabinet woods were used by colonial manufacturers. The coin, as already mentioned, stimulated trade; and while it was used mostly to pay for European and British manufactures, its presence nevertheless favored local industries, for ready money and manufactures go together. Moreover, in Rhode Island, silversmithing and the manufacture of jewelry received their first encouragement from the supply of bullion provided by the active West Indian trade. As this commerce extended to the coast of Africa, whence slaves were supplied to the sugar planters, it afforded a market for rum and, in a lesser degree, for the iron bars used as currency on the Guinea Coast. The trade with the Wine Islands, on the other hand, stocked the colonies so plentifully with Madeira that this was accounted some discouragement to colonial brewers and cider makers; but in early times, among the returns from the latter traffic were Spanish wool and salt, important industrial commodities for the colonists.

THE INDIAN TRADE AND THE FLEET TRADE

The fishing and merchant fleet on the coast and the Indians on the frontier also made demands upon colonial manufactures. The fleet took provisions, principally rum and beer; but various ship supplies—anchors, cordage, and possibly sailcloth—were made for this market. The rough, durable homespuns of the colonists appear to have been in request by the fishermen in preference to imported fabrics, and there is at least a suggestion that they found their way to the depots of the western fur trade. The Indians trafficked for colonial rum and, like the frontiersmen, preferred the leather goods, axes, and firearms made in America. In the lists of wares supplied the eastern Indians by the Massachusetts truck-masters in 1703, in addition to woolen and cotton cloth, knives, combs, thread, and shirts, the following articles are mentioned, all of which may have been of colonial origin: Indian meal, tobacco (sold by the fathom), biscuits, pork, hats, kettles, axes, and hoes. Kalm says the kettles sold the Indians were of copper or brass, as iron was too heavy and fragile to be used on their journeys. English goods, being cheaper than French manufactures, were employed for the Indian trade even in Canada and Louisiana, in spite of the stringent laws enacted by New York to prevent the sale of British manufactures through Albany to the French. On the southern Mississippi, these traders brought British goods from New York and Philadelphia merchants to traffic with the Creeks, Choctaws, and other southern tribes. Such supplies at times, and usually in case of certain articles, were supplemented by the products of colonial industry, which thereby found their way into the western country more extensively than they otherwise might have done.

Manufactures for the Home Market

Manufactures thrive better with an expanding than with a stationary market, and expansion remarkable beyond that of most other nations has been a chief characteristic of American consumption from the founding of Jamestown and Plymouth to the present time. The growth of population and consequent flow of settlement westward into new country, where the entire energy of the people was absorbed in clearing land and making homes, favored the extension of domestic manufactures adapted to the peculiar needs of these pioneers. Certainty of an increasing demand for their productions gave confidence to the projectors of new undertakings. These same conditions exercised a counteracting influence, by diverting capital and labor from manufactures to the development of unexploited resources; but the total effect, as evidenced by history, has been favorable to industrial growth.

The expansion of the domestic market during the colonial period may be viewed under three aspects: the growth of population, the development of natural resources, and the rising standard of living.

Expansion of Markets due to Growth of Population

Our knowledge of the total population of the colonies at different periods is based on estimates rather than enumerations, but these are sufficiently accurate to measure markets. It is supposed that by 1640, there were 25,000 white settlers in the English colonies and that this number more than trebled during the next 20 years. As early as the Revolution of 1688, the colonial population was thought to have increased to 200,000, of which New England and the Virginia–Maryland district each accounted for 75,000; the colonies between these two sections, for something over 40,000; and the Carolinas, which included the present territory of Georgia, for less than 10,000. The 18th century opened with something over 250,000 white settlers in English America, and this number appears to have doubled in about two decades. Again, the population doubled in about 20 years, the million mark being reached between 1740 and 1745. The colonists already formed a nation numerically important, whose clothing and conveniences well might employ in the age of handicrafts a small army of manufacturers; but the babe of 1745 had hardly attained his majority before these numbers again were doubled, and 2 million people were demanding and assisting to sustain the multiplied wants of a community whose needs grew more complex as it expanded. In 1775, Congress, in proportioning the Continental money among the states, estimated the total population at 2,243,000 whites and nearly half a million blacks. The first federal census, in 1790, which gave the population of the Union as 3,929,214, confirmed the approximate accuracy of this estimate.

At the outbreak of the Revolution, therefore, the population of the colonies was more than 12 times as great as a century previously; and for reasons that will presently be shown, their consumption of manufactures had risen faster than the number of inhabitants. Meanwhile, every reason leads us to believe that a constantly smaller proportion of the settlers in the colonies north of Maryland were producing commodities for export. The decreased area of merchantable timber near the coast alone would suggest this. Wheat raising was on the decline in New England before the close of the 17th century and had "almost passed out of cultivation with the third generation of farmers." This was due partly to the opening of new lands in the central colonies, which assumed in the 18th century the same agricultural relation to New England that the Mississippi Valley and the prairie states assumed to the Atlantic states after 1850. In Pennsylvania and New Jersey, though export farming was extended, the growth in industries, relative to their small beginnings, was even more rapid. These considerations, and others to be presented later, indicate that the growth of population was an index not only of the general demand for manufactures, which conceivably might have benefited British industries without affecting those in America, but also of a specific demand for homemade goods.

The rapid growth of colonial population during the last decades before the Revolution suggested some ambitious industrial enterprises, which it did not under existing competitive and transportation conditions provide a body of consumers large enough to support. As late as 1789, according to a Pennsylvania writer: "Most new works have been begun too large in this country. If we built a slitting mill it was made sufficient to slit as much iron in a week as we would sell in half a year. If we built a glass house, it was at the expense of thousands, and calculated to cover all that part of the Country with glass which was not covered by the houses." Nevertheless, this statement, which probably referred to Baron Stiegel's ill-advised enterprises in Pennsylvania, did not truly characterize most colonial undertakings. Local manufacturers well understood their inability to command their whole home market. The industrial development of Great Britain more than kept pace with the growth of her dominions. That country produced manufactures in such abundance that they sometimes were forced upon colonial markets in advance of a demand. Consequently, an oversupply of manufactured goods, such as seldom or never occurred during the early years of settlement, is frequently recorded during the latter half of the 18th century. Intercolonial trade helped to regulate this competition by drawing off surplus commodities to places of better demand. A condition resulted from this that at first glance might not have been anticipated. The colonial ports that thus formed warehouses, whence foreign manufactures were distributed to remoter markets, themselves became centers of manufactures for those markets. In the wake of their other commerce followed the products of their domestic industries; and the geographical area these industries supplied was widened by the very condition that limited their sales to local consumers.

Expansion of the Home Market due to Development

Even in the longest settled countries, new natural resources are constantly discovered; internal improvements make it possible to assemble for manufacture materials that previously were too remote from each other to be used together; and from these conditions, new industries arise, and old ones are extended. The internal development of the colonies, especially in the 18th century, presented all these features. It is not improbable that between 1750 and the adoption of the Constitution, despite the wars that intervened, as much land was brought under cultivation, with corresponding improvement of ways of communication, as during the entire previous period of settlement. This extension of agriculture carried with it mill building and village handicrafts, which in turn made a demand on other local industries. The progress of settlement westward from the coast revealed new resources—mountain ores producing better grades of iron than had been made hitherto in the colonies, coal and lead in Virginia, and saltpeter from the Appalachian caves. The forest and the sea continued to be important fields for colonial enterprise but were less dominant than formerly. The British policy of encouraging the production of raw materials in America itself reacted upon industries. That these occupations supplanted home manufactures competing with those of England was true only with qualifications. Makers of pitch and tar, hewers of timber, and smelters and forgemen, all depended in part upon the manufactures of the country in which they lived. Even the plantation colonies began to diversify their products, as settlement penetrated to the grain and flax lands of the interior and mill towns arose along the fall line of the southern rivers. In Virginia the culture of tobacco declined or ceased to increase about the middle of the 18th century, though the population was growing and new lands were brought under cultivation. Petersburg and Richmond were becoming mill towns, and Baltimore was enriched by the growing trade of the interior uplands.

The isolation that fostered these manufactures prevented their growth beyond a rudimentary stage until western migration carried the frontier to the tributaries of the Mississippi and the Great Lakes; then the rivers that bore products to the interior themselves, by an adverse current, barred the way to competing manufactures. Settlements began to be formed on the western waters as early as 1748 but did not become numerous enough to support manufactures until the Revolution. In 1784, Pittsburgh was making lumber, bricks, and iron for the Ohio trade, and supplied the materials for building Louisville. Before the adoption of the Constitution, its pioneer newspaper advertised the shops of gold- and silversmiths, lockmakers, other metalworkers, cabinetmakers, and manufacturers of farming tools. Throughout the colonies the growth of varied industries made a varied market, and in such a market the local manufacturer had more advantage over his foreign competitor than where the same demands, repeated without change from season to season and year to year, caused a pulsation of trade reaching the remotest countries. The repair of machinery and implements, the supply of facilities for transportation, especially after boats and vehicles took the place of packtrains, emergency demands for the tools of trade and the arms of protection, and growing interchange of local supplies as district became differentiated from district in response to varying resources and situations, all enlarged the call for local manufactures.

ARTICLES CONSUMED IN THE COLONIES

Colonial consumption embraced most of the articles of use or luxury found among the prosperous classes of England, and the variety of the demands that custom and caprice made upon industry was almost as great as at the present day. For purposes of rapid survey, we may divide this market into four groups—clothing, furniture (using the word, as was the custom of the time, for all household articles), tools and implements, and luxuries. The last class included many objects serving purposes of display or refinement, seldom made in the colonies and largely imported even at present. They embraced, to quote from an advertisement of a Burlington merchant, in 1764:

Common pressed dolls, carts, chairs, horses for children; fiddlers for children, sorted toys, three and four joint hazel, dogwood and bamboo fishing rods, and three and four joint solid rods, kirby and common hooks, silk and hair lines, flies and gut, six and eight stave reels . . . straw, Japanned, and carved ivory tooth pick cases, playing cards, morocco pocket books . . . paste necklaces and earrings, silk and velvet needle cases, . . . backgammon tables . . . fine paper maché snuff boxes; engraved ditto.

The Market for Clothing

In colonial days, clothing indicated rank and occupation more than at present; and in this respect, the colonists may be divided into two classes—those who used imported garments and fabrics, and those who used homespun. This distinction did not follow the same parallel in all the colonies, northern settlers of independent station often wearing homespun, while southern slaves were clad in rough cloth of English make. In general, however, rank and vocation set fashions and created habits that modified the influence of competition upon the respective consumption of domestic and imported textiles. A New England farmer might, by prejudice and unquestioning wont, use homespuns when foreign cloths were selling at the lowest prices; while a city gentleman, even in financial distress, would hardly wear the product of family industry. Competition existed rather between the finer colonial manufactures and those imported; and in respect to these two only, during most of this period, can we speak of a market involving exchange. That market was dominated by British goods, except when business depression or political agitation disturbed the normal course of trade. Nor was the boundary between homespun and commercial consumption inflexible. Merchant manufactures encroached upon the manufactures of the household from time to time, or permanently when new trade conditions were established.

The imported fabrics used in the colonies were, in order of importance, woolens, linens, and cottons; and of these, only the first were mainly of British manufacture. Among the woolen cloths that figured most prominently in the American market was broadcloth, which continued throughout this period the principal and the most expensive carded woolen fabric used in the colonies. This cloth was seldom manufactured in America for sale, though it was sometimes dyed and finished by colonial clothiers, especially when it became necessary to adapt an old stock to changing taste or fashion.

Linens, using this term to include fabrics made of either flax or hemp, supplied many uses now served by cottons. As they were not manufactured extensively in England, those brought from abroad were at first mostly of Dutch and German manufacture and, after the bounty on Irish linen was established, from that island. Sheets and napkins generally were made of linen, but sometimes of cotton, which was higher priced than either linen or worsted. Fine muslins, cambrics, and lawns were imported; and though their consumption must have been relatively more limited than at present, they appeared in the stocks of most colonial merchants.

The use of Indian cottons was prohibited in England for the protection of local manufacturers, but was permitted in America; and the importation of these goods, especially calicoes, was extensive. They were commonly used for women's dresses, and were so cheap and plentiful, compared with other similar fabrics, as to be considered a discouragement to home manufactures. In wealthier circles, silks were worn by both sexes, silk stockings and waistcoats often appearing in men's wardrobes. Acrelius says that satin was used still more widely "all over the country." Damasks and expensive fancy cloths and plushes found a market in the cities and among the large planters.

Of hats and caps, the common consumption was supplied largely by American makers, but those imported continued to be preferred by the more exacting custom of the cities. Heavy boots and shoes found their way to the southern colonies from both New England and the mother country; the rural trade of the provinces north of Maryland was supplied chiefly by those of domestic manufacture. The value of leather goods imported was only one tenth the value of the woolens and included harness, saddlery, and minor articles, as well as fine and plantation shoes. In 1721 the recorded imports of the colonies that might by a liberal definition be classed as clothing were valued at somewhat under $1.5 million. Assuming the population at this time to have been 500,000, the foreign expenditures of the colonists under this head annually would have been about $3 per capita. In the 18th century, textiles cost more than at present, and leather goods nearly as much, so that even allowing for a relatively numerous child and servile population, and for the difference between English official and colonial retail valuations, it is evident that a large fraction of the home consumption was supplied from local sources.

THE MARKET FOR FURNITURE, TOOLS, AND LUXURIES

The needs of the colonial household, though not so elaborate as those of the modern home, brought into request an even greater variety of articles. Domestic handicrafts called for their respective implements, the entire process of food preservation and preparation was conducted in the family, and other specialized services which are now the concern of outside agencies were supplied then by the industry of the fireside. In colonial homes of the better sort, as we know from examples that have come down to us, the furniture equaled in solidity, grace, and variety that with which we are familiar. The difference in the market of that period was its restriction to a smaller class, relative to the whole population, than at the present time. The home of the merchant and planter alone afforded these conveniences; the mass of the laboring and farming people was far more scantily supplied.

Writing of Massachusetts in 1763, Governor Bernard said: "Most of the furniture in the homes of the trading towns is of British manufacture: nails, glass, lead, locks, hinges, and many other materials for homes are wholly imported from Great Britain." But even in the towns, this was true only to a qualified extent of bulkier articles of furniture, such as tables, lounges, bedsteads, and chairs. Walnut tables, invoiced at $4 a foot, and chairs by the dozen, occur in the ladings of New England schooners trading with the southern colonies. The ironware in the kitchen was largely of American make; and earthenware and pottery were not infrequently of colonial manufacture. Porcelain was replacing pewter, which had been made to some extent in New England, and cheaper whiteware was gradually substituted for the wooden trenchers that had satisfied the taste and consulted the thrift of the earliest settlers.

The table furnishings of the better class of colonial homes may not have equaled in elegance those of the rich West Indian planters; but the merchants found custom, among other things, for glass tumblers, cruets, salts, mustard pots and cream pots, decanters, wine and jelly glasses, beer glasses and mugs, jars, and four vase syllabubs "in waves"; for porcelain dishes, plates, cups, coffeepots, decorated cups, coffee and patty cans, fruit and salad dishes, and blue Nankeen tea sets; and for silver salts, castors, cream jugs, tablespoons, soupspoons, and teaspoons, and waiters.

Agricultural implements were made at home, often with imported ironwork. The Virginia planters purchased cartwheels from England but made the remainder of the vehicles in their own shops. Edge tools, and in general all steel manufactures, were usually imported. But the extremely rapid growth of the demand for tools and implements used in clearing lands and settling and cultivating new country, especially during the decades immediatly preceding the Revolution, caused American iron manufactures to be extended and improved. Though Great Britain shipped to the colonies ironwork as well as cordage and sailcloth for vessels, home industries also supplied a part of this demand.

The colonies were purchasers as well as sellers of raw materials. During the first half of 1770, Boston imported from Great Britain between

400 and 500 tons of hemp; also, nearly 20 tons of brimstone, 13 tons of alum, and approximately an equal amount of copperas came from the same source to supply the powder mills and dye pots of the New Englanders and their colonial customers. Nearly 20 tons of gad steel, 180 boxes of tinned plates, 17 blocks of tin, and 2,224 bars, sheets, or casks of lead were imported for local whitesmiths. To meet the needs of homespun industries, which were stimulated by political opposition to Great Britain, Boston, during these six months, took from the mother country about 780 dozen wool cards and 34 dozen cotton cards.

6. COLONIAL COMMERCE, ENGLISH MERCANTILISM, AND ECONOMIC DEVELOPMENT*

Although the British navigation acts are well known for the restrictions they placed on colonial trade, these acts, which were merely a part of England's prevailing mercantilist policy, had a number of beneficial effects. Of particular significance was their impact on colonial shipbuilding and shipping. Colonial vessels enjoyed the same privileges as English ships, and the New England colonies obtained their previously mentioned control of coastal shipping. Mercantilism and its effects notwithstanding, roads and waterways carried a substantial amount of intercolonial trade. This was true despite the inadequacies of the currency substitutes necessitated by a chronic shortage of gold and silver coin.

THE SLANT of the 17th and 18th centuries toward mercantilist doctrines overemphasized the importance of foreign trade. The pamphlet writer, the economic theorist, the manufacturer, the merchant, the statesman were all busy scrutinizing, as if they were matters of life and death, the receipts of the customhouses, the arrival and departure of vessels, and the totals of imports and exports. Such subjects were thought vital. This obsession induced an ignorance of internal trade and occasionally created a contempt for it. But as an actual fact, England's internal trade in the 18th century far exceeded her overseas commerce. And the same generalization seems to have held true of Holland and France, the other European nations with a foreign trade and a mercantilist complex. In the case of the British colonies in North America, overseas trade probably played a greater part than domestic commerce. But even here, mercantilism has destroyed the proportions of the picture by its failure to chronicle an extensive intercolonial traffic.

INTERNAL TRANSPORTATION AND COMMERCE

The crude trails and roads of the British colonies effectively curtailed land transport and internal commerce. On very few products could pro-

* Reprinted from Edward C. Kirkland, *A History of American Economic Life* (3d ed.; New York: Appleton-Century-Crofts, Inc., copyright, 1951). Reprinted by permission of Appleton-Century-Crofts, Inc.

ducers or forwarders afford to pay the excessive charges such journeys involved. Such handicaps were peculiarly severe in frontier regions of dispersed settlement and long distances. The Philadelphia fur traders, for instance, added 20 to 30 percent to the prices of the goods they shipped over the mountains to cover the cost of the transportation. Even when roads were cut through to the Ohio during the French and Indian wars, and the dispatch of packtrains from the East to Pittsburgh became a considerable business, only a few goods could be carried profitably. Iron products and salt were shipped westward; furs and whisky, valuable articles of small bulk, were brought back on the return journey.

Nearer the coast the situation altered. Here, there was a relative density of population. Boston, Newport, Providence, New York, Philadelphia, Charleston, and Baltimore furnished considerable markets and impressed observers with their settled air. Around Boston, there grew up a considerable land transportation, particularly in the winter, when the snow remedied and concealed the deficiencies of the highways. In the middle colonies, land transportation was more common. Over the route between New York and Philadelphia a regular wagon traffic in goods was started in 1732 to bridge the land barrier in Jersey between the Delaware and the Raritan. Around Philadelphia, improved highways made possible the transportation of grain for some 50 or 60 miles; and the Conestoga wagon, rounded at the bottom to prevent the contents from spilling, covered with a linen top, and crammed with a diverse cargo, drove down to the urban markets. In every colony where there was a trail, the peddler was both scourge and blessing. In the pack slung over his own back or saddled upon his horse was a stock of "notions": combs and brass buttons, dyes and drugs, small wooden articles. He was an indispensable distributor and middleman. But unsavory commercial practices—he gained an almost mythical reputation for cunning—impaired his usefulness. The irritation of cheated patrons and the opposition of local merchants injured by peddlers' competition led to provincial legislation for their restraint. Even in Connecticut, the traditional home of the slick Yankee trader, peddlers' fees were placed in 1765 at £20, a prohibitive figure.

As contrasted with land carriage, water transportation was startlingly cheap. In shipping wheat from the Connecticut Valley to Boston, it cost a shilling a bushel to cart it from Northampton, Massachusetts, to Windsor, Connecticut; thence the rate by the river to Hartford was only twopence, and by river and sea from Hartford to Boston sixpence more. Thus the total freight from the farm was 1s. 8d., of which by far the larger part was for the short land carriage. It is small wonder that waterways became the arteries of domestic commerce. In this respect, New England was poorly endowed, for on the chief rivers, running through settled country, the fall line interrupted navigation near the sea. Without improvements, therefore, the Merrimac and the Connecticut were not successful channels of communication between the coast and the interior. In New York, there was no poverty of natural waterways. The Hudson was a magnificent artery; and by 1770, well over a hundred vessels were engaged in the trade between Albany and New York. Philadelphia combined the trade following the Delaware and that following the Schuylkill, and drew overland by transshipment a part of the Susquehanna traffic which flowed down to Baltimore. South of the Potomac, the streams are too numerous to chronicle. A nondescript flotilla of rafts, pole boats, and small sailing vessels plied these interior waterways.

The coastwise traffic between the Thirteen Colonies, however, was the largest item in domestic commerce. Although its value never equaled that of the direct trade with Europe or the West Indies, it employed a tonnage in 1769 which gave it a high rank among the branches of colonial commerce. To be sure, this coast traffic ministered to foreign commerce. It collected products at a few important American entrepôts for shipment to Europe or to the West Indies, and it distributed articles imported from both these sources to scores of smaller ports. Nevertheless, domestic commodities formed an indeterminable portion of the cargoes of these coastal vessels. In spite of the prevalence of self-sufficing agriculture, New England shipped to the middle and southern colonies butter, salted meats, cider, fish, and rum. New York in 1714 was sending "Wheat & Flower to Boston and Road Island as well as to South Carolina." The Chesapeake region dispatched wheat and flour to the New England ports and to the southern plantations. The tobacco and to a lesser extent the rice and naval stores of the South were a return current to the northern colonies. The coastal traffic in manufactured articles was bewildering in variety and extent. Before the end of the colonial period, Massachusetts was drawing pig iron from Pennsylvania for its forges and iron ore from Maryland for its furnaces, and was sending its woodenware to Maryland; Philadelphia was sending paper to all the colonies, and Rhode Island, candles and tow cloth to the South. The New England peddling instinct could not be suppressed even on the high seas. During the winter, when the fisheries were at a dead end, the fishermen loaded their sloops with a cargo of salt, rum, sugar, molasses, iron- and woodenware, hats, caps, cloth, handkerchiefs, and stockings, which they peddled from place to place in the southern colonies.

BARTER, CURRENCY, AND BANKING

This commerce was retarded and confused by the absence of a stable and uniform medium of exchange. Here the colonies had run into difficulties. As soon as communities have emerged from a primitive organization, some form of currency has been designed to serve as a common measure for the relative value of different commodities and thus to remove the complexities attendant upon bartering goods. Athough the purpose of money has been obvious enough, there has been a continuous dispute as to the nature of a suitable currency. For centuries the precious metals, gold and silver, seemed to meet most proper requirements. In the last 250 years, however, various forms of paper money—individual notes, bank notes, government notes, and checks—have appeared in the Occident. Until very recently, it was thought that the amount of this paper currency ought to bear some clearly defined relation to the amount of gold and silver. Governments have therefore promised to redeem their paper in gold and silver, or in gold alone; banks have been required by law or experience to hold certain coin reserves for the redemption of their notes or for the support of their checks. Certain devices, like the clearing-house, commercial practices, and above all confidence in the government or bank, have contributed to make the coin reserve a fraction of the total amount of notes or checks used in business transactions.

A realization of this evolution in financial experience is necessary in order to appreciate the financial experiments of the American colonies. It was unthinkable that they should at once adopt a gold and silver currency. Supplies of the precious metals in adequate amounts for commercial transactions could be obtained only from mines within the colonies or through foreign trade. The colonies had no gold and silver mines; and it was unwise for a new country, craving development, to reduce its expenditures, export a large commodity surplus, and thus obtain the precious metals through foreign commerce. The colonies therefore reverted to barter. Although the transaction was clothed in a money terminology, goods were exchanged not for coin but for each other. At the store the merchant credited his customers with the products—cider, eggs, cheese, yarn, flax, and the like—which they brought in and set off against their value the goods which he gave them. College bills were paid in a variety of articles, and one Harvard student in the 17th century discharged his academic obligations with an old cow. This system was early modified by the use as a medium of exchange of articles other than gold or silver. Indian wampum (highly polished beads, manufactured from shells and then strung together) served for currency. Massachusetts made corn and beaver legal tender; the Carolinas used tar and rice. In 18th century Virginia the certificates of deposit issued by warehouses where tobacco had been appraised and stored formed the currency. The ingenuity of the colony was taxed, however, to preserve this currency at a uniform standard, since the market value of tobacco fluctuated wildly. In fact, the sudden and unforeseen changes in the value of these barter currencies were one of their many serious disadvantages.

Through the avenues of foreign trade, metallic coins crept in, largely from the Spanish and Portuguese colonies; of these, the Spanish dollar and its fractions were the most important. The exact equivalent of the Spanish dollar in English money varied from place to place. In 1704, Newton assayed it at the English mint as worth 4s. 6d. So avid were the colonies for such coins that legislative enactments overvalued them in the hope of enticing or retaining them within their boundaries. A result of this unusual rivalry was that the Spanish dollar had different values from colony to colony and even from time to time. Massachusetts raised it to 5 shillings and then to 6 shillings; South Carolina put it at 4s. 8d., while North Carolina pegged it at 8 shillings; the middle colonies favored 7s. 6d. Some colonies forbade the export of this commodity to other colonies, and the chests of departing travelers were subjected to harrowing scrutiny lest they smuggle away metallic contraband.

Meanwhile, some 17th-century thinkers were toying with the idea of a paper money whose value was to be supported not by precious metals but by other forms of security—land, goods, or the personal worth of the issuers. Even in England, these novel proposals met with a hearing. But the contagion of such ideas easily seized colonies which sought funds not only for commercial transactions but for investment in the multifold projects whose ultimate profitableness was undeniable. Soon a variety of experiments was under way. The first and less important form of paper currency was "bills of credit." In the issue of these bills, Massachusetts was the pioneer, but at least eight other colonies followed her example by 1755. These bills of credit were the result of some emergency in the colonies' financial arrangements. Since these govenments had either gone into debt or undertaken projects for which their taxes were insufficient, they anticipated the tax returns by issuing bills of credit. These naturally were to be redeemed when the taxes were collected. The real value of such currency as measured in terms of gold and silver depended upon the confidence of the public in their redemption, which in turn depended upon the size of the issue and the nearness of the date of redemption. Since colonial governments tended to overissue and gradually to lengthen the period before repayment, the specie value of bills of credit steadily declined.

More important were the issues of colonial "loan bills." Sometimes, such currency was issued by banks, if they can be called such, formed by individuals who contributed land or other property as a basis for bills which they hoped to keep afloat by their own credit, by an agreement to accept them as payment in all transactions, or by a promise of redemption at some future date. Generally, the colonial governments were suspicious of such private enterprises and preferred to supply such credit facilities on their own account. In Massachusetts, these loan bills were simply issued by the state on real estate or other security, and their repayment with interest by the borrowers was provided for over a series of years. Extravagant issues were made repeatedly after the first issue in 1711. In Pennsylvania the device was handled with greater skill. In 1722 the colony established a public loan bank. Among the agitators for this institution was Benjamin Franklin, whose *Modest Inquiry into the Nature and Necessity of a Paper Currency* anticipated modern thinking in its argument that the currency of a nation must bear some relation to the value of its trade and the number of its business transactions, and advocated the use of paper money as a flexible instrument of adjustment. The security taken by the Pennsylvania bank for its loans was land, double in value the amount of money loaned, and a bond and attachment upon the borrower's whole property. The debt was to be repaid in 12 annual installments with interest at 5 percent. Not more than £200 could be loaned to any one person.

Every colony except Virginia issued loan bills. One danger of all these colonial issues was the underlying nature of the security upon which they were based. To use land, the most common form of wealth in agricultural colonies, as a basis of note issue was logical but inexpedient. No single note was secured by a specific piece of property; land could not be converted quickly into cash for redemption of an issue. A greater defect in the colonial enterprises was the inability or unwillingness of loan commissioners or colonial officials to stay the flood of notes. In some colonies, as in Rhode Island and the Carolinas, they were poured forth without stint or limit. When the borrowers could not pay their installments, the period of repayment was extended, and the payment of interest was commuted. Rascality and political favoritism corrupted arrangements already loose enough. The result was extravagant inflation.

As notes and bills of one sort and another were issued by the colonies, their value declined. By 1750 in Massachusetts and Connecticut the paper currency was valued in English sterling at 9 to1. Part of Rhode Island's paper money finally sank as low as 23 to 1. Such depreciation profoundly affected the welfare of different classes of the community Debtors were benefited. Inflation brought higher prices for the products they sold, and they were therefore more easily enabled to earn the money to discharge those obligations they had previously assumed. On the other hand, persons who received a fixed income from mortgages in land, investments in securities, or payments on insurance found no increase in their incomes to match the increase in living expenses. This creditor class, whose incomes in Massachusetts the governor calculated had been halved within eight years by the inflation of the currency, naturally regarded paper-money schemes as a conscious fraud promoted by ragamuffins, blackguards, and knaves. In turn, the advocates of paper money regarded its opponents as animated by a sordid self-interest. In the colonies, both sides rushed into a pamphleteering war which was often conducted with great ability. From writing, the controversy worked its way into colonial politics, class interests were fanned into a flame, and the currency controversy eventually aroused the attention of the mother country.

Alarmed by the flood of paper, parliament in 1751 singled out New England for restraint. It forbade these colonies to issue bills of credit and make them legal tender. As the disease of currency experimentation spread southward, the arena affected by this prohibition was enlarged. In 1764, parliament applied it to all the colonies and provided for the gradual retirement of outstanding bills. In both enactments, however, there was a loophole allowing the issue of notes which were to be redeemed after a brief period from the proceeds of taxation.

THE ACTS OF TRADE AND NAVIGATION

In colonial times the welfare of America depended to a degree never since equalled upon foreign commerce. Without it, the thin fringe of settlement along the Atlantic coast could have existed—but only on a primitive and simple economic scale. A higher degree of comfort and material development would have arrived only after a longer period of self-sufficing agriculture and manufacturing. With foreign trade, on the other hand, specialization by the colonies in the products most suited to their circumstances was possible. Their natural resources could be rapidly exploited and shipped abroad in a crude or semimanufactured form in exchange for the products which were more advantageously produced in other countries. Whereever there was an abundance of material prosperity, there was foreign trade. The export of tobacco built the mansions of the Virginia tidewater, equipped them with pictures, furniture, and plate, and supported its courtly social life. Rice and indigo performed the same legerdemain farther south. In New England the merchant and the shipbuilder owed their higher standard of life to overseas trade. And the cities of Boston, New York, Philadelphia, Baltimore, and Charleston were built upon foreign commerce. Everywhere the exchange of goods across the water quickened and enriched colonial economic life.

The mercantilist policy of the mother country consciously mapped the channels for this commerce and dictated the nationality of the vessels that should follow them. Legislation of this sort had been passed as early as the end of the 14th century. Orders in council of a mercantilist cast had been issued during the reigns of the first Stuarts, but the great period of mercantilist legislation was the second half of the 17th century. The first navigation acts of 1650 and 1651 came during the Puritan supremacy of Oliver Cromwell; a whole series of acts—1660, 1662, 1663, 1673—was passed by the parliament of the restored Stuarts; and the maze of regulation was clarified and summarized by the act of

1696 in the reign of William and Mary. At first glance, it is surprising that a continuity of policy should persist through the alternations of sovereigns supporting such different religious and political programs. But under-officials influential in shaping this policy were on two occasions, at least, adroit enough to hold office under rulers or kings of different stripes; the economic classes benefited by this legislation were always vocal; and mercantilism was the unquestioned formula for empire building. Great Britain applied it naturally to the structure she was erecting in the face of Dutch and then French opposition.

So comprehensive were the statutes passed in this era to regulate imperial trade and navigation that after 1700, there was a pause in legislation which was interrupted only by the Molasses Act of 1733. This dealt with a specific problem within the imperial structure. But the Peace of Paris in 1763, ending as it did the competition of the French, gave occasion for a reorganization of the whole commercial system. Act succeeded act in Great Britain as ministry succeeded ministry. This later legislation was still inspired by mercantilist theory. There were, however, shifts of emphasis. Markets had become more important than sources of supply. Also, Great Britain, in the Townshend acts, the Grenville acts, and the North acts, was interested less in regulating colonial commerce than in raising money through taxation to support a colonial system for which she believed her own finances to be inadequate.

The provisions of these various acts from 1650 to 1764 were a monument of complex legislation, but their purposes were comparatively simple. The first was to create a national merchant marine such as would furnish business for shipbuilders, employment for seamen, and profits for shopowners. Legislation from Richard II to Elizabeth had been aimed at this target. Now, since the American colonies had been planted, there was a larger field from which foreigners could be excluded. At first, there was no settled policy. The colonizing companies more or less enforced their monopoly against foreigners and other Englishmen; colonial governors occasionally put the clamps upon trade in foreign vessels; and the king issued orders and instructions. In 1624, for instance, James I forbade the importation of tobacco into England in "forrayne bottoms"; and since a previous order had required all tobacco, whether destined for foreign markets or not, to be brought to England, this later royal pronouncement in theory prevented foreign vessels from handling the most important export of the North American colonies. Other scattered instructions attempted to exclude them in a similar fashion from the import trade. The years of domestic confusion in England attendant upon the struggle between king and parliament tore loopholes through such tentative measures; and the Dutch, whose success in the European trades had been irritating enough, began to invade the English colonial routes. Their vessels crowded to the ports of Barbados, Virginia, Maryland, and Massachusetts, and colonial impediments to their reception were removed.

In 1650, parliament abruptly intervened. An act forbade all foreign ships "to come, or Trade in, or Traffique with" any of the English colonies in America without a license. This policy of exclusion was soon inserted in the more formidable Navigation Act of 1651. In its regulations for the carrying trade, that act provided that European goods might be imported into England, Ireland, and the colonies only in English vessels or in vessels belonging to the place of production or to the port from which such goods were usually shipped. All goods from or produced in Asia, Africa, and America might be imported into the mother country or into the colonies only in ships which belonged to "the people of this Commonwealth or the Plantations thereof, and whereof the masters and mariners are also for the most part of them of the people of this Commonwealth." Although the main object of this act was the transfer of the carrying trades from Dutch to English hands, its precise effect upon colonial shipping was uncertain. Were the people of the colonies included in the phrase "the people of this Commonwealth"? The Navigation Act of 1660, the Magna Charta of the English sea trade, brought greater clarification. It declared that all exports from and imports to the English colonies in Asia, Africa, and America must be carried in English vessels or those which had been built in and belonged to the colonies. The master and at least three quarters of the crew of these ships had to be English. Two years later, an act gave final definition to the nationality of the crew. The term "English" was to include "His Majesties subjects of England, Ireland, and his plantations."

These acts definitely admitted colonial shipping to the privileges and monopolies, including the trade between Europe and England, accorded to the English merchant marine. There were a few exceptions, but the generalization holds true. Such an inclusion was naturally of the greatest benefit to the colonies. For the metropolis, it was likewise advantageous. The plantation trade was a great stimulus to the English merchant marine, for the transatlantic journey was a long one, and colonial cargoes were bulky. A larger number of vessels was therefore required for this commerce than for shorter hauls of more valuable commodities. The commissioners of the customs in 1678 wrote with enthusiasm that "the Plantaĉon trade is one of the greatest Nurseries of the Shipping and Seamen of this Kingdome, and one of the greatest branches of its Trade."

A second purpose of these statutes was to make sure that the colonial products desired by the metropolis should be delivered to her or her satellite settlements and not elsewhere. The charters of the early trading companies to Europe had contained the germ of this principle; and in America, it was first applied in the laboratory of the tobacco trade. By

1621 the tobacco crop was far too large for absorption by the English market, and the Virginia Company meditated dumping its surplus in various continental ports. This procedure was abruptly terminated by an order of the privy council declaring that Virginia tobacco must first be shipped to England. Other acts followed. The Stuarts were all the more eager for this form of regulation since these imported products paid duties upon their arrival in England and thus helped to alleviate the financial perplexities in which these sovereigns were continually involved.

With the Restoration, this early policy was placed upon a firmer basis by enumerating in the various acts of trade or Navigation the products which must be shipped only to England, Ireland, Wales, Berwick-upon-Tweed (whose location on the Scottish frontier had given it an unusual political status), or the other plantations. The act of 1660 designated as enumerated articles sugar, tobacco, cotton, ginger, indigo, and various other dyes. Of these products, only tobacco at the time was of importance to the American continental colonies. Their other products might go wherever they wanted—in the proper shipping. Later acts extended the enumerated list. Naval stores and rice were added in 1704. The latter article, however, might go directly to any European port south of Cape Finisterre. In 1722, beaver and other skins joined the group. With the readjustment after the Seven Years' War, the enumerated list was greatly extended by the inclusion of products from both tropical and temperate colonies. In the latter category were hides and skins, potash and pearl ashes, iron and lumber. This was such a considerable restriction that exceptions were soon allowed. Iron and lumber might be shipped to any place in America, Africa, or Asia; and in 1765, direct exports of colonial lumber were allowed to Europe south of Cape Finisterre. In the previous year the American rice colonies had even been permitted to ship their product to any part of America south of these colonies. In this fashion the trade with Guadeloupe and Martinique was preserved.

This series of regulations was confronted by numerous difficulties. For one thing, Ireland and Scotland occupied an anomalous position. They were not constituent parts of the kingdom, like England, Wales, and Berwick-upon-Tweed, nor could they be regarded as colonies or independent nations. By the act of 1660, Ireland was treated like any other plantation; but this favorable position was whittled away by later legislation. Although Scotland was generally excluded from the sacred circle of these enactments, her economic competition was so embarrassing to England that the Act of Union in 1707 joining the two nations was in part inspired by the desire to give both nations a common commercial policy. The position of the colonies was equally confusing. Since enumerated articles in the trade between the colonies paid little or no duties, the colonial consumer purchased them at a lower price than his fellow in England. An act of 1673, by levying export duties on enumerated commodities shipped from one colony to another, sought to give both purchasers similar treatment.

One explanation for this policy of enumeration was the requirements of the English market. The crying insistence of her merchant marine and royal navy amply explain the enumeration of naval stores and ship timbers. The expansion of the English textile manufacture placed a premium on dye supplies. A more varied, generous, comfortable standard of living, at once cause and effect, required the importation of tobacco, foodstuffs, and other commodities from the colonies. But enumeration was designed for broader purposes than satisfying domestic needs. Beaver skins, hides, naval stores, sugar, rice, tobacco—all were reexported. Even if they left England in their crude state, they often redressed an unfavorable balance of trade. But the mercantilist planned that these colonial products, whose original cost was small, should be transformed by the artisans and manufacturers of the metropolis into articles whose value for reexport was much greater than that of the imported raw material. Everyone was benefited by this arrangement. English employers were given profits and English workers employment. English merchants had the business of forwarding the products, and English shipowners had more numerous voyages. Finally, the government would collect customs which would have been lost if the products had been carried directly to the European markets. The full amount of these customs did not always accrue to the government. In order to encourage the reexport trade, drawbacks on the import duties were paid when the goods again left England. These varied. In general, tariff acts remitted one half the duties as a drawback; but on the most important enumerated products (tobacco and sugar), all import duties were eventually repaid. Nevertheless, so dearly was this form of revenue cherished that when the carriage of rice to Europe south of Cape Finisterre was permitted, the commodity, even though it did not pass through Great Britain, paid the English import duties less the drawback.

The tobacco trade, of all the commerce from North America, best illustrated the influence and implications of this policy of enumeration. Tobacco exports to Great Britain increased enormously. As early as 1685, the revenue derived by the Crown in duties was between £100,000 and £130,000. The ocean carriage gave employment in the same year to "200 sail of ships." In England, hundreds were engaged in manufacturing pipe tobacco or snuff; and tobacco merchants, shippers, colonial planters, and English statesmen were cooperating to enlarge the European markets for the product. By the end of the 17th century, three quarters of the tobacco imports into England were reexported. Holland consumed 8.22 million pounds, a quantity larger than that used by English smokers. Ireland and Germany were other important markets. Spain, whose colonies produced the best tobacco in the world, even imported the

English product. The considerable exports to Sweden were regarded with special favor as a redress to England's customary threatening balance of trade with the Baltic regions. Particular attention was paid to Russia, where a large population had a "passionate love of tobacco." The privilege of entering these markets was eventually won from the czar, only to be lost again. In spite of such reversals, the continental markets grew. In the years before the American Revolution, only one fifth of the exports shipped from Virginia and Maryland were consumed in England.

The third aim of the acts of navigation and the laws of trade reversed the enumeration process. Goods destined for the colonies must be shipped thither from England. This was obvious in the case of English products, but such European and Asiatic goods as the American colonies insisted upon consuming were in general to be transported to the colonies only by way of the metropolis. The first act which formulated this principle was that of 1663. It provided that all European goods for the colonies must first be shipped from England, Wales, or Berwick-upon-Tweed in vessels legal under the Navigation Act. The purposes of this Staple Act were manifold. It was designed to give the English rather than the European merchant the profitable business of supplying the colonies with the goods which were needed; it was hoped to stimulate "the further imployment and increase of English shipping and seamen" by establishing two voyages, one from Europe to England and a second from England to America, rather than a single direct voyage; it would increase the customs revenue through the payment of duties; and it would increase "the vent of English woolen and other manufactures and commodities" at the expense of their European competitors.

The exceptions to this general legislation prove even more precisely the sway of mercantilist motives. The direct importation of certain European articles was allowed by the act of 1663. Salt, obtained largely from southern Europe, could be brought directly to the colonies in order that their fisheries might not be hampered in the rivalry with the French and the Dutch. Scotland and Ireland could ship provisions and horses without a detour through England. Some consideration was also shown to Portugal, which was gracefully included for many purposes within the English system because of its economic dependence. Wines from the Portuguese islands, the Madeiras and Azores, were allowed the privilege of a direct voyage. In the readjustment of the trade system after the Peace of Paris, the English ministry attempted to shift this commerce into the lines of the general pattern. A heavy duty was placed upon wines imported directly into the colonies, a low one on wines imported from England. In view of this arrangement, it was hoped that the Portuguese beverages would in the future flow to the colonies by way of the metropolis. Some of the disadvantages of using England as a staple were eased by the drawbacks paid upon imported European goods which were reexported from England to the colonies. On some foreign commodities, manufactured iron and steel, cordage, and sailcloth, these drawbacks were not given. Here, apparently, the English government was determined to give even greater favors to its own industries.

"A MANIFEST VIOLATION OF SACRED RIGHTS"

Some have regarded these provisions of the navigation and trade acts as a triple-headed hydra. Adam Smith set the fashion as early as 1776. "To prohibit a great people from making all that they can of every part of their own produce, or from employing their stock and their industry in the way that they judge most advantageous to themselves, is a manifest violation of the most sacred rights of mankind." Most thinking in the 19th century, particularly in America, took its cue from this utterance. The English colonial system was a dismal straitjacket or a heavy shackle upon American trade. This modern condemnation would have found little sympathy, if indeed it would have been understood, among generations contemporary with the regulations themselves. To them, the navigation acts were "the guardian of British prosperity," a "most glorious bulwark, the best acts that ever passed for the benefits of trade." The discrepancy of judgment is startling.

Undoubtedly, these acts cost somebody something. Under their provisions, goods were not bought in the cheapest or sold in the dearest market. But the acts of trade and navigation prevented this halcyon form of exchange for the citizens not only of the colonies but also of the metropolis. Take the matter of enumeration. By sending his product to Europe via England, where it was burdened with customs duties and extra freight rates and commissions for handling, the colonist received less for it than he could have received by sending it directly to its destination. The balance of this simple statement, however, is at once upset by a number of compensations. Certain products, such as indigo, which had to be shipped to England, could not have been produced in the colonies without the bounty which was paid upon their arrival in England, Wales, or Berwick-upon-Tweed. In the case of these enumerated products, the burden was upon the English consumer and taxpayer rather than upon the colonist. Other articles from the colonies were admitted into the metropolis duty-free or at low rates, while competing products from other nations were charged heavily. Finally, certain colonial commodities were given a virtual monopoly of the English market. The English consumer was literally compelled to use colonial tar, colonial sugar, and colonial tobacco.

In the case of tobacco, the colonial producers received even further consideration. Tobacco growing in England was forbidden. James I felt that the soil of England should be put to some nobler purpose. As time went on, other considerations reinforced this policy. The Virginia planters were none too content that their product had been placed on the enumerated list and that they had been deprived of their European markets. By 1652, parliament prohibited the planting of tobacco in England on the ground that it tended "to the decay of Husbandry and Tillage, the prejudice and hindrance of the English plantations abroad, and of the Trading, Commerce, Navigation and Shipping of the Nation," and authorized any person to enter the tobacco fields and destroy the plants. In spite of these prohibitions, however, the cultivation of the plant continued and became a profitable business in the southwestern counties of Gloucester and Worcester. The planters threatened violence to anyone who attempted to destroy their crops and issued a defiance against the county justices who had been commanded to carry out the governmental policy. But the central government was obdurate in its devotion to the interest of colonial planters and the importers who flourished on that trade. During the Restoration, such vigorous measures were taken that by the end of the century the English tobacco-growing industry had been extirpated. Fifty years later, an English writer thought that the prohibitions upon iron manufacturing in the colonies "will not be a greater hardship upon them than the Prohibition of the Planting of Tobacco in Great Britain is to us."

On the surface the colonists were likewise penalized by the Staple Act of 1663 and other acts compelling them to obtain most of their European goods from England rather than from Europe itself. Such legislation normally would have extorted higher prices from the colonists than those paid by the English consumer. On the other hand, the colonial consumer was often favored as compared with the English purchaser. Certain products, notably calicoes, which could not be legally imported into England for sale there, could be shipped to the colonies. Certain British products, moreover, when shipped abroad, received bounties in order to encourage their manufacture. These bounties not only were paid from the British treasury and hence were a tax upon the English people, but enabled the manufacturers to sell these articles in the colonies at a price below that obtained in the metropolis. British and Irish linens benefited by this arrangement.

Still another item operates to confuse the question of whether the colonies or the mother country was more constrained by this legislation. The preamble of the Staple Act stated that one of its purposes was to make navigation to and from England and the colonies "more safe." This was not a pious platitude. Ocean trade was subject to all sorts of dangers. The frequent wars of the period let loose a flood of privateers and warships to prey upon commerce. Protection had to be accorded to national vessels by proper convoys. Then there were swarms of pirates.

One group of buccaneers infested the West Indies and on occasion used the continent, especially North Carolina, as a base of operations. In Algeria, Tunis, and Tripoli was a second nest of more professional pirates—the Barbary corsairs. Refusing to confine their operations to the Mediterranean, they penetrated on occasion to the English Channel and interfered with the tobacco ships sailing from Virginia. Intermittent punitive expeditions were dispatched against them, and naval vessels had to be stationed in the Mediterranean to enforce such agreements as the corsairs could be compelled to sign. The concentration of trade routes sought by the English acts of navigation and trade made easier the protection of commerce. And the cost of that protection, which was enjoyed by the colonists as well as by the English, was assumed solely by the latter.

Any discussion of the relative burden imposed by these acts upon colonies and metropolis must not overlook the fact that their results might be evaded through failure to obey them. Smuggling is a considerable and profitable undertaking even in the 20th century. The profit was no less in the 17th and 18th centuries, and the operation was easier. Long sea voyages, unfrequented coast lines, and scanty navies facilitated the evasion of the laws. The extent of evasion in the colonies has been the subject of much murky disputation. The provisions of the acts dealing with shipping were almost never violated. There was little reason for disobedience. As for enumerated articles, most of them were probably taken to England. But the profits to be gained by an illegal and direct trade in tobacco to other destinations were so attractive that the colonies sometimes neglected to observe the formalities. Before the Act of Union, Scotch ships and Scotch merchants had invaded the trade. They paid good prices for tobacco; their ships easily evaded the European patrols; and Glasgow had laid the foundations of its future eminence as a great tobacco merchandise center at a time when the commerce upon which it was based was prohibited. In the 18th century the violation of the enumerated provisions seems to have decreased.

The regulations most frequently set at naught by the colonies were those requiring the importation of European and Asiatic goods through Great Britain. One avenue of evasion was the permission given to import wines from the Madeiras and the Azores. This clause was so obscurely worded that the colonists affected to believe that it allowed also the importation of the wines from the Spanish islands of the Canaries. If they doubted the validity of this legal exegesis, colonial shippers placed a few casks of Madeira near the hatchway and depended upon the customs officers to sample these and ignore the Canary wines stored below. A second smuggled commodity was tea. In 1765 a rather generous estimate placed the colonial consumption at 1.5 million pounds. The recorded annual imports were 150,000 pounds. The difference naturally was not grown in this country. Tea, silk, linens, brandies might be brought to this country directly from Holland, Spain, or Portugal by English or American vessels, which simply but dangerously neglected to touch at Great Britain with these commodities; or else they might be secured in the West Indies at St. Eustatius, St. Thomas, or Curaçao.

In spite of these evasions, the acts of trade and navigation so far discussed were not extensively violated. The reason was simple. In the main, the regulations expressed in the acts coincided with the natural conditions of trade. The colonies benefited by their inclusion within the world of British shipping; they were protected in the English market; and as for European goods, they would have had them from England anyway. England manufactured most articles as cheaply as any nation in Europe, and Americans would have imported their woolens and their hardware from her whatever the legislation. Even the goods not produced advantageously in England and drawn by the colonies from Europe would probably have gone through the former in transit. England served as a great warehouse into which commodities from all parts of the world flowed. A vessel could obtain at London or other ports a diversified cargo; it was spared the expense and trouble of collecting it from all quarters of the world. Even in the 19th century, England still played the same role for America and the other new countries of the world.

Any judgment which approaches the acts of trade and navigation from the angle of the colonies only is based upon the wrong premise. The aim of such legislation was the creation of a powerful economic state and empire, and in the light of this purpose it must be appraised. After the passage of the acts, undoubtedly, the prosperity of Great Britain increased, and the economic importance of her rivals relatively declined. What proportion of this success can safely be attributed to England's mercantilist legislation is uncertain. Since the other nations were following similar policies and thus theoretically cancelling the advantages bestowed upon Great Britain, it would seem that many factors created the supremacy of the latter.

7. CREDIT IN A RAPIDLY GROWING COLONIAL MARKET*

The vital role of credit in the economic life of the time can be appreciated by examining its use in colonial Philadelphia. Credit oftentimes originated with the British merchant-capitalist and extended through the chain of importer, wholesaler, and retailer (functions sometimes performed by the same firm) to the ultimate consumer. As is true today, all social and economic groups availed themselves of credit—the wealthy as a matter of convenience and others out of necessity. Because coin was scarce throughout the colonial period, book credit actually served as a substitute medium for exchange. The widespread use of credit had a stimulating effect on the general welfare of the colonists. It allowed production and consumption on a scale which would otherwise have been impossible. There were abuses in those days, also, and voices raised by such notables as Thomas Jefferson and Benjamin Franklin against the excessive use of credit.

CREDIT, including credit to the ultimate consumer, was a constitutive factor of colonial economic life. Lord Sheffield said that at least four fifths of the importations from Europe into the American colonies at all times were upon credit. Current exports from the colonies were not used to pay for current imports but rather to pay debts that had been contracted in making previous purchases abroad. Current imports were to be paid for in the future.

The credit the American importer received from the exporter abroad was passed on to the city shopkeeper (sometimes the importing, whole-saling, and retailing functions in Philadelphia were performed by the same firm), the backcountry storekeeper, and the Indian trader, who in turn extended credit to the ultimate consumer. The Indian, the farmer, the artisan, the clerk, the professional person, and the businessman, in their capacity as ultimate consumers, were at the end of a chain of credit that extended from them back to British merchant-capitalists.

In the matter of credit, Philadelphia differed somewhat from the rest of the country, in that it was less dependent upon credit from abroad.

* Reprinted from Wilbur C. Plummer, "Consumer Credit in Colonial Philadelphia," *Pennsylvania Magazine of History and Biography*, Vol. LXVII (October, 1942), pp. 389–409.

This is another way of saying that the merchants of Philadelphia had accumulated a larger supply of their own capital which was available for use in financing themselves and their customers. As Philadelphia became more wealthy, the local merchants to an increasing extent took the place of foreign capitalists. A similar situation prevailed in other cities of the North. New York, Boston, Newport, and Providence were also commercial centers, each with its wealthy and influential merchants. The South did not have a comparable native merchant class.

A study of colonial business, professional, and personal records reveals quite strikingly the fact that there was a large amount of credit extended for the purchase of all kinds of commodities and services for consumption purposes—so much, in fact, that it seems certain that credit rather than cash was the rule. All economic and social groups used consumer credit, although not for the same reasons. The wealthy did so as a matter of convenience, and others as a matter of necessity.

Selling on credit involves costs which in the long run are borne by the ultimate consumer. While there is no way of knowing how much was added to prices by retailers because of their granting credit, there is some information on how much was added by foreign merchants to the prices of goods sold to American importers on credit. Robert Morris said that with ready money, importers might have made their purchases "ten, fifteen, twenty, and perhaps in some articles, thirty per cent cheaper than on credit." Continuing, Morris said:

> It is true that the merchants in England usually shipped goods on one year's credit, without charging interest for that year. But it has been always said, and in some instances proved upon trials in the courts of law, that the year's interest is amply compensated by the advances put on the real cost of the goods, besides other benefices derived by the English merchant, by means of drawbacks, discounts, etc., etc. And if the American importer cannot pay at the expiration of the twelve months, an interest account commences, and is continued in such manner, that he pays at the rate of compound interest, until the debt is discharged. Under these disadvantages, the credit, obtained in Europe, at a rate of interest equal to fifteen, twenty, or perhaps thirty per cent has been the foundation of that prosperity which we behold in America.

There was some cash lending for consumption purposes in colonial times, but it was not quantitatively important in comparison with sales credit. Although pawnbrokers were to be found in Europe from the later Middle Ages, there were none in Philadelphia in colonial times. Also, the various types of specialized cash-lending agencies of the present time are a more recent development. The chief sources of cash credit in 18th-century Philadelphia were the relatives of the borrower and the merchants from whom he customarily bought goods on credit.

Credit terms in respect to the time the debtor was supposed to pay were customarily indefinite but liberal. "Our laws and habits countenance long credits, and afford slow methods for recovering debts," it was said. In 1727, Samuel Power, Jr., a Philadelphia merchant acting as agent for a London firm, wrote his principal that he had sold his wares "tho it may be a pretty while befor I can be in cash for these goods." The next year, he wrote to one of his correspondents that there was a prospective market in Philadelphia for linen goods of various types, "including a few diapers," but that "little or none of the pay will be had in less than 12 months and some of it longer." A letter of this same merchant written in 1739 tells in short space a great deal of the customary credit and other trade practices of the time. He wrote: "When we have sold our European goods and trusted them a while, we are obliged to take a great part of the pay in bread, pork, flour, wheat or any goods that are the produce of the country, and most of these goods we send to the islands in the West Indies where they are sold and from thence the effects are sent to England per exchange, gold, silver, or sugars." In individual transactions, time limits sometimes were set, such as six months or a year, but these were the exception rather than the rule. The customary practice appears to have been for the debtor to pay in whole or in part as he was able if he was poor, and at his convenience if he was a man of means.

Collections of accounts receivable were slow in those days as judged by present-day standards. Unfortunately, there are too many dates of collections missing on the books of colonial business and professional men to compute overall averages for the length of time their accounts receivable were outstanding. However, there are complete data for many individual accounts. Aitken's books show that Benjamin Franklin paid in 9 months and 21 days, on an average. Francis Hopkinson, whose purchases were considerably larger than those of Franklin, paid in 2 years, 3 months, and 13 days, on an average. The accounts of James Burd show that the average monthly collection percentage for the eight-month period May to December, 1765, was 14 percent. This means that the average length of time Burd's accounts receivable were outstanding was slightly over seven months. Bad-debt losses on the whole were high in comparison with those of the present time.

There was a great deal of what today would be called refinancing, that is, changing the form of the debt—liquidating one debt by contracting another. Book accounts were settled after they had been standing for some time—six months, a year, or longer—by the debtor giving his promissory note or bond, usually with interest, which was negotiable and could be used by the creditor to pay his own debts.

A noteworthy and significant fact from the standpoint of economic science, although it does not seem to have been pointed out heretofore, is that book credit was actually a medium of exchange—a substitute for money. This arose from the practice of balancing accounts against each other, or paying accounts in kind, or refinancing the book account into a debt evidenced by a promissory note or bond. The credit instrument, in turn, was used by the creditor to buy goods or pay his debts, or by the creditor drawing an order, more formally called a bill of exchange or draft, on his debtor, and using this to buy goods or to pay his own debts. If a debt is paid in cash, the original credit transaction does not eliminate the use of money entirely; it simply postpones its use. However, if the debt is paid in kind, or if accounts are balanced against each other, or if the account is changed into a form of debt evidenced by a negotiable instrument that is itself used in exchange, goods are exchanged for each other, and the use of money as a medium is not necessary.

Book credit and the promissory note, bond, and bill-of-exchange credit growing out of it, as media of exchange, deserve notice in the development of economic institutions. The lack of an adequate medium of exchange has a retarding effect on the growth of trade and prosperity. Specie was always scarce in the colonies because it was drained off as fast as it was received to meet an unfavorable balance of trade. As badly as the colonists needed gold and silver for monetary purposes, they wanted even more the necessities and luxuries gold and silver would buy in Europe. The issuing of paper money was prohibited by parliament in 1764. Previous to that, its use had proved unsatisfactory because of too abundant issues, although Pennsylvania was one of the most conservative of the colonies in this respect and avoided the excesses of some of the others. Tobacco in Virginia and Maryland, and furs in New England, were media of exchange. But they, like other commodities used as money at one time or another in the colonies, were not very satisfactory because they lacked some of the essential qualities of good money. Demand deposits, as a circulating medium, like banks themselves, were unknown in the colonies. Book credit and the notes, bonds, and orders growing out of it may not be considered very efficient as media of exchange when judged by modern circulating media, but they were the best available and filled a need of the time.

The use of credit, on the whole, helped to increase the productivity of the country. This was true of the credit extended for consumers' goods as well as for producers' goods. The cooking utensils, blankets, and clothing that were given to the Indian had very much the same effect as the firearms and traps. They made him a more efficient hunter and trapper. One may be sure that if this were not the case, he would not have been given such articles on credit. The object of the Indian traders and the merchants who financed them was not to promote the welfare of the Indian but to secure the pelts he brought in from the hunt and the profits to be derived therefrom. The salt which was sold on credit to the farmers for their table use and to cure their pork for home consumption had the same economic effect as the salt which was used to feed their stock and to cure the pork which was sent to Philadelphia for export. The nails bought on credit that went into their homes had the same effect as those that went into their barns. The medicines and services of the physician rendered to those unable to pay cash—and there were many such—tended to make people more healthy, and able-bodied workmen were as essential to the development of the country as the tools with which they worked. It would be farfetched, of course, to apply the same reasoning to some consumer credit—for example, that which enabled some of the planters of the South to purchase luxuries and to live extravagantly beyond their means—but there is no question that on the whole, consumer credit in colonial Pennsylvania tended to increase the productivity of the country.

Robert Morris recounted the favorable effects of credit, explaining how America had risen to "opulence" by means of the credit she obtained in Europe. He said: "That credit has been extended by the importer to the country shopkeeper; and through him, to the farmer and mechanic, who being thereby enabled to pursue their labors, have drawn produce from the surface and bowels of the earth, which has not only defrayed the whole of the cost and charges, but enriched the industrious."

In contrast with the views of Robert Morris are opinions attributed to Benjamin Franklin and the recorded views of Thomas Jefferson. Dr. Benjamin Rush quotes Franklin as saying in 1786 that credit produced idleness and vice and that he wished all debts should, like debts of honor or gambling debts, be irrecoverable by law. At another time, Franklin is quoted as saying that interest was 30 percent per annum in China and that this promoted industry, kept down the price of land, and made freeholds more common. His point in the latter case apparently was that the rate was so high that it discouraged borrowing, and thus the ill effects of credit were avoided. In 1787, Jefferson wrote:

The maxim of buying nothing without the money in our pocket to pay for it, would make of our country one of the happiest upon earth. Experience during the war proved this; as I think every man will remember that under all the privations it obliged him to submit to during that period he slept sounder and awaked happier than he can do now. Desperate of finding relief from a free course of justice, I look forward to the abolition of all credit as the only other remedy which can take place. I have seen therefore with pleasure the exaggerations of our want of faith with which the London papers teem. It is indeed a strong medicine for sensible minds, but it is a medicine. It will prevent their crediting us abroad, in which case we cannot be credited at home.

In this study a number of generalizations have been drawn which may be restated briefly by way of summary. A detailed examination of business, professional, and personal records reveals the fact that in colonial Philadelphia, the largest and most rapidly growing city in pre-Revolutionary America, there was a large amount of credit extended in connection with the sale of all kinds of commodities and services for consumption purposes. In fact, it seems certain that credit rather than cash was the rule. There was also some cash lending for consumption purposes. The chief sources of cash credit were the relatives of the borrower and the merchants from whom he customarily bought goods on credit. There were no pawnbrokers in colonial Philadelphia nor any of the other various types of specialized cash-lending agencies of the present time. In Philadelphia and in the rest of Pennsylvania, with whose economy that of Philadelphia was interdependent, consumer credit was at the end of a chain of debt that extended from the Indian, the farmer, the artisan, the clerk, the professional person, and the businessman, in their capacity of ultimate consumers, back to British merchant-capitalists. Credits were long, collections slow, and bad debts high in comparison with those of the present time. The use of credit, including consumers' credit, generally speaking, had beneficial effects, in that it helped to increase the productivity of the country. Especially noteworthy from the standpoint of the development of economic institutions is the fact that book debt, the usual form of credit, and the promissory note, bond, and bill-of-exchange debt growing out of it, were media of exchange, substitutes for actual money, and as such filled a pressing need of the time.

PART I

Marketing in Colonial
America, 1607-1790

B. MARKETING AND ITS
   ENVIRONMENT:
   A TWO-WAY FLOW

1. THE MARKETING ENVIRONMENT OF MASSACHUSETTS BAY COLONY*

Efforts to regulate marketing practices in 17th-century Massachusetts reflected not only the economic and religious aims of the colony but its cultural and social heritage. Though it is not generally recognized, the philosophy of Saint Thomas Aquinas had a considerable impact on the legislation adopted in this colonial community. Despite a political and theocratic structure that encouraged attempts to control prices, wages, foreign trade, and even dress, domestic markets continued to be governed largely by supply and demand conditions.

THERE HAS BEEN much dispute as to the impact of Protestant theology on the commercial and industrial development of western Europe. Whatever the relationship in Europe between Protestantism and capitalism, in New England material success was not accepted as evidence of one's election to eternal bliss. Saint Thomas Aquinas had more effect on the economic thinking of Massachusetts Bay Colony than John Calvin. The officials of this theocratic commonwealth accepted the medieval doctrine of the "just price" and attempted to regulate rather than to stimulate business enterprise. Social and economic life was to be carefully ordered in the interest of the common good.[1]

In 1639, Robert Keayne, a wealthy Boston merchant, was accused of notoriously oppressing the buyers of his wares. At Keayne's ecclesiastical trial, John Cotton contrasted the true principles of trade with some existing misconceptions.

Some false principles were these:

1. That a man might sell as dear as he can and buy as cheap as he can.
2. If a man lose by casualty of sea, etc., in some of his commodities, he may raise the price of the rest.

* Reprinted from Stanley J. Shapiro, "Marketing in Massachusetts Bay Colony: 1629–1685," *Economics and Business Bulletin, Temple University School of Business and Public Administration,* Vol. XVI (December, 1963), pp. 3–10.

[1] Samuel E. Morison, *Builders of the Bay Colony* (Cambridge: Houghton Mifflin Co., 1930), pp. 160–62. Morison's viewpoint, however, is not universally accepted. See A. W. Griswold, "Three Puritans on Prosperity," *New England Quarterly,* Vol. VII, pp. 475 ff.

3. That he may sell as he bought, though he paid too dear, etc., and though the commodity be fallen, etc.
4. That as a man may take the advantage of his own skill or ability, so he may of another's ignorance or necessity.
5. Where one gives time for payment, he is to take like recompense of one as of another.

The rules for trading were these:

1. A man may not sell above the current price, i.e., such a price as is usual in the time and place, and as another (who knows the worth of the commodity) would give for it if he had occasion to use it.
2. When a man loseth in his commodity for want of skill, etc., he must look at it as his own fault or cross, and therefore must not lay it upon another.
3. Where a man loseth by casualty of sea, or etc., it is a loss cast upon himself by providence, and he may not ease himself of it by casting it upon another . . . but where there is scarcity of the commodity, there men may raise their price; for now it is a hand of God upon the commodity, and not the person.
4. A man may not ask any more for his commodity than his selling price, as Ephron to Abraham, the land is worth thus much.[2]

Unlike many ruling classes, the Puritan clergy and the country squires were not opposed to trade so long as it was regulated in the public interest. Despite the emphasis on a just price, they recognized the effect of supply and demand conditions on wage rates and price levels. Most early Puritan merchants found that success in trading was not incompatible with church membership.[3]

Cotton's rules for trading had a limited impact on the commercial life of the colony. As early as Keayne's civil trial, the magistrates gave the following reasons for reducing the fine levied against him by the delegates to the general court: No law was in force limiting profits; Keayne was not the sole offender and had followed the accepted practices of other lands; and a perfectly equitable price could neither be determined nor be prescribed. In 1640, Governor Winthrop complained that most men were attempting to buy as cheap as they could and to sell as dear.[4]

The commercial prosperity of the second half of the 17th century increased the wealth, the prestige, and the social and political influence of the colony's merchant class. Second- and third-generation Massachusetts merchants challenged the hitherto unquestioned leadership of a clerically

[2] John Winthrop, *History of New England,* edited by James Savage (Boston, 1853), Vol. I, pp. 316–17.
[3] Morison, *op. cit.,* p. 163; Bernard Bailyn, *The New England Merchants in the Seventeenth Century* (Cambridge: Harvard University Press, 1955), pp. 39–44; E. A. J. Johnson, *American Economic Thought in the Seventeenth Century* (London: P. S. King & Son, Ltd., 1932), pp. 123–36.
[4] Daniel W. Howe, *The Puritan Republic* (Indianapolis: Bowen Merill Co., 1899), pp. 140–44.

led oligarchy. The merchants obtained considerable representation in the lower house of the general court, where they were usually able to protect their interests. The majority were not doctrinaire Puritans, and they sided with the forces of liberalism and religious toleration during the theological struggles of the period. Business connections with England and Anglican leanings made some sympathetic to attempts to increase the degree of royal control over Massachusetts. This was true even though the same merchants had grown rich violating English navigation acts.[5]

PRICE AND WAGE CONTROLS

In the period under examination, frequent efforts were made to regulate prices and wages. Such action was in the English tradition. In England, however, regulation began on the local level and subsequently became national policy. In Massachusetts the control of prices and wages became a local responsibility only after regulations passed by the central government proved ineffective.[6]

In 1630, maximum wages were established for those employed in the building trades. This legislation was repealed six months later, but the principle of wage fixing was not repudiated. Because of the "exorbitant" demands of the laboring class, a much more extensive system of wage controls was soon introduced. In 1633, statutory limits were placed on the amount that could be earned by skilled artisans. The same act gave town constables and two other men selected by these officials the right to regulate the wages of day laborers. This legislation proved ineffective, and it appears that current wages exceeded the specified levels by some 50 percent. Wage regulation became a local responsibility in October, 1636. More effective control was anticipated, since the elders of the local churches could employ a combination of spiritual and legal power. The new policy, however, met with very limited success. Labor was scarce, and artisans who felt oppressed would either move elsewhere or take up farming.[7]

The statute passed in 1636 made wage regulation a local matter. In 1641, however, the general court ordered that laborers reduce their wages in accordance with the decline that had occurred in the value of the commodities they produced. An abrupt end to immigration caused a sharp break in prices, and workers were expected to share in the general misfortune just as they had previously benefited from a high level of prosperity. The basic law of 1636 against oppression in wages remained in effect until 1675. At that time the labor shortages associated

---

[5] Bailyn, *op. cit.*, pp. 94–111, 134–42, 154–62.
[6] Richard B. Morris and Jonathan Grossman, "Wage Regulation in Massachusetts," *New England Quarterly*, Vol. XI (September, 1938), pp. 473–74.
[7] *Ibid.*, pp. 470–78.

with King Philip's War and sustained agitation for new controls resulted in legislation increasing the regulatory powers of town selectmen. Court records show that town and colony officials frequently, albeit sporadically, prosecuted workers for violating existing wage regulations. A most noteworthy case was that of Edward Palmer, who was found guilty of overcharging in the construction of the Boston stocks. Palmer was fined and sentenced to sit in those same stocks for one hour.[8]

Price regulations were a necessary corollary to wage controls. In 1633 the Massachusetts General Court passed legislation limiting the price of imports to one third more than the cost of similar goods in England. Because of the risk involved in importing perishables, such merchandise could be sold at whatever rate was agreed upon by buyer and seller. Merchants who exceeded the bounds of moderation in pricing other commodities were to be severely disciplined. This law was repealed in 1635 and replaced by one which made the charging of unreasonable prices a crime punishable by fine or imprisonment. Robert Keayne was brought to trial under this statute. In the early years of settlement the use of corn as currency resulted in its price often being fixed by the general court. In 1641 the towns were given the authority to regulate the prices of commodities as well as wages. Price, quantity, and quality controls were imposed on bread, casks, leather, wood, and bricks, and violators were prosecuted. Generally, it was the prices charged by artisans rather than by merchants that were regulated. As was mentioned earlier, the lack of skilled workmen resulted in the sporadic enforcement of wage and price restrictions placed on this group.[9]

17TH-CENTURY MERCANTILISM

Historical insight and new developments in economic thought have combined to point up the inadequacy of mercantilist policies. In the 17th century, such policies were adopted by all the leading nations of Europe. Colonies were desired because they could serve as markets for products manufactured at home and provide raw materials that would otherwise have to be purchased abroad with valuable bullion.

The ideal empire, according to the Mercantile Theory, would embrace the home country, which, aside from the production of certain raw materials, was, in the main, the source of credit, the seat of manufactures, the selling agency to the world for the whole empire, the centre of administration, and the protective power to guard the system. The colonies in the temperate zone were to supply the typical products of their regions, the East and West Indies materials found in the tropics, and the African stations the supply of Negro

---

[8] *Ibid.*, pp. 479–97.
[9] Howe, *op. cit.*, pp. 138–40.

labor . . . . The English Empire was the most complete embodiment of the ideal.[10]

The New England colonies were the only possessions in the Empire that competed with rather than complemented the commercial and industrial activity of Old England. Observers recognized the threat to English commerce, agriculture, and manufacturing posed by colonies with very similar resources. Oliver Cromwell's attempt in 1655 to induce migration from Massachusetts Bay to Jamaica was due in part to the colony's position as a disturbing element in England's mercantilist empire.[11]

Early English acts of trade contributed to the commercial development of Massachusetts Bay colony. In 1644 the trade of New England was specifically exempted from the payment of English import and export duties. The first Navigation Act, passed in 1651 by a Puritan parliament favorably disposed to New England, gave English and colonial vessels a monopoly on all shipping to or from any part of the Empire. This exclusion of the Dutch from the carrying trade greatly benefited Massachusetts Bay merchants, who could construct and operate ships more cheaply than their English counterparts.[12]

Legislation passed after the Stuart Restoration in 1660 made England the sole market for many colonial goods. European manufactures could not be imported directly into the colonies, and some types of merchandise could be purchased only from England. Certain qualifying provisions mitigated the harmful effects of these acts. Many products shipped to and from Europe were exempted from regulation, and no restrictions were placed on intercolonial commerce. Also, protected markets were often established for colonial products which could be sold only in England.[13]

These early navigation acts appear to have achieved their objectives. The volume of English shipping soon surpassed that of the Dutch, colonial trade and commerce increased, and the Empire prospered. The government of the bay colony and private citizens petitioned for relief against the features of the Stuart legislation considered most harmful. The undesirable provisions had a limited effect on the colony's commerce, however, as they were frequently violated by Massachusetts merchants and indifferently enforced by sympathetic public officials. That the laws were not flaunted with impunity was apparent from the

---

[10] James T. Adams, *The Founding of New England* (Boston: Atlantic Monthly Press, 1921), pp. 284–85.

[11] *Ibid.*, pp. 278–88; Johnson, *American Economic Thought*, pp. 35–49; E. A. J. Johnson, "Some Evidence of Mercantilism in the Massachusetts Bay," *New England Quarterly*, Vol. I (July, 1928), pp. 371–79.

[12] Bailyn, *op. cit.*, pp. 90–94.

[13] Adams, *op. cit.*, pp. 298–300; Bailyn, *op. cit.*, pp. 112–14.

fact that repeated evasions of the navigation acts caused Massachusetts to lose its charter and become a royal colony in 1685.[14]

England's commercial policies conflicted with a form of native mercantilism practiced within the Massachusetts Bay colony. In many respects, the leaders of the colony considered it a free and independent state, and local mercantilism was a corollary to such thinking. The authorities urged the domestic production of goods that would otherwise have to be imported. In the 1640's, for example, bounties were paid to increase the manufacture of textiles. In the following 20 years, sheep production was encouraged, a protective tariff against the importation of wheat was passed, and the exportation of lambs and various types of raw material was forbidden. Mercantilist tendencies were also demonstrated by the establishment of a mint, the passage of regulations against the export of specie, the levying of tonnage duties on ships owned outside the jurisdiction, and widespread concern with the colony's unfavorable balance of trade. The wage and price regulations mentioned earlier and the sumptuary legislation yet to be discussed were also consistent with mercantilist doctrine.[15]

FOREIGN COMMERCE

The development of the bay colony's foreign trade was hastened by the economic crisis of 1640–41. Fish and fur had been shipped to Europe in the preceding decade, and many of the ships used in this trade had been built locally. The bulk of the earlier colonists, however, had prospered by selling food, livestock, and labor to new arrivals. When immigration to New England fell off sharply during the English Civil War, the resultant oversupply of agricultural commodities caused prices to drop to a third or even less of the previous levels. Trade became necessary if the bay settlement was to prosper and continue to grow.[16]

The colony's maritime efforts met with phenomenal success. By 1650 a contemporary historian commented upon the speed with which prosperity returned, the growth of Boston from a poor country village to a small city, and the many nations with which Massachusetts traders dealt. Twenty-five years later, another observer reported on the commodities most frequently being shipped.

In exchange of fish, pipe staves, wool, and tobacco, they have from Spain, Portugal, and the islands, the commodities of these countries (cotton, wines, silver, and gold); their wool they carry to France and bring thence linen; to England they bring beaver, moose, and deer skins, sugar and logwood, and carry hence cloth and ironwares; to Barbadies in exchange for horses, beef,

---

[14] Bailyn, *op. cit.*, pp. 143–70.
[15] Johnson, "Some Evidence," pp. 379–95.
[16] Herman F. Clarke, *John Hull: A Builder of the Bay Colony* (Portland, Me.: Southworth-Anthoensen Press, 1940), pp. 39–41; Morison, *op. cit.*, pp. 143–44.

pork, butter, cheese, flour, peas, biscuit, they have sugar and indigo; when they trade with Jamaica, as they do sometimes, they bring home pieces of eight, plate, and pigs of silver. . . . As to cloth, . . . the better sort of linen is brought from England. . . . Salt they get from Tortugas.[17]

Molasses was imported from the West Indies at the end of the period, when the manufacture of rum became an important New England industry. Some Indian captives and Negro slaves were sold to the plantation owners of these islands. All during the period, Massachusetts boatwrights built ships for their own merchants and for English traders.[18]

Merchant life in the 17th century was not without its risks. Dutch and French privateers captured trading ships during the period when England was at war with these nations. Any vessel seized as a war prize would be a complete loss, and such seizures occurred quite frequently. Also, Algerian pirates were active in the Mediterranean. In an attempt to spread risk, merchants would often obtain part interests in many ships rather than complete ownership of a lesser number. Uncertainty as to future market conditions in foreign ports made it necessary that considerable leeway be given ship captains. They were even empowered to sell the ship if this appeared profitable.

"I leave it to you from first to last in everythinge to doe with vessele and cargo whatever may conduce in your best judgement for my reale benefitt and advantage." (The captain who received this message was also given specific instructions to worship God daily, to sanctify the Lord's day, and to suppress all profanity.) Judgment appeared necessary in the selection of agents with whom to deal in foreign ports, as long-term credit was the rule and barter transactions were common.[19] For this reason, intercolonial and international trading arrangements were frequently established by merchants related through blood or marriage.[20] A safe return home solved many but not all of the merchants' problems. Many warehouses were burned in the great fires which ravaged Boston in the 1670's and 1680's.[21]

Despite the many risks of the business, sizable profits on goods safely delivered made 17th-century Boston merchants wealthy men. These merchants were all of English origin, and their homes were as fine as any in England. Many had estates of £4,000 to £18,000 in a country where one was considered rich if he was worth much less. A merchants' exchange was established by a Boston ordinance of 1664 in order to facilitate "the

---

[17] Cited in George F. Dow, "Shipping and Trade in Early New England," *Massachusetts Historical Society Proceedings, 1930–1932*, Vol. LXIV (Boston, 1932), p. 191.

[18] *Ibid.*, pp. 190–94; Clarke, *op. cit.*, pp. 39–46, 101–12.

[19] Clarke, *op. cit.*, pp. 72–75, 101–11; Morison, *op. cit.*, pp. 171–75.

[20] Bailyn, *op. cit.*, pp. 87–91.

[21] Carl Bridenbaugh, *Cities in the Wilderness* (New York: Ronald Press Co., 1938), pp. 57–61.

more convenient and expeditious dispatch of Merchant affairs." Close relationships existed between the 40 full- or part-time merchants active at the end of the period.[22] Personal ties were strengthened by the considerable intermarriage that had occurred between the limited number of merchant families. In later years, one's commercial prospects depended in large part on the quality of his connections with individuals of authority and influence at the court of Charles II. Well-placed friends could obtain profitable government contracts for their colonial associates and also recommend them for local sinecures.[23]

DOMESTIC MARKETING

The colonists' fur trade with the Indians can be considered the earliest form of domestic marketing. This trade was the major source of revenue for the Plymouth colony, and it soon became an important industry in Massachusetts. Traders would offer wampum, liquor, guns, or almost anything else requested by the Indians in return for beaver and other skins. By 1640, the local supply of furs proved inadequate. Efforts to obtain pelts from more remote tribes brought the New England colonies into conflict with French, Dutch, and Swedish settlements. In 1657 the general court declared the fur trade a state monopoly and issued exclusive trading rights in return for payments into the colony's treasury. Fur-trading companies licensed in Massachusetts attempted to interpret that colony's charter in a manner that would sanction trading posts on the Hudson and the Delaware. First the Dutch and then the royal governor of New York objected to such action, and these companies were unable to establish inland trading posts. Geography and political considerations combined to prevent Massachusetts interests from gaining direct access to the valuable western fur trade.[24]

Public markets were established in the Massachusetts Bay colony in the early 1630's. The code of laws of 1648 authorized markets on different days at Boston, Salem, Lynn, and Charlestown. Semiannual fairs could be held in Salem, Watertown, and Dorchester. The first market, at Boston, was held on Thursday, since the "country people" would be in town to hear the church lectures given on that day. In 1649 the town meeting of Boston appointed "Clarkes of the Market" to supervise trading. In 1658, this market was moved from an open-air location to an area beneath a public building bequeathed the town by Robert Keayne.[25]

---

[22] Dow, *op. cit.*, pp. 191–92; Bridenbaugh, *op. cit.*, pp. 27–28.

[23] Bailyn, *op. cit.*, pp. 134–38, 170–77.

[24] *Ibid.*, pp. 49–60; Arthur H. Buffinton, "New England and the Western Fur Trade, 1629–1675," *Transactions of the Colonial Society of Massachusetts, 1915–16*, Vol. XVIII (Boston, 1917), pp. 160–88.

[25] *The Laws and Liberties of Massachusetts, 1648* (Cambridge: Harvard University Press, 1929), pp. 21–22; Bridenbaugh, *op. cit.*, pp. 27–28.

The colony also acted to standardize weights and measures, and to regulate the amount of malt in beer. The prices to be charged for food and drink by licensed alehouses were specified, as were the procedures for tanning leather. Also, inspectors were appointed by the general court to assure the quality and to maintain the reputation of New England products shipped abroad. The system of apprenticeship and the temporary licensing in 1648 of shoemakers' and coopers' guilds were motivated in part by a desire to protect the public from inferior work.[26]

Seventeenth-century Boston was the most important wholesale market center in North America. This position followed logically from the town's role as the major seaport in the English colonies.

The only town to extend its economic control beyond nearby hamlets to the hinterland in the seventeenth century was Boston. By 1680, Newfoundland, Maine, New Hampshire, Massachusetts, Rhode Island, and the River towns of Connecticut all paid tribute to the Bay town's commercial leadership. In 1640, cattle began to move overland from the Piscataqua, and after 1660, Hampshire County, Massachusetts, specialized in grass-fed cattle for the Boston market. . . . [From Newport,] Peleg Sanford sent overland his flocks of sheep in 1667, and received in exchange clothing and dry goods by pack horse. . . . From Milford [Connecticut] came beaver pelts and grain; peas and pork were shipped from the River towns to Boston, whence they went to feed the fishermen of Salem and Marblehead. . . . Clement Corbin of Woodstock carried produce by oxcart over the hills into Boston, and returned with dry goods, liquor, ammunition, and 'other necessaries' for his general store.[27]

Boston's commercial leadership grew ever more marked despite efforts in the Connecticut and New Hampshire legislatures to limit the activities of Massachusetts traders. Rhode Island farmers and Maine fishermen also attacked the high prices the Boston merchants charged for English goods.[28]

Much of the retail trade of Boston was carried on by merchants who sold imported goods and domestically produced items accepted as payment in earlier transactions. All the leading merchants of the town operated such stores. "The shops were valuable to the merchants not only because retail sales to the growing Boston trade were lucrative but also because these retail stores provided a necessary outlet for the odd lots of goods left over from wholesale exchanges."[29]

In 1651, George Corwin established a shop in Salem for the sale of fabrics and hardware. He carried a very extensive line of textiles as well as a great variety of ladies' accessories and sewing supplies. Among the hardware items available were locks, children's toys, combs, white-haft knives, barbers' scissors, flour boxes, carving and carpenters' tools, door

[26] Morison, *op. cit.*, pp. 163–66.
[27] Bridenbaugh, *op. cit.*, pp. 32–33.
[28] *Ibid.*, pp. 30–34; Bailyn, *op. cit.*, pp. 94–99.
[29] Bailyn, *op. cit.*, p. 100.

latches, brushes for horses, and a considerable supply of earthen- and woodenware.[30] Boston appears to have had a number of small shops owned by people "who buy to sell again" and frequented by townsfolk making small individual purchases. These embryonic general stores stocked such diverse articles as looking glasses, candlesticks, gloves, tin lanterns, rattraps, dry goods, imported groceries, fishing tackle, bottles, and trays. By 1675, shopkeepers as well as merchants were accused of charging exorbitant prices. A shopkeeper's journal available for the years 1685 to 1689 reveals a rural as well as a town trade, customer purchases in exceedingly small quantities, and a majority of barter and/or credit transactions.[31]

CURRENCY PROBLEMS

The bay colony suffered from an inadequate monetary system all during the period under examination. Lack of a medium of exchange complicated domestic trade, and foreign commerce was hindered by a shortage of specie. Since the supply of currency brought into the colony by settlers was insufficient, a variety of substitutes was employed. During the first 20 years, corn, fur, and wampum were used as a currency within the province, and beaver skins were sent to London as a form of foreign exchange. Since corn and wampum were legal tender, laws were passed to stabilize their value. During the depression of 1640, the general court ruled that all debts, however contracted, could be paid in corn, cattle, fish, or other commodities at rates specified by the court or by disinterested parties. As late as 1649, wampum was legal tender in payment of debts up to 40 shillings. An attempt in 1661 to prohibit its use as currency was only partially successful.[32]

By 1650 the increasing volume of foreign trade had brought into circulation a considerable amount of miscellaneous coin, much of it debased, counterfeit, or clipped. On May 27, 1652, the general court authorized the establishment of a mint, which continued in operation for more than 30 years. A conscious policy of overvaluing Massachussets pine tree shillings to keep this currency at home met with limited success. An unfavorable balance of trade with Europe caused these shillings to be exported, despite the legal restrictions on such action and their circulation at a discount abroad. Also limiting the supply of currency were policies that made it more profitable to ship foreign coin and bullion to Europe than to send it to the Massachusetts mint.[33]

Within the colony, taxes were paid in kind, and barter was the rule in domestic trade. Merchants would exchange imported goods for crops,

---

[30] Dow, *op. cit.*, pp. 194–95.
[31] Bridenbaugh, *op. cit.*, pp. 41–42.
[32] Clarke, *op. cit.*, pp. 39–40, 53–55.
[33] *Ibid.*, pp. 56–57; Morison, *op. cit.*, pp. 150–53.

animals, fish, and percentages of ships or of current voyages. In the 1680's an attempt was made to establish a land bank, and there was some agitation in favor of paper money.[34]

SUMPTUARY LEGISLATION

From the time of earliest settlement, many inhabitants of the bay colony were fashion-prone and style-conscious. Officially, however, such traits were condemned. In 1634 a law was passed against the making and buying of elaborately decorated clothes, slashed sleeves, and gold and silver accessories. This and much subsequent legislation on the subject proved ineffective, and moral suasion was only of limited usefulness. The elders of the church could do little to suppress the dangerous new fashion, "for divers of the elders' wives, etc., were in some measure partners in the general disorder." Court prosecutions for the wearing of "wicked apparell" took place as late as 1675. The most liberal clergyman of the time preached against ungodliness in female attire and became indignant at hearing a "Gentledame inquire what dress the Queen is in this week." Devout Puritan merchants imported the clothing desired by such women and their husbands with considerable reluctance. The wearing of wigs by the men of the Puritan smart set was also frowned upon by more conservative citizens.[35]

Class distinctions were quite marked in the colony, and some of the sumptuary legislation was designed to preserve these differences. In 1651 the general court recorded its displeasure at the fact that men and women of mean condition, education, and calling were dressing in the garb of ladies and gentlemen. A statute passed in that year limited the wearing of fancy apparel to those whose estates exceeded £200. Puritan laws against idleness and statutory limitations on wages were also designed in part to preserve class lines. Wage contracts were introduced in 1633, after Governor Winthrop complained that high wages enabled workers to spend their time in idleness and their surplus money on tobacco and liquor. The desire to keep the wages of laborers at a subsistence level was also consistent with the mercantilist doctrines prevailing at the time.[36]

---

[34] Johnson, *American Economic Thought*, pp. 159–202; Bailyn, *op. cit.*, pp. 99–100, 182–89.

[35] Henry W. Lawrence, *The Not-Quite Puritans* (Boston: Little, Brown & Co., 1928), pp. 3–26; Clarke, *op. cit.*, pp. 101–3.

[36] Lawrence, *op. cit.*, pp. 1–7; Morison, *op. cit.*, pp. 162–66; Johnson, *American Economic Thought*, pp. 206–13.

2. COLONIAL NEWSPAPER ADVERTISING AND FREEDOM OF THE PRESS*

The popularity of the newspaper as an advertising medium made it possible to convert the early weeklies into semiweeklies and then dailies. Equally if not more significant, advertising revenues enabled newspaper editors and publishers to free themselves from the need for political subsidies or the support of political parties. This reading illustrates how advertising contributed to the early struggles of journalists to assure freedom of the press. The history and editorial policies of eight newspapers which operated between 1690 and 1750 are briefly traced. One of the earliest newspaper editors, Benjamin Franklin, recognized from the start that a sizable circulation, a journalistic layout, and improved typography were necessary prerequisites for success.

IT IS FREQUENTLY said that the newspaper of today is printed on the backs of advertisements because the price the reader pays usually does not cover the printing cost and the publisher has to depend upon the sale of advertising space for his principal revenue. The partnership between journalism and advertising is so close today that the quality and quantity of editorial matter supplied to the reader depend upon the amount of advertising that can be sold.[1]

In the study of the historical development of journalism and advertising, it is interesting to note that the first daily established in the United States came not because of a demand for fresh news but as a result of the pressure of advertising. The first newspapers were weeklies, and it was only when these weeklies could not handle the increasing volume of advertising that they were converted into semiweeklies. Then, as advertising volume grew still heavier, these publications were published triweekly, and finally on a daily basis.[2]

* Reprinted from Steven J. Shaw, "Colonial Newspaper Advertising: A Step toward Freedom of the Press," *Business History Review,* Vol. XXXIII (Autumn, 1959), pp. 409–20.

[1] George B. Hotchkiss, *An Outline of Advertising* (3d ed.; New York: The Macmillan Co., 1950), p. 22.

[2] Frank Presbrey, *The History and Development of Advertising* (Garden City, N.Y.: Doubleday, Doran & Co., Inc., 1929), p. 161.

The history of newspaper advertising also reveals the remarkable fact that it was largely through the development of profitable advertising that editors in England and the United States were finally able to free themselves from the subsidy and control of governors and political parties.[3]

However, the development of newspaper advertising into a profitable undertaking came only after a long, determined struggle. The colonial printer-editors did not have to discover newspaper advertising, since English pioneers such as Houghton, Addison, and Defoe had already experimented and proved its effectiveness. But the colonial economy was largely agricultural, and the few potential business advertisers were naturally skeptical of the untried medium and had to be won over gradually. The colonial printer-editors strove to overcome this skepticism by running stores on the side and advertising their own merchandise. Thus, by example, they demonstrated to commercial interests the value of advertising.[4]

Moreover, before advertising patronage could be built up substantially, the crude newspaper advertising technique borrowed from England had to be refined. Save for their headlines, the first advertisements were set up like regular reading matter and buried on the back page.[5]

The most formidable obstacle faced by the colonial editors was that of developing adequate circulation in order to make their papers effective carriers of advertising. This was difficult to accomplish, since strict censorship was exercised over the early colonial newspapers. Frank publication of news events in the colonies meant almost certain imprisonment for the editor and suppression of his paper. To be on the safe side of authority, an editor practically had to have his paper edited by the ruling governor.[6] A newspaper so edited was more an organ of official propaganda than an unbiased common carrier of news. To keep out of trouble with the authorities, most of the early colonial editors followed the custom of reprinting news from leading English newspapers. Consequently, much of the editorial matter was stale, and it was difficult for editors to build and maintain a circulation of several hundred paying subscribers.

This study covers the first 60 years of colonial journalism, a period roughly from 1690 to 1750. It was during this period that freedom of the press was fought for and won, and newspaper advertising was built up to the point where editors could begin to divorce themselves from dependence on political subsidy, postmasterships, job printing, and other revenues except copy sales. Specifically, this article gives a brief biographical sketch of eight early colonial newspapers, and evaluates the contributions of their editors to the development of advertising and free

---

[3] Times (London), *The History of the Times*, Vol. I, p. 20; also Alfred M. Lee, *The Daily Newspaper in America* (New York, 1937), p. 181.

[4] James M. Lee, *History of American Journalism* (Boston, 1923), p. 72.

[5] Alfred M. Lee, *op. cit.*, pp. 31–32.

[6] George H. Payne, *History of Journalism in the United States* (New York, 1926), p. 57.

journalism. The development of advertising and the development of a free press must be studied together, as both are essential ingredients of a healthy newspaper.

HARRIS' *PUBLICK OCCURRENCES*

As in England, the forerunner of newspapers in colonial America was the newsletter. This letter was prepared either by a writer who wandered from one coffee house to another to pick up the news or by the postmaster, who handled the few copies of newspapers which came from abroad, and who had contact with the captains and passengers of incoming ships. As soon as the requests for this paid letter service became too numerous to be handled by pen, the writer was forced to employ a printing press.[7]

The first such printed newsletter was *Publick Occurrences*, published on September 25, 1690, by Benjamin Harris, a refugee who had fought unsuccessfully for a free press in England. Without fanfare or preliminary advertising, Harris came out suddenly with the first and only issue of his paper. *Publick Occurrences* was to be published once a month or oftener, depending upon the amount of news. From the standpoint of journalism, it was an excellent conveyor of news, carrying a vivid account of a battle waged by Governor Winthrop with the French and Indians and of the barbarous treatment of French prisoners of war. Its was this account that angered the authorities and caused the immediate suspension of the paper.[8]

What Benjamin Harris' intentions were with regard to advertising are not known. The lone issue contained no paid announcements, and his first-page statement of objectives carried no mention of advertising.[9] Even though *Publick Occurrences* contained no advertising, it is important because it challenged the authorities and began the fight for a free press in the colonies. Following its suppression, the governing council quickly passed a resolution to the effect that any person or persons wishing to set forth anything in print must first obtain a license from the local authorities. This drastic action made it clear to other aspiring publishers that a free press would not be possible without a long and hard fight.

CAMPBELL'S *BOSTON NEWS-LETTER*

The quick suppression of *Publick Occurrences* and the passage of the licensing law discouraged the founding of a second newspaper until 1704, when John Campbell began the publication of the *Boston News-Letter*.

---

[7] James M. Lee, *op. cit.*, p. 18.
[8] Payne, *op. cit.*, p. 21.
[9] Presbrey, *op. cit.*, p. 122.

Mindful of the fate of the first newsletter, Campbell was careful to publish his paper "by authority" and to print nothing that would offend the Council. For the most part, he followed the practice of reprinting material from back issues of the *London Flying Post* and the *London Gazette.* His coverage of local news was largely restricted to the recording of deaths and the announcement of sermons.[10]

Campbell was aware of the success Houghton and other English publishers were having with newspaper advertising in England, and he was anxious to develop his *News-Letter* into a profitable advertising medium. On the back page of the very first issue, he printed the following announcement:

ADVERTISEMENTS

This News Letter is to be continued Weekly; and all Persons who have any Houses, Lands, Tenements, Farms, Ships, Vessels, Goods, Wares or Merchandizes, etc. to be Sold or Let, or Servant Run away; or Goods Stole or Lost; may have the same Inserted at a Reasonable Rate; from Twelve Pence to Five Shillings, and not to exceed: .   .   .   .[11]

Campbell's bid for advertising was viewed with great interest by New York's earliest printer, William Bradford. To see for himself what response a newspaper advertisement would bring from a public not yet accustomed to it, he sent in the following real estate announcement, which appeared in the third weekly issue of the *Boston News-Letter,* and which is considered to be the first American newspaper advertisement.[12]

AT Oyfterbay on *Long-Ifland* in the Province of *N. York,* There is a very good Fulling-Mill, to be Let or Sold, as alfo a Plantation, having on it a large new Brick houfe, and another good houfe by it for a Kitchin, & work houfe, with a Barn, Stable, &c. a young Orchard, and 20 Acres clear Land. The Mill is to be Let with or without the Plantation: Enquire of Mr. *William Bradford* Printer in *N. York,* and know further.

Slaves, runaway apprentices, lost articles, books, and real estate were the most frequent subjects of advertisements in the early issues of the *News-Letter.* Of these, shocking as it might appear to the modern reader, slaves constituted a large percentage. In the seventeenth issue of Campbell's paper, the first American store advertisement appeared. It ran as follows: "At Mr. John Miro Merchant, his Warehouse upon the Dock in Boston, There is to be Sold good Cordage of all Sizes, from a Spurn-yard to Cables of 13 inches, by Whole-sail or Retail."[13]

---

[10] Payne, *op. cit.,* p. 26.
[11] Presbrey, *op. cit.,* p. 126.
[12] *Ibid.*
[13] *Ibid.,* p. 127.

In colonial times a store was sometimes referred to as a "warehouse," since families were largely self-sufficient, growing and making their own products, with the exception of a few imported necessities which were frequently stored in a warehouse at the port of entry.

Now and then, cloth merchants used the *News-Letter* to announce the arrival of new merchandise from England; and occasionally, someone would advertise made-up frocks. But store advertising was a small part of a small total of advertising that appeared in the *News-Letter*.[14]

At the end of three years a total of 5 inches of advertising was a heavy run for the *News-Letter*, and some numbers appeared without a single advertisement. That Campbell had expected greater support from retail advertisers is evident from his petition to the governor for a subsidy. In this petition, he complained "that the post office was paying him very little and that despite the fact that a number of merchants had promised to contribute to the support of his weekly *News-Letter*, he had not made anything by it."[15]

John Campbell's failure to obtain a greater volume of advertising was largely due to the scant circulation of his *News-Letter*. Even after 15 years of publication its circulation was only 300 in a city with a population of about 10,000.[16] Ever conscious of the fate of *Publick Occurrences*, the editor played down local news, and his paper contained mostly stale reprints from London newspapers. Usually, the *News-Letter* was from 5 to 13 months behind with the news.[17]

Small wonder, then, that the public was reluctant to subscribe to the *News-Letter* and that business people were reluctant to advertise in it. Rather than read dull accounts of past events in Europe, the populace preferred to continue the custom of getting news of events in the colonies through coffeehouse gossip and private newsletter.

Probably another reason for Campbell's failure to attract a larger volume of advertising was his lack of enterprise and ingenuity.[18] He did not try to devise ways of making each advertisement resultful. The publicized product was not illustrated, and the only display was the word "advertisements." Otherwise, all of the *News-Letter*'s announcements were set up like regular reading matter and appeared inconspicuously on the back page.[19]

Campbell's journalistic career suffered a severe blow when in 1719 he was replaced as postmaster by William Brooker. With the loss of the

---

[14] *Ibid.*, p. 129.

[15] Payne, *op. cit.*, p. 26.

[16] *Ibid.*, p. 27.

[17] Anna J. DeArmond, *Andrew Bradford, Colonial Journalist* (Newark, Del., 1949), p. 51. See also Payne, *op. cit.*, p. 27.

[18] Presbrey, *op. cit.*, p. 129.

[19] Elizabeth C. Cook, *Literary Influences in Colonial Newspapers, 1704–1750* (New York, 1912), p. 8. See also Presbrey, *op. cit.*, pp. 128–29.

post-office revenue, he found it extremely difficult to continue the publication of his *News-Letter;* and on January 7, 1723, it passed into other hands.[20]

JAMES FRANKLIN, THE *BOSTON GAZETTE*, AND THE *NEW ENGLAND COURANT*

On December 21, 1719, Brooker, the new postmaster, brought out the first number of the *Boston Gazette* at the request of several Boston merchants who apparently were completely fed up with the ineffective *News-Letter*.[21] James Franklin, older brother of the celebrated Benjamin, was the printer of the *Gazette* for one year.[22] To supplement his meager income as printer, Franklin printed and sold cloth at his printshop. He was an enthusiastic advertiser of his own products. On April 25, 1720, for instance, he inserted this advertisement in the *Gazette*: "The Printer herof prints Linens, Calicoes, Silks, etc., in good Figures, very lively and durable colours, and without the offensive Smell which commonly attends the Linens printed here."[23]

While its founding had been encouraged by disgruntled *News-Letter* advertisers, the *Boston Gazette* failed to introduce any new advertising techniques during its early years, possibly due to its frequent change of ownership. It was approximately the same size as the *News-Letter*, used the same soggy typography, and carried the same type and paucity of advertisements—mostly of slaves, lost articles, books, and real estate—on its back pages.[24]

On August 6, 1721, shortly after his dismissal as printer of the *Boston Gazette*, James Franklin began to publish Boston's third newspaper, entitled the *New England Courant*. He was well prepared for this venture, having studied in London, where he observed firsthand the work of the English masters, Addison and Steele.[25] While the *Courant* was the liveliest and most literary of the early colonial newspapers,[26] it lasted less than five years, for James Franklin was another Harris and constantly clashed with the authorities. Most of the space in the *New England Courant* was absorbed in frank criticism of the conduct of colonial affairs

---

[20] Clarence S. Brigham, *History and Bibliography of American Newspapers, 1690–1820*, Vol. I (Hamden, Conn.: Shoe String Press, Inc., 1947), p. 327.

[21] DeArmond, *op. cit.,* p. 42.

[22] James Franklin was replaced after one year because Brooker lost both the postmastership and the *Gazette*. Between 1719 and 1739, this paper was owned and operated by no less than five postmasters. In spite of this shaky start, the *Gazette* was published continuously until 1798.

[23] James M. Lee, *op. cit.,* p. 72.

[24] Presbrey, *op. cit.,* pp. 131, 133.

[25] Payne, *op. cit.,* pp. 30–31.

[26] DeArmond, *op. cit.,* p. 216.

and in attacks against inoculation for smallpox.[27] It carried very little news and but few advertisements.[28]

While James Franklin's journalistic career was short-lived,[29] he contributed in at least two ways to the development of colonial journalism. First, his fearless criticism of the colonial government revived the fight for a free press. And secondly, he trained his brother Benjamin in newspaper work and prepared him for his influential role in colonial journalism.

ANDREW BRADFORD'S *AMERICAN WEEKLY MERCURY*

It is interesting to note that the first issue of the *American Weekly Mercury* appeared in Philadelphia on December 22, 1719, one day after the *Boston Gazette*'s first number was published.[30] Andrew Bradford, the founder, was especially well qualified for the task of publishing a colonial newspaper, and he developed his *Mercury* into the most influential newspaper of the 1720's.[31]

Bradford knew from the experiences of the first colonial journalists that the development of a wide circulation was crucial to the success of his undertaking. Therefore, before launching his paper, he made careful arrangements for its distribution. To insure the widest possible circulation, not only in Philadelphia and Pennsylvania but in all the middle colonies and even in parts of the South and New England, he contracted with nine business associates to take in subscriptions and to collect news and advertising.[32]

To please subscribers, Bradford printed both foreign and domestic news. He strove particularly hard to serve business people and thereby gain their advertising patronage. His *Mercury* regularly published commodity prices and shipping news of Philadelphia, New York, and Boston.[33] Bradford's method of appealing to the self-interest of business people is well illustrated by the following announcement, which appeared in the ninth issue of the *Mercury*.

The Design of this Paper, being to Promote Trade it is hoped, that it will be Incouraged by the Merchants of this City, by Acquainting Us with the true price Current of the Several Good's inserted in it, which we presume may be Serviceable to All concern'd in Commerce, Especially to them, that have any of those Good's to Sell, who will find a quicker Sale, by Our Informing those

---

[27] Payne, *op. cit.*, p. 32. See also DeArmond, *op. cit.*

[28] Isaiah Thomas, *The History of Printing in America*, Vol. I (Albany, 1874), p. 111.

[29] DeArmond, *op. cit.* The *Courant* lasted from August, 1721, to June, 1726.

[30] *Ibid.*, p. 12.

[31] *Ibid.*, pp. 1–6, 25. He inherited from both sides of his family the tradition of the press. Both his grandfathers were well-established printers and publishers in London, while his father, William Bradford, was New York's first printer.

[32] *Ibid.*, p. 41.

[33] *Ibid.*, pp. 40–41.

persons that want them where they may be Supplied: We likewise Desire those Gentlemen that receive any Authentick Account of News from Europe, or other places, which may be proper for this paper, that they will please to favour Us with a Copy.[34]

With such able business management, the *Mercury* prospered from the start. By the end of the first year, it had a wide circulation and carried several advertisements from distant colonies.[35]

In his early years as publisher, Bradford had several clashes with the authorities; but later, he became circumspect and avoided the publication of controversial political matters.[36] By such judicious avoidance, he was left free to develop his newspaper into an effective organ of commerce.[37]

Besides his newspaper, Bradford was engaged in several other business ventures.[38] The enterprise that was the most helpful to his newspaper business was his retail store. It was the custom, almost the necessity, for the printing shop to sell all sorts of commodities, for as James M. Lee states, "the colonial printer was willing to take almost anything in exchange for subscriptions" and often "sold over the counter the goods accepted in payment."[39]

Bradford contributed to the development of retail advertising, in that he regularly advertised merchandise that had accumulated in his print shop. Thus, by his own example, he undoubtedly influenced other merchants in Philadelphia to try newspaper advertising. In the early issues of the *Mercury*, Bradford's own advertisements announced for sale such items as molasses by the barrel, whalebone, live-goose feathers, Barbadoes rum, chocolate, Spanish snuff, tea, pickled sturgeon, and beaver hats, as well as a variety of patent medicines.[40] As his retail business developed, he added imported merchandise; and from about 1726, his advertisements in the *Mercury* announced the importation from Europe of such articles as spectacles, compasses with dials, leather, English brandy, clothing, and books.[41]

By such astute business practices, Bradford gradually built up his advertising volume to the point where in the mid-thirties it reached one and a half to two pages regularly.[42] Business people from all the middle colonies, as well as some from New England and the South, frequently

---

[34] *Ibid.,* p. 41.
[35] *Ibid.,* p. 43.
[36] Payne, *op. cit.,* pp. 40–41.
[37] DeArmond, *op. cit.,* pp. 20, 44. By staying out of politics, he was able to keep the lucrative job as government printer; and in 1728, he was awarded the postmastership, which post enabled Bradford to circulate his paper free of charge.
[38] DeArmond, *op. cit.,* pp. 20, 34. Bradford also had a financial interest in an iron foundry and speculated in real estate.
[39] James M. Lee, *op. cit.,* pp. 68, 72.
[40] Payne, *op. cit.,* p. 40. See also DeArmond, *op. cit.,* p. 21.
[41] DeArmond, *op. cit.,* pp. 22–23.
[42] *Ibid.,* p. 48.

announced their wares, which included food and clothing, utensils and machinery, houses and land, ships and wagons and horses, musical instruments, jewelry, and chinaware. Also, the *Mercury* advertised services of different sorts, not only the professional assistance of doctors and lawyers, but also of skilled artisans who offered such services as sharpening of sickles, dry-cleaning and dyeing.[43]

Unlike Campbell of the *Boston News-Letter*, Bradford was constantly experimenting to improve newspaper advertising technique. In addition to employing a considerable variety of type, he was the first of the colonial printers to use cuts to identify the advertised product. His first such illustration was a crude picture of a book beside the notice for the sale of an almanac in 1721. Later in the same year a cut illustrated the notice of an unclaimed bale of goods.[44]

By the early thirties, cuts became a regular part of the makeup of the *Mercury*'s advertising pages. During the later years, other improvements in advertising format were made. Advertisements were set in varied type, boxed separately, and carefully spaced to catch the eye. Bradford frequently employed rows of type ornament to divide the news section from the advertising section.[45]

Finally, Bradford was probably the first of the colonial journalists to start classified advertising. As early as 1730, the *Mercury* carried help wanted announcements which called for carpenters, joiners, bricklayers, tanners, and hatters.[46]

While Bradford's distinguished journalistic career ended with his untimely death in 1742, his wife continued to publish the *Mercury* until May 22, 1746. Thus came to an end, after a notable history of 26 years, Pennsylvania's earliest newspaper.

WILLIAM BRADFORD'S *NEW YORK GAZETTE*

William Bradford was one of the first printers in America, having come to Pennsylvania with the Quakers in 1682 for the purpose of printing the laws of the colony. Here, he was frequently in trouble with the authorities for printing seditious materials; and after 11 years of discouragement, he moved his press to New York in 1693 and became the governor's printer at a very attractive salary. From this time on, he was most careful of what he printed.

It was not until November 8, 1725, that William Bradford, at the age of 62, began to publish the *New York Gazette*, New York's first newspaper,[47] six years after his son's *American Weekly Mercury* appeared in

---

43 *Ibid.*, p. 157.
44 *Ibid.*, pp. 47–48.
45 *Ibid.*, p. 48.
46 *Ibid.*, pp. 157–58.
47 John W. Wallace, *An Address Delivered at the Celebration by the New York*

Philadelphia. At this advanced age, William Bradford lacked the drive to promote his newspaper aggressively. He was content to publish a news sheet like Campbell's *Boston News-Letter*; and like the latter paper, it carried mostly foreign news. Invariably, the *New York Gazette* was poorly printed, due to the fact that William Bradford had used his type for a long time before he began to print his newspaper. Circulation was limited, and the printer frequently had to appeal to delinquent subscribers.[48]

Advertisements in the *New York Gazette* were few in number, and the subjects were mostly slaves, runaway apprentices, lost articles, and real estate. Since William Bradford was a land speculator and developer, he at times ran his own real estate announcements in the *Gazette*.[49]

The *New York Gazette*, which was published continuously until October 29, 1844, contributed little to the advancement of journalism and advertising. However, its publisher in his earlier years as a printer fought staunchly for freedom of the press; trained his son Andrew for his role on the *Mercury*; and in his later *New York Gazette* days, took in the immigrant Zenger and taught him the newspaper business.

BENJAMIN FRANKLIN'S *PENNSYLVANIA GAZETTE*

As a matter of historical fact, the *Pennsylvania Gazette*, the state's second newspaper, was started by Samuel Keimer on December 24, 1728. According to Franklin, it was his idea to start a paper in competition with the *Mercury*; but Keimer, upon getting wind of Franklin's plan, hurriedly made arrangements to forestall him. Keimer, however, proved unequal to the task; and after struggling along for nine months with less than 100 subscribers, he sold out to Franklin for a trifle.[50]

Since Andrew Bradford had a monopoly of all the profitable printing in the colony, it took great courage on Franklin's part to take over the insolvent *Gazette*. Some of the difficulties that could befall a printer not in the subsidy and grace of the colonial authorities are vividly described in this editorial piece, published by Keimer as an explanation for an interruption in the publication of the *Gazette*: "It certainly must be allowed somewhat strange that a person of strict Sincerity, refin'd Justice, and universal Love to the whole Creation, should for a Series of near twenty Years, be the constant But of Slander, as to be three Times ruin'd

---

Historical Society, May 20, 1863, of the Two Hundredth Birthday of Mr. William Bradford, Who Introduced the Art of Printing into the Middle Colonies of British America (Albany, 1863), p. 86.

[48] James M. Lee, *op. cit.*, pp. 37–38.

[49] It will be remembered that the first American newspaper advertisement was William Bradford's Oyster Bay real estate announcement that appeared in the third number of Campbell's *Boston News-Letter*.

[50] D. H. Montgomery (ed.), *The Autobiography of Benjamin Franklin* (Boston, 1927), p. 73.

as a Master-Printer, to be Nine Times in Prison, one of which was Six Years together."[51]

That Franklin was able to surmount all obstacles and establish the *Gazette* within a few years is proof of his genius. Having been a personal witness of the struggles of both Keimer and his brother James, he realized the futility of open resistance to authority. From the very start, he strove to sell his ideas through tactful persuasion.[52] In the conduct of the *Pennsylvania Gazette*, he was careful to exclude material of a scandalous or libelous nature. At the time, it was common strategy for politicians to injure the reputation of rivals by paying to have fabricated, defamatory information printed.

However, from time to time, Franklin used the editorial pages of his *Gazette* to criticize mildly the public conduct of certain citizens of high standing. The story is told that when some wealthy patrons tried to suppress his plain speaking, Franklin invited them to his house for dinner and served them nothing but pudding made of coarse cornmeal and a pitcher of water. Franklin ate heartily; but upon seeing his guests' inability to do likewise, he arose and said: "My friends, anyone who can subsist on sawdust pudding and water, as I can, needs no man's patronage."[53]

Benjamin Franklin succeeded where Keimer failed because he was thrifty, plowed back profits into his paper, and constantly sought ways and means of improving it. Editorially, the *Gazette* was of uncommon brightness. Its pages were illuminated with the quiet humor to be found in all of Franklin's writings. His lucid style of writing and the excellence of his typography at once attracted attention throughout the colonies. He put in new and larger type, watched paper and ink and presswork, and got better printing. Good use of leading and white space helped further to make the *Pennsylvania Gazette* the best-looking paper. The circulation of 90 copies per issue quickly went into the hundreds. To increase his circulation, Franklin originated the practice, still popular today, of writing letters to the editor, creating a number of imaginary characters and engaging in disputes with himself in order to draw the public into the editorial circulation-building net, wherein they write letters and buy many copies of the paper in which their names are printed.[54]

It was in the advertising that Franklin's typographic skill found its chief opportunity. He opened up soggy columns by separating each advertisement from its neighbors above and below with several lines of

---

[51] John C. Oswald, *Benjamin Franklin, Printer* (New York, 1917), p. 98.

[52] In his autobiography, Franklin describes in detail his plan for self-improvement. His method is still used today in sales training courses. During his first year with the *Gazette,* he won from Andrew Bradford the printing of the laws through personalized sampling of his work.

[53] Montgomery, *op. cit.*, p. 74.

[54] Payne, *op. cit.*, p. 64.

white space. A 14-point heading for each advertisement was another innovation. Franklin's combinations of type were pleasing, and his typography as a whole was ahead of that used in London newspapers of the period.[55]

Franklin, along with Andrew Bradford, pioneered in the use of cuts for better identification of advertised products. His first illustrations were 1¼-inch stock cuts of ships, which were set into the announcements of cargo space and passenger accommodations. As retail advertising developed, Franklin used stock cuts of scythes and sickles in advertising these products for hardware dealers. He used clockfaces to identify the watchmaker's advertisement. Later, he used stock cuts of horses and other objects to identify at once the nature of the advertisement.

Franklin's gift as a writer is reflected in his advertising copy. Much of his copy has a modern ring, with a factual presentation of the qualities of the product. For instance, the following advertisement of soap carries a strong appeal and sounds quite modern:

Super Fine Crown Soap

It cleanses fine Linens, Muslins, Laces, Chinces, Cambricks, etc. with Ease and Expedition, which often suffer more from the long and hard rubbing of the Washer, through the ill qualities of the soap than the wearing.

Like other colonial publishers before him, Franklin took merchandise in exchange for subscriptions and advertised it for sale in his newspaper. Thus, as his retail operation grew, he advertised a wide variety of goods, which included wine, coffee, chocolate, tea, mathematical instruments, codfish, and even two quack medicines, the "True and Genuine Godfrey's Cordial," and "Seneka Rattlesnake Root, with directions how to use it in the Pleurisy, etc."[56]

Keimer, during his proprietorship of the *Gazette*, occasionally but not often published enough advertisements to fill one page. Franklin had from the start more advertising in each issue than any other paper in the colonies had been able to develop after 3 to 20 years of effort.[57] Some of the *Gazette's* early issues contained paid announcements occupying two of its four pages. As the volume of advertising increased, the paper's size had to be expanded from two short columns to three deep columns, making the *Gazette* about the size of one of our 20th-century tabloids. Finally, the pressure of advertising broke the long-standing tradition that advertisements should appear at the bottom of the back page and work forward; the *Gazette* began to carry paid announcements on every page.[58]

---

[55] Presbrey, *op. cit.*, p. 133.
[56] *Ibid.*, p. 137.
[57] *Ibid.*, p. 133.
[58] *Ibid.*, p. 136.

Besides setting an example in good newspaper work with his own paper, Benjamin Franklin also contributed greatly to the growth of journalism by financing the establishment of six other colonial newspapers. To ambitious apprentices, he supplied the press and a font of type and took a one-third interest in the profits. The *South Carolina Gazette* and the *New York Post Boy* were two colonial newspapers set up with the financial assistance of Franklin.[59]

When Franklin was elected to the assembly, he turned over the publication of the *Pennsylvania Gazette* to a partner, David Hall, who in 1766 became the sole proprietor. With the exception of a brief interruption during the Revolutionary War, the *Gazette* was published continuously throughout the remainder of the 18th century. It was finally discontinued in 1815.

ZENGER'S *NEW YORK WEEKLY JOURNAL*

John Peter Zenger is perhaps the best known of the colonial printer-publishers because of his fearless and successful fight for a free press. On November 5, 1733, after serving an apprenticeship of eight years on William Bradford's *New York Gazette*, Zenger launched his *New York Weekly Journal*, which from its first issue began to carry frank criticisms of the provincial government. As a result of these attacks upon the authorities, Zenger was jailed but continued to edit his paper from prison.

Of his famous trial in 1735, nothing need be written. The immediate effect of Zenger's victory was to increase his popularity and the prestige of his paper. People were tired of the British rule, and Zenger's seditious *Journal* was popularly subscribed.[60]

Unlike the wealthy Bradford, who had a monopoly of all the choice printing in the colony for over 30 years, Zenger desperately needed revenue to defray the cost of printing his *Journal*. For this reason, he went after advertising aggressively; and since his paper enjoyed a much wider circulation than Bradford's *Gazette*, it was not difficult to increase advertising patronage. Within a few years the *Journal* carried four and five times as many announcements as the *Gazette*. Moreover, Zenger's paper attracted a wide variety of advertisements, whereas Bradford's sheet carried mostly the lost and found variety.

As for innovations in advertising technique, Zenger is credited with publishing the first American half-page advertisement. He was also the first to use broken column rules in newspaper advertising.[61] Along with Andrew Bradford and Franklin, Zenger also contributed to the development of display technique.

In 1737, two years after his victorious trial, Zenger was made public

---

[59] Payne, *op. cit.*, pp. 65–66; and Presbrey, *op. cit.*, pp. 144–45.
[60] Presbrey, *op. cit.*, p. 56.
[61] *Ibid.*, pp., 142–43.

printer for New York, and the following year for New Jersey. These positions contributed much-needed revenue for the support of his financially hard-pressed *Journal*. Although many other remunerative printing opportunities now tempted him, Zenger continued to apply himself energetically to the development of his newspaper until his death in 1746, after which his family continued its publication for another five years.

CONCLUSION

The development of an adequate circulation was one of the most pressing problems faced by the early colonial journalists. Andrew Bradford and Benjamin Franklin led the way out of this dilemma. Through careful planning and organization of distributive agencies in key population centers, Bradford proved that a newspaper could be circulated widely throughout most of the colonies. Franklin demonstrated that newspaper readership could be greatly stimulated when stale foreign news was rewritten and a lively sense of humor was injected. In addition, both journalists experimented and discovered many ways of improving the crude newspaper techniques borrowed from Europe. They pioneered in the use of illustrations and developed a variety of type to improve the appearance and readability of copy.

The colonial journalists were ingenious and resourceful. To build circulation, they took merchandise in exchange for subscriptions and then advertised the accumulated stock for sale in their newspapers. By engaging in retailing, and by advertising their own merchandise, they gradually overcame the skepticism of other businessmen about newspaper advertising.

Harris, James Franklin, and Zenger fought the all-important battle for a free press. However, even after the victorious Zenger trial in 1735, newspapers still could not stand alone on their youthful advertising legs. The economy was largely agricultural, and there were simply not enough potential advertisers. Even the most able of the colonial journalists continued at least partially to finance the publication of their newspapers by such activities as job printing, retailing, and politicking.

Nevertheless, the struggles of the pioneer colonial journalists were not in vain. Through their sacrifice and dogged persistence, they freed the press and introduced many of the technological improvements that were needed to develop the newspaper into an effective carrier of advertisements.

3. THE REGULATORY PRACTICES OF THE TIME[*]

The economic prosperity of the colonies depended on their ability to export agricultural products, lumber, and fish. This article describes the efforts made to preserve the reputation of colonial commodities in foreign markets. Laws were passed requiring that such staple goods as tobacco, lumber, beef, fish, and flour be examined as to quality and quantity by duly licensed inspectors prior to export. Such abuses as short weight, quality misrepresentation, and adulteration were the principal targets of this legislation. Although not 100 percent effective, the inspection system greatly facilitated the marketing and trade activities of the period.

THE COLONIES usually provided for the inspection of their staple articles for export, while occasional provision was made for the inspection of other articles. The chief purpose of these laws was to raise or preserve the reputation of the commodities in the foreign market, for it was not at all uncommon that "deceit and fraud" were practiced as to the quality or quantity of the articles exported.

The inspection laws become more detailed as a rule as we approach the Revolution—and even more so from the Revolution to the adoption of the federal Constitution. The laws were quite uniform to the extent that they required the articles to be examined by officials provided for in the acts. They also prescribed the fees the inspectors were to receive in the performance of their duties. Naturally, there were radical differences of detail as to the amount of the fee, the extent of the inspector's duty, and the articles inspected.

The only article (besides lumber) the inspection of which was provided for by law in each of the colonies was meat, i.e., beef and pork. The packer, as the inspector of beef and pork was ordinarily designated, was required under oath to see that these commodities were properly packed. None could be exported until the inspection had taken place. Even when imported into a colony for reexportation or for sale, the beef and pork were frequently repacked. Massachusetts provided for the

[*] Reprinted from Albert A. Giesecke, *American Commercial Legislation before 1789* (Philadelphia: University of Pennsylvania, 1910), pp. 74–80.

134

gauging of the casks for beef, pork, and other commodities as early as 1641; and New York had a similar provision in 1665. In both cases the cask was to be "London" size and of well-seasoned timber. In the later act, as was the general practice, the gauger was to mark the barrel as evidence that it had been inspected.

The inspection of fish was provided for in all of the New England colonies and in New York. The fishing industry developed early in the New England colonies and was a factor of economic importance to them throughout the colonial period, for it furnished them with a needed staple for foreign trade. The administrative provisions for the inspection of fish were quite similar to those for the inspection of beef and pork.

Timber was inspected at one time or another in every colony. The earlier laws usually regulated in detail the size and quality of staves exported; later acts added shingles, boards, planks, and other kinds of lumber. From the very beginning the vast resources of the forests furnished the colonists with a ready and cheap article of export, especially for the trade to the West Indies, Spain, and Portugal. England had admitted it duty-free early in the 18th century and also placed it among the enumerated articles. Pennsylvania and the southern colonies did not provide inspection laws for timber until about the middle of the 18th century, although it was exported from these colonies prior to that period. There is one law on record which specifically provided for the inspection of staves, headings, and shingles exported to the Madeira Islands and the West Indies. Such a procedure in the inspection laws was very unusual, even though the legislators doubtless knew the markets for which the lumber from their province was intended and perhaps enacted provisions with that thought in mind.

Flour and bread were regularly inspected by New York, New Jersey, Pennsylvania, and Maryland. Pennsylvania was especially active in the export trade in flour. Unmerchantable flour was not permitted to be exported; nevertheless, this prohibition was not always heeded. The southern colonies began the inspection of these commodities just a few decades before the Revolution.

The commodity which received the most detailed regulation was tobacco. Inspection laws for tobacco were provided by Connecticut, Pennsylvania, Delaware, and the southern colonies. Pennsylvania, Maryland, and Virginia began to secure the inspection of tobacco quite early in their colonial existence, but the laws of the two last-mentioned colonies are by far the most important and detailed. Tobacco was the mainstay of Virginia and Maryland, and consituted the greatest single export from the continental colonies. Inspectors of tobacco were provided by law; and later the southern colonies, except Georgia, provided public warehouses to which the tobacco was brought for inspection. Bad or "trashy" tobacco, usually defined in the act, was rejected and was not to be exported; and in some instances, tobacco could not be exported in bulk. The cask in which the tobacco was exported was also regulated as to size and even quality of timber. Masters of vessels were to give oath that the tobacco was duly exported and properly inspected. Moreover, Virginia prohibited the sale or shipment of North Carolina tobacco in her territory.

The gauging of casks for liquors was commonly practiced in the New England and middle colonies, but not in the southern colonies. At first, they were often made London size; but subsequently, gauging according to Gunter's rule became the practice. The necessity of a standard was due to the fraud which could be practiced by exporting liquors in smaller casks and the consequent effects of such a violation in foreign markets.

Naval stores were early subject to inspection in the southern colonies; they were also inspected in Massachusetts and Connecticut shortly after the parliamentary bounties had been offered upon naval stores. Governor Cornbury of New York at the same time informed the assembly that he had been instructed by the Queen to recommend suitable acts to make the parliamentary act effective; and accordingly, a bill was actually drawn up to prevent frauds and abuses in the exportation of naval stores to England. Their exportation was of some importance in the southern colonies, the bounties proving comparatively ineffective in the northern colonies. Other articles were inspected at various times in some of the colonies for the same reasons that the commodities already mentioned were inspected; these commodities included butter, flax, hemp, horses, indigo, grain and provisions, leather, malt, rice, and sometimes even commodities in general.

The administrative effects of these various inspection laws cannot be gauged with any degree of accuracy for the policy of inspection as a whole. There was a tendency upon the part of planter and merchant, in the case of some commodities at least, to mix in the unmerchantable or bad portions with the good, or to adulterate articles intended for export; and there is evidence to show that this practice was carried out to some extent. Experience occasionally proved the inefficacy of these laws, whereupon an amendment was passed to increase the efficiency of the administrative provisions. On the whole, however, the inspection laws must have been very beneficial in preserving the reputation of the colonial products in foreign markets, though at times individual preferences were expressed for the staple from one colony rather than from a neighboring colony. The inspectors were under oath to perform the duties prescribed in the acts, and at times were prohibited from buying the commodities inspected by them. Their compensation was upon the fee system, which was specifically regulated by law.

4. POLITICS, ECONOMICS, AND THE INDIAN TRADE: THE NORTHERN SETTLEMENTS*

The political policies of the rival English and French settlements in North America were primarily influenced by commercial considerations. In the earliest periods, commercial activity centered around the fur trade and fishing. The various Indian tribes aligned themselves with the English or the French, with their choice depending on which group provided the most satisfactory trade agreement. Though the French had a head start in the commercial and political struggle for the interior, their established position contributed to their eventual failure. Having their own trading posts, the French did not need the aid and assistance of the Iroquois. Consequently, this group sided with the English and played an important role in the eventual conquest of all the major French settlements.

THE CHIEF EARLY ECONOMIC INTEREST of Englishmen in America were in turn gold, fish, and furs. The interest in gold perforce soon disappeared. The fishing industry reached large proportions at a very early date. The transition from fishing to trading, though its history is obscure, was an easy one, and it occurred remarkably early. Before the Armada, Richard Whitbourne, primarily a fisherman, was sailing along our eastern coast, "proposing there to trade then with the Savage people (for whom we carried sundry commodities) and to kill Whales."

Thus, in Mr. Biggar's phrase, the "great fishing industry . . . in turn became the mother of the fur trade." Evidences of the importance of this early Indian trade become more numerous as time goes on, and indicate a trade at once significant in amount and important in the eyes of contemporaries. The surprising thing in these records is the fact that, go back as far as we may, in the very earliest recorded voyages we find that the Indians had collected stores of skins in anticipation of trade with the Europeans, and that the voyagers in turn had invariably brought with

---

* Reprinted by permission of the publishers from Peter Wraxall, *Wraxall's Abridgement of the New York Indian Records, 1678–1751*, edited by Charles Mc-Ilwain (Cambridge: Harvard University Press, 1915), pp. xii–xvi, xl–xliv.

them goods for this traffic—"Hookes, Knives, Sizzers, Hammers, Nailes, Chissels, Fish-hookes, Bels, Beades, Bugles, Looking-glasses, Thimbles, Pinnes, Needles, Threed, and such like," as Purchas records of the voyage of Martin Pring to the New England coast in 1603. More surprising still is the fact that as early as 1616, the Indians, in order to collect these stores of skins, had to penetrate the interior probably as far as the lakes. It seems remarkable that the trade had developed to such a degree and had already covered so great an area before a single permanent English settlement had been made within the present United States north of the James River.

After settlements were made, the story is the same. The records of the ill-starred Sagadahoc colony are full of the subject. With the coming of Plymouth settlers, we might expect something else. Their motives in coming to America were mixed, but fishing was no small ingredient. In the beginning, they knew nothing of the fur trade, but proved very apt learners; and this trade soon became one of the foundations of their prosperity, one of the chief means of lifting the financial burdens which threatened the little colony, and it is hardly too much to say one of the principal factors which enabled the struggling settlement to survive. But the Pilgrims were not the only settlers on the Massachusetts coast before the great migration to the bay. Of the others, one has left a most interesting account, which shows that he and his fellows were there for one purpose, and that the trade in furs.

The leaders of the great bay colony itself have left unmistakable evidence of the importance of the Indian trade to them and of their appreciation of it. Much of the jealousy which divided the New England colonies one from another, as well as their common opposition to external enemies which produced the New England confederacy, is directly traceable to the fur trade and the early extinction of the beaver in New England. In the southern colonies, we might indeed expect the trade to be unimportant, but the records do not bear out that expectation.

As the beaver country near the coast became exhausted, the conditions of the trade changed, and those colonies which had direct access to the lakes and the Mississippi Valley acquired a virtual monopoly of the English trade. Thus, New Jersey, which had once enjoyed a prosperous trade, was deprived of it by Pennsylvania, though Pennsylvania herself was for a half century or more at a disadvantage compared with New York, on account of the lack of water routes to the West; Virginia was handicapped in the same way, and New England saw herself, notwithstanding desperate efforts, cut off by the new English colony of New York from her share of the receding trade. The earlier Dutch, Swedish, and English settlements along the coasts of the middle colonies had been made in large part on account of the fur trade and had drawn much of their sustenance from it. The history of the fur trade in these early settlements is much the same as is found to the north and south of them. By the time of the consolidation of all these middle colonies in English hands, however, the beaver supply east of the "endless mountains" was practically exhausted, and all the furs came from the tributaries of the Mississippi or the lakes. From this time onward, therefore, the geographical position of Pennsylvania and New York made these colonies the center of a trade which had reached proportions unheard of before in the English colonies, though the southernmost English colonies retained a fair share. Albany was far the best situated English town in America for this trade, and it enjoyed the largest part. But the tireless efforts of the Pennsylvania traders under far greater handicaps secured to them even in this period a trade which was great and growing. The shifting of the field of the trade had consequences of the greatest international importance. It led to that competition for the interior, for its trade, and for alliances with its Indians which played so great a part in the great struggle of France and England for this continent, in many respects the momentous struggle in our history.

Really to understand what Winsor means when he says that "trade was on the whole the most important influence now at work in the struggle for a continent," we must appreciate two things: First, what was the real aim of the French and English in all their relations with the interior; by what means and under what relative conditions were they striving to accomplish it? Second, what influence upon such aims, means, and conditions was given to the Iroquois by their unique geographical position? In the 18th century, trade with an Indian nation meant an alliance with it, and an alliance meant trade. The nations that traded with New France would fight against the English colonies, and the ones who brought their furs to Albany instead of Montreal could be counted on to fight the French. "The ultimate question for the rival whites," as Winsor says, "as well as for the intermediary natives was: Who should supply the rum to the distant Ottawas and Miamis?" Trade and policy were inseparable, but trade was the ultimate end of all policy; it was also practically the sole means in all Indian relations. The endeavors of the contending whites were thus directed to the control of the interior and its trade, and the interruption so far as possible of all communication between the interior tribes and their own enemies, white and red.

The English entered this competition for trade and for peace under great handicaps. The French were far in advance of them in the trade with the interior. To this must be added the abuses of the English traders themselves. During the whole history of the English fur trade, the evidence indicates that most of these traders were the very scum of the earth, and their treatment of the Indians was such as hardly to be suitable for description. The lack of adequate regulation of these lawless and unprincipled men was no doubt a serious disadvantage of the English colonies, and it was one hardly likely to be amended while there was such rivalry for the trade between the different colonies themselves. Against these handicaps, serious as they were, and sometimes threatening the very continuance of the English trade, were two important and closely related influences. One was the fact that with the exception of powder alone, the English goods were so much cheaper than the French that at Albany and Oswego, twice as much could be given for beaver as the Indian could get at any of the French posts. This is the reason always given by English, French, and Indians for the English share in the trade. There is no doubt that it is the correct one, practically the sole one. The second fact derives its importance entirely from it: The only route from the interior to Albany, the center of distribution of these cheap goods, lay directly through the country of the Iroquois. These two interrelated facts furnish the secret of the Iroquois alliance, the enduring and sufficient cause of their practically unbroken friendship with the nation that held Albany. The reasons for this are plain. The great role of the Iroquois was that of middlemen between the "Far Indians" and the English, a role which enabled them not only to obtain material benefits but to retain that position of superiority over the Indians of the eastern half of the United States which they had probably first secured through their knowledge of the white man's firearms, but could now no longer hope to hold by mere force alone, since their fighting men had so diminished in numbers and their enemies had obtained weapons as good as their own. They hoped to retain by peaceable means what they could not expect any longer to keep by force of arms. This could be done by alliance and by trade alone, and by English trade alone. They could not possibly hope to enjoy the same importance as intermediaries between the French and the western Indians, because the French themselves already had their own trading posts as far west as the lakes extended, with hundreds of *coureurs de bois,* who collected the furs in the interior and brought them directly to Canada. Besides, the Canadian Indians were strong enough to prevent any interference, notwithstanding their defeats by the Iroquois. It was clearly good policy on the part of the Iroquois to stick to the English, particularly as their friends had no posts farther west than Oswego.

The Iroquois were fully alive to the great advantages their situation gave them. It became, therefore, a consistent part of their policy to do their utmost to induce the nations of the interior to desert the French and accept the English goods. The very existence of the Five Nations depended on this. There were no beaver left in their own country. As early as 1671, we have a French memoir to the effect that hardly a single beaver could be found south of Lake Ontario. The Iroquois had to get their beaver from the Indians farther west or get none; and beaver they must have or lose the rum, clothing, guns, and ammunition which had become necessary to their happiness and even to their existence. To induce these other Indian tribes to take English goods often meant to induce them to take up the hatchet against the French. It was at times a part of Iroquois policy to bring this about, and the alternatives offered were usually trade or war. Particularly important to them at one period were the Hurons and the Tobacco Nation, who were in such a position geographically that they could intercept all furs coming from the West to Canada. To intercept trade there was to turn it southward, where it must pass through the Iroquois country to Albany.

5. POLITICS, ECONOMICS, AND THE INDIAN TRADE: THE SOUTHERN SETTLEMENTS*

In the southern colonies as well, the fur trade and other ties with the Indians were important elements of economic life, with both political and commercial implications. Evidence of this is found in numerous acts passed by colonial legislatures, notably in Virginia and South Carolina, regulating Indian trade and barring nonresidents from their areas of commercial influence. In the lower Mississippi Valley, political control was inexorably linked with the Indian trade, where success depended on the adeptness of rival French and English interests in cultivating Indian allegiances. By the end of the colonial period the fur trade had facilitated the development of marketing channels that stretched from the wharves of England to the wilds of North America.

FROM THE BEGINNING of settlement the Indian was an important element in the economic life. In the early years of the several colonies, food obtained from the Indians supplemented the meager supplies of the colonists and in some instances prevented starvation and abandonment. The colonists also employed Indians for hunting and fishing, paying them bounties for hunting wolves and other predatory animals. The Indian trade, an important stage in the evolution of economic life, was closely coordinated with agriculture. Not infrequently, both were carried on by the same persons. The Indian trader, ranging hundreds of miles in advance of settlement, explored new territory, brought back news of choice lands, and inspired enthusiasm for agricultural expansion. The trails opened up were subsequently highways of agricultural expansion and commerce. The Indian trade was a potent influence in allaying the hostility of the natives against pioneer settlers, and the traders frequently gave warning of native outbreaks. The profits of the trade supplied capital for agricultural development and sustained the infant colonial establishments until agriculture could gain a foothold. Finally, the rich prizes of the trade were the bone of contention in the international struggle for empire, and the superiority

* Reprinted from Lewis C. Gray, *History of Agriculture in the Southern United States to 1860*, Vol. I (Washington, D.C.: Carnegie Institution, 1933), pp. 129–39.

of British commercial organization was a factor in the ultimate achievement of British supremacy in the territory between the Atlantic and the Mississippi. The traders also gradually introduced the arts of civilized life and improved native agriculture, teaching the Indians to produce European crops and encouraging them to raise livestock. Some of the traders kept herds of their own. In the latter part of the 18th century, some of the Indian chieftains in the Gulf colonies were maintaining large herds of cattle, and some of them possessed a considerable number of slaves.

After the struggle between Baltimore and Claiborne to control the Indian trade of the Potomac and Susquehanna had resulted in the exclusion of the Virginia traders, the trade was for some years the dominant concern of the Maryland colony. In 1638 the principal settlers were more interested in the trade than in planting, and roanoke and beaver were employed as currency. Maryland was at a geographic disadvantage, however, for Indian trade. The local tribes were gradually reduced in numbers and their hunting grounds restricted by white settlements. Virginia and the Carolinas were better situated to control the trade of the Southwest. In 1659 the Virginians were complaining that neighboring English plantations (Maryland) and the Dutch were allowing northern Indian tribes to come down to the heads of the Virginia rivers, thus cutting off trade to the westward. Moreover, the Virginians' commercial rivals were practicing unfair competition by supplying the natives with powder and shot, which compelled the Virginia Assembly to authorize similar practices by Virginia traders. A Virginia law of 1662 excluded Maryland and other northern traders from Virginia territory. New York, and later Pennsylvania, intercepted Maryland trade with the northwestern tribes. The Marylanders were hard put to it even to prevent encroachment on their own territory. In 1662, they negotiated a treaty with the Nanticokes, who agreed to exclude Dutch traders on demand of the English. In 1683, Maryland found it necessary to establish a fortified post at Christine Bridge, in Newcastle County, to exclude Pennsylvania traders. As early as 1678, it was stated that the Indian trade of Maryland was not very considerable. Miss Morriss estimates the value of the exports of skins in 1695 at only £648, principally the product of local trapping on the eastern shore.

In Virginia the frequent wars of the early decades were serious interruptions to systematic trade, and it was necessary at times to prohibit it. Gradually, a specialized class of traders developed. Henry Fleet, who played a part in the conflict between Claiborne and Baltimore, was one of the earliest. In 1652 Claiborne and Fleet, again making common cause in spite of ancient rivalries, and their associates were granted trading privileges for 14 years to explore and trade in territories where Englishmen had not been. A similar privilege was granted to Captain Abraham

Wood, who before the middle of the 17th century made Fort Henry, at the falls of the Appomattox, the center of an important Indian business, mainly toward the South and Southwest. He and his associates sent out packtrains consisting at times of as many as 100 horses to trade with the Tuscaroras, the Catawbas, and finally the Cherokees. As early as 1650, Wood and Edward Bland penetrated to the region of the upper Roanoke. In 1671, William Byrd (I), backed by his merchant uncle, Thomas Stegg, was a strong competitor with Wood for the southeastern trade. In that year, Wood sent two traders, Batts and Fallam, as far as New River; and in 1673, Wood's representative, Needham, went as far, probably, as the Little Tennessee. By 1675 the great trading route from Virginia southwestward to the Cherokee tribes had become fully established. As early as 1690, a Virginia trader named Daugherty had taken up his residence among the Cherokees. After 1718 the Virginians began to develop considerable activity in the trans-Allegheny trade to the Northwest, where, however, they came into keen competition with the Pennsylvanias, as well as with the French. The settlement of South Carolina, however, seriously restricted the Virginia trade.

Some of the Carolina proprietors were interested from the beginning in the fur trade and largely monopolized it during the first two decades of the colony. In fact, they fitted out the first expedition with an equipment of goods for the trade. Shaftesbury arranged for the establishment of his estate on Edisto Island to serve as headquarters of a large Indian trade. The settlement was scarcely a year old before a bolt trader, Dr. Henry Woodward, was among the Indians in western South Carolina. Four years later, he crossed the middle Savannah and visited the Westoes, and in the next three years became acquainted with the tribes still farther west. By 1685, he was on the Chattahoochee and had established trading relations with the Lower Creeks. The Spaniards made the mistake of attempting to compel the tribes to resist English encroachments, but the lure of trade gained for the English a preponderant influence. Soon, they were among the Alabamas and the Chickasaws. In 1677 a group of the proprietors formed an association for the exploitation of the more distant trade, restricting the colonists to the trade within 100 miles of Charleston. The South Carolina trade was rapidly extended. The statement was made in 1719 that for over 30 years the South Carolinians had traded with the Indians along the Coosa, 700 miles from Charleston. Some years before the beginning of the 18th century, South Carolina traders had penetrated to the Mississippi and probably beyond—perhaps following in the footsteps of hardy Virginia traders who left no historical record.

As early as 1698, the question of prohibiting the Virginia traders was discussed by the South Carolina lower house. In 1708 the Virginians complained to the British Council for Trade and Plantations that the

South Carolina authorities had seized goods being carried by the Virginians to the southwestern tribes. South Carolina had placed an export tax on furs, and the authorities of the colony had interpreted this as applicable to furs carried out of the province by Virginia traders. After considering the problem, the Council for Trade and Plantations recommended that the application of the duty to Virginia traders be discontinued, and it was so ordered. The jealousy on the part of the Carolinians was doubtless increased by the fact that at that period the Virginians enjoyed an advantage in the price of Indian goods obtained from Great Britain by reason of the greater "Conveniency of Shipping" to that colony. The Carolinians also believed the Virginia traders guilty of encouraging the tribes to make war on the Carolinas. Accordingly, South Carolina passed another act in 1711, requiring Virginia traders to come to Charleston and take out licenses, pay the fees, provide the bonds, and conform to the police regulations required of South Carolina traders under the act of 1707. Governor Spotswood vigorously protested to the British authorities, who proceeded to veto the act.

In spite of the geographic advantage enjoyed by the Carolina traders, they continued for many years to be subject to keen competition. Some of the more reputable Virginia traders were duly licensed in South Carolina, but the looser sort refused to subject themselves to the regulations. Gradually, however, the Carolinians ousted the Virginians from the trade. By 1751 the share of the latter was probably small, for in that year a delegation of Cherokees, who as a result of French intrigue had become disaffected against the Carolinians, visited Williamsburg, seeking a treaty. They were kindly received and given to understand that a regular trade would be opened. In 1757, and again in 1765, the Virginia Assembly appropriated £5,000 sterling to carry on a trade with the Cherokees, proposing to sell goods at cost, and providing for appointing a resident factor. The Virginia policy led to a strong protest by Governor Glen of South Carolina, who also took vigorous measures to placate the Cherokees.

The settlement of Georgia tended to divert much of the trade from South Carolina. By the middle of the 18th century, Augusta was the great entrepôt of southwestern trade, although its business was built up mainly by South Carolina Indian merchants. In 1741, it was estimated that 49 men and 314 horses were engaged in the Augusta trade with the Lower Creeks, and 46 men and 305 horses in the trade from Augusta with the Upper Creeks and the Chickasaws. It was claimed that the South Carolinians, chagrined at the diversion of their trade, even tried to incite the tribes to war against the Georgians, and raised money to defray the legal expenses of defending South Carolinians who violated the Georgia acts of regulation.

When the British obtained control of Pensacola, that point, being more strategically located than Augusta, became the center of a trade amounting to 500,000 pesos annually. Mobile was another point from which the English dominated the trade of the interior of the Southwest.

Far more significant economically and politically than the English intercolonial rivalry was the prolonged struggle between the French and the English for the control of the southwestern trade, a struggle involving 60 years of intrigue, bribery, and organized murder. The Cherokees were too remote for the French traders to bring their goods cheaply by river, and consequently remained tributary to the British interest until toward the middle of the 17th century, when they began to be alienated by French intrigue and British blunders. Although the French succeeded for a short time in detaching the Chickasaws, the British early achieved a superior influence over them, which was later strengthened and, except for occasional lapses, permanently maintained. After a brief struggle in the early years of the 19th century, the British were compelled to abandon trade with the tribes of the lower Mississippi. The French early developed a preponderant political influence among the Choctaws, but not so much as entirely to prevent English traders from dealing with them, for it was the policy of the Choctaws and Creeks to play one party against another. Both parties were compelled to establish interior trading posts. In order to neutralize the influence of British posts among the Choctaws and Creeks and to intercept their traders on the Chickasaw trading path, the French built Fort Toulouse on the Coosa River, four miles above its junction with the Tallapoosa, and Fort Tombecbee, 140 miles above Fort Louis de Mobile. As early as 1719, Carolinians maintained a fortified and garrisoned trading post on the Coosa River, 700 miles from Charleston and only a short distance from the French Fort Toulouse. In 1734, they established the fortified post of Okfuskees among the Upper Creeks, 400 miles from the sea.

To offset the geographic advantage of the French for all but the Cherokee trade, the English had the great advantage of manufactured goods that suited the Indians much better than those which came from France, and a much better European market for peltry. It is true, there were short periods when the French appeared to have the advantage. About 1719, Spotswood wrote that the current prices of peltry in England and the high duties thereon had temporarily placed the English traders at a disadvantage. At times, also, the French deliberately sold goods to the Indians at less than cost in order to meet British competition. Sometimes the greed of British traders led them to injure their trading connections by charging the Indians excessive prices for goods. Taking the period as a whole, however, the greater cheapness and adaptability of British goods and the superiority of the British market for peltry, particularly for disposing of inferior grades for which there was no demand in France, were recognized as important advantages. The French overcame their disadvantage in part by purchasing goods from British ship captains and selling their peltry to them. The veteran Indian trader James Adair asserted that the British traders always found the French influence more difficult to meet in times of peace than in times of war, for in the latter periods the French suffered from shortages of goods hitherto obtained from British sources.

In spite of their economic disadvantage, the French brought to the problem of Indian relations their traditional superiority in diplomatic negotiations with native tribes. In the earlier part of the period the British allowed themselves to be outmaneuvered. While the French were skillfully applying the arts of flattery, the Carolinians were employing domineering methods, charging excessive prices, and committing excesses and atrocities, including wholesale enslavement. The result was the Indian coalition of 1715, which nearly overwhelmed the Carolinians, and the temporary loss of more than half their trade. The necessity of observing the amenities forced the British to adopt French methods of dealing with the Indians, and the former shortly regained much of their earlier trade and influence. In 1746, they succeeded in detaching a large section of the Choctaws from the French interest. On the other hand, the French had brought a part of the Chickasaws under their influence and gradually undermined the traditional friendship of the Cherokees with the British, finally bringing on war in 1760 between the Cherokees and the English colonists. The French also succeeded in achieving the disaffection of some of the Upper Creeks, and their concerted action with the Cherokees. Both sides cultivated the natives by giving lavish presents annually and by playing on intertribal jealousies. The more influential Indian leaders were regularly subsidized. Legislative efforts were made to prevent the abuses committed by the traders and to discourage the granting of credit (an important source of friction). While the selling of liquor to the natives was a recognized evil, competition forced both the contending parties to supply them with rum.

To a large extent, the more distant trade was promoted and financed by the commercial and capitalist influences which early developed the plantation system—that is, by British colonial merchants, associated at times with influential courtiers and politicians. A number of the proprietors of South Carolina belonged to the group of merchants and courtiers who promoted the Hudson Bay Company and brought about the seizure of New Amsterdam with its rich fur trade. British tobacco merchants were deeply concerned in the trade by reason of the supplies furnished colonial merchants.

The British interests operated through merchant planters of the colonies, who received supplies from their British correspondents on credit or in partnership, fitted out traders, and employed political influence to control Indian policy. In this regard, their interests were not always consonant with those of pioneer settlers. About 1716, for instance, there was much opposition by the small planters and pioneer farmers of Virginia to the policy of the Indian trading monopoly set up under Spotswood's encouragement. It was alleged that the government was much too tender with the Indians, that the sale of arms to the natives facilitated the murder of frontier settlers, and that the conduct of the traders bred contempt for English authority. Colonial merchants who combined the functions of planter, wholesale merchant, Indian merchant, and politician included such men as William Byrd (I), Cadwallader Jones, Colonel Abraham Wood, and the Carys of Virginia; Colonel James Moore and Governors Blake and Boone of South Carolina; and James Spaulding of St. Simons Island, Georgia. Other important merchants—for instance, John Musgrove, Lachlan McGillivray, and his son Alexander McGillivray —combined the advantages of a large Indian influence acquired by intermarriage or blood relationship and profitable commercial connections with British mercantile firms. The Revolutionary War, breaking up the commercial connections of the colonies, created the opportunity for the establishment by Tory refugees of the Indian trading firm of Panton, Leslie and Company at Pensacola, which, partly through its connection with Alexander McGillivray, dominated for many years the Indian trade of the Southwest.

The traffic itself was carried on by traders sent out by colonial merchants. If the Indian trade was important to the whites, it became of vital concern to the Indians, and their interest in obtaining European goods enabled the traders to travel hundreds of miles in comparative safety. Some of the traders were men of parts; a number of them became councilors or governors. All too many, however, were desperadoes, reckless, cruel, profligate, and unscrupulous, "the most abandon'd Wretches in the World." Such men gave untold trouble to the colonial authorities. Very early, it was found desirable for the trader to take up a permanent residence among the tribes in order to maintain his trading goodwill, prevent competing traders from undermining his influence, and determine more accurately the kind and quantity of goods required. Some traders established stores, which occasionally grew into trading posts at which a number of men were stationed or where many traders congregated. Some firms, like that of James Spaulding, in East Florida, maintained an extensive chain of stores.

The delicate character of Indian relations early led the various colonies to undertake regulation of the trade. Traders were required to have licenses and give bond to observe certain requirements. For a time, efforts were made to prevent the sale to Indians of guns and ammunition, but it was found impossible to stop the practice. As early as 1658/9, Virginia officially authorized free trade in arms and ammunition, since the Indians were obtaining them anyway from neighboring colonies. Efforts were made to prevent the indiscriminate giving of credit. The traders were held responsible under bond for misdemeanors and crimes committed in the Indian country, and commissioners were appointed to regulate their conduct. The problem of prices for skins in terms of British goods gave much trouble. When the traders charged excessive prices, the Indians became resentful; whereas when prices of skins were too high, the natives hunted less and became independent and dangerous. At times, it was found necessary to fix legal rates on Indian goods in exchange for peltry, but it was difficult to compel adherence thereto. Excessive competition among the traders sometimes resulted in the collapse of prices and the demoralization of the trade. To prevent this, South Carolina tried the experiment of assigning each trader to one or two villages, or exclusively to a definite range. Maryland, Virginia, and South Carolina forbade traders going among the Indians, attempting to confine all trade at certain frontier posts. Virginia, in 1714, and South Carolina, in 1718, created trading monopolies, but these acts led to much protest by independent traders and were vetoed. The policy of establishing monopolies as a mode of regulation should be distinguished from the various attempts to monopolize the trade mainly for purposes of profit.

6. CURRENCY PROBLEMS
DURING CONFEDERATION*

Lack of a suitable medium of exchange was a major problem throughout the colonial period. After the Revolutionary War, hard money was very scarce and the paper currency of the day virtually worthless. As a result, both domestic and foreign marketing was seriously hampered. Retailers also had to be constantly alert lest they be paid in counterfeit currency or "clipped" coins. After the Constitution was adopted and Alexander Hamilton's efforts provided an acceptable medium of exchange, marketing and commercial activity could again flourish in the new country.

A TRADER keeping a general store, who had had the good fortune to survive the War of the Revolution, might have felt reasonably safe about his political liberties after the surrender of Lord Cornwallis at Yorktown in October, 1781. About his material well-being—the value of his ledger accounts, of the bills and notes in his strongbox, of his stock of goods, his oxen, sheep, and barns—that remained a matter clouded with anxiety and uncertainty for a considerable time after the victory was won.

Some 10 turbulent years were to pass before a man who "kept store" in any settled part of northern or eastern United States could view the future of storekeeping with any confidence. Behind him lay the ruinous years of war and inflation. During this time the state governments and the Congress of the Confederation seemed to have made every possible financial mistake that would tend to make goods dear and destroy the public faith in the money they issued. The pockets of the ordinary citizen and the tills of the merchants were crammed with paper money, the purchasing power of which diminished to almost nothing. Refined sugar, in the cone shape of colonial days, went to 7 shillings per pound, hay to $9 per hundred, lime to $30 a hogshead. A clock cost £21, milk 15 shillings a quart, potatoes 96 shillings a bushel, pork 60 shillings per pound, rum 45 shillings per pint, corn $40 per bushel. If a man wanted to buy a cow, it took at one time around $1,200 to interest the seller.

It is not surprising, in these circumstances, that the countrypeople turned to other mediums of exchange which represented real values.

---

* Reprinted from Gerald Carson, *The Old Country Store* (New York: Oxford University Press, 1954), pp. 5–9, 18. Reprinted by permission of Willis Kingsley Wing. Copyright, 1954, by Gerald Carson.

Small cubes of indigo would pass in a day when every house had a fireplace, and every fireplace had beside it a dye pot or indigo tub. Unofficial values were recognized in a bushel of salt, required in vast quantities in the days before refrigeration for pickling and preserving beef, pork, and fish. In western Pennsylvania a gallon of whiskey could be exchanged for "European goods," meaning glassware, hardware, dress goods, bar iron, thread, powder, and shot; or for "West India" goods—salt, molasses, sugar, tea, coffee, spices, rum, and various vegetable dyes. Often, in the border counties, imported goods were not to be had at any price.

The economic difficulties connected with the Revolution were a matter of recent and bitter personal experience. But any trader could have heard from his father or grandsire, as a racial memory, equally dark tales of wild inflation during the interminable French wars and how in those times, too, the money got poorer and poorer, the debtors more and more reluctant to pay.

> The country maids with sauce to market come,
> And carry loads of tattered money home.

The dread of a worthless currency was a deep and wasting worry. Once the disease got the upper hand, the cure seemed even worse; for when the necessary steps were proposed for redeeming the paper, a new difficulty arose. Instead of poor money, there would be none, with the hard money, what there was of it, draining out of the country to pay for exchange. The doggerel writers sang a sad good-bye to the departing coins:

> To foreign lands they'll be convey'd
> Then what's our fate—the silver gone,
> The paper burnt—and we undone.

During the confederation, that loose association of friendly but sovereign states, while the ideas of delegated powers and a strong central government were germinating, the plague of paper money continued without relief. No one knew whether the national debt would be paid or repudiated. Such hard money as there was came from England, Spain, France, and Germany. It did not stay long. While it was here, it carried different values in different states. A man of large affairs might be paying bills in Spanish dollars worth 6 shillings in New England, 8 shillings in New York, 7s. 6d. from New Jersey to Maryland, and 4s. 8d. in South Carolina and Georgia. Adding to the confusion, counterfeiters were industriously occupied in turning French sous into Spanish moidores, an ingenious alchemy by which copper became gold, and was worth 36 shillings. Coppers washed with silver passed off as English sixpences. The British, delighted to compound American difficulties, manufactured counterfeits of their own English ha'pennies on a large scale in Birmingham and exported them to the United States in casks marked as "hardware."

Nor was the imitation of the paper money of the several states beyond the talents of our own native rascals who operated covert engraving shops and presses. The ethics of the keeper of a general store in matters of money and coinage was unvarnished self-preservation. When tainted money appeared in the day's cash, the first rule of the country was—get rid of it quickly. Usually, the junior clerk was the agent appointed to pass it out again so that if the gesture was discovered, the responsibility would be diluted.

It was no time for a country merchant to relax when he saw a debtor count out gold coins of high face value and reputable origin—joes, half joes, doubloons, Spanish pistoles, English and French guineas. They had been sheared and clipped so long and so severely that gold coin was acceptable only by actual weight. George Washington himself said that unless the United States soon had a coinage of its own or could find some way to stop the cutting and clipping of dollars and pistareens, a man would have to travel with a pair of scales in his pocket, or run the risk of receiving gold at a fourth less by weight than by count.

There was a problem of another kind which might have persuaded a storekeeper of the 1780's that he was in the wrong line of work. The young country, bursting at the seams, with few manufactures of its own, and few imports for nearly 10 troubled years, acted with the pull of a powerful magnet on the markets of the old countries once trade was resumed. The American market was soon flooded with merchandise, and the storehouses of the importers were piled high with barrels and boxes as supply outran the ability to buy. Prices dropped, and a chain reaction set in. The farmer could not settle up with his crossroads trader. The country dealer could not meet his obligations to the wholesaler and importer. The importer had to call for extensions from his correspondents overseas. Debtors everywhere could not pay. The courts could not enforce payment.

The turn for the better came with the adoption of the Constitution and the beginning of government under it in 1789. Here was assurance of a stable and responsible government on a federal basis. In 1790, Alexander Hamilton, as Secretary of the Treasury, presented a plan for the payment of the foreign and the domestic debt. There were also state debts, incurred in the same cause. These were also to be taken over by the federal government, a happy circumstance for the farmers and mercantile classes who held the paper. Congress adopted these measures and went on to pass a national coinage act based on the decimal system. The United States mint was projected and in operation within two years after 1790.

And so it came about that a man with a store on his mind had every reason to "chirk up." He could look around in the year 1791 and see peace, plenty, and a future as sound as wheat. The measures of the government were popular in the North and East, where tradesmen and merchants, good Hamiltonians all, were now in a position to collect their debts and to be paid in sound money. Trade quickly responded. Packets were loaded down with freight. Loaded oxcarts and farm wagons appeared on the roads, for farmers were now eager to part with their produce. Commercial treaties were made. A patent office was established. The mails bulged. Courthouses were rising to serve new counties, canals dug, roads laid out. Schools, bridges, and docks were under construction. Powder mills became paper mills.

In the closing decade of the 18th century an energetic young merchant with a good stand might have dwelt on the fact that the first census of the United States showed that there were 3,929,214 American people to be clothed and equipped, though this statistic, had he known it, would probably have seemed academic to a trader whose fortunes were tied up with those of a particular four corners. Yet, it was an underlying reason why, all in all, 1790 was a good time to be alive. A country dealer with a brisk run of trade, who applied the advice stamped on the Franklin penny —"Mind Your Business"—had a good chance to grow up with the country.

PART I

Marketing in Colonial America, 1607-1790

C. MARKETING INSTITUTIONS, AGENCIES, AND PRACTICES

1. TOBACCO MARKETING
IN COLONIAL AMERICA*

The importance of organized markets, established standards, and specialized middlemen in the buying and selling of basic commodities is demonstrated by the history of tobacco marketing. Seventeenth-century tobacco production and distribution began as an extremely risky business. There was no mechanism to bring buyers and sellers together on a continuing basis. As a result, this commodity was subject to price manipulation and other abuses. Gradually, a more orderly market developed as merchants in this country and in England assumed the specialized functions of exchange, storage, standardization and grading, risk taking, information, and financing. However, intermittent surpluses caused by the inability to adjust agricultural production to demand existed much as they do today. Monopoly agreements among English merchants, legislative price fixing, and restrictions on output were of little avail in dealing with these surpluses.

CORRESPONDING TO the commercial mechanism in Great Britain for the marketing of tobacco, there also developed a commercial mechanism in the colonies. In the first place, many of the larger planters who maintained wharves of their own early began shipping tobacco for smaller neighboring planters not located on navigable water or not possessing wharves. Thus, there developed a class of merchant-planters who found the joint function advantageous. As a planter, the expenses of marketing were reduced and some of the elements of exploitation removed. It was also possible to control somewhat the time of marketing his crop and to be in closer touch with marketing conditions. Servants to stock his plantations could be transported cheaply on return voyages, and the headrights provided a means of acquiring large landholdings. As a merchant, there was greater certainty of obtaining a cargo; and if such could not be obtained, plantation slaves could be employed in preparing a cargo of pipe staves, clapboards, and other timber for shipment to the West Indies. By reason of his British connections, the colonial merchant-planter enjoyed unusual facilities for obtaining capital, which he invested not only in planting but in various other enterprises; and thus, there were many colonial merchants who, like William Byrd (I), at one and the

* Reprinted from Lewis C. Gray, "The Market Surplus Problems of Colonial Tobacco," *Agricultural History*, Vol. II (January, 1928), pp. 13–34.

same time were planters, colonizers, wholesale exporters and importers, retail storekeepers, lumbermen, Indian traders, millers, and prospectors for ores.

The merchant-planter operated in various ways. These are well illustrated by the activities of William Fitzhugh. To a large extent, he served merely as a resident factor representing one or more British firms, for whom he developed a permanent clientele of planters whose business he solicited, and collected indebtedness due his British correspondents. However, when he saw a chance of profit, Fitzhugh bought on his own account tobacco from neighboring planters; and at times, he wrote apologetically to his correspondents in England because of the smallness of his consignment business, and continued to ship small quantities merely as a means of maintaining their goodwill.

In the latter part of the colonial period, there developed a specialized class of merchants in the tobacco colonies, some of whom were acting as junior partners of British firms or as salaried representatives, and in some cases as independent merchants with foreign correspondents. As the tobacco industry expanded westward, some of these mercantile agencies developed chains of stores in the backcountry for selling goods and slaves on long credits of nine months or more in exchange for tobacco and other products.

CONDITIONS RESPONSIBLE FOR INELASTICITY OF PRODUCTION

The long periods of price depression were due in large part to the great inelasticity of production, that is, the failure to adjust volume of production quickly to the quantitative demands of the market. In part, these elements of inelasticity are inherent in the very nature of business enterprise, whether agricultural or industrial. In part, the inelasticity arose from conditions peculiar to agriculture, such as the connection between the business and the home, the large proportion of the family income obtained in kind from the farm, the general lack of adequate accounting, the lack of control over volume of production due to the weather and other uncontrollable influences, the inability to exert any purposeful control over prices or to employ concerted methods of restricting volume of production, the practice of selling "at the market" instead of producing in accordance with prearranged orders, etc.

In part, however, these elements of inelasticity were intensified by conditions of production in the tobacco colonies. In general, tobacco was produced by two quite different classes. One class consisted of pioneer or backwoods families operating largely by their own labor. In general, this class of farmers were largely self-sufficing, but produced a little tobacco as a means of satisfying by purchase a few simple wants that could not be provided for directly by their own labor. Prices influenced the behavior of these producers mainly through the direct balancing of the utility of things obtained against the disutility involved in producing the market crop, rather than indirectly through considerations of expenses, profits, and return on investment. Their reaction to price changes was likely to be very tardy.

The second class of producers consisted of established planters employing servant or slave labor, having debts and expenses to meet, and relying largely on production for sale to meet their obligations—in other words, a commercial and capitalistic system of farming. Having their fixed charges to meet, it was observed that for a considerable time after the beginning of a depression period the planters actually increased the acreage planted, trying by the production of a larger quantity to make up for the smaller price. In time, however, loss of profits had its influence on the production policy of this class. While there was no other available staple to which they could turn, for in every one of these depression periods attempts to develop such staples as silk, wine, flax, hemp, and cotton proved futile, they could at least produce a larger part of their own supplies, particularly clothing; and when the depression lasted long enough, there was a strong tendency toward greater self-sufficiency.

The maladjustment of production to price was promoted by the consignment system, under which the planter was compelled to wait as much as two years before learning the results of the sale of a particular crop. It was further promoted by the general use of tobacco as a medium of exchange in the colonies and to some extent as a standard of value, and particularly by the legislative provisions for paying taxes, fees, quitrents, and other public charges at certain fixed rates.

Undoubtedly, another factor which interfered seriously with the adjustment of supply and demand was the large proportion of the consumers' price which consisted of fixed charges for customs duties, cost of transport, and various market costs. In 1720, it was estimated that, not counting customs duties, a price of 4 pence in Great Britain would yield but 1¾ pence in Virginia. For Maryland tobacco a British price of 3 pence would yield the planter only a penny. The addition of the duty, which at that time was 6½ pence, meant that for the Virginia planter to receive 1¾ pence, tobacco must sell in Great Britain at 10½ pence, and for the Maryland planter to receive a penny, his tobacco must sell at 9 pence. It is true that most of the duty was recovered on reexportation; but in continental markets, other heavy charges were again imposed.

ATTEMPTED SOLUTIONS OF THE PROBLEM

Many attempts were made to deal with the problem of marketing the tobacco surplus more effectively so as to bring greater advantages to the producer, including a vast amount of legislation, probably more than has ever been devoted to any other crop, with the possible exception of sugar.

ATTEMPTS AT MONOPOLY

The first decade of tobacco growing in the American colonies was on the basis of an abnormally high price level. It was an age of monopoly; and consequently, the attempts to uphold this abnormally high level took the form of a series of monopolistic concessions calculated to maintain unity of control in merchandising the product. There was also sufficient practical recognition of the laws of supply and demand to lead to provisions in the earlier proposals for restricting the quantity brought to market from the colonies and from Spain, and later to restrict the quantity grown in the colonies.

While the colonists opposed these various attempts at monopolistic concessions, except that of the Virginia Company, which was a matter of controversy both in the company itself and in the colony, this opposition was due less to antagonism to the monopolistic solution than to the fact that the various proposals were made largely for the special benefit of the Crown and of a persistent group of courtiers who sought to fatten their purses at the expense of the planters.

Long after the idea of fiscal monopolies as a royal prerogative had been swept overboard by the civil wars and the accompanying changes in British constitutional principles, some interesting private attempts were made to employ monopoly in marketing as a means of coping with the problem of price depression.

In 1690, some adventurer who had traveled in Brazil and had learned the methods of curing tobacco in that country proposed the formation of a monopolistic company under royal charter for the production and marketing of "sweet-scented" tobacco cured by Brazilian methods. The scheme met with little encouragement by the Virginia authorities.

During the long depression which began in 1725, a notable attempt was made to bring about concerted action on the part of the London merchants in the handling of tobacco. The impulse for this attempt was largely the preponderant advantage enjoyed by the agent of the French fiscal monopoly of tobacco in purchasing annually 15,000 hogsheads of the dark variety of Oronoke tobacco.

The French, it was alleged, consistently took advantage of their position to play one merchant against another and thereby beat down the price. Not content with purchasing for the requirement in France, the shrewd French buyer bought whole shiploads, which he dumped on the Dutch market at less than cost in order to demoralize prices; and then, on the basis of prices thus established, he came into the London and outport markets to purchase his annual supply. By these methods, it was estimated that he deliberately incurred a loss of about £2,000 on tobacco shipped to the Dutch market but saved about £50,000 on tobacco purchased for use in France. The evil was all the greater because the price determined for the French purchases tended to establish the market level for other classes of tobacco. Furthermore, the London merchants had been losing business to the outport merchants because their former clients, dissatisfied with the results of the consignment system, were turning to the method of selling in the colonies to the outport merchants.

A number of times previously, the London merchants had organized for concerted action, and for some years had deducted 3 pence on each hogshead, which was supposed to be devoted to a common fund to pay the expenses of the tobacco lobby in parliament and the other expenses of the merchants' organization. Apparently, this charge had been made with the tacit consent of their colonial clients in the hope of substantial benefits, but the attempts of the merchants at concerted action in the market had always failed through inability to hold all the members in line. Yet the charge still continued, and it was claimed that much of the proceeds had never reached the treasury of the organization.

The principal leaders in the movement for reorganization in 1727–29 were Henry Darnall, a Maryland merchant resident in London, and John Falconer, another London merchant. They developed a plan which involved provision for a salaried secretary, and meetings by all the London merchants on the first Thursday of each month and by a board of 12 managers on the third Thursday of each month. Certain annual contributions were to be made by each merchant, from which he was allowed certain refunds for prompt attendance at meetings. Unused funds were to be employed to provide a dinner once or twice a year "to beget a good Friendship and Harmony among the Merchants; which Eating together, does more often produce among Mankind than bare Drinking."

It was proposed that careful statistics be collected of stocks on hand and shipments of tobacco to and from Great Britain. The merchants agreed to act in concert in dealing with the French; and in order to prevent them from turning to the outports for supplies, it was proposed to open correspondence with the outport merchants with a view to obtaining their support. In order to hold the London merchants in line, the promoters expected to rely on the pressure of opinion among their clients in Maryland and Virginia. In order to solidify opinion in the colonies, it was suggested that correspondence be opened with the various planters' clubs, of which, it was said, there was at least one in every county "for talking over affairs."

The organization was formed in April, 1728, according to these plans, and the agreement was signed by all the London tobacco merchants, 29 firms in all. A minimum price for tobacco was agreed to. Very soon, however, some of the merchants were accused of dealing surreptitiously with the French. Then, still others openly broke over on the ground of self-defense. Letters were written to the colonial planters; and for a time, charges and countercharges flew thick and fast.

Nearly a decade later, in 1737, another proposal was made by a group of merchants (probably Scotch outport merchants) headed by Daniel McKircher, Esq., for a monopolistic selling agency to confront the buyers' monopoly enjoyed by the French tobacco concessionaires. Not only were British merchants at a great disadvantage in dealing as separate individuals with the French buyers, but the merchants themselves were put to unnecessary expense, in that they were compelled to send their ships out to the colonies "by Way of Adventure, to procure their Lading," involving expensive delays in the colony of five or six months, and other great expenses in soliciting tobacco, the transportation at times of incomplete cargoes, storage in England until sale could be effected, and various charges and losses involved in holding and merchandising the tobacco. The proponents estimated these unnecessary costs in England at £1 7s. 11d. per hogshead of 732 pounds net weight.

It was proposed to have a single company which would arrange in advance for the required amount of tobacco and have it ready when the ships came out, thus effecting an economy in freight charges estimated at 25 percent. The proponents of the plan had obtained the consent of the French buyers to purchase their usual quantity on the quay in London, paying 2 pence sterling per pound cash. It was estimated that this was a quarter penny less than the average price, but would involve economies in marketing and transport that would make the total net gain to the planter 13s. 8d. per hogshead.

The proposal met determined opposition in the colonies, probably largely on the part of the old-line British commission merchants, whose trade would have been largely displaced by the arrangement; and apparently, the proposal was not put into effect.

LEGISLATIVE PRICE FIXING

In the early decades of the industry, some attempts were made at crude legislative price fixing. Two such acts were passed in 1632, two others in the following year, and other acts in 1639 and 1640. These were acts fixing the general price level for tobacco and prohibiting by penalties its exchange at a lower price. They are to be distinguished from the numerous rating acts, necessitated by the use of tobacco as currency, to determine the ratio of tobacco to sterling in payment of taxes, fees, quitrents, tavern rates, and ferry charges. In 1641 a royal ordinance inspired by the merchants put an end to these attempts at legislative price determination.

Our forefathers are not to be charged with complete ignorance of the laws of economics in the passage of these acts fixing the general price level of tobacco. In the first place, the several acts were associated with attempts at stinting, or restricting the volume of production. In the second place, they were more or less justified by the uncertain conditions of marketing and the imperfection of marketing machinery. At a time when no general price level had as yet developed and when the individual planter was largely at the mercy of the merchant who chanced to call for his crop, the legislative enactments served to define crudely the limits of bargaining and to supply a price criterion for the application of the laws against engrossing, forestalling, and regrating.

RESTRICTION OF VOLUME OF PRODUCTION OR OF EXPORTS

As suggested above, from an early period, attempts were made to solve the surplus problem by stinting, or restricting production, usually by allowing so many plants for each household, for each tithable or other unit of labor. Various arrangements for stinting were included in the later monopolistic contracts, as well as in connection with the price-fixing acts just described. In the legislation of 1639–40, designed to retrict production and fix prices, it became apparent that such legislation would be largely futile without an intercolonial agreement with Maryland. This was the beginning of a succession of attempts to achieve such agreements.

There is evidence that Virginia legislation for stinting existed in the latter part of the 17th century and the early part of the 18th. The depression beginning in 1725 resulted in renewed attempts at control of volume of production. Virginia renewed an act in 1727, which had expired in 1725, for improving the staple of tobacco, probably involving destruction of inferior grades and stinting. A stinting act passed at the special session of the Maryland Assembly in 1726 encountered the opposition of the council because of the provision for scaling fees and debts by reason of the expected rise of prices. Another attempt in 1727, in which a compromise was effected on the scaling problem, was vetoed by the proprietor. The continuing distress, which culminated in an outbreak of plant-cutting riots in Maryland, finally led to the successful passage of a stinting act in 1730, which, however, lapsed in 1732. The Currency Act of 1733 provided for the enforced destruction of 150 pounds per taxable during each of the two succeeding years. During this period, also, negotiations were carried on between Maryland and Virginia looking to mutual legislation for restricting the latest date of planting tobacco, in the interest of curtailing production.

The restriction of volume of production was also intrinsic in numerous acts passed from time to time in both colonies, partly for the purpose of improving quality, such as prohibitions against the packing of ground leaves and suckers, and the tending and packing of second-growth crops ("seconds"). In some of these acts, it was provided that viewers should annually inspect the fields in their respective localities and insure the destruction of second-growth tobacco. To some extent, restriction of quantity was also achieved by the various acts against packing inferior tobacco and the destruction of such tobacco found in tobacco hogsheads. Restriction of quantity was also involved in the practice of stemming tobacco, which was strongly opposed by the British government because of resulting loss of revenues and was prohibited in 1722 by act of parliament. However, the act led to vigorous protest by the colonies, Virginia sending John Randolph to London especially to obtain its repeal, which he succeeded in achieving.

The aim of restricting the quantity of tobacco was also more or less present in the various acts in the early colonial period requiring the production of food crops (the two-acre acts), acts to exempt new settlers from taxation for a time on condition that they refrain from tobacco cultivation, and certain temporary legislation against the importation of slaves.

ATTEMPTS AT STANDARDIZATION AND IMPROVEMENT OF MARKETABILITY

Probably more effective than the attempts at direct control of price and restriction of output were the efforts to improve the marketability of the product.

PROHIBITION OF SHIPMENTS IN BULK

Among these measures, we may include the long struggle to restrict the shipment of tobacco in bulk instead of in the hogshead. The former custom increased greatly in the latter part of the 17th century and early decades of the 18th by reason of the expansion of the industry into frontier regions where facilities for prizing in hogsheads were lacking, and by reason of the practice of pioneer farmers of trading small miscellaneous lots of tobacco at neighborhood stores in exchange for goods brought by the outports ships.

The practice of shipping in bulk, which had increased rapidly with expansion of the industry into the backcountry, was strongly opposed by the administrative authorities, by the old-time commission merchants, and by the larger planters, because it was favorable to smuggling; because it was an obstacle to the standardization of quality; because a smaller number of ships for transportation were required, which did not appeal to the mercantilist ideals of the period; and because the earlier arrival of the bulk tobacco tended to disorganize the market, besides lending itself to cutthroat competition by small and irregular dealers. We may suspect that in part the opposition grew out of the general resistance of the old-line commercial agencies to the encroachments of the aggressive outport merchants, whose new and vigorous methods were tending to displace them in the trade.

The practice was defended on the ground of smaller cost of transport and because it was essential to the welfare of the poorer classes on the frontier and to the profits of the small outport merchants; and for many years, this democratic resistance defeated attempts at prohibition in the colonies. The practice was prohibited by parliament in 1698, but there was much evasion until the practice was prohibited by the inspection acts hereafter mentioned.

ATTEMPTS TO REGULATE SIZE AND SHAPE OF HOGSHEADS

There was also a long struggle to regulate the size and shape of the hogshead and the time of shipment. Both of these points were of special concern to the merchants, for hogsheads of irregular shape and size were costly to transport because they required an undue amount of cargo space. Carelessly made hogsheads came to pieces or warped apart in transit. Maryland long held out for a larger hogshead than was specified by Virginia laws on the ground that the character of Maryland tobacco did not admit of such close packing as in Virginia, while the Virginians attributed the difficulty to slovenly methods of packing in Maryland. Even an order by the Queen annulling the Maryland act and requiring that the Maryland specifications be made identical with those of Virginia did not settle the problem.

ATTEMPTS TO REGULATE TIME OF COMPLETING HOGSHEADS

The great and costly delays encountered by merchants in collecting tobacco in the colonies led to a great deal of legislation to require coopers to have hogsheads completed in sufficient time and other acts to confine shipment within certain specified periods. The practice of hurrying the completion of hogsheads by using unseasoned staves and headings necessitated also the passage of acts to compel the early cutting of timber for the purpose.

PROVISIONS FOR OFFICIAL INSPECTION BEFORE SHIPMENT

It early became apparent that none of these measures for improvement of quality would be effective without a system of standardization by thorough inspection before shipment. As early as 1619, there was developed the practice of employing sworn viewers to inspect tobacco.

From this time forward, various temporary or partial measures for inspection were provided for. No permanently effective system was achieved until the passage of the Virginia Act of 1730, which marks an important milestone in the evolution of agricultural marketing machinery and practice.

The foundation for this important measure was laid by the Warehouse Act of 1712, which provided for the establishment of public warehouses at convenient points not more than one mile from navigable water. Though these warehouses might be privately owned, they were made public utilities. The rates and conditions of storage were fixed by law.

An inspection law was also passed in 1713 providing for licensed inspectors to enforce certain minimum standards, issuing warehouse receipts against tobacco. However, the measure excited tremendous opposition, including that of such important merchant-planters as William Byrd (II), who reflected the attitude of the conservative consignment merchants, such as Micajah Perry of London. These influences obtained in 1717 the royal veto of the measure.

Fortunately, the Warehouse Act, slightly amended in 1720, still remained to serve as a nucleus, and the serious and protracted depression beginning in 1725 brought public sentiment to the support of the act of 1730. Variously amended from time to time, this act and the cognate Warehouse Act constituted the backbone of the colonial system of marketing until the Rovolutionary War.

The system involved several licensed and bonded inspectors stationed at public warehouses. They were authorized to open each hogshead; with the consent of the owner, to sort out and destroy inferior tobacco; and lacking his consent, to destroy the entire hogshead. The class and grade of the tobacco were then marked on the repacked hogshead. For the purpose of issuing warehouse receipts, a distinction was made between "transfer" tobacco and "crop" tobacco. Against the former, general negotiable receipts were issued which did not entitle the owner to any particular hogshead, while the receipts for crop tobacco were specific in character, representing largely the consignment tobacco. When the receipts in course of circulation reached the hands of the exporter, he could demand delivery and at that time require a second opening and inspection of the hogshead; and in case the tobacco was found below the standard, he could enforce judgment against the inspector for compensation and costs. A scale of allowances for shrinkage was provided, and tobacco stored in public warehouses was publicly insured against loss by fire and other causes.

This was probably the most constructive type of marketing legislation passed in the colonial period, and its influence was profound. It contributed to improving the average quality of exports, standardized the commodity as a medium of exchange and of public payments and as a standard of deferred payments, and improved the system of customs administration. It gave Virginia growers and merchants a great advantage over those of Maryland. In 1743, Daniel Dulaney wrote that Maryland factors were moving to Virginia where they could buy better tobacco, though at a higher price. The French "regie" buyers also were turning more and more to Virginia to obtain their supply. The council and governor of Maryland informed the proprietor that unless Maryland took similar action, the whole trade in tobacco would be lost to Virginia.

Maryland experimented for about a quarter of a century with a vacillating policy comprising acts against tending of seconds, suckers, and ground leaves, and acts imposing heavy penalties for false packing, enforced by the offer of rewards to informers. Finally, in 1747, the colony was forced to adopt the Virginia solution by the adoption of an inspection law closely modeled after that of the sister colony.

SUMMARY

Through more than a century and a half, great progress was made in the marketing of tobacco along the lines of more complete commercial organization and greater standardization. It is probable that this progress accounts in part for the comparative freedom from protracted depression during the last three or four decades of the colonial period; but the market surplus problem, as we know it today, remained unsolved in spite of the numerous and varied efforts at solution which have been described. It continues as one of the outstanding economic problems of our own time.

2. MARKETING IN COLONIAL VIRGINIA*

The trade and marketing practices of Virginia differed appreciably from those of northern colonies like Massachusetts and Pennsylvania. Since the large planters tended to buy both for their own needs and for their smaller neighbors as well, no strong merchant class grew up. That northern marketing institutions failed to develop was due in part to the lack of urban centers in Virginia. Also, a plantation culture encouraged all-pervasive relationships between the planters and London tobacco merchants. Despite some important causes of friction, the commercial ties between the two groups remained close throughout the colonial period.

THE VIRGINIA TRADERS never got beyond the stage of neighborhood storekeepers. They lived along the greater rivers, buying large quantities of goods for their own estates and somewhat more for the neighbors who lived on smaller plantations; and in the fall, if there seemed to be any chance to make money by the speculation, they bought tobacco in the country and sent it to England in the ships which came in the winter. They were traders and planters; and not seldom, they added to these activities that of one of the learned professions. Thus the colony merchants, so far as they existed at all, were not a distinct feature of colonial life.

The trade, on the other hand, was immediately from the hands of the Londoner to those of the planter. Into the rivers the ships came early in the winter, loaded with goods which had been ordered the preceding spring either by the large planters or by the scattered smaller traders. These goods were slowly disembarked as the ships moved leisurely from wharf to wharf. The captains, in the meantime, were making engagements for tobacco with which to make their return loads. They proceeded about their business leisurely enough, and in the course of some weeks returned for the tobacco they had agreed to take.

About this trade, there was much indirection. The London merchant was not a merchant in the sense that a merchant is one who buys and sells commodities. He was more of a commission merchant than a dealer. The only article he handled directly was tobacco. This he disposed of to the

---

* Reprinted from John S. Bassett, "The Relation between the Virginia Planter and the London Merchant," *American Historical Association Annual Report for 1901*, Vol. I, pp. 551–75.

best advantage when it was received in England, deducted from the receipts the necessary expenses of the transaction, and placed the balance to the credit of the planter. This balance was rarely remitted to the colony, but it was laid out in goods of one kind or another to be sent to the planter by the ships which returned in the following season. Each ship which brought tobacco brought also orders for goods. These goods were bought from various shopkeepers in the city by the Londoner to whom the tobacco was consigned. If there were complaints, and such there frequently were, there was no easy redress for the person who bought the goods. The shopkeepers were so far away that it was a difficult matter to reach them. Frequently, the orders sent over with the tobacco amounted to more than the crop realized. The result was that debts were contracted by the planter. How much irritation came of these debts one may easily imagine. They served to produce some harsh feeling on each side of the water. The Londoner was apt to feel that his debtor was a little anxious to escape from his obligations; the planter was often led to think that his creditor was a Shylock. Each may have been to a certain extent right, but the fact that such feelings existed was unfortunate in its effect on the state of commerce.

This form of trade was expensive. The commissions of the London factor had to be paid in the first instance. Although he may not have charged anything for his services in buying the articles the planter ordered, it is reasonable to think that he did not fail to include in his commissions enough to repay him for this trouble. Moreover, he was not interested enough in his purchases to buy with the same care for prices and for quality of goods as the planter would have done in person. It is evident, too, that there was opportunity for corrupt collusion between the factor and the shopkeeper; and it is not very improbable that it did sometimes occur. The item of freight was somewhat more expensive when goods had to be put ashore at the various landings than if they had been sent in bulk to one place.

The most permanent social result of this was that it prevented the development of a strong trading class. It served to turn the commerce of the colony away from the normal channel in other colonies of a trade through one or more strong trading centers, and it scattered the commerce in a thousand smaller parts among the richer planters themselves. Such a state of trade was a social disadvantage. It no doubt gave a certain modishness to colony manners, because it put the wealthy people into close touch with the best London shops; but it deprived the people of the more compact society which exists when strong trading centers have developed.

It is natural to ask ourselves why there did not develop trading cities in Virginia. The people who settled there were in no material sense different from those who settled in Massachusetts. Why, then, did they not build towns? It was not, as some have said, on account of a social prejudice against trade. Such a prejudice, which may have existed after the Revolution, did not exist in the formative period of Virginia. There was no more influential family in Virginia than that of the Byrds, and they not only originated from a family of traders but were engaged in trade themselves. William Fitzhugh was also a trader, and his social position was the best. In fact, there was hardly a family of social and political importance in the first century of the colony which did not have some kind of a connection with commerce.

Neither could the existing system have grown up because it was cheaper than a trade through the usual channels. It is probable that large dealers, buying in quantities in England, could have undersold the traders following the usual method. This view is supported by the strong opposition of the Londoners to the attempts which were made to establish towns in Virginia. They feared that such a move would lessen the profitableness of their trade. The planters, it is true, believed that they would pay more for their goods if they were to lose the direct trade with England, but they could hardly have realized how much they would have gained in cheaper freights for their tobacco, which would probably have offset all the loss in this other way. This condition refers only to the very rich planters. The smaller and less influential planters, who were not themselves buyers of tobacco, could have had no advantage in the existing system as compared with the trade through towns.

A more probable reason for the existing system was the extreme profitableness of tobacco planting in connection with slave labor. It is doubtful if ever a surer road was opened to the man of industry to go on to wealth and respectable influence. So strongly did it attract men that it was never possible for commerce to take a firm foothold in the colony. How strongly it drew the people is seen from the fact that there were very few people of professions other than farming who did not combine farming with those other callings. Physicians, lawyers, and clergymen frequently were planters as well; and not infrequently, the professional life was allowed to dwindle into insignificance, while the plantation was made more and more the chief support of the family.

The disadvantages the colony suffered from lack of towns were not unknown at the time. In 1662, 1680, and 1691, acts were passed to establish towns, but it was too late. The rural system was so well established that it was impossible to overcome its influence. The last of the laws may furnish us an illustration of how the conditions of town building presented themselves to the people of the day. By it, a large number of towns were created as ports of entry. They were given privileges, and the people were commanded to trade in them. The law was passed at the instance of Lieutenant Governor Nicholson. It aroused the opposition of the London merchants, who saw that their trade would be seriously injured. It aroused also a strong opposition in the colony; first, from the large planters, who foresaw that their own plantation trade would be interfered with, and secondly, from the people at large, who knew nothing of the advantages of town life and considered the restriction which sought to bring the trade into the proposed towns a hardship. So strong was the opposition that the law was repealed a few months after it was sought to put it into operation.

One of the most serious features of colony trade was transportation. It was especially serious in Virginia. The system which came into use was slow and expensive. The ships which were sent to take the tobacco crop to England usually arrived late in the fall or early in the winter. The slow method of collecting freight, which has already been noted, delayed their return till late in the spring. The long period in the colony was a source of heavy expense to the planter. In 1659, it cost £7 to send a ton of tobacco to England. This was 17.9 percent of the gross sales. At the same time the planter received, after paying the expenses of customs, commissions, freights, and other charges, 35.1 percent of the gross sales. Thus, he paid for his freight half as much as his crop netted him.

High as these freights were, there was continued and general complaint about the difficulty of getting opportunities of shipping. There often was a dearth of ships. The fault was usually charged, in Virginia, to the merchant. What the merchant would have said about it, we do not know, for his evidence is not at hand. It seems probable that each side was partly responsible. The planter sent home in late spring or in summer reports of what kind of crops would be made. It was natural for him not to overestimate the yield, for that would mean low prices. The merchant was careful not to send more ships than would accommodate the crop. It was for his interest to send too few ships rather than too many. Moreover, the ships which came were chartered, frequently by the merchants; and if they did not take enough tobacco to repay the outlay, the loss was the merchants'. Thus the normal condition was one of scarcity of ships.

The planter was obliged to allow to his English correspondent much discretion in disposing of the tobacco shipped and in buying goods out of the proceeds. This was frequently due to the uncertainty of the selling price of tobacco. Thus, Fritzhugh writes to Cooper that if the tobacco and bills of exchange he is forwarding shall come to more than the goods he has ordered, Cooper is to send the overplus in linen. At the same time, Fitzhugh wants a bricklayer and a carpenter for service on his building, and gives instructions for having them sent to him. It might happen, also, that the proceeds would not be sufficient to pay for the goods ordered. In such a case the merchant might exercise his discretion about filling the order. It thus came about that many planters were slightly in debt to the merchants. A sagacious planter would avoid this state of affairs, since it gave the merchant a right to expect that such a debtor would continue to send tobacco to him.

The relations between such a prudent person and the merchant might be very satisfactory, for as long as the planter was not in debt, he was a man to be courted. In such cases, it is noticeable that terms of intimacy between the two were frequent. On the other hand, the relations between these two parties might be anything but pleasant. The very nature of the trade was such that it fell into the credit system from the beginning. When once a merchant had brought goods to America, it was no practical thing to carry them back to England because the Virginia market was overstocked. He sought some other way to dispose of them. He might leave them in the hands of an agent, or he might sell them on credit and take a lien on the forthcoming crop of tobacco. In fact, each method was followed. Thus the credit relation got a deep hold on the economic life of the colony. It was the beginning of the expensive system of fall credits in the South. Between the most reliable of the planters and the merchants, it might not lead to complications. But there were always people among the Virginians, as among all other peoples, who were not thrifty. Here were causes of the merchant's continual losses. Here was the source of the planter's bitter feelings. The result was a certain jealousy of foreigners of means which struck deep into the community's consciousness.

Besides this open disadvantage, there were a number of unavoidable inconveniences in the trade. One often recurring was the slowness of the planter in finding out how his balance stood. This might happen through accident when the merchant was careful to forward reports, as by the loss of letters. It would more frequently happen through the carelessness of the merchant in not making prompt returns by the ships which took the goods back to Virginia. The slowness of intercourse might well make it two years after the tobacco was shipped before the planter knew certainly what it had netted him.

A similar inconvenience was the irregularity of the mails. The post office was introduced into Virginia in 1692. Before that time, letters were left to the rather uncertain accommodations of the merchant ships. Sometimes the letters went astray through being forwarded in any chance ship which came to Virginia. By this means, they might be sent in a James River ship and be as difficult to get on the banks of the Potomac as if they were still in London. This condition of affairs evidently produced serious trouble when, as in 1693, there was not a London ship in the Potomac. Such an occurrence could not have happened often.

All kinds of commodities were ordered by the planter; and in the complexity of articles the Londoner must select in order to fill the orders sent to him, a high order of shopping skill must have been developed by the merchant and his assistants. All kinds of furniture for the planter's house, all kinds of clothing and dress goods, books, various tools, saddles, servants, orphan boys to be bred up as secretaries, and a hundred other similarly miscellaneous articles were to be looked after. A merchant who had this trade was a true factor. Besides orders for goods, he might be directed to look up family relatives, or to have an old wig made over or an old sword exchanged for a fashionable rapier.

In conclusion, it ought to be mentioned that not all of the Virginia trade was conducted by the English merchants. There was from an early day in the history of the colony quite an important trade with New England and with the Dutch. Later, as the colonies of Maryland and Pennsylvania came to be settled, they too were admitted into the trade relations. From New England came slaves and rum and miscellaneous goods. Fitzhugh bought slaves and paid for them in tobacco according to a stipulated rate of so many pounds for each slave, the exact rate varying with the age of the slave. For the New England traders, in the later period at least, the Virginia planter had but little respect. Most of them seem to have been small dealers who came into the Virginia rivers trading with such of the inhabitants as would come aboard their vessels. To the planters, this was of the nature of chapmen. They complained also that such ships traded in a clandestine manner with the servants of the planters. It cannot be denied that the planter had a certain disdain for the average New Englander. Byrd expressed it in his characteristic way when he referred to them as the "Saints of New England." "They have a great dexterity," he added, "at palliating a perjury so well as to leave no taste of it in their mouth, nor can any people like them slip through a penal Statute."

3. THE "CHARLESTON FACTOR": A SOUTHERN MARKETING INSTITUTION*

In the Carolina country, marketing activities were dominated by a highly integrated, multifaceted institution known as the "Charleston factor." Such firms acted principally as agents for English merchants but oftentimes bought and sold for their own account as well. The Charleston factors operated as importer-wholesalers for foreign merchandise, as assemblers for agricultural goods being shipped to their overseas principals, as agents in the sale of slaves and the handling of indentured servants, and as the directing force in the fur trade. These firms were able to monopolize the shipping business and used their position as sole financial representative of the powerful English merchants to control the credit system of the region.

SINCE CAROLINA was a new country of colonial status, overseas business was carried on almost exclusively by means of credit and was directed by factors or commission merchants who acted as agents of British firms. Those representatives of the British merchants who dominated the external trade of the Charleston district seem to have been generally called Charleston factors, and it is the name which will be applied to them in this work. The internal trade of the district was in the hands of retailers, who acted principally as agents of the Charleston factors, but also as independent traders. The most important group of retailers were called country factors.

The Charleston factor was not only a merchant but a banker and broker as well. In his character as merchant, he sold merchandise sent out to him by the British firms and bought rice, indigo, deerskins, naval stores, and other produce for his British correspondents; in his character as financier, he managed the fiscal system and controlled the financial life of the country. The Charleston factor derived his importance from his connection with the British merchants, who gave him a year's credit for merchandise, paid him a commission (usually 5 percent) for selling merchandise and buying rice and indigo, and furnished him in the bill of exchange a medium by which he could purchase cargoes in any part of the world with which he was allowed to trade.

---

* Leila Sellers, *Charleston Business on the Eve of the American Revolution* (Chapel Hill: University of North Carolina Press, 1934), pp. 50–59.

As a merchant proper, the Charleston factor was interested in selling goods in wholesale quantities to the retailers; in monopolizing and supervising the shipping business; in selling slaves, chiefly Negroes, sent to him directly from Africa; in participating in the immigrant and indentured servant business; and in directing the skin trade. As a financial representative of the British merchants, he was chiefly concerned in operating the credit system of the country, in recommending and making investments for his customers in Great Britain and America, and in manipulating means of exchange to the advantage of the British merchants and incidentally to his own advantage.

The wholesale trade, then, of the Charleston district was largely in the hands of the Charleston factor, whose chief stock in trade was naturally derived from England and Scotland or from the East Indies and Europe through the channel of England. In addition to being a factor, he was often an independent trader, importing and exporting on his own account, with correspondents not only in Great Britain, but in the West Indies, the Wine Islands, Portugal, Spain, and the cities of Flanders, Holland, and Germany.

The wholesale dealers were the great advertisers of the time. They advertised their merchandise in terms of the current exchange. Since £700 currency was equal to £100 sterling, selling goods at 7 for 1 was selling at prime cost. Goods were advertised to be sold for cash or ready money, for produce, for short or long credit. Short credit seems to have been for one, three, or six months; long credit anything beyond six months, usually a year. The following is an example of the terms advertised by wholesale dealers:

> Selling off at
> Prime cost.
> Whole at 7 for 1 with 9 months credit without
> interest, and Payments will be made easy.
> To any person taking three thousand Pounds,
> 8 for one with six months credit.
> To anyone taking Five Hundred Pounds, 8
> for one with 3 months credit.
> 250 Pounds 8½ for one 3 months credit.
> For sums under, 8 & Half for one cash.   ISAAC MOTTE.

The chief requisites for holding the much envied and profitable position of factor to the big British firms were capital and successful experience as a clerk, extending over a series of years, with some merchant firm, preferably in England or Carolina. Capital was required for the numerous cargoes of slaves, which were the most valuable merchandise handled by the English and Carolina firms; to provide for the housing and marketing of the great quantity of goods sent out for the Indian trade, the plantation trade, the backcountry trade, and the coastal trade; to buy partnerships in vessels, for the English merchant secured the interest and fidelity of his Charleston factor by allowing him partnerships in overseas ships. Also the entire or partial ownership of inland and coastwise vessels was absolutely essential to the prosperity of the business of the Charleston factor.

The Charleston factor invested in lands and slaves, and operated plantations to such an extent that it was often difficult to determine whether his dominant interest was planting or merchandising. He frequently resided like a country gentleman on a plantation along the banks of the Ashley or Cooper, where the seats of the oldest and wealthiest families lay, in a colonial mansion appropriately set amidst acres of cultivated parks and gardens. It was through the Charleston factor that the British investors received the information and obtained the means to make investments in the Charleston district. These investments often assumed the form of a partnership between the British investor and the local merchant.

The great importing merchant found it as profitable to own the boats that transported rice and indigo to market as the railroad baron finds it to his interest to own the railroad operating in the coal district; but in his efforts to monopolize the shipping business, he encountered rivals in the great planters who owned plantations scattered through Carolina, Georgia, and even as far south as East Florida, and were therefore interested in boat ownership, as well as in the country factors and country merchants whose business could not go on without boats. Besides, there was a considerable class, including shipmasters and seamen, shipbuilders and repairers, the keepers of rope walks and fishermen, who earned their livelihoods because of the several hundred ships that entered and cleared at Charleston each year, and on account of the numerous vessels employed in the inland and coastwise trade of the province.

There were three classes of vessels employed in the Charleston trade: Inland boats of a few tons burden carried on the interior trade of the province because of the danger of large vessels being grounded on the shoals in the rivers. The largest vessel of this type had trunk masts that had to be folded when they passed under a bridge. In the maritime parts of the province, where most of the great plantations lay, rice and indigo were conveyed to market in vessels with standing masts, decked to protect the produce from the weather. These "decked periaugers" drew too much water to pass far up the channels of the inland waterways. They were essentially coasters, some of them of 50 tons burden, which collected produce from the landings of the plantations and from the depots of the port towns. Vessels of the same type, some of them, however, of 70 tons burden, carried on the coastal trade.

The inland boats and the decked periaugers were probably owned principally by Charleston businessmen. Some of the West Indian coasters were owned by Charleston merchants and some in partnership by Charleston and West Indian merchants. The ships employed in the European trade ranged from 200 to 500 tons burden, although a 500-ton vessel was considered a very large ship. The great majority of the vessels carried from 1,000 to 1,200 barrels of rice, that is, they were from 250 to 300 tons in capacity. The *South Carolina Gazette* of April 10, 1775, reported the arrival of a new ship, the *Maria Wilhelmina*, burden 800 tons, the largest ship that had ever been built in New York and that had ever entered Charleston harbor. Most of the overseas ships were owned by British merchants, who allowed their Charleston factors a sufficient partnership in vessels to make it to their interest to be faithful and efficient partners. Laurens wrote during the Revolution that before the war, about 400 "sail of vessels" were usually employed in the trade of South Carolina, one tenth of which were owned in the state.

Perhaps the greatest part of the trade of the Charleston district was conducted by first- or secondhand barter; and for this reason, an indispensable part of the merchant's equipment for business, in addition to his store of goods, consisted of storehouses to contain produce brought in by the farmer or planter, which the merchant paid for partly or wholly in merchandise. In fact, in the early colonial period, it had been necessary for the treasurers, like Pharaoh of Egypt 3,000 years before Christ, to keep granaries and cattle pens, in which to receive taxes and from which to make payment of public debts; and in the troubled period following the war, Virginia was obliged to pass acts declaring tobacco, flour, grain, and skins acceptable in payment of taxes, and to construct warehouses for the reception of such commodities. It was the custom in Carolina for merchants, in advertising their goods, to specify what commodities were acceptable in exchange; and the prevalence of barter sometimes caused a merchant to publish a long advertisement in which he gave a list of all he had for sale and all he wished to exchange, of which the following is an example:

> To be sold by the Subscriber,
> Forty large Hogsheads and 30 Tierces of New Rum—
> Ten Hogsheads of Jamaica Rum—Six Half and one Whole
> Chests of Bohea Tea—Twenty Dozen of Women's Black
> Callimance Shoes, made at Lynn near Boston in New
> England—Twenty half quintals of very Best Isle
> of Shoals Table Fish—with a quantity of Wooden
> bowls, Racks, and Mast Hoops, Also, a few
> Barrels of Train Oil and Blubber.
>
> JOSIAH SMITH, JUN.

Wanted immediately, By said Smith
And for which he will Barter any of above-mentioned articles:
Twenty Thousand weight of the best Water-rotted Hemp, clean & bright.
Fifteen hundred weight of very best Copper and Purple Indigo, in large
    and dry Squares.

Sixty Barrels of Rice, to be very clean, bright, and whole grains.

Two Hundred Sides of thoroughly tann'd, well cur'd Soals.

Twenty Barrels of thick and large Corn-fed Pork, well cur'd, in tight strong Casks.

Twenty Kegs of white, & clean saved Hogs' Lard, to weigh from 60 to 100 lb. each.

One Hundred Barrels of Good Tar,—in tight strong Casks, to be full hoop'd, and free from Water.

Twenty Chaldrons of Smith Coals.

Other means of exchange were furnished by hard money, paper money, and bills of exchange. Hard money consisted mostly of foreign coin brought in by trade with southern Europe, the West Indies, and South America, especially Spanish and Portuguese coins. This specie was hard to retain. Some of the silver left the country for the payment of the King's duties, especially under the operation of the Townshend Acts. Then, Carolina tourists who liked to summer in Rhode Island, Philadelphia, New York, or Boston found it convenient to use hard money on their travels, particularly half johannes and dollars. Also, traders from the northern colonies carried out much foreign coin, for the chief object of their quest was not Carolina produce but hard money with which to make remittances to the mother country. And finally, all the trading people at Charleston found hard money a very satisfactory remittance to Great Britain, in that it was present cash. Not only was there no discount on it, but there was often a premium, although freight on it was an item to be considered.

The traders in Charleston, as elsewhere in the colonies, tried to remedy the chronic scarcity of hard money by placing a high value upon it. Thus, in 1771 the moneylenders and merchants entered into an agreement to receive foreign gold and silver at advanced rates. The agreement was not confined to milled money alone, but extended to unmilled of sufficient weight, with certain exceptions. Foreign coin was to pass at prescribed rates. The presence of unmilled money gave great opportunities to the counterfeiters, and there were frequent accounts in the newspapers of villains passing off base, cut, and clipped coins on the unwary.

There was little English money in the colonies; and the hard money of the different European nations, particularly of France, Spain, and Portugal, passed at par with sterling as the value of the metal warranted. While foreign money was of the same value as sterling in all the colonies, it was rated differently in the different colonies. For example, the commonly used silver coin known as the Seville piece of eight passed at 4s. 8d. in South Carolina and Georgia, at 6 shillings in New England, and at 8 shillings in New York and North Carolina. In English sterling, however, the same coin was equivalent to 4s. 6d. Queen Anne attempted to bring order out of the confusion resulting from the existence of colonial currencies of different values by issuing a proclamation in 1704, which was enacted into parliamentary statute in 1707, creating what was known as proclamation money. By this law, a person was forbidden to accept foreign money as worth more than a third of the value of his colonial money; that is, the ratio of proclamation was fixed at 4 to 3; in other words, £100 sterling was equal to £133 proclamation. This legislation failed, however, of its purpose, which was, as the statute recites, to prevent foreign money "being drawn from one plantation to another to the great prejudice of trade." Hard money was in such demand that it was impossible to prevent businessmen of the different colonies from entering into agreements to receive it at advanced rates.

4. BUSINESS PRACTICES ON THE EVE OF THE REVOLUTION*

Business activities which facilitated marketing in colonial America were readily observable in New York prior to the Revolution. Standards covering quality, sizes, and weights and measures had been established. Methods and modes of transportation had markedly improved. Use of advertising as a marketing tool increased as the newspaper notice grew in popularity. Current market information on commodity prices and on supply and demand conditions became far easier to obtain. Bookkeeping practice developed steadily during the period, with the large merchants using a double-entry system. The attitude of caveat emptor *continued to prevail, however, obligating buyers to purchase goods either by sample or by actual inspection.*

To a generation accustomed to mail-order houses, trade at a distance presents no particular difficulty; but the matter was complicated in the 18th century by the incomplete standardization of goods. The ease with which such enterprises are now carried on has been made possible by the development of accurate and uniform standards of quality, fineness, and manufacture, a process which had barely begun in 1750. Complaints are frequent in the letter books of differences in measure and indefinite meanings of terms.

Some progress had of necessity been made in reducing confusion to order. A certain amount of standardization may have been obtained through the concept of "merchantable goods," a term in use also in England and comparable to the *Kaufmansgut* of the German cities. It must not be inferred, however, that this concept had developed in response to the greater need for such a yardstick consequent upon the spread of purchase and sale at a distance, for it is found in the German cities of the 16th century as fully matured as it was in London or Amsterdam in the 18th. Nor did it apparently imply in either Europe or America an absolute standard, but seems rather to have originated as the agreement of a small group upon certain details. The qualities demanded in goods if they were to be "merchantable" were simply those which ex-

* Reprinted from Virginia D. Harrington, *The New York Merchant on the Eve of the Revolution* (New York: Columbia University Press, 1935), pp. 79–104.

perience had shown to be desirable for sale under given conditions, not necessarily either the most or the least exacting. The term served to establish certain norms for particular markets rather than to standardize products, and to furnish one method of grading goods. The attitude of the merchant toward the term was one of conformity not to an objective measure but to the demands of his customers. Goods accounted merchantable in one locality were not always satisfactory to another. Even where the term was not actually employed, it is clear that a general informal agreement on the characteristics of acceptable goods prevailed. Good indigo should be "light as a Cork, of good copper and Purple color, scrape it and it resembles polished copper." For wine, "*stout* and *pure* are the two grand requisitions." "The older it is the better, admitting the Quality equally good. . . . The Straw Colour we most esteem, of a good body without a sweetish Taste."

One further guarantee of quality was found in certain staple exports, such as tobacco from Virginia, and wheat, flour, bread, beef, pork, and lumber from New York, which had to be inspected before export to ascertain that they complied with the law. Regulations concerning the measurements of lumber, the fineness of wheat and flour, and the weight of barrels of bread, beef, or pork were on the statute books of the province all through the English colonial period, and, insofar as they were well enforced, insured a dependable product. If the produce passed inspection in New York, the barrel was branded "New York." Although a simple minimum requirement was thus established, uniform quality was not always assured, as it is in modern "brands."

The most usual method of making sure that the merchandise should be exactly as ordered was to send samples—another characteristic practice of the 18th century. This procedure was used especially for cloths, both woolen and linen, the samples being pasted or pinned to the order. The practice was not confined to textiles. Samples of tobacco, candles, flour, indigo, and even clay pipes were sent from New York to Boston, Rhode Island, and Philadelphia to demonstrate in tangible fashion the quality desired. The sample system, of course, had its drawbacks. It was bulky. Some products did not lend themselves easily to such a method, and it was often impossible to match the sample because of unevenness of manufacture. Protests and demands for rebates accordingly were frequent.

Methods of marketing goods differed most obviously from modern practice. No cohorts of salesmen roamed the country in quest of customers. No blatant advertisements assaulted the eye on every side. Large-scale production had not yet made it necessary to convince people that they had needs of which they were unaware. It is true that the germs of modern usage were present; clerks and factors were the 18th-century counterparts of present-day salesmen, but the actual business of selling fell with greater weight than it does today on the shoulders of the merchant himself. Defoe's *Complete Tradesman* advocated the daily presence of the merchant in his store, and letter books of New York merchants evince a close familiarity with detail which would indicate such diligence.

Advertising, while it had been constantly improving in variety and technique, occupied but a small place in the provincial businessman's budget. By 1750, English advertising had developed three outstanding media, the signboard, the handbill, and the newspaper notice. Signboards lined the streets of London, taking the place of house numbers and thus becoming important landmarks as well as attracting business. In the competition for something new and distinctive, glaring incongruities were perpetrated, and eminent artists like Hogarth were drafted into the service. Indeed, the period has been dubbed "the great Pictorial Signboard Era." Signboards had not the same vogue in New York, however, because the smaller community found them less necessary. Inn signs and tobacco-shop Indians were fairly common. An occasional merchant established himself at the "Sign of the Golden Key" or "Crosshand Saw," but most of them directed their customers by reference to other landmarks—Hunter's Quay, Cruger's Wharf, or "opposite Mr. Walton's house." The beautifully illustrated handbills or tradesmen's cards which were so widely used in England do not seem to have been adopted by the colonies.

On the other hand, newspaper advertising equaled if it did not surpass that found in English journals. A few of the old "reader" type of business notices, which were simply paragraphs about 2 inches long resembling our modern want ads in appearance, persisted; but most printers had adopted newer methods, at least to the extent of separating the merchant's name from his goods and using decorative font marks. One of the less well-known contributions of Benjamin Franklin, in a distinctively American line, was the improvement of the technique of advertising. Not only did he use illustrations before they were introduced in England; but by varying the type and breaking up the paragraph by the use of leads and space, he introduced emphasis into the old reader advertisement so that it caught and held the attention. New York newspapers were equally up to date and enterprising. By 1765, about half the space or more of an issue was given over to advertisements, most of which used headlines varying from 10- to 18-point capitals. Many had broken away from the old 2-inch length and ran to a quarter or half a column. Milligan's "Woman's Shoe Store" inserted a cut of a shoe with the name running around in the frame much like a signboard. Pictures, however, were chiefly used to advertise the sailing of vessels, runaway slaves, horses, and an occasional house for sale.

The most progressive advertiser in New York and, indeed, in North

America was Gerardus Duyckinck, who conducted a general store containing everything but dry goods and perishable foods, which he called the "Medley of Goods." Beginning with a quarter column which used headlines and was decorated with font marks (*#!, etc.), he gradually worked into a "display type." By 1769, he was employing what was probably the earliest all-enclosing border used in American newspaper advertising. Patterned on the lines of some English shopbills, it was a highly ornate design resembling a carved mirror frame, but topped with a mortar and pestle instead of a scroll. Inside it were listed his wares in centered display lines using a delicate roman and italic face, which, according to a later-day opinion, was inconsistent with his merchandise. Duyckinck, in fact, was so much ahead of his age that his advertisements have been called "an isolated instance of twentieth century display methods in the eighteenth century."

Few merchants, however, used advertising in a modern way. No one advertised regularly every week. Most of them inserted notices only sporadically—some often, some seldom. A few, mainly wholesale houses, scarcely ever advertised. Vendue houses were the most regular. Although most merchants thought one paper a sufficient expense, about a third of those in New York, not all of them the largest houses, advertised in both the *Mercury* and the *Post Boy*. The third quarter of the century, furthermore, saw an increase in the amount of advertising, for in the seventies a special single-page supplement was often required.

The Lilliputian scale of provincial business made modern selling methods unnecessary, but the absence of certain aids to marketing which have been developed in our time was a real, though unrealized, handicap to the merchant of 1750. Trade journals, house organs, and stock market reports inform the 20th-century businessman of the fluctuations in prices and demand for goods, analyze the condition of the market, and predict the future. Such information was not available to the provincial merchant. New York weekly journals printed entries and clearances, prices current in town, and a column of miscellaneous data from abroad, chiefly concerning vessels, brought in by ships' masters. Any one of these features might be omitted, for they were regarded, especially the prices current, as filler, not as news of first importance. Occasionally, a list of prices from some other port, such as Charleston, might appear. For any real information concerning the state of the market, however, the merchant had to depend upon his correspondents, who sent him "advices" about profitable cargoes and the course of affairs. A wide and regular correspondence was thus invaluable. Letters, on the other hand, arrived a week or a month after they were written, depending on whether they came from other continental colonies or from across the Atlantic, and during that time the complexion of affairs might have altered considerably. Progress in this respect had to wait upon the improvement of communication. The merchant himself was partly responsible for this situation, for trade information was still considered confidential and the development of organs for its dissemination was retarded by the persistence of the old idea. Nor was this unnatural when profits depended on having first knowledge of a market and arriving before the crowd.

The normal demand of the community probably took off a good part of the merchant's stock, for his first effort naturally was to satisfy this market. Unfortunately, there is little or no record of this type of buying. Beyond the notices of stocks in the papers, no special effort seems to have been made to attract local purchasers. The enterprising wholesale merchant, desiring to increase his profits by extending his sphere of activity, had to make a real effort to sell his goods. In the disposal of large quantities, definite orders accounted for a good share of the business, especially in the case of goods sold to retailers in the country or materials for which there was a steady demand in England or the West Indies. William Hawxhurst, indeed, contracted to supply country stores with imported goods. Beyond this, the merchant had three courses open to him; to send his goods out to be sold on commission, to ship them in ventures or trading voyages, or to put them up at auction or public vendue. The method chosen was the one that seemed most likely to be successful under the circumstances.

The general attitude in selling was summed up in the ancient phrase *caveat emptor.* Constant attempts were made to pass goods off for better than they were, and complaints multiplied that wares were not as represented. Even the most reputable merchants raised the proof of rum by adding spirits and "mended" poor wine by coloring it. This was probably not considered reprehensible. Actual fraud, however, was contemplated when stone blue was made to sell for indigo; and a modern ring can be heard in Van Cortlandt's protest that in the last Virginia tobacco he had bought, both ends of the casks were covered with a fine grade while the middle was not merchantable. On the other hand, a reputation for fair dealing demanded a certain amount of honesty, and there are many instances of allowances being made for goods not up to specification, and of rebates for Carolina indigo represented as French, for short weight, and for poor quality. Damage introduced a new element—the carrier. The dangers of shipping were as omnipresent as the dangers of the seas. It was to the seller's interest to claim that the goods had been in proper condition when they left his hands, and to the master's to insist that he was not responsible for stowage. Unless he could recover from the carrier, the loss was borne by the purchaser. Where a dispute could not be settled, the practice was to submit the question to the arbitration of "indifferent persons," usually three. Arbitration was widely used to compose all kinds of differences, not only concerning goods, but also to determine the liability of insurers, rates of salvage, freight, disputed accounts, whether or not a contract existed, who should bear the cost of towing a ship off the bar, and even the ownership of land. Men found it "the most speedy and just determination" and far preferable to "two or three lingering Law Suits that may be Spun out for Years in the way the Law is Here." When the Chamber of Commerce was founded, in 1768, one of its expressed aims was "the adjusting of disputes relative to trade and navigation," and in pursuance of this end a committee was appointed each month to hear and decide any question that might be submitted to it. It appears that these arbiters received a fee for their services; and doubtless, that procedure was usual. Compulsory arbitration, however, had little support, for a motion to enjoin it upon the members of the chamber was tabled.

In the conduct of business, New York merchants generally followed English practices regarding both forms and policies. Bills of lading, freighting conditions, marine insurance policies were all copied from English models, as was natural, since English law was in force. Insofar as it was possible, the maxims of business administration were also imported from "home."

The financial policy of a firm is revealed in its books. Unfortunately, no complete set of books has survived from this period, nor are existing scattered volumes satisfactory. Both single- and double-entry bookkeeping were used, according to inclination. Although in England single entry was reserved for retailers and traders who had little business, the same distinction was not made in New York.

Most wholesale houses apparently used double-entry bookkeeping, and a fairly high level of proficiency must have been maintained. The accounts of New York merchants with English houses were kept in both provincial currency and sterling, and all other currencies were translated into New York money. No instance has been found, for example, of accounts kept in Spanish dollars. A customer's regular account was kept separate from his consignment account, and personal and partnership accounts were differentiated. Careful bookkeepers noted the invoice number of all goods sold, but to find out how much of a particular invoice had been sold required a troublesome search through several books. In 1786, Benjamin Booth, "late of New York and now of London," brought out "A Complete System of Book-keeping by an improved mode of double entry," which offered as the fruit of his experience in New York a solution of this difficulty. This was a special arrangement for recording sales on the same page as the invoice—in reality, a new method of keeping the salesbook—which enabled the merchant to tell at a glance how much of a single shipment had been sold.

The English custom was to balance accounts of stock and of profit and loss at least once a year; individual accounts it was recommended to balance once a month. It is not at all clear that either of these things was done in New York. At intervals of no special length, creditors were supposed to furnish a customer with a trial balance called an "account current." Eighteenth-century freedom of spelling rendered this in one instance "Account Currant," which, since the balance was "in the red," was especially apt. As the proceeds of bills of exchange and cargoes seldom amounted to the exact sum owed, accounts over several years continually showed a small balance due or credited. Ordinarily, to close out an account entirely meant the cessation of the connection.

Early in the 18th century, Defoe had counseled young merchants that "few goods and a quick sale is the beauty of a tradesman's warehouse or shop." This he considered the basis of success, for overstocking was one of the chief causes of failure. New York merchants were compelled to carry a fairly large stock because of the "long credit for dry goods and Slow payment." From the incomplete records at our disposal, it is impossible to compute accurately the rate of turnover of the merchant's stock. It seems clear from the letter books and from the semiannual orders to England that goods were supposed to be off the shelves in about six months; but in many cases, turnover was slower.

Profits are supposed to have been high, at least on English manufactures. In provisions, prices were adjusted by the operation of the law of supply and demand. The published price current possibly had a tendency to keep charges reasonable, although there was no survival of the medieval idea of the just price except in the municipal assize of victuals. Profits were probably low on foodstuffs. The average profit on imported goods, according to Governor Bellomont, was 90 percent in 1699; while in 1706, English woolens sold at 200 percent advance, and in 1715, 100 percent was considered low. This general average was still true in 1750. Philip Cuyler wrote to his father in 1755 that "dry goods sells very well here at 150 per cent advance." It should be borne in mind, however, that this advance was over the prices charged by English houses, not over the total cost to the importer. To the initial cost must be added many charges such as packing, freight, insurance, advancing cash in some instances for purchasing part of the invoice from other houses, and so on. All this combined to raise the price of the goods when delivered in New York anywhere from 10 to 25 percent. Furthermore, the practice of selling on credit made it necessary to charge higher prices in order to make the part of the returns which would be in early cover the amount due to the English wholesaler.

Competition, especially when the community was overstocked with goods, undoubtedly kept profits low, and price slashing was evidently practiced. In the issue of the *New York Mercury* of November 4, 1771, Leigh & Price announced "that they ask no more than a cent [1 percent] retail on the Manufacturer's Price."

They cannot think [they continued] that the Candid Part of Gentlemen in Trade will Censure them for this Determination, when the many Precedents, the many living Instances are considered of People who have done all in their Power to hurt the fair Tradesman, and prove destructive to Trade in general— Every Man who pretends to sell under a Cent, must either make (to use a mercantile phrase) a Salt-Water Invoice, put rotten Goods at Vendue, or use some sinister Means to delude the Town, deceive their Customers and impose on the credulous Part of Mankind.

A week later, one Timothy Fagwell announced in the same paper as the *reductio ad absurdum* of this price war:

None of your Cents, nor under Cents, but Goods given away Gratis. The subscriber having (of late) seen a number of advertisements in the news-paper, in which the public are offered goods at prime cost and under—now take notice—that he being moved by such laudable examples, has determined within himself not to be backward in serving his community, as well as some of his fellow citizens; he therefore takes this method to inform the respectable public that he has imported in the last vessels from Europe a large and general assortment of all kinds of goods to the amount of One Hundred Thousand Pounds Sterling, which he proposes—observe well—to give away gratis, to any person or persons (in small quantities) who chuses to apply; and as his plan is one of the most beneficial, perhaps, that ever was offer'd to the public, he don't doubt but this advertisement will attract the attention of many, and that he shall have the pleasure of bestowing his charity to numbers of his fellow Creatures, which will be a great satisfaction.

All New York merchants extended credit under varying conditions. Selling goods on time had been widely practiced in Europe for a long while; but nowhere was it so extensive as in England, where, it was claimed, four fifths of all sales were made on credit. New York customers were generally allowed 12 months by English merchants. The Dutch theoretically allowed three months; but in practice, payment had to be made upon demand, or further credit was not extended.

Opinion differed as to the proper policy in the matter of credit. Some criticized only the folly of giving too long credit and thus of not insuring that returns should be in before payment must be made. For example, a merchant who was allowed 12 months by his creditors should grant only nine months to his purchasers. Others, while admitting that credit was useful and prudent when extended only to retailers and beginners, felt that for wholesale merchants to purchase on time and expect to pay for their purchases with the returns on the same goods, especially when the goods were exported, was unjustifiable and had an injurious effect upon trade. "It tends to force trade and glut foreign markets with greater quantities of merchandise than is ordinarily required, whereby the price of commodities comes to be abated to the prejudice not only of the fair trade but also of the nation in general." Trading for cash, on the other hand, made it possible for a man to buy cheaper and, by avoiding the necessity for immediate payment, to wait for the best prices.

Among the New York traders, dry goods, which included even deerskins, were always sold on credit. Six to 12 months' credit was usual, while as low as four was considered a very good bargain. On the other hand, West India goods (sugar, molasses, rum), flour, and tea were considered "cash articles"; but three months were sometimes allowed for payment on these commodities, or occasionally, by special dispensation, six months. In some instances, where actual cash was not demanded, interest was charged from the day of delivery. Nevertheless, every effort was made to encourage people to pay cash rather than to take credit. Prices varied in direct ratio to the length of time allowed.

While it is clear that a great deal of business was done on credit, and Watts asserted that the greater part of the merchants in New York lived on credit, it is impossible to indicate definite ratios. The proportion may be estimated at perhaps one half to three quarters of a man's business, depending on the amount of local trade he had. Even purchasers in the city frequently paid at the end of the month rather than when buying. Ledgers and letter books show that practically all of the distant trading was done either on credit or on commission. Very seldom did a man send the money to pay for his merchandise with the order, although New York merchants did this occasionally for European firms. The nearest approach to cash payment was when the purchases were to be made from the proceeds of a cargo.

In fact, one noticeable feature of New York business before the Revolution was the persistence of direct barter, not of the primitive type, since value was measured in money, but nevertheless as actual payment for goods by goods. It is a platitude to say that all trade is at bottom barter, but the actual exchange of one commodity for another has been many removes separated in modern times. This was not true in 1750. Storekeepers advertised that produce or "country pay" would be accepted in return for merchandise. Even in sales at a distance, returns were made in wheat, sugars, rum, peach brandy, flaxseed, or any other commodity acceptable to the creditor. This condition was apparently far less true of Europe, and was due in America to the inadequacy of financial organization, and to the lack of a sufficient currency and of institutions which might facilitate exchange and extend credit.

5. COLONIAL NEWSPAPER ADVERTISING*

By the middle of the 18th century, tradesmen, itinerant peddlers, and merchants were advertising in newspapers. Although the advertisements of the day were largely informational in character, some contained a persuasive ingredient extolling the virtues of either the product or the seller. The arrival and departure of sailing ships was frequently advertised to alert those segments of the community interested in commercial affairs. The importer advertised to describe the variety of items he had for sale. The extensive use of newspaper advertising during this period indicates its effectiveness in communicating information and stimulating demand.

THE ECONOMY of North Carolina in the last half of the 18th century was founded on the growth, production, or extraction of raw materials, chiefly agricultural and forestry products. The commodities produced were to a large degree natural ones, at best only partly modified by a low order of industrial processing. These commodities, supplying raw material requirements of users and manufacturers elsewhere, gave North Carolinians access to an ever-increasing diversity of goods and merchandise that satisfied material needs and appetites. The economic cycle was not completed until the raw materials were exchanged for goods and services.

Advertisements reflecting practices and activities relating to trade, commerce, and industry nearly equal in number and space those relating to other forms of property. There were announcements of provincial and state governmental regulations, notices concerning the availability of various businesses or services, a few industrial or manufacturing items, advices concerning ships and shipping, descriptions of goods wanted for purchase or exchange, notices of partnership dissolutions and settlements of merchants' accounts, and finally a rash of advertisements heralding long and complex lists of imported goods and merchandise offered for sale. Running throughout these paid newspaper notices is evidence that North Carolina in economic development was not far removed from the barter stage.

* Reprinted from Wesley Wallace, "Property and Trade: Main Themes of Early North Carolina Newspaper Advertising," *North Carolina Historical Review*, Vol. XXXII (October, 1955), pp. 471–82.

Advertisements of governmental regulation of trade in the extant issues of North Carolina newspapers from 1751 to 1778 are not numerous, but the few which remain shed light on the commercial problems of the times. In an advertisement originating with the "Customs-House" in London, bearing the internal date of November 25, 1763, the customs authorities were obviously concerned about reports of collusion between shippers and local customs officials in America. The advertisement, which does not appear to have been published in North Carolina until August, 1764, noted that the "Honorable Commissioners of His Majesty's Customs" had been informed that "Compositions have been frequently enter'd into for the Duties . . . payable to His Majesty at the Ports of *America.*" Anyone who knew of such connivance and so informed any port official, "except the Port where such Fraud was enter'd into," would receive a third of the duties involved upon conviction of the guilty parties.

The New Bern town inspector, John Williams, early in 1765 put on notice all shipmasters not to accept for loading any of a long list of commodities which had not been properly inspected according to law and which did not have "the Inspector's Brand or Stamp thereon." The shipmasters guilty of breaking the law would be fined £100, and any port collector of customs who cleared an uninspected ship would be fined half that amount. In addition, any unstamped commodities found aboard any vessel would be confiscated.

Navigational aids were an absolute necessity for shipmasters who had to pick their way through North Carolina's torturous and dangerous coastal waterways. If John Bragge is to be believed, however, not everyone appreciated the value of these safety devices. According to Bragge's advertisement, "Masters of Vessels and other Persons make a Practice" of running over and otherwise destroying "Stakes and Beacons fixed in the Channels from *Newbern* to *Occacock* Bar." Obviously, this sort of thing would not do at all, as it resulted in "great Prejudice of the Navigation, and the manifest Injury of the Subscriber, who is employed by the Commissioners of the Navigation to keep the same up." Bragge concluded by offering a reward to anyone who would help him catch and convict the guilty parties.

A few tradesmen and craftsmen advertised in early North Carolina newspapers, and the various services they offered reveal something of the customs of the times. A potash maker named Stephens placed an advertisement in the New Bern paper in 1757, calling attention of "all Those concerned in making POT-ASH" to the fact that he was then in Savannah, Georgia, but planned to return to Williamsburg, Virginia, stopping at various places along the way presumably to assist in this specialized work. In addition to visits in South Carolina, Stephens planned to be at Brunswick, Wilmington, New Bern, Bath, and Edenton in North Carolina. The advertisement listed the date and exact location where he could be consulted at each place, with the trip to commence about April 12 and to conclude at Williamsburg on May 25.

Thomas Brown, a "Copper-Smith from Philadelphia," announced he had "set up his business in Wilmington," for the purpose of making and selling various items of copper, including "Stills, brew-kettles, wash kettles and tea kettles, also all other kinds of copper work." Brown also wanted his public to know that he was an importer of a "variety of tin-ware and sheet-tin, which he will sell very low." But the important part of his announcement seemed to be the concluding portion of his sentence: a warning that "he likewise acquaints his friends & customers that he is determined to give no credit for repairing any old copper ware."

By no stretch of the imagination could North Carolina of the late colonial and early Revolutionary days be considered an industrial or manufacturing region; yet, newspaper advertisements occasionally recorded such activity. There were, of course, numerous references to saw- and gristmills, a mention of a "Tar-House," and information concerning copper stills. In this latter connection, an advertisement in the *Cape-Fear Mercury* revealed that Cornelius Harnett and William Wilkinson owned a company operating a distillery in Wilmington. Harnett and Wilkinson used the advertisement to inform the public that they had bought the stock formerly owned by John Murgatroyd and Richard Rundle and as a result wanted to get all the distillery company accounts settled. Some three and a half years later, Harnett and Wilkinson terminated their association and offered to sell all the property and equipment, including "three Stills, with Worms and Tubs, the largest Still quite new, and will hold near 200 Gallons." They reminded prospective purchasers that they had "every . . . Apparatus necessary for carrying on the distillery Business, situated in a very convenient Place, and at a Distance from other Buildings."

The industry of North Carolina was not limited to distilleries—though that line of endeavor may be presumed to be one engaged in by numerous citizens of the state throughout its history; there were also advertisements of a state-owned "iron works" in Chatham County put up for auction at a superior court session in Hillsboro, a fulling mill in Pitt County where cloth might be treated and dyed, and a mention of shipbuilding.

An advertisement quite revealing in its comments on economic and social conditions was the notice of the erection of a paper mill at Hillsboro. The advertiser reminded his readers that because normal trade was being interrupted by "our unhappy Contest with *Great Britain*," paper was very scarce in North Carolina and other southern states. The operators, constructing the mill "To remedy this Evil, and throw in their Mite towards the Perfection of American Manufactures," were ready to begin work, and promised that "if a sufficient Quantity of Rags can be had, they will be able to supply this State with all Sorts of Paper." To get the rags, the millowners needed the cooperation of the womenfolk in particular, "whose more peculiar Province it is, to save all their Rags and Scraps of Linen of all Sorts." Fearing that such a task would be beneath the dignity of many women, the advertisers appealed in terms of patriotism, flattery, and self-interest, noting that "the young Ladies are assured, that by sending to the Paper Mill an old Handkerchief, no longer fit to cover their snowy Breasts, there is a possibility of its returning to them again in the more pleasing Form of a Billet Deaux [*sic*] from their Lovers."

An integral part of the process of carrying on trade and commerce in North Carolina was the shipping necessary in the transportation of imported and exported goods. From advertisements of imported merchandise, it is frequently possible to learn the name and classification of the vessel, its master, its port of origin, and sometimes its route. Before the Revolution, most of the shipping originated in British ports. There were advertisements announcing the arrival of "the Snow MARY, Captain Cor[sie?], from Leith; and the Ship CAESAR, Captain Hume, from Glasgow." From Bristol came the brig *Sally* and the schooner *Sally and Betsey*. London was the port of origin for the ship *Spencer*, the brig *Peggy*, and the *St. Andrew*, which had come "*last from* Boston." One exception was a "slaver," the schooner *Hope*, advertised as arriving at New Bern "from Africa," with a cargo of slaves for sale.

Following the outbreak of fighting, the advertisements reflect a shift in point of origin. One announced the arrival of the sloop *Nancy* from Martinique; another spoke of "A French vessel lately arrived from Bordeaux." Other vessels which arrived from France included "the *frigate* FERDENAND," the ship "PENTHIEVRE," and the "*Ship* DEANE, Capt. Bernard Margolli." The sloop *Success*, bound for New Bern from Bermuda with a cargo of salt, ran ashore on Cape Hatteras; and the ship *St. Germain*, from Cape Francois, suffered a similar disaster, having been "lately stranded at Occacock bar."

Notices devoted to ship sailings usually indicated when the vessels were expected to sail, what cargo space was still available, whether there were accommodations for passengers, the ships' destinations, and other items of interest. John Scott, captain of the sloop *Tryal*, was about to sail "For ANTIGUA, Directly," and he wanted the public to know that his vessel was "very well accommodated for Passengers." Anyone who wanted to book passage or to ship freight could see Scott "at Richard Ellis's, Merchant, in NEWBERN." Captain English, of the schooner *Charming Molly*, had space for passengers who wanted to go from Wilmington to Kingston, Jamaica. He also gave notice that "Any letters for the above Port, may be left at the Bar of Mr. Rogers's Tavern, where they will be received."

The activities of the port of Wilmington are nowhere more clearly pictured than in the *Cape-Fear Mercury* for December 29, 1773. No less than six vessels were referred to by name, and several of these were mentioned more than once. The brig—or brigantine, depending upon which advertisement is read—*William* had just entered Wilmington "directly from Bristol," and was expected to sail again in about a month. Passage or freight, the latter limited to "Flaxseed and Flour," could be arranged with John Burgwin or the vessel's master. The ship *Good Intent* had come in from London, with a cargo of merchandise which Jonathan Dunbibin and George and Thomas Hooper offered for sale. At the same time, the firm of Hogg and Campbell announced that the *Good Intent* had a portion of her cargo space already contracted for and would be ready to sail again for London "in Four Weeks from this Date." Josias Walker advertised the imminent sailing of the brigantine *Adamant* for Bristol and announced there was space for both passengers and freight. The ship *Grenada Packet* had just come in from Grenada with some slaves. The sloop *Dolphin* was moored "at the Market-Street wharf," where some slaves would be sold "for Cash or Lumber." Finally, there was a notice concerning indentured servants who had run away from the brig *Roger*. There seems little doubt that the riverfront presented a busy sight to anyone chancing to stroll down Market Street in the village of Wilmington late in 1773.

Newspaper advertisements demonstrate beyond question that goods and merchandise in very great variety were brought into North Carolina between 1751 and 1778. Perhaps only a few North Carolinians had the financial resources necessary to acquire and enjoy the niceties of life, but the niceties were available in wider variety and larger quantity than is popularly thought to have been the case. Wealthy eastern residents, and possibly the wealthy ones living farther west, did not have to lead primitive lives of unrelieved hardship. Comforts, conveniences, and even luxuries were obtainable, if the buyer could pay the price, and if he followed the advertising columns of the New Bern and Wilmington newspapers.

In addition to what was made for his use by local craftsmen in town, or on his plantation by his own workmen, a North Carolina aristocrat could buy imported farm tools, milling equipment, and rigging and other "furniture" for his ships. There were both plain and fancy building materials and fixtures for his house, which could be equipped with choice and decorative draperies, rugs, curtains, and furniture. There was almost no end of fabrics for wearing apparel for himself and his wife. He and she could wear the latest in shoes, hats, wigs, buckles, watches, ornaments, fancy buttons, and laces. Sometimes, he could buy a few books to read; medicines, such as they were, were available in large quantities. For his sport, there were fine saddles, bridles, stirrups, and other accoutrements for the horseman; and there were guns, powder, and shot to aid his effectiveness in hunting. Delicacies for his table could be obtained to supplement and give variety to the sturdy fare produced locally. And in his lighter, more relaxed moments the North Carolina "gentleman" could play cards; take a pinch of homegrown snuff from an imported snuff box; or bend an elbow in conviviality well stimulated by many kinds of beer, rum, cordials, brandies, wines, and other spirits.

Many North Carolina merchants used considerable space in listing the goods they had "just imported." Samuel Cornell used 13 column-inches in the *North-Carolina Magazine* (New Bern), October 19, 1764, to advertise in small print more than 290 items. In addition to common fabrics, Cornell offered "diaper table cloths," in 4-foot widths and ranging in length from 6 to 8 feet. There were "boys[,] youths, and mens felt hats," as well as "castor and beaver" hats for men. Rugs came in four colors— "blue, green, red and spotted"—and in four sizes, all 4 feet wide by 6, 7, 8, and 9 feet long. The lady of the house could dress to her heart's content in such fabrics as "bombazine," various taffetas, brocades, figured silk, ribbons, and "silk and worsted ferreting and gartering." Nor were the men to be drab in their dress, for their "breeches patterns" came in "red, blue, and black knit." The necessary buttons were available in five different kinds: "silk and hair twist . . . common metal . . . gilt and pinchbeck."

For household use, a quantity of pewter ware was included, consisting of "plates, dishes, basons," two sizes of pots and "tankards," as well as pewter "porringers, table and tea spoons." There were knives for the table, besides "common and very neat penknives, cuttoe and clasp" knives. Other tableware included "white stone plates and dishes . . . crates of common yellow ware [as]sorted . . . stone mugs, delf[t] bowles . . . double flint wine and ale glasses, with tumblers and vinegar cruets." Neither was the kitchen neglected; Cornell's customers could obtain "frying pans, gridirons, and chafingdishes, tea kettles, iron pots sorted from one to 20 gallons, fire tongs and shovels."

Tools and plantation working equipment were not overlooked. Cornell had available two kinds of axes, several sorts of saws, "carpenters, coopers, and shoemakers tools," three kinds of gimlets, a variety of spades and "iron-bound shovels," seven different weights of "flat-pointed nails," two kinds of hinges, some grindstones, and "reap hooks and scythes."

In the riding and hunting department, the customer could choose from "snaffle and short hunting bridle bits, swivel and plain stirrup irons, with sundry other sadlery . . . twig horse whips, half and whole hunters [whips] . . . plain and fringed saddle housing." In firearms, there were "common trading" and "neat walnut stocked guns," while the accessories included "gun locks . . . gun powder, shots of all kinds, with bar lead . . . [and] best oil gun flints."

Among many miscellaneous items, Cornell advertised "sewing needles and pins, a large assortment of writing paper . . . playing [cards] . . . window glass" in two sizes, "sad irons . . . wire mouse traps . . . [and] razors." He lumped together his medicines and kitchen seasonings, and listed "brimstone, allom, copperas, and saltpetre, bohea tea, pepper and allspice, cinnamon and nutmeg." Then the description of the newly arrived merchandise ended with "slates and pencils, bibles, testaments, spelling books, psalters and primmers, gloucester cheese and bottled beer."

In spite of the very large number of items Samuel Cornell advertised, he by no means covered the field. Just a week after Cornell's notice, Robert Williams listed a quantity of merchandise which would be sold "*at the Store of* John Williams," in New Bern. Williams went into greater description of his items, many of which differed from those of Cornell. There were 11 different kinds of saws, as well as files, rasps, "with choice coopers jointer irons, [and] bricklayers and plasterers trowels." Besides these, Williams called attention to useful items like "rosinstrainers, and wire seives [*sic*] of different finesses [*sic*] for rice, wheat, corn meal and flour." To aid in writing, there were "brass inkpots and fountain pens."

Williams listed different patent medicines, "fresh and new, from the original warehouse, and true preparers in London," an indication that publicizing brand names is not a recent development in American advertising and that "patent" medicines did not originate in the western hemisphere. Customers were invited to buy "*James's* fever powder, *Lockyer's* pills, *Turlington's* balsam, *Bateman's* drops, *Hooper's* pills, *Frauncess's* elixir, *Ratcliff's* purging elixir, *Anderson's* pills, *Godfrey's* cordials, antimony and flour of sulphur."

The needs of craftsmen were reflected in Robert Williams' advertisement and in one by William Watkins of Wilmington. Williams stood ready to supply a "great variety of watchmakers working tools and utensils," along with 10 different kinds of watch parts, "and a couple of sound WATCHES." Watkins, on the other hand, had "an assortment of hair, cauls, ribbons, & c. for peruke-makers."

Under the impact of the Revolution, North Carolina merchant advertising exhibited some changes. First, wartime advertisements of sales of merchandise were fewer in number and shorter in length. In the second place, the notices increasingly advised the public that the goods would be sold at auction. Thirdly, the advertisements seemed to concentrate on fewer items, many of which were staples (salt, sugar, flour), tools, and other necessities. And finally, in apparent but not real contradiction, there were some few notices which advertised sales of truly luxurious items.

The employment of a warship as a cargo vessel is somewhat out of the ordinary, to say the least. North Carolinians who chanced to be in the vicinity of Cape Lookout in the spring of 1778 were favored with such

a sight, and the New Bern *North-Carolina Gazette* in March announced
that there had *"Just arrived . . . from France, the frigate* FERDE-
NAND, *mounting 36 guns, with 200 men, Monsieur de Gatinau, one of
the king's officers, commander, who has imported . . . goods, which
will be sold at the town of Beaufort."* Sixty-two items made up the list of
goods, which ranged from "NAILS of all sizes" to "gold and silver shoulder straps for officers." Among the more unusual items were "shirts and
sheets for hospitals, umbrelloes . . . harpsichord and violin strings
. . . [and] paintings of all colours."

The Edenton firm of Savage and Westmore advertised a long array
of luxuries just brought in "in the last vessels from France," and the
public was advised that the merchandise would be sold at auction. A few
of the delicacies included raisins, currants, anchovies, olives, capers,
truffles, and brandied fruits. Grouped together were boxes of *"white soap
. . . mould candles . . .* [and] *manna."* A large portion of the
shipment consisted of fancy brandies, liqueurs, and "Frontenac Malaga
and Muscadel [sic] *wines,"* as well as *"scented waters."* Arriving in cases
of a dozen bottles each were such uncommon items as *"orgeat . . .
cappalaire . . .* [and] *ratifea."* Near the end of the advertisement
was a single beverage not now considered a luxury but so regarded in
1778. The discriminating customer could, if he wished, buy *"sarsaparella."*

PART II

Marketing in America, 1790-1860

A. TOWARD A NATIONAL MARKET

1. THE DEVELOPMENT OF A NATIONAL ECONOMY*

The dramatic growth of the internal commerce of the United States between 1815 and 1860 was a tremendously important marketing development. It gave rise to regional specialization, contributed to the growth of metropolitan areas, and diminished the country's dependence on trade with Europe. In short, it marked the transition of the United States from a colonial to a national economy. The interdependence of the three principal sections of the country—the East, the then "West," and the South—was of particular significance. Although these regions developed along very different lines, what happened in each was in large measure related to developments in the others.

THE PURPOSE of this paper is to present a survey of the part internal commerce played in the economic development of the United States before 1860.[1] In essaying this task, it will be necessary (1) to review in broad outlines the streams of commerce between the three great sections of the country—the food-producing West, the plantation South, and the shipping-manufacturing-banking East—and (2) to consider the influence of internal trade on regional specialization and the development of a national economy.

The several streams of commerce between the different sections of the country were (1) the trade on the western rivers, consisting for the most

* Reprinted from Louis B. Schmidt, "Internal Commerce and the Development of the National Economy before 1860," *Journal of Political Economy,* Vol. XLVII (December, 1939), pp. 798–822, by permission of the University of Chicago Press.

[1] The foundation of this study is my paper, "The Internal Grain Trade of the United States, 1850–1860," *Iowa Journal of History and Politics,* Vol. XVIII, No. 1 (January, 1920), pp. 94–124. The reader is also referred to the following papers which have a bearing on various aspects of this subject: R. B. Way, "The Commerce of the Lower-Mississippi in the Period 1830–1860," *Proceedings of the Mississippi Valley Historical Association,* Vol. X (1918–19), pp. 57–68; George W. Stephens, "Some Aspects of Early Intersectional Rivalry for the Commerce of the Upper Mississippi Valley," *Washington University Studies* (Humanistic Series, Vol. X, No. 2 [April, 1923]), pp. 277–300; John B. Appleton, "The Declining Significance of the Mississippi as a Commercial Highway in the Middle of the Nineteenth Century," *Bulletin of the Geographical Society of Philadelphia,* Vol. XXVIII, No. 4 (October, 1930), pp. 267–74; and J. W. Scott, "Internal Trade of the United States," *Hunt's Merchants' Magazine,* Vol. VIII (1843), pp. 321–30, 447–58; *ibid.,* Vol. IX (1843), pp. 31–47.

part of the farm products of the Middle West which were shipped down the Mississippi River to the southern planters, in return for which the principal plantation products sent up the river were molasses and sugar; (2) the coastwise trade, consisting of manufactured goods from eastern to southern ports, with return cargoes of southern staples for the East or for export, supplemented by shipments of western food products for the New England states; and (3) the trade over the canals, the Great Lakes, and the railroads, consisting of eastern and imported manufactures shipped westward to supply the western farmers or to be sent down the river to the planters; while the East, at first dependent on its own food supplies supplemented by the coastal trade, began to receive direct shipments of western produce over the Erie Canal which were swelled to large proportions after the entry of the railroads into the Middle West in the fifties. Let us consider first the internal commerce between the Middle West and the South.

A history of the commerce between the Middle West and the South before 1860 is largely an account of the commerce on the Mississippi. Obstacles to the development of the Middle West before 1815 were overcome after 1815 by the introduction of the steamboat on the western rivers and by the extension of cotton culture into the Southwest. These two events led to a division of labor between the farmers of the Middle West and the planters of the South, and gave rise to an important trade on the western rivers comparable to the coastwise trade between the northern colonies and the West Indies before the Revolution.[2] The Middle West, therefore, found its first important market in the South, which devoted itself to the production of cotton and other plantation staples for the rapidly expanding markets in the East and abroad.

The steamboat became the symbol of western development, the importance of which was reflected in the rising tide of immigration into both the upper and lower regions of the Mississippi Valley and the rapidly

---

[2] "This commerce between different agricultural communities in America has played a more important role in our economic history than seems to have been appreciated. It began in colonial times and shows itself in the trade between the Northern Colonies and the West Indies which was reckoned by the colonists themselves to be of vital importance to their prosperity. It appears again in the first part of the nineteenth century when a trade grew up on our western rivers between the lower South and the new states of the West of exactly the same character as that which went up and down the Atlantic coast between the West Indies and the Northern Colonies during the eighteenth century. It was in both cases a trade between a community of planters using slave labor to produce a few valuable staples which found a ready sale in the markets of the world on one hand, and a community of small farmers (who in many cases were partly fishermen) producing food and trade supplies on the other. The basis of the trade in both cases was the fact that the planter found it more profitable to devote his slave labor to the production of valuable staples to be sold in the markets of the world than to use it in producing the food and other supplies which he needed. So long as there were other agricultural communities ready and willing to furnish these supplies, it was cheaper to procure them by trade than by direct production" (Callender, *op. cit.*, pp. 300–301 n.).

expanding shipments of extractive products down the river. Frontier towns on the western rivers sprang into life and became commercial centers, and numerous commercial towns situated on the navigable tributaries of the Ohio–Mississippi river systems.[3] The decade of the fifties was the golden age of river commerce, and the year 1859–60 records the maximum of river prosperity.[4]

The rapid growth in the receipts of raw and processed products from the interior was accompanied by significant changes in the relative importance of commodities which had an important bearing on the economic and political development of the United States. The Mississippi carried a much larger volume of traffic but a smaller percentage of the entire commerce of the valley. The loss was most marked in western produce, which was diverted eastward and southeastward over the railroads to the Atlantic seaboard for domestic consumption or for export to Europe and the West Indies. The products of the Ohio and upper Mississippi valleys shipped to New Orleans were no longer for export but were for consumption on the plantation. This does not represent, however, the full measure of the market for western produce in the South. The West supplied the South with livestock as the latter turned its attention more exclusively to the production of cotton, sugar, and tobacco in response to domestic and foreign market demands. This dependence of the South on the West became very pronounced after 1830.

There was a considerable upstream traffic in western produce originally shipped to New Orleans and then reshipped to the plantations of Mississippi, Louisiana, and Arkansas. This amounted to as much as one half of the downstream trade. New Orleans became an export center for southern staples, but it was an import center for eastern and foreign goods only to a minor extent. At first an export center for western produce, New Orleans later lost this trade, which was diverted eastward and southeastward over the railroads.

It was not until a southern market demand was created that the West definitely entered upon the era of commercial expansion. The heavy demand, both domestic and foreign, for cotton, sugar, and tobacco, and the strategic position of the South in meeting this demand, led the people of the South Atlantic and Gulf states in particular to devote themselves to the production and marketing of these staples and to neglect other

---

[3] There were no cities of any importance in the Mississippi Valley before the War of 1812, with the single exception of New Orleans, which in 1810 had a population of 24,562. Pittsburgh had but 4,768 and Cincinnati only 2,540. The rapid rise and growth of commercial cities constitutes one of the most significant features of American economic development after 1830.

[4] J. D. DeBow, *The Industrial Resources of the Southern and Western States* (1852), Vol. II, pp. 134–43, 146–47, 149–50; William F. Switzler, *Report on the Internal Commerce of the United States* (Washington, D.C.: U.S. Government Printing Office, 1888), pp. 199–202, 209, 210, 215–24; Callender, *op. cit.*, pp. 313–21. The flatboat slowly went out before 1860.

branches of agriculture for which the Middle West possessed natural advantages. The South therefore became the first important market for the grain and the livestock and animal products of the Middle West.[5] The prosperity of those two sections in turn influenced profoundly the East, which underwent a great economic transformation.

The commerce between the South and the East was predominantly a coastwise trade, which expanded with remarkable rapidity after 1830 as the "American system" was developed.[6] It was far more valuable than either the internal or the foreign commerce of the United States. The most important products of the South entering into this trade were cotton from the South Atlantic and Gulf states; tobacco, rice, and naval stores from the Atlantic states; and sugar and molasses from Louisiana. These products were shipped to the northern ports for distribution in the eastern states for domestic consumption or for export abroad. The coastwise traffic was supplemented by large quantities of produce from the upper Mississippi which were shipped by way of New Orleans to the Atlantic seaboard states. The East, in return, shipped all kinds of manufactured goods of both domestic and foreign production to the South. This trade was an important factor in the commerce of all the seaboard cities, and certain of those cities became competitive shipping points for the collection and distribution of commodities destined for domestic and foreign consumption.[7]

The most significant feature of the commerce between the South and the East in the fifties was the diversion of a large volume of traffic from the sea to the railroads. The farm and mineral products of the Middle West which had formerly been shipped to the East by way of New Orleans were now shipped directly eastward over the new transportation routes which tapped the river markets.[8] The westward extension of the railroads in the South effected a further diversion of produce from the southern to the eastern routes. Another important feature of the commerce between the South and the East to be considered is the fact that the Mississippi River and the Atlantic coast were both being paralleled by railroads, which were already beginning to secure an increasing volume of both local and through traffic, thus indicating that the time was near

---

[5] Switzler, *op. cit.*, pp. 191, 192, 205.

[6] *Ibid.*, pp. 285–87; E. R. Johnson, T. W. Van Metre, G. G. Huebner, and D. S. Hanchett, *History of Domestic and Foreign Commerce of the United States* (Washington, D.C.: Carnegie Institution, 1915), Vol. I, chap. xix.

[7] See *Hunt's Merchants' Magazine*, Vols. I–XLII (1839–60), for accounts of the rise of "commercial cities." Each volume contains an account of one or more cities which rose to commercial importance during this period.

[8] The steamboat and the eastern canals and railroads had already by 1850 begun to effect the diversion of some of Cincinnati's trade from New Orleans and other downriver ports to upriver ports and eastern markets (see DeBow, *op. cit.*, Vol. I, pp. 253–54; Vol. II, p. 145).

at hand when the river and the coastwise trade would be relegated to an inferior position.[9]

The South exported a larger surplus than any other section of the country. It supplied the wants of the East and swelled the exports of the Union to impressive proportions. It was estimated by T. P. Kettell that the East in 1859 purchased southern products of every kind for domestic consumption to the value of $200 million, while the value of southern commodities received by the East for export abroad amounted to $246.5 million, thus bringing the aggregate receipts of the East from the South to $446.5 million, which, it was observed, was "probably an undervaluation" of the products sent north by southern owners and producers.[10]

What did the East give to the South in exchange for this large volume of trade? Kettell goes on to make the following pertinent observations:

This is a vast trade which approximates the sum of the dealings between the North and the South. The transactions influence the earnings, more or less direct, of every Northern man. A portion of every artisan's work is paid for by Southern means. Every carman draws pay, more or less, from the trade of that section. The agents who sell manufactures, the merchants who sell imported goods, the ships that carry them, the builders of the ships, the lumbermen who furnish the material, and all those who supply means of support to them and their families. The brokers, the dealers in Southern produce with the long train of persons who furnish them with houses, clothing, supplies, education, religion, amusement, transportation, and so forth, are dependent upon this active interchange by which one thousand millions of dollars come and go between the North and the South in a year.[11]

The commerce of the Middle West was the prize for which the South

---

9 In 1850, nearly all the 475,702 bales of cotton shipped to the eastern mills were transported by the coasting vessels to the eastern seaports. In 1855, but 7,661 bales were shipped east on the railroads. By 1859 the overland movement had assumed considerable proportions, 106,678 of the 786,521 bales being transported to the eastern factories by rail (Joseph Nimmo, *Report on the Internal Commerce of the United States* [1879], pp. 122, 128).

The internal slave trade, although extensive, is omitted from consideration in this paper, since it was carried on wholly in the southern states. It may be observed, however, that while no statistics on the slave trade are available, Olmstead estimated in 1856 that more than 20,000 Negroes were sent annually from the border states of Virginia, Maryland, Delaware, Kentucky, Missouri, Tennessee, and North Carolina to South Carolina, Georgia, Alabama, Mississippi, Louisiana, Arkansas, and Texas, and that this trade approximated $30 million a year (F. L. Olmstead, *The Cotton Kingdom* [1861], Vol. I, p. 58).

10 Quoted from T. P. Kettell, *Southern Wealth and Northern Profits* (New York, 1860), in Callender, *op. cit.*, p. 282. For a review of Kettell's book, see *DeBow's Review*, Vol. XXIX (1860), pp. 197–215. Kettell's statistics and conclusions are not altogether reliable and consequently need verification, although they are generally in accord with the established facts.

11 Quoted from Kettell, *op. cit.*, in *DeBow's Review*, Vol. XXIX (1860), pp. 206–7.

and the East contended.[12] This prize was first won by the South in accordance with the old theory that "trade will follow the rivers." The South and the West were bound together in interests, sentiments, and sympathies by the unifying agency of the Mississippi River system and by geographical separation from the Atlantic seaboard states.[13] This trans-Appalachian solidarity was threatened by the East when it entered into competition with the South for the trade of the Middle West by its extension of direct lines of transportation, which diverted the traffic from the southern to the eastern routes, with the result that the West, no longer dependent on New Orleans as an outlet for the surplus products of its mines and fields, now looked to New York City. The interests of the West were united with those of the East, while the bonds between the West and the South were weakened.

New York City was isolated from the West until the Erie Canal, which George Washington envisioned, was constructed.[14] It opened a direct line of transportation between the Middle West and the East, and made New York City the leading commercial metropolis of the country—a position it has since retained by virtue of water, rail, highway, and airway connections with the West. Prior to 1835, practically all the eastbound shipments originated in western New York, but by that time the construction of the Ohio canals began to make the surplus products of the Middle West available for the eastern markets. Buffalo became the gateway between the East and the West. Then came a tide of grain with shipments of meat, dairy products, wool, and lumber from Ohio, Indiana, Michigan, Illinois, and Wisconsin. The return trade consisted of manufactured goods of many kinds and exotic articles: textiles, boots and shoes, hardware, and machinery; paper, drugs, and medicines; sugar, molasses, coffee, and tea; tobacco, salt, and fish. This direct trade gave rise to great commercial centers on the Great Lakes: Cleveland, Toledo, Detroit, Chicago, and Milwaukee as primary markets for the concentration and shipment of the

---

[12] Christy observed in 1856 that "This active commerce between the West and the South, however, soon caused a rivalry in the East, that pushed forward improvements by States and Corporations, to gain a share in Western trade. These improvements as completed, gave to the West a choice of markets, so that its farmers could elect to feed the slave who grows the cotton, or the operatives who are engaged in its manufacture. But this rivalry did more. The competition for Western products enhanced their price and stimulated their more extended cultivation. This required an enlargement of the markets; and the extension of slavery became essential to Western prosperity" (quoted from D. Christy, *Cotton Is King* [1856], in Callender, *op. cit.*, p. 297).

[13] Callender, *op. cit.*, pp. 290–301. The selections here given are from R. Mills, *Statistics of South Carolina* (1826), pp. 153–55; F. L. Olmstead, *Seaboard Slave States* (1856), pp. 378–79; Buckingham, *op. cit.*, pp. 203–4; Russell, *North America: Its Agriculture and Climate* (1856), pp. 265–66; J. Stuart, *Three Years in North America* (1838), Vol. II, pp. 191, 239; and Christy, *op. cit.*, pp. 62–64, 137–38, 142–46, 159, 163.

[14] *Hunt's Merchants' Magazine* may be consulted to advantage for accounts of the rise of New York City as the leading commercial metropolis of the East.

grain and flour, the meat and dairy products, and the mineral and lumber products which swelled the export trade of the Middle West.

The Atlantic seaboard cities—New York, Boston, Philadelphia, and Baltimore—became engaged in a desperate competition to reach the Middle West by the construction of east and west railroads.[15] These roads tapped the western rivers at many points and effected a diversion of traffic destined for the East or for export abroad from the southern routes to the eastern lines. It was estimated in 1845 that one half of the shipments of western produce to the Atlantic seaboard were sent to market by way of the canals, railroads, and other means of transportation to the East and the other half by way of New Orleans. The lead trade of Iowa and Missouri was diverted from the river to the railroads by 1852. The produce trade of Cincinnati, which had formerly been sent down the river for the East, was now sent in large part to Pittsburgh, or direct by rail to New York, or by canal to Cleveland, Buffalo, and thence to the Hudson River for Boston and New York.[16] St. Louis occupied a strategic position.[17] It was the center of concentration for the farm products of Missouri, Illinois, and Iowa which were shipped down the river; a distribution center for manufactured goods from the East and the staple products from the South; a transshipment point for western produce to the East when rail connec-

[15] Callender, *op. cit.,* pp. 326–37. "It is well known that the greater portion of the merchandise of the west has ever been and will continue to be supplied from the eastern markets, so that the possession of what is denominated *the western trade* has already become an object of competition with our principal Atlantic cities; and the east in return is supplied by the staple western agricultural products. Should the country arrive at that period when these products are exported abroad, the eastern cities must be the depots of shipment for the produce of the west to foreign markets, as they now are and long will be the distributors into the interior, of all imported foreign goods" (*Hunt's Merchants' Magazine,* Vol. III [1840], pp. 22, 40).

[16] The destination of specified articles shipped from Cincinnati for the year 1850–51 is presented in DeBow, *op. cit.,* Vol. I, pp. 253–54. The southern trade of Cincinnati was still very important in 1860, as shown by the fact that the South continued to take more than half of the exportable surplus of a number of specified commodities: 71 percent of the candles, 73 percent of the cooperage, 85 percent of the furniture, over 60 percent of the sundry mrchandise, 63 percent of the whiskey, and more than 50 percent of the iron castings. On the other hand, the South took only 11 percent of the boots and shoes, 19 percent of the flour, and 16 percent of the merchandise in packages. But the South took 54 percent of the pork packed in barrels, nearly half of which was for home consumption, while the remainder was exported (C. R. Wilson, "Cincinnati, A Southern Outpost in 1860–1861," *Mississippi Valley Historical Review,* Vol. XXIV [1938], pp. 480, 481).

[17] The importance of St. Louis as a commercial emporium is reviewed in *Hunt's Merchants' Magazine,* Vol. IX (1843), pp. 154–60. The leading articles of export consisted of lead, tobacco, furs and peltries, hemp, pork, bacon, lard, flour and wheat, horses and mules, hogs and cattle, potatoes, and cod; while the imports from the East consisted of hardware, chinaware, cotton, woolen, and linen goods, and wines and liquors. One hundred and fifty steamboats were employed in the St. Louis trade. The exports from St. Louis to New Orleans by steamboats, keelboats, and flatboats consisted of flaxseed, tobacco, wheat, whiskey, shot, hides, hemp, castor oil, cornmeal, buffalo robes, beeswax, rope, butter, baggage, beans, furs and peltries, green fruit, dried fruit, tallow, bacon, beef, dried corn, lard, lead, oats, potatoes, onions, and cattle.

tions were established in 1856; and a point of departure and arrival of the growing overland trade to the Far West. Pittsburgh was the leading manufacturing city and commercial emporium of western Pennsylvania. It occupied a commanding position on the upper Ohio River and in the midst of the great coal area.

The diversion of the grain trade from the southern to the eastern routes constitutes one of the most important features of the internal commerce of this period. As stated in 1860 by the superintendent of the United States census:

The artificial channels of trade, canals and railroads have tapped the west and carried its products eastward across the continent. The grain trade of Illinois, Iowa, Missouri, Wisconsin, and even the greater portion of that of Indiana and Ohio, have been limited almost entirely to the lakes, the Erie Canal, the St. Lawrence River, or the six great trunk lines of railroads that lead from the heart of the west to the seaboard. The Mississippi River has been bridged at Rock Island, and another bridge is just being completed at Clinton, farther up. The lines of railroads which extend from Lake Michigan to this river are being pushed forward with great rapidity to the Missouri River, and into Kansas and Nebraska, and there is every probability that the grain of these frontier states will also find a market by way of the lakes. Even now grain is being received at Chicago from Kansas and Nebraska *via* the Missouri River, the Hannibal and St. Joseph Railroad, and the Chicago, Burlington, and Quincy Railroad. As an outlet to the ocean for the grain trade of the west, the Mississippi River has almost ceased to be depended upon by merchants.[18]

The comparative advantages of the eastern over the southern routes in the competition for the commerce of the Middle West led J. D. DeBow to declare in a speech at Nashville in 1850 that northern "energy, enterprise and an indomitable spirit had rolled back the mighty tide of the Mississippi and its ten thousand tributary streams until their mouth, practically and commercially is more at New York and Boston than at New Orleans."[19] The advantages in favor of the eastern routes, as reported in 1860, were the uncertainties of river navigation and the vexations and ruinous delays that occurred in consequence; the risk of damage to grain and flour shipped during the summer months through the southern latitudes; the speedy transportation by the safer and more economical canals and railroads as compared with transportation by river to New Orleans, and thence by ocean ships around the Atlantic coast; the superior advantages of New York City as an importing and exporting center; and the rapid growth of the cotton, sugar, and tobacco trade of New Orleans to the exclusion of almost every other branch of commerce.[20]

The old theory that "trade will follow the rivers" was disproved. South-

---

[18] Schmidt, *op. cit.*, p. clvii.
[19] *Op. cit.*, Vol. II, p. 484.
[20] *Eighth Census of the United States* (1860), "Agriculture."

ern leaders became keenly conscious of this fact and urged that the South be aroused to the situation. The Memphis convention of 1845 emphasized the importance of the river trade. Railroads linking the seaboard South with the Middle West were proposed,[21] and direct trade with Europe was demanded.[22] DeBow and others urged the South to industrialize and to patronize home industry.[23] Some progress was made in these directions, but it was slow compared with the rapidly advancing East and West. But all to no avail. Economic reorganization and adjustments were postponed by the Civil War and its aftermath to the end of the century.

There was another stream of internal commerce which began to be developed during the period: the commerce between the Mississippi River and the Far West.[24] First came the fur trade. By 1840, practically all the western furbearing country had been exploited. The Santa Fe Trail became the great highway of commerce with the Southwest after the establishment of Mexican independence in 1821.[25] The Mormon settlements in Utah opened up another avenue of trade after 1848.[26] The mining camps of the West called for supplies which were freighted across the plains; but there was no overland freight traffic between the Mississippi Valley and the Pacific Coast. By 1860 the value of merchandise freighted west to the Missouri River amounted to $10.5 million.[27] The center of this trade was Kansas City.

The rapid rise and growth of the internal commerce of the United States from 1815 to 1860 was accompanied by a relative decline of the foreign trade. It was estimated by Robert J. Walker, Secretary of the Treasury, in his report for 1847–48, that "the value of our products exceeds three thousand millions of dollars. . . . Of this $3,000,000,000

---

[21] DeBow, *op. cit.*, Vol. II, pp. 452–56,

[22] "Two-thirds of the shipping built in 1857 was owned north of Maryland; in the same year, while the South supplied at least half of the exports, it handled less than one-seventh of the imports" (Ingle, *op. cit.*, p. 96). Cf. *DeBow, op. cit.*, Vol. III, pp. 1–13, 92–120; Herbert Wender, *Southern Commercial Conventions, 1837–1859* (Johns Hopkins University Studies in Historical and Political Science, *Series XLVII*, No. 4 [Baltimore: Johns Hopkins Press, 1930]), pp. 133–36, 159–60; and see also Robert R. Russell, *Economic Aspects of Southern Sectionalism, 1840–1861* (University of Illinois Studies in the Social Sciences, Vol. XI, Nos. 1 and 2 [Urbana, 1924]).

[23] See a series of brief articles on "Southern Patronage to Southern Imports and Southern Industry," in *DeBow's Review*, Vol. XXIX (1860), pp. 77–83, 226–32, 494–500, 623–31, 771–78. See also Ingle, *op. cit.*, chap. iii, "Phases of Industry," which gives a survey of industrial development in the South in the antebellum period, showing the possibilities of further development, if only initiative and enterprise to promote manufacturing were provided. Cf. DeBow, *op. cit.*, Vol. II, pp. 107–21, 130–31.

[24] Ernest L. Bogart, *Economic History of the American People* (2d ed., 1935), p. 350; *Hunt's Merchants' Magazine*, Vol. XXXVIII (1858), p. 353.

[25] Switzler, *op. cit.* (1889), pp. 565 and 566.

[26] *Ibid.*, pp. 123, 124, 373, 853.

[27] Bogart, *op. cit.*, p. 350.

only about $150,000,000 are exported abroad, leaving $2,850,000,000 at home, of which at least $500,000,000 are annually interchanged between the several states of the Union." Israel D. Andrews, in his report for 1851–52, estimated the value of internal commerce at $1.461 million, divided as follows: commerce on the Great Lakes, $157 million; on the rivers, $170 million; on the canals, $594 million; and on the railroads, $540 million. It will be noted that Andrews gave no estimate of the value of traffic on the highways; consequently, his figures do not include products consumed at home or entered into local trade. The annual value of internal commerce, excluding the local trade, probably approximated $1.5 billion by the close of the decade of the fifties. The American people were absorbing a larger proportion of the total annual production. Colonial dependence on Europe was diminished. The nation was becoming economically more independent of Europe.

What, then, is the importance of the rise and growth of internal commerce during the antebellum period of American history? Is it an important event or not? Is it merely of passing interest to the historian, the statistician, and the economist? What bearing does it have on the relations between the sections, on the relations between agrarianism and industrialism, on the development of national economy? These questions go to the very heart of the problem, and they cannot be answered without taking into consideration the economic conditions of the country as a whole and the changes that internal commerce effected in the life of the American people. The traditional treatments of this subject are largely of an analytical and descriptive character which deal with limited aspects of the problem. Callender has pointed out the nature and importance of the problem and has suggested the lines of inquiry. There has been no attempt, however, to synthesize the several streams of commerce and to interpret the meaning of the whole pattern. What is the significance of the facts that have been presented?

The significance of the rise and development of internal commerce during the period before 1860 lies in the fact that it marks the introduction into American life generally of the practice of the division of labor which Adam Smith urged as the most important factor contributing to the ability of a community to produce wealth.[28] The division of labor refers to two distinct yet closely related lines of development: (1) the separation of laborers of a region into distinct occupations or industries and (2) a territorial division of labor based on regional differences and aptitudes. One is intraregional; the other is interregional. These features of American economic life had not been developed to any considerable extent before 1815, except in the tidewater areas, where it was possible, owing to the existence of domestic and foreign markets, for a large number of people to devote their labors to a few industries for which they had an abundance

---

[28] *The Wealth of Nations* (1776), Book III, chap. iii.

of natural resources and to depend on the labor of others to produce whatever else they required. The absence of markets in the backcountry—the hinterland—compelled each family to produce most of what it consumed, exchanging a very small amount of produce with other families of the same region. There were no towns over the larger part of the country. Division of labor was practically unknown over considerable areas before 1815. This does not mean that families were entirely self-sufficient, for there was always some trade which enabled each household to produce a surplus which was exchanged for necessities and comforts or sold for cash to pay taxes. As trade developed, towns sprang into life with division of employment, and self-sufficiency gave way to interdependence between town and country, and between the sections as markets were expanded and transportation facilities were developed.

The rise of internal commerce after 1815 made possible a territorial division of labor between the three great sections of the Union—the West, the South, and the East. The markets which were developed for various products opened the way for the division of labor in regions where it had been practically unknown before. Each section tended to devote itself more exclusively to the production of those commodities for which it was best able to provide. There was fostered a mutual economic dependence between sections and the establishment of predominant types of industry in each, which were in turn dependent on foreign commerce. The South was thereby enabled to devote itself in particular to the production of a few plantation staples, contributing a large and growing surplus for the foreign markets, and depending on the West for a large part of its food supply and on the East for the bulk of its manufactured goods and very largely for the conduct of its commerce and banking. The East was devoted chiefly to manufacturing and commerce, supplying the products of its industries as well as the imports and much of the capital for the West and the South, while it became to an increasing extent dependent on the food and the fibers of these two sections. The West became a surplus grain- and livestock-producing kingdom, supplying the growing deficits of the South and the East.[29]

---

[29] It should be emphasized again that the South became the first market for the produce of the Middle West, while the reopening of the British West Indian trade in 1830 and the repeal of the English corn laws gave rise to an important export trade; but it was the rise of manufacturing and the growth of an industrial population in the East that supplied the principal market for western agricultural products. To what extent the tariffs of 1824 and 1828 promoted the growth of manufacturing in the United States has been a debatable question. The influence of this legislation has been exaggerated (see F. W. Taussig, *The Tariff History of the United States* [8th ed.; New York, 1931], Part I, chap. ii). It may be noted that manufacturing continued to expand rapidly after the tariff was reduced to almost a revenue basis. Granting the influence of the tariffs of 1824 and 1828 on the development of manufacturing, the tariffs of 1846 and 1857 were governed more by considerations of revenue. Consequently, the complaints of southern leaders that the tariff was responsible for their commercial ills had little or no validity.

The triangular character which internal commerce had assumed by 1830 was analogous to the triangular maritime commerce before the American Revolution. The West purchased more from the East than it sold to that section, whereas its sales to the South exceeded the purchases from it. The South bought most of its manufactured goods from the East in exchange for its staple products, the bulk of which was exported to Europe. This created an intersectional indebtedness, the West paying for its manufactures from the East with its sales to the South in somewhat the same manner that New England paid for its manufactures from the mother country during the colonial period by the sales of its commodities to the West Indies.[30] This triangular trade was at first a lopsided or unsymmetrical trade that moved in one general direction down the Mississippi to New Orleans, eastward and northeastward along the Gulf and Atlantic seaboard to the northern seaports, and westward into the Ohio Valley and the Great Lakes region. The entry of the railroads into the West in the fifties modified this pattern by diverting western products from the South to the East. Increased market demands and the extension of improved water and rail transportation facilities brought the three great sections of the country into a closer and more interdependent economic relationship.[31] Regional specialization was intensified, and the triangular or circular pattern of internal commerce gave way to a more direct exchange of commodities between the agrarian South and West and the rising industrial East. Had the nature and significance of this interdependent relationship been better understood, the South, the West, and the East each might well have continued on their respective courses of development, sectional differences might have been settled in the natural course of economic evolution, and the Union might have been preserved without recourse to arms. Led by agitators, timeserving politicians, and mercantilists who overcame the more conservative plantation and farming groups, the agrarian South and the industrial East supported by the food-producing West drifted into a conflict which was not "irrepressible."

[30] "The proceeds of the Southern crops came North simply *to pay Southern debts*. Take an illustration of this on a grand scale. Every year the value of merchandise going West over the Erie Canal, New York Central and Erie Railroads exceeds that coming East over the same routes by $100,000,000. This is a puzzle to many persons who do not reflect upon the course of trade in this country. They look upon the enormous excess of western-bound freight as a proof of the extravagance or unsoundness of the West. It is simply the process by which that section gets pay for the products which it sells to the South. These debts cotton pays. The Northern shipper takes it to Europe, brings back the proceeds, which are distributed by Northern merchants and factors to the creditors of the South, throughout the length and breadth of the land. It is not convenient for the West to receive its pay through Norfolk, or Charleston, or Savannah, or New Orleans, but through *Northern cities*, and over interior routes of communication" (quoted from Lord, *op. cit.*, in Callender, *op. cit.*, p. 289).

[31] This interdependence was emphasized by *Hunt's Merchants' Magazine*, Vol. XLIII (1860), p. 442.

2. THE COSTS OF INTERNAL TRANSPORTATION*

A fundamental limiting factor in the development of the nation was the high cost of overland transportation. A U.S. Senate report of 1816 states "that a ton of goods could be brought 3,000 miles from Europe to America for about $9, but that for the same sum it could be moved only 30 miles overland in the country." The development of the turnpike and the construction of canals in certain areas helped to reduce freight costs, but it was the railroad that brought about the sharpest reduction in rates. The time required to move goods was a second major problem. Speeds were incredibly slow as team wagons and canal boats averaged only two miles an hour. With the development of railroads and steamboats, however, freight could move at 10 to 14 miles an hour.

FUNDAMENTAL AS IS THE STORY of the rise of the new agencies of transportation to an understanding of American economic development, attention must first be directed to the core of the revolutionary change in transportation itself: the cheapening and facilitating of the movement of goods and persons.

FREIGHT RATES BY LAND

At the close of the War of 1812, heavy wagons drawn along common roads or turnpikes by four- and six-horse teams provided the only means of moving bulky goods over appreciable distances by land. It is hard to realize how prohibitively expensive such transportation was. A U.S. Senate committee report written in 1816 points out that a ton of goods could be brought 3,000 miles from Europe to America for about $9, but that for the same sum it could be moved only 30 miles overland in the country.[1] Little wonder that under such conditions, foreign trade flourished, while domestic commerce developed only very slowly.

Any summary of the cost of land transportation presents unusual difficulties because charges depended on many factors, including the condition of the road, the season of the year, the presence or absence of

---

* Reprinted from George Rogers Taylor, *The Transportation Revolution, 1815–1860* (New York: Holt, Rinehart & Winston, Inc., 1951), pp. 132–40. Copyright, 1951, by George Rogers Taylor. Reprinted by permission of the publishers.

[1] *American State Papers: Miscellaneous*, Vol. II (1834), p. 287.

backhaul, the level of wages and prices, and competitive conditions; nevertheless, a fairly clear picture emerges. Between 1800 and 1819 the ton-mile rate for wagon transportation appears to have varied from about 30 to 70 cents. At freight rates of 30 cents or more a ton-mile, none but the most valuable commodities could be carried very far; and farmers, unable to market their bulky produce at a distance, lacked the ability to purchase lighter manufactured products, even though such items could be transported without prohibitive price increase. With costs for teaming at 30 cents a ton-mile, the mere charge for carting wheat to Philadelphia equaled its whole selling price if it was drawn 218 miles; for corn, this was true for a distance of 135 miles. The month before the Erie Canal was authorized—March, 1817—a committee of the New York State Legislature found that the cost of transportation from Buffalo to New York City was three times the market value of wheat in New York City, six times that of corn, and 12 times that of oats.[2] It is not surprising that under these conditions the industrial revolution lagged in America.

Between 1819 and 1822, rates for hauling goods by wagon fell drastically. Before 1819, westward from Philadelphia and Baltimore, they had ranged from 30 cents a ton-mile to more than double that figure. During 1822, they were quoted as low as 12 cents. Thereafter, charges ranged down to 7 and as high as 20 cents a ton-mile, although charges between about 12 and 17 cents were most common.[3] This sharp reduction finds its chief explanation in the general price deflation of 1819–21. The spread of the turnpikes during this period may possibly have helped reduce costs by as much as 50 percent.

Actual charges for wagon carriage show wide variation even within given sections of the country. At the time when railroads were first introduced, 20 cents a ton-mile appears to have been regarded as the average wagon charge. By the fifties, 15 cents was considered the usual rate on "ordinary highways."[4]

On even the earliest railroads, rates were appreciably lower than those charged for wagon transportation. When the railroad from Boston to Worcester began operation in 1833, its charge between the two terminals was 6.25 cents a ton-mile as compared to 17.5 cents on the turnpike.[5]

---

[2] Israel D. Andrews, *Communication from the Secretary of the Treasury* (Senate Executive Document No. 112, 32d Cong., 1st sess., [1852]), p. 278 (hereafter referred to as the *Andrews Report*).

[3] Berry, *Western Prices before 1861*, pp. 74–77, 81–83; Hunter, *Steamboats on the Western Rivers*, p. 658.

[4] George L. Vose, *Handbook of Railroad Construction: For the Use of American Engineers* (Boston: James Monroe & Co., 1857), p. 3; Logan G. McPherson, *Railroad Freight Rates in Relation to the Industry and Commerce of the United States* (New York: Henry Holt & Co., 1909), pp. 148–49; C. E. MacGill, *et al.*, *History of Transportation in the United States before 1860* (Washington, 1917), p. 223 n.; *Hunt's Merchants' Magazine*, Vol. V (September, 1841), p. 284; *Andrews Report*, p. 380; Ringwalt, *Development of Transportation Systems in the United States*, p. 28.

[5] Taylor, "The Turnpike Era in New England," p. 319.

As railroads improved and iron rails linked the chief commercial centers of the country, land transportation became so cheap as to permit long-distance shipment of bulky products. Rail freight rates varied from one part of the country to another and present difficulties of comparison because special class and commodity rates were soon adopted by each railroad. Also, rates fluctuated with the business cycle and according to competitive conditions. Nevertheless, a strong trend downward to the time of the Civil War is clearly indicated. For bulky products moved over long distances, rates went even lower than the average ton-mile charge. Just before the Civil War the charge on all-rail shipments of wheat from Chicago to New York was 34.8 cents a bushel, or about 1.2 cents a ton-mile.[6] When these rates at the end of the period are compared with those for 1815–20, it will be seen that for shipments by land of bulky products over appreciable distances, freight charges had been reduced by approximately 95 percent. Less than half of this decline merely reflects a decline in the general level of prices; the remainder represents a real reduction in the cost of land transport. The magnitude of this change was so great as to permit a major revolution in domestic commerce.

FREIGHT RATES BY RIVER AND CANAL

During the period covered by this study, steamboats facilitated and cheapened the carriage of freight, especially upstream, and canals created new routes over which low water rates replaced the high cost of land carriage. The effect of the steamboat in reducing shipment costs was greatest on the chief navigable rivers. Even for downriver trade, flatboat shipments were not as inexpensive as might be expected, for on most large rivers the clumsy wooden craft could not make the return trip and had to be sold at a substantial loss at their destination. On the Mississippi–Ohio system, freight costs declined almost as sensationally as the decline shown above for land routes. Most of the decline came in the early twenties, thus by the third decade of the century freeing the landlocked central valley from high freights on its bulky exports and, more than any other single factor, promoting the rapid development of the trans-Appalachian frontier.[7]

A very substantial reduction in charges appeared for coastwise shipments and on the Great Lakes, although it is uncertain to what extent the

---

[6] Berry, *op. cit.*, pp. 71 ff.; W. M. Grosvenor, "The Railroads and the Farms," *Atlantic Monthly* (November, 1873), p. 597; *Report on the Internal Commerce of the United States* (House Executive Document No. 6, Part II, 52d Cong., 1st sess. [1891]), p. xxxiii; Ringwalt, *op. cit.*, p. 132; Charles W. Turner, "Railroad Service to Virginia Farmers, 1828–1860," *Agricultural History*, Vol. XXII, No. 4 (October, 1948), pp. 244–45.

[7] Berry, *op. cit.*, pp. 42–70, 557–61; Hunter, *op. cit.*, pp. 374–77, 658–59; Frank Haigh Dixon, *A Traffic History of the Mississippi River System* (National Waterways Commission Document No. 11 [Washington, D.C.: U.S. Government Printing Office, 1917]), pp. 26–28.

steamboat was responsible. As late as 1860, sailing vessels were still giving a good account of themselves in both areas despite strongly increasing steam competition.

The canals made their contribution by permitting relatively cheap water transportation to be substituted for high-cost movement by land. Little is known as to the rates of carriage on the least prosperous of the canals; but their very failure, except where they were subjected to severe railroad competition, suggests that they may not have greatly lowered transportation costs. At any rate, we do know that such moderately successful artificial waterways as the Pennsylvania Main Line and the Blackstone charged rates substantially below those for wagon carriage. And the most successful artificial waterways, by their ability to offer extremely low-cost transportation, greatly stimulated trade.

SPEED OF FREIGHT SHIPMENTS

The time necessary for moving heavy freight in the turnpike and canal era seems extremely slow by later standards. Teams drawing loaded wagons did well to average 20 miles a day, or 2 miles an hour. This was also about average time for heavily laden canalboats, though if traffic was dense or locks were frequent, even this rate might not be achieved. From 1853 through 1858 the average rate of speed for through flour shipments on the Erie Canal was about 1.8 miles an hour.

Steamboats and steam railroads greatly speeded up freight movement. By the end of the period the fastest packets on the Ohio and Mississippi were able to average up- and downstream about 15 miles an hour, but the usual rate for western steamboats was probably under 10 miles an hour. Steam tugboats greatly facilitated the movement of sailing vessels in harbors and rivers. They often saved sailing vessels two or three days' delay in entering or leaving New York harbor. And with unfavorable winds, vessels often required weeks to ascend the river to New Orleans. As early as 1815, steamboats were used to reduce greatly the time for this passage.

Massachusetts railroads included in their official reports of 1860 the average speed of freight train movement. Minor roads, probably reporting for combination freight and passenger trains carrying very little freight, reported average speeds as high as 20 or even 30 miles an hour. But the more important lines claimed a rate of only 10 to 12 miles an hour. A New York State report for 1858 gives the average rate of speed of freight trains, including stops, as 10.69 miles an hour, and the average speed while in motion as 13.95 miles an hour. For the country as a whole, the speed of railroad freight shipments over appreciable distances certainly did not by 1860 exceed that on New York lines, and in all probability was less.[8]

[8] Durrenberger, *Turnpikes*, p. 118; *Returns of the Railroad Corporations in*

Thus, by 1860, steamboats and steam railroads were moving freight approximately five times as fast as was usual by wagon and canalboat. Though figures for the average rates of speed are helpful in showing the changes which took place, it is well to point out that they do not present the whole story. In the first place, average speeds are typically available only for single railroad lines and so may take no account of transfer delays en route for shipments over appreciable distances. In addition to the ordinary delays incident to switching and transfer, nonuniformity of track gauges often made necessary the actual transfer of goods from one freight car to another. In the second place, average rates of speed do not take account of the relatively direct, shorter distance routes which were often available for rail as compared with water shipment. Thus the river distance from Cincinnati to Pittsburgh was 470 miles, by railroad 311 miles. In the late fifties, water shipments averaged about 3 days and 6 hours between these two cities, but only 1 day and 12 hours by rail.[9]

In order further to facilitate shipments, express companies sprang up in nearly every part of the country during the forties and fifties. They were service organizations designed to secure the rapid and safe delivery of money, important papers, and especially valuable or perishable freight. First appearing in the East in the latter part of the thirties, these companies spread rapidly with, and even ahead of, the railroads. By the fifties, they were active everywhere east of the Rockies, had established service to Europe and Canada, and were doing a tremendous business carrying gold dust by stagecoach in California. In 1860 the celebrated Pony Express made its first trip nearly 2,000 miles across mountains and deserts from San Francisco to St. Joseph.

At first, agents traveling with carpetbags easily handled all of the traffic, but the volume and character of the business expanded rapidly. Soon, special express cars became common on railroad trains. Stagecoach lines were organized to do an express business; and for local delivery the horse-drawn express wagons, still a familiar sight on American streets in the first quarter of the 20th century, began to appear on city streets. Even bulky products were accepted for express shipment; and by the middle fifties, fast freights were operated by express companies between Chicago and New York. Business was extended to include money-order, collecting, and letter-of-credit services. Agents would even accept a Negro slave, attach a waybill to his clothing, transport him in the express car, and deliver him to his proper destination.

A tremendous number of express companies sprang up as soon as the

Massachusetts, 1860 (Massachusetts Public Document No. 46 [Boston, 1861]), unnumbered folding table; Harlow, *Old Towpaths*, pp. 124, 142; Morrison, *History of American Steam Navigation*, pp. 560–71; Hunter, *op. cit.*, pp. 23–24; *Niles' Weekly Register*, November 4, 1815, p. 171; Robert G. Albion, *The Rise of New York Port* (New York: Charles Scribner's Sons, 1939), pp. 147, 158; *Hunt's Merchants' Magazine*, Vol. XL (1859), p. 501; *ibid.*, Vol. XLII (1860), p. 118.
   9 Hunter, *op. cit.*, p. 490.

business was shown to be profitable. Though a large number of small, local firms continued in existence, five companies, through consolidation and expansion, controlled most of the long-distance express business by 1860. These were the American, Wells Fargo, Adams, United States, and National companies. Some indication of their importance may be derived from the following statement made by Henry Wells in 1864:

[The] annual expenses of the Adams, American, and United companies, incurred in the transportation of freight and the salaries of agents and messengers, amount to not less than *ten millions of dollars*; . . . the single carpet-sack of 1839 has now grown into more than thirty cars forwarded daily from the East by the American Express Co. alone, while the Adams and United States Co's each require at least an equal amount of transportation; . . . the American Express conveys freight over 9,000 miles a day in a *direct* line, while its messengers travel daily more than 30,000 miles, and wherever on this extensive route there is a village with a post-office, this company has an agency at that point.[10]

---

[10] Henry Wells, *Sketch of the Rise, Progress, and Present Condition of the Express System* (Albany: Van Benthuysen's Printing House, 1864). See also Alvin F. Harlow, *Old Waybills: The Romance of the Express Companies* (New York: D. Appleton-Century Co., 1934), passim.

3. COMPETING METHODS
OF TRANSPORTATION*

During the early 19th century, turnpikes and canals competed fiercely for the freight business of the era. Later, the principal rivalry was between the steamboats that traveled the Ohio and Mississippi River system and the railroads that ran from Chicago to the eastern seaboard. Prior to 1840, railroads transported far less freight than the inland waterways. By 1860 the two methods, carried equal tonnage, with the value of goods shipped by rail far exceeding that moved by water. The rapid development of a national transportation system made interregional trade economically feasible. It also facilitated geographic and economic specialization—an industrial North, a cotton-producing South, and a West that exported its grain and wheat.

TURNPIKE VERSUS WATER AND RAIL TRANSPORTATION

EACH NEW METHOD of transportation had to establish itself in a bitter competitive battle against previously existing devices, and each new traffic route had to meet competition from established ones. This competitive struggle provides one of the chief characteristics of the period, and it profoundly affected the rate and nature of American industrial development.

Turnpikes were chiefly built over routes where water transportation was not easily available, so that for the most part they served to supplement rather than to compete with water routes. Thus, in New England, they led inland in a generally east and west direction and avoided to a considerable extent paralleling the coast or the Connecticut River; in New York, they radiated out from Hudson River towns; and in the Middle Atlantic states, generally, they ran at right angles to water routes or led westward over the mountains.

For travelers, stagecoaches were faster, although more expensive and much less comfortable for long journeys than sailing packets. But where coastwise journeys were very roundabout, stagecoaches secured considerable patronage.

The steamboats on their advent quickly absorbed most of the parallel turnpike traffic which had survived previous river competition. Their

* Reprinted from George Rogers Taylor, *The Transportation Revolution, 1815–1860* (New York: Holt, Rinehart & Winston, Inc., 1951), pp. 153–75. Copyright, 1951, by George Rogers Taylor. Reprinted by permission of the publishers.

competition actually hurt only a few stage lines and stimulated many others, which began running so-called "accommodation" stages timed to meet the steamboats at such ports as Hartford, Connecticut; Albany and Newburgh, New York; and Richmond, Virginia. But for the transportation of goods, turnpikes could compete successfully with carriage by sea or river only under very special conditions.

Most turnpikes, especially those in New England and the South, were not faced with important canal competition; but where such competition did appear, results varied. At least in the case of the Middlesex Canal, the waterway won the freight business away from the teamsters only after an extended struggle. Not until the late 1820's, after repeatedly lowering its rates, did this canal succeed in overcoming important turnpike competition not only in carrying raw materials and manufactured goods for the textile mills of Lowell, Massachusetts, but also for transporting such bulky county produce as ashes and grain from tributary farming areas as far as 160 miles northward in New Hampshire.[1] This struggle merits attention because it reveals the fundamental shortcomings of canals and emphasizes those factors in land transportation which later proved so advantageous for the railroads.

The one clear advantage of the canal was its lower ton-mile rates; but the superintendent of the Middlesex Canal, in a report submitted in 1822, pointed out the following considerations, which, unless rate differences were sufficiently great, led shippers to prefer wagon transportation:

1. Practically all goods had to be carried from the farms to the canal by wagon. The teamsters, having a monopoly of this business, charged very high rates. The same carriers greatly reduced their ton-mile rates when they carried goods all the way to Boston.

2. Through shipment by team permitted avoidance of truckage charges between the canal and the warehouse in Boston.

3. The country trader who personally accompanied his shipments, supervised the sale of his produce in Boston, and actually purchased his return load did not have "to wait in town after making his purchases nor at home for his goods" if he used turnpike transportation.

4. The trader who conducted his operations from his store in the country and shipped by turnpike dealt with a single teamster, who made a round trip for him and who was held responsible for delays or damage to goods. If the merchant used the canal, he dealt at a distance and often through intermediaries with canal agents, Boston teamsters, and merchants. This was inconvenient and frequently gave rise to difficulties in fixing responsibility for delays or damage to shipments.

5. The time of arrival of goods sent by canal was unpredictable, and country traders were often put to the expense of sending teams to secure freight at the nearest canal port only to find that their shipments had not arrived.[2]

[1] Roberts, *The Middlesex Canal, 1793–1860*, pp. 148–54, 166–70.
[2] *Ibid.*, pp. 149–51.

Of course, these difficulties arose in part from the lack of fast communications and from the imperfect commercial organization of the time. But they illustrate the superior flexibility and convenience of road over canal shipment.

The canals of the Middle Atlantic states promptly took away from the turnpikes most of their long-distance freight. Nevertheless, the teamsters continued to do a large local business and, until the railroads came, to operate over their old routes in the winter when ice closed the canals. In middle western states the periods of canal and turnpike building coincided; and to a considerable extent, roads were built to facilitate movement of goods to and from canals or rivers.

In the transportation of passengers the turnpikes suffered little from canal competition. Most American canals did little or no passenger business. In fact, the more successful canals, like the Erie, actually stimulated turnpike traffic. Impatient of the slowness of canalboats, many persons chose to travel by coach on New York turnpikes which paralleled the waterway. Turnpikes which led to the canal often became canal feeder lines, and their traffic increased with the growing population and wealth of the region.[3]

When the railroads appeared, they quickly captured the passenger business and thus took over the chief remaining turnpike traffic. Even less could the wagon lines compete effectively for freight with parallel railroad lines, though for a few years, until rail freight rates were considerably reduced, wagon routes offered occasional competition where rail lines were unusually roundabout and charges high. But for freight shipment of 15 miles or less, railroads were at a disadvantage as compared to the more flexible wagon. In most areas the railroads actually added to the business of the teamsters, for the increased demand for short-haul movements more than made up for the long-distance traffic lost to the railroads.[4]

COMPETING WATER ROUTES

The phenomenal growth of overland commerce between the Atlantic states and the West during the decades preceding 1860 should not be permitted to deflect attention from what was in 1816 and remained in 1860 the most important trade route in the country, that along the Atlantic coast. This coastwise shipping lane was challenged by the development of an extensive inland waterway system paralleling the coast.

[3] Durrenberger, *Turnpikes,* p. 142; Holmes, "The Turnpike Era," Vol. V, pp. 270, 290–393; Lane, *From Indian Trail to Iron Horse,* pp. 161, 263; Leland D. Baldwin, *Pittsburgh: The Story of a City* (Pittsburgh: University of Pittsburgh Press, 1937), p. 188; McKelvey, *Rochester: The Water-Power City, 1812–1854,* p. 94; Oliver W. Holmes, "The Stage-Coach Business in the Hudson Valley," *New York State Historical Association Quarterly Journal,* Vol. XII, No. 3 (July, 1931), p. 246.

[4] See Kistler, "The Rise of Railroads in the Connecticut River Valley," pp. 185–89; Kirkland, *Men, Cities and Transportation,* p. 202.

But long-distance shipments by this inland passage did not seriously rival those by sea. Naval stores from North Carolina and flour and tobacco from the Chesapeake region continued for the most part to move to New York and New England markets by coastwise vessels, the manufactured products of the northern states and Europe furnishing valuable return cargoes. Nevertheless, the canals were utilized for some long-distance shipments.

But it was over the shorter distances and primarily between Philadelphia and New York that the canal system so successfully challenged the sea route that only the bulkiest products were left for coastal vessels. Of course, a little later the railroads in turn took the most valuable freight away from the canals, and the inland and sea routes were left to divide the less valuable business between them.

The prosperity of the western states depended upon their ability to exchange the products of their farms for needed manufactures and other outside products like salt, sugar, and coffee. At the beginning of this period the high cost of transportation erected a wall around the states west of the Alleghenies which seriously blocked the economic development of that area. In a sense, this barrier was overcome by the spirit of a pioneering people who, defying or ignoring difficulties, crowded into the broad western valley. Three great developments in the technique of transportation—steamboats, canals, and steam railroads—helped to raze this wall and to justify frontier optimism. The part played by steamboats and canals is here briefly summarized; the role of the railroad is examined in the following section.

At the beginning of this period the transportation to and from the Ohio River Valley moved counterclockwise in an irregular circle more than 3,000 miles in circumference. Upcountry produce moved southward by flatboat to New Orleans on the river arc of the circle. Transportation on this section was far from satisfactory. Also, trade moved almost exclusively in one direction. Upriver shipments were almost prohibitively expensive even for the most light and valuable merchandise.

From New Orleans, some upriver products were exported to Europe and the West Indies; but in large part, they flowed around the second and longest arc of the circle, i.e., by coastwise vessels to Atlantic ports. Though much the longest of the three parts of this circular route, it presented the fewest problems. Costs of ocean transportation, even on this long sea route, were remarkably low. Also, trade could move as easily in one direction as the other.

In order to overcome the delays and costs of breaking cargo at New Orleans, in the first decade of the century a considerable number of seagoing vessels had been built on the Ohio River, loaded with produce for eastern or foreign markets, floated down the river to New Orleans, and then sailed to their destination. Despite many discouragements, attempts of this kind were still being made in the years immediately following the War of 1812. But the hazards of river navigation by seagoing vessels and the rapid development of the river steamboat soon gave the *coup de grace* to this unique development.

Finally, the circle was closed by the routes across the Appalachian highlands from Philadelphia and Baltimore over which the West received, in return for its downriver exports, textiles, hats, shoes, hardware, china, books, tea, and so on. This overland stretch of about 300 miles proved the least satisfactory arc of the whole route, for transportation by wagon over this short distance cost more than shipment by sea and river all the way from Pittsburgh to Philadelphia.[5] Moreover, as on the river route, freight moved chiefly in one direction, for the cost of turnpike carriage eastward across the mountains effectively discouraged return loads made up of the bulky produce of the frontier.

Developments during the four and one-half decades of this study greatly affected the flow of commerce on each of the three arcs of the circle described above. The introduction of fast, regularly sailing packets added materially to the speed and dependability of shipment on the coastwise sector. On the river, steamboats greatly reduced the time and cost of shipment and made upriver traffic little more expensive than downstream. And on the bottleneck arc across the Appalachians, canals and then railroads performed a similar miracle.

By making possible upriver trade and greatly reducing transport costs both up and down the river, the steamboat gave the first great impetus to western growth. An increasing flood of western products came down the rivers; while northward from New Orleans, there began to move a growing stream of eastern and European merchandise which frontiersmen could now afford to purchase.

No sooner had trade adjusted itself to changes wrought by the river steamboat, than canals, penetrating the barriers on the short Appalachian route, further stimulated western commerce and influenced the direction of its flow. The first effect of these new waterways was greatly to stimulate traffic from the landlocked areas through which they passed, although before long the commerce of the whole Great Lakes area and the Ohio Valley began to feel their influence.

For the first time the bulky products of the West began to flow directly eastward. By connecting with the Great Lakes, the canal system of New York had tapped the finest inland waterway in the world. The immigrants who crowded the Erie canalboats and settled first in Ohio, Indiana, and Michigan, and later in the more western lake states, soon sent back over the route they had traveled an increasing flow of flour, wheat, and other frontier products.

In the Ohio Basin, produce, which from the first settlement of the

---

[5] Berry, *Western Prices before 1861*, p. 81.

West had gone down the river to market, now began to reverse its flow. Produce was carried to Lake Erie by either the Miami or the Ohio Canal and thence via the Erie Canal to the New York markets. Grain and flour from Pennsylvania, Kentucky, and southern Ohio and even some Kentucky tobacco moved to eastern markets by way of the Ohio Canal. Neither of the two canals across Ohio ever developed a large through traffic, despite the fact that low rates were instituted in order to encourage long-distance traffic. Apparently, through traffic was discouraged by the large number of locks and the slow rate of movement possible. Nevertheless, in 1846, James L. Barton claimed that the northern route was to be preferred because of the danger of souring and other damage to the flour on the southern route.[6]

The alternative direct route eastward—up the Ohio and over the Pennsylvania Main Line Canal—also provided an outlet for a number of western products. About 20,000 hogsheads of tobacco annually passed eastward over the Main Line Canal; and by 1850–52, total shipments of pork and pork products by this route were almost as large as those sent down the river. But the total volume of through traffic eastward via this Pennsylvania canal, though considerable, fell well below that on the Erie. In 1844, it amounted to less than 75,000 tons, while that on the Erie for the same year totaled over 350,000 tons.[7]

A third direct water route to the East—through British North America by way of the Welland Canal, Lake Ontario, and the St. Lawrence River—constituted another outlet for the bulky products of the West. Much money was spent on digging canals and in improving navigation on the St. Lawrence River. Hopes ran high that a good deal of American trade would be attracted to this northern route, but it was never able to compete effectively with the Erie Canal–Hudson River outlet. Although the cost of shipment from Chicago to Quebec was less than that to New York via the Erie Canal, the ocean freights from Quebec to Liverpool were much higher (nearly double in 1856) than from New York to the great English market. The port of Quebec was closed during the winter, lacked the excellent port facilities of its rival to the south, and held out scant promise for inbound cargoes.[8]

---

[6] *Lake Commerce: Letter to the Hon. Robert M'Cleland* (2d ed.; Buffalo: Jewett, Thomas & Co., 1846), p. 18.

[7] Ernest L. Bogart, "Early Canal Traffic and Railroad Competition in Ohio," *Journal of Political Economy,* Vol. XXI, No. 1 (January, 1913), pp. 58–65; E. R. Johnson, T. W. Van Metre, G. G. Huebner, and D. S. Hanchett, *History of Domestic and Foreign Commerce of the United States* (Washington, D.C.: Carnegie Institution, 1915), Vol. I, pp. 230–37; Berry, *op. cit.,* pp. 83–90; William F. Switzler, *Report on the Internal Commerce of the United States* (Washington, D.C.: U.S. Government Printing Office, 1888), pp. 210–11; Louis B. Schmidt, "The Internal Grain Trade of the United States, 1850–1860," *Iowa Journal of History and Politics,* Vol. XVIII, No. 1 (January, 1920), pp. 94–124.

[8] Samuel McKee, Jr., "Canada's Bid for the Traffic of the Middle West: A Quarter-Century of the History of the St. Lawrence Waterway, 1849–1874," *Report of the Annual Meeting of the Canadian Historical Association,* May, 1940, pp. 26–35.

Despite the tremendous volume of commerce developed by the canal routes, the Mississippi trade showed no slackening in its growth. The rise in the value of receipts at New Orleans from the interior is shown in Table 2. For 1860 the value was the greatest in river history up to that time, and from 1820 to 1860 the total value of commerce at New Orleans from upriver had about doubled in each successive decade.

TABLE 2

VALUE OF RECEIPTS AT NEW ORLEANS FROM
THE INTERIOR FOR SELECTED YEARS, 1816–60

(In Thousand of Dollars)

Year	Value
1816	$ 9,749
1820	12,637
1830	22,066
1840	49,764
1850	96,898
1860	185,211

SOURCE: William F. Switzler, *Report on the Internal Commerce of the United States*, Part II: *Commerce and Navigation: Special Report on the Commerce of the Mississippi, Ohio and Other Rivers, and of the Bridges Which Cross Them* (Washington, D.C.: U.S. Government Printing Office, 1888), pp. 199, 209.

But it should not be concluded that river traffic was unaffected by the competition of canals, beginning in the thirties, and of the railroads in the fifties. The whole West was growing so rapidly that for the time being, there was more than enough business for all channels of trade. The tremendous tonnages reaching Buffalo from the lake region consisted largely of new production made possible by the Erie Canal. At the same time that produce was being diverted eastward from the Ohio Valley, states tributary to the upper Mississippi—Illinois, Missouri, Iowa, Wisconsin, and Minnesota—were rapidly increasing their shipments down the river. Moreover, the lower Mississippi Valley was one of the most rapidly developing sections of the country, with the result that receipts of cotton and sugar at New Orleans tremendously increased.

Although the rate of growth of commerce on the Mississippi did not slacken, major changes in its nature were taking place. New Orleans became much less important as a distributing center for the manufactured products of the East. The value of eastern products reaching the interior in 1851 was about twice as great by the Hudson and canal as by coastwise shipment and the Mississippi. At the same time, the upriver shipments of certain products grew greatly as western population increased and the canals of Illinois, Indiana, and Ohio opened up new markets for southern, Caribbean, and South American products.

Significant changes also took place in the character of the downriver trade. Though the total value of river commerce continued to increase, the major part of this growth was due to increased receipts of southern staples. In 1819–20, western products had constituted 58 percent of the total value of receipts at New Orleans. By 1849–50, they were about 41 percent of the total. It is significant that even before 1852, when through railroad connections were made with the Ohio River at Cincinnati, shipments to New Orleans of most of the major Ohio Valley products had already begun to decline in volume. Thus, tobacco receipts at New Orleans reached their peak in 1843, wheat and flour and corn in 1847, butter in 1848, and pork in 1849.[9] Though upcountry produce arriving in New Orleans increased during the fifties, it was largely consumed in local delta markets or exported to the West Indies. Coastwise shipments of western products to the East showed a marked decline. Hence, by 1860 the canals and railroads had almost completely substituted direct trade across the Appalachians for the old indirect route via New Orleans and the sea.[10]

RAILWAYS VERSUS WATERWAYS

Before 1840 the amount of traffic carried by American railways was negligible as compared with that moving on all inland waterways. By 1860 the total volume carried by the two methods was probably about equal, and the value of goods transported by railroad greatly exceeded that carried on the internal waterways. As the railroads were opened over new routes, they almost without exception immediately took away from competing waterways most of the passenger and light freight business. Except for the Erie Canal, which long provided cheap water passage for impecunious immigrants, passenger traffic on canals collapsed as soon as rival railroads were completed. The decline was just as sharp for other water routes, though a few long coastwise passages or shorter overnight sailings long retained a part of the passenger business because of their convenience.

Before through rail lines were completed from New York City to Lake Erie at the beginning of the fifties, the Erie Canal had developed a tremendous business in transporting westward the manufactured goods of the East. This trade reached its peak in 1853 but, as a result of railroad competition, was more than cut in half by 1860.[11] Even in the carriage of the heavier and bulkier commodities, the railroad proved an unexpectedly successful competitor. Confronted by railroads, such weak ca-

---

9 Berry, *op. cit.*, pp. 580–81; Switzler, *op cit.*, pp. 209–15; Frank Haigh Dixon, *A Traffic History of the Mississippi River System* (National Waterways Commission Document No. 11 [Washington, D.C.: U.S. Government Printing Office, 1917]), p. 16, 24–26.

10 Berry, *op. cit.*, pp. 90–91, 107; Dixon, *op. cit.*, p. 34.

11 S. P. Chase, *Foreign and Domestic Commerce of the United States* (Senate Document No. 55, 38th Cong., 1st sess. [1864]), p. 181. This document is hereinafter referred to as the *Chase Report on Foreign and Domestic Commerce* (1864).

nals as the Middlesex and the Blackstone had collapsed before 1850. Most of the western canals rapidly lost the cream of their traffic to the railroads during the fifties.

River traffic was also adversely affected. Most of the trade on the upper Connecticut simply disappeared soon after rails paralleled the river. After 1852 the volume of goods shipped down the Ohio River to New Orleans declined because of railroad competition; but as far as Ohio River traffic was concerned, this loss was more than compensated for by increased upriver shipments to the railheads at Pittsburgh and Wheeling, a growing traffic with St. Louis and the upper Mississippi River area, and greatly increased coal shipments.[12]

Railroads, which, beginning in 1853, were rapidly completed across Illinois and Wisconsin to the Mississippi River, had no trouble in getting all the business they could handle. But commerce on the upper Mississippi also continued to increase during this decade. At St. Louis, the great distributing center for the whole upper Mississippi area, goods were transferred from the steamboats of the lower Mississippi built to operate in 4 to 6 feet of water to steamboats of the Missouri and upper Mississippi which might navigate in 30 inches or even less.

In the long run, the river could not retain much traffic in competition with the railroads. The difficulties of navigation on the upper Mississippi and the long journey via New Orleans, on which goods were especially likely to damage and spoilage, proved much more costly than that directly eastward by rail or rail and water. But during the fifties, settlement was advancing so rapidly in Illinois, Wisconsin, Minnesota, and Iowa that both the rivers and the railroads were taxed to carry the growing traffic. So both increased in absolute tonnage carried; but from about 1847, and especially after 1852, the rivers transported a decreasing proportion of the total trade of the upper Mississippi area.[13]

In tonnage terms, most of the domestic commerce still moved by water in 1860. The direct trade between the West and the North Atlantic seaboard expanded so rapidly during the fifties that the railroads, the lakes, and the Erie Canal were all needed to deliver western products to the East. The tonnage carried by the Erie Canal grew tremendously despite railroad competition and did not actually reach its peak until 1880. The Great Lakes served as a gigantic extension of the Erie Canal; and during the fifties, railroads, pushing westward from Chicago and Milwaukee,

---

[12] Cf. Berry, *op. cit.*, pp. 39, 90–93; Johnson *et al.*, *op. cit.*, Vol. I, pp. 244–47; Hunter, *Steamboats on the Western Rivers*, pp. 484–88.

[13] John B. Appleton, "The Declining Significance of the Mississippi as a Commercial Highway in the Middle of the Nineteenth Century," *Bulletin of the Geographical Society of Philadelphia*, Vol. XXVIII, No. 4 (October, 1930), pp. 267–84; Isaac Lippincott, *Internal Trade of the United States, 1700–1860* (Washington University Studies, Vol. IV, Part II, No. 1, Second Study [St. Louis, October, 1916]), p. 136.

acted as feeders to the Great Lakes trade, so that its volume, swollen by the corn of Iowa and the wheat of Illinois, Wisconsin, and Minnesota, grew from year to year in almost geometric ratio.

The railroads also rapidly increased their eastward shipments. The tonnage of through freight carried eastward by the Pennsylvania, Erie, New York Central, and Baltimore & Ohio railroads was not yet quite equal to that transported by the Erie Canal. But it was much more valuable, for the rails transported practically all of the merchandise and livestock, most of the packinghouse products, and about two thirds of the flour. As a result, the heavier and bulkier products, such as grain and lumber, made up an increasingly large percentage of lake and canal traffic. But in terms of tons of western produce moved eastward to tidewater, the Erie Canal was still the predominant agency in 1860. Through freight moving eastward by the New York Central, Erie, and Pennsylvania railroads appears to have been about half the canal tonnage.[14]

Railroads had little effect on the coastal trade between New England and the southern Atlantic states. But trade with the West was appreciably altered. Textiles and other merchandise destined for the Ohio Valley had formerly been sent by coastwise vessel to Philadelphia and Baltimore, and thence overland to market. With the completion of the Western Railroad to Albany in 1841, these products began to move directly westward by rail and canal, and later all the way by rail. Also, with the opening of the Erie Canal, much flour had moved by sloop from Albany directly to New England coastal markets. The Western Railroad gradually secured this business, so that little was left of this coastwise trade by 1860.[15]

The coastwise trade between the South Atlantic and the middle states was also largely unaffected by the coming of the railroads. Rail lines extended north from Washington, D.C., along the coast to Boston and beyond. But south from the capital city the only coastal railroad connecting with the east and west roads of the Carolinas and Georgia was the stem extending 325 miles from near Washington to Wilmington, North Carolina. Unfortunately, this route was comprised of several independent railroad companies and, as late as the Civil War, had three gaps, places where rolling stock could not pass from the rails of one road to those of another. Passengers were transported across these breaks in the line without great difficulty; and as a result, the railroads were able to compete fairly effectively with the coastwise packets for the passenger business. But the cost of reshipping freight was prohibitive. Not until well

---

[14] Johnson *et al., op. cit.,* Vol. I, p. 238; Pierce, *A History of Chicago,* Vol. II, p. 494; and Schmidt, *op. cit.,* pp. 91–124; *Chase Report on Foreign and Domestic Commerce* (1864), pp. 138, 140–41; *Hunt's Merchants' Magazine,* Vol. XLIII (December, 1860), p. 701.

[15] Robert G. Albion, *The Rise of New York Port* (New York: Charles Scribner's Sons, 1939), pp. 128–29.

after the Civil War did the railroads begin to offer important competition for seaboard shipments south of Washington.[16]

Hope had run high that the line extending northward from Mobile and connecting with the Illinois Central at Cairo would promote inter-sectional rail traffic. In 1860 the lack of direct physical connection between these two rail routes still made necessary a 20-mile shipment by ferry between Columbus, Kentucky, and Cairo, Illinois, and little through business had developed. The rail route connecting Cincinnati and New Orleans was opened in 1859, too late to permit much traffic to develop before war closed such intercourse. The overland movement of cotton to northern markets was inconsequential until the very end of the period. The railroad system of the South gave great assistance in moving staples to southern seaport markets, but not until the very end of the period were southern rail lines beginning to be sufficiently integrated with those of the North as to encourage long-distance rail shipments between the North and the South.[17]

THE PATTERN OF TRADE

The rapid settlement of the West, the great increase in population, and the phenomenal improvements in transportation which have been emphasized made possible the territorial specialization upon which rested the striking growth of American domestic commerce during the period of this study. The direction and magnitude of this commerce was largely determined by the growth of New York City as the great center for foreign importations, and the development of manufacturing in the Atlantic states lying north of Chesapeake Bay. The fundamental pattern of this trade was very similar to that which existed between Great Britain and this country in the colonial and early national period. The South, which in colonial days had sent its great staples directly to England and received manufactured products in return, after 1815 found a growing market for its raw materials—in the manufacturing East. The West, an exporter of grain and meat, carried on a similar direct trade with the manufacturing states; but it also provided the South with food products, receiving in exchange drafts on the East which were used to pay for manufactured imports. In similar manner, before the Revolution, fish from New England and grain from the Middle Atlantic states had been exported to the West Indies to help permit payment for British imports. But this earlier trade had involved only the fringe of states along the Atlantic, whereas the

---

[16] Howard Douglas Dozier, "Trade and Transportation along the South Atlantic Seabord before the Civil War," *South Atlantic Quarterly*, Vol. SVIII, No. 3 (July, 1919), pp. 232–34.

[17] Pierce, *op, cit.,* Vol. II, pp. 45–46; Joseph Nimmo, *Report on the Internal Commerce of the United States* (1879), pp. 122, 128.

domestic commerce rapidly developing during the 19th century presently involved a whole continent.

Though the essential pattern of American domestic trade was determined by this exchange between the agricultural West and South and the increasingly industrialized East, there were many special or subsidiary traffic movements of great importance. A few of these merit at least brief mention. As firewood grew scarce in the vicinity of the larger towns, a brisk trade in coal developed, which, from a small start at the beginning of the century, grew to major importance as Virginia and Pennsylvania coal was moved northward by coastwise sloop, by canalboat, and even by rail to provide warmth for homes and fuel for factories and gas plants. Thus, in 1856, no less than 42 percent of the total tonnage of the Pennsylvania Railroad consisted of coal.[18]

Resourceful Yankees developed a number of bulky products to fill the holds of coasters which brought coal, cotton, and flour to Boston and other New England ports. To their export staples, they added ice, which provided a backhaul for many a returning Philadelphia coal schooner or for farther-ranging vessels to southern or even foreign ports. Other bulky items moved southward in large quantities to coastal markets.[19]

Equaling and at times exceeding coal as an important item of domestic trade was lumber. South from Maine and New Hampshire, north from South Atlantic and Gulf ports, eastward via the Great Lakes and the Erie, and down the Susquehanna River, hundreds of millions of feet of lumber moved annually to eastern markets. As the loggers moved into the forests of Michigan and Wisconsin, lumber vied with grains as the leading item of trade on the lakes. Down the upper Mississippi River, also, tremendous quantities of lumber moved southward from the pine forests of Wisconsin and Minnesota to the prairie farms.[20] In both the East and the West, other building materials, usually destined for nearby markets, provided heavy cargoes for thousands of canal- and riverboats.

Finally, there was the trade with the Far West. Though at first a mere trickle over the Santa Fe Trail, it quickly became of considerable importance following the discovery of gold in California. This historic route, the Santa Fe Trail, connected Franklin, and later Independence, Missouri, with the Mexican frontier trading town of Santa Fe. Traders first essayed this difficult journey on a large scale with wagon trains in 1824. Despite

---

[18] Richmond E. Myers, "The Story of Transportation on the Susquehanna River," *New York History*, Vol. XXIX, No. 2 (April, 1948), p. 163; H. Haupt, *The Coal Business on the Pennsylvania Railroad* (Philadelphia: T. K. and P. G. Collins, Printers, 1857), p. 9.

[19] Johnson *et al., op. cit.*, Vol. I, pp. 340–43; Richard O. Cummings, *The American Ice Harvests* (Berkeley: University of California Press, 1949), *passim*.

[20] Pierce, *op. cit.*, Vol. I, pp. 67, 103–5; Merk, *Economic History of Wisconsin during the Civil War Decade*, pp. 79–86; Agnes M. Larson, *History of the White Pine Industry in Minnesota* (Minneapolis: University of Minnesota Press, 1949), chap. vi.

Indian attacks and difficulties from suspicious Mexican customs officials, the trade continued, except for the years of strained relations with Mexico, 1844–48, until the appearance of railroad competition after the Civil War. Westward the slowly moving wagons carried chiefly cotton goods and hardware; returning, they brought specie, Mexican blankets, beaver skins, and buffalo robes. The total value of the merchandise sent westward over this route was small before 1844. After 1848, following the annexation of Texas and the cession of Mexican territory, this trade, now for the first time strictly a domestic one, assumed really large proportions.

Following the Mormon settlement in Utah, and accompanying the growing military and mining developments in the Rocky Mountain region during the fifties, a considerable trade grew up over a number of more northern routes. Though Pony Express lines carried small packages to the West Coast, and though postal service was developed, the great distance and the difficulties of mountain and desert travel prevented the development of an overland freight trade to the West Coast. Even camels, introduced on the southern route by the United States Army during the latter part of the fifties, failed to solve the problem.[21]

As a result, the exchange of goods with the Pacific Coast, which grew rapidly after 1848, was chiefly carried on by coastwise vessels sailing all the way around Cape Horn, perhaps the longest domestic trade route in the world. The shorter route, involving transfer across Panama or Nicaragua, was important chiefly for passengers, for specie, and, after the completion of the Panama Railway in 1855, for light and valuable freight. This was the fastest and safest route to the Far West. Of the total emigrants to California from 1849 to 1859, about one fifth went via the Panama route.[22]

Statistical treatment of the growth in the total volume or value of domestic commerce is most unsatisfactory. In the first place, detailed statistics, such as are available for foreign trade, do not exist; in the second place, the defining of domestic trade presents many pitfalls.[23] As a consequence, perhaps the best understanding of the growth of this commerce is to be obtained from the kind of description contained in

---

[21] Lewis Burt Lesley, *Uncle Sam's Camels* (Cambridge: Harvard University Press, 1929); LeRoy R. Hafen and Carl Coke Rister, *Western America* New York: Prentice-Hall, Inc., 1941), chaps. xiv and xxvi; R. L. Duffus, *The Santa Fe Trail* (New York: Longmans, Green & Co., Inc., 1930), pp. 85 ff.; Glenn Danford Bradley, *The Story of the Santa Fe* (Boston: Richard G. Badger, Gorham Press, 1920), chap. i; Johnson *et al., op. cit.,* Vol I, pp. 248–50; Everett Dick, *Vanguards of the Frontier* (New York: D. Appleton–Century Co., 1941), pp. 342–43, 367; Josiah Gregg, *The Commerce of the Prairies* (Chicago: R. R. Donnelley & Sons Co., 1926); Winther, *The Old Oregon Country,* especially chap. xi.

[22] John Haskell Kemble, *The Panama Route, 1848–1869* (University of California Publications in History, Vol. XXIX [Berkeley: University of California Press, 1943]), pp. 205–9.

[23] See, for example, *Chase Report on Foreign and Domestic Commerce* (1864), pp. 118–22.

the preceding pages. Nevertheless, it is worthwhile to note some comparisons of the total value of goods moved over particular routes and to summarize the estimates of the total value of domestic trade which have been made for this period.

A number of rough statistical comparisons are possible between trade in the 1820's and 1850's. As the general level of prices for these two decades was roughly the same, value data are not appreciably influenced by price changes. The value of goods carried by wagon from Philadelphia to Pittsburgh in 1820 was estimated at $18 million. This appears high, but it may be compared with the total receipts by river at New Orleans, 1821–22, and the annual value of traffic on the Erie Canal, 1825–30, each of which totaled about $15 million.[24] The total value of downriver trade on the Susquehanna was estimated at $4.5 million in 1826.[25] In contrast to these totals, it should be noted that the annual value of foreign trade varied from $109 million to $181 million during the twenties.

The estimates for the last decade of the period covered by this volume are of a different order of magnitude. Through traffic westward on the Erie Canal was valued at $94 million when it reached its peak in 1853. Two years later the total value of all Erie Canal traffic was reported to be over $204 million. Receipts from the interior at New Orleans were valued at $185 million in 1860.[26] Estimates of the value of trade on the Great Lakes for 1856 are $450 million and $608 million. The latter sum is slightly larger than the total value of American foreign commerce in that year.[27] Treasury computations for 1862, two years beyond the close of the period, evaluate the through freight passage westward over the Erie Canal and on four railroads—the New York Central, Erie, Pennsylvania, and Baltimore & Ohio—at $522.5 million.[28] The total value of American foreign trade was $687 million in 1860.

One of the earliest estimates of the total value of domestic commerce was made by a writer in *Hunt's Merchants' Magazine* in 1843, who placed it at $900 million.[29] Secretary of the Treasury Robert J. Walker, making an estimate in 1846, reported that the value of American production exceeded $3 billion, of which that part "interchanged among the several States of the Union" was worth at least $500 million.[30] A more elaborate estimate, published in the *Andrews Report* of 1853, is reproduced in

[24] Johnson *et al.*, *op. cit.*, Vol. I, pp. 218 and 220.

[25] Ringwalt, *Development of Transportation Systems in the United States*, p. 13. But compare *Niles' Weekly Register*, December 30, 1826, p. 283.

[26] *Hunt's Merchants' Magazine*, Vol. XXXV (1856), p. 358; Dixon, *op. cit.*, p. 165; *Chase Report on Foreign and Domestic Commerce* (1864), p. 181.

[27] *Hunt's Merchants' Magazine*, Vol. XXXVI (1857), p. 89. An official Canadian estimate of the value of the lake commerce for the same year placed it at $450 million (*Hunt's Merchants' Magazine*, Vol. XXXVII [1857], p. 233).

[28] *Chase Report on Foreign and Domestic Commerce* (1864), p. 136.

[29] *Hunt's Merchants' Magazine*, Vol. VIII (1843), p. 322.

[30] *Report of the Secretary of the Treasury*, December 9, 1847 (House Executive Document No. 6, 30th Cong., 1st sess.), p. 22.

Table 3. The values shown in this report were secured by multiplying tonnage data (partly estimated) for important routes of trade by the estimated value per ton over each route. In order to avoid duplication and thus secure the "net" figures shown in the table, the "gross" figures were merely divided by 2. The resulting totals were, as Israel D. Andrews

TABLE 3

TOTAL VALUE OF DOMESTIC COMMERCE

	Net		Gross	
1851	*Tons*	*Value*	*Tons*	*Value*
Lake commerce	1,985,563	$ 157,246,729	3,971,126	$ 314,473,458
River commerce	2,033,400	169,751,372	4,066,800	339,502,744
Aggregate	4,018,963	$ 326,998,101	8,037,926	$ 653,976,202
Estimate of 1852:				
Coasting trade	20,397,490	$1,659,519,686	40,794,980	$3,319,039,372
Canal commerce ...	9,000,000	594,000,000	18,000,000	1,188,000,000
Railway commerce ..	5,407,500	540,750,000	10,815,000	1,081,500,000
Aggregate	34,804,990	$2,794,269,686	69,609,980	$5,588,539,372

was careful to point out, computed in "a very unsatisfactory way," but they are the best we have.[31] Table 3 points to two important generalizations: By the fifties, domestic trade had become much greater than foreign, and coastwise commerce was much more important than that over any other domestic route. Both of these conclusions fit well with what other knowledge we have and appear sound enough. On the other hand, the exact figures presented by Andrews will have to be carefully restudied before they can be taken very seriously. It must be borne in mind, moreover, that Andrews' data are for the early fifties. In the decade 1851–60, domestic commerce, at least on rivers, on the Great Lakes, and by railroad, experienced extremely rapid growth.

It must not be supposed that the domestic commerce grew at a constant rate from year to year, unaffected by the great cyclical disturbances of the period. Each of the major commercial crises put a damper on the growth of internal commerce; but in each period of prosperity, trade expanded rapidly to totals much higher than their previous levels. In major depressions such as that following 1839, tonnage totals might actually decline for a year or more. Thus, New York State canal traffic declined slightly over the previous year in 1837, 1840, and 1842; but tonnage, which had reached a prosperity peak in 1836, had more than doubled by 1847. Similarly, the value of Mississippi River trade, although declining slightly in 1839, 1841, 1842, and 1845, very nearly doubled

---

[31] *Communication from the Secretary of the Treasury,* (Senate Executive Document No. 112, 32d Cong., 1st sess. [1853]), pp. 903–6 (referred to in text above as the *Andrews Report*).

between 1836 and 1847. Ton-miles of traffic on New York railroads increased by more than 100 percent between 1853 and 1860, but suffered a slight decline from the 1856 level in 1857–59. Nevertheless, the irregularities in the growth of domestic commerce should not be overemphasized, for at least before the fifties, fluctuations were repeatedly much less extreme than those experienced by foreign commerce.[32]

The tremendous growth of American internal trade during the 45 years ending in 1860 was, of course, the result of many interacting factors. Fundamental was the adoption of the new instruments of transportation: canals, steamboats, and railroads. But many other influences played a part, especially the rapid settlement of the West, the growth of manufacturing, and the increase of foreign trade. Each was partly cause and partly effect; all were mutually interacting forces which, taken together, produced the transportation revolution and at least the beginnings in America of that whole series of rapid changes which has come to be termed the industrial revolution.

---

[32] Dixon, *op. cit.*, pp. 199, 215; W. B. Smith and A. H. Cole, *Fluctuations in American Business, 1790–1860* (Cambridge, 1935), pp. 72–73; 104–5; Bureau of the Census, Department of Commerce, *Historical Statistics of the United States, 1789–1945: A Supplement to the Statistical Abstract of the United States* (Washington, D.C.: U.S. Government Printing Office, 1949), p. 218; Albion, *op. cit.*, p. 411.

4. THE MARKETING IMPACT OF THE ERIE CANAL

Completion of the Erie Canal was one of the major achievements of the period and had a profound effect on the economy of the young nation. The canal made it possible for western farmers to ship cash crops to the East and with their proceeds to buy goods manufactured at home or in Europe. Also, the canal strengthened the position of the port of New York as the logical destination for European imports and markedly increased the size of the hinterland which New York served as wholesaling center. Both the early history of the Erie Canal and its marketing impact are discussed in the following selection.

BACK IN THE INLAND COUNTIES, where men never smelled salt water and probably would not recognize a brig if they saw one, the country store-keepers carried on an activity almost as essential to the success of the port of New York as were the movements of its shipping.

A farmer in our period would drive up to the store with 60 bushels of wheat, for instance, in his wagon. After a dicker with the storekeeper, he would sell the grain and then make purchases from the variegated stock of the general store. When he started back home, he might be carrying in place of his wheat a few yards of calico, some bushels of salt, a scythe, a kettle, a bag of coffee, and a gallon or so of rum, or some similar assortment. No cash had changed hands; the storekeeper had simply set down the grain in his ledger on the credit side of the farmer's account and the various articles taken away on the debit side, which was generally the heavier of the two.

Such an episode represented the alpha and the omega of the port's commerce. The farmer was the original producer of many of the articles the port offered as exports in the world of commerce, while he was also the ultimate consumer of the goods collected by the port's merchants from beyond the seas. The shipowners and merchants had already taken their import profits on the calico and hardware brought from Liverpool, the salt from Turks Island or Cape Verde, the coffee from Rio or Samarang, and the rum distilled from Caribbean molasses. They could antici-

---

° Selections from Robert G. Albion, *The Rise of New York Port* (New York: Charles Scribner's Sons, 1939), pp. 76–92, are used by permission of the publishers. Copyright, 1939, Charles Scribner's Sons.

pate further profits from selling the wheat, once it was ground into flour, either to Boston or to some port beyond the seas.

The country storekeeper, consequently, served an invaluable function in collecting goods for export and distributing the imports. No port could grow great simply by catering to the needs of its own inhabitants. Its success would depend to no small extent upon the number of such little storekeepers who might be persuaded to trade through its merchants rather than through those of some rival port. It naturally had first call upon those who lived close at hand in its immediate backcountry or hinterland, to use the German equivalent less grating to inland ears.

New York's original hinterland consisted of the valley of the Hudson and other upstate regions, together with adjacent parts of Long Island, New Jersey, and Connecticut. In the Hudson Valley, there was no serious threat of outside competition, but some of the trade of the southwest portion of the state was drained down the Susquehanna toward Philadelphia or Baltimore, while the counties of the "north country" had an easy natural outlet through Montreal and Quebec. Until after 1800 the population of New York State had lagged behind that of Pennsylvania, where a more liberal land policy had attracted settlers to Philadelphia's hinterland. By 1810, New York State ranked second to Virginia in population, with 959,000 inhabitants to Pennsylvania's 810,000.

When pushing its commercial activities sideways into New Jersey and Connecticut, New York naturally encountered competition. The two college towns of Princeton and New Haven were disputed outposts of New York's sphere of influence. New Jersey, then as since, was a "cask tapped at both ends." East Jersey traded through the Raritan and New Brunswick with New York, and West Jersey through the Delaware River towns with Philadelphia. The Connecticut towns and western New England in general represented a three-cornered dispute between New York, which had the advantage of proximity and the convenient Sound approach; Boston, which had a considerable trade with the region in spite of its remoteness; and finally, the local maritime enterprise of New Haven and New London along the coast and in the Caribbean. Altogether, if one combines the population of New York State with half of New Jersey's and a third of Connecticut's, the population of New York's hinterland numbered about 1.17 million in 1810 and 1.6 million in 1820, roughly one sixth of the national total in each case.

That had previously been about New York's share of the nation's commerce; but by 1820, it already handled more than a third of the total imports and would steadily increase its proportion of the country's commerce. That was largely brought about by two clever strokes which greatly increased the number of country storekeepers whose wares came and went through New York. The "cotton triangle" added a considerable part of the South to New York's sphere of influence, while the Erie Canal gave the West as well.

The story of the Erie Canal has been told so often that it does not seem necessary to follow it here in any detail, but the high points must be mentioned because it was one of the vital factors in New York's commercial ascendancy.

Even before the Revolution, settlers from the seaboard colonies were beginning to pass beyond the Alleghenies to take advantage of the opportunities offered by the apparently limitless tracts of rich land in the West. By the end of the Revolution, they were so numerous that George Washington and others began to consider the problem of communications between the coast and the new settlements.

The most pressing economic problem of the frontiersmen was the marketing of their products. Even in the absence of good roads, it was practicable to carry imported goods, representing high value in small bulk, over the mountains on packhorses, but there could be no trade in such wares unless the western farmers could pay for them with some sort of "cash crop." Wheat, ashes, and other agricultural products could not pay their way—it cost $100 or so to transport a ton of goods from the Great Lakes to New York and about $70 from Pittsburgh to Philadelphia. That was more than those bulky articles were worth when they finally arrived at market. The only feasible way to reach the sea was to send the stuff in rafts or boats down the Mississippi to New Orleans; but even after that port passed into American hands in 1803, it was not perfect as an outlet. Most of the products came down with the spring freshets and, arriving more or less all together, found the market so glutted that the wares had to be sold at sacrifice prices. Until a more satisfactory outlet developed, the frontiersmen were forced to live on a primitive subsistence basis, denying themselves the outside products which they had no means of purchasing. There was no point in raising wheat which could not be sold, and the best they could do was to convert their corn into pork or whiskey which could be transported more easily. At the same time, both they and the Easterners knew that the rich virgin soil beyond the Alleghenies could produce excellent wheat if it might only be brought through to the coast at a rate which would not be prohibitive.

Geographical considerations gave New York a tremendous advantage over its rivals for easy communication with the West. The "water-level route" from Albany westward to Lake Erie was the one point where the Appalachians could be taken in flank. As early as 1724, the surveyor general of the province had pointed out the possibilities of this route, and the matter was already being discussed by the eve of the Revolution. In the last years of the century a corporation actually constructed some locks to make the navigation of the Mohawk River easier, and numerous proposals were being made for improving the waterways to provide communications with Lake Erie or Lake Ontario.

The more ambitious proposal to construct an artificial canal all the way from the Hudson to Lake Erie, rather than simply to improve natural waterways, might be dated from 1810, when the state legislature appointed a commission to investigate the possibilities. The ultimate success of this plan may be attributed largely to the vision and tireless energy of one of the commissioners who made the arduous trip over the proposed route that year. This was DeWitt Clinton, of prominent Old New York stock, son of a general, nephew of a governor, and at the time mayor of New York City, a man of wide cultural and scientific interests. Two years later, he would give James Madison a close run in the Presidential election, and he was involved in many ups and downs in state politics. Through all that, however, he maintained his eager interest in the canal project. Temporarily postponed by the War of 1812, the issue was brought to the fore again in 1816 by Clinton. He persistently pointed out how New York would benefit from the opening of communication not only with its own western counties but also, by way of Lake Erie, with Ohio and the regions further west. The project gained such widespread support that even the seasoned politicians, who disliked Clinton thoroughly, felt it wise to back the idea.

Early in 1817 the legislature received the canal bill, drawn up largely by Clinton, who had mastered both the technical and the financial aspects of the problem. The state of New York was to pay for the canal, build it, and operate it. The bill passed both houses and became law on April 15. On the fourth of July, three days after he first became governor, Clinton lifted the first spadeful of earth at Rome (Fort Stanwix), on the upper Mohawk River.

It was a stupendous undertaking for that day, considering that America had few trained engineers and that the steam shovel had not yet been invented. Even on the simpler, straightaway stretches of the middle section, there were forests to be cleared away and miasmic swamps which threatened fever to the workers. Though the route was relatively level, 83 regular locks, each 90 feet long, had to be constructed of masonry. Such things offered problems enough to inexperienced contractors, but the canal also involved several more arduous engineering feats, such as the 750-foot aqueduct to carry the canal over the Genesee River at Rochester; the great embankment, nearly a mile long, to carry it across the Irondequoit Valley; and as a final difficulty, the piercing of the ridge at Lockport. There, just east of the Buffalo terminus, a double series of five locks had to be constructed to raise the level of the canal nearly 60 feet within 2 miles. The total length of the canal from Buffalo to Albany was 363 miles.

The middle section, because it was the simplest to build and politically the most expedient, was tackled first. Three thousand men, 500 horses, and 200 yoke of oxen were kept steadily at work; and by the spring of 1820, traffic was opened on the 96-mile stretch from Utica westward. The eastern section came next; and on October 8, 1823, the canal was open for 280 miles for through traffic from Rochester to Albany and on to New York. On November 16 the schooner *Mary & Hannah* reached New York from Hector Falls at the head of Seneca Lake with a cargo of wheat and butter. "We hope our citizens will pay some attention to this arrival," said one newspaper, "it being the first vessel that has reached this city through the Great Western Canal."

With the Erie or "Great Western" Canal thus partly open, we might note the opening of its junior partner, the Champlain or "Great Northern" Canal. Authorized on the same day in 1817 as part of the state program, it was designed to connect Lake Champlain with the Hudson and thus provide an outlet for the northern regions which were being lured toward Montreal. It was 64 miles long, following natural waterways part of the distance. Since it entailed much less work, it was naturally finished first. About 10 weeks before that first boat arrived from the Erie Canal, the "sloop-rigged boat *Gleaner*, Capt. Mills," came from St. Albans, Vermont, with 1,000 bushels of wheat and 35 barrels of pot ashes, "the first that has come through the whole distance of the Northern Canal." Since this was New York's first tangible evidence of canal activity, the *Gleaner* got a rousing welcome. A pleasure craft, decked out with flags, rode up the Hudson to greet her; she received a salute from the veteran corps of artillery and the "cheers of the multitude assembled on the Battery."

That, however, was mild compared with the celebration of the final opening of the Erie Canal in October, 1825. With the ridge at Lockport finally pierced, water from Lake Erie was let into the western end of the canal, and a procession began its 10-day triumphal progress over the route of more than 500 miles from Buffalo to New York. Cannon, placed at intervals, served in lieu of a telegraph to spread the news. The first boat entered the canal from Lake Erie at 10:00 a.m. on October 26; and New York, more than 500 miles away, learned of it 100 minutes later. DeWitt Clinton, once again governor, was the hero of the group on the canalboat *Seneca Chief*, receiving tremendous ovations as she passed eastward through Rochester, Syracuse, Rome, Utica, Schenectady, and on to Albany. There the steamer *Chancellor Livingston* took her in tow for the final stages of her trip down the Hudson to New York City. The eventual arrival made November 4, 1825, one of the red-letter days in the history of the port. Twenty-two steamboats, gaily decked with bunting, participated in the welcome—a flotilla which scarcely another port in the world could muster at that time. The city fathers, on the steamer

Washington, rode out to meet the procession from upriver. They hailed the *Seneca Chief:* "Whence come you and where are you bound?" "From Lake Erie—bound for Sandy Hook!" came the reply. Off Sandy Hook, Clinton poured into the sea a keg of water from Lake Erie, symbolizing the completion of the great task which he, more than any other man, had pushed through to success in 15 years of tireless promotion. That night, New York celebrated with fireworks, and three nights later with a great canal ball. All these things impressed the Erie Canal upon men's minds as the chief cause for New York's rise—overshadowing the equally significant development of the "cotton triangle" which had already tremendously extended New York's sphere of commercial influence without the attendant blare of trumpets.

The canal naturally wrought tremendous change in the hinterland of New York port. The western counties of New York, along the route of the canal, quickly replaced the Hudson Valley as the center of the flour industry. The virgin lands of the Genessee Valley could produce far richer wheat crops than the long-used fields closer to New York. The Mohawk Valley, which had long thrived on wheat and flour production, turned to dairying and began to offer tons of cheese instead. The city which most immediately profited by the change was Rochester. On October 29, 1822, the first canalboat load of Rochester flour left for Little Falls; and the following spring the local paper remarked, "10,450 barrels of Rochester flour were shipped on the canal from this village during the last ten days. So much for 'Clinton's big ditch.'" By 1840, Rochester, with 20,000 inhabitants, was the leading flour-milling center of the country, with its closest rival, Oswego, located just north of the canal on Lake Ontario, where it had access to the Canadian grain supply. It, like numerous other points, was provided with a "feeder" canal which connected it with the Erie. Another short branch, to the state saltworks at Salina, helped to relieve the previous dependence upon salt imports from Turks Island, Portugal, and the Cape Verdes.

Along with Rochester, Buffalo also underwent an immediate expansion, not so much as manufacturing center as from its strategic relation to the lake trade. Westward on Lake Erie lay Cleveland, the natural northern outlet for the Ohio region. A brisk lake trade between Buffalo and Cleveland rapidly sprang up, partly with steamers and partly with schooners. Within a few weeks after the opening of the canal at Buffalo, in October, 1825, 15 vessels sailed with cargoes for Ohio, chiefly with material which had come from New York. The following year, Ohio products began to arrive at tidewater.

Financially, the Erie Canal's success was clear, for tolls soon totaled more than $1 million a year. The state was before long reimbursed for the initial cost, some $7 million, and for the subsequent charges for maintenance and enlargement, which were needed because of an increasing volume of traffic. As for the effect upon the commerce of the port of New York, it would seem that while the canal had a very definitely stimulating influence, the western trade did not for some time rise to equality with the southern trade developed by the cotton triangle. The chief importance was not in the flour and other articles brought eastward, for New York's exports were always relatively less important than its imports. The main significance was the rapid growth of the number of little country stores which came under New York's influence in the hinterland as distributing points for the imports which the port brought from Europe, China, and Latin America. As far as the physical transportation of the goods went, they represented sufficient value in small bulk to have paid their way under the older and more costly system of transportation. The chief influence of the Erie Canal upon the growth of the port of New York apparently lay in the opportunity it gave to the westerners to send to the seaboard the "cash crops" wherewith to pay for the imports they desired. Eventually, even though they might ship their produce to tidewater at other eastern cities or at New Orleans, they were apt to buy their imports and domestic manufactures through New York.

Unfortunately, there is no adequate yardstick for measuring the regional distribution of New York's offerings to the interior. Unlike flour barrels and cotton bales, which make computations and comparisons easy, dry goods, hardware, and similar wares were too diversified. In view of the fact that New York was before long handling two thirds of the nation's imports, it would be interesting if we might trace the distribution of a Liverpool packet's cargo, to see how much was consumed at New York itself, how much was spread among the adjacent coastal ports, and how much found its way into the little country stores of the South and of the West. Until 1840, probably, westbound shipments by the Erie Canal were overshadowed by the cargoes which went southward along the coast. The latter included merchandise not only for southern consumption but also for many of the western storekeepers as well.

We may, however, draw more definite conclusions about the trade in flour. The influence of the Erie Canal in making New York the principal flour market is clear. We have, for example, the statistics of flour inspection at the chief ports during the twenties. In 1820, Baltimore led with 577,000 barrels, followed by Philadelphia with 400,000, and then New York with 267,000. By 1823, when part of the canal was already open, New York had passed Philadelphia, but Baltimore was still in the lead. In 1827, however, the western flour put New York in first place, with a score of 625,000, followed by Baltimore at 572,000, and Philadelphia at 351,000. New York's lead increased steadily after this.

5. NEW YORK PORT AND ITS DISAPPOINTED RIVALS*

Although its spremacy was continually resented and occasionally challenged by Philadelphia and Boston, the port of New York emerged as the most important in the nation. By 1860, it handled two thirds of the country's imports and one third of its exports. The port's easy access to growing western markets was the major factor underlying its success. We have already shown how it benefited from completion of the Erie Canal in 1825. But the Hudson River was frozen during much of the winter; and the railroad from Albany, eastern terminal of the canal, to New York was not completed until 1851. Although vulnerable to competition in the interim, New York port retained its commercial leadership. The merchants and civic leaders of the other eastern seaports failed to develop alternate methods of transportation that would enable their cities to capture the trade of the West.

ALL THE WAY from Canton to Chicago, New York encountered the stubborn opposition of rival ports as they sought to stem the increasing concentration of American commerce at Manhattan wharves. The other ports had missed their chance in 1815; late in 1823 the New England Society toasted "The City of New York—The emporium of America; commerce her glory, rivalship hopeless." Yet, those rival ports hopefully struggled for a quarter century or so, if not to wrest the primacy from New York, at least to retain a fair share of the nation's commercial transactions. The rivalry spread out over the seas to many distant regions, but its most conspicuous feature was the fight for the western front. Each port raced to spread rails beyond the mountains to draw the rich trade of the interior toward its own wharves.

The rivalry aroused, particularly during the second quarter of the century, an outpouring of pamphlets, newspaper and magazine articles, and oratory. The main theme of each promoter was the alarming threat that unless his port supported his project, grass would soon be growing on the wharves, and merchants would be making reservations at the poorhouse. The "decayed ports" of earlier times were paraded time and

* Selections from Robert G. Albion, *The Rise of New York Port* (New York: Charles Scribner's Sons, 1939), pp. 373–86, are used by permission of the publishers. Copyright, 1939, Charles Scribner's Sons.

again to emphasize this point. While neither Boston, Baltimore, nor Philadelphia ever sank to such a state, there was a striking example of what might happen to a port which lacked initiative and foresight. Norfolk, close to the mouth of Chesapeake Bay, had been endowed by nature with advantages second only to those of New York. In the late colonial period, it had ranked, like Newport, among the leading ports of America, at a time when Baltimore did not even have a customhouse. Then, like Newport, it fell behind to such a degree that its commerce and shipping in the 19th century were not only relatively but actually lower than they had been in colonial times. Such an example was enough to scare the merchants of other ports into buying stock in one canal or railroad after another.

Turning to the more general and to the internal aspects of the rivalry, we might notice the various successive stages between 1815 and 1860. A search of the London archives revealed some interesting comments of the British consuls stationed at the various Atlantic ports. They were naturally inclined to be more objective about the trade than were the local residents, and they show clearly that New York's rivals had been caught napping during that first decade after 1815. In 1822 the consul at New York reported that "while the commerce of Boston, Philadelphia, Baltimore, and the other principal ports has fallen off, that of New York has increased." In 1819 the widespread slump was reflected by the Baltimore consul, who declared that "the trade of this city was never more depressed, pecuniary embarrassment beyond anything ever before known, many failures, more expected, and no one knows who to trust." One year later, some signs of initiative at Charleston were summarized by the consul there as "these do not amount to much." The consul at Philadelphia remarked: "There is a spirit of enterprise in the State of New York for improvements which has not been followed up by its neighbors, . . . at the same time there is in Philadelphia a manifest superiority as regards manufactures." As late as 1824, this same consul declared that the commerce of Philadelphia was "on the decline in all its branches. . . . Commercial men here seem to have lost all their accustomed enterprise."

The completion of the Erie Canal aroused the rivals from their lethargy and saw the beginning of that flood of propaganda which would continue for years. Not all were as generous in spirit as Hezekiah Niles of Baltimore, who wrote: "The New Yorkers *deserve* success for their enterprise. There is a good spirit among the citizens to advance the business of New York. Let it be imitated—not envied." Whether the motive was emulation, envy, or fear, there was widespread conviction that something must be done, and done quickly. Boston and Philadelphia had already started packet lines to Liverpool, but the opening of the Erie Canal centered attention on the western front. The rivalry of the seaports thus became a major factor in the development of the nation's transportation systems.

Legislatures, cities, and individuals were ready to spend millions to divert the golden stream from New York and to engage in any means, fair or foul, to check the efforts of rival ports.

The situation was complicated by the fact that in September, 1825, just one month before the Erie Canal was finished, George Stephenson had run his pioneer locomotive over the Stockton & Darlington Railway in England. As early as 1812, John Stevens of the Hoboken family had urged railroads as the proper method of communication with the West, but the canal idea seemed easier to grasp at the moment. Now, however, as one consul reported, the "rage for canals" had become mixed with the "Rail Road mania." New York, enthusiastic over the success of the Erie Canal, did no more than toy with the idea of railroads for many years to come. Boston, after drawing up a comprehensive and very intelligent analysis of the situation created by New York's initiative, wisely rejected any project for a canal to the West and bided its time for its successful railroad venture.

New York's pioneer work in the first decade of peace may be called the "first act" in the rivalry of the ports. What we might term the "second act" centered in the efforts of Philadelphia and Baltimore, during the next decade or so, to cross the Alleghenies to the Ohio.

Philadelphia was alarmed at the situation. Its prestige, if not its prosperity, seemed to be at stake. In volume of trade, it had dropped in 30 years from first to fourth place. It had, moreover, given place to New York in population. Officially, fears were expressed that unless Pennsylvania "awakes to a true sense of her situation . . . she will be deprived of the sources of public prosperity . . . and instead of regaining the high commercial rank she once held, she will be driven even from her present station in the system of the Confederacy."

The state set to work to remedy the situation by undertaking the task of connecting Philadelphia with Pittsburgh on the Ohio. Between 1827 and 1835, it spent some $14 million, double the cost of the Erie Canal, in building its 395-mile "Main Line" between those two cities. It bungled the affair badly, however, by failing to appreciate the relative merits of canal and railroad. A canal had well served the purposes of New York, as it had been able to take the Alleghenies in flank; but Philadelphia's route to Pittsburgh had to go over mountains at 2,200 feet above sea level. Those $14 million might have been spent to excellent advantage on an all-rail route, which might have done wonders, in the formative years, in diverting the western trade from New York. Instead, the Main Line was a mongrel compromise between rail and canal. The first stage was a railroad from Philadelphia to Columbia on the Susquehanna. Then came a series of canals to the foot of the Alleghenies. The mountains were, of course, too steep for canals; too steep even, it was believed, for the crude locomotives of the day. The unusual solution for spanning the crest between Johnstown and Hollidaysburg was the 36-mile Allegheny Portage Railroad, in which stationary engines hoisted the cars up and lowered them down steep "inclined planes." The rest of the way to Pittsburgh was completed by canals through river valleys. The mixed system was both costly and slow, and was never a particularly formidable rival of the Erie Canal.

Baltimore proved more successful during this "second act." While Philadelphia was declining in importance, Baltimore was definitely a port "on the make." Its growth, both in commerce and in population, was surprisingly rapid. Merely a hamlet in the colonial period, it had begun, after the Revolution, to concentrate the rich grain and tobacco trade of the upper Chesapeake region, until then widely scattered. By 1800, it ranked third among all the cities of the Union in population. Its chief asset in this rivalry was the fact that it lay closer to the West than any of the other ports and that it had an excellent approach up the Potomac Valley to Cumberland on the western border of Maryland. Beyond there, to be sure, were the Alleghenies to be crossed at a half mile above sea level, which was even higher than on Pennsylvania's route. George Washington, in his keen interest to develop this "natural pathway to the West," had warned that if New York or Philadelphia were to get into contact with the West first, Baltimore would face "the difficulty of diverting trade after connections are once formed." This route had been selected for the national project of the Cumberland Road, begun in 1811, which had for some time given Baltimore a considerable advantage over its rivals. Baltimore now met with energy and intelligence the threat of the Erie Canal, which, despite its greater mileage, was a cheaper and easier route to the West.

Instead of copying Philadelphia's muddled compromise between rail and canal, which was less satisfactory than either system alone, Baltimore was quick to grasp the possibilities of the railroad. Two of its prominent businessmen visited England in 1826 to examine what Stephenson was doing. On their return, they organized the Baltimore & Ohio Railroad. Unlike the Erie Canal and the Main Line, which were state undertakings, this was a private venture; but the city of Baltimore contributed generously to the stock. On July 4, 1828, Charles Carroll of Carrollton laid the "first stone" of the B.&O., remarking afterwards: "I consider this among the most important acts of my life, second only to my signing the Declaration of Independence, even if it be second to that." At almost the same hour that day, however, John Quincy Adams was officiating at the opening of the Chesapeake & Ohio Canal near Washington, and both were designed for that same route up the Potomac to Cumberland. From the outset, the Baltimore & Ohio thus ran into the rivalry which was to hamper the whole course of its construction. Maryland supported both ventures, but Baltimore was more interested in its railroad. Many fights took place among lawyers and laborers before the Baltimore & Ohio received the right to parallel the canal route up the Potomac. By 1835, when the Main Line had been put through to Pittsburgh, the Baltimore & Ohio had progressed as far as Harpers Ferry and was tapping the rich wheat fields of the Shenandoah Valley. But another seven years were to elapse before it reached Cumberland; and beyond, there lay the rough Alleghenies and hostile, jealous states whose grudging permission was necessary before further extension was possible.

In addition to the rich but distant prize of western trade, the exploitation of the immediate hinterland was a source of port rivalry also. Baltimore, as well as Philadelphia, struggled for the prosperous business of the nearer Susquehanna Valley. In this competition the Chesapeake & Delaware Canal, built in 1829, was a score in Philadelphia's favor, for it gave access to Chesapeake Bay and the Susquehanna outlet. Baltimore, however, successfully countered by pushing a railroad to York, Pennsylvania, and thereby tapping one of the most flourishing agricultural regions in the country. New York likewise invaded Pennsylvania territory by building the Delaware & Hudson and other canals to bring anthracite direct to New York without having recourse to the port of Philadelphia.

The panic of 1837 might be taken as the end of the "second act," for it temporarily retarded further developments along the western routes. Neither Philadelphia nor Baltimore had succeeded in offering dangerous competition to the Erie Canal. Philadelphia had, to be sure, been connected with the Ohio River, but by means of a mongrel and inefficient system, whereas Baltimore's railroad had gone only halfway. Baltimore had caught up with Philadelphia in exports by 1832 and was to outdistance the latter port still further; but both, in spite of the millions they had sunk in communications, lagged far behind New York.

In the "third act," during the decade following 1837, New York's source of anxiety lay to the eastward. Seagoing Boston had quietly bided its time during the earlier stages of the competition. Now, it suddenly blossomed forth as the first of the four rivals to enjoy through rail communications with the West, and at the very time that the Cunard liners were giving it the best connections with Europe. Boston, moreover, had weathered the panic of 1837 better than the other three ports. The British consul there wrote in 1842 of "the superior situation in Boston in almost all matters of business, in comparison with New York, Philadelphia, and other rival cities which are suffering under great commercial depression." The real cause for this, he continued, lay in Boston's financial policy, "based on specie and steady principles of banking." As a result, Boston was in a position to drive energetically ahead in the railroad race.

Its immediate objective was Albany, which was not only the eastern terminus of the Erie Canal but also of a series of short railroads running parallel to the canal. The initiative in the building of these parallel roads, which would one day be joined into the New York Central, came chiefly from upstate New York. The state, in granting the charters, made many stringent restrictions to prevent freight competition with the canal; for some time the roads were pretty much limited to passenger traffic. As yet, however, no railroad connected New York and Albany, which meant that during the winter, when the Hudson was frozen, flour and other commodities accumulated at Albany with no outlet to the port.

The shrewd Bostonians wanted to tap this supply and realized that they would be able to do so if they pushed rails across the Berkshires to Albany. They hoped to lure the Erie Canal traffic away from New York; and anyway, they could give Boston and its surrounding manufacturing region a cheaper supply of western products and an outlet for their own wares by such a rail link. They began with a railroad to Worcester and then extended it by the Western Railroad to the New York state line, where another short road connected it with Albany. As a result of this enterprise, Boston, by 1842, had through rail service to Buffalo. Traffic on this future Boston & Albany road increased all through the forties and resulted in good dividends.

For almost the only time in the whole period of port rivalry, New York was definitely worried. Long overconfident in its canal, it had neglected railroads. The enterprise and initiative of its great decade seemed to have passed to its rivals. One particularly bad dream haunted New Yorkers during the mid-forties. They knew that England was planning to repeal its corn laws, which would naturally mean a tremendous boom for American grain and flour in the opening of such a new market. They could also foresee that this news might reach America in December or January, when the Hudson would be in all probability frozen, and that the Cunarders would undoubtedly be the bearers of the news. Boston would thus not only hear of it first but might capture all the initial advantages of the boom by rushing through all available western grain by rail to its wharves at a time when 150 miles of river ice would leave New York hopelessly at one side.

The New York legislature, acting in the same spirit which most of the other state bodies showed throughout the rivalry, continued to hamper the rail route from Albany to Buffalo as much as possible by hostile legislation, while New York financiers refused to subscribe to the stock of the Western Railroad. Yet, in constructive work, New York did little. The Erie Railroad, chartered in 1832, was even then described as a matter of "delays and disappointments"; and $1 million invested in its original stages was wasted from a faulty system of building the railroad on wooden piles. The Hudson River Railroad, designed to link New York with Albany, existed only on paper in 1845. Freeman Hunt, editor of *Hunt's Merchants' Magazine*, sounded a warning to New York in that year:

The rapid increase of the city in population, wealth, trade and commerce during the last fifteen or twenty years is attributable, for the most part to the opening of the Erie Canal and other internal improvements. At the present moment, the tide of prosperity threatens to be checked by the superior enterprise of other cities on the seaboard, which are beginning to share in the advantages of those improvements, and thus to draw away much of the trade that flowed in this direction. Without great outlays of capital and enterprise, beyond what has already been made, New York must soon lose her proud pre-eminence among the cities of the Union, and add another example to the many the world has already seen, of the rapid decline of a commercial mart, by the operation of a decayed spirit of enterprise and successful competition in other places.

The Massachusetts menace lasted until about 1847, when New York, Philadelphia, and Baltimore all resumed the rivalry in the "fourth act." By 1852 the three cities had their own through rail communications with the West, four great systems all being completed within two years.

We left the Baltimore & Ohio stranded at Cumberland, at the head of the Potomac and on the western edge of Maryland, in the early forties. Financial stringency and the tough ridges of the Alleghenies were not its only sources of trouble. New York and Philadelphia were able to build their systems to the West entirely within the boundaries of their respective states. Cumberland, however, was the farthest point to which Maryland might extend support to the Baltimore & Ohio. To reach the Ohio River from there, it was essential to gain the permission of Pennsylvania to run the road up to Pittsburgh, or of Virginia to push it through the Alleghenies to Wheeling. Both states were jealous and hostile. In the Virginia legislature, Baltimore was referred to as a "foreign" port, while Philadelphia naturally fought such an attempt to divert Pittsburgh's business to Baltimore. Not until 1847 did Virginia finally give its consent; and the Baltimore & Ohio engineers began to wrestle with the problem of piercing the ridges, with their irregular contours and 2,600-foot maximum altitude.

Even when that obstacle was overcome and the objective was being approached, Pennsylvania once more interfered in the interesting "Wheeling Bridge case." Stanton, Lincoln's future Secretary of War, led the argument that the proposed railroad bridge over the Ohio, necessary in order to reach Wheeling on the far bank, would interfere with river navigation. To demonstrate the point, steamers with abnormally high stacks paraded the Ohio, but the Baltimore & Ohio finally won the case. The last rail was laid and the last spike driven in on Christmas Day, 1852, more than 24 years after Charles Carroll had laid the first stone. It had taken some $20 million to build the 379-mile line. Wheeling in itself was not an important terminus; but the road, after emerging from the mountains, sent off a branch further sought, which led to an excellent through route from Baltimore to Cincinnati and St. Louis. Baltimore ultimately gained a fair share of western trade; but just before that final spike was driven near Wheeling, Philadelphia had completed its through rail route to Pittsburgh, while New York had finished two rail lines to the West.

Indirectly, the approach to the Baltimore & Ohio through the mountains had hastened Philadelphia's move. The inhabitants of Pittsburgh were angry with the Pennsylvania legislature for denying them the opportunity to have something better than the Main Line for an outlet to the sea. They had no love for Philadelphia and, not being permitted to trade with Baltimore, even flirted with New York.

At any rate, shortly after this, the legislature incorporated the Pennsylvania Railroad, which began in 1847 to connect Philadelphia with the West by a real railroad over the route of the mongrel Main Line. The original railroad to Columbia was utilized; but along the previous canal routes, rails were laid. This was completed, except for the mastering of the crest of the Alleghenies, during 1852. The Allegheny Portage was continued in use for six years more; but eventually, the through regular rail connection was completed between Philadelphia and the Ohio River and beyond. In 1857 the old Main Line was put up at auction, and the "Pennsy" purchased it at half its original cost. This new connection proved disappointing to Philadelphians, for they found that their port was not getting full advantage of it. Much freight from the West simply snubbed Philadelphia and continued by rail to New York, which thus acquired an extra western route in addition to two of its own.

The two New York rail connections had put that port ahead in the western race the year before Baltimore and Philadelphia completed their long quest for rail connections across the mountains. President Fillmore had come north for the formal opening of the Erie Railroad on May 14, 1851, while the first train over the new Hudson River Railroad ran up to Albany on October 1 of that same year.

The Hudson River road followed the river up to Albany, where it connected with the series of roads running parallel to the Erie Canal westward to Buffalo. Such a road had been discussed for some time; but nothing definite happened until 1847, the same year which saw the start of the Pennsylvania and the renewed advance of the Baltimore & Ohio beyond Cumberland. The route ran along the river's east bank all the way, involving slow and costly work in cutting through the flinty rock of Anthony's Nose and Breakneck Hill, but resulting in a "water-level route" almost without grades. The first train made the run in five hours, whereas the fastest of the steamboats required more than seven hours. Just after our period, in the sixties, Cornelius Vanderbilt would weld this new run with the old Albany–Buffalo roads into a single New York Central & Hudson River Railroad; but in the meantime, New York enjoyed its new all-year connection with Lake Erie over the route by which the Erie Canal traffic had come for more than a quarter century.

The other New York venture, which reached completion a few months earlier, was the Erie Railroad. Instead of being a gradual assembling of little lines, it had been planned from the first as a single system. From the beginning, it had encountered constant financial difficulties. Its route was shorter than the Hudson River one, for it skirted the southwestern edge of the state. Almost no other towns except Binghamton and Elmira lay along the whole 446 miles of the Erie's route. This meant that there would be little local freight for the road, which would consequently be chiefly dependent on through business. In order to avoid the jealous action of the legislatures of Pennsylvania and New Jersey, the Erie's original route lay entirely in New York. At Piermont, a great stone pier ran out into the river so that the steamboats might pick up the passengers and freight for New York City. Later, the railroad secured a place on the New Jersey waterfront across the Hudson from New York City. It was also extended along the lake shore beyond Dunkirk to Erie, Pennsylvania. The road suffered from chronic financial troubles which made it a byword in railroad circles. Nevertheless, it gave New York port a good, direct freight route to the Great Lakes.

These various roads to the West did not stop at their original objectives. By 1852, when the four big lines were completed, connecting ones were being extended to Chicago and to other centers of importance.

Once more, New York had triumphed. The Baltimore & Ohio and the Pennsylvania had not been completed in time to divert the long-established western connections with New York. The New York railroads simply took over gradually the traffic which had traveled the Erie Canal.

The West was not the only direction in which New York was sustaining its commanding position. Boston and Philadelphia found themselves sidetracked as the termini, respectively, of the Cunard and Inman steamship lines. In 1848, it was New York's good fortune that the Cunard Line was shifted from Boston to meet the coming competition of the Collins Line and that of other American steamships. This loss of the advantage it had enjoyed as the sole western terminus of the Cunarders put Boston behind in the port rivalry. Philadelphia, too, suffered when the British line of iron-screw Inman steamships, which had been coming there for a while in the fifties, extended their western terminus to New York before that decade was over.

Thus, on the eve of the Civil War, New York's prosperity had reached a point which was certainly enough to incite the envy of its rivals. In spite of all they had been able to accomplish, its lead had increased steadily. By 1860, New York was handling two thirds of all the nation's imports and one third of its exports. The combined imports of Boston,

Philadelphia, and Baltimore were less than New York's imports of textiles alone. Those three rivals together exported less grain and meat products than did New York, whose hold on the West had not been seriously affected by the Baltimore & Ohio, the Boston & Albany, and the Pennsylvania roads, all of which had been begun with such high hopes. In the value of its imports and exports, as well as in the volume of shipping which entered and cleared, New York not only stood an easy first among American ports; but in all the world, only London and Liverpool exceeded it. Although the decline of American shipping, already under way, would gravely affect the little ports down east after the Civil War, New York would still retain its commanding share of the nation's commerce, under whatever flag the cargoes might arrive or depart. World primacy still lay 60-odd years in the future; but in the meantime, New York waxed steadily greater in trade, wealth, and population, thanks to the well-timed enterprise of its citizens in the decade following 1815.

6. ECONOMIC ASPECTS OF SOUTHERN SECTIONALISM*

Twenty years prior to the Civil War, southern businessmen resented their subservience to northern commercial interests. Southern ports had languished as the harbors of New York and Boston received an increasing proportion of European imports. Even when agricultural exports were shipped from southern ports, title passed to English firms through some northern intermediary. The region's storekeepers purchased mainly from northern wholesalers, who could offer credit terms far more liberal than those available from local importers and jobbers. A series of state and sectional conventions was held in 1837, 1838, and 1839 to discuss how these problems might be resolved. Although little was accomplished at these meetings, this selection provides considerable insight into the marketing patterns and economic thinking of the period.

THE COMPARATIVE GROWTH of northern and southern seaports, the tendency to concentration of the importing business of the United States in northern cities, especially New York, and the disparity between the shipping industries of the two sections—in short, the "commercial dependence" of the South upon the North—were matters which received considerable attention in the antebellum South, not only from citizens of the seaports themselves but from the section as a whole. Southern men quite generally looked upon commercial dependence as an evidence of the failure of the South to prosper as it should. They gave consideration to the relation of commercial dependence to the comparatively slow accumulation of mobile capital in the South and to the inadequacy of credit facilities, because of which they were handicapped in their efforts to construct internal improvements and to develop the varied resources of the section. They canvassed commercial dependence as a cause for the slower increase of population in the South than in the North—a matter of much concern because of its bearing upon the sectional struggle over slavery. The causes of commercial dependence were sought, therefore, and efforts were made to devise and apply remedies.

The whole subject was first thoroughly discussed; and the first efforts

* Reprinted from Robert R. Russel, *Economic Aspects of Southern Sectionalism, 1840–1861* (University of Illinois Studies in the Social Sciences, Vol. XI, Nos. 1 and 2 [Urbana, 1924]), pp. 16–32.

were made to effect a revolution in the manner of conducting southern commerce, by a number of direct-trade conventions which met in Georgia, South Carolina, and Virginia in 1837, 1838, and 1839.

The direct-trade convention originated in Georgia. While the financial crash of 1837 deranged the currency and the exchange and credit operations of the country, it seems not to have affected the Old South as disastrously at first as it did other sections of the Union. It was seized upon as affording a good opportunity for attempting to effect the establishment of direct trade and a change in the method of marketing cotton. With these objects in view, William Dearing and other gentlemen issued a call for a convention to meet in Augusta in October, 1837. The call stated that a crisis had arrived in the commercial affairs of the South and Southwest, "the most favorable that has occurred since the formation of the American government, to attempt a new organization of our commercial relations with Europe." The first Augusta convention was followed in April and October, 1838, by a second and third; and in April, 1839, by a fourth in Charleston.

Each of this series of conventions was composed of from 100 to 200 delegates, elected by local meetings. The great majority in each case was from Georgia and South Carolina; and an attempt was made to enlist as many southern states as possible. Although the state-rights, antitariff men gave tone to the proccedings, the conventions were bipartisan in composition; they were not got up for partisan purposes, and party politics played a minor part in their deliberations. Among the delegates were bankers, merchants, and planters, as well as men active in politics. The presence and active participation of such men are sufficient to indicate the deep interest in the objects of the conventions.

There was substantial agreement in all of the conventions in regard to the manner in which southern commerce was conducted, the evils attendant thereon, and the benefits to follow the establishment of direct trade with Europe. The staple-growing states were described as being in a "state of commercial dependence, scarcely less reproachful to their industry and enterprise than it is incompatible with their substantial prosperity." What would be more natural than that those who furnished the nation's exports should also receive its imports? Yet, while the South furnished two thirds of the exports, she received directly only one tenth of the imports of the United States. Francis Mallory estimated that nine tenths of the exports went directly to Europe, while five sevenths of the imports from abroad came indirectly by way of northern seaports. The direct imports of Charleston were said to have amounted to several millions in 1807; by 1833, they had dwindled to $500,000; since that time, they had gradually increased but were still insignificant. The same was said to be true of Virginia. At the time of the Revolution, exports and imports had been equal; from that time to 1831, imports had steadily declined; since 1831, there had been some, though not marked, improvement. Though southern exports went directly to Europe, the business was not conducted by home merchants, but chiefly by agents of northern and English firms. Southern seaports were described as mere appendages of northern seaports, "places where their agents and factors do business, and who, having but little local interest, withdraw from them after a few years' residence, with all their gains, to swell the wealth of the place of their early affection and attachment." In Virginia, northern steamboats often went up the rivers buying and selling directly to the farmers, the lumbermen, and the country merchants; the cargoes were paid for by bills on New York, and the money never entered Virginia. Interior merchants purchased their stocks in New York, Philadelphia, or Baltimore without the intervention of jobbers in southern ports.

The profits northern merchants and shippers made from conducting southern commerce were believed to be very great and to account in large measure for the prosperity of northern cities, while the loss of those profits explained the impoverishment of the cities of the South.

At Charleston, Robert Y. Hayne quoted a report of a committee of the Alabama legislature in which it was estimated that over one third of the price of cotton went to New York agents and shippers. Hayne himself was content to put the tolls at 10 or 15 percent. George McDuffie thought the "voluntary tribute" paid annually to the North for carrying southern commerce amounted to $10 million. A Virginia delegate said the state could save $1 million annually by importing directly. But this direct annual drain was not the only loss occasioned the southern people; there were also the "consequential losses," that is, the capital which would have accumulated had the South conducted her own commerce. Commercial dependence had operated to prevent the accumulation of capital in the South, and the deficiency of capital had handicapped enterprise.

The greatness of New York City was pictured—all said to have been built upon southern staples and southern trade. "You hold the element," ran the address of one of these conventions, "from which he derives his strength, and you have only to withdraw it to make him as subservient to you, as you now are to him. You have but to speak the word, and his empire is transferred to your own soil, and his sovereignty to the sons of that soil." But the benefits were not confined to New York; the virtual monopoly of southern commerce had "either directly or indirectly made the whole of the North and Northwest what they are," according to the call of the first Augusta convention. Because of it, "the one people has risen like the rocket, and the other has fallen like its stick—their positions must have been reversed, if the southern people had maintained their foreign trade." Glowing descriptions were given of the prosperity of southern states and cities after direct trade should be restored. Were direct trade established, according to the address calling the second Augusta convention:

[There] would be an end to the unequal barter of which we have spoken. The doleful cry for northern funds would be hushed. The speculators upon southern distress would cease. The disorders of the currency would be healed. The relation of the commercial agency would be changed. They would be acquaintances and friends, identical in feeling and interest; enjoying mutual confidence, and interchanging mutual favors . . . . The fountain and the streams of commerce lying all within our land, would enrich it to an extent that none can foresee. Our works of internal improvement would receive a new and ever-accelerating impetus. Our drooping cities would be revived —our creeping commerce winged; and all the blessings, physical, moral, and intellectual, which invariably accompany affluence and independence, would be ours.

In regard to the causes for the decline of the shipping and the import trade of southern ports, the conventions exhibited differences of opinion. First, there was the view that for many years the North had possessed great advantages over the South for these lines of business by reason of its superior wealth and larger accumulations of capital. Not only must shipowners and importers be men of large capital, but they must have the backing of wealthy communities.

And men of the South Carolina school, the followers of Calhoun and McDuffie, were ready with explanations for the more rapid accumulation of capital in the North than in the South. It was, they said, because of the unequal operation of the federal government. The tariffs had long enriched the manufacturing sections at the expense of the agricultural. Furthermore, while the people of the South had paid their proportionate share of the federal revenues, these revenues had been disbursed chiefly in the northern cities; and this process, going on year after year, had transferred a staggering total from the one section to the other. A minority report in the Richmond convention rehearsed the old story of the assumption of the state debts by the federal government and the refunding of the national debt carried out under the guidance of Alexander Hamilton. The refunded debt had been distributed between the North and South in the ratio of 3 to 1 and, because of this inequality of distribution, had acted as a mortgage of the one section upon the other, great sums having been transferred from the South to the North in the form of interest paid to northern bondholders from the common treasury. It was claimed, also, by men in these conventions, that for long the funds of the federal government had been deposited almost altogether in northern banks, thus giving northern businessmen a decided advantage over southern in the ability to secure financial assistance. Those who held these views of the causes of southern decline saw a basis for hope for revival in the gradual reduction of the tariff, according to the provisions of the compromise tariff law of 1833, the recent extinguishment of the national debt, the destruction of the United States Bank, and the evidence of a new policy in distributing deposits of the public funds.

Another alleged cause for southern commercial dependence, closely related to the one just mentioned, was the inadequacy of credit facilities. An examination, however cursory, of business methods in the South in that period makes it clear that a successful importing firm would have to command very great resources of capital or credit, or both. It was proverbial that the planters lived each year upon the prospective income from the next year's crop. The country merchants, who extended them long credit, could not buy, therefore, except on long time. Importers, who bought on 60 or 90 days' time, had to sell to the merchants upon from 6 to 12 or 16 months. Country merchants were sometimes unwilling to give negotiable notes; they considered a request to do so a reflection upon their business integrity. Southern importers and jobbers did not, unaided, possess the means, and southern banks were unable to lend them sufficient support, to enable them to extend to retail merchants the long credits the latter received in the North.

A correspondent of the *Charleston Courier* attributed the loss of foreign trade to the fact that country merchants began to buy of northern jobbers because of the longer credits obtained. McDuffie said he confidently believed that if the planters would "adopt the system of expending, in the current year, the income of the year preceding . . . . it would dispense with one-half of the capital that would otherwise be necessary for carrying on our foreign commerce by a system of direct importation."

It is to the credit of the men of these conventions that they recognized other causes for southern commercial dependence than the action or nonaction of the federal and state governments. They recognized that agriculture had in the past proved more attractive to capital than the shipping or mercantile business; land and Negroes had been considered the best investments. The existence of a prejudice against other pursuits than agriculture and the professions was admitted. Some were willing to credit the people of the North with habits of industry not possessed by their own people and with superior commercial enterprise; they spoke of the "voluntary tribute" the South paid the North. A committee in the Charleston convention reported that the consumption of domestic goods had increased greatly, was still increasing, and was estimated by merchants to extend already to one third of the whole consumption. The committee believed, however, that the quantity of foreign goods consumed in the South was sufficient to justify merchants in southern seaports embarking in the importing business and to enable them to compete with northern importers, who, of course, supplied a larger demand.

It was generally denied that northern seaports possessed any natural or physical advantages over southern seaports for conducting foreign commerce. The direct course of trade was the natural course, and the indirect the unnatural. Direct trade would save one set of jobbers' profits, the cost of shipping coastwise, the difference between the discount of southern notes in New York and Charleston (or the cost of whatever other mode of payment was employed), and the expenses retail merchants incurred in going North to lay in their stocks. Southern harbors were said to be as good as northern. However that may be, it is certain that oceangoing vessels entered southern harbors to receive their exports. These ships often came in ballast and, it was reasonably argued, would be willing to carry imports at low freights. Shipping was considered adequate, though there was recognition that regular packet lines were needed. The South was said to have timber for shipbuilding; but in the thirties, not much was said about the desirability of promoting shipbuilding or shipowning: The big object was to save the "importers' profits." Now and then, someone suggested that the importing business in southern cities was rendered precarious by visits of yellow, or "strangers'," fever; but residents of the South were generally ready to defend their coastal cities against the prevalent belief that they were unhealthy.

Various plans and measures were suggested for promoting direct importations of foreign goods. Some were intended to overcome the obstacle to direct trade which lay in the lack of mercantile houses with sufficient capital to enable them to embark in the importing business. The first Augusta convention took the view that while individual merchants were not possessed of resources necessary, the requisite capital could be got together by associations of individuals; and to that end, it appointed a committee to memorialize the state legislatures in behalf of limited copartnership laws. In response to the committee's memorials, the legislatures of Virginia, South Carolina, Georgia, Alabama, Tennessee, and Florida Territory enacted the desired legislation, and subsequent conventions urged men of means to avail themselves of the opportunity thus afforded. The opinion was expressed that there was an overproduction of cotton in the South and that planters could profitably invest a portion of the proceeds of their crops otherwise than in land and Negroes. If for a few years the planters would apply one half their net income to commerce, abundant capital would be supplied to conduct the whole foreign commerce. This suggestion, however, could not carry great weight. The question of capital, it was considered, would be a serious one only while the revolution in trade was being effected, for, once established, the profits of direct importations would supply the capital requisite for their continuance.

Other recommendations of the direct-trade conventions dealt with the great obstacle to direct trade which lay in the inadequacy of credit facilities in the South. The second Augusta convention was especially detailed in its recommendations. It requested banks to form European connections so that they might be able to assist importers with letters of credit. It recommended that the banks in the seaports discount paper from the interior for the importing merchants—paper for periods longer than six months as well as for shorter periods. The banks of the interior were requested to cooperate by collecting and remitting the proceeds of such paper to the coast with as little delay as possible. "It is not to be concealed that without the aid and support of the banks, the difficulties in our way will be greatly multiplied. It will depend upon them, in great measure, to determine the fate of our great measure."

Many other suggestions designed to promote direct importations were made. Individual citizens were urged to be more enterprising. It was declared a sacred duty to buy of those merchants who traded directly in preference to those who bought foreign goods from northern jobbers. Interior merchants were requested not to go North for their stocks until they had investigated the possibilities of making their purchases in their own seaports. A local Virginia convention, in 1838, recommended the organization of an association of retail merchants pledged to deal after September 1, 1839, with the importing merchants of Virginia cities only, "provided those merchants would sell as cheaply as the Northern merchants"; and 60 or 70 citizens actually signed a pledge not to patronize any merchant who would not join the association. The pledge system was advocated in the Norfolk convention, but the convention refused to recommend it. Complaint was made that the tax laws of the states discriminated against commercial capital in favor of land and slaves. Some southern states and cities taxed sales; port and wharf charges and fees were said to be too high. The Charleston convention adopted a resolution requesting the state legislatures to repeal discriminatory taxes. A motion introduced at Norfolk to ask the legislature of Virginia to exempt direct imports from taxation was defeated. The prejudices of the people against mercantile pursuits were deplored: "The commercial class must be elevated in public opinion to the rank in society which properly belongs to it." It was recognized as an evil that the great majority of the merchants, commission merchants, and factors in all the seaport cities of the South (and interior towns too, for that matter) were either northerners or naturalized citizens. Commercial education was recommended to train southern youth to enter the field. Manufacturers and exporters of foreign countries were asked to establish agencies in southern cities for selling their goods, as they had done in New York and other northern seaports. The Norfolk convention considered this quite important; it appointed a committee of seven to get in communication with European firms.

The direct-trade movement of these years was very closely related to efforts being made in the South Atlantic states to establish connections by railroads or canals with the Ohio Valley. All of the direct-trade conventions very heartily endorsed these projects for connecting the South and West as most promising measures for securing direct trade. The West sold to the South, it was said; if it could also buy in the South, such a demand for goods would be created in southern seaports that there could no longer be any question of their ability to import directly. "We must contend for the commerce of the West," read Mallory's report; "the section that gets that commerce will get the commerce of the country." A resolution adopted by the Norfolk convention declared internal improvements to be the foundation of an import trade. The general committee of the second Augusta convention said that direct trade was inseparably connected with the extension of intercourse to the West. "And when the great West shall find a market and receive their supplies through the seaports of the South, a demand will be furnished, the extent and value of which *cannot* be too largely estimated." Calhoun, who took a deep interest in both projects, believed that direct trade could not be established until railroads had been extended to the West. On the other hand, discussion of the establishment of direct trade with Europe would stimulate interest in projects for connecting the seaboard and the Ohio Valley. Many of the members of the direct-trade conventions were closely associated with the internal improvement projects; and though it would be inaccurate to say that the former were got up to give impetus to the latter, that was undoubtedly one of the objects of the conventions.

Although the money panic of 1837 was the occasion for the convening of conventions which proposed to attempt to change the course of southern trade, the movement cannot be considered the outgrowth of depressed economic conditions. In 1837 and 1838, it was believed that business had received only a temporary, although sharp, check, and that enterprise would soon be in full swing once more. As was the rapid building of railroads, canals, and turnpikes, the direct-trade movement was a manifestation of the spirit of progress and enterprise which had seized upon East, West, and South alike. The movement came to a temporary close when general stagnation of business settled upon the country in 1839 and continued for several years thereafter.

It is noteworthy that these direct-trade conventions were concerned almost exclusively with economic conditions and means for improving them. The slavery question, which was being given considerable prominence about this time, both in Congress and out, by reason of the debates in Congress upon the exclusion of abolition literature from the mails and the treatment of abolition petitions in Congress, was rarely mentioned. A decade later, no direct-trade convention could be held, no plan for achieving commercial independence proposed, nor, for that matter, for erecting a cotton mill, building a railroad, opening a mine, or in any way promoting the material progress of the South, without consideration of, or due advertence to, its relation to the sectional struggle over slavery and the extension thereof. The argument would then without fail be advanced that the South must develop her strength and resources, and achieve commercial and industrial independence, in order to be prepared to defend her rights and honor in the Union, or, if worst came to worst, her independence out of it; but as yet, such considerations were very infrequently advanced, at least in public. The direct-trade conventions of the thirties were in the main what they purported to be, namely, bona fide efforts on the part of southern men to promote the prosperity and progress of their states and section, and particularly their seaports.

The direct-trade conventions accomplished no tangible results in the way of changing the course of southern commerce. They afford evidence of discontent in the older states of the South with their material progress. They show that the belief was held, and no doubt they contributed to its spread, that commercial dependence was an evidence and, at the same time, a cause of "Southern decline." It is unnecessary to point out the common element in the view that the East was being enriched at the expense of the South because of the commercial vassalage of the latter and the quite prevalent belief that the operation of the federal government had been unequal in its effects upon the material progress of the two sections. The direct-trade conventions were another manifestation of the economic discontent of which evidence had been given during the nullification controversy.

7. THE GENERAL STORE: A MARKETING AXIS OF THE PERIOD*

The contribution of the general store to the development of New England industry is reviewed in this article. The storekeeper opened new markets for his community's artisans, helped farmers exchange their goods for needed manufactured products, and found distant outlets for the products of local factories. For a brief but nevertheless crucial period, he served as focal point of the entire distribution system, facilitating the transition between handicraft production and large-scale manufacturing.

ATTENTION HAS BEEN CALLED to the functions of the itinerant New England tin peddler as an agency in the opening of inland trade routes for New England manufactures. Even more ubiquitous, almost as picturesque, and of considerably greater significance in the development of most New England manufacturing industries was the village general store, whose importance in this connection seems to have remained all but unnoticed. Any study of village life in the northern states during the closing decades of the 18th century and the opening years of the 19th will reveal in this common village institution a focal point for several lines of economic activity related to the growth and development of manufacture. The account of them here given is limited to New England, but the first part of the story is repeated with only slight variation during the first third of the 19th century in many communities in the eastern half of the Ohio Valley–Great Lakes region, wherever New England village life reproduced itself.

Before manufacture can develop in any community, there must exist, of course, not only "simple division of labor" but—that which develops division of labor—a sufficient contact between the possessor of skill in the making of manufactured goods and other persons who need his wares, who have means of payment acceptable to him, and who may therefore constitute his market. In 18th-century New England, down to the period of the Revolution, the market for manufactured goods, as is well known, was almost purely local in each producing community. There were a few

* Reprinted from Harvey Wooster, "A Forgotten Factor in American Industrial History," *American Economic Review*, Vol. XVI (March, 1926), pp. 14–27.

exceptions. The activities of the tin peddler had already begun. For the few luxuries and indispensables which the community could not produce at home, it relied upon foreign ports, just as each frontier farm household, depending upon its own skill and energy to satisfy its wants, relied upon peddlers and occasional trips to the village store, when one was accessible, for such goods as its members could not produce themselves. In every village community the local general store was the chief source of supply for these few goods from outside.

The storekeeper had three lines of contact that, taken together, gave him a strategic position for dominance in the development of manufacture as soon as a market outside the community was opened up. Indeed, he was the only person in the community in a position to lead in the opening of outside markets. If located in a maritime town, he was likely to be in contact with foreign merchants. He was sure to have relations with coastwise merchants in other colonial ports. If he was located in an inland village, he was in contact with the merchants of these larger coastwise towns and could secure some of the same connections with only one intervening step. The storekeeper was thus in a position to market in other communities, either in nearby cities or in more distant ports, any surplus of manufactured commodities which might be wanted elsewhere and which the resources of the community and the skill of its local craftsmen (or housewives, in the case of textiles) could produce.

At home, he was in contact with two different sets of customers— different, that is, in their relation to the manufacture of domestic goods. He sold chiefly to the villagers, bartering with them the "English and West India goods" that in the earlier years constituted his chief stock in trade. He had some customers, however, among the farmers in outlying districts who came to town occasionally—sometimes as infrequently as once or twice a year—to purchase salt, iron, glass, powder and shot, and perhaps a very meager supply of the miscellaneous lot of imported goods he kept for sale. This trade was even more exclusively a barter trade than that which he carried on with the village folk. From these farmer customers, he had to take such products of farm and fireside labor as they could offer. He had thus two sets of local contacts of significance in connection with manufactured goods. He served as a distributing agent for country-made products which many villagers were glad to buy, and for village-made manufactures which the country farmers needed and were only too glad to obtain in this way. From these three points of contact—the outside market in nearby city or distant port, the outlying farm population surrounding his village, and the villagers themselves—the storekeeper constructed the beginnings of a manufacturing system that replaced the older handicraft organization and the still older household industry, as later paragraphs will show, only to give way in turn to the "merchant-capitalist" of the city and the yet more highly capitalistic factory system.

This system, variously named, but here referred to as merchant-manufacture,[1] established itself throughout most of southern New England during the period intervening between the end of the Revolutionary War and the end of the War of 1812, or not long thereafter. It was, needless to say, of much briefer duration in America than in England. In some industries, it was swallowed up by the factory system almost as soon as it was introduced. It commonly existed side by side with the older handicraft organization, which broke down as it appeared, and quite regularly overlapped the coming of the factories. It had all but disappeared by 1860, however, except in boot and shoe manufacture, where it was rapidly declining, and in the ready-made garment industries, in which traces of it still remain. Except in the boot and shoe industry, it was hardly more than a transitional step between the specialized artisan, with his purely local market and custom-made goods, and the factory, with its increasingly distant market and ready-made product. But it was a necessary transition as internal commerce developed, except in the textile trades, in which machinery and the factory were introduced coincidently with the improved means of transportation that made an immensely larger market accessible, and in iron manufacture and flour milling, in which the germs of modern machinery were already present. Even these industries felt its influence and utilized to some extent the services of merchants as entrepreneurs, so that for about two decades, from 1800 to 1820, merchant-manufacture could be found breaking out in spots, unevenly, all over southern New England.

The mosaic of that transition from handicraft to full-fledged merchant-manufacture has been pieced together from incomplete records and shows a fairly definite pattern, with the village storekeeper as the basic starting point. It is the purpose of this paper to show his functions in this connection.

The village store had rivals in the creation of the new system. One of them was the tin peddler, referred to above. They were probably numbered in thousands the country over, far-traveling Yankee traders, who covered the roads and trails from Cape Cod to the Great Lakes and the Mississippi, and from Maine to Louisiana, shrewd distributors of many lines of household wares to housewives in village and countryside wherever horse and cart or wagon could go. The peddler's part was an impor-

---

[1] This term is preferred to others because it so easily comprehends the two fundamental characteristics of this mode of organization, viz, that the organizing and directing entrepreneur is primarily a merchant, and that the commodities involved are handmade and for a market. The exact date of its introduction into any given community or industry is usually difficult to establish. Dates vary, of course, and are not everywhere included within the period specified here. Shoemaking, shipbuilding, and lumbering appear to have reached at least the early phases of this form of organization in some communities earlier than the Revolution. In more remote villages, its appearance might be delayed for a decade or more and only the later phases ever appear.

tant one. He rendered especially valuable service as agent for the opening of new channels of inland trade and for the introduction of new goods, some of them later to become staples, whose purchase was primarily of concern to women. His influence was especially potent in the development of the brass, clock, silver-plate, and hardware industries of central and western Connecticut. Outside of a limited area, however, embracing but little more than the narrow strip of country between the Naugatuck and the Connecticut rivers, his activities could have had but little effect on the growth of manufacture, except as a pioneer trader in general, for this region was the center of the peddler organization, and the bulk of his supplies came from it. Further, the tin peddler, passing from house to house, dealt almost entirely with women, as the wares he carried plainly indicated. Doubtless, he had more or less to do with the men of the farms and villages where he visited, since arrangements for payment, often in kind, or in board and lodging, must frequently have been made with them or have been consummated after family consultations in which they took part. But his wares, after all, almost wholly lay in the housewife's province.

The storekeeper, on the other hand, was to be found all the year round in every town, village, and hamlet in New England. He ministered to the needs of male and female alike. He made contacts that were permanent. He served the wants of whole communities rather than of isolated families, and he aided by his very numbers not only a vastly wider area but a greater diversity of industries than the tin peddler. In time the peddler succumbed to his competition, but not until after the storekeeper himself had been driven out of every form of control over manufacture.

Another rival of the storekeeper was the craftsman who went into manufacture and marketed his own goods. As markets were opened, some of these in nearly every community broadened their activities, set up as merchant-manufacturers "on their own," and so became competitors of the storekeeper. Yet, these men seem more often to have followed his lead than to have preceded him, to have entered the trade with outside markets after the storekeeper had already demonstrated the possibilities of profit in such markets than to have originated the contacts with them. This was to be expected, because of the storekeeper's threefold line of contact within and without his community, already referred to. His very occupation gave him an advantage the local craftsman could hardly obtain. Often the craftsman who became a "manufacturer" did so by establishing a store through which to pay his employees and market his product, thus turning merchant in order to succeed in manufacture. Storekeeping was not the only source from which the merchant-manufacturer sprang, but the storekeeper was so situated as to make the step easier for him than for anyone else; and this was true to such an extent that others who wished to compete with him on the ready-made market were likely to undertake storekeeping as a means of carrying on manufacture. He was the first and most important source from which the earlier "manufacturers" came.

There is abundant evidence as to the nature of the storekeeper's position in his community near the beginning of the period under discussion. For example, in 1804, a merchant of the then village of Worcester, Massachusetts, advertises that he has to sell "West India goods and groceries, viz: best cognac and Spanish brandy; West India and New England rums; real Holland gin; Madeira wines; flour, molasses; loaf, white, and brown sugar; teas, coffee, chocolate, spices, raisins, copperas, alum; rock and fine salt; dried and pickled fish; glazed china tea sets, crockery and glass ware, violins and flutes." Significant for our purposes is the added statement that he offers to give cash for country produce. This produce he must have marketed to a considerable extent, at least, to his customers in the village. He could hardly have sent much of it to any large town so early in the century as this.

An advertisement in the local newspaper published in Danbury, Connecticut, in 1805 runs as follows: "Those indebted to the subscribers, on Book or Note (now due by agreement), may have the opportunity of canceling the same by payment in Walnut, Oak or Maple Wood, Wheat, Rye, Corn, Oats, Buckwheat, Flax Seed, Hats, Saddles, or Shoes, at their full value, if delivered soon, but if delayed cash will be the only substitute which will be accepted by Joseph F. and E. M. White."

Illustrations of this nature might be multiplied, though there are not many so detailed as these. Here are village storekeepers, one of them offering for sale a considerable range of imported goods of interest to both men and women, and willing to buy for cash the products of his farmer customers, the other offering to take payment for goods previously purchased in country produce or in the products of local handicrafts. To secure a complete picture of the village storekeeper of this period, these two advertisements should be combined. The Worcester merchant must have been willing to receive in payment of indebtedness to him the country produce for which he advertised to pay cash. The Danbury firm must have had for sale a line of goods other than the miscellaneous lot of products they were willing to receive. Both would unquestionably have been found exchanging farm and village products for other similar products of the community along with the selling of wares imported from outside.

The picture is all but completed, in fact, by one of the local historians of Haverhill, Massachusetts, who writes of the beginnings of shoe manufacture in that city. "In the course of time, storekeepers began to keep a few shoes on hand for sale. This naturally grew out of the barter system of trade, then so common. They bartered with shoemakers for their shoes, bartered the shoes with the back-country farmers for produce; and then bartered the produce for English and West India goods." Haverhill was fortunately situated on a river, navigable for many of the small vessels in use at that time, and its merchants were evidently able to send a part of the country produce they received to the larger cities on the coast.

To bring to full completion the story of the village storekeeper in a prosperous community at or near the beginning of the 19th century, we need only glance at another picture drawn by the same artist. "This town [Haverhill] was for a long time the headquarters of trade for a large back-country. . . . The goods and articles of trade were transported to and from the interior wholly by oxen, hundreds of which were constantly employed in the business." Oxteams were loaded in Haverhill with imported goods from English or West Indian ports and brought back "pearl-ashes, linseed oil, flaxseed, grain and various other articles of export and exchange." One Haverhill merchant, we are told, built a potash works and a mill for grinding flaxseed in Lebanon, New Hampshire, and "sent over $90,000 worth of goods to his store in Lebanon . . . during a single period of twenty-six months."

Haverhill was a Merrimac River town favorably situated for the river commerce of the time. In other towns not so favored by nature, a similar development took place, differing only in the degree of its advancement at this early time and in the slower rate and the ultimate extent of its progress. Thus, in Boscawen, New Hampshire, we learn that there were, quite early, two hatters who, working separately, "purchased mink and muskrat skins of the farmers and also made silk and wool hats, finding a market at the country stores, or manufacturing to a citizen's order." It is not improbable that mink and muskrat skins found their way to the village store on more than one occasion, and so into the hands of the hatters. Again, James Byers and Company, in Springfield, Massachusetts, advertised as early as December, 1788, that they had for sale at their furnace and store various tools and utensils "for which Pearl and Potashes . . . Beef, Pork, Woolen and Linen Check, Country made Hats and Shoes, Old Pewter and West India Goods will be received in payment."[2] These illustrations will suffice to make clear the three lines of contact described earlier. English and West India goods, violins and flutes, china teasets, etc., may stand for the contact with foreign ports and seaboard city merchants; the wood, grain, flaxseed, potash, etc., represent trade with nearby farmers; while hats, shoes, saddles, and the like are for the most part the work of village craftsmen.[3] It should be noted that some of

---

[2] Cited by Miss Blanche E. Hazard, *Organization of the Boot and Shoe Industry in Massachusetts before 1875*, pp. 31–32. See comment on this book below. Other country store advertisements or descriptive accounts illustrating the functions of the storekeeper in the earliest phases of his contact with local manufacture appear on pp. 55–56, 81–82, and 183–200 of this work.

[3] Some of the "country" produce may of course have been brought in by villagers, most of whom did some farming even when they engaged largely in some other occupation. The use of the term "country-made" in connection with hats and shoes would at this time have meant "locally-made" or "village-made" as distinct

the country produce included raw materials for possible local manufacture and that most of the manufactured goods mentioned, and not obviously imported, were such as pioneer farmers could secure only with difficulty, if at all, when not purchased at the store. Thus, potash and pearl ashes were utilized in glass manufacture, and in bleaching and dyeing cloth, as well as for household soapmaking. Furbearing skins were used in making felt for men's hats. The woolen and linen check might come from either farm or village. Farmers sometimes brought tallow candles, tow cloth, butter, cheese, home-wrought nails, flax for the manufacture of shoe thread, and indeed a surprising variety of goods in exchange for what the store carried. Likewise, the local artisans left with the storekeeper a considerable variety of manufactured goods, their nature depending upon the available resources of the community and the location of the town with respect to trade currents. Here, then, was the necessary beginning for a manufacturing organization that depended upon more than merely casual sales of farm-produced materials and locally manufactured products. It needed for development only better means of inland transportation to connect the westward-moving population with the seaports and the growing river ports of the West and South, and to make easier the shipment of goods between the New England ports and the inland towns of that region. Water transportation was already well developed.

It was not long before the taking of local manufactures in the course of trade became a regular practice in every town which had easy access to the outside world or to a growing backcountry region. In shoemaking, this has been admirably described by Miss Blanche E. Hazard.[4] One illustration from another source will suffice to show how the transition from the earliest phase to the next one took place in at least one community. In Georgetown, Massachusetts, about 1810, Benjamin and Joseph Little

opened a store and shoe factory [*sic*] . . . and began by various devices . . . to attract travel from the old Haverhill road. . . . They kept an extensive stock of salable goods, were ready to barter, taking in exchange odd lots of coarse shoes by the dozen pairs, which farmers brought there from Newbury and other places, some coming a long distance on foot, with shoes under their arms, the work of their off-hours, rainy days, and evenings.[5]

---

from imported or city-made hats and shoes. It would not mean "farm-made." Later, it did acquire this latter meaning in the shoe industry.

[4] Hazard, *op. cit.* This monograph is without equal as a study of a specialized industry in a more or less specialized industrial area. Every phase of the development described in this paper can be found in this much written-about industry in Massachusetts.

[5] Nelson, in D. H. Hurd, *History of Essex County* (Philadelphia, 1888), p. 834. Shoe manufacture had progressed farther away from simple handicraft organization at this time than any other nonfactory industry in the United States, with the possible exception of hatting. The form of organization here described had a

How regular exchange between merchant and artisan developed in shoe-making from beginning to end may be read in Miss Hazard's monograph.

In hat manufacture, regular contacts between storekeeper and crafts-man hatter were early established, at least in Danbury. Indeed, regular connections seem to have existed from the first. Such connections can be read in the advertisement of Joseph F. and E. M. White of Danbury, cited above. In the same year in which this advertisement appeared (1805), there appeared another, signed by "White Brothers," which ran as fol-lows: "The subscribers have for sale a quantity of good Muskrat Skins, very low for cash, or will exchange them for good unfinished Knapped Hats. Also all kinds of Hatters' trimmings. WHITE BROTHERS AND CO. N.B. The skins will be sold for 2s. 3d. cash (York currency) or 2s. 5d. in ex-change for hats." This firm may have been the same as that referred to earlier. We are told that White Brothers employed about 40 hands and that "their factory [*sic*] was the largest of any in the country at that time." Some light is thrown on the situation by the statement that about 1808–09, "there were fifty-six hat shops in the township of Danbury averaging from three to five men each." One may guess that the 40 hands of White Brothers and Company got other supplies than those for making hats from their employers. At any rate, it is clear that there existed a regular trade in hats and hat materials, involving hatters on the one side and merchants on the other, hats being exchanged for materials, and prob-ably for groceries and other supplies, at a fixed rate in at least one case. Such a situation amounts to a piece-wage contract between a merchant who has become, in fact, an employer of workmen and an ostensibly in-dependent worker who has, in reality, lost all control of the price-fixing function in his trade.

Other industries furnish clearer illustrations. In Lee, Massachusetts, in the western part of the state, "lumber constituted the chief article of export, the farmers transporting it by horse power to Hudson [N.Y.?] and bringing back salt, molasses, sugar, and other groceries." This was a regu-lar trade in which other communities shared. Similarly, in Exeter, New Hampshire, which, like most New England towns at one time or an-other, engaged in the lumber industry while the forests lasted, "the traders . . . bought the timber and paid for it in merchandise. . . . The owners of farms that might have been profitable, failed to raise products enough for their own subsistence and lived upon Virginia corn and pork, which they bought from the traders." The lumber-cutting "farmers" of Exeter and vicinity even bought hay from outside through

---

counterpart in many towns in eastern Massachusetts about this time. The form of farm manufacture it implies spread a little later well up the coast of New England and inland, wherever a "manufacturer's" wagon could pass without too great difficulty to pick up the finished product and leave new uppers and soles for sew-ing and lasting before its next appearance.

the traders. Here again was an industry dependent upon regular exchange with the village merchants.

A similar development apparently overtook the coopering trade in Hingham, Massachusetts. Since it was involved in the New England fisheries, it felt the effects of the West India trade and, by the beginning of the 19th century, had developed a coopering trade of some consequence which seems to have followed the usual course. Apparently, handicraft coopers, making tubs and barrels for the local fisheries, began early in the century to sell their wares outside the town. The products of the coopers' shops were gathered by the local traders, shipped by them to Boston, or sold in the backcountry by the producer or the local storekeeper.

Even in carriage making, the influence of the storekeeper may be found a little later. "In the early years of the nineteenth century," writes Thomas in *One Hundred Years of American Commerce*, "business in the old carriage towns was done on what is called the 'dicker' system." Woodworkers, blacksmiths, trimmers, painters, each did business on his own account, and swapped parts, as they termed it, the final settlements being made in finished carriages. The dealer in materials also took carriages in payment. Many storekeepers carried carriage trimmings along with groceries, took payments in carriages, and sometimes went from storekeeping into the manufacture of carriages under the merchant-manufacture system. Success in carriage making—in Amesbury, at least—was evidently dependent upon a barter trade with a merchant who had connections with possible customers not known to the craftsmen by whom the actual work of manufacture was performed. This becomes more evident when we consider the alternative methods utilized both in Amesbury and in the neighborhood of New York City.

In Amesbury, it was long the custom for the smaller carriage manufacturers to drive their finished vehicles, peddler fashion, through the surrounding countryside, offering them for sale as they went. Indeed, this practice lasted until after 1850, when Amesbury firms began to establish repositories in Boston. In the twenties, it was the practice of country chaise makers, in the vicinity of New York City, including many from Connecticut, to drive each completed vehicle to the city, where it was auctioned from sidewalk stands in front of Trinity Church and in the general vicinity of Wall and Water streets. This practice was too inconvenient to last, however; and the larger manufacturers, who began to establish repositories as early as 1823, drove out the smaller independent traders here, as they did later in Amesbury.

In this industry the village storekeeper appears as a dealer in specialties related to the trade along with his business as a general storekeeper or grocer. Here also, he serves as a distributive channel for the finished product as well, but he seems to have been less important in this respect to the development of the carriage industry than he was in the history of shoe manufacture. Carriages constituted too bulky and too valuable a product to be handled to any extent on any large market and for any long period by small nonspecialized dealers. Their manufacture involved both too much working capital and too large a supply of labor for the small dealer on a large competitive market.

The second phase of the transition from handicraft to merchant-manufacture thus brought the village storekeeper into a position of dominance, so far as his own community was concerned. He was in reality, however, at the parting of the ways. In shoemaking, hatting, and carriage making, we have seen him engaged in specialized merchandising of the materials and products of the dominant industry of his neighborhood, along with his general or grocery store business. It appears to be characteristic of this phase of development in other industries as well that the storekeeper begins to specialize in the interests of manufacture. As merchant-manufacture developed to its fullest form, specialization became the rule. Markets for the new ready-made goods grew rapidly. Men from various walks of life began to enter the manufacturing business as capitalist entrepreneurs, and competition became exceedingly keen. It became a necessary requisite for success to cut the costs of manufacture in every possible way.

The average village storekeeper was as ill-suited to meet the new needs as the average inland village was to become a great manufacturing center. Small towns and small stores alike dwindled in relative importance as the seaboard and river cities expanded; and many of the manufacturing enterprises they had fostered moved away to the rising factories in the larger towns or fell into the hands of larger merchants, who used the storekeeper only as a distributing agent for the "putting out" of materials and the collecting of goods from workers in his neighborhood, the storekeeper being no longer in reality an entrepreneur in the industry. In some of the larger towns the local manufacturing capitalists arranged with him to serve them as a kind of paymaster, through the use of a system of "store pay" by which the workers were paid in orders on some more or less subsidiary store for such supplies as they needed rather than in cash. Storekeepers who became primarily manufacturers, as many of them did, frequently kept their stores alive for this latter purpose, undoubtedly turning an extra profit in most cases by this practice, since they bought at wholesale and sold to their employees at retail.

The village storekeeper thus found himself confronted by three alternatives. He might give up storekeeping as his major occupation and become primarily a manufacturer, either in his own town or in some neighboring and more promising location. He might give up manufacturing and go back to storekeeping as his primary business. Or he might occupy an intermediate position, remaining partly a general storekeeper and becoming in part a local distributing center for some large manu- facturer in a larger town. In most communities, he had been obliged to make his choice some time before the panic of 1837. His part in the de- velopment of manufacture was thus a transitory one; but if beginnings are important, it was an important one. How did the decline of handicraft begin? Through dealings between the storekeeper and his village and farmer customers. How did it continue? Through the development by the storekeeper, acting with the seaboard merchants and followed by local workmen from many sources, of markets outside the community. His brief ascendancy represents the beginning of industrial control by mercantile rather than craft skill, the entry of profits as against wages, and the be- ginning of the decline in economic and social status of the handworker in industry. His own decline might be said to mark the beginning of the ascendancy of "big business" over "little business," if the analogy between conditions a century ago and those of recent years be not pressed too far.

8. THE SANTA FE TRADE*

The Santa Fe trade flourished between 1821, the year of Mexican independence, and 1843. It illustrates the ways in which a marketing system is both conditioned by and influences its environment. As early as 1804 an attempt was made to open a trade route between Santa Fe and St. Louis, some 300 miles closer than the Mexican port of Vera Cruz. Because of restrictive Spanish policies, no trade of any consequence could develop until Mexico won its freedom. Considerable ingenuity and enterprise were displayed in developing the Santa Fe market. The 700–mile trip was fraught with peril, and government officials in Santa Fe were either hostile to Americans or interested in enriching themselves at the traders' expense.

THE "COMMERCE OF THE PRAIRIES" was unique in American history and owed its origin to the condition of commercial isolation which existed in New Mexico prior to the coming of the Americans. In spite of the extreme paucity of geographical knowledge of the country between New Mexico and the Missouri in the earlier years of the century, in spite also of the jealous surveillance of the Spanish government over the domestic affairs of her colonies and the careful exclusion of all knowledge concerning them from the outside world, certain facts had become known to the American merchants of St. Louis and the settlements along the lower Missouri. It was clear that the Missouri River near the mouth of the Kansas was much nearer to Santa Fe than was Vera Cruz, whence all imported fabrics reached that inland town. Inasmuch as there was continuous navigation from American and foreign ports to St. Louis and even to the mouth of the Kansas, nearly 300 miles farther west, it was an obvious proposition that traders from the Missouri could import goods to Santa Fe more cheaply than could the Mexicans themselves by way of Vera Cruz. The only uncertainty in the matter related to the duties the Spaniards might levy upon imports. If these were reasonable, then it was evident that the advantage of trade would lie with the Americans. These considerations led to attempts, as early as 1804, to open trade relations between St. Louis and Santa Fe. They were renewed at intervals, but always unsuccessfully, until the overthrow of Spanish power in Mexico. The trade then began to develop rapidly into a flourishing commerce which continued with little interruption until Santa Fe became an

---

* Reprinted from Hiram M. Chittenden, *The American Fur Trade of the Far West* (2 vols.; New York: Francis P. Harper, 1912), pp. 519–29.

American city. It will be considered here in reference to the character of the traffic, the method of conducting the caravans, and the conditions encountered in Santa Fe.

"The town of Franklin on the Missouri river . . . seems truly to have been the cradle of our trade," says Josiah Gregg, the historian of the Santa Fe Trail. Franklin was the first town of importance in the celebrated tract of western Missouri known as Boone's Lick. It has now been entirely washed into the river, while on the opposite shore has arisen the thriving town of Boonville. At the time when the Santa Fe trade commenced, Franklin was the most important town of Missouri west of St. Louis, and the first to establish a newspaper. It was 205 miles by river above the mouth of the Missouri and 187 below the mouth of the Kansas. The earlier expeditions to Santa Fe after 1820 nearly all started from this locality, and were made by residents of the Boone's Lick country. But as the trade grew in importance, as steamboats began to ascend the Missouri, and particularly as traders from other points began to engage in the trade, the starting place was gradually transferred to that point on the Missouri which was nearest to Santa Fe. Independence, Missouri, near the mouth of the Kansas, began to be an outfitting point as early as 1827. In the course of the next six years the Missouri River destroyed the steamboat landing, and the boats had to go farther up where there was a convenient and permanent bank. Here arose Westport Landing, and a few miles back, Westport itself, which from that time began to draw a share of the outfitting trade from Independence. By 1831, Franklin had almost entirely lost its hold as the starting place for the caravans, which thenceforth was permanently fixed in the neighborhood of the mouth of the Kansas. The trail to the mountains also started from this point, and the growing volume of the mountain trade still further augmented the importance of this early rendezvous.

The goods taken to Santa Fe in trade comprised almost every variety that are made use of in everyday life. There were dry goods, silks, hardwares, calicoes, velvets, drillings, shirtings, etc.; but domestic cottons constituted fully half the cargo. The trade extended beyond Santa Fe, and in later years a large portion of it was carried to Chihuahua, and some even to California. From this last region were brought horses and mules, which thus found their way from the distant Pacific to the Mississippi Valley and possibly even farther east. The furs from the Colorado mountains were frequently brought in by way of the trail either by traders who had purchased them or by the trappers who joined the caravans for protection. The most important item in the return cargo was specie, both gold and silver, which was transported in large quantities to the states. The magnitude of the Santa Fe trade at one time rose to about $450,000 per annum. For the 22 years from 1822 to 1843, inclusive, it averaged over $130,000, or nearly $3 million for the period.

In a business of so hazardous and uncertain a character the profits must necessarily have been large to justify a pursuit of it. The goods were mostly bought in eastern markets and were sold at a great advance, often more than 100 percent upon the first cost. But by the time the sales were accomplished and the various expenses and losses in transporting them so far were deducted, the net profits rarely exceeded 40 percent and were frequently as low as 10 percent. There were, of course, occasional instances of actual loss.

A striking characteristic of the Santa Fe trade was its division among a great number of proprietors. It was a business of small dealers, and no "American Fur Company" followed the Santa Fe Trail. Not infrequently, individuals took with them all they possessed; and as the enterprises were generally profitable, the trade was undoubtedly a great benefit. Often, individuals would secure credits by mortgages upon their property until their return in the fall. If, as occasionally happened, the Santa Fe market proved dull and it required considerable time to get rid of one's cargo by retail, these home obligations enforced a resort to the less profitable method by wholesale in order that the business might terminate in time for the trader to get back home and satisfy his creditors.

While there is no reason to doubt the substantial accuracy of the figures heretofore given concerning the Santa Fe trade, there were those at the time who ridiculed its importance. To give a fair hearing to both sides, however, the following comments will be of value. They are the substance of a spirited protest which appeared in the *Missouri Republican* of St. Louis, February 16, 1830, against a statement which had been made upon the floor of Congress that the trade of 1829 had amounted to $200,000 and was deserving of government protection. The writer had procured an estimate from those who alone knew anything about it; $133,000 and 900 of the 1,200 mules which were brought back belonged to Spanish refugees who were with the caravan and were daily expecting a decree for their return. The specie amounted to between $20,000 and $30,000, about twice the cost of the military escort, which did not prevent the loss of an estimable trader who was killed by the Indians. The furs belonged mostly to traders who came in with the caravan for protection and whose property represented the fruit of two or three years' toil.

A majority of the traders invest in the trade from $100 to $600; these *capitalists* live cheaply upon buffalo meat, and improve their habits and morals among the, in every way, vicious and lascivious inhabitants of Santa Fe. . . . *It will not be denied* that most of the traders are professedly smugglers. Others deceive the ignorance, or overcome by bribes the conscientious scruples, of the custom house officer, the agents of the republic of Mexico. Ought this trade to be protected by the government?

Nevertheless, the trade was one of considerable magnitude and genuine importance. It was as honestly conducted as any business could be which had to do with Spanish officials. It was an unquestioned blessing to the isolated community penned up in the mountains, and it was a source of revenue to a great many worthy American citizens. So important had it become to the New Mexicans that when a decree prohibiting it was promulgated in 1843, Gregg predicted that unless the decree was speedily withdrawn, revolution would follow.

The most interesting feature of the Santa Fe trade was that which related to the long journey over the plains. The distance from Independence to Santa Fe was over 700 miles; and except for the last 50 miles, no permanent abode of civilized man greeted the eye of the traveler. Much of the intervening territory was prairie country, some of it a barren, sandy, trackless desert, where lack of water was an ever-present peril. All of it, except a narrow strip at either end, was infested with some of the most treacherous and restless Indians to be found west of the Mississippi. So real were the perils of these long journeys that it was extremely hazardous for small parties to undertake them alone. The traders early formed the practice of banding together for mutual protection, over at least the most dangerous part of the journey. Hence arose the custom of forming caravans which every year crossed the plains in each direction.

The traders, being of a very independent class, were averse to sinking their individuality in a general organization except when danger positively compelled it; and they therefore deferred the caravan formation to the latest possible moment. From Independence, they set off by themselves and went on in this way 150 miles to Council Grove. Here, for many years, the caravans were organized, for beyond this point attacks might be looked for from the savages.

The first step in the organization was to select officers. In the larger caravans the list was quite extensive, including captain, first and second lieutenants, marshal, clerk, pilot, court (three members), commander of guards, and chaplain. For captain, it was customary to select an experienced plainsman, bold and fearless, yet of cool judgment. These qualities, however, were rarely so conspicuous as to indicate any one man for exclusive choice; and as a result, there was a goodly amount of electioneering. The American of the plains could not shake off the training of his native country, and these elections usually proceeded by the most approved American methods. "One would have supposed," says Gregg, "that electioneering and party spirit would hardly have penetrated so far into the wilderness; but so it was. Even in our little community we had our office-seekers and their political adherents, as earnest and devoted as any of the modern school of politicians in the midst of civilization."

Not only in the work of effecting an organization, but in the organization itself, the patriotic trader patterned after the institutions of his beloved country. Augustus Storrs, referring to the expedition of 1827, says: "Our government is almost as complete and perfect as though we composed a republican government; we can never forget the blessings of our own institutions; and I have no doubt that the longer we are absent the more forcibly this idea will occur to us." In truth, the fires of patriotism burned ever brightly on the prairies and in the mountains, and no wandering band was so benighted as to forget to render honor to the institutions of their country wherever the anniversary of its natal day overtook them. Upon such occasions the entire resources of the party were called into requisition—artillery (when there was any), oratory, and games of skill—while the celebration was rounded off in true prairie style with the most ample feast and frolic which buffalo meat and alcohol could produce.

The authority of the captain was very limited, and his orders were obeyed only according to the whim of the individual, who generally considered himself as good a captain as anyone. There was a notable absence of anything like discipline except in the matter of guards, and the captain's functions were practically limited to fixing hours of starting and stopping and the location of camp. The result was that these organizations were always subject to greater danger from the Indians than would be a similar body of troops. Although the members were generally armed, there was no system of inspection to compel them to keep their arms in order, and they were likely to be found *hors de combat* when suddenly required for use.

The caravans, if large, were organized into divisions, each under charge of a subofficer whose duty it was to superintend the details of the march, select the best creek crossings, and look after the arrangements for the evening camp. Guard duty was relentlessly enforced; and no members of the party, except officers and invalids, were exempt.

The composition of the caravans was the most heterogeneous imaginable. The vehicles consisted of heavy wagons, carts, and light carriages. There were occasionally elegant outfits on the road. "It has the air of romance," says an early writer, "to see splendid pleasure carriages with elegant horses journeying to the Republic of Mexico! Yet it is sober fact." The draught animals were horses, mules, and oxen. There were always a large number of saddle horses. In personnel, the caravans were composed of all sorts. There was first the plain man of business, intent only on the prosecution of his enterprise. There were the rough denizens of the plains who, in long years of living in these unsettled wilds, had become half Indian in dress, habits, and general appearance. There were pleasure seekers, health seekers, scientific travelers, and now and then ladies. Then there was always the picturesque Mexican, with a dress peculiarly his own, even when, as was generally to some extent the case, there was a marked absence of any dress. The equipment of the party was likewise of no common pattern; and there were as many varieties of dress, saddles, and firearms as there were of men, wagons, and animals. "The wild and motley aspect of the caravan," as Gregg well observes, "would have formed an excellent subject for an artist's pencil."

The progress of these huge caravans was always slow, and rarely averaged more than 15 miles a day. The location of springs and creeks determined the length of march, for water could not be found wherever wanted. At night the caravans were generally parked in some form suited to the ground and the necessities of defense. The danger from Indians was always a serious one to small parties, but never to large ones, except when small groups were carelessly permitted to get away from the support of the main body. Gregg says that "in the course of twenty years since the commencement of this trade I do not believe there have been a dozen deaths upon the Santa Fe route, even including those who have been killed off by disease as well as by the Indians." While this may have been strictly true of the Sante Fe traders, it is certain that the casualties upon the plains among the smaller parties greatly exceeded this number.

The scene of bustle and confusion during the hasty preparation of each morning for the day's march, when animals were being saddled or harnessed, fastened to the wagons, and everything gotten ready for the start, was something to be long remembered by those who had once seen it. As a general thing, the best of spirits prevailed among the party, and there was a friendly rivalry not to be the last in the performance of duty. All writers agree that the sight of these huge caravans in motion was a most interesting one—truly American in its individuality, variety, and independence. The line, when in single file, often stretched out for more than a mile in length. At other times, upon the broad, even prairies, where the whole country was one vast road, the caravan would form in three or four parallel columns, thus giving the appearance of greater compactness and strength. The motion of this large body, with the scattering groups of horsemen on its flanks or in advance, the shouting of the drivers, the incessant cracking of the whips, and the jolting and creaking of the wagons, all combined to form a medley of sights and sounds that never failed to excite the enthusiasm of the beholder.

The election of officers having taken place at Council Grove, everyone exerted himself to get into the best possible state of preparation for the long journey that lay before him. The goods perhaps required repacking, and the greatest ingenuity was shown in placing the packages in the wagons so that they would not jolt with the constant shaking of the several hundred miles of travel. Wood was gathered from the ample supply in Council Grove and strapped underneath the wagons for use in case of breakages. Over the tops and sides of the cargoes were spread sheets of thick canvas to resist rain in the driving storms of the prairies.

The caravan, upon arrival in the buffalo country, subsisted largely upon game, and the universal testimony is that these long journeys were health restorers which might have rivaled the fabulous fountains of youth which so appealed to the credulity of the early Spanish adventurers. The only really serious problem of subsistence en route related to provision for water in crossing the Cimarron desert. There was stretches of the journey where from one to four days had to be passed without water, depending upon the speed of the traveler and his knowledge of the location of springs. All the later caravans carried enough water with them from the Arkansas to get them safely through this region.

The first evidence of approach to the Spanish settlements would usually be the meeting of some lonely cibolero, or Mexican buffalo hunter. The picturesque costumes of these denizens of the prairies was in itself an attraction that made the meeting of more than passing interest, but the fact that they brought news from Santa Fe made their welcome one of genuine enthusiasm. The great subject of inquiry from these prairie news agents was the state of the customhouse administration, for upon this depended in no slight degree the success or failure of the enterprise. A few of the most experienced traders generally posted ahead as soon as it was safe to leave the caravan, in order to arrange all this troublesome business in advance of the main arrival.

The entry of the caravan into Santa Fe was, of course, an event of very lively interest. The long sojourn in the uninhabited prairies was in itself enough to make an approach to civilized abodes a matter of no ordinary importance. It was the end of a long and tedious journey, and the beginning of a long and luxurious rest; for the life of the caravan employees while in Santa Fe was a continuous round of conviviality. Before entering the city, one—even to the lowest employee—did his best to improve his personal appearance. He subjected his hair and beard to such barbering as the rude conveniences of the plains afforded and made himself as irresistible as possible in the eyes of the dusky maidens of Santa Fe. Even the animals, as Gregg observes, caught the spirit of the occasion and however much they might have lagged of late, now pricked up their ears and bent forward under their heavy loads with quick and elastic step.

The joy of these sunbrowned travelers was reciprocated by the inhabitants of Santa Fe, to whom the caravan was like the arrival of a ship at some solitary island of the sea. Pouring out into the streets, they would announce the event with shouts of "The wagons! The Americans! The arrival of the caravan!" And at once, in a spirit of fraternity which knows no frontier lines or national jealousies, they would join with their American visitors in joyous celebration of the event.

The traders attended at once to the serious business of their visit. The goods were entered at the customhouse with the least possible delay and were then exhibited for sale. They were generally closed out at retail, but it often became necessary in a dull market to sell in bulk in order to get ready for the return caravan. Many of the traders were compelled to stay more than a season and often went to other points, so that the return caravans were rarely more than half as large as the outgoing.

The Santa Fe end of the business was thoroughly characteristic of the government and people of that country. Both the Spanish and the Mexican authorities always exhibited a jealousy of their northern neighbors that would gladly have interdicted the trade altogether, but the extreme isolation of the remote northern province made commerce with the United States almost indispensable to the domestic welfare of the people, while it was a source of considerable revenue to the government. The customs restrictions upon the trade were always heavy, often capricious, and were a never-ending source of annoyance to the traders. They were the subject of most anxious inquiry as the caravans approached Santa Fe, for changes might have transpired since the latest information which would make or ruin an enterprise. The extreme venality of the customhouse officers led to all kinds of peculation and bribery, and it has been estimated that not more than one half of the revenue receipts found their way to the public treasury. It was a common saying that the duties on American goods went one third to the traders, one third to the officials, and one third to the government. Between smuggling and bribery, the trader must have felt that he had left behind him in his native land all semblance of virtue in the transaction of business.

In 1839, Governor Armigo conceived the brilliant idea that by placing an arbitrary impost on each wagon that entered the territory, regardless of its cargo, he would avoid the official corruption and smuggling which diverted from its proper destination so much of the revenue. This impost he fixed at $500. But however carefully he may have figured out the proper amount to charge, he totally failed to foresee the consequences of his act. Traders at once increased enormously the size of the wagonloads by using stronger wagons and more teams to each, rejecting largely the bulky, coarse stuffs of small value and loading with fine fabrics of higher value. The impost was thus made to operate as a great reduction of the former tariff and was quickly abrogated by the governor.

The customs regulations, which had shifted about so often in the course of 20 years, and which had already excluded many articles of great importance to the trade, finally in 1843 prohibited the trade altogether. It was a blind and fatal error, an expiring effort to stay the tide of destiny. It only served to make the people of New Mexico more dissatisfied with so capricious and oppressive a government and caused them to accept with greater readiness the always difficult change from one sovereignty to another.

9. MIDDLEMEN IN DOMESTIC TRADE, 1800–1860*

Middlemen operating during this period served a predominantly agricultural society that was experiencing rapid population growth, increased urbanization, and marked improvements in transportation. At the opening of the 19th century the principal forms of retailing included general stores, public markets, and peddlers. General stores predominated, but almost any community of size had a public market. The peddlers were oftentimes artisans selling their own wares in nearby rural areas. The majority of merchants sold at wholesale and retail, for insufficient volume generally precluded specialization. The auction developed in some lines of trade and threatened the established channel of importer–jobber–retailer. Similarly, other marketing institutions underwent considerable change or development during the next half century.

THE SYSTEM OF MIDDLEMEN that existed in the United States at the opening of the 19th century was designed to serve a country whose markets were small, whose transportation and communication facilities were undeveloped, and whose industrial organization was in the household stage. Agriculture was by far the most important economic activity. As a result, the large majority of manufactured goods were obtained from those countries whose industrial development was more advanced. The volume of goods required from these countries was sufficient to permit some merchants to sell at wholesale only; but a great many merchants found this not to be the case, and consequently they sold at retail and wholesale. In some instances the volume of business was sufficient to permit the merchants to take advantage of the economies of specialization; and in the case of dry goods, some merchants went so far as to specialize in kinds of dry goods. The retail merchants, however, were supplying a market which was too small to permit any specialization. To make up the assortments desired by the retailers, there existed a class of middlemen known as jobbers. Thus the trade channel for a great deal of foreign textiles was importer–jobber–retailer–consumer.

The auction system that developed after the War of 1812 seriously challenged this trade channel. The restrictive policy followed by the

* Reprinted from Fred M. Jones, *Middlemen in the Domestic Trade of the United States, 1800–1860* (Urbana: University of Illinois Press, 1937), pp. 64–68.

government both before and during the war shut off from the domestic markets most of the foreign supplies. Consequently, the condition of the market was such that it could absorb a large amount of goods. The quickest method of sale for the foreign merchant or manufacturer was to have an agent accompany the merchandise; upon his arrival, the agents placed the goods in the hands of an auctioneer for sale. The auctions were well attended by the retailers, and the consequence was a tendency to eliminate the importer and the jobber.

Merchants and manufacturers preferred the auction method of sale because of certain advantages it offered over others. In the first place, it offered the advantages of a quick sale of large quantities of goods, and thus the advantages of a larger scale of production could be realized. Capital was released and was ready for a new turnover. It was not necessary to assume the risks of bad debts, and the risks of style obsolescence and physical depreciation were reduced. Moreover, it was not necessary to maintain a continuous sales organization. Likewise, it was not necessary to incur certain other expenses which were connected with maintaining a permanent establishment. Also, the auction was a convenient method for disposing of end-of-season stocks and for closing out consignments. For short periods, it was probably more economical to continue production and sell at auction than to cease operations. The auction method also offered an opportunity to test the market both for price and for new styles.

The importers and jobbers, however, did not sit idly by and watch this serious inroad on the business it had been customary for them to control. From 1817 to 1830, particularly in New York City, they opposed auctions with petitions, pamphlets, and ballots. After 1830, however, the movement against auctions subsided. In the first place, the opponents were not successful in getting a bill passed by Congress to prohibit or seriously restrict auctions. Furthermore, some of the importers and jobbers had been eliminated in the struggle, and others switched their attention from foreign to domestic products. The products of the domestic textile industry were sold through selling agents; and consequently, fewer American goods were sold at auction. Interior cities began to develop as wholesale centers, and this had a tendency to keep business from going to the auctions in the eastern cities. Improvements in transportation and communication brought about by steam navigation made it easier for foreign merchants and manufacturers to establish contacts with jobbers in the United States. Buyers, too, preferred to buy at private sale because of the longer term of credit available. All of these causes—and in addition, the fraud or alleged fraud practiced at the auctions—contributed to reduce the importance of auctions.

The factor, like the auctioneer and broker, was an agent-middleman. Factors were more numerous, however, than either auctioneers or brokers.

The number of auctioneers was limited by the state legislatures, and since the function of the broker is merely to bring buyers and sellers together for purposes of negotiation, there were but few of them at the opening of the 19th century, for most of the markets were not so large that buyers and sellers could not easily establish contact with each other. When the producer or merchant was at a distance from the wholesale markets and made infrequent trips to them, there was an economy in having an agent who had information as to the location of buyers and sellers, their credit standing, the market price, places and rates of storage, transportation facilities, and sources of financial aid. The factor or commission merchant furnished this information.

The textile industry early made use of commission merchants, who in this industry came to be known as selling agents. Their method of operation in 1860 still resembled very much that of general commission merchants. At first, they usually had possession of the merchandise they sold; later, this was not always the case. As a whole, they were probably more efficient distributors of textile products than general commission merchants were or could have been, as they specialized in the distribution of textiles. They usually charged only 1 percent as a selling commission, whereas the commission merchants charged 2½ percent. They were in a better position to know the demands of the market than were the general commission merchants. On the other hand, they got control of the companies for which they acted as selling agents; and in some cases, they manipulated them in such a manner that the stockholders were not benefited. They did not subject themselves to much risk except when they made advances to their clients and when they determined the style and patterns their clients were to produce. In such a case, if they interpreted the market incorrectly and had the wrong styles produced, they were faced with reduced commissions and an impairment of any investment they had in their client companies.

At the opening of the 19th century the principal means for selling at retail were general stores, public markets, and peddlers. The general store was designed for small markets that were served by slow means of transportation. The principal method of sale was exchange of goods for goods. In many cases, there was no other outlet for the surplus products of a community. This, of course, gave the general store an advantage; but this advantage was balanced, to an extent at least, against the increased risk it was necessary to assume. If the general storekeeper accepted grain for his merchandise, he had to assume the full risk of price declines as long as he held it. The same was true of cotton and other products, as facilities for hedging did not exist. A heavier risk also accompanied the relatively longer period of credit, which often extended from one crop to another. If the crops failed, the storekeeper might fail. In the earlier years of the century the country storekeeper often transported not only the produce he collected from the farmers but also the merchandise he purchased in the wholesale centers, thus assuming the risks of transportation. But as common carriers such as steamboats, canals, and railroads developed, more of the transportation risk was shifted. Common carriers were regarded as insurers of the property entrusted to them and were held responsible for all acts against the merchandise, acts of God and the public enemy only excepted.

Some specialty stores existed in the commercial and agricultural economy that prevailed in the United States at the opening of the last century; and with the development of domestic industry, more appeared. Previous to 1860, some attention had been given to departmental organization, but department stores would thrive only in an economy that required large-scale retail distribution. Chain stores were also created but could not exist without a relatively fast transportation system, intense competition which would induce economies in organization, and facilities for accumulating large amounts of capital.

Public markets and peddlers were two other methods of selling at retail. By the opening of the 19th century, every town of any size had at least one public market, but by 1860 the importance of public markets had begun to decline. At other points, meat shops were beginning to establish themselves because the cities had grown so large that the location of public markets had become inconvenient for many consumers.

Some artisans found that the most advantageous method of distributing their products was to carry them, either personally or by agents, directly to the customer. Peddling was carried on not only by land but by water as well. It was well adapted to a community that lacked roads and to one whose inhabitants were for the most part located along the waterways.

The chief kind of legislation affecting middlemen was licensing laws. In some instances the license fees charged peddlers were so high as to amount to a prohibition. Public markets were established, administered, and regulated in detail by the municipal governments. The time when business could be conducted by auctioneers, as well as the place at which they might carry it on, was regulated. Limitations in some instances were placed on the rate of commission that could be charged. It was also customary to tax sales at auction.

During the period covered in this study, the various middlemen attempted to adapt themselves to the changing economic conditions. The factors that had the greatest influence in this adaptation were changes in the source of supply, changes in the markets, and improvements in transportation and communication facilities.

PART II

Marketing in America, 1790-1860

B. THE CHARACTER AND COMPOSITION OF RETAIL TRADE

1. RETAILING DEVELOPMENT AND PRACTICES*

In this selection the author discusses the operations between 1800 and 1860 of the general store, the specialty store, the department store, and the chain store. Trade relationships with supply sources, sales promotion practices, the number of retail outlets, and the legislative framework of retailing are described. Of particular interest is the review of conditions facilitating establishment of the specialized retailing firms and dry goods stores which were forerunners of department stores. Among the environmental factors and economic conditions affecting retail sales promotion were the popularity of auctions as a method of wholesaling, the absence of production standards, the changing role of advertising, and the sporadic availability of merchandise. The selection portrays the adaptive, even opportunistic, character of retailing during this period.

In the opening years of the 19th century the general store was the typical retail store in the United States. In the back settlements and western country, rarely was any other kind found. As its name implies, its stock consisted of a wide range of articles. Thomas Ashe, traveling in western Pennsylvania in 1806, observed:

> These storekeepers are obliged to keep every article which it is possible that the farmer and manufacturer may want. Each of their shops exhibits a complete medley; a magazine where are to be had both a needle and an anchor, a tin pot and a large copper boiler, a child's whistle and a pianoforte, a ring dial and a clock, a skein of thread and trimmings of lace, a check frock and a muslin gown, a frieze coat and a superfine cloth, a glass of whiskey and barrel of brandy, a gill of vinegar and a hogshead of Madeira wine, &c.

The stock of the general store was necessarily of this nature because of the character of the demand of the local market. The wants of the villagers and settlers were relatively few, and these they often satisfied by fireside and home industries. The demand for any particular class of commodities was insufficient to permit specialization in one or even a few lines.

While these early stores carried a wide variety of articles, their entire stocks, if the stores of St. Louis were typical, were relatively small. "A

* Reprinted from Fred M. Jones, *Middlemen in the Domestic Trade of the United States, 1800–1860* (Urbana: University of Illinois Press, 1937), pp. 44–58.

place occupying but a few feet square would contain all of their goods, and indeed, during the period of the first growth of St. Louis, a merchant kept all of his goods in a chest or box, which was opened whenever a purchaser would appear. Sugar, coffee, gunpowder, blankets, paint, spice, salt, knives, hatchets, guns, kitchen-ware, hunting-shirts, and every variety of coarse dry goods, were stored together." Finery such as millinery could not be carried to any extent. The reason for this and the smallness of the stock as a whole was the difficulty and expense of transportation. In 1819 the cost of transporting merchandise from Baltimore to Zanesville, Ohio, was $10 per hundredweight, and at any time from the first settlement of the Ohio Valley to about 1820 the cost per hundredweight from Philadelphia to Pittsburgh was from $5 to $7.50.

The scarcity of money in the West was almost proverbial. Ashe writes: "I do not conceive that I assert too much, though it may be surprising to you, in saying, that the entire business of these waters is conducted without the use of money." Money which did come into the hands of the villagers and settlers soon found its way to the hands of the storekeeper, who remitted it east to make payments; and since the balance of payments was usually against the West, the money did not return. In addition, the inhabitants were afraid that what money was presented to them for acceptance might be counterfeit. Consequently, the operations of the stores were largely on the basis of exchange of goods for goods, but to say that their entire business was transacted on this basis would be to overstate the fact. There were certain articles that were called cash articles and could not be purchased except with money. A pioneer stated: "These were mostly tea, coffee, etc. Leather, iron, powder, lead and like articles were also of this class. These things could not be bartered for with the produce of the country, except a few products that were treated as of cash value. Among them were linen, cloth, feathers, beeswax, deerskins, and furs, which were not too heavy to transport, and would be taken by wholesale dealers for goods."

As a result of their bartering operations, the storekeepers found that when it came time to replenish their stocks, they had little cash and much local produce with which to pay the importer or manufacturer. The merchants and manufacturers, if they were to distribute their products to the general stores, necessarily had to accept as pay the goods the general stores had to offer.

The general store continued to be the typical store of the thinly populated districts, and its method of operation did not materially change. Fifty years after Ashe made his observations, the general store was much the same as he had found it. It still did business on a barter basis, although probably not to the same extent as formerly. Manufacturers, however, were no longer confronted with the problem of accepting country produce in exchange for their products. This practice, common in 1830, had largely disappeared by the decade of the fifties. It was now customary for the general store to send produce to the so-called "produce merchants" in the larger cities.

The functions performed by the general store during the period from 1800 to 1860 were relatively more important than at a later period. With the exception of the peddler, the inhabitants of the thinly settled regions had no other source of supply, "besides rare accidents," for those goods which they required and could not produce by their own efforts.

Another function performed by the general store was that of assembling country produce. In many cases, there was no other outlet for the surplus products of a community. This, of course, gave the general store an advantage; but this advantage was balanced, to an extent at least, against the increased risk it was necessary to assume. If the general storekeeper accepted grain for his merchandise, he had to assume the full risk of price declines as long as he held it. A heavier risk also accompanied the relatively longer terms of credit which might extend from one crop to another. If the crops failed, the storekeeper might fail.

In addition to the marketing risks, the general storekeeper often bore property risks of fire and theft, for at the opening of the 19th century, there were only about 14 fire insurance companies. Outside the cities, it was many years before fire insurance became a recognized factor in commercial life.

THE SPECIALTY STORE

The tendency for the retailer to specialize had progressed to the point that by the opening of the 19th century, stores existed which handled chiefly the four lines of groceries, dry goods, hardware, and queensware. Stores handling some combination of two or three of these lines were numerous, but retail stores handling only one of the four lines were scarce. This was more true of the stores handling queensware and hardware than of those handling dry goods and groceries. The reason is probably to be found in the nature of the demand for the different articles. A more steady and larger demand exists for articles of food and clothing than for hardware and queensware. Then, too, the local blacksmith often supplied the articles of hardware.

Retail drugstores were of frequent occurrence at the opening of the century. The special knowledge required for drugs is at least a partial explanation of the appearance at this time of the retail drugstore.

The retail bookstore had also appeared, but bookstores were probably not so numerous as drugstores. The publisher of the local newspaper often conducted a book and stationery store, but most books were imported and sold by the importer at retail or in lots to the general storekeeper.

In the opening years of the century, articles of men's wear such as hosiery, hats, and handkerchiefs were often handled by any store which had a dry goods stock. In the cities, tailors made greatcoats, surtouts, vests, and pantaloons to order; while in the country, most families manufactured their own clothing. In some of the seaports, stores existed which supplied sailors with ready-made clothing; but in 1816, there were only two such stores in New York City. It was not until 1831 that a store existed in New York which dealt exclusively in men's furnishings. Until about this time the great majority of men's clothes continued to be made to order by the tailor, but this was often inconvenient. Shortly afterwards, ready-made clothing was more often found in the stocks of general stores; and a decade later, men's clothing stores were of common occurrence.

A retail shoe store at the opening of the century was a decided exception, if any were in existence. Shoes were commonly sold at retail by general stores and local shoemakers. This continued to be true until 1860. During most of this period the industry was operating under the domestic system of production. The village shoemaker gradually lost ground as more and more shoes were sold by clothing and general stores. Toward the end of the decade of the fifties the industry began to operate under the factory system of production. A few strictly retail shoe stores could be found in the larger cities, but the clothing and general stores were still dominant in the retail sale of shoes.

A retail jewelry store in the year 1800 was more an artisan's shop than a store. The work of the proprietor of such a shop involved the making of fine mechanical instruments, the repairing of watches and clocks, and the production from the precious metals of different articles of personal adornment. Because the production of such articles required a large element of skill, the trade was one that yielded only slowly, although inevitably, to factory methods of production. As the industry adopted factory methods, the craftsman manufactured less and repaired more. By 1835 the business of the local jeweler was primarily that of selling at retail and repairing watches.

The early furniture dealer was also a craftsman. Along with chairs and tables, he manufactured coffins as needed. It was only one step further to the business of an undertaker, and some early cabinetmakers added this to their regular business. Between 1815 and 1825, steam-driven machinery began to be employed in some factories, but the retail furniture store did not appear with any regularity until about 1855.

From this description of the development of the retail specialty store, it can be seen that retail dry goods, grocery, drug, hardware, and book stores could and did exist in the commercial and agricultural economy which prevailed in the United States at the opening of the last century; but such stores as retail clothing, shoe, jewelry, and furniture stores could exist only as markets widened and an industrial society developed. The specialty store was likely to have a buying advantage over the general store because the proprietor of the specialty store could make purchases in larger quantities; and also, not having as many lines to give attention to, he could become more adept in seeking out advantageous sources of supply. Likewise, it was possible for such a retailer to have a better knowledge of the merchandise itself and not only to buy but also to sell more advantageously. As a result of his being better informed both as to merchandise and as to sources of supply, risk was eliminated to a certain degree, and this aided the specialty store in offering lower prices than the general store.

THE DEPARTMENT STORE[1]

Although the department store did not exist at the opening of the 19th century, its development can be observed. Some dry goods stores and some general stores, instead of listing one item after another in their advertisements, as was common practice, arranged the articles according to groups. These groups would be indicated by a larger and different typeface, thus suggesting that retailers were thinking of departmentizing. If they arranged the merchandise according to a particular classification in their advertisements, they probably had a similar classification within the store. Until the early forties, little more was done than to classify articles and arrange them in the store according to classification. By 1847, however, one dry goods store in Philadelphia had been so systematized and departmentized as to approximate closely the modern department store.

A contemporary account says:

The amount of sales made at this store, is about $300,000 annually; each department in the store is alphabetically designated. The shelves and rows of goods in each department are numbered, and upon the tag attached to the goods, is marked the letter of the department, the number of the shelf and row on that shelf to which such piece of goods belongs. The cashier receives a certain sum extra per week, and he is responsible for all worthless money received. Books are kept, in which the sales of each clerk are entered for the day, and the salary of the clerk cast, as a per centage on each day, week and year, and, at the foot of the page, the aggregate of the sales appear, and the per centage that it has cost to effect these sales, is easily calculated for each day, month or year. The counters are designated by an imaginary color as the blue, green, brown, &c., counter. . . . The proprietor's desk stands at the farther end of the store, raised on a platform facing the front, from which he can see all the operations in each section of the retail department. From this desk run tubes, connecting with each department of the store, from the garret to the cellar, so that if a person in any department,

---

[1] For the purpose of this discussion a department store will be defined as a retail store which handles a wide variety of lines such as women's ready-to-wear and accessories, piece goods, small wares, and home furnishings, and which is organized into departments for purposes of promotion, service, accounting, and control.

either porter, retail or wholesale clerk, wishes to communicate with the employer, he can do so without leaving his station. Pages are kept in each department to take the bill of parcels, together with the money paid; and return the bill receipted, and change, if any, to the customer. So that the salesman is never obliged to leave the counter; he is at all times ready either to introduce a new article, or watch that no goods are taken from his counter, excepting those accounted for.

This store had some of the characteristics of a department store. It was organized by departments and controlled by departments, and there was some accounting by departments, but it does not appear that this store was any more than a departmentized dry goods store. Nor does it appear that even the largest retail store in New York City, Stewart's, was any more than a dry goods and clothing store organized by departments. As late as 1870 the 15 departments of Stewart's store handled only articles which were products of the textile industry.

What appears to have been a general store evolving into a department store operated in Springfield, Illinois, in 1851. Instead of heading the different classes of products simply dry goods, grocery, hardware, queensware, etc., the different groups of commodities were headed dry goods department, grocery department, and provision department. Hats, shoes, and furnishings were included in the dry goods department, while queensware and hardware were included in the grocery department. If this store had had accounting and control by departments, it could correctly have been called a department store.

It would almost be accurate to say that the department store had not appeared previous to 1860. The increased competition among retail stores was causing more attention to be given to internal economies such as departmental organization and management, but stores with a departmental organization were more likely to be general stores or dry goods stores rather than department stores. Department stores would thrive only in an economy that would require large-scale retail distribution. This could hardly be expected in a nation that did not yet have more than 10 cities of over 75,000 population.

THE CHAIN STORE

In the opening years of the last century, it was not unknown for a group of stores to be operated under a common management. Andrew Jackson, for instance, seems to have operated three or more stores in different parts of Tennessee. In the same year, 1803, James and Archibald Kane were operating a store in Albany and others in three nearby villages. These two groups of stores were general stores. They had a common ownership and management, and there was a uniformity of operation, insofar as all general stores at that time were operated alike.

A more ambitious undertaking was that of the Worthington Manufacturing Company of Worthington, Ohio, incorporated in 1811, which, in addition to operating stores, also manufactured woolen cloth, furniture, hats, caps, and other articles. Besides, it issued paper money of a kind. The stores of this company were numbered from 1 to 9. In November, 1818, price reductions of from 10 to 15 percent were offered at certain of the stores.

A chain of retail stores previous to 1860 was a decided exception. Large-scale retailing could not exist in an economy characterized by slow transportation, small markets, and small-scale production.

SOURCES OF SUPPLY

At the opening of the last century, retailers resorted chiefly to the importers and jobbers for their merchandise. They also obtained goods from auctions, craftsmen, commission merchants, manufacturers, and peddlers. After the close of the War of 1812, auctions became more important as a source of supply for retailers and for 15 years retained this importance. The rapidly fluctuating prices in the auction room required the retailer to be ever on the alert to buy at the most advantageous prices. The founder of the largest retail store previous to the Civil War, A. T. Stewart, in the early part of his career followed the auction sales closely. At the auction sales the retailers would sometimes form buying clubs. Clubs were also formed by the retailers when they purchased from the importers.

For the retailers located in the large cities the task of seeking out the various wholesale middlemen and other sources of supply was relatively less difficult than was the task of the country retailer. The retailers in the towns and villages usually had to make an annual or semiannual trip to Philadelphia, Baltimore, Boston, Charleston, New Orleans, or New York to secure fall or summer goods; but the growth of such interior cities as Cincinnati, Chicago, and St. Louis, as well as the development of the traveling representative of manufacturers and wholesalers, rendered it steadily less necessary for the western retailer to make trips east for his merchandise.

In the earlier years of the century the western retailer usually assumed more risk in connection with the transportation of his merchandise from the place of purchase to the place of sale. If the retailer provided his own means of transportation, he assumed all risks of transportation. If he employed a private carrier, some of the risk was shifted, but a private carrier could be held liable only for ordinary diligence and care. As common carriers such as steamboats, canals, and railroads developed, more of the transportation risk was shifted. Common carriers were regarded as insurers of the property entrusted to them and were held responsible for all acts against the merchandise, acts of God and the public enemy only excepted.

SALES PROMOTION

The devices used by retailers to promote the sale of merchandise during the first 60 years of the last century, although the same as those used at a later period, were decidedly undeveloped. Personal salesmanship was of course used; but if there is any truth in the great number of anecdotes related, much improvement was to be made in the ethics and efficiency of the retail salesman. In the earlier part of the century, when the quality of foreign manufactures surpassed—or at least this was the common belief—that of American manufactures, there was a temptation on the part of retail salesmen to use deception in disposing of American-made products. The lack of definite standards in production also contributed to the inefficiency of the retail salesman. Without these standards, it was difficult for the salesman, had he been so inclined, to investigate the merits of the various products handled and thus be able to serve his customers better.

Probably a more important function performed by the salesman was that of negotiating price. As a rule, at the opening of the century, retailers had no established price for their merchandise but charged what the traffic would bear. It was up to the salesman in every sale to obtain as high a price as possible; consequently, much of the time of the salesman was consumed in negotiating terms. It was some years before the one-price policy was generally adopted by retailers; its adoption by A. T. Stewart did much to secure more general acceptance for it.

Advertising in the local newspaper was another device used by the retailer to promote sales. At the opening of the century the advertisements of the retailers were nothing more than an announcement of the place of business and a more or less long list of the products kept in stock. This list of merchandise was often followed with the name of specific articles of country produce which would be accepted in payment. Almost without exception, the advertisements were confined to one column in width, with no illustrations, and the same advertisement sometimes appeared week after week. Prices almost never appeared with the articles. These advertisements, however, probably attracted as much attention as their more pretentious successors of a century later, since at the opening of the century there was less to read and the advertisements usually enjoyed a back- or front-page position.

About 1830, as a result of the lower price of paper, more illustrations began to appear in retail advertising. These illustrations, however, served to identify a particular class of stores rather than to picture a particular product. (For instance, appearing with the advertisement of a grocery store, or a store that handled groceries, would be an illustration of a barrel of liquor and a chest of tea; with the advertisement of a drug store would appear the illustration of a mortar and pestle, and with that of a bookstore an open book. When jewelry stores used an illustration, it was that of a watch.)

There appeared to be a slight tendency for advertising to become a little more aggressive in its attempt to induce readers to visit stores. In a general way, a small attempt was made to stimulate desire, but practically nothing was done toward giving a prospective buyer detailed information about a particular product. In the fifties, retail advertising was reflecting the establishment of the one-price policy. More stores were announcing its adoption and mentioning prices for particular products. Nevertheless, the newspaper advertising of retail stores remained relatively undeveloped. This was partially due to the restriction in size of individual advertisements enforced by the publishers, partially to the fact that the mechanical facilities for producing better advertisements did not exist, and partially to the fact that the competition of retailers was not such as required better advertisements.

At the opening of the century, there was not much window display. In fact, the windows were not designed for this purpose; they were equipped with shutters which in most cases were closed at night. It was not unknown, however, for windows with merchandise displayed in them to be lighted at night; but without plate glass, which was not manufactured in this country until the fifties, store windows were likely to remain unpretentious affairs.

NUMBER OF RETAILERS

The federal government passed a law in 1813 that required retailers to obtain licenses. In 1814, there were 46,021 of these licenses issued, but this does not mean that there were so many retail stores as that in the United States at that time, since the law defined as a retailer "every person who shall deal in the selling of any goods, wares, or merchandise, except such as are the growth, produce, or manufacture of the United States, and except such as are sold by the importer thereof in the original cask, case, box, or package wherein the same shall have been imported." This would seem to require those importers selling at both wholesale and retail to obtain a retail license. The law also could have applied to peddlers. It is highly improbable that there were any retailers of domestic products who could have benefited by the exception provided for them. Of the licenses issued, 15,018 were issued to retailers of wines and spirits alone.

In 1816, it was estimated by the commissioner of revenue that the duty on retailers amounted to about 1 percent of sales. On that basis the volume of retail sales for 1816 was about $81,265,000.

The only attempt by the federal government previous to 1930 to ascertain the number of retail stores in the United States was made in connection with the census of 1840. Information concerning the amount of capital invested by these stores was also secured. The results of this census show that in 1839 there were 57,565 retail stores in the United States, with $250,301,799 of capital invested. Slightly over 51 percent of both the number of stores and the amount of capital invested was in the five states of New York, Pennsylvania, Ohio, Massachusetts, and Virginia. The average amount of capital invested per store was $4,350. For the United States as a whole, there were 3.4 stores per thousand population, but there was considerable variation from this in different parts of the country. In the southern states the number per thousand population was usually less than for the United States as a whole. The reason for the smaller number of stores per thousand population in the southern states was the plantation system. Supplies were bought in large amounts when the crop was sold; and then, too, the economic condition of part of the free population was not a great deal better than that of the slaves, and they thus had little use for the services of a retail store.

LEGISLATION

The only federal legislation affecting retailers, other than retailers of liquor, passed previous to 1860 was the law of 1813 referred to above. This law was a licensing law and provided for license fees varying from $10 to $25. It was also provided that this act should remain in force until the termination of the war with Great Britain. Before that time, however, the duties were increased 50 percent. The act was finally repealed on December 23, 1817. Its purpose was to provide extra revenue required as a result of the war with Great Britain.

Among the states that had passed laws previous to 1825 requiring retailers to obtain a license were Pennsylvania, Virginia, Maryland, Missouri, Tennessee, and Louisiana. The original laws of the first three of these states applied only to retailers dealing in foreign merchandise, but subsequent legislation extended the laws to include retailers of domestic merchandise. The object of this legislation was clearly not to regulate but rather to provide additional revenue for the operation of the various state governments.

2. URBAN RETAILING IN 1850*

This short article presents an overview of retailing practices between 1800 and 1850. The most pronounced characteristic of the period was the tendency toward extreme specialization. This specialization was found not only by merchandise line, i.e., stores handling such narrow lines as hosiery and gloves, silks and ribbons; but also by function, i.e., importing firms, commission houses, wholesalers, and retailers. Other developments of the period included the emergence of the one-price policy and the gradual adoption of the "return goods" privilege by the more progressive firms.

I PROPOSE TO INTERPRET my subject rather liberally and to concentrate upon what seem to me to be some fundamental changes in retailing— ranging the whole of the 19th century, but focusing attention especially upon the years form 1850 to 1875, a period of great innovation. And please note that all my remarks have to do with American experience.

To start, then, let me sketch briefly the retailing picture in the larger American cities about 1850. In general, the principle of specialization dominated the scene: Both retail and wholesale trades were split up, by types of merchandise, into single-line or specialty stores. If you examine the advertisements and business directories of the period, you will find a really astonishing array of stores, each of which confined itself to a narrow range of goods.

Let me give some of these specialized lines by way of illustration: books; boots and shoes; carpetings; china and glassware; clothing; combs and fancy goods; cutlery and hardware; drugs; dry goods; feathers and mattresses; furniture; "gent's furnishings"; groceries; hats, caps, and furs; hosiery and gloves; house or kitchen furnishings; india rubber goods; laces and embroideries; millinery; saddles, trunks, and harness; silks and ribbons; tea and coffee; tobacco and snuff; upholstery; watchmaking and jewelry.

We have so many specialty shops today that this list may not seem significant until we realize that the dividing lines were quite sharply drawn. A drugstore confined itself to drugs in those days. Sometimes, it also carried flavoring extracts and toilet goods; and in St. Louis, it fre-

---

* Reprinted from Ralph M. Hower, "Urban Retailing 100 Years Ago," *Bulletin of the Business Historical Society,* Vol. XII (December, 1938), pp. 91–95.

quently carried varnish, paintbrushes, and window glass. But it did not sell icecream sodas, books, toys, kitchenware, groceries, and even clothing, as the corner drugstore does today. Nor did tobacco stores sell razors, books, and candy!

Sometimes, one or two lines were combined if local circumstances warranted it. The old firm of William Sherman & Co. of Providence had long carried both dry goods and crockery. Lord & Taylor had combined carpeting with dry goods, as did a few other dry goods stores. As a general rule, however, stores specialized in particular lines of merchandise.

The absence of anything like the modern department store is especially noteworthy. In small towns and villages, of course, there was the general store—a type still familiar to anyone who is acquainted with rural communities today; but by 1850, it had already disappeared from such large cities as Boston, New York, Philadelphia, and St. Louis.

Urban firms in 1850 also tended to specialize in marketing function as well as in lines of merchandise. There were importing firms, commission houses, wholesalers, and retailers, each operating in its own sphere of action. True, there were houses which combined the retailing and wholesaling functions, and others which united importing and wholesaling; but such combinations were becoming much less common than they had been in 1800.

This leads me to my first generalization. During the first half of the century the tendency in marketing was toward specialization, both as to the goods handled and as to the function performed. Prior to 1800 the dominant or typical unit had handled many lines of merchandise and combined importing, wholesaling, and retailing as well as such functions as transportation and banking. Here and there, some tendency to specialize could be observed, but it had not gone far.

Why this drive from nonspecialized toward specialized business enterprise? The whole story is too long to tell here, but the marked changes in production and transportation which came after 1800 were accompanied in this country with a rapid expansion of markets, both geographically and in terms of population. The new problems which developed, plus the growing capital requirements, forced men to specialize in order to succeed. At the same time, the great increase in volume of business enabled them to reduce the scope of their operations and still earn a living. A "gent's furnishings" store could thrive on Broadway in 1850, but in a small community in 1800 the owner of such a specialized store would have been idle and hungry most of the year.[1]

---

[1] For a good sketch of the entire marketing scene at this time, see Fred M. Jones, *Middlemen in the Domestic Trade of the United States, 1800–1860* (Urbana: University of Illinois Press, 1937).

By 1853, specialization had gone so far that a New York observer sounded a half-facetious note of alarm:

The tendency is to a still more minute division, and thus we have a dealer in hosiery, a dealer in lace, a dealer in perfumery, a dealer in pocket handkerchiefs, a dealer in shawls, and a house is just starting to keep nothing but suspenders! We suppose in ten years more there will be an establishment for spool cotton, and another for corset-laces, if such instruments of torture shall then be in vogue.[2]

In Philadelphia, another commentator asserted: "Division of trade into distinct branches appears to be in the natural order of things. Even where two or more branches are yet united in the same establishment, there is an avoidance of incongruity—as when fur robes are kept for sale in a hat store."[3]

A major tendency like the specialization just noted seldom goes far without a reaction setting in, and this is true of retailing in the period under observation. Before the outbreak of the Civil War, a counter-movement began toward combination in a single institution both of lines of merchandise and of marketing functions. But before examining that development, let us look further into the retail stores of the mid-19th-century period.

For the most part, they seem to have been relatively small with respect to capital investment. The only statistics available on this point are from the census of 1840, which reveals an average investment of $4,350. It also shows an average of 3.4 stores per thousand inhabitants for the country as a whole. Of course, these averages would undoubtedly be different for urban districts. Some light is thrown on this point by a statement that Boston's Oak Hall, which was supposed to be the largest clothing store in the country, boasted an annual volume of $500,000 in the late 1840's.

How different the typical retail stores of 1850 were from the ones we know today!—small quarters, with selling largely confined to the street floor; goods piled on shelves, with no attempt at attractive display; cheap and ugly fixtures; no heat in cold weather, except in the proprietor's office, and stifling temperatures in the summer; very little window dressing, if any; a dingy interior during the day and gas or oil-lamp light at night. Here, as in so many other aspects of life, the "good old days" are not really so attractive when we tear aside the kindly veils of time and legend and look closely at the facts.

Most of the retail concerns seem to have employed men as attendants; but in dry goods stores, at least, women clerks were gaining in numbers,

---

[2] *United States Economist*, May 28, 1853, p. 92.
[3] *Hunt's Merchants' Magazine*, Vol. XXXII (1855), pp. 776–77.

especially in Philadelphia. One contemporary writer objected strenuously to the spectacle of able-bodied men in New York stores—"he biddies," they were sometimes called—in the act of "measuring out a yard of ribbon or tape or descanting on the color or shade of a piece of silk," a task for which he felt a female attendant was much better suited.

Contemporary discussion of this topic of men versus women in retail stores emphasized the point that women were naturally better adapted to handling dry goods and waiting upon women customers. It was urged, too, that their employment would release men for "more athletic and useful employments."

A. T. Stewart, however, is said to have employed the handsomest men he could obtain because he observed that women liked to converse and even to flirt with male clerks.

Certainly, the salaries paid should have discourged men from entering retail employment. In 1849 a young man was lucky to get $600 a year, and a frequent complant was that too many youths from the country drifted into jobs in city stores where opportunities for advancement were very limited. It was asserted that "with the exception of the retail dry goods business, there is not one that holds out less encouragement to clerks than the jobbing business . . . the young man who goes into the dry goods store with any other view of making money than that of saving it from his salary, makes a mistake that will cost him the better part of a lifetime to get over."

The retail workday was invariably long, even after the Civil War. In 1857, many Boston stores were regularly open from 13 to 16 hours a day, and this seems to have been true in other cities at the time.

Most observers agree that selling methods in the 1850's and 1860's left much to be desired. Misrepresentation of quality, short measure, and other sharp practices were frequently encountered, and selling prices almost everywhere depended upon the customer's ability to bargain with the salesman. A change for the better was under way, however, for A. T. Stewart had inaugurated the one-price system in New York at a very early date, and a number of stores in New England (among them R. H. Macy's in Haverhill) regularly advertised that they had only one price for all customers. Moreover, the idea was making headway that the customer should be satisfied with his purchase. Thus a Haverhill store advertised in 1853 "all goods as represented or the money refunded"; and in 1855 the clothing store of Smith & Strong, of Oswego, New York, pledged "that we guarantee every article sold to be what it is represented, and that we cheerfully return the money when any dissatisfaction exists." Macy's made a similar guarantee as early as 1859; and a few years later, John Wanamaker began to emphasize one price and satisfaction guaranteed to such an extent that it soon became the standard practice of all self-respecting retailers.

The retail advertising of the 1850's contrasts strongly with that of today. Many firms did none at all, apart from the signs over their storefronts, while those that did advertise usually confined themselves to a column-inch or so in the classified advertisement sections of the newspapers. Dull statements of the firm's main items of merchandise and its place of business were usual, and only a rash newcomer like George Simmons of Boston's Oak Hall or R. H. Macy in New York ventured to use sprightly copy in a personal vein or to present the merits of his store as an institution. When prices were mentioned, however, even such concerns as Lord & Taylor and Arnold Constable did not hesitate to claim that their merchandise was priced at least 25 percent under the market.

3. THE ROLE OF THE WESTERN MERCHANT*

The contribution of the merchant to the development of his community has generally been overlooked. It was only with the establishment of its first store that a town could function. The availability of merchandise from the East and Europe was itself a spur to western economic development. Since farmers no longer had to be economically self-sufficient, they could concentrate on raising the most profitable cash crops. In addition, the merchant also assumed the double burden of banker and dealer in agricultural crops. The merchants of the pioneering towns were generally more sophisticated than their neighbors, more widely traveled, and frequently better educated. They used their position of leadership to encourage the adoption of new agricultural methods and to spearhead both commercial and industrial development.

IN THE LATE 1830's, John Beauchamp Jones—sometimes listed under the pen name of Luke Shortfield—engaged in merchandising at Arrow Rock, Missouri, a village on the Missouri River some 200 miles above St. Louis.[1] For him, merchandising was but a means to accumulate sufficient wealth to sustain a literary career. His lack of interest in business did not blind him to the significant part merchants were playing in the transformation of western society, however, for in the preface of his book, *The Western Merchant,* he stressed the services performed by the mercantile class:

The merchants of the West, and particularly of the Far West, constitute a distinct class of society. This class is not only important from its numbers,

---

* Reprinted from Lewis E. Atherton, "The Pioneer Merchant in Mid-America," *University of Missouri Studies,* Vol. XIV (April, 1939), pp. 7–17.

[1] William Barclay Napton, *Past and Present of Saline County, Missouri* (Indianapolis and Chicago, 1910), p. 314. Armistead Churchill Gordon's biography of Jones in the *Dictionary of American Biography* omits all mention of his mercantile career. Napton's identification of Jones as a pioneer merchant adds great value to Jones's writing on western merchandising by establishing the fact that the author was actually engaged in the mercantile trade. The urge to write accentuated Jones's appreciation of details which would enliven any theme he might undertake. At the same time, this purpose marred his efforts, since he continually strove for effect, a feature which helps to explain the lack of attention accorded him by historians, who perhaps have tended to ignore a too florid account. Jones must needs dress up his scenes and characters; consequently, his descriptions often impress students as merely costume pieces. In reality, he came very close to reporting the frontier life of his time as it existed.

but powerful and influential from its intelligence, enterprise, and wealth. . . . He[the merchant] is a general locum tenens, the agent of everybody! And familiar with every transaction in his neighborhood. He is a counselor without license, and yet invariably consulted, not only in matters of business, but in domestic affairs. Parents ask his opinion before giving their consent to their daughters' marriages; and he is always invited to the weddings. He furnishes the nuptial garments for both bride and groom, and his taste is both consulted and adopted. Every item of news, not only local, but from a distance, —as he is frequently the postmaster, and the only subscriber to the newspaper —has general dissemination from his establishment, as from a common center; and thither all resort, at least once a week, both for goods and for intelligence.[2]

The records of the time fully support this estimate; but the ebullient language Jones employed suggests overstatement. Regarded as a eulogy of the western merchant, his description has received little notice; and in the years since the publication of his book, students of western history have neglected the leads he provided. In consequence, the services of the mercantile class in transforming western society have received little attention.

Only when one considers the highest type of civilization these frontier classes could erect does the full significance of Jones's emphasis on the mercantile class become apparent. If the story of the frontier is to be told solely in terms of classes like the cowboy and the farmer, the process of transforming such an area into a modern specialized community will remain a closed book. At one period or another, all America was in the pioneer stage. How the transition to a specialized economy occurred has not been studied, and the story of this transition should prove as valuable as the descriptions of other western developments in explaining American life. When told, it will be in terms of the merchant class and professional groups—lawyer, doctor, and teacher.

Jones's estimate of the services of the mercantile group grew out of his experiences in Missouri in the late thirties. James Hall held the same view as the result of his own observations in Ohio in the forties, contending that the prosperity of the West was due in large part to the mercantile class. Hall felt that merchants had been criticized and neglected by those who swayed the political power of the country, and suggested that more emphasis be placed on education and culture as a means of lessening any prejudice against the power of mercantile wealth. He wanted merchants to concentrate less on moneymaking; but their wealth, social standing, and leadership in community charities and kindred enterprises was fully recognized in his discussion of their problems.

In a description of the West as early as 1817, E. P. Fordham had expressed similar views. He pictured western society as composed of

---

[2] John Beauchamp Jones (pen name, Luke Shortfield), *The Western Merchant* (Philadelphia, 1849), Preface.

four classes: the hunters who lived by the rifle; the first settlers, who did some hunting but devoted most of their time to farming; the true farmers and the enterprising men from Kentucky and the Atlantic states, who founded towns and trade, speculated in land, and began the fabric of society; and a fourth class of old settlers, who were really the third class in its maturity. This classification recognized both the complexity of western society and the modifying influence of the business and professional men.

Fordham's list also placed the different groups in the approximate order of their arrival on the frontier. Hunters, farmers, and land speculators naturally preceded the business classes, a market for their services being necessary to attract the latter groups. Of these, the merchants were the most numerous and frequently the first to arrive in point of time. A new town attracted professional men, and a store was the most important element of western towns. Real estate promoters, anxious to start a new town, realized the imperative necessity of attracting merchants and often offered town lots free to those agreeing to erect store buildings. The promoters' advertisement in 1825 of the new Missouri River town of Rocheport listed the general advantages of the location, closing with the statement: "And as it is the desire of the proprietors rather to promote improvements than to realize cash from the amount of sales, no lots will be sold except subject to certain improvements to be made within 18 months from purchase, say at least a log house 18 by 20 feet, on each lot. To merchants or mechanics, who wish to become settlers & make extensive improvements, donations of Lots will be made." If two or three merchants could be attracted by such inducements, the nucleus of a town was formed; and the promoters then hoped to draw teachers, doctors, and lawyers to the new location. In many cases, merchants took the lead in establishing towns, motivated by the desire either to follow frontier trade west or to profit from the sale of town lots. Thus the Lammes, Missouri merchants from the early twenties, sought to create a new town in what is now Livingston County, Missouri.

New towns soon attracted doctors, but it was often difficult to differentiate between their merchandising activities and professional practice. Frequently, they operated a drugstore, which generally meant the sale of paint and glass as well as the practice of medicine. An advertisement of Doctors Crews and Benson of the town of Fayette, Missouri, in 1830, announced that they were conducting a wholesale and retail drugstore, with a large stock of drugs, paints, surgical instruments, and patent medicines. Such men could well be classified as merchants in the early stages of transition to a specialized community life.

In analyzing the western merchant, it should be borne in mind that frontier conditions demanded a type of business more varied than that found in the East. Merchandising was only one of the merchant's activities. Ninian Edwards of Illinois owned and supervised five stores in Illinois and three in Missouri, practiced law, engaged in farming and real estate speculation, operated saw- and gristmills, served as governor of Illinois while it was in the territorial stage, and as governor and United States senator after Illinois entered the Union as a state. Varied interests were the rule rather than the exception; and in this respect, merchants were conforming to the pattern of western life; but their activities were of such a nature that other residents of their communities were able to specialize to a greater degree than had formerly been the case. As a result, the western merchants speeded up the process of developing a modern economy by remaining entrepreneurs of varied interests when they first entered a pioneer community.

As a citizen of the small western village, which he helped to create, the merchant's first, and most obvious service was the retailing of manu-factured goods and groceries. In this capacity, he offered escape from the self-sufficient stage in which the community lived when he first appeared. In his varied stock of dry goods, hardware, groceries, and drugs was the power to liberate the resident of the West from the necessity of being a jack-of-all-trades and a master of none. He brought to the West the products of the more specialized communities of the East and Europe and, with these, the challenge to the West to lift itself to a higher degree of economic organization.

If the merchant had been satisfied to stop with this service, the West would have taken a much longer period of time to reach economic maturity than proved to be the case. Money was scarce, and the most bountiful supply of goods was worthless unless some medium of exchange was available. Banks and a market for western crops would solve the problem, but neither existed. Faced with this situation, the merchant had no choice but to assume the double burden of banker and dealer in agricultural crops.

The simplest and most pleasant banking operation consisted of caring for the funds of farmers who feared to keep their money at home. Cus-tomers withdrew the money as needed or took it out in goods, the merchant profiting both from the additional sales and the use of the money as capital on which to operate. Here the usual process was reversed, however. As a rule, the merchant supplied the capital for busi-ness operations and rare indeed was the customer who had money credit at a store.

The merchant's chief contribution in the way of capital came from whatever credit standing he had in the wholesale centers where he traded. Credit was obtained without great difficulty from wholesale houses, the usual terms being 6 months' credit, payable in 12, with inter-est ranging from 6 to 10 percent after the 6 months. In turn, a large percentage of the sales to customers were made on a credit basis. Thus the western merchant obtained from one to two years' supply of credit from the East throughout the period from 1820 to 1850 and, through credit sales, permitted western farmers to share in the benefits with him. The procedure was undoubtedly expensive, sales on credit being much higher than those for cash; but the West was developing and could stand high prices for what it bought.

Furthermore, the merchant soon realized the need for banks. Many bought their goods directly in the eastern cities, a practice which called for annual remittances of large sums of money. A storekeeper in a village without banking facilities had to send paper money through the mails to the largest western cities in order to purchase bills of exchange with which to make remittances. Such a procedure was dangerous, the uncertainty of the mails making the transfer of money by that means extremely hazardous. Even more of a problem was the transfer of specie. This often was moved to the larger cities in the wagons of freighters hauling goods for merchants, or concealed in shipments of produce—the consignee being instructed to remove the money at the end of the trip. Such difficulties demonstrated the value of banks to the mercantile class, and many of them ultimately entered the banking business.

The mercantile barter system also helped to ease the money situation. Farmers exchanged their crops for groceries and dry goods, thereby escaping the necessity of purchasing with currency. Through this means the storekeeper could dispose of his wares to a population that lacked ready cash with which to buy. All over the West, this pattern of bartering goods for produce was practiced, the merchant serving as a middleman to a much greater extent than is the case today. The farm crops taken in exchange for goods were consigned to commission merchants in the larger western cities and in New Orleans, the proceeds from the sale settling the merchant's bills to the eastward. The produce trade grew rapidly, and competition among commission houses for a share of the business caused them to adopt a policy of advancing money on goods deposited for sale, a practice which added still more to the small supply of money available in the West.

The value of this system to the western farmer is made apparent in a pitiful and indignant letter of a Missouri farmer to the editor of his county paper in 1821, a letter inspired by the refusal of Franklin, Missouri merchants to take depreciated paper or farm crops in payment for goods. He berated the Franklin merchants for advising farmers to take their crops to New Orleans and exchange them for sound money with which to purchase goods. His father had warned him against the evil of running off to New Orleans with produce and leaving his farm to the whims of fortune in the interval. If four farmers did join together and get their pork ready by the middle of December, they could not get it on board for New Orleans before the first of April. And apparently, the dangers of navigating the Missouri and Mississippi rivers were as nothing compared to the bewildering and fearful experiences waiting these rural people in New Orleans: bells ringing day and night; rumors of fever, plague, smallpox, and death; thousands from Kentucky, Virginia, Pennsylvania, Ohio, Illinois, Indiana, Tennessee, Mississippi, Arkansas, and Missouri lining the shores with produce, and no one to buy. Then probably in the end a Franklin merchant, in New Orleans to purchase groceries, might come along and buy the load for less than the expenses of the trip down the river. The four farmers returning home might find their farms "gone to wreck" and only half a crop under way. The writer was undoubtedly indulging in exaggeration, but such a trip was no light undertaking for an untraveled country farmer.

Many merchants were interested in farming and operated farms of their own. Better read and more widely traveled than the average western farmer, they exhibited an interest in scientific farming and took the lead in fostering it. Through such activities the merchant aided in increasing the value of the yearly output in the West, a service of great significance in view of the fact that the balance of trade was always in favor of the East.

Furthermore, the mercantile class played a prominent part in developing manufacturing. The Aull mercantile firm owned a rope walk at Liberty, Missouri. Operations were started in the autumn of 1829, with Aull shipping between 60,000 and 70,000 pounds of bale rope to New Orleans in the first year. The shipments increased in size in succeeding years, with New Orleans as the chief market. In enterprises of this type the merchant achieved his most advanced position in the pre-Civil War period. Goods from the Atlantic seaboard were bartered to the western farmer for his leading crop. The farm crop was then processed by the merchant, which enabled him both to reduce the bulk and to increase the value before paying freighting charges. The commodity was often sold in the South, fulfilling the West's place as the source of supply for the South in the three-cornered trade so typical of that period. Through the process, credit was built up in New Orleans, and this was transferred to the eastern cities to meet the wholesale bills the merchants contracted in the winter months.

While the mercantile group will be judged primarily on the basis of these material contributions to western life, they did perform certain services of a social nature, services generally credited wholly to the professional groups. Western stores constituted a social center for the farming classes, and the storekeeper came in contact with such people much more frequently than did the lawyer, doctor, or preacher. Sometimes the merchant resented the fact that his store was used as a loafing place, and advertised his resentment in the papers, as did a St. Louis merchant in 1825:

Mr. Printer—I am a storekeeper, and am excessively annoyed by a set of troublesome animals, called Loungers, who are in the daily habit of calling at my store, and there sitting hour after hour, poking their noses into my business, looking into my books whenever they happen to lie exposed to their view, making impertinent inquiries about business which does not concern them, and ever and anon giving me a polite hint that a little grog would be acceptable.

Do, Mr. Printer, give this an insertion; some of them may see it, and take the hint. If it should not, however, answer the purpose, I shall certainly be under the necessity of disposing of my goods the best way I may, shutting up my shop, mounting a Vide Poche Cart, and crying "Marche donc," take myself off to some more favored country where I shall not be bored to death by loungers.

Yrs. T. WILL YARDSTICK.

For regular customers, however, merchants often kept a barrel of whiskey in the back room, with a tin cup tied at the side to provide every convenience. And because of his education, business connections, and travel over the country, the merchant was called upon to perform various services for customers and friends during the course of the day's business. James Aull, at Lexington, Missouri, must have written 25 letters a year ordering periodicals for his customers, the *Missouri Republican, Saturday Evening Post, Quarterly Review, Nashville Banner,* and *Nashville Whig* being among the favorites in his locality. Subscribers disliked to send money through the mail, and the use of drafts and bills of exchange was far too expensive and time-consuming for such small transactions. So it was easier to bother the merchant; let him write the letter and do the worrying about getting the money to the paper. On the merchant's part, such favors constituted good business, and he was better equipped to do such work than anyone else in the West. For example, Aull made remittances for newspaper subscriptions through his agents, thereby eliminating the necessity of sending money through the mail.

Saw- and gristmill owners generally asked Aull to write their letters when ordering equipment, his wide business connections giving them confidence in his ability to get the best service possible. If county residents built a flatboat, Aull was asked to see about insurance.

A local resident traveling in another state thought of the merchant first of all when in difficulty. And men at home, faced with problems beyond the grasp of their own education, came to the merchant for a solution. A poor, illiterate citizen of Lafayette County chopped and ricked a large supply of wood near the riverbank in 1831. The steamer *L. B. Yellowstone* took on a supply of wood for its engines, without inquiring about the ownership of the rick, which was some distance from any house. An appeal to James Aull for help resulted in a letter to Tracy and Wahrendorff at St. Louis to collect for the wood when the steamboat arrived there.

Merchants also facilitated travel for those visiting the West. Students of history are familiar with Francis Parkman's description of Westport and the services he obtained there, as portrayed in *The Oregon Trail.* Less distinguished men did not hesitate to call on western merchants with letters of introduction in the hope of obtaining employment in the new country. Some advertised for positions through the columns of local newspapers, but fully as many sought work through the use of personal letters. Typical of these is a letter from Peter Cartwright to John O'Fallon in 1827:

> To Col. John O'Fallon at St. Louis and all others it may concern—This is to certify that I have been long and intimately acquainted with Mr. Carlton R. Galton, and after transacting a great deal of Business with him and being intimately acquainted with his manner of life, and mode of conducting business: I feel no hesitancy in recommending him as a gentleman of sound, *Moral, Honest* principles and well qualified to transact business in the line which he has been accustomed to, i.e. merchandising. This is the character he has Borne in Kentucky and Springfield, Illinois, from early life—much more might be said of Mr. Galton by way of commendation but it is unnecessary as a small acquaintance with him will satisfy any candid man—and faviour bestowed, or, attention paid to him will be greatfully acknowledged by me. . . .

The frequency of such letters in mercantile records attests their efficacy in aiding men to obtain employment.

Nor were such services always performed in the hope of ultimate economic gain. The comments of one merchant show that the proprietors of frontier stores sometimes sensed the effect of a drab and lonesome existence on women in their localities:

> I have often seen a hard-worked country lady come into a store and inquire for all the handsomest goods in the stock, and admire them, comment on them, take out great strips of pretty patterns, and with her knotted fingers fold them into pleats and drape them over her plain skirt, her face illumined with pleasure at the splendor of such material could she wear it. It was really pathetic and deserving of sympathy. The love of what is beautiful was as intense in her soul as in that of her more fortunate sister who could afford to wear it. Bright, harmonious colors, and fine fabrics, over which she would draw her tired hands caressingly, soothed and gratified her. Who could grudge her such a privilege?

Storekeepers of this type helped to mitigate the bleakness of frontier existence for those who came before community life was fully developed.

When all these services by the mercantile class are totaled—the building of towns, wholesaling and retailing, banking, the development of a market for farm crops, the promotion of agriculture, and the start of manufacturing—they are seen to be of the same general significance. They were the services which had to be performed if the West was to pass from a self-sufficient economy to the stage of economic specialization. Without them, an advanced economic order was impossible; with them, the West rapidly worked itself out of the pioneer stage. It is because of its leadership in this transition period that the mercantile class deserves a place in the story of the frontier.

4. THE FRONTIER STORE: ITS PLANT AND OPERATION*

The typical country general store was a large log structure or a cluster of buildings. Windows and doors could be bolted to afford maximum security. The products handled met the basic needs of the rural community. The arrangement of the inventory was rather bewildering, and much of the merchandise was suspended from the rafters. As would be suspected, assortment or range of choice within a given class of goods was practically nonexistent. Hours were long, with the store typically opening at dawn and remaining open to accommodate farmers who arrived late at night. Barter and price higgling were widely practiced and considered an ordinary part of doing business. The store was also a social center where news was exchanged and people called to pass the time of day.

STORE BUILDINGS, of course, varied according to the location. The largest and most expensive stores in mid-America were to be found in St. Louis and Chicago. Around 1835 a merchant arriving in St. Louis chose a location in the business section best suited to the type of store he wished to open. If his capital was too small for wholesaling, he found the riverfront a poor location. Front Street in that section was open on the riverside. The ground, sloping from the street to the riverbank was paved with cobblestones and brick, and all day long the rumble of carts and the hoofbeat of horses indicated the rush of business. Importing, wholesaling, and commission firms dominated Front Street, proximity to the wharf enabling them to move goods back and forth from the river to their four-story limestone warehouses, which faced away from the wharf and gave an imposing appearance to the river section. The wholesale dry goods firms extended into the next block, just beyond Front Street and the river wharf. Still farther on were the stores of the retailers, men who engaged only in the local trade, but who lived in hope of some day emulating their more successful business associates along the river.

By the fifties, St. Louis could boast of some very imposing business structures. Nicholson's store claimed to be the "largest retail and jobbing

---

* Reprinted from Lewis E. Atherton, "The Pioneer Merchant in Mid-America," *University of Missouri Studies*, Vol. XIV (April, 1939), pp. 32–46.

family grocery" in the United States. It occupied a pretentious building of Renaissance style, four stories high and three rooms wide, engaged columns adding to the impressiveness of the facade. The name Nicholson stood out in large letters at the top of the fourth story and again at the level just above the ground floor. In between these displays of the firm's name the nature of the company was revealed by the words "Tea, Coffee, Sugar, Wine and Liquor Warehouse." But few stores, even in St. Louis, rivaled Nicholson's size or architectural triumphs. In 1820, Asa Wheeler rented a store at the corner of First and Main streets from Auguste Chouteau for $40 a month, the premises containing a grocery with two rooms on the back, a bakehouse with two ovens, a yard, and a cellar. And this was in the best business location available! In 1823, Chouteau gave James Lansdell and Joseph Branson an even better bargain by renting them a house and lot fronting on Market Square for $10 a month. At the time the men were using the house as a cabinetmaker's shop and grocery store, but the new contract stipulated that they should build a log cabin to house the cabinetmaking business. The structure was to become Chouteau's property at the end of a four-year period.

In the smaller towns and frontier outposts, store buildings were even less costly. The reason for this becomes apparent when one examines the structure of such a store more in detail. J. B. Jones described a frontier store building in his book on western merchandising, a picture drawn from his own observations while engaged in storekeeping at Arrow Rock, Missouri. The framework was of hewed logs, laid lengthwise, and with the chinks between filled with clay and lime. The structure itself consisted of two rooms, each about 20 feet square—one to be used for a salesroom and the other for storing goods. Door and window in the salesroom were equipped with locks and bolts as a precaution against robbers. Located in a clearing of trees, where rattlesnakes and deer could be observed occasionally, the building appeared little different from the scattering of log-cabin homes in the surrounding territory. Interior walls were whitewashed, except in the salesroom, which was shelved on all four sides. A counter of boards 30 inches wide and 12 feet long extended from the window to the partition wall between the two rooms, dividing the salesroom into two triangular sections, the larger of which could be entered by the front door. The smaller section opened into the storeroom, giving easy access to supplies not on the shelves, and providing an area in which the clerk could conduct the business of selling goods without hindrance from customers. A large shoe or hat box served as a desk, and the cash register was nothing more than a drawer under the counter, with a small hole cut through the top for convenience when business was heavy.

Some stores were even smaller and less well equipped than the one described by Jones, the first store in Davenport, Iowa, being a single-room, shingled log cabin, 16 by 20 feet in size. As competition increased in the original location, the merchant might send a younger member of the firm farther out on the frontier to open a smaller store and thus gain the benefits of an exclusive market. Such stores were even smaller and less well equipped than those in the villages along the rivers and highways, Jones citing an example of one located in a log hut originally used as a henhouse by some settler.

Merchants provided their stores with locks and bars, a precaution that frontier settlers as a whole found unnecessary. Business establishments seemed to attract thieves, an advertisement in an Arkansas paper in 1836, headed "Stop the Thieves," illustrating the difficulties faced by merchants in that respect. Robbers had broken in the door of a store near Fort Smith by using a fence rail, and had made off with considerable merchandise and $800 or $900 in cash. Notes and other valuable papers also were taken, the advertisement warning the public against trading in any of these. The thieves were trailed 15 miles into the Cherokee Nation territory, but there the trail was lost. All other resources having failed, the merchant was now offering $100 for the apprehension of the guilty parties, and an additional $50 if the property was recovered.

It was a great event in the life of a western community when a steamboat began to unload the boxes and barrels of goods for a new store. People came from miles around to observe the occasion, a result prompted only in part by backwoods curiosity. Such institutions enabled farmers to concentrate on the most profitable line of activity and thereby end the days of economic self-sufficiency, for these early stores attempted to carry everything needed by the community.

In the grocery line, package goods were as yet unimportant; and the bulk of the groceries, therefore, consisted of tea, coffee, sugar, flour, and liquor. James Aull, of Lexington, Missouri, occasionally ordered 20 barrels of rye whiskey at one time to care for the demand at his four establishments. He also sold peach brandy and Jamaica rum, but whiskey was the common liquor all over the West. Frequently purchased for as little as 25 cents a gallon, it retailed at a price that gave maximum satisfaction on a small outlay by the customer.

Coffee frequently was purchased green by the merchant, the roasting being left to the customer. Only two or three grades were sold, which permitted the merchant to keep a supply in a limited space in the storeroom, probably in small kegs. The same was true of tea, a few standard names, like Imperial and Young Hyson, dominating the field. Standard names did not guarantee uniform quality, however, as Young Hyson tea might vary, for example, from very good to very bad. Brown sugar was kept in open barrels near the counter, as it sold more readily than the expensive white variety. A supply of soap, spices, flour, and salt completed the grocery stock of the average western store. Hardware and leather goods shared floor space with the groceries. Axes, log chains, kettles, pots, pans, kegs of nails, and other articles of like variety, being durable in nature, could be piled down in some unoccupied space or suspended from the rafters on cords. Shoes, saddles, and harness added to the bewildering variety of goods on display.

Dishes, drugs, books, and dry goods occupied the shelves around the sides of the building. In the matter of dishes, queensware was considered standard. Originally imported from foreign countries, it was made in the United States before the Civil War, and the name had probably ceased to have more than a general significance. The drug supply was limited principally to patent medicines, physics, and sedatives. E. D. Sappington's store at Jonesboro, Missouri, purchased licorice balls, pillboxes, oil of sassafras, calomel, camphor, Godfrey's Cordial, Bateman's Drops, laudanum, paregoric, rhubarb, asafetida, turpentine, sweet oil, and opium in Philadelphia in 1835. If one adds Epsom salts to the list, it is representative of the range of drugs offered for sale by the general store.

In the dry goods and clothing field the stock was so varied that one can do no better than list the goods offered for sale, as revealed in the newspaper advertising. John Collier and Company at St. Charles, Missouri, advertised the following items in 1820: "Superfine and common Cloths, superfine and common Cassimers, Callicoes, Ginghams, Irish Linen, Brown Holland, India, Book, Mull, Jaconet, Cambrick, Leno and Figurd Muslin, Nankeens, Senshaws, and Sasanets, Shawls and Handkerchiefs, Plain and Figured Canton Crapes, Hosiery and Gloves—Straw Bonnets, Seersuccer and Cotton Cassimers, Bombazetta & Diapers— Vestings, Ribbons, Steam Loom Shirtings, Russia Sheeting, Plaids and Stripes, Sheeting, Shirting & Bed Ticking, Shoes and Boots, Morocco Hats and Skins."

Most of the dry goods consisted of coarse and serviceable cloth, but fashion played its part even in the West. Leghorn bonnets were especially fashionable at one time. Big Shoal Creek Meeting House in Clay County, Missouri, a church of the Primitive Baptists, was so noted for its display of these hats and new dresses on the second Sunday in May each year that the occasion was dubbed the "Bonnet Show."

Items in the amusement line were included in the varied assortment of merchandise. No wonder, then, that the store attracted customers, for along with the many necessities it offered something in addition for every member of the family—liquor for the men, fine cloth for the women, and a bit of peppermint candy or a lump of brown sugar for the children.

Stores opened at dawn, and it was not unusual for a clerk still to be selling goods at 10:00 o'clock at night by the feeble glow of candles. Farmers living nearby arrived in the forenoon to dispose of produce and do their trading. Those at a distance reached the store later in the day, and some did not arrive until bedtime. As they were anxious to be on their way again early the following morning, it was necessary to care for their produce and put up their bill of goods before the store closed for the night. In addition to the confirmed loafers, who were the biggest problem, the merchant received long visits from his regular customers. A trip to town was often an all-day affair, no matter how close to the store one lived. Although lacking money or credit to purchase goods, some came merely to participate in the political arguments and exchange of gossip around the stove. Women were as frequent visitors as men, Gottfried Duden warning his German friends not to come west with the expectation of making a living peddling goods, as people waited to buy at the stores where they could also obtain free gossip—"most of the girls and women would very reluctantly forego the opportunity occasionally to ride to the stores of the cities, or even to the country stores, where there is usually a concourse of strangers."

The younger women made merchandising more palatable for the clerk who was working and saving to get ahead. The men, however, constituted more of a problem. Barter and higgling were universally practiced in the West, the one-price system not becoming popular until after the Civil War.

Price debates were less disturbing to the routine of the business day than the occasional appearance of some individual looking for trouble. Jones included such an incident in his account of the first day's business. Two characters of unsavory reputation entered and inquired the price of brown domestic cloth, a bolt being out on the counter at the time. The clerk priced it at 20 cents, meaning a yard, but his customers insisted that he had sold them the whole bolt for 20 cents. One clerk went for the constable, who could not be found. The argument continued, the remaining clerk hitting one of his tormentors over the head with a yard-stick. Enraged, that individual prepared to wreak vengeance with an ax, but the clerk knocked him down with a two-pound iron weight.[1] Once a merchant demonstrated his ability to handle such problems, he could expect a peaceable future.

The average business day was much less exciting, however; and because it was, the records for reconstructing it are less numerous. All stores kept blotters or daybooks for immediate entry of sales, and these matter-of-fact records give the best available picture of the run of business. Stores facing little competition and located in out-of-the-way places were able to demand high prices. This is well shown from a representative day's business for the firm of F. Frisel and Company, at Jackson, Missouri Territory, in 1818. Nine customers visited the store on March 25 of that

[1] John Beauchamp Jones, *The Western Merchant* (Philadelphia: 1849), pp. 60–61.

year, and all paid high prices for what they bought. The day's business totaled $53.92$7/_{12}$, excluding a few entries certifying collection for goods sold on time at earlier dates.

Records of daily sales are voluminous, but further illustration would add nothing to the explanation of merchandising, insofar as typical transactions are concerned. The sales of this firm illustrate the records of most other stores in a number of ways. For one thing, they show that purchases were not limited solely to the necessities of life, a practice that was true in a general way, but far from the extent often thought. People did buy ribbon and combs and plush cloth all over the West as soon as the store appeared as an institution. Everyone apparently possessed luxury goods to some extent, even though such items might be limited to a pair of silk gloves or a silk handkerchief. And one cannot turn many pages in a merchant's daybook without realizing that such goods were in steady demand. Again, these accounts illustrate the general nature of the stock of goods carried by western stores. In one day, this firm sold dry goods ranging from gingham to plush and ribbons, groceries, hardware, shoes, and glassware—a typical situation as revealed by the entries in most daybooks. Furthermore, purchases as a rule varied as widely in amount as did the nine sales made by Frisel and Company. People living at a distance from the store might buy $50 worth of goods, with the next item recorded being a 10-cent purchase. The total sales for the day, reaching a little over $50, are also typical of the amount of business transacted by the western store in the early period. This would make the weekly sales total between $200 and $300, a figure which agrees with the estimates of merchants that business ran from $100 to $300 a week. Jones estimated average sales at $10,000 to $12,000 a year. James Aull bought from $35,000 to $45,000 worth of goods a year in Philadelphia for his four stores in Missouri, and supplemented this by many purchases by letter during the next 12 months. At times, Joseph Hertzog visualized Christian Wilt doing a $100,000-a-year business in St. Louis, but letters of a more realistic mood set the total at from $180 to $200 a week.[2]

Some qualifications need to be made in accepting Frisel and Company's sales as typical, however. The general retail price of coffee certainly was far below the price charged by this one store. Coffee retailed for 25 cents in the unidentified town of St. Helena in 1832 and at the same figure in Jonesboro, Missouri, in 1835. Similar prices prevailed in Iowa and Wisconsin. Sugar was even cheaper, frequently selling for as little as 12 cents a pound. And tea would not have sold elsewhere at the exorbitant price of $3.00 a pound.[3] The other prices were more in keeping with the scale charged in the West at the time, although one finds wide variations in the charges for dry goods, the result of differences in quality

---

[2] *Letters from Joseph Hertzog, 1811–15.*
[3] Figures compiled from various daybooks.

and nomenclature. Although the tendency to charge one customer double
the rate at which an article was sold to another seems to bear out Jones's
assertion that prices were made according to the customer's likelihood to
pay, an investigation of some other daybooks reveals little of this in the
sale of staples. Perry Wilson and Company, an Iowa firm, sold sugar
at prices ranging from 15 to 18 cents in the 12-month period ending
November 7, 1837. Furthermore, the 3-cent variation was not a matter
of day-by-day change, but developed over a period of time and without
reference to individual customers.[4] Certainly, the practice of varying
prices according to individual customers was not universal in the sale
of staple articles, unless we limit the classification to cash and credit
customers—cash customers frequently receiving a reduction in price.
Still one other qualification needs to be made—sales did not run at a
uniform volume. Good weather and good roads meant increased purchases, and bad weather practically halted business. Thus, Frisel and
Company did not do $40 worth of business every day. Solon Robinson's
daybook contains only two entries for Saturday, February 29, 1840, John
Cochran buying one-half plug of tobacco at 25 cents, and H. S. Pelton
one gallon of molasses at $1.[5]

---

[4] Perry Wilson and Company, *Day Book, November 4, 1836, to August 25, 1838.*
[5] *Solon Robinson's Account Book, 1840–43.*

5. EARLY RETAIL ADVERTISING*

Mercantile advertising during the period stressed primarily the availability of products rather than their attributes. Oftentimes the source of the merchandise was given, particularly if it was purchased in the East, since this fact enhanced its salability. Quantities on hand were frequently mentioned, perhaps reflecting the general scarcity of goods in particular locations. Newspapers were the primary media, but other means were widely used, including handbills, small cards, and city directories. Early retail advertising rarely mentioned specific prices, for barter was frequent, the cost of credit depended on the standing of the purchaser, and higgling took place even on cash sales. As the author concludes, "early advertising was dreary, matter-of-fact reading, served a limited purpose, and was completely devoid of all the customer appeal of modern advertising."

Advertising played a smaller part in mercantile life in the pre–Civil War period than it does today. Then, its primary aim seems to have been to give the location, business, and services of a store, or to acquaint the public with any unusual changes occurring in the life of the firm. Little effort was spent in trying to increase sales through creating new desires for goods. Mother's Day, and all the other sacred modern observances, which mean so much to special business groups, were left untouched by the pioneer merchant. Such matters remained for a more enlightened period. Because of this situation, the unique character of early advertising stands out fully only when compared with the modern form.

Perhaps the most marked contrast of all is the almost complete absence of prices in early advertising. Merchants frequently advertised goods cheap for cash or stated that prices were as reasonable as those to be found anywhere, but neglected to give a schedule which could be used for comparison. John Beauchamp Jones's explanation gives a logical reason for this. Cash prices were made as uniform as possible, reductions being given only in cases where a quantity of goods was purchased. Because credit sales involved a risk, the merchant charged in proportion to this. Dr. Greenleaf might be worth $25,000 and Mr. Gates $1,000; but even though both were good men, Mr. Gates could more easily fail than

* Reprinted from Lewis E. Atherton, "The Pioneer Merchant in Mid-America," *University of Missouri Studies,* Vol. XIV (April, 1939), pp. 121–25.

Dr. Greenleaf. Consequently, he would be charged a slightly higher price for the goods bought on credit, both men being told the prices were confidential as a means of preventing hard feelings. (Mercantile business records do not substantiate Jones's explanation, however.)

Another explanation frequently given for the absence of prices in advertisements is that much of the business in the West was on a barter basis. Under such a system, there was a tendency to shift prices to meet each transaction. This is hardly a full explanation, for eastern merchants, where the barter system was fast disappearing, also omitted mention of definite prices from their advertisements. If the barter system had been the full reason for not stating prices, eastern merchants would have been free to list their rates in the newspapers long before the Civil War. It is probable that storekeepers feared to announce prices lest some other merchants should undertake to undersell them. As long as others refrained from the practice, there was no need for any one individual to pursue such a course. More than likely, such activity was regarded as slightly unethical—unfair competition contrary to the rules of the game. This policy was so widespread that not over one advertisement in a thousand before 1850 mentioned definite prices.

In three notices, we have early examples of the modern practice of advertising "leaders" as a means of attracting trade. It is worth noting, however, that occasional advertisements of this type did not stampede other merchants into following the same practice. In none of the three cases did other merchants reply by advertising their prices. Nor did these firms seem to prosper greatly by their variations from the established custom, none of the three increasing his advertisements in later issues. Price quotations and the use of leaders were to wait until after the Civil War period for their day of prominence.

Merchants were much freer from the influence of manufacturers than is the case today. Now, even small-town merchants find it necessary to carry several brands of breakfast food, customers buying the brand promoted by their favorite radio star or comic strip. But "standard" brands were unknown in the early period. Coffee and tea were sold under general trade names, every wholesale center carrying supplies of Imperial, Young Hyson, and Gunpowder tea, for example. A merchant could buy these from any wholesale grocery house, none promoting a special brand. The same condition prevailed in the dry goods line, manufacturers and wholesalers leaving the advertising in the hands of the local merchants, and customers selecting their purchases without previous bombardments in favor of some particular brand.

The patent medicine field was the only exception to this practice. The general policy there was for the owner of the remedy to write the advertisements and obtain the testimonials to accompany them. Joseph Hertzog arranged for his nephew at St. Louis to handle Dr. Dyott's patent medicines, the doctor paying the cost of manufacture, freight, and advertising, and giving the retailer a profit of 20 percent on all medicine sold. And no group was more willing to spend money on advertising than the patent medicine manufacturers. Benson and Company at Franklin, Missouri, in 1829 advertised a supply of "Swaim's Genuine Panacea" with directions printed in Spanish, and suitable for sale in the Santa Fe trade. Like other merchants, they limited the advertisement to as small a space as possible in order to lessen printing expenses. A week later, however, a full three-column announcement of "Columbian Syrup" appeared on the front page of the local paper, paid for by the manufacturer. The description of the medicine revealed its marvelous curative powers in any and all diseases, and established the fact beyond argument by giving testimonials from grateful users of the product. Benson and Company were listed as the sole agents for the medicine in the state of Missouri, the product retailing at the moderate price of $3 a bottle. The issue of the paper for September 25 carried a full-page advertisement of the same product. Such extravagance could never be charged to a western merchant; but patent medicine salesmen apparently found the practice profitable, their advertisements alone making no endeavor to save space.

In some respects, the rudimentary nature of advertising could be charged to conditions over which the merchant had no control. This was especially true in the matter of advertising goods suitable for the various seasons and holidays. Merchants in smaller towns made little endeavor to publicize goods which might serve as Christmas presents or for other occasions. Even in towns like St. Louis, very few merchants sought to increase their business through such means. The largest newspaper in St. Louis, the *Missouri Republican,* carried only a few small notices headed "Christmas and Holiday Goods" in its December issues in 1834. In part, this was due to a limited conception of advertising, merchants seeming to have little idea of the possibility of increasing sales by appealing to latent desires of customers. Newspapers in such cities had a wide circulation in the surrounding territory, however, and the advertisements were directed only in part to local trade. Many rural subscribers received their papers a month or six weeks late, and advertisements had to be written in a manner to appeal to customers reading them long after they were published.

Furthermore, goods were not received as frequently as today, and an advertisement of the supply of merchandise on hand could be written so as to cover the full stock of goods for sale several weeks or months in the future. This, of course, saved money by leaving the notice in the same form for a longer period. And this was even more true in the smaller areas. Merchants visiting the East bought the greatest part of their merchandise in one lot. Slow communication and long periods intervening between orders made it hard to synchronize advertisements with the seasons. Consequently, the storekeepers contented themselves with advertising "spring and summer" and "fall and winter" goods. And even here, the notices did not coincide closely with seasons or events. Goods "just arrived" were frequently advertised three months later under the same caption.

Another marked contrast with modern advertising was the infrequent use of pictures. Even two- and three-column notices regularly appeared without any illustrations to break the monotony of the reading matter; and where pictures did appear, they were generally only a symbol of the business advertised. A cut of the same pestle and mortar was used by merchants throughout the Mississippi Valley to head notices of drugs for sale. Leatherworkers frequently used the picture of a boot or a saddle. Metalworkers employed the design of a still. As it was easier for skilled tradesmen than for merchants to obtain some design symbolic of their business, such formalized pictures were limited mostly to the skilled trades. A chair, a stove, a hat—anything that the workman produced was used to head the announcement.

In general, the early advertising was dreary, matter-of-fact reading, served a limited purpose, and was completely devoid of all the customer appeal of modern advertising. Personality was lacking; one advertisement was like all others. Between the dead level and the modern form of individuality in advertising were many merchants who experimented with new techniques, some of them in this early period. Such a man was L. Deaver, who based his announcements on an appeal to fashion. His "Emporium of fashion" obtained "elegant ready made clothing" directly from the markets in New York City, Philadelphia, and Baltimore, an arrangement with merchants in those cities enabling him to import goods once a month. In this way, he planned to keep St. Louis supplied with the latest fashions, an extensive stock permitting purchasers a wide choice in making selections. The appeal to fashion was successful, for Deaver continued to advertise in the same vein over a period of years. Mark Murry at Belleville, Illinois, advertised goods at only a 20 percent advance on Philadelphia prices, an adherence to low charges resulting from his desire to see Belleville advance as a city. John Hogan, in the same state, expressed the belief that "a nimble six-pence is better than a slow shilling"; consequently, he intended to sell at a low price and rely on a large volume of trade for his profits. And even the most extravagant claims sometimes appeared in the newspapers of the day. O'Hara opened a tailoring establishment in Franklin, Missouri, in 1820 and immediately announced a 20 percent reduction over all former prices prevailing there. Country produce would be accepted the same as cash. O'Hara defied "even prejudice" to show that he could not execute work as well as any man in the territory, an experience based on work in 42 European cities, five years in Philadelphia and New York, and two in Lexington, Kentucky, eminently fitting him for his trade. An occasional quotation of prices and the mention of some special advantage of location distinguished some advertisements from the usual run. But beyond this merchants did not go. Custom and difficulties created by frontier conditions served to hold advertising to very circumscribed purposes.

6. THE INDOMITABLE PEDDLER*

Between 1790 and 1860 the itenerant peddler supplied his rural customers with inexpensive fabrics, a limited assortment of convenience goods, and a few feminine frills. Although the peddlers' backgrounds were as divers as their merchandise, all were generally considered "Yankees" with highly questionable business ethics. On the average, the peddler's prices were no higher and his ethics no lower than those of the country storekeeper. Moreover, the arrival of the peddler at an isolated farmhouse was welcomed as a diversion from routine chores and as a source of information and gossip about the outside world. As was true in the case of auctions, it was not the efforts of competitive marketing institutions to further their own interests, but changing economic conditions that caused the eventual decline in importance of peddling. As Carson states, "solid services were rendered by thousands of wayfarers who ventured where stores were few, among a people scattered thinly over an unfriendly and half-conquered land."

A MAN WHO KEPT a country store any time between 1790 and 1860 had plenty of problems to occupy his mind, but competition was not usually one of them. Among his chief difficulties were acquiring a stock of goods, transporting them, disposing of the country pay that came into his store, and raising the cash necessary to meet his obligations. Trading areas were established by the distance a farm family could travel by horseback, oxcart, or wagon. A circle with a five-mile radius would represent a fair estimate of the amount of geography in which a country dealer could take a serious commercial interest. In the absence of a large town or city nearby, the storekeeper got nearly all of the local run of trade; nearly all, but not quite all. No spot was too remote for the pack peddler.

We have contemporary testimony that it was scarcely possible to step out along a traveled highway from spring to fall in the first half of the last century without running into a man carrying a tin trunk, or perhaps a pack wrapped in black oilcloth. He would be a young man, canted forward under a 100-pound load, with a sharp eye out for a trade that might reduce his burden. This was the Yankee peddler, so called; and

* Reprinted from Gerald Carson, *The Old Country Store* (New York: Oxford University Press, 1954), pp. 37–63. Reprinted by permission of Willis Kingsley Wing. Copyright, 1954, by Gerald Carson.

though he might be a Connecticut man or a Vermonter, he could easily be a Jew from Germany, an Armenian, or Syrian, or for that matter, a Murphy or a Cosgrove.

The peddlers were out in force as soon as the ice disappeared from the dog pan. Though his expeditions, or depredations, in the Deep South have been chronicled in the most detail, the pack peddler was equally "all over the place" in the eastern and North Central states. Nor did he always require dry ground under foot, or mild temperatures. If the peddler was a "carting gentleman," he went right on touring in the wintertime, traveling any road that would take a cart, gig, or old thorough-brace wagon. The peddler worked the canalboats. He "ventured" in sloops through eastern coastal waters, with bayberry candles, Yankee rum, cheese, and codfish. He floated down western rivers on flatboats that served as stores, moving on to another landing place when trade languished.

If the pack peddler felt able to take a step up in the world, he bought a horse. Occasionally, very occasionally, a team of horses drew his bright red or blue wagon as it jangled over the rough roads with a rattle of tinware, the squeak of stiff leather springs, brooms sticking up behind like grotesque plumes, feathers, and bags of wool lashed onto the rear, growing bulkier with each day's trading. The cart was set high, so it could traverse the deeply rutted roads, with plenty of clearance for rocks, fords, stumps, and swampy places. The sides, hinged so that they could be dropped down, often bore a descriptive legend such as "Enameled Ware." Great double doors opened up the whole of the back. Many of the carts, as several generations recalled them, looked like the stagecoaches, with the oval bodies made familiar to the present generation by the movies, though they were lighter in draft. Some resembled a hearse. Others were half wagon, half carriage.

"Yankee" was sometimes a term of contempt or of fear, sometimes merely a descriptive expression used without prejudice, sometimes an affectionate and proud appellation, especially if self-applied. Much depended on who was doing the talking. In the West the Yankee was considered to be "too quirky." When used as a verb, "Yankee" meant to cheat. In conjunction with "peddler," the word was sufficient notice that a fraud was in the making. All of these connotations appear together in a newspaper piece published in the *Newark Daily Advertiser* before the Civil War—the heyday of peddling—and reprinted by the *Hartford Courant*, the venerable newspaper which still flourishes at the capital of the Yankee notions state:

We may laugh at the Yankees as we will, but they are the most thriving people in the world, and "let those laugh that win." . . . It is unfair to judge of a race by the emigrant portion, who if the most adventurous are also the least steady; but even this portion, including the whole procession of pedlars

which annually stream southward, like emmets from an ant hill, there is something good to be said. Take your stick, and walk out on the highway: you will
not have fairly warmed yourself with the exercise before a gaily painted
equipage, snug and light, drawn by a sturdy pair of Vermont horses, will come
in sight. The driver is a healthy, ruddy, happy-looking fellow, comfortably
wrapped up, and with a shaggy buffalo skin gathered around his feet. You
see at a glance that the master's eye has had its well-known effect on the
cattle. When he alights to bait, you will easily get into conversation with him.
His eye is even more inquisitive than his tongue, which is saying much; but
beyond this he is not disrespectful. He has a book in his pocket, and has been
taught to lay aside his cap in a Christian house. He does not drink, and he
does not blaspheme, and he carries no bowie-knife. . . . In a few months
he will return to the banks of "the river," with money enough to stock his tiny
farm. During his thousand miles of travel he will be sneered at, taxed for his
license, hustled at court houses, brow-beaten at inns, blasphemed at barbecues,
but never cheated, never beaten, never goaded into an assault, and never
seduced from his main point.

In 1850, there were 10,669 peddlers on the road in the United States;
in 1860, there were 16,594. New York State licensed 302 peddlers in
1841, of whom 227 traveled on foot and paid $20 a year for the privilege;
71 drove a single horse, and one traveled by canalboat—for $30 paid to
the Secretary of State; and three opulent peddlers were drawn by a two-
horse team, which cost them $50 in license fees. Peddling dropped off
to a low mark during the Civil War, made some recovery in the 1870's—
New York licensed 80 in 1871—and thereafter the decline was rapid as
the railroads brought the expanding rural population nearer to markets
and stores. How many persons peddled on a part-time basis or took the
risk of selling goods without a license, there is of course no way of
knowing. At any rate, with more and more country stores opening up, the
peddlers' opportunities shrank, though some continued to make their
rounds well into the 20th century.

Much of the economic thinking of the middle 1800's still followed
mercantilist lines. Trade barriers were set up by states, of which the
licensing of peddlers is an instance. It was considered desirable to keep
a firm hand on "foreign goods," which included merchandise brought in
from outside the state by the peddler. Pennsylvania, Connecticut, Georgia,
Tennessee, Illinois, and Ohio all required the peddler to take out a license
which specified that the migratory salesman could not dispose of his
goods at auction under any circumstances. Pennsylvania, Georgia, and
Tennessee added the provision that the license was available only to
those who were "disabled from procuring a livelihood by labour" due
to age, the loss of an arm or leg, or other bodily infirmity.

Many other obstacles were thrown in the way of the peddler. The
language of the New York licensing statute was severe. A penalty of $25
was "incurred by every person found traveling and trading in foreign

goods without a license, and $10 for refusing to produce a license when requested by an officer or citizen, and he may be apprehended and detained by any citizen and carried before a justice of the peace." The overseer of the poor of each town was charged with enforcement. "This notice is given that persons engaged or about to engage in the business of pedlars, may know the penalties to which they are exposed." The names of the authorized peddlers were struck off on sheets and distributed to local authorities. The secretary of state's office advised county clerks to circulate copies of the lists "in such a way as will be likely to cause the same to be most generally known." Appropriate agencies for this dissemination were suggested. The justices of the peace, who profited from the fines, comprised one such agency. Publishers of country newspapers, who of course received no advertising from peddlers, "are sometimes willing to give publicity to the list of peddlers holding licenses as a matter of general interest to their readers." Retail merchants were also suggested.

In plain words, the natural enemies of the peddler were alerted and set on his heels. We can imagine the virtuous zest of a country merchant in posting the list of peddlers on his post-office bulletin board, alongside notices of reward for the capture of bank robbers and horse thieves.

The peddler was reputed to be a sharp, slashing trader, a "cute one," who was always making a snug trade with his rustic customers. It was believed, and the belief often repeated, that if he did not cheat them on his pins, needles, or tinware, then he would certainly do so in bartering for the feathers, skins, and wool he accepted in lieu of money; and most probably, he would take them over the jump both going and coming.

The peddler's cheats made folklore. His lies were not little ones, such as ordinary men told, but monumental, impudent, and imaginative. The truth about the peddler's methods probably occupies a middle ground. Those who dealt with the same customers year after year would find honesty the best policy. The peddler making a once-around tour, never to return again, might be sorely tempted to adopt a free and easy brand of commercial honesty, especially when far from home. Sometimes, he sold goods for resale to other peddlers, to country merchants, or whoever wanted to trade.

The peddler knew just when to lay out a tablecloth of linen for the farm lady to feast her eyes on, or when cotton would be better, just as he had some extrasensory perception of what neighborhood would be in need of clocks. One Yankee "calculator" described the signs of a homestead that required a clock. If the house had glass windows, if the man of the house did not wear a cap but a hat, if he had boots on—the clock was as good as sold. If the wife appeared in calico and a checked apron, the peddler knew she had had a taste of buying from another traveling merchant and would be easily excited by a gaudy ribbon or a shining pair of scissors. Like his eastern counterpart, the western peddler was "the beatingest fellow"; and often, he was the same fellow. With an excellent memory and an ingratiating manner, apt in recalling who had been sick on his last trip, whose daughter was ready for long dresses, who would welcome advice—and who wouldn't—the loquacious peddler clipped the purses of the women with shining scissors or thread and ribbons and papers of pins which he drew from a well-packed coffee pot.

With all the disapproval and fear the peddler inspired, he was at the same time recognized as a kind of natural symbol for the American aggressive spirit when applied to business. His tenacity, his defiance of fatigue, danger, and even murder—many stories come down the years of peddlers killed and robbed on lonely wooded roads—was accepted as a recognizable self-portrait of the commercial American. Solid services were rendered by thousands of wayfarers who ventured where stores were few, among a people scattered thinly over an unfriendly and half-conquered land.

In singular antithesis to the peddler as a sharper was the reputation his goods had of being cheap. This, too, was not wholly deserved. Peddling was an expensive way to get goods to the customers. The economics of peddling scarcely supports the idea that it was a highly profitable occupation. How many calls could a peddler make in a day? Obviously not many. His business was mostly in small wares, and mostly with farm women who had little money or truck to trade with. The wagon peddler started out with a stock of merchandise worth from $300 to a top of $2,000, and he turned his stock in a period of two or three months at a gross profit of 100 percent, more or less. That was generally in line with what the country storekeeper made in selling a considerably larger volume of goods. There was a living in peddling for the man who had plenty of git-up-and-go. Those peddlers who accumulated a fortune did it by abandoning their itinerant way of life and applying their sharp minds to urban merchandising or new fields such as railroading, manufacturing, and finance.

Contemporary prints repeatedly show the whole family—the farmer, his wife, and all the children—eagerly gathered around the visitor as he spreads out an astonishing quantity of wares nested in his pack. He bought the housewife's rags, weighing them out carefully on the old steelyard. Discarded horseshoes and other scrap iron which the boys had been collecting from around the barnyard went into the peddler's van. All was paid for either in cash or in goods, while the peddler kept up an enthralling commentary on his offerings, passed out the news and gossip, speaking generously and frequently of his calico, fine "woosterds," and remarkably cheap prices.

It requires an effort of the imagination now to understand what the visit of a peddler once meant to a farm family. Battered as we are today by mass communication, with more contacts and impressions than we can deal with adequately, we are unfamiliar with the effects of solitude and long hours of grinding toil. The monotony, the empty silences, left the rough edges on character, making a woman as skittish as a woods creature. A man became a "regular original." The unstable slipped over into a world of fantasy, "teched" in the head.

Imagine, then, a plodding figure at the dooryard. It is the stocky form of a man who brings with him a flash of color and vivacity, a little taste of civilization, a man with a ready tongue and a miniature store on his back. He made his trades right there, settled up, and never dunned his customers, as the credit merchant did. His arrival was an event, not of the day, nor of the week, or month. It was a memory for the years, to be told and retold, the droll things he said and what was displayed when he unrolled his pack.

It is not strange that the peddler should have been fixed in the national memory as a sharp bargainer by these shy and lonely people. Tied to the farm, they would naturally look with a touch of suspicion at a man so worldly and so different, who had seen towns and even cities, and traveled hundreds of miles in a season. Or we may advance the scene to a later and more settled period, when the road was good enough for horse-and-wagon travel most of the time. A peddler's wagon would lumber into the barnyard, bristling with rakes and hoes, a wreath of tin dishes and milk pans arranged around its sides. The rear doors opened with a delicious jingling and rattling. There came a whiff of mingled smells, the sizing on cotton print goods, the smell of paint from the toys, sweetenin', and the all-pervasive horse odor.

The peddler had a knack of seeming to be everywhere, and always at the right time. Once a year came the country fairs, with the people assembled off the farms in a mood for a frolic, to see the biggest pumpkin, eat gingerbread, and inspect the newest marvel of a horsepowered mower or thresher. The traveling "doctor" would be on hand in full Indian costume, speaking eloquently against ill-health. There, too, would be the peddler, with his notions and his gift of gab.

If the militia mustered for a training day, the peddler would be on hand, declaring his views on light-infantry tactics, circulating up and down the line of temporary booths and stands. From time to time, he would compliment the captain on the brave appearance his men made as they performed the 18 prescribed maneuvers in the manual of arms from the *present* to the *shoulder arms*. He would be loud in his admiration as the men in the company fixed and unfixed their bayonets, assuming that there were some militiamen present who possessed bayonets and had remembered to bring them. Nearby would be the sedentary merchant's permanent store. We can imagine the proprietor of a country store sourly watching the peddler go in and out of the tavern, "working" the holiday crowd, jingling the coins in his pocket—the thrivingest fellow you ever saw.

Hawthorne sketched a peddler who auctioned a miscellany of small articles at a Williams College commencement, of all places.

There was a peddler there from New York state, who sold his wares by auction, and I could have stood and listened to him all day long. Sometimes he would put up a heterogeny of articles in a lot—as a paper of pins, a lead-pencil, and a shaving-box—and knock them all down, perhaps for nine-pence. Bunches of lead-pencils, steel pens, pound-cakes of shaving-soap, gilt finger-rings, bracelets, clasps, and other jewelry, cards of pearl buttons, or steel, "there is some steel about them, gentlemen, but my brother stole 'em, and I bore him out in it," bundles of wooden combs, boxes of matches, suspenders, and in short, everything—dipping his hand down into his wares, with the promise of a wonderful lot, and producing, perhaps, a bottle of opodeldoc, and joining it with a lead-pencil—and when he had sold several things of the same kind, pretending huge surprise at finding "just one more," if the lads lingered; saying, "I could not afford to steal them for the price; for the remorse of conscience would be worth more,"—all the time keeping an eye upon those who bought, calling for the pay, making change with silver or bills, and deciding on the goodness of banks; and saying to the boys, "Fall down, roll down, tumble down, only get down"; and uttering everything in the queer, humorous recitative in which he sold his articles.

Turning from the literature of humor and imaginary incident to the journal of James Guild of Tunbridge, Vermont, we find a real-life peddler no rascal, but a youth of sober sentiment. As he started on his first expedition, Guild confided to his diary: "No one knows the feelings of my heart when parting with my little all for a trunk of goods and losing my caricter, if I had any, by being a pedler."

Guild need not have exclaimed quite so vehemently about parting with his all, a note for $70, for it was uncollectable. Nor did everyone take as mean a view of peddling as did young Guild. A fellow Vermonter, Oren Wiley, who manufactured tinware, set his brother up to peddle it, remarking with better feeling than syntax: "Whoever may think the office of a Tin Pedler a petty office will do well to make themselves experimentally acquainted with its duties before they decide."

Another authentic peddler differs from the Yankee "calculator" of folklore as he reveals himself in the diary of William C. Holbrook. Holbrook wholesaled tinware and matches to country merchants, with a sideline in silverware and dry goods. As he sold his merchandise, Holbrook took in trade the rags the country dealers had collected, and pelts, fleece, socks, horn, and hair for mattresses. He was thus a part of the mechanism of the country store, a transitional type in that he was a peddler; yet, he anticipated the modern traveling salesman. He took orders sometimes, like a salesman, and the goods were shipped via railroad freight. He received and paid out substantial amounts of cash in addition to the barter trade he handled. He shipped money by express and used the new electric telegraph.

Some peddlers were specialists, such as Fred Ellis, who traveled through the Missouri mud behind a wiry team with home remedies, extracts, and spices. Like many of his colleagues, he was a versatile fellow who could graft an apple tree, sharpen scissors, half-sole shoes, call a square dance, or hang wallpaper. Other specialized lines were Bibles and baskets. Peddlers of patent medicines were legion and closely related to the itinerant doctors, such as the Indiana irregular who doubled in brass as an "eclectic physician and part-time farmer." Some dealt in heavier articles such as chairs, corn shellers, spinning wheels, and patent washing machines. There were even peddlers who pulled after them a train of wagons or sleighs, repaired and renovated from a stock of old stray parts, "Yankeed over" with shiny new paint—canny forerunners of the used-car merchandiser of today.

Sometimes the goods belonged to the peddler. At other times the peddler was in the employ of a wholesaler, as was Holbrook, or of a manufacturer trying to find a market for his product.

There were even women peddlers. Elizabeth Covey of Wilmington, Vermont, recalls that women with dark skins, wearing cheap jewelry, who were possibly Armenians, came through that part of Vermont, wearing small brightly fringed woolen head shawls and dresses of rusty black, green, or brown material with tight-fitting basques and full skirts of calico. Their articles of sale were necessarily small, though their packs seem to have weighed nearly 100 pounds at times, crammed with rolls of lace, doilies, pins, needles, thread, and cheap jewelry.

"The valise was wrapped in a square of black oilcloth and was fastened on the women's backs with leather straps. Like the men who wore packs, the women were always bent over under their heavy load. . . . No one recalls that the peddlers ever molested or stole from the farmers who were their customers." Armenian or Syrian women peddlers were also known and received with hospitality in Maine in the nineties. They wore a red handkerchief over black hair, gold earrings, and bright necklaces, "a huge oil-cloth-covered pack on each hip fitted with embroideries and notions."

After the Civil War the peddler appeared in a new form, as manufacturer's "agent" for the endless stream of new inventions that appeared as the country improved its techniques for mass production. The new breed of peddler was highly specialized. The canvassers made sales directly to the customers, delivered the goods, collected the money, and departed for parts unknown. Famous among all the manufacturers' representatives for their numbers and persistence were the agents who popularized the sewing machine and sold the cash register idea to small retailers. Magazines and newspapers were full of advertisements for agents. Men and women were needed to sell patent wire clotheslines, parlor organs, washing machines and wringers, parlor matches, stationery, new kinds of kerosene lamps with patented chimneys or no chimneys, grinding apparatus for farms, and books, books, books.

By the eighties the old-fashioned peddlers were greatly reduced in numbers. Only 15 held licenses in 1881 to follow their trade in New York State, while the "agents" were numbered in the thousands. Peddling had always been a marginal occupation, something to do for a time, to get experience, a way to learn about human nature, meet people, see the country. The young, the adventurous, the ne'er-do-well, the defeated, the immigrant, or the "mover" drifted in and out of peddling. Anyone could get into the peddling way with a tiny investment.

When the Lincolns and the Hankses and the Johnstons got restless in southern Indiana and "lit out" for Illinois, Tom Lincoln's gangling boy, Abe, put his little capital of $30 into pins and needles, knives and forks, buttons, thread, and other notions, and peddled along the way. We have already noticed how James Guild acquired his stock—by turning over a dubious note for $70. Jared Warner of Canfield, Ohio, set himself up as a wagon peddler at Pittsburgh at a cost of $324.71 for merchandise. His horse cost $45; his harness $14 and wagon $6. All he had to put up in cash was approximately $200, the rest being advanced on credit. A man with a sharp eye, such as Warner, traveling and trading as he went, jogging along at 6 to 20 miles each day, covered a lot of territory. In a single tour, he would move over hundreds of miles of roads and cross several states, talking to all kinds and conditions of men, from the woodsy coon hunter to a lawyer on his way to being a judge. He had excellent opportunities to spy out the country.

For many young peddlers the way ahead in the world was to pitch on a promising spot and set up as a country storekeeper at a permanent stand. That is precisely what Jared Warner did, what many another long-headed youth did, such as Dexter Knowlton. Knowlton left the old family farm in the hills of Chautauqua County, New York, for a peddling trip to the western prairies. At Freeport, Illinois, he exchanged his pack for the counter, ruler, and slate of the sedentary merchant. Within a few years, he owned a private bank as well as a store, and sat as a director of the Galena & Chicago Union Railroad; and was nominated, though not elected, for governor of the state. In his last years, still bubbling with enterprise, Knowlton reappeared in New York State as a substantial capitalist, and purveyed Congress Water to the ailing who took the cure at Saratoga. Carting gentleman, storekeeper, banker, politico, promotor, and entrepreneur—peddler's progress, indeed!

In becoming a merchant with a home, family, and stake in the community, the peddler acquired a new respectability and regard. He escaped from the physical discomfort and loneliness of his old calling; embraced the opportunity to settle down and become a sound judge of Monongahela rye and the burgoo pot; and if he had something of the promoter in his makeup, he talked expansively of plats, additions, and town lots. As a merchant, he saw more cash in a year than most of his customers would ever handle in a lifetime of planting and harvesting. With his own store, a likely son coming along, the country growing up, the ex-peddler found himself a man of consequence; his prayer for his son, as one merchant expressed it, "that he become a good, honest man and grow up to love his country and keep out of the Democratic party."

New vistas were opened up to the peddler-turned-storekeeper. Almost anything could happen. He might become school trustee, captain of the militia, or supervisor of the town, or even make the race for the lower house in the state legislature. It was a better life, if also a more complex one; but a man who had cut his eyeteeth selling from a peddler's pack, and thrived on it, could also surmount the trials and complexities of storekeeping.

PART II

Marketing in America, 1790-1860

C. THE WHOLESALING SYSTEM

1. THE PERILS OF PEARL STREET*

Many country merchants traveled to New York to purchase their stock, and Pearl Street was the focal point of that city's wholesaling activities. This selection presents in all its color and excitement the scene we would have observed in the 1850's accompanying a backwoods merchant on his journey. Attention is focused in turn on the role of the drummers who represented competing wholesale houses and the attractions of the city which the shopkeepr might enjoy. The author also provides an impressionistic picture of the business practices of the period. This colorful era in American marketing was to disappear within a few years. Even in the 1850's, some merchants preferred to stay at home and purchase their requirements from commercial travelers who, at that time, were transporting themselves and their samples by steamboat, railroad, and even lumber wagon.

A COUNTRY MERCHANT, seated in a New York omnibus, handed his fare up to the driver through a hole in the roof. The door flew open, and he stepped out into the Broadway of a hundred years ago. Glancing at the iron-fenced city park with its pleasant fountain in the near corner, and at Barnum's Museum, its front covered with great gaudy paintings, noticing the signs of the wholesale houses across the way on Park Row, he turned and passed through the swing door of Coleman & Stetson's imposing Astor House at 221 Broadway, grateful to escape the slow crawl of New York traffic.

Taking a firm grip on his carpetbag and satchel, the visitor walked slowly up the steps which led to the lobby on the second floor. It was not easy to make his way through the piles of luggage and swarms of people who clogged the way. His manner was diffident, but his eye missed nothing. He saw the house porters, leaning easily against the marble pillars, waiting for orders. As he traveled toward the desk, he caught a glimpse down long corridors of the eating saloons, one for ladies and families, the other for single male guests like himself, the "long table" set for dinner at 3:00 o'clock in the afternoon. Luxurious parlors gave off the vast hallways, awash with velvet, lace, Turkey carpets, and gilded

* Reprinted from Gerald Carson, *The Old Country Store* (New York: Oxford University Press, 1954), pp. 135–58. Reprinted by permission of Willis Kingsley Wing. Copyright, 1954, by Gerald Carson.

mirrors, satin couches, rocking chairs, pianos, and ottomans. Where in tunket could a man get rid of a chew of "fine cut" that had been "used up considerable"? Nowhere in there, he noticed, was there a suitable place to deposit a black quid except under the sofa. Children rolled hoops and flew about the corridors, darting in and out among the boys who hawked newspapers, one more trial to a travel-weary country merchant. It was a great distance—in every sense of the word—from his backcountry store to these pile carpets and brilliantly lighted girandoles.

The countryman passed a factotum at a wicket who tended greatcoats and parcels. There was another niche where soiled boots were cleaned and burnished. A clerk sat in a little sentry box beside the magnetic telegraph, which now connected New York with Boston, Buffalo, Washington, and intermediate cities. He sensed the existence of other recesses: a closet with basins of water, and furnished with towels; a desk for writing, with pens, ink, and paper. The merchant put his satchel and flowered carpetbag down on the marble floor. While he waited for the room clerk's attention, he observed among the novel conveniences a wirepull by which a guest could signal for a waiter from the seclusion of his own room.

The arrival of a country merchant at the Astor House, say in the year 1852, or at any of the other New York hotels of the first chop, did not go unnoticed—at the Irving, the Prescott House, the St. Nicholas, or the United States Hotel. Lounging in the lobbies at almost any hour were men who took a keen interest in arrivals, their eye trimmed for the western merchant who held a good bill of eastern exchange or carried in his pocket a letter from the squire back home, endorsing him as a good risk. One of the great hazards among Pearl Street jobbers who were "in the country trade" was the lack of reliable credit information regarding the character, ability, and financial circumstances of the southern and western country traders who came to the city in an open-to-buy position. The West was filling up. Businesses of all kinds multipled. As the frontier fell back, the lines of communication grew constantly longer and more attenuated, the need for credit information more urgent, the information harder to get.

In 1841, Lewis Tappan created a new kind of business in New York to meet the needs of an expanding economy—the commercial agency for impartial credit reporting. Tappan's new enterprise, styled the Mercantile Agency, met a pressing need successfully and was not alone for long in its field. Among the competitors was Bradstreet's Improved Commercial Agency. Both have had a continuous existence down to the present through a succession of proprietorships, coming together finally in today's corporation of Dun & Bradstreet, Inc.

Tappan described the purpose of his agency as

procuring, by resident and special agents, information respecting the standing, responsibility, etc. of country merchants residing in the States of New York, Ohio, Michigan, Illinois and the New England States, New Jersey, parts of Missouri and Pennsylvania and the territories of Iowa and Wisconsin, for the benefit of such merchants in this city as approve the object and become subscribers to The Agency. . . . The information obtained is from attorneys, cashiers of banks, old merchants and other competent persons. It is not a system of espionage, but the same as merchants usually employ—only on an extended plan—to ascertain whether persons applying for credit are worthy of the same and to what extent.

There were certain signs by which the New York commercial gentlemen sauntering through the lobbies of the hotels could recognize a visitor who intended touring the wholesale district. He would have a memorandum book of his needs which he consulted frequently, making erasures, alterations, and additions, and probably right in public; for a man who had traveled hundreds of miles and had already spent upward of $100 must be ready on the instant to give his memory every possible assistance. He had to recall the state of his inventory exactly. As he judged the market and demand, so would he prosper in the year to come.

Those who had made a study of the country merchant as a type or "character" would expect him to have his hair cut in the old Brutus fashion, ragged and shaggy and brushed down over his forehead. His pantaloons were about a decade behind the mode in their cut, being made in the old comfortable fashion of large seats and plaited fronts tapering entirely too much toward the bottom, with straps underneath his boots which should not be there at all. The cowhide boots were coarse and clumsy, the right one exactly like the left, and there was a huge blanket coat topped by a long beard and a fur cap. The neckcloth was too full and looked untidy. Although his clothes were all old in cut, perhaps the most remarkable fact about them was that they looked quite new, as though worn only on special occasions, as briefly as possible, and then laid aside quickly after each churchgoing or ceremonial. There was a pleasant suggestion about such a man that if he treated his clothing with such care, he could probably pay his bills.

So there was a rush to the hotel register to inspect the name and residence of the stranger and verify his occupation from the clerk. The merchant, refreshed, could no sooner step into the lobby with the thought of a stroll down Broadway toward the Battery and Castle Garden than he would be greeted by men with whom he was not acquainted, offering an oyster supper, theater tickets, a visit to Barnum's American Museum, just across the way, and as a starter, would he care to step into the Astor bar for a dollop of brandy or a mug of flip?

Thus the trader from western Pennsylvania or the valley of the Ohio, the ancestral butter-and-egg man, came up against a New York sharper, the drummer of Pearl Street. Narrow, crooked Pearl Street was the wholesale business center for importers and jobbing stores in all lines 100 years ago, standing as Worth Street does today to the textile trades. For 50 years, approximately from 1800 to 1850, Pearl Street was the most important, as well as the most irregular, business street in the city, lined with warehouses, pennants fluttering over the retail shops, and the red flag hung out in front of auction rooms where the jobber and his retail customer might both find themselves bidding for a piece of Calcutta cotton goods or a lot of Birmingham hardware. "Pearl Street contains all the large warehouses," said Baron Axel Leonhard Klinckowstrom of Sweden after his visit of 1818. "Here everything is sold wholesale. The shops are well supplied with goods and this street is considered the richest, though its appearance is less brilliant than Broadway."

Ten years later, Charles P. Forbes, compiler of *The Merchant's Memorandum and Price Book,* listed the wholesale dealers who sold merchandise of interest to a country merchant, the hardware firms, dry goods, crockery, and West India goods, which included groceries. All were located in Pearl Street or nearby. "It is very narrow, and the houses are very high," wrote Lady Emmeline Stuart Wortley in her account of her American travels in 1849–50. "Waves and billows of merchandise of every description and denomination seem pouring over from the brimming stores and warehouses, into the inconveniently narrow street."

Here the jobbers bought by the bale or the package from importers or manufacturers, broke the big bales and boxes to make up small lots, and sold by the piece to country traders. For this middleman function the reputable warehouses charged an advance of 6 to 8 percent on a fair valuation. Some followed the principle of "One price, and no deviation," like Nelson & Co., which dealt in men's clothing at 51 Cedar Street, permitting the customers to examine the goods at their leisure and providing them with a catalog which gave printed figures for every item—the sack coats of Kentucky jean; blue blanket coats, sack and half sack; cottonade pants of French, English, or American make; the figured vests of Farmers' satin; the white cotton shirts with muslin or linen bosoms. Other houses followed the policy of letting the buyer look out for himself. There, every price was negotiated.

Not every jobbing house drummed trade with a staff of high-pressure salesmen, but most of them did. A treatise on merchandising noted in 1856 that drumming was "now almost universal." The system continued to expand up to the time when commercial travelers took to the "road" and the country merchant stayed at home. The corps of Pearl Street drummers was made up of young men, shrewd, genial, droll storytellers, adroit at flattery and quick at accommodation to the prospective buyer's mood. A man far from his own stamping ground, and a little bit lonesome,

The Perils of Pearl Street   337

could not help liking them, with their free cigars, wine, and tickets. Each one wove all this hospitality in smoothly with the address of his own place of business. There, he had prints of a splendid style on view, a very desirable article that sold like hot cakes in the country trade, priced at only two-and-six, undoubtedly the cheapest goods in Pearl Street.

When country merchants met on the cars, in stages, on the boiler deck of a river steamboat, to talk of trade and jobbing, some said that there were more sharpers in New York than in Philadelphia and that the New York market was more unstable. They cited the auction watch swindle, in which the rustic paid a bargain price for a good watch, which was then switched for a worthless one during the wrapping up of the parcel. They warned of tricks in the wholesale trade. The jobber left out part of the order, some important country staple such as blue cloth. When questioned, he promptly credited the item, with profuse thanks for having the matter called to his attention. Correcting the "mistake" built character and so made the country customer less suspicious of overcharges elsewhere, usually made on goods the actual value of which was hard to determine. The custom of drumming came in for heated discussion, with some defenders, who pointed out that the drummers did show their lines, introduced new ideas, that the retailer did not have to buy unless he wanted to—and that anyway the custom was universal.

The country dealer, resting in his room at his hotel, was not without warning of importunities yet to come, for the business cards of the drummers were already streaming up to his room, with lithographed circulars, catalogs, and printed price lists. When he returned to the second-floor lobby, he was ambushed. The drummer presented in his person a piquant contrast to the general store owner. He had about him the air of the town. In fact, in many instances, he lived at the hotel, his employers paying the difference between the cost of living at a good boardinghouse and the $2 a day it cost to board and lodge, American plan, at the Astor. The drummer was also sometimes known as a borer, "probably from some resemblance in qualities to a worm that infests fruit trees," according to a Philadelphia newspaper. The drummer dressed in the height of style. His trousers had the full-cut leg, in checks or plaid, and were trimmed with braid down the side seams. He was shod not in boots but in the new lace-up shoes, his neck dressing smooth, not dowdy, topped with a green flat scarf; his hat was of beaver. He wore a moustache and side-whiskers and made a dashing figure with his walking stick and shawl of a rich wool plaid gracefully draped over his shoulder—an art in itself and one not to be mastered without hours of practice.

The borer was expert in his knowledge not only of cottonades and calicoes, but he was also required by the exigencies of his occupation to be something of an epicure in tasting the town. He knew the city, from the Battery to the new Washington Square Park, with its young trees and the look of the country about it. He could guide a wondering visitor to Fowler and Wells's Phrenological Cabinet containing busts and casts "from the heads of the most distinguished men that ever lived . . . Mummies, Pirates, Robbers, Murderers, and Thieves, living and dead"—where a country tourist could also get his own head examined. The New Yorker who drummed successfully in Pearl Street was also, if required, a discreet guide to the temptations the city afforded. If a countryman desired to be separated elegantly from his cash at a gambling dive, the drummer knew all the places where a man could throw a card. He knew where the cozy saloons and "retreats" were, under the stoops of old brick or brownstone dwellings, a proper setting for serious drinking. A part of the borer's value to his employers was his acquaintance among "waiter girls" and such of the city's ladies of light virtue as had not yet been rounded up by the police or the Magdalen Female Benevolent Asylum.

"The country merchant is booked on his arrival, is captivated by courtesy, is attracted by appeals to each of his appetites and passions," wrote the author of a mercantile guide of 1850, "is coaxed, decoyed, and finally ensnared or captured." Yet, so skillful and ingratiating were the drummers in their art that they could and would guide the trader as readily to a church as to an assignation, and praise him loudly, too, for his preference, provided only that he be responsive when told of the A–1 articles the drummer sold for cheap prices. "I keep at number so-and-so Pearl Street," he would say, slipping his arm through that of the man in country dress.

The drummer was always most familiar and affable. He inquired with keen interest about "the times" in the dealer's part of the country, probing carefully about the amount of hard cash he had with him, supposing that he did a dashing business in his store, fishing for the quality of his business references. Earnestly, the nimble borer warned his new-found friend against rascality and shook his head more than once over the business ethics of his competitors. "I grieve to say it, in Pearl Street a great many persons, who while they sell goods and merchandise by wholesale, also cheat and deceive by wholesale." An attentive young drummer in the jobbing line would warn most particularly against the iniquitous system of selling goods at auction.

It was a great temptation to any honest Johnny Raw, in the city from some little crossroads Paw-Paw or Stovepipe Corners, to sidle into Water Street as he heard the dulcet voice of the crier say, "Once, twice, going— gone," or cocked an ear to the neat tap of the auctioneer's hammer. Here were kerseys and flannels, Liverpool hardware, East India cottons, a chest of tea, a case of shrub, all presumed to be going for a song, at 15, 20, or even 50 percent under what the regular jobber would charge him. The auction system had a solid reputation with the interior merchants of Indiana, Missouri, Tennessee—all the western and southern regions—for bargain prices, especially in regard to imported goods. The auctions did in fact turn over merchandise faster, at lower overhead cost. They gave the established wholesalers and the little United States mills a stiff run of competition, starting with the boom days after the second war with Britain. It was the fond hope of certain British politicians—Lord Brougham, Robert, the second Earl Grosvenor, Lord Folkstone, and Sir Robert Peel, heir to a great calico-printing works in Lancashire—that they might make the United States such a vast dumping ground for British goods that they could smother American industry while it was still in its trundle bed, choking off its breath with millions of yards of English alpacas and balmorals. During the 1840's a new set of conditions ameliorated the struggle, as changed conditions—steam navigation, establishment of the bonded warehouse, the stunning success of American manufacturing—favored the native middleman as against the "foreign" agents.

The fight was a hot one while it lasted. As an early uprising of the middleman issue, it recalls the acerbity of later controversies over mail-order selling, and the independent retailer's tussle, still going on, with the modern drug, grocery, and auto-supply chain stores. American importers tagged the auction system as "foreign" because it represented foreign goods, for the most part, and foreign interests. They organized mass meetings and fought the auction rooms with pen, pamphlet, and the use of the boycott.

The part taken by the country merchant under these circumstances comes out clearly in an auctioneer's letter to an English friend which said that the hundred crates of "ware" had arrived safely by the *Lucilla,* but they had found the market so poor that "we must endeavor to retail the residue by single crates to country dealers as we find them come into the market. The Dealers in this city of your acquaintance are not pleased with your making consignments to us and will not do anything that will assist in making advantageous sales on your account."

A country trader must often have heard it said against the auctioneers that they were a menace because they had a monopoly. It was said that the auctions simply drew a special class of inferior goods to the United States, expressly manufactured for the auction market; that the United States was becoming the dumping ground for all of Europe's seconds, damaged or "tender" goods, contraband and distress merchandise. Less was said on the other side. Lower prices had their own kind of eloquence. The psychology of the city jobbers, interested in maintaining the status quo, was bad; for the protests of these indignant, righteous men, that goods were going for less than production cost, or that they might have been smuggled down from Canada or up from Bermuda, only added zest to the retailers' speculative spirit, as some 200 men gathered to peer in the twilight of the auction rooms at the packages and pieces. What if it was true that each lot represented a loss to the seller, and to the United States Customs House? So much the bigger bargain for the successful bidder!

If a country dealer was adept at evading the plots of the drummers to get him under some kind of an obligation, not wishing to be be-drammed, be-dinnered, and be-suppered, he might gaze upon various metropolitan wonders at little or no cost. Supposing that the time was early March, 1852, he could step out on the street knowing that a full moon was due; but if it clouded over, he could watch the lamplighters on their rounds of lighting New York's 8,000 oil lamps and 6,000 gaslights. On Thirty-third Street, there was a sight, the city's first iron bell and watchtower, where a policeman twirled in his chair, 100 feet up in the air, keeping an eye out for chimney fires. The out-of-town visitor could ride uptown, by hackney coach, for 25 cents a mile, to Reservoir Park to look at the distributing reservoir for the Croton water system at Fortieth Street, or he could hire a carriage for $2, "within the lamp and watch district."

A country merchant from the back settlements did not endure the long trip to eastern seaboard markets for goods alone, but for the excitement, too, of seeing the world, and the nourishment of the imagination to be found in viewing Miss Fanny Wallack's Rosalind at the Bowery Theatre or in showing up at Metropolitan Hall at "7-½ o'clock" to hear Professor Williams' astonishing lecture on mental alchemy. The physical trials of a long journey were formidable, often involving a start on horse-back, then a river steamboat for another leg on the way, with a finish in the steam cars or in unheated stages, jouncing over frozen, rutted roads. For days on end the traveler got little or no sleep, risked catching pneumonia in the wet and cold. It is not surprising that a merchant, before undertaking such a journey, consulted the almanac, made his will, and recorded a preference about whether his casket should be displayed open or closed.

Hotels were crowded at even the stiff price of $2 a day. The expense of travel was so considerable that even allowing for favorable prices in the eastern markets, a man would have to maintain a brisk run of trade to offset the costs incurred and the time lost while he was away from his stand. Once launched on the way, it was agreeable to savor in advance the welcome he knew he would receive upon his return home. A local citizen who had walked familiarly in the streets of Boston, Baltimore, or New York, who had sniffed salt water, whose boxes of goods bore the marks of the country's most respected wholesalers, could stand on an even footing with any judge, colonel, or politico in his home county.

In a day when the greatest shortage of all was the lack of news, the returned merchant would be endlessly cross-examined on his experiences; and he would be expected to deliver a lively account of the ways of travel, of how Philadelphia looked, of the crowds, the gaiety, the scandals, the snow and rubbish in the streets, the very atmosphere of New York. The men back home would want to know that it had been a cold, late spring; that collections were slow, buyers cautious; that the jobbers were heavily supplied and able to move only small lots. Personal contact and experiences endowed the goods of the merchant who bought in the East with intangible values that could not be matched by retailers who were served by the jobbing trades of interior cities such as Cincinnati, Louisville, or St. Louis.

The neighbors and customers would want to know, as a very practical matter, the trend of trade for the products they had to sell, and for store goods. Were goods going to be high or low? The answer settled the home market for the season. The storekeeper was expected, as a result of his six weeks of mingling with the great world outside, to bring back new ideas which would benefit the whole township—about the new patent cooking stoves; about new varieties of apples, pears, and cherries. Was there a promising kind of flint or dent corn well calculated for the manufacture of whiskey? What was the trader's opinion of the latest fanning machines and cultivators? What about the new "power"—meaning a treadmill or capstanlike arrangement operated by horses to convey a flow of power through tumbling rods to a grain separator.

The buying trip of 100 years ago would perhaps be unique in this respect: There might be no necessity of taking it again. With the rapid extension of the railroad network across the country, the stay-at-home drummer was about to be superseded by the traveling salesman, and it was the merchant's turn to stay at home. The Scovil Manufacturing Company of Waterbury, Connecticut, made a pioneering experiment in sending out a button salesman, Merit Welton, through the Middle West in 1832. Not a peddler, Welton had the distinguishing characteristics of a modern commercial traveler; he did promotion work, carried no stock, sold from sample cards, took orders according to sample, accepted no barter goods, and the company made delivery later by freight. The results of this novel effort, as it happened, were disappointing. Nevertheless, Welton hung pictures of the Scovil factory in the public rooms of countless hotels, gave a set of firemen's buttons to the head of the Cincinnati Fire Department, collected useful information about credit ratings of customers, and learned more than had been known before about the kinds of buttons the public wanted.

The practice of sending out commercial tourists had been well established by the eve of the Civil War by manufacturers in search of their markets and by the jobbing houses of all the wholesaling cities, with the addition of a husky newcomer, Chicago. The Chicago drummer became quickly the personification and byword for hustle and pereseverance. He bobbed up beyond the reach of steamboats, beyond the railheads, his trunks loaded on lumber wagons. He found his way to the store, any store. One irrepressible Chicago wholesaler, John V. Farwell, even hired billposters to precede his drummers as they worked their way through Chicagoland, and posters lettered in red were slapped up on the walls of stores and barns, announcing "Our Travellers Will Soon Be Here!"

At the same time, business practices were changing. Freight rates were falling. The postal service was improving. Stocks of goods could be filled in at any time, and so less capital was tied up in inventory. Turnover speeded up. Credit terms began to shorten. The discount for cash became general, with the result that the country dealer had to look more critically at the customer he was in the habit of carrying from one year's end to the next.

With the drummer appearing punctually at regular intervals, the storekeeper purchased smaller lots but stocked a wider variety. The country merchant put in perishable goods for the first time and even gave a little bow to fashion. "Shelf goods" in consumer packages were still few, confined to medicines, hard soap, tobacco, and the new novelty of canned foods. The cracker barrel was supreme as a fact and as a symbol of an age in which the clerk weighed, measured, and hand-wrapped every purchase. Yet change was in the air. Home manufacture was fast disappearing. The old wool wheel and the flax wheel had been sent to the attic. United States manufactures were gaining in volume and in repute against European imports. Connecticut, Massachusetts, and Rhode Island poured out a torrent of thread, cloth, nails, buttons, jewelry, clocks, and brass goods. A farmer could get hold of more tools and light hardware than he had ever seen before.

New inventions were a matter of such general interest that the daily newspapers often devoted half a column—an important amount of space in the 1850's—to listing and describing the patents issued by the U.S. Patent Office for the current week: patents for an improved reverberatory furnace, a carbonic acid gas engine, a new safety valve, a water meter, new chucks for lathes, a new way to feed logs into a sawmill, better methods for panning ores, new seats and running gear for railroad cars. Slowly, but with gathering speed, the "American system," with its emissaries, the "knights of the grip," worked its changes on country life and the institution of the country store. Old Jed Barber, his gray hair, long-skirted coat, high beaver hat, and ivory-headed cane, all tokens of the age that was passing, wrote indignantly to a friend, without pausing for punctuation: "Travelling by cars the telegraph oil gold silver and iron are exciting people."

The merchant on a buying trip had a serious piece of business before him, the laying out of about $5,000 in wanted merchandise, mostly staples, but also including specialties suited to his particular community, such as military goods or Masonic regalia. He had to investigate new categories of merchandise as they came on the market, such as the new vulcanized fabrics, sold by specialized jobbers, the "india rubber" warehouses. In New York, Molyneux Bell, at 58 Canal Street, was the sensation of the dry goods business, because he had the novel idea of manufacturing ladies' cloaks, talmas, and mantillas before a buyer had appeared. The rise of the ready-to-wear industry meant that the country storekeeper could stock ladies' garments made from the same stylish and *recherché* patterns as those worn by women of high position in the centers of fashion.

The visitor also needed a sharp eye for novelties that might "go"—dollar clocks, for example. There were a rage for gold pens and the new self-sealing envelopes. A retailer from the backcountry who had been thinking of sprucing up his store might drop around at Fraser's Manufactory, corner of West Broadway and Reade Street, to see the latest style of showcase. If he needed a safe, the old reliable was Herring's Patented Salamander Safe. Fire in the country usually meant total destruction. Yet, when A. M. Cable's general store at Deposit, New York, burned down, and all the heavy timbers and double floors fell in on his Herring safe, heating it up like a retort, Cable found his books and papers safe and still legible.

Stationers printed and bound up memorandum books for country dealers listing the articles a general store handled, with room at the left margin for the owner to put down the quantity he wanted before he visited the markets, a wise protection against the blandishments of the Pearl Street drummer, with his smooth tongue and tempting loss leaders.

At the right side of the page, there was a space for jotting down the prices paid. Being made of all-rag paper which would stand repeated erasures, the book could be kept and used for years.

One such memorandum book, bound in scuffed old leather and marbled boards, has the title *The Merchant's Memorandum and Price Book.* The Preface brings to our eyes the country retailer at work in the wholesale trade, still feeling the fatigues of his long journey and the novelty of being in a great city. The hurry and confusion, the noise, all were upsetting—so much coming at a man all at once. In such a situation the book was his friend, "A General Remembrancer for Mercantile Gentlemen . . . embracing the leading articles of merchandize in common use for the country trade." The merchant could choose from among nine kinds of coffee. Thirteen teas were listed by type. Spermaceti oil, candles, and flasks of olive oil were listed, as well as 5 brandies and 15 wines; rum from Jamaica, Santa Cruz (St. Croix), the Leeward Islands; also, New Orleans and Yankee rum. Sugars included the refined loaf and lump, Havana white and brown, and Muscovado, the latter raw, coarse, and lumpy, requiring a portable mill and a boy to break up the lumps before it could be sold.

Braids, ribbons, and gimps are a reminder that much of the clothing of country families was always cut and sewed at home. All the tools a shoemaker or cobbler used were in the book, showing clearly, as the mail-order catalogs did 50 years later, just what goods people actually bought and used. Shoemaking, or at least shoe mending, evidently went on in every household as a matter of course. Drugs and medicines were listed in English and Latin, classified in the pharmacology of the time as balsams, berries, barks, extracts, flowers, gums, oils, roots, seeds, salts, and elixirs.

For his own needs the merchant would find money scales and till locks, iron or brass and plain or fancy; also account books, books for ciphering, bills of exchange, and bills of lading; blanks for leases, powers of attorney, and deeds. An interesting section, and a significantly long one, listed military goods, serving especially the ceremonial side of the military arts, a reminder again of the social importance of muster day. Plumes, lace, gilt, and spurs appear; eagles and tassels, swords and epaulets, as well as pistols, horse or pocket; and powder flasks, flints, shot pouches, and gun worms.

When a country merchant had thoroughly canvassed the buying opportunities of Pearl Street, stepped around his last sidewalk blockade of goods boxes, bumped into his last self-important clerk, peered into the dark interior of his last jobbing store, shaken off the last drummer, written the initials of the supplier beside his last purchase, it was said in the commercial lingo of the day that his memorandum book was "ticked off." Then he had no more to do except book his passage home and visit with other country retailers of his acquaintance, comparing invoices and discussing the prospects for trade. Perhaps an advertising display for the local *Paladium*, with lots of black type to announce its importance, began to take shape in his mind, something along this line: "The Subscriber respectfully informs friends, customers, and the public generally, that he has just returned from the City of New York, where he has personally selected an entirely *New Stock of Fall and Winter Goods,* suitable in every respect for this part of the country. Fall suits from 7 to 12 dollars."

The merchant looked forward eagerly, we may suppose, to his welcome home—home, where a man could sit at his ease on his own nail keg and clean his fingernails with his Barlow knife, scratch his stomach without embarassment as an honest American freeman should be able to do, and chew his "fine cut" without concern for ankle-deep Turkey carpets or silken ottomans.

2. THE EARLY HISTORY OF AMERICAN AUCTIONS*

In the early part of the 19th century the auction was a prominent marketing institution. Among the many factors contributing to its importance were the following: a desire on the part of sellers for immediate cash payment, the growth of major market centers containing many buyers, an abundance of available imported merchandise, the eagerness of foreign manufacturers to discourage domestic industry, and an attempt by middlemen, particularly retailers, to circumvent established channels of distribution. Domestic manufacturers and competing middlemen generally regarded the auction as a force that disrupted orderly marketing, with numerous harmful effects. Many attempts were made to obtain legislative protection against this allegedly "illegitimate" marketing institution. Such restrictions were sponsored by those with vested interests; and characteristically, they were designed not only to curb abuses but to place this method of distribution under a severe competitive disadvantage. The eventual decline in importance of the auctions, however, was due primarily to a maturing economic system, which required more comprehensive and continuing marketing effort.

DURING THE EMBARGO and the War of 1812 the English manufacturers resorted to auctions to sell their products both in London and in America. This innovation hurt the London and provincial tradesmen, and it was bewailed that "a commercial nation should have fallen into the mistake of suffering the sale of manufactured goods" through the "numerous and increasing progeny of auction marts . . . academies of trick and chicanery," causing bankruptcies by underselling and by rapid selling of goods bought on credit.

The American ports being closed to direct importations from Europe, the volume of imports declined, and only through neutral ports or Canada did goods enter to stem the rising prices; and in this trade, several houses were often jointly interested in the same importation. For this reason, quick sales were desirable; consequently, package sales at auction were introduced as the most expeditious, as well as the most profitable, mode

* Reprinted from Roy B. Westerfield, "Early History of American Auctions: A Chapter in Commercial History," *Transactions of the Connecticut Academy of Arts and Sciences*, Vol. XXIII (May, 1920), pp. 159–210.

of disposal. Boston, during the war, had been practically free from blockade by the British, and so this city and its hinterland had continued to receive relatively plenty of British products in the old way. But New York, Philadelphia, Baltimore, and other ports depended upon blockade runners and indirect importations. "During the war the British merchants established extensive depots of goods in Halifax, Bermuda and other British possessions, that they might be ready to supply the American market on the declaration of peace. Immediately after the close of the war these goods were sent" into the more destitute ports, but chiefly New York. For a time the competition among buyers was very keen, and the British found auctions the most profitable and quickest method. Fresh goods from Europe began to pour into the country. Since the practice at this time was for the auctioneer to advance the cash for the sales immediately, the importer enjoyed a very high rate of turnover. "Merchants, finding that they could sell their goods at auction with such facility, and be ready for another venture so soon, ordered twice as many as they would have done had they continued to sell all their goods in the old way." Auctions therefore soon glutted the market; the extraordinary demand was satiated by the autumn of 1816, and prices started to decline that winter. Prices fell till they scarcely covered the duties. A severe crisis broke upon the importers and jobbers; almost all failed or were seriously crippled.

During this period of distress, American importers ceased ordering from Europe. British manufacturers determined to rid themselves of their accumulating stocks. They dispatched agents to America, who found auctions the readiest means of sale. The prices prevailing in England were very low, lower than in America. It was alleged at the time that the prices in both places were below the cost of production. However that may be, the low prices in England appeared on the invoices which were genuine; and the fact that the tendency was for prices to decline further gave excuse for fictitiously invoicing shipments at less than the prevailing English prices; and the low invoice prices greatly reduced the ad valorem tariff duties in the United States, to the advantage of the British manufacturer and the American auctioneer. As a consequence, auctioneers increased in number, wealth, and influence in all the commercial cities. A course of trade which had thus been begun partly from temporary causes was found by experience to insure the British a very decided advantage in the competition with the American importer.

THE MENACE OF PEACE

The Embargo of 1807, the Non-Intercourse Act of 1809, the higher tariff duties, and the restrictions on trade during the War of 1812 had caused a mushroom growth of manufactures of cottons, woolens, iron, glass, pottery, and other articles. The continuance of these war-born industries after 1815 depended largely upon the maintenance and extension of protection. A very distinct feeling had arisen in favor of manufactures, and Congress made clear concessions in the tariff act of 1816 to protect textiles and other needy lines; this was in addition to the high level of duties for strictly fiscal purposes. Despite this measure, the importations of British manufactures during 1816 and 1817 were excessively large. Exporting speculators and manufacturers found good markets in the United States until the fall of 1817 and thereafter found this the least costly mart in which to sacrifice their glut of wares. Not only did the sales net them more, but sacrifices in America tended also to work an ultimate benefit; for as Lord Brougham said, "it is well worth while to incur a loss upon the first exportation in order, by the glut, to stifle in the cradle those rising manufactures in the United States which had been forced into existence, contrary to the natural course of things." It was the common talk of the day that the British manufacturers were making a concerted, open, and studied effort to defeat our rising manufactures by buying out and suppressing inventions and makers of machinery, by buying up our sheep, by dumping their manufactures on our market regardless of cost and pooling their losses, which amounted to "several hundred thousand pounds sterling."

The machinery used to dump their wares was an arrangement by which agents of foreign manufacturers and merchant-exporters (1) received consignments on more or less fictitious invoices and therefore largely evaded import duties; (2) paid the duties by signing customs bonds indorsed by fellow agents or auctioneers; and (3) sold the goods by private treaty or, more usually, at auctions, for cash advanced by the purchaser or the auctioneer or on long credits of 6, 9, or 12 months.

The auction system tended to defeat the protective tariff. Before 1816, auctions had played such an unimportant role that their evils were not mentioned in the memorials of manufacturers and chambers of commerce praying for protection to domestic producers. The first petitions listed in the annals of Congress, complaining of auctions and pleading for protection, were two presented in February, 1817, one from "sundry inhabitants of the city of New York" on behalf of domestic manufacturers and a similar petition from the merchants of that city, and recommending a 10 percent tax on auction sales. This movement started naturally in New York, where the abuses were most extensive and severe, and spread rapidly to all commercial cities, even towns far inland. The manufacturers asked Congress for further protection in three ways: (1) to abolish customs credits on imports; (2) to alter and increase the duties on imported goods; and (3) to impose a restrictive, if not prohibitory, tax on sales at auction. The auction system was opposed with great fury for many years. The distress wrought by dumping after 1816 was a chief factor in inspiring the demand for a secure and stable "home market." The antiauction movement was affiliated with the "American system" movement.

Through the rise of auctions the native American importing merchants were placed in a most peculiar position relative to the tariff. Normally, they would oppose the tariff, since it was to their interest to have large importations; and the higher the duties, the stronger would be their opposition. The rise of domestic industry would shift trade from the importing merchants to the jobbers. Some persuasion was needed to ally the merchants with the protectionists. But this alliance was effected because the system of foreign agents selling through auctioneers diverted a considerable trade to new groups of middlemen and gave them competitive advantages which tended to rob the merchants of their business. The merchants were therefore in the dilemma of losing business either to domestic jobbers by the stoppage of foreign trade as effected by the tariff and the abolition of auctions, or to British agents and auctioneers by the consignment and auction sales system. The diversion of trade to the British agents and auctioneers was more obvious, direct, sudden, and offensive; and the merchants therefore supported the tariff program and its counterpart, the abolition of auctions.

VOLUME OF AUCTION SALES

Except for the city and state of New York, the statistics of sales at auction are wanting. The petitioners from other cities often made rough estimates of the total auction sales or of the proportion of the total sales of merchandise that were done by auction. Such estimates are questionable and probably exaggerate the importance of auctions. In New York, where auction duties were imposed, certain relatively authentic statistics exist. It was common to assert in petitions (1) that the proportion of auction sales to private sales was increasing; (2) that the proportion of sales done on foreign account, i.e., by British agents on consignment, to sales done on domestic account, i.e., by domestic importing merchants, was increasing; and (3) that the auction business tended to become concentrated in relatively few houses, thus creating an idle mercantile class and making possible monopolistic abuses. Available figures understate the auction sales, inasmuch as various devices existed for evading duties and not reporting sales correctly. Practically all auction sales in the state occurred in New York City. Taking the year 1817 for illustration, the auction duties amounted to 1.6 percent of dutiable sales; and in 1828, to 1.5 percent. The largest auction revenue producers were English and French dry goods; the next largest were teas and silks from China; and then, sugars, groceries, and ardent spirits. Added to this were the customs duties paid to the federal government.

THE AUCTION SYSTEM

An auctioneer is a person who is authorized to sell at public auction, for a commission. He differs from a broker, who may buy as well as sell, whereas an auctioneer, generally speaking, may only sell; and a broker may sell at private sale, but an auctioneer only at public vendue. The auctioneers in New York City had very early settled along what is now Water Street; and their buildings, opposite the old Coffee House, were known (about 1780) as the "Merchants' Promenade or Auctioneers' Row."

The system was for the British manufacturer or exporter to consign his goods to an agent or an auctioneer, who would bond the goods, have them landed and sold at auction for promissory notes which were discounted at the banks, and, having deducted the commission, remit the proceeds to the British principal; the proceeds thus included the duties for which the government allowed a credit of 8, 10, and 12 months without interest; and until maturity of the customs credits, the collected duties formed additional capital in the Britisher's hands. The following very detailed description of the system is contained in a defensive memorial of the auctioneers to Congress in 1821:

Sales of dry goods are made at auction by package or by piece; and this is the only important distinction to be observed in all the varieties of the trade. Package sales, being more important in amount, more attractive by the assortments of merchandise they combine, excite most interest, and are attended with greatest competition. When the sale is of magnitude, it is generally advertised in the principal commercial cities, with an enumeration of the articles to be sold. Printed catalogues are prepared, specifying the terms of credit, with other conditions of sale, and detailing the contents of each package, the number of pieces, the varieties of quality, by number or otherwise, and the lengths; all of which is guaranteed to the purchaser. The widths are are also in some instances specified, but always with a reservation expressed in the conditions of the sale, on the printed catalogues, or published by verbal explanation, that there is on that point no warranty, except that the goods not exhibited shall correspond in this as well as in every other respect with the samples shown; . . .

The packages are arranged in lots corresponding with their numbers on the catalogue, and are exhibited sometimes two entire days before the sale, sometimes but one; the length of the exhibition being regulated by the magnitude of the sale. When the goods are prepared for inspection, the purchasers are invited by public notice in the papers to examine them. Where it is necessary for an advantageous examination, whole packages are displayed; where it can be made with more convenience from samples, one or more pieces of each quality are exhibited; and where there are many packages exactly corresponding one only is shown.

Pattern cards are exhibited displaying the assortment of colors, etc. The purchaser receives every information and facility that can contribute to his convenience and protect him from mistake. The goods are arranged with so much attention to the accommodation of the purchasers, that three or four hundred packages may be examined with care and accuracy in one day.

On the day of sale the purchasers assemble, each prepared with a catalogue marked with his estimate of the value of the articles wanted; a practice that not only guards the buyer against any disadvantageous excitement which competition naturally produces, and refers him to the deliberate opinion formed upon careful examination before the sale, but also promotes a general knowledge of merchandise in every variety, and creates a useful register of the fluctuations of the market, as these catalogues are generally preserved, with notes in the margin of the prices at which every article has been sold.

At the commencement of the sale the conditions are recapitulated by the auctioneer, among which is a provision that no allowance will be made for damage or deficiency after the goods have left the city (a regulation at once equitable and necessary), as otherwise there would be no protection for the auctioneer in the settlement of his accounts, or for the seller against the fraudulent claims of strangers. This being however, a declared condition at all times, the publicity of the rule insures the prompt examination of the goods.

Package sales are resorted to when entire cargoes are to be sold, or where the quantity of goods is too great to be disposed of in detail. Large assortments of merchandise are daily offered at the piece sales, where packages are opened, and the goods sold in small or large lots, as may most tend to the interest of the seller and the convenience of the purchaser. These sales are regular and systematic, being held by each auctioneer of extensive business on two or more specified days in each week, and are principally depended upon by the retailers as well as the larger dealers for their uniform supplies; they are held under the same implied regulations which govern sales by package. Every article is opened and exhibited on shelves on the morning of the sale; a sample piece of every package, as it is offered by the auctioneer, is displayed upon the counter for examination, and several others distributed among the company in original folds; the rest of the packages, if of similar quality, is sold in order; but the same process takes place whenever any difference in value exists, or where the accommodation of the purchasers makes it necessary. Ample time is given during the sale to examine accurately every article as it is offered.

A credit of three, four, or six months, is usually given on sales by the piece, where the amount purchased exceeds $100, and approved security is always required by the auctioneer. Legal interest is allowed for cash payment; and men of limited means, by a combination of their purchases, secure the credit which is at all times convenient, and frequently necessary—their united responsibility being admitted for amounts for which either individual would not be accepted. When it is considered that these transactions take place daily, and that the supplies so obtained are essential to the support of numerous inferior establishments, the importance and value of the accommodation will be evident.

As the auctioneers grew in number and wealth, they became a powerful influence in the money market. They were directors in nearly every bank in New York and obtained almost indefinite lines of credit. A report by a citizens' committee in 1828 put it this way:

As auctioneers in many cases give their own notes in payment for goods sold by them while at the same time they have use of the very large amounts which they receive from those who buy from them, an increditable capital is thus accumulated in the hands of a few persons, who form a moneyed aristocracy, influencing the banks, controlling by the fear of their displeasure, the free expression of public opinion, and hostile to the genius of republican government.

Since they took such precautions to have good names on the notes they accepted for merchandise, their paper was accepted by the banks as prime; when a buyer became insolvent, he commonly assigned his whole effects to protect his indorser, and the auctioneers thus virtually absorbed the whole estate, to the detriment of his other debts by private sale. "Relying on this preference, they are proverbial, as a body, for trusting many dealers who, among merchants, are not considered trustworthy," and "give ruinous facilities to rash young men to begin business without experience, character, or capital; and multiply failures to an extent that could not otherwise happen."

The rate of commission was determined by private bargain but tended to uniformity as among the auctioneers; the rates differed with the kind of goods and services performed. In a calculation for 11 New York auctioneers in 1829, a writer used 3½ percent as the normal rate on foreign goods sold. In a schedule of rates recommended for adoption and allowed by the New York Chamber of Commerce, when no agreement subsisted to the contrary, about 1820–25, the rate for sale of merchandise for foreign business was 5 percent and for inland business 2½ percent. The profits of some auction firms were considered very large, the net to one firm exceeding $100,000 a year.

An examination of the auction duties paid by the auctioneers of New York, Philadelphia, and Baltimore confirms the justice of persistent criticism that the auction markets were dominated by relatively few and powerful auctioneers; but the further charge that they were monopolistic seems questionable, for the number of auctioneers was large, and a comparison of the lists of auctioneers paying the largest amounts of auction duties shows not only radical changes in rank but also the appearance of new names in very short interims. These facts would indicate that competition was at work.

Increasingly, after 1816, auction sales of imported goods were done for foreign account. British manufacturers and exporters consigned their goods directly to auctioneers or, more commonly, to agents sent to our ports. These "foreign agents of manufacturing and mercantile establishments of Europe" were "most of them—single men, and aliens,—in the habit of living at boarding houses, neither hiring houses, stores, nor employing clerks." "On the arrival of their goods, their general practice" was "to hand over their invoices and endorsed bills of lading to their auctioneer, leaving it to him to enter their goods at the custom house and give bonds for the duties." The auctioneers were "in the habit of making advances on goods so placed under their control, to an amount equal to two-thirds of their value, and to pay the balance on sales as soon as they" were made out, and thus enabled "the agent to make an immediate remittance to shippers." It was frequently charged that these agents interfered in American elections, contributing substantial "sums of money for electioneering purposes . . . as well as for printing of pamphlets, &c., about the tariff, and for the support of agents at Washington when it was under discussion."

Besides the general advantages to the British principal of tending to stifle our manufactures and of finding a market for his goods, the agent auction system gave him the certainty of an immediate sale and immediate remittance. It gave him the benefit of the customs credits and thus increased his working capital; the auctioneer became his bondsman for the duties at the customhouse, as the law required that the sureties should be American citizens. The expenses of selling were greatly reduced compared with those which were unavoidable to a regular mercantile establishment—house and store rent, stationery, fuel, insurance, clerk hire, family expenses, taxes, bad debts, expenses of collections, fall in value of the goods left on hand—expenses which were estimated to amount to $7\frac{1}{2}$ to 10 percent. His agents tended to become experts, "and by constantly attending public sales, and becoming perfectly acquainted with the market, kept their friends advised of every change; so soon as any article sold at a profit, it was instantly ordered, and transmitted with great rapidity." They were said "to be always on the alert to obtain copies of orders sent to England by the old and experienced American importers, and the articles directed by them to be furnished as suitable for our market" were "hastily prepared and sent off, to anticipate such orders, and supply the market before the goods on account of such orders" reached this country.

Customhouse practices, as well as the ease of concealment, made it impossible to determine what proportion of imported goods were handled on foreign account. It was, in 1817, "supposed that more than one-half of the goods subject to ad valorem duties . . . imported into the United States" were "entered by . . . the mere representatives of the owners of the goods." In 1819, an estimate based upon "a careful examination of the weekly abstracts of merchandise entered at the custom house in New York" was that three fourths of the importations were on foreign account. The New York Mercantile Society, in a petition to Congress in 1820, stated that the proportion ranged between two thirds and three fourths; and of dry goods from England, Scotland, and Ireland, four fifths. In 1824, it was claimed it could be "substantiated by a reference to official papers, that about three-fourths of all British and French goods imported into New York" were on foreign account.

COMMERCIAL EFFECTS OF THE AUCTIONS

It has been shown above that the auction system tended to reduce the efficiency of the protective tariff; this fact gave auctions a political as well as economic and fiscal importance. The auction system produced some important commercial effects. Auctions facilitated the introduction of new foreign and domestic products; goods were forced on the market by rank price cutting, and in time the prejudices that opposed their introduction and advancement were overcome; this was true of both foreign and domestic goods. The auctions were a solvent and revolutionary factor that broke down the too staid traditional methods of commerce and consumption; the changes in dress, for instance, were toward "cheap but showy fabric" and were noticed by contemporaries. The auctions served particularly the humbler domestic manufacturers with a means of reaching the market, and some who were too small to maintain a sales organization did all their selling through auctions.

The auction system affected the business of the importing merchants and the jobbers very materially. The passage of the auction law in New York in 1817, with its moderate duties on auction sales, gave New York City a comparative advantage over Boston and Philadelphia, where "the free and absolute sale of goods at auction was not encouraged." East India goods, which formerly all went to Boston, were thereafter sent to New York. Of course, other factors were tending to give supremacy to New York, such as the establishment of the first regular packet line between New York and Liverpool in 1817, the construction of the Erie Canal in 1825, and the natural advantages of New York.

The interior merchants and retailers resorted increasingly to auction sales at New York; they came from Ohio, Indiana, Tennessee, Missouri, and other states, and the compelling motive was said to be the cheaper prices; the periodicity and dependability of the auction sales were a great convenience to the visiting buyers; and they found the jobbers became more accommodating in the face of the competing auctions. The overstocking of the seaports tended to force the goods into the interior, "generally on extended credits"; in the mercantile world the East tended to become creditor to the West. It was complained at the time that the New York auction tax had the effect of making the consumers of taxed goods in all states subject to New York tax laws. The

American manufacturers did not object so much to wholesale sales of foreign goods, provided they were made through the regular jobber channels, but sales at auction obstructed their distributing system by eliminating the jobber.

Besides the country merchants, the small city retailers were advantaged by auction sales. They were able to procure their supplies without the necessity of paying the intermediate jobbers' profits, which were commonly estimated at 15 or 20 percent. A contemporary estimated that in New York City in 1831, there were about 7,000 persons engaged in the retail dry goods business, most of whom made their purchases at auction piece sales. The retailer with small capital, either on his sole account or jointly with others of his class, was able to buy direct and free himself from jobber monopoly. A common complaint, however, of the retailer was that he had to spend so much time in auction rooms.

The two middlemen who were hurt most were the importing merchants and the jobbers. A majority of the American dry goods importing merchants, formerly the most numerous and important of the mercantile class, gave place to, or became themselves, agents of British manufacturing houses. If an American merchant sent an order with description or samples, the British manufacturer frequently sent by the same ship a large quantity of the same goods to be sold at auction by his agent, thus defeating the merchant's market. On account of this and other devices, the old importing houses failed, and new houses were restrained from beginning. The general decline of the American merchant marine after 1815 was a leading factor in this tendency to mortality of mercantile houses.

The jobbers, as distinguished from retailers on the one hand and importing merchants on the other, were opposed to seeing their old customers go to auctions and were loud in their condemnation of the auction system. The auctioneers, replying to the jobbers' demand for legislation prohibiting auctions, urged the danger of class legislation, that other classes of tradesmen might be abolished or regulated once such legislation had been initiated. Their efforts to abolish their new competitor having failed, there arose an "intermediate grade of merchants" who purchased largely at auctions, at the package sales, from wholesale importers, and in such other ways as they could obtain merchandise on reasonable terms, and who sold to local and country retailers. One of these New York houses, Reuben Vose, shoe and hat store, was the first to introduce the one-price plan, which has come to characterize American business; Vose published a catalog describing some 100 different articles, with all prices marked against them; he gained and kept the ascendency over all other New York jobbers in sales to western and southern merchants; his business was conducted on a strictly cash basis, and he won from the credit houses their cash business. There arose at this time in New York a company of young men, called "Prime Ministers," who were the junior partners and confidential clerks of the jobbing houses; they had entire control of all country buyers who visited the city for the first time; they were men of education and polished manners, superior to the merchants who employed them; and they soon acquired a powerful influence in the mercantile world.

By these devices (purchase by package at auction one-price cash sale, employment of expert salesmen, and entertainment of visiting buyers) and others, the jobbers withstood to a good degree the competition of the auction houses.

OBJECTIONS TO THE AUCTIONS

Many of the objections to auctions have been stated above. These and others will be summarized here.

1. Auctions tended to defeat the American protective policy. They facilitated dumping by foreign manufacturers, made customs credits more advantageous to importers, and abetted the evasion of duties by undervaluation.

2. Auctions hurt certain vested interests, particularly the American importing merchants and jobbers; disturbed the accustomed channels of trade; and diverted a large part of foreign commerce to foreign agents and consignees resident in America.

3. The auctioneer was less responsible than the merchant and retailer for dishonest practices and frauds, such as short lengths, deficient numbers, defective materials, etc.

4. Auctions tended to concentrate a considerable proportion of the trade in a few hands and draw away the customers of merchants and retailers, and were therefore attacked as "monopolistic." But it was a perverted use of the term, for the earmarks of monopoly are limitation of supply, higher prices, discriminations, and excessive profits, none of which characterized the auctions. Indeed, they tended to make trade more competitive, to break the hold of jobbers and retailers on their customers, and to give open publicity to prices and profits. The concentration of auction sales at fewer places was to the convenience of buyers and very likely intensified competition among buyers. Auction sales made it possible for small local and interior retailers, whom the jobbers refused or hesitated to encourage, to get a start. The complaint against auctions was that against big business and plutocracy; they were held to be "unjust, by giving a few, that which ought to be distributed among the mercantile community generally. A single auction house does as much business as would support fifty respectable firms in private trade, each consisting of two partners, maintaining two families, and two or three clerks. The evident tendency of this monopoly is to crush the

middle ranks, and to divide the society into the very rich and the poor."
Evidently, the case is exaggerated and the economic doctrine questionable. The only basis for a charge of monopoly was that the auctioneers
were under license by the state and their number was limited, and no
other persons were allowed to sell in this way; but as there were every
year some auctioneer licenses not taken, it is evident that New York
was not suffering from the restriction on the number of auctioneers. Nor
were good evidences of monopoly the common charges that certain goods
could be found only at auctions, that some stores refused to sell certain
goods by private treaty but only through auctions where higher prices
might be gotten, and that buyers at auction had frequently to buy more
than they wanted.

5. In proportion to the amounts of goods imported and sold, the
agents, consignees, and auctioneers did not hire as many houses, stores,
and clerks and did not, therefore, contribute as much to the public coffers
as the generality of resident merchants, jobbers, and retailers. So they
were alleged to hurt the city and escape their due burden of public expenditure. But on the other hand, the revenue derived by the state of
New York from auction taxes constituted one of the principal items in
the canal fund—"a revenue which grew out of a business which drew
merchants or purchasers from all parts of our widely extended country,
which tended directly to enhance the value of houses, stores and lots,
multiply the business of the shipper, importer and jobber, and which has
filled our city with palaces, and made our merchant princes."

6. Auctions tended to concentrate the whole trade of the country in
a few large cities, to the extinction of all other wholesale markets. The
importers of such places as Richmond, Petersburg, Charleston, Savannah,
and Augusta disappeared within a few years. Goods bought at auction
in seaboard cities were carried by itinerant dealers to interior towns and
offered for sale at auction day after day and night after night in some
rooms adjoining the local retail stores; such operations tended to disrupt
and destroy the local retail trade. Some of these interior auctioneers were
resident and maintained purchasing agents at the seaboard city.

7. It was argued that the foreign agent auction system hurt the country because it tended to cause the export of money which would otherwise be expended inside our boundaries. An estimate of the profits of
foreign agents in 1825 was $2 million, which, it was pointed out, would
employ 500 principal merchants, with their 1,000 clerks and assistants,
together with their families; and require stores, warehouses, and dwellings, fully 1,000 houses, with rentals of $250,000; and would percolate to
advantage through mechanics, dependent branches of business, farmers,
etc.

8. Auction sales disturbed the regularity and dependability of commerce and industry. Dumping by foreign manufacturers had that very

purpose. That steadiness of market which is required to yield a reasonable profit and regular employment was adversely affected. Prices fluctuated widely, and speculative purchases were fostered.

9. A charge against auctions, reiterated without end, was that they injected into use a poorer quality of goods than the people were wont to buy by private treaty and than they thought they were buying. It was a period when, the world over, people began to wear cheaper clothes, introduced and made possible by the industrial revolution, particularly cotton goods. Auctions probably did facilitate this change of custom in costume by breaking the rigid trade channels and giving the manufacturer a competing outlet for his new products. But the enemies of the auction system charged the manufacturers and auctioneers with fraudulent activities. It was alleged that manufacturers prepared *"on purpose for auctions,* goods defective in every respect—in length, width, quality, color, and pattern, which no reputable house would venture to import and to offer at private sale—and which would be dear at any price"; that they used auctions to force the sale of refused and damaged goods; and that they artfully made and packed the poor-quality goods so that none but good judges could discriminate. Auctions were supposed to facilitate these deceptions because the time and conveniences allowed to examine the goods were entirely inadequate. Auctions caused a decline in the "distinctive character of goods," that is, they could no longer be bought simply by name and brand and number, but only after personal inspection. These allegations were probably somewhat exaggerated, for most of the goods sold at auction were sent there from the stocks of importers and retailers, and the difficulty of examining the goods in the short interval at time of sale was "in some measure removed by the previous exposure of the goods for examination (1 to 3 days) and also by the three days allowed after each sale, as allowed by common custom for the examination, within which time, goods sold as perfect, and of specific lengths, breadths and qualities, if found to differ from the terms of sale, in either of these respects," might be returned, or retained by the purchaser, "receiving such deductions as may be agreed upon at his option." That so few claims were made for deficiencies is evidence that the frauds were not rank.

10. Various undesirable social results were ascribed to auctions. They were thought to lower private morals. Deceptions, frauds, irresponsible sellers, etc., alleged to prevail at auctions, were said to be subversive of "the mutual confidence and courtesy that subsisted, in our better days, between the responsible importer and his customers," "subversive of all the milder and kindlier charities of our nature, and unavoidably conducive to progressive and infinite depravity." The spirit of gambling was supposed to be excited by bidding at public sales, and resulted in overbuying, bankruptcies, and misery. The auctioneers claimed that their

business was conducted on a high moral plane and that credit extensions by private-treaty sellers encouraged overbuying to a greater extent than auction sales.

11. In this connection, certain business practices were criticized. Fictitious bidding at auctions was alleged, false news was published, the market was rigged, etc. To evade auction duties, small quantities of a certain commodity were offered at auction to determine the price, and then large sales at this price were made in private; false reports of sales were used; the auctioneers sold their commissions, conducted sales at other places than their regular place of business, and did other irregular things.

CAMPAIGN AGAINST THE AUCTIONS

The opponents of auctions tried openly three methods for ousting or restricting them. One was a vehement publicity campaign exposing their evils and shortcomings in violent and exaggerated language. This was done through newspapers, pamphlets, and mercantile associations. The campaign was nationwide but largely concentrated in the seaboard cities. Alliances between cities and with the protectionists were effected. The auctioneers fought this by a counter publicity campaign and by threats to withdraw their advertisements from hostile newspapers.

The second device was to boycott the auctions. The members of merchant associations agreed to purchase no goods at auction and to deal with no one who did. The United Dry Goods Association of New York in 1821 adopted unanimously a strong resolution against auctions but found after a short trial that its boycott was not respected by its members and repealed by close vote so much of the resolution as bound them to boycott. In 1830, 165 dealers in New York pledged themselves for one year not to purchase at any sale by auction where endorsed notes were required because they believed auction sales should be on an equality in this respect with private sales. Another large list of dealers pledged themselves not to deal with auctioneers who at a package sale exhibited dry goods in lots or parcels of less value than $150, except in original packages, or who offered for sale duplicate packages not declared in the catalog, or who refused to sell a sample lot that had been exhibited. And a third long list of signers agreed not to attend or be concerned in any purchase made at auctions after 2.00 p.m. Boycotts of this limited nature which sought to correct specific abuses were more successful than omnibus boycotts against the whole auction system.

The third method of opposition was legislation by the state and federal governments.

3. THE TOBACCO WAREHOUSE AUCTION SYSTEM*

The history of the warehouse auction system of marketing tobacco demonstrates how marketing practices and institutions are conditioned by the physical specifications of the product, its sources of supply, rival channels of distribution, and the characteristics of the ultimate market. Also illustrated is the manner in which an institution evolves in response to modification in the above factors. Early in the 1800's, purchases were typically made on the basis of inspection. Hence the need for warehouses where the product could be stored and examined. Buyers would physically inspect the tobacco and purchase it one of three ways: directly from the planter, through a commission merchant, or from a state-licensed inspector-auctioneer. As the century developed, purchasing on the basis of sample became more common. This practice was violently opposed by the inspector-auctioneers, who were not as well qualified as commission merchants to operate in such a manner. This was just one of the rivalries that had a significant effect on how an important agricultural product was marketed.

WHEN THE 19TH CENTURY OPENED, the colonial practice of sale by mere display of the tobacco note was still common in Virginia. By 1860, there had evolved a system of warehouse auctioning only slightly removed from the modern method.

DECLINE OF THE TOBACCO NOTE

In the early days of Virginia the merchant usually purchased tobacco notes, carried them to the warehouses, collected the hogsheads, and shipped his cargo. Backed by the oath of a bonded officer, the tobacco note became a circulating medium, for it certified a definite quantity and quality of a salable staple. Although it was customary to purchase tobacco in this manner, sight unseen, as late as 1800, the consideration given by the buyer to the reputation of both planter and warehouse sharply curtailed indiscriminate buying. Lax inspecting, which occasion-

---

* Reprinted from Joseph C. Robert, *The Tobacco Kingdom: Plantation, Market and Factory in Virginia and North Carolina, 1800–1860* Durham, N.C.: Duke University Press, 1938), 104–17.

ally suffered the passage of worthless leaf, aroused careful manufacturers to demand that their tobacco be reinspected by responsible agents. Following the loss of faith in the inspectors' guarantee, it was natural for buyers to frequent the state-regulated warehouse and there observe the official sampling. Thus, they could intercept the better hogsheads and purchase on the spot from the planter.

At the beginning of the century, personal inspection before buying was occasional rather than habitual. Of all the hogsheads up for sale, those inspected in rural warehouses and then brought to market towns for sale were most subject to requests for reinspection. The planter's reluctance to yield to this demand was based only in part on his natural conservatism. Damage to the tobacco and usually the loss of the sample were entailed, all with no guarantee that the prospective buyer would close the deal. A planter always liked to sell his whole "parcel."

It should be kept in mind that during the first years of the 19th century, there was a demand for tobacco merely by virtue of its having passed the official inspection; the "common market price" was for such. Existing letters indicate a conflict between the new demand for quality and the older method of sale. To avoid the difficulties of reinspection, some shippers in the lower country began sending buyers to the smaller inspections during the tobacco season.

The new system of sale as it had developed in Lynchburg by 1810 was described at the time by one obviously critical of the innovation:

One or more hogsheads are opened and a public signal is given, by the sound of a trumpet, that the gentlemen speculators may attend. As many as may be in readiness come forward. The tobacco is broken open, and each one present inspects for himself, and makes up his own private opinion of its quality. The planter must then instantly sell to one of the persons present, for if the sale be deferred, he will be subjected to another inspection. It follows, of course, that one of four, six or eight men, sometimes one of two or three, must be the purchaser. None others having seen it, they only are prepared to judge of its value. Possibly the planter may think the offers made him are illiberal, yet it is dangerous to reject them, for if once the gentlemen who attended the inspection turn their backs upon him, he may hawk it up and down the streets in vain. The men who are considered the best judges and who are always ready to buy that which they approve, have seen and refused it, and therefore those who have not seen, cannot act prudently to buy it at all. And as but few men can devote their whole attention to the warehouses, the competitors are but few; insomuch that the buying of tobacco has almost become a monopoly. Still, however, it must be admitted that these men act judiciously, and as they ought to do, under existing circumstances.

Strict regard is had to the qualities of tobacco when carried to any foreign market. Judicious shippers, therefore, reinspect all their purchases, before they send them on board their vessels. And there are houses in this town, which expend four or five hundred dollars a season in re-opening their tobacco on that very account. It therefore clearly follows that respect must be had to that circumstance in the first purchase. But this mode of doing the business is new to the planters, and many of them are so embarrassed by it as to receive real injury.

The writer of the article believed that classification of tobacco by inspectors would restore the old method of sale, which allowed planter and merchant to meet on more equal terms.

By its very nature, the custom of actual examination of the hogshead, once started, grew rapidly. With buyers culling the inspections of choice tobacco, purchasers of tobacco notes in the old way naturally found that they had been presented with claims on less desirable leaf, perhaps barely able to pass a lenient inspection. The intense speculation after the War of 1812 attracted buyers in large numbers to the principal inspection points, resulting in a further expansion of the market towns and obliteration of smaller warehouses which had not evolved into markets. By the second decade of the century, sale at the warehouse was a well-established practice.

RISE OF THE AUCTION SYSTEM

Warehouse sale of the leaf preceded the development of a definite auction system. Although an impromptu type of auction sale was probably in existence before the War of 1812, its widespread adoption came about after the conflict. The amount of tobacco disposed of in this manner during the second decade of the 19th century is problematical; but by the middle of the third decade, selling at auction had become sufficiently well established for the inspector to be taken to task for assuming the role of auctioneer.

With the growth of actual examination by the buyer before purchasing, the inspector suffered a temporary eclipse, for his tobacco note was no longer considered a certificate of real quality. However, with buyer and planter together in the warehouse, the inspector acted sometimes as auctioneer, sometimes as commission merchant, and sometimes as both. Incidentally, as precedent for the auction system, there had been legally directed public sales of transfer and waste tobacco, presided over by the inspector.

The Virginia tobacco law, if obeyed, would have prevented the inspectors from connecting themselves with the actual sale of tobacco. In the first place, they were expressly forbidden to receive any fees other than those provided by law for performing the duties of inspectors; and in the second place, the list of prohibitions for inspectors and their assistants included the restriction that they should not "in any manner, for themselves, or for any other person purchase, sell, stem[,] manufacture, barter, lend or exchange any tobacco, inspected at their said warehouses. . . ." While the inspectors might have claimed exemption from the first restriction under the fiction that their activities as auctioneers or commission merchants were foreign to their duties as inspectors, only the flimsiest reasoning could absolve them from violating both letter and spirit of the second law. At least, so thought the committee of the House of Delegates appointed at its 1825–26 session to examine abuses in the state tobacco warehouses.

With a cautiousness demanded by the important character of the subject, the committee remarked the violation of the law, granted that there were differences of opinion as to whether the new practice worked to the planter's disadvantage, and recommended provisions to guarantee obedience to the letter of the rule. The report, which dealt more particularly with the Richmond situation, contained a paragraph concerning the newly grown appendage of the inspection system:

The inhibition of the inspectors from dealing in, or deriving any emolument from the sales of tobacco, although founded in wisdom, has not been very strictly observed in Richmond. It was the opinion of several witnesses, that the violation of the law in this respect, had frequently produced an improper lenity and preference in favour of those planters who allowed to the inspectors an emolument upon their sales; and although other witnesses equally respectable, were of a different opinion, your committee recommend an efficient provision to ensure a strict observance of that valuable feature of the inspection law.

If not among the witnesses actually examined by the committee, certainly in agreement with those who differed from the committee was James Caskie, who had been "constantly a dealer in tobacco for almost twenty years, regularly attending at the inspections for the purpose of making purchases." Caskie declared that the system of public auction which had become established was highly beneficial, and believed that the inspector, frequently the most suitable person to "cry" the tobacco, should not be prohibited from auctioning the hogsheads at his own warehouse.

In the same legislative session an unsuccessful effort was made to separate the two functions the inspector was exercising, the original one of inspecting and the newly assumed one of selling, by the creation of a new state position of auctioneer. The act which finally resulted from the agitation ignored the major complaint; and by default of additional legislation the inspectors continued their selling, disregarding the prohibitory features already in the law.

The warehouse auction system became firmly established, as did the practice of inspectors participating in the sale whenever they had opportunity. With the revision of the Virginia laws in 1849, there was added to the old prohibitory section, customarily violated, a proviso recognizing the *fait accompli*. The inspectors' *sub-rosa* custom now had legal sanction.

Note the second sentence in the new phraseology: "If any inspector shall directly or indirectly buy, or sell, stem or manufacture, any tobacco inspected at his warehouse (other than tobacco grown on his own plantation), he shall forfeit ten dollars for every hundred pounds of tobacco so bought, sold, stemmed, or manufactured. But this section shall not prohibit any inspector from acting as crier or agent for any owner in selling tobacco by auction at his warehouse."

In addition to the fees provided for him by law, the inspector received 12½ cents for each hogshead he sold as public crier, and $1 for each he sold as agent or "commission merchant." Naturally, the regular commission merchants, operating on a standard 2½ percent fee, resented this cut-rate competition from a state officer whose original function had been that of impartial judge.

The evolution of the inspector's position aggravated the once mild rivalry among the warehouses. With their income now largely proportional to the amount of business attracted to their establishments, inspectors devised ingenious schemes for presenting the advantages of their own warehouses. In the competition, more acute as the warehouses declined in number and grew in size, the planters were promised high prices, and the wagoners, whose influence might be decisive, convenient facilities. Rivalry among the warehouses was tempered by the necessity for agreement on the order in which breaks—inspection and sale of the hogsheads—would be held. In the market towns an established custom was for the breaks to rotate; the warehouse having first break one day would come second the next, and so on. This arrangement, when functioning smoothly, allowed buyers to go from one warehouse to another as the hogsheads were exposed for sale.

A feature which increased the similarity between the antebellum and the modern warehouse was the sale of loose tobacco—tobacco cured but not prized into the traditional hogsheads. Certainly, by the early 1830's, and probably before then, new loose tobacco was being brought to market and taken by local manufacturers for immediate use and by an occasional rehandler who packed it into hogsheads. At the 1833–34 session of the Virginia General Assembly, in recognition of "the growing traffic in unprized or loose tobacco, carried on in towns or elsewhere, without being either inspected or weighed at the public warehouses," an attempt was made to force the passage of a bill prohibiting the sale of loose tobacco at or near the public inspections. At the next session the town of Lynchburg received permission to appoint weighers of loose tobacco; and the assembly of 1841–42, in establishing an inspection at Centre Warehouse in Petersburg, specified that a portion of the building be set aside for the reception of loose tobacco. Obviously, the traffic in the loose leaf spread to all state warehouses. Finally, in the Virginia Code of 1849 the custom found legal sanction in the requirement that all inspectors receive, weigh, and inspect such unprized tobacco as was submitted to them. Thus, loose tobacco gained formal admission to the warehouses, where it became part of the auction system already established for prized tobacco.

The supply of loose tobacco steadily increased, and just before the Civil War the amount sold in the principal market centers fluctuated in weight between one fourth and one fifth of the entire Virginia hogshead inspections. The expansion of tobacco manufacturing within the Virginia district contributed to the growth of loose tobacco sales. While shipments from distant points to centers of marketing and manufacturing required prizing for compactness and keeping, the planters within easy distance could deliver loose tobacco to manufacturers buying for early processing. The many small Dan Valley entrepreneurs constituted a ready market for planters; and accordingly, in that section, loose tobacco sales, though rarely of the warehouse auction variety, were especially common. Since the sale of loose tobacco allowed the omission of the last laborious phases in plantation management, the marketing of the unprized leaf took place in the late fall, winter, and early spring. Thus began a movement which eventually was to draw the main marketing period a half year nearer the actual harvesting. Through the antebellum period, however, firsthand sale in hogsheads continued to be the usual practice; and certainly, from about 1825 to 1860, the major marketing months were in the late spring and in the summer.

THE RICHMOND TOBACCO EXCHANGE

Although the planter jealously guarded his right to administer personally the marketing of his crop, he found less necessity for accompanying his tobacco as methods of transport and sale became more stable. When deputizing the sale of his tobacco, the planter might use either the inspectors or the commission houses. Commission merchants for the sale of tobacco were comparatively rare within the Virginia district at the beginning of the 19th century; sale was more frequently direct to a merchant or shipper by the planter himself. After the War of 1812 a great increase in middlemen of all types took place, much to the dismay of the old-time merchant, who sold goods to the planter and took his tobacco crop in payment, or obtained the leaf by outright purchase and shipped it to foreign countries. The newly emerged commission merchant, however, did not always satisfy the planter. In 1831 an agrarian speaker in the Virginia House of Delegates remarked the evolution in the tobacco trade: "Formerly the planter, when he had his tobacco inspected, was his own seller. But now, from the change in the manner of doing business, the commission merchant was the seller and his profits were another burthen on the planter."

The system of warehouse auction sales became exceedingly offensive to Richmond commission merchants and buyers, especially the former, in the 1850's. In the first place, both commission merchants and buyers objected to the tediously long breaks which involved an actual sampling of each hogshead, and to the weary trek from warehouse to warehouse, a situation aggravated by the ever-increasing concentration of selling in the capital city. In the second place, the regular commission merchants were angered at the commission business which inspectors enjoyed. One of the Richmond inspectors declared in 1858 that "he and his brother Inspectors represented *at least* one fourth of the Planters who send their tobacco to this market." The commission merchants charged—and presented witnesses in proof—that time and again, inspectors favored tobacco consigned to themselves over that presented through commission merchants.

Both the inconvenience resulting from citywide scattering of sales and the evil of inspectors acting as commission merchants would be alleviated by establishing a central salesroom. Accordingly, on Wednesday, May 26, 1858, there was formally opened the Richmond Tobacco Exchange, where buyers and commission merchants congregated for the sale of tobacco by sample, the hogsheads having been previously opened and left in the warehouses. As originally planned, the Tobacco Exchange was to have taken all the sales away from the warehouses, although the legal inspection was to continue, since at the official break the sample to be later used for sales was extracted. A week after its foundation the Richmond Tobacco Exchange was declared a "fixed institution."

Naturally, the Richmond inspectors, having for a generation profited as intermediaries in the sale of tobacco and having only recently obtained explicit legal recognition of their roles, were the first to object to the Exchange. Colonel McDearmon, inspector at Shockoe Warehouse and the most vigorous opponent of the new institution, declared that he and his fellows were required by law to sell at their warehouses tobacco entrusted to their care. As has been pointed out, the legislation he referred to was at most only a recognition of an assumed privilege and was merely permissive in its nature. The Bush and Briery Agricultural Club of Prince Edward County led the resistance from rural districts. Fearing that the Exchange aimed at transferring supervision of all sales from the planter to the commission merchant, the members, by unanimous resolution, sturdily vowed that while they might use merchants *at their own option,* they would not be compelled to do so against their will. To ward off such criticism, the Tobacco Exchange, on the very day of the Bush and Briery resolution, agreed to a rule which allowed the planter to attend and to have his tobacco sold by the Exchange auctioneer for 12½ cents per hogshead, the same fee which had been allowed the inspector when confined to his auctioneering activities.

The *Richmond Daily Dispatch* attempted to soothe the rural section, and the *Southern Planter* vigorously defended the Exchange. Justification of the innovation gave an opportunity to air long-standing complaints against the inspector and the inspection system. It was pointed out that the selection of inspectors was merely a phase of political patronage, that buyers let the inspectors' verdict influence their decision not one whit, and that inspectors could hardly be impartial judges, as originally intended, as long as they were agents for one party in the trade. The *Southern Planter* showed that even without fees from auctions, the inspectors made handsome wages, and stated that commission merchants, with the choice of several modes of sale, had advantages over inspectors, who could only sell by auction at their own warehouses.

Though the "large majority of Planters" were congratulated for acquiescing in the reform, it was but natural that many looked with suspicion on the innovation, revolutionary in its suddenness as compared with the evolutionary warehouse auction sale system. Richmond inspectors continued to sell at the warehouses such tobacco as was consigned to them, the purchasers being those who still made the laborious rounds. Even after the Exchange had been in operation for nine months, the inspectors of Shockoe Warehouse advertised that attendance of buyers was as full as ever. On the other hand, so prosperous and successful was the Exchange that the Tobacco Exchange Building was erected in 1860.

The establishment of the Richmond Tobacco Exchange marked the only serious departure from the Virginia warehouse auction system in places where once that mode of selling was practiced. But even in the inspection warehouses, sellers or their agents did not always patronize the public auction. When buyers were present in small numbers, that method might be tried, the offering withdrawn if bids were insufficient, and the tobacco eventually sold by private negotiations. An appreciable business was conducted by displaying samples in the counting rooms of commission merchants. These "indoor" sales, as they were called to distinguish them from the regular warehouse business, included the disposition of a large number of hogsheads sent from one market to another for resale. The indoor trade enjoyed most patronage at the close of the busy season for warehouse breaks.

In many small towns and in country districts, selling was informal and independent of the state warehouse inspection system. Tobacco might be sold direct to a country merchant in settlement of an account, at a public street auction, or by private negotiations at the planter's curing barn. In the last 30 years of the antebellum period, extra-warehouse trading commonly included loose tobacco bought by manufacturers from planters. As already suggested, informal sale was especially prevalent in the Dan River section, a region of numerous small factories. Manufacturers of Danville and vicinity, where few establishments were over medium size, were purchasing loose tobacco almost exclusively by 1850, and this without the aid of official warehouses. Of North Carolina tobacco towns, Milton alone made appreciable use of the warehouse auction system.

TYPES OF BUYERS

Those who purchased firsthand the planter's tobacco may be divided roughly into the following six classes: (1) the general merchant, who took his customer's tobacco in payment for goods advanced during the year; (2) the upland dealer, or the dealer in a small market, who sent the leaf for resale to larger markets within the Virginia district; (3) the occasional speculator proper, who bought and sold in the same market; (4) the local manufacturer, who purchased raw material for his own establishment; (5) the agent, who bought for foreign houses or for contractors holding government monopolies; and (6) the shipper, who invested his money in exporting tobacco for foreign resale.

The first type of tobacco buyer, the general merchant, was more common in the earlier part of the 19th century than later, and always more characteristic of the country than the town. Direct purchase by the general merchant varied inversely with the frequency of warehouse auctions. Sale to him was of a distinctly informal character. In an extension of the colonial practice, it was customary early in the century for the general merchant to deal in tobacco, for by selling his goods on credit, he received from the planter tobacco in payment. Sometimes the merchant became a shipper and sent the tobacco taken in settlement of accounts, perhaps with other hogsheads, to foreign markets for sale, applying the proceeds to the purchase of foreign goods with which to stock his shelves.

Dependent on the staples of the section, tobacco in particular, for balancing their debtors' accounts, the merchants were embarrassed by an interference with the planters' ability or inclination to deliver their crops. In 1802, low water prevented shipments down the James and caused overcrowded warehouses at Lynchburg.

A parching summer meant hardships to the merchant as well as to the planter, for it prohibited full payment of accounts. During Jefferson's Embargo, many planters refused to deliver their tobacco to merchants for the prevailing low prices. At other times, in order to make their collections, merchants were compelled to buy tobacco, sometimes paying a premium on the current price to clear the account. Even if the quoted price was considered by the merchant too high, it had to be met; otherwise, the debtor might refuse to pay.

With the rise of the warehouse auction system, about 1820, the general merchant in the market towns had less immediate connection with the sale of tobacco; but he looked forward to the time of selling, for then his customers would settle their accounts. Now, although the planter received cash from the auction of his tobacco, he usually kept up his charge account with the merchant. The planter, according to John Hartwell Cocke, because of the long period elapsing between the initial preparation for his tobacco crop and its final sale, was always involved in the credit system. The general merchant in the interior sections, which were removed from the warehouse auctions, continued to buy tobacco directly from the planters to satisfy charges for supplies advanced during the year.

The second type was the buyer in the smaller or upland market, who shipped tobacco to a larger market for resale to shippers, manufacturers, or speculators. Usually, a dealer of this type bought leaf in Danville, Milton, or Lynchburg and, like many others in the tobacco trade, at one time or another dabbled in nearly all its phases. About 1850, he was principally engaged in buying tobacco in Lynchburg and sending it down the canal for sale at Richmond. The price difference between the two cities generally, though not always, yielded him a profit for his trouble in selecting the best bargains in his own market, in sometimes reprizing to improve the appearance of the hogsheads, in transporting to the lower market, and in there executing the sale through commission houses.

When tobacco came down from the upper inspections, it might be either stored in a state-controlled inspection warehouse or, as was more frequently the case toward the close of the antebellum period, in a private warehouse. In the private warehouse the commission merchant gave the upland tobacco a reinspection and a private breaking and sampling. Buyers might be present, and a warehouse auction might take place—a private edition of the regular inspection auction. Usually, however, the commission merchant merely extracted a sample and kept it in his "sample box" for examination by prospective buyers. The "indoor" sales by commission merchants, as the private sales of upland tobacco were called, became more common when the season for heavy breaks at the public inspections closed, freeing the buyers from that attraction. Incidentally, an advantage of the private sale was that purchasers could buy without public knowledge of what they were willing to give for tobacco.

The commission merchants charged the upland dealers the regular 2½ percent commission, in addition to fees for drayage and sampling. As the custom had developed, the price at these private sales was understood to mean with 60 days' credit. Any variation was figured at 6 percent: If cash was paid, a deduction of 60 days' interest was allowed; and if purchasers asked for 90 days instead of 60, they were charged for the extra 30 days at 6 percent. A guarantee of the debt by the commission merchant cost the upland dealer at the rate of 6 percent per annum. A common arrangement was for the upland dealer, even before the tobacco was sold, to draw drafts against the commission merchant of Richmond so that purchases in the upper market might continue.

Also important was a third type of buyer—the speculator proper. This category contains those who bought primarily because they expected to profit by reselling in the same market. The line is vague between the speculator proper on the one hand, and the upland dealer and the shipper on the other. The business of the latter two, buying outright in one market and selling in another, with the time of transportation intervening, was speculative in its very nature. A certain amount of chance taking entered into all transactions involving outright purchase rather than agency. Upland dealer, shipper, and manufacturer, when expecting a general rise in tobacco prices, naturally purchased more heavily than usual, for the speculative spirit sometimes caught the entire tobacco trade. The role of the speculator proper is well illustrated in the following description of Richmond tobacco trading in July, 1815:

The price of all kinds has improved greatly since you left us, say from 2 to $3 pr. hundred. As small as the quantity is bound to be, that quantity will not get into the European market for some time. It is in the hands of middle speculators, who make it change owners frequently, but not to the shippers, hence you may discover an unwillingness in shippers to ship more at the high prices.

The fourth type of buyer was the local manufacturer, who sought leaf for his own establishment. He offered a 12-month demand for tobacco, and during the winter months was sometimes the only buyer in the market. The antebellum maker of chewing tobacco, the product in nearly all the factories of the Virginia district, did not age his raw material. In fact, much of the buying was a hand-to-mouth affair, the manufacturer purchasing only what he needed for the month, week, or even day. Of course, some of the entrepreneurs with sufficient capital took advantage of the season of heavy firsthand sales to lay in a year's supply.

Manufacturers used all qualities of the leaf, from the meanest to the finest, but the great bulk of their product was prepared from low-grade and average tobacco. In the earliest part of the 19th century, when domestic manufacturing was but an incidental item in the Virginia industry, it absorbed much of the tobacco unable to pass the inspectors, and that "ducked" (water-soaked) because of boat accidents. Until 1826, it was illegal to export the leaf refused by inspectors; always, it was dangerous to ship water-soaked hogsheads which might arrive mouldy and spoiled. Although the purchase of higher qualities of raw material by manufacturers after 1830 received great publicity, so persistent were the Virginia and North Carolina manufacturers in their attempt to make a cheap article that they, using worthless leaf, for a time almost ruined their market for the lower grades of chewing tobacco.

At the top of the price quotations was the grade "fine manufacturing." The paying of extra sums for selected lots of tobacco was one form of advertising for both market and manufacturer. It was good business for Cosby and Winfree of Richmond to buy fine tobacco at extra prices when that fact was published as news, with the additional item that the particular tobacco was intended for use in the famous brands, Rock Candy, Pride of Virginia, Golden Pomegranate, and Palmetto Twists.

The fifth type of buyer was the agent, purchasing for export to foreign markets and occasionally to northern manufacturers. His distinguishing characteristic was that he did not invest his own money in the venture but worked on a commission or contract basis. There were buying agents from the first of the century, but they became more numerous in the period just prior to the Civil War.

Those buying on large foreign orders usually managed their purchases so that they would not be forced to pay high prices. Though they did not make public property the specific commission with which they were entrusted, the trade soon guessed the cause of large purchases. Commission merchants, in part dependent on private sale of tobacco consigned to them, appear to have courted the favor of agents for European monopolies. Independent tobacco dealers, jealous of the large orders executed by contractors in a way which did not allow them a share, were quick to join in any movement which attacked the monopolies.

The sixth type of buyer was the shipper, the true tobacco merchant, who invested his capital in purchasing the leaf outright and in sending it to foreign markets for resale. As has already been indicated, the general merchant of the earlier period, as well as the upland dealer, sometimes became a shipper. Incidentally, both upland dealer and shipper might send leaf to northern ports to be purchased by manufacturers there, but this trade became less important with the competition supplied by western tobacco in those markets. The tactics of the shipper as a buyer were similar to those of the fifth type, the agent, in that he was particularly averse to competing with the manufacturer in bidding for leaf, choosing rather to buy those types for which the Virginia and North Carolina manufacturer had little use.

The planter was prone to suspect all the buyers of mysterious and crooked methods. According to him, a favorite device of the purchasers was to spread false reports in an effort to depress prices and, at the same time, to employ agents for the procuring of every available hogshead.

Even as there are today accusations of secret agreements by supposedly competitive buyers, so there were before the Civil War. In 1809 the illegal exporters of refused tobacco were accused of adding to their crimes by combining in purchase. A writer in 1810 described the Lynchburg buyers and pointed out their opportunities for combining, noting the fact that while country merchants had been in town increasing competition, there were higher prices than before—in his opinion a suspicious coincidence. In 1846, Richmond buyers felt called upon to contradict a rumor that they had agreed not to pay over $12 per hundred for tobacco, no matter how fine the quality. They vowed: "There has not been, nor could there be, any *combination* among them, as their interests conflict too much."

4. THE MIDDLEMEN OF THE WOOL TRADE*

Although this selection discusses the emergence and growth of wholesaling middlemen in the wool and textile industries, it illustrates what happened in many other fields during the same period. Before 1800, mills produced almost exclusively for local markets. Increases in the industry's productive capacity, however, made it imperative that distant markets be cultivated. Marketing agencies that originally arose to meet this immediate need were soon making a more positive contribution to the industry's further development. Mass production of woolens was possible because of technological advances. But it was the ability of marketing institutions to sell what was produced that made growth of the industry economically feasible.

THE EXPANSION of the market for domestic wool manufactures, with the decline of importations and of household production, and with the change in factory production to the lower quality fabrics, had its more tangible side in the rise of agencies for the distribution of wool goods. While this development is to some degree confused by the intermingling of the cotton with the wool textiles, sufficient evidence is available to trace the general course of evolution in the latter industry and to picture the situation as it obtained around 1830.

The early mills apparently enjoyed but a rather narrowly restricted local market for their products. These operations, supplemented frequently by direct sales at the mills themselves, sufficed for local distribution; but the thriving concerns soon found it necessary to establish wider contacts.

The initial step in this development came through the patriotic spirit of the times. Persons interested in aiding the new American industries established warehouses for the disposition of manufactures in several of the larger cities, institutions which also made advances upon these products. The Philadelphia Society for the Encouragement of Domestic Manufactures seems to have been the pioneer in this movement. It was incorporated in 1807 with a capital of $10,000 and empowered to make advances either in cash or in raw materials upon American manufactures, especially textiles, to the amount of half their value. The goods were to

* Reprinted by permission of the publishers from Arthur H. Cole, *The American Wool Manufacturer* (Cambridge: Harvard University Press, 1926), pp. 208–18.

be deposited at the Society's warehouse; and after their sale, the balance above the advances was to be paid over, with deductions only of the legal interest on the loan and a 5 percent commission. Similar institutions were soon erected at Baltimore and Alexandria. That they proved to be among the most useful investments of patriotic zeal is indicated by their financial success or by the growth in their sales. The Philadelphia Society during its first six years of existence paid dividends of 6 and 8 percent; and the volume of transactions at the warehouse of the Athenian Society at Baltimore rose from a value of $17,000 in 1809 to one of $80,000 in 1812.

But the success of these enterprises is perhaps still better illustrated through the imitation of their efforts by purely business concerns. Commercial undertakings of this character were also stimulated by the dislocation of normal international commerce in the period after 1807. Such new concerns—organized to sell on commission any sort of manufactures, but especially cotton and wool fabrics, and, by reason of the example or competition of the earlier societies, to make advances upon goods deposited with them—were quickly established in such centers as Philadelphia, New York, Baltimore, and Boston, and had become quite numerous before the close of the war. Perhaps as ambitious an undertaking as any was the so-called Commission Company of New York, incorporated in 1812 with a capital of $600,000. According to its announcements, it dealt in all the textiles—wool, cotton, flax, and hemp—upon which it agreed to make "liberal" advances. Agencies were erected in various cities "in such a manner as to form a Chain of Connexions, and open Channels for the Disposal of Goods to every Point of the Union"; goods received in New York were forwarded to the "appropriate and best market"; and traveling agents were employed "to exhibit Patterns and Samples of Goods in the Ware-Houses of the Company." The increasing scope of business done by such companies is also suggested by the fact that the possession of a partner "generally well acquainted" with Ohio and the western country was considered a point worth calling to the attention of possible clients.

After the close of the War of 1812, and more particularly after the period of distress which followed hard upon the peace, came a development of even greater significance, the transference of various enterprises from the distribution of foreign cloths to that of domestic fabrics. A case in point is that of A. & A. Lawrence, for years thereafter a famous house in the cotton and wool textile trade. Previously, it had been engaged over a considerable period solely in the sale of foreign goods; but after 1816, it came gradually to deal in American fabrics, cotton and woolen, selling on commission. Merchants began to turn their faces away from the sea and to find in the increasing industrial development of the country an ever-broadening field for their activities. Probably not unconnected with this change was the rise of the agent auction system in the sale of imported fabrics.

Now the establishment of new commission houses proceeded rapidly. Most of these firms had their head office in Boston, nearby the important wool-manufacturing centers, but some commission merchants located in other cities. When Bela Tiffany, who had been connected with Samuel Slater in the cotton manufacture at Dudley, entered the commission business together with his brother Lyman and one Samuel Wyman, they established their central office in Baltimore and had branch houses in New York and Boston. Tucker, Sayles & Hitchcock also had a New York office. However, up through 1830, Boston maintained a distinct leadership in the systematic distribution of domestic cloths, and not for some years thereafter did New York begin to draw ahead.

The early mills seem at first to have sent their products to several commission houses, the number of such houses employed and the quantity of goods sent to each varying from year to year. But from this practice, it was an easy and wholly reasonable step to the employment of a single merchant for the sale of a mill's total output. In fact, I am inclined to think that by 1830 this practice was by no means uncommon in the American industry.

Among the various points of contact between the factory and the commission merchant or selling agent, none is of so great significance in the present connection as the credit relation. Apparently, the earlier practice of making advances on goods consigned for sale continued without change throughout this period. Advertisements of commission houses frequently carried the formula "Cash liberally advanced on consignments." But this was only one of the great liaisons. A less satisfactory type is described by Mr. George W. Bond. When the demand for wool was particularly keen—as in the period 1824–28, according to Mr. Bond —"Manufacturers had to go into the country to secure their supply for the year. This could be bought only for cash. To enable themselves to do this, many were obliged to mortgage their mills and machinery to their selling agents. . . . Sooner or later nearly all of these mills failed and their agents were obliged to take possession under their mortgages." Illustrations of this result are not wanting, though probably causes other than that given by Mr. Bond contributed to the same end. Finally, in the floating of new companies the commission merchants played an important part. According to Mr. Bond, the stock of such concerns was largely taken by these houses. In at least one case, the formation of the Middlesex Woolen Company, the evidence is quite clear. Here the trading house of W. & S. Lawrence was the prime mover in the enterprise and remained for years closely allied to that concern.

But commission houses apparently did not confine themselves always to selling on commission alone. Merchants of somewhat similar position in the importing field had been accustomed to purchasing goods outright; and presumably, this example had influence in the distribution of domestic fabrics. A case in point concerns one of the earliest commission houses, that of Mr. Joshua Clapp. "During the summer of 1821," Mr. Clapp said in later years, "commission No. 3, the proprietor's own, furnished the largest part of our business. Having ascertained the probable amount of importations in plaid worsted goods for the coming autumn, and finding the quantity limited, the merchant [Mr. Clapp] exercised his full credit and bought up in advance the stock due in Boston and largely in New York. As the season advanced, these goods were sold at a profit." Probably this was not a conspicuous feature in the business of commission houses; and indeed, such a practice might easily lead to a situation of conflicting interests. However, perhaps we have here an indication of the manner in which commission houses changed into more independent concerns.

Meanwhile, agencies other than the commission houses and selling agents were springing up. With the extension of the market for wool fabrics, it became necessary or advantageous for selling houses, located chiefly in the larger cities, to turn over a portion of their work to others, to concerns who would make it their business to be familiar with the varying conditions of the divers smaller communities, and who would act as relayers in the transmission of goods to the increasing number of retailers. This elaboration of the distributive system apparently did not occur before the twenties; at least, there is no trace of it prior to that time. In that decade, however, one finds a merchant dealing with regular customers, and others, who are described as "prosperous and solid jobbers, influencing and holding largely the country trade." A committee of the New York Legislature likewise includes them in a brief description of the dry goods sales organization it incorporates in one of its reports. The jobbers, it says, "are an intermediate grade of merchants, between the wholesale and importing merchants and the retail shopkeepers." But seemingly, the distributing system had not as yet settled into what was later to be its normal form; for, as the description continues, these jobbers "purchase largely at auctions, at the package sales, from wholesale importers, and in such other ways as they can obtain merchandise on reasonable terms. Some of them are also importers to a limited extent, and others occasionally receive goods on consignment." Still, it is obvious that, generally speaking, a commercial organization of somewhat modern character has developed to take care of the growing internal trade in wool manufactures.

That the degree of development in this system would differ between the several sections of the country need hardly be suggested. Just as the industrial organization in the West went through many of the stages which had earlier formed the course of evolution in the East, so in a measure did the western commercial organization tread in the footsteps of eastern experience. As late as 1832, many of the factories in the middle states were still selling largely to local consumers—and sometimes not even for cash. Indeed, considerable local distribution of their products was for many years thereafter a feature in the operation of many western mills.

Before we leave this phase of our subject, however, something must be said of that type of distributive agency—"auctions" and "package sales"—mentioned just above, and discussed in connection with the import trade. The auction system was, in fact, *l'enfant terrible* of the whole distributive organization. It was a serious disturbing factor, not only on account of the instability it gave to values, but because it broke in upon the arrangements made and being made by the other agencies. The import trade was most seriously affected, since there the auction method of sale played directly into the hands of the foreign merchant, relieving him from the necessity of maintaining any considerable organization within the country; but the commerce in domestic goods was also embarrassed to a very considerable degree. Dealers in American fabrics found themselves faced with a severe competition, and a competition which tended to make all their business extremely speculative. Moreover, they could not control the jobbers, who instead sought bargains in the auction sales. Unless these jobbers were purchasers, remarked the New York legislative committee above mentioned, these sales "would be but small, compared to what they now are." And again, these jobbing houses complained because their business, too, was seriously disrupted: Country dealers and shopkeepers went over the jobbers' heads and bought directly of the auctioneers. So prevalent did this become that the retail trade was itself rendered subject to violent fluctuations. Speaking of a certain type of cotton fabric—but there is no reason to suspect different conditions in the woolen trade—a retailer wrote:

I have known prints to sell at 28 cents and go down to 21 cents in less than five minutes. I have known an article that was not very plenty, to advance in a few days from 35 to 65 cents, by the competition in the auction room. And that article in a few weeks after sold in large quantities at 22 to 25 cents; and had it not been for the auctions, they would never have been higher than 35 cents, as they could be well afforded at that price."

These fluctuations, he said, kept the retailer always with one eye on the auction sales instead of both on his legitimate business, and always readjusting his prices lest his competitor across the street, who had just replenished his stock at the auctions, should undersell him. While these accounts are probably exaggerated, for suppression of these sales was a subject of much debate in this period, there can be little doubt that the system was a cause of substantial disturbance and unsettlement in American commercial transactions.

Yet, despite condemnation of the system by various advocates of

American manufacturing development, it is interesting to note that domestic manufacturers and merchants of textiles came to utilize this method of distribution in increasing volume. Certainly, references to the sale of domestic wool fabrics at auction become more frequent as the years approach 1830. It is, of course, impossible even to estimate the proportion of American wool fabrics which was marketed through the auction sales; but the evidence points to a substantial, and during this period an increasing, importance of this sales method in the American trade.

Yet the alternate and better organized system of distribution was making headway even during these years, whatever the disturbing influences of the auction system. And the steady evolution of a better articulated system is of special significance in the history of wool manufacturing. The auction method, unorganized as it was in this period, was distinctly the sign of an immature market for wool fabrics. It suggested a lack of regularity in the demand for such goods and the failure of woolen factories to provide an even and orderly flow of products to the consuming areas. The elaboration of the newer system was a natural result of the growing maturity of wool-cloth manufacturing and marketing; while the development of that "intermediate grade of merchants," the jobbers, indicates the increasing geographical expansion of the trade. That the complete modern system of distribution had not been worked out before 1830 is not surprising. The manufacturing end had not as yet reached full maturity, nor had the commercial agencies had time to work out entirely their relationships with the mills and among themselves. The feature most noteworthy in the development before 1830 was that the marketing organization manifested the effect of a widening trade in wool fabrics, the same widening trade which made possible the establishment of manufacturing upon the factory basis.

5. TEXTILE SELLING AGENTS*

The increased scale of manufacturing and the need for specialized knowledge of the market explain the key role played by the selling agent in the distribution of textiles between 1840 and 1860. These middlemen rendered a wide range of necessary services which manufacturers could not have obtained in any other manner. In addition to furnishing sales and financial assistance, the sales agent provided his principal with market information and advice on such issues as the methods of transportation to be employed. Indeed, the selling agents frequently owned stock and had considerable influence on the overall management of the manufacturing companies they represented. This selection also discusses at some length the marketing practices characteristic of the textile industry at that time.

AN AGENCY HANDLES PEPPERELL'S SALES

FOLLOWING THE CUSTOMARY METHOD of large textile companies in New England, apparently originated by the Boston Manufacturing Co., Pepperell sought an independent organization to handle sales. William Dwight, the firm's treasurer, selected an agency from a group of sales organizations which in the preceding three decades had been growing in Boston. Some of these agencies had formerly carried on a mercantile business at their own profit or loss, but they had given up their functions to specialize in one—the handling of goods for mills on a commission basis. Other sales agents had started in a small way as retailers, jobbers, or combining a number of functions, but had grasped the opportunity to become specialized sales agents. Dwight chose one of the latter, Francis Skinner & Co., a partnership which had already demonstrated its ability in many ways. Francis Skinner & Co. continued as Pepperell's distributing agency until 1870, when for a few months a successor partnership continued the selling. Then, in the autumn of that year, Pepperell's management as well as its selling arrangements changed considerably, bringing to a close the first period of Pepperell's history.

Although Francis Skinner & Co. was not legally a part of Pepperell, it was in fact an intimate part of its business organization and must be

---

* Reprinted by permission of the publishers from Evelyn H. Knowlton, *Pepperell's Progress* (Cambridge: Harvard University Press, 1948), pp. 73–97.

treated as such. For many years, Francis Skinner & Co. was among the leaders in the business life of Boston. Starting in a small way, this selling house grew, particularly after the panic of 1837, when the senior partner, Francis Skinner, acquired a reputation for acting boldly when others hesitated. This reputation he increased by gaining the accounts of several promising textile companies in the 1840's and by being one of the first to have a partner in New York. He did not rest there; until his death, he sought to expand the business, adding the accounts of other new companies from time to time. These companies required capital, both permanent and working, which he was willing to advance in order to have their accounts. Thus, he contributed to the prosperity of New England not only by selling the woolen and cotton goods but by assisting in the expansion of manufacturing through the loaning of working capital.

Of the partners in the selling house, Francis Skinner was the most important. He was born into the petty capitalist class of New England, which saw in the new specialization in business an opportunity for success with a small initial capital. Although he was the son of a successful doctor in a small community in Massachusetts, he had to assume responsibilities at an early age; his father died in 1810, leaving a widow with four children. The two older sons had already left home to work in country stores. The younger of them returned to help Francis run the family farm for a few years. Then they sold it. Perhaps Francis accompanied his brother Henry to Andover and sought employment in one of the small woolen mills there. In 1821, however, when 24 years old, he was living in Boston. Probably in this year, he formed a partnership to handle domestic goods with James C. Dunn, under the style of Skinner & Dunn, despite the fact that he seems to have had little or no business experience. In 1825 or 1826 the partners separated, each finding a new partner. Skinner set up the house of Francis Skinner & Co., whose title remained the same in the following decades, although partners changed from time to time.

Just when the partners turned to selling on a commission basis is uncertain; probably they added a few accounts to a combination of retail and wholesale business. Then, when sufficient accounts had been obtained, they dropped the earlier functions. This had occurred by 1831, according to a Boston directory of that year. From the beginning of his business life in Boston, Francis Skinner seems to have devoted all his energies and money to building up his firm.

At this time, there were few or no salesmen who scoured the country with trunks of textile samples from the commission houses. This was an era when the Boston businessmen expected the customers to go to them. In fact, a committee of commission merchants and jobbers reported in 1858 that they had "been bred to believe that the seller should keep his goods at home, and allow the purchaser to come to him." This policy meant that the commission houses expected the distant jobbers to make trips to Boston once or twice a year, in the spring and fall, to see the goods and to place orders. As for the local jobbers, there could be more frequent visits with more frequent ordering of goods.

As the years went by, Francis Skinner & Co. was able to offer more and more goods to the buyers. Whereas in 1832 this firm had handled the products of a few small mills, by 1850 it had acquired the accounts of a few large cotton textile companies—the James Steam Mill, the Naumkeag Steam Mill, and the Pepperell Manufacturing Company. By 1870 the house was handling the goods of additional large companies, including Laconia, Androscoggin, and Continental.

In order to get many of these large accounts, it was necessary for the selling house or the partners to subscribe to stock or to advance funds for working capital. During the years when these textile companies were being organized, such subscriptions to stock by Francis Skinner & Co. and by the partners must have reduced tremendously their current personal income. By the middle 1860's, however, the partners were benefiting from their earlier sacrifices. They were getting good dividends from the companies as well as large commissions on sales. From Pepperell alone in 1865 the selling house received more than $60,000 in commissions. If we multiply this several times to compute the commissions from all companies, it is evident that the agent received an enormous income for several years. Thus, at last the partners were repaid for the risks they had taken earlier. By 1865, Francis Skinner was worth $1 million, having multiplied many times the small capital he had inherited from his father about half a century earlier.

WORKING WITH PEPPERELL

The relations of Pepperell with its selling agent were much more complicated than appeared on the surface. Some of the terms of doing business together were stated in the contract between the company and the agent. Other terms can be pieced together from other bits of evidence. On the whole, the evidence is scanty, chiefly since much business was transacted by word of mouth. Some material remains in the correspondence of the New York partner with Dwight and of various partners with Haines, but only for a few of the score of years. Other evidence can be secured from sales journals, which cover the distribution of the goods for most of this period.

On September 4, 1850, Pepperell's directors determined the initial terms of selling by Francis Skinner & Co. They approved a commission of 1 percent on all sales and a reimbursement to the selling agent for all charges involved in selling, such as freight, storage, and insurance of the goods. These were customary payments to agents of large companies. In one way, however, Pepperell's arrangement was slightly different. Other selling houses had distributed part of their goods through subagents in New York, Philadelphia, and Baltimore, and the textile companies had allowed the subagents an additional 2 percent. But Francis Skinner & Co. had a partner in New York, and Pepperell agreed to give 2 percent additional on business done there, with the proviso that the total commissions to Skinner were not to average more than $1\frac{3}{4}$ percent. To subagents in Philadelphia and Baltimore, Pepperell allowed the customary 2 percent additional. Also, Pepperell granted one fourth of 1 percent additional on colored goods, an extra commission which was usual at this time.

Pepperell's first arrangement with Francis Skinner & Co. continued until the spring of 1853, when the commission to the agent was changed to $1\frac{1}{2}$ percent on all sales, while that to the subagents remained the same, 2 percent in addition. It came as a result of the well-known and heated controversy the outstanding cotton textile house, A. & A. Lawrence & Co., had stirred up among the treasurers of textile companies in the fall of 1851. Then the partners in the Lawrence firm announced that they were planning to open an office in New York and that they were raising the commission on all goods sold directly in Boston and New York to $1\frac{1}{2}$ percent; or if the companies preferred, they would continue the previous 1 percent for sales in Boston and add 2 percent for those in New York. To stop such action, the treasurers set up a committee, with William Sturgis as chairman. This committee reported at the beginning of 1852 that the Lawrence proposal would move the principal place of sale of dry goods from Boston to New York and that 1 percent was ample for selling the goods in either city. The controversy raged until the spring of 1853, when a compromise was reached—$1\frac{1}{4}$ percent on sales in Boston and New York, and not more than 3 percent in all in Philadelphia and Baltimore. Although the Lawrences gave way slightly in the rate of commission, they gained their point about the importance of a New York office. As a result of this and other moves, business in dry goods in Boston was to decline, while New York was to become not only the center of imports but the "great emporium of trade." Boston's "commodious warehouses," railroads, and other facilities, provided for making it "the headquarters for the sale and distribution of manufactures" of New England, were no longer needed.

It should be remembered that Pepperell took no part in this controversy and had no representative at any of the meetings to protest the Lawrences' proposals. Furthermore, the fact that the company had chosen a selling house with a New York partner indicates that it viewed the Lawrence move as a wise one, despite the possible adverse effects on Boston as a business center.

In the contract, must was left unsaid about other financial arrangements between Pepperell and Francis Skinner & Co. Of great importance was the question as to how much stock the selling house was willing to subscribe. The selling agent agreed to take half the stock left on Dwight's hands. During the following years the holdings declined. The firm transferred title to some stock as collateral for long-term loans and sold the remainder of its holdings on Black Friday, October 13, 1857. In the 1860's the agent acquired stock which again it disposed of—sold and transferred as collateral. By the middle of 1870 the house of Skinner was again without stock. At the same time, the partners individually held small blocks. After the selling house had helped Pepperell by subscribing to stock at the beginning, it disposed of these holdings to tide itself over periods of distress.

Nothing was said in the contract about the provision of working capital by the selling house. In 1851, Francis Skinner & Co. did loan $75,000 to the company on a short-term basis. Later the agent aided in securing loans from Massachusetts savings banks, which were prevented by state regulations from loaning money directly to a company incorporated outside the state. It was necessary to resort to the artifice of loaning to William Dwight, Francis Skinner & Co., and Francis Skinner. During the Civil War the agent assisted the company to a great extent, when to get government business it was necessary to take certificates which matured in one year or notes which did not mature for three years. In particular, the agent held U.S. government notes to the amount of $885,000 for about three years. During these war years the agent loaned to the company large sums as, for example, nearly $1 million in short-term loans in 1865. In the following years the agent continued to aid the company but not to such an extent as in the war years.

For the major part of this period the sales agent did not take the responsibility for collecting the sales notes from Pepperell's customers, as some agents did for their clients. At times, however, Skinner did assist in collection, particularly after the panic of 1857 and during the depression which preceded the Civil War. During the war, when terms of sale grew shorter for many customers, the selling house took over the collection of the short-term paper, leaving to Dwight only the notes for longer periods. This division of duties continued throughout this period, with the selling house collecting the short-term paper and the treasurer the long-term notes, which were received from large customers for both the domestic and the foreign markets.

Although the sales agent's role was minor in finances, it was major in many aspects of production. Since many of the transactions between Dwight and Skinner were made orally, the full extent of this influence cannot be ascertained. We gather that Skinner suggested the types of goods which would be advisable for the mills to make. From early letters, we find also that the agent suggested the number of looms to be put on each particular width of goods. Besides, the agent designed the various marks to be put on goods sold in the brown. Skinner & Co. did not seem to urge the practice of putting Pepperell's name on all domestic goods, but it did on the exports. The sales agent also directed the sending of goods to the bleacheries and the method of shipment, whether by boat or by rail.

In the determination of Pepperell's general policies, the selling house also took a part, since it was represented on Pepperell's board of directors. From 1851 to 1870, there is no evidence of any controversy over selling. Inasmuch as there were many difficult years when the directors might well have questioned the sales agent's methods, this record seems remarkable.

Pepperell, then, in many ways was tied to the selling house of Francis Skinner & Co. Between them was a contract as well as other agreements. Pepperell paid commissions and charges, while the sales agent helped in the determination of policies, subscribed to stock, assisted in getting loans and in collecting sales notes, planned changes in production, and directed the disposal of the goods. But the selling agent's chief job was always to find markets for Pepperell's goods, which is the subject to which we now turn.

GETTING CUSTOMERS FOR PEPPERELL

From 1850 to 1870, Francis Skinner & Co. and its successor partnership were successful in getting customers for Pepperell, not only dealers in the domestic market but also exporters to South America, the Near East, and particularly the Far East. Since these two types of customers operated quite differently, we shall consider them separately.

One reason why Francis Skinner & Co. proved so helpful to Pepperell was that it steered Pepperell along the line of specialties. Comparatively few textile concerns were manufacturing specialties, such as the shirtings, drills, and jeans made by Pepperell's first two mills. In 1854, Francis Skinner & Co. proved to be even more daring in selecting wide sheetings as a product for Pepperell's third mill. This was all the more notable in that only recently had New England mills attempted to produce wide goods. Although other companies later turned to the manufacturing of such products, Pepperell had been given a head start and was thereby well established in the market.

On the first of April, 1851, Francis Skinner & Co. sold the first bales of Pepperell's shirtings to jobbers in New York. The selling agent thus began a practice in the distribution of Pepperell's goods which continued with little change for nearly three quarters of a century. In the domestic market, Skinner distributed largely to wholesalers, or jobbers, as they called themselves at that time. Some of these distributors still combined jobbing and importing of dry goods, since as yet, even in Boston and New York, the leading centers for dry goods, specialization had not separated these functions. In addition, the agent sold to a few others such as manufacturers of clothing and of industrial products.

The tedious work of identifying, classifying, and locating customers and compiling sales for each from the daily postings in the sales journal for the first full year of selling for Pepperell—July, 1851, through June, 1852—has produced some definite information. We find that Francis Skinner & Co. reached 240 domestic customers. Of these, the vast majority were located in New York and Boston. In Philadelphia and Baltimore the sales agent distributed through three subagents as well as to 10 accounts directly from its offices. Elsewhere in the United States, there was a scattering of outlets.

Francis Skinner & Co. sold most of Pepperell's goods to domestic customers in New York and Boston. In Philadelphia and Baltimore the subagents distributed 3 percent, while to customers there the agent sold 5 percent directly. Elsewhere in the North the agent sold 2 percent, and in the South and West 10 percent, of the total domestic sales. Only 2 percent cannot be located. Thus, New York ranked first in number of domestic customers and in dollar sales. Boston ranked second in both respects, but proportionally closer to New York in sales than in number of customers. The rest of the United States was of little importance.

Among these domestic customers in 1851–52, there were a few who took large amounts. In New York, there were three firms that took goods worth over $10,000, but none of them continued to be important in later years. In Boston, in 1851–52, the two companies which took more than $10,000 worth of goods were J. M. Beebe, Morgan & Co. and Jordan Marsh Co., both outstanding wholesaling houses.

When business was becoming dull and finished goods were accumulating, Francis Skinner & Co. resorted to an earlier method of disposing of goods—sale by auction. The auctioneers were given 4 percent of sales for their commission and for guaranteeing the collection of customers' notes, in all almost $3,000 in one case. In addition, Skinner paid the charges incurred for the catalog and advertising. Sales by auction, however, were not favored except when deemed absolutely necessary, since the costs of distributing were higher, prices might be lower, and as a result the market in the following months might be depressed.

By the fiscal year 1859–60, Francis Skinner & Co. was selling Pepperell's goods in larger amounts to fewer domestic customers, estimated at about 200 in all, still concentrated in New York and Boston, but with a greater scattering than earlier in the South and West. By that time the selling house was reaching customers in Chicago, Nashville, and Richmond, so that there were 25 customers in nine cities in the South and West. This decrease in the number of customers from the 1851–52 figure may have come as a result of the panic of 1857; also, by this time, Skinner could be more selective in customers for Pepperell's goods and was able to choose larger accounts than at the beginning.

During the following years, when the pattern of sales was disturbed by the Civil War, Francis Skinner & Co. was fortunate in securing government contracts and other war business for Pepperell's mills. In 1861–62, Skinner obtained orders from the government for Pepperell duck which amounted to over $25,000 in value. The house also secured contracts for military supplies from other dealers in duck, and from several other companies, which in 1861–62 totaled almost as much as direct government contracts. In the third war year, 1863–64, Pepperell's agents sold still more goods for war purposes, over $600,000 worth. In addition to ducks, it sold drills, jeans, and flannels. Three reasons for this success in getting business were the promise of early delivery, reasonable prices, and willingness to wait from one to three years for the maturing of certificates and notes which were given for these goods.

For the pattern of sales after the Civil War, we have little information—the last surviving sales journal of this period ends in 1867. From the journal, we learn that the majority of customers in 1866–67, as well as the major part of the sales, were in New York and Boston. We also find that the subagents were more important than earlier. Skinner was reaching more jobbers in the South and West than formerly; indeed, it was selling to 9 in St. Louis and 11 in Cincinnati.

Thus, we can conclude that the original pattern for selling to domestic customers changed somewhat between 1850 and 1870. Francis Skinner & Co., while continuing to concentrate in Boston and New York, turned over more and more of Pepperell's goods to subagents. Skinner sold to jobbers in a larger group of cities throughout the United States, but still gave much attention to the large houses in Boston and New York, which distributed not only to retailers but also to smaller jobbers in their regions.

During the first period, 1850–70, the selling agent planned to have part of Pepperell's production go abroad; but during these years, there were disturbances, domestic and foreign, which prevented the development of a steady foreign market. There was the Crimean War from 1854 to 1856; the war involving China, Great Britain, and France from 1856 to 1858; and the internal war in China, the Taiping Rebellion, which lasted from 1848 through 1864. In 1858, when more treaty ports were opened in China, many more American goods were exported, among them Pepperell's Dragon drills. During our own Civil War, trade was cut off for about five years because American cottons were priced too high to be disposed of abroad.

In the first full year of selling, 1851–52, Francis Skinner & Co. sold goods for export to 15 merchants in Boston, 9 in New York, and 1 each in New Bedford and Philadelphia. During this year the foreign business amounted to 34 percent of the total sales. Almost $140,000 worth of Pepperell's goods for export were handled by Boston merchants and about $44,000 by those in New York.

In the following years, Pepperell's exports waxed and waned. In 1852–53, exports reached over $270,000 in value, from which they declined to a low of $10,000 in 1854–55. After this year, exports increased again, reaching a high in 1860–61 of $580,000 in value. In the following year, little went abroad; and in the next three years, none. In 1865–66 the selling agent arranged for a smaller volume of exports, which was increased to $360,000 worth in the financial year 1866–67. For the last six months of 1867 the total was over $130,000.

In the records of Dane, Dana & Co., one of the Boston houses doing business with China, are found some of the details of the hazardous export business. We find, for example, that in 1852 this company arranged for the export of 300 bales of Pepperell's drills and 84 bales of Stark's and Suffolk's drills, the latter purchased at an eighth of a cent a yard less than Pepperell's. The company consigned the drills to a representative in Canton and Shanghai, "or in case of absence or accident" to another in Canton. Some of the drills damaged in shipment were sold at auction in Shanghai, and the remainder were sold at the price of Pepperell's drills in Boston. Thus the merchants, even on the perfect goods, did not make money; in fact, they did not recover charges for shipping. We find also that during the 1850's the merchants did not agree as to the advisability of exporting. On the whole, N. L. & G. Griswold, one of Pepperell's customers, probably did not lose because of its bold policies, as the nickname "No Loss & Great Gain" indicated.

Nevertheless, in this period the selling agent laid the foundation for an excellent foreign as well as domestic demand for Pepperell's goods. Since international affairs upset foreign trade, Francis Skinner & Co. could not build up the steady demand for Dragon drills which a later agent achieved. Fortunately for Pepperell, Skinner had other markets and other goods for Mill No. 2 to produce, thus enabling the company to maintain a good record of sales. Skinner increased gross sales from over $500,000 in 1851–52 to a prewar high point of almost $1.3 million in 1860–61. While in the following year, sales dropped to about half, they rose to new heights during the Civil War, to $4 million in 1864–65. A large proportion of these rises came not by increases in volume but by higher prices, as we shall see in the following pages.

SETTING PRICES AND TERMS

For Pepperell's several types of goods, Francis Skinner & Co. established prices, discounts, and lengths of credit. Although there was some variation in all three, depending on the particular customer, there were more significant differences by types of customer and over periods of time. The domestic varied from the foreign customer; the early years differed from those during and after the Civil War.

Since there are no early price lists available, a set of prices, using actual sales in January of each year for each type of goods, has been compiled. From 1852 through 1861, variations were slight as compared with those in the following nine years. In 1852, Francis Skinner & Co. quoted prices of shirtings lower than in later years, perhaps to induce various jobbers to take Pepperell's goods. By 1854, it had increased prices to within a few percent of the high point of 1860. For sheetings, introduced by the agent in March, 1856, we find that lower prices were not offered at the beginning; in fact, in January of the following year, prices of sheetings were higher than in the subsequent two years.

The pattern of prices was upset by the scarcity of cotton during the Civil War. From 1860 to 1865, prices of shirtings and sheetings increased about 400 percent, while that for jeans rose almost 600 percent. The price of duck in 1854, when Skinner had sold it before, had been 11½ cents a yard, but in 1865 the prices varied from 88 cents to $1.98 a yard. To be sure, the duck sold in 1854 weighed only 8 ounces per yard, while during the war it weighed 8, 10, and 12 ounces. When the price of cotton dropped after the war, the prices of finished goods did likewise. As one would expect, the drop was greatest during 1865 and 1866. By 1870, prices of Pepperell's goods were still lower, but wages had risen in many industries, so that there was a good potential domestic market.

In the tabulations of prices per yard during January of each year, there are some variations, which in the prewar years were generally less than a cent a yard for shirtings, drills, and jeans and from ½ to 2 cents for sheetings. This variation was tied in with discounts and with the size of the orders.

At the beginning, Francis Skinner & Co. sold goods for the domestic market on credit of eight or nine months; and by 1855, this firm had established the normal term as eight months. After the panic of 1857 the partners cut the terms of credit in many cases to cash or to four, six, and eight months. By 1859, six months had become the accepted length. Then, to civilian customers during the Civil War the selling house gave terms of net 30, 60, 90, and 120 days, with 30 days the usual period. During the war, as we have noted already, government business was on a basis of long-term paper—one to three years. After the war the selling agent continued 30 days as the usual period for credit to domestic customers.

To the export trade, Pepperell at first extended credit for 12 months, sometimes with the additional charge of 1 or 2 percent for interest for the period. Later, after the crash of 1857, it was customary to grant credit for a shorter period, eight or ten months. Interest was not charged, but discounts were given on the prevailing prices. When exports were resumed after the Civil War, the selling agency did not grant the old terms. Instead, credit was granted for four or six months, with interest for the months after the first at 7 percent. Also, it added a charge (hitherto not exacted) for boards and hoops on the bales. This implies that credit for either market, before an interest charge, was 30 days and that it was a seller's market for Pepperell's wares.

Although, on the whole, Francis Skinner & Co. was very fortunate in its choice of customers and subagents for Pepperell's goods, the firm had several who were caught in the panic of 1857 and in the depression of 1861. The resulting losses were not too great for Pepperell to bear, since each year it had been the practice to set aside 2 percent of sales as a guarantee and insurance fund. Losses did reduce the accumulated funds considerably in 1857–58 and 1861–62; but on the whole, Pepperell's losses were less than the reserves set up. At the end of this period, Pepperell did suffer a great loss, not directly from individual customers but from the selling house itself.

In this first period of operations, then, the pattern of prices and terms is complicated by the different treatment of domestic and foreign customers. The former type was accorded much shorter terms of credit than the latter. Both received about the same treatment as regards prices and discounts. The greatest change of all was the drastic reduction in length of credit to civilian customers during the Civil War—from dealing in months to days. Then, 30 days became the usual period for credit; although this was to be modified in the following period, the dry goods trade did not go back to the former terms of six and eight months.

We have followed in some detail the operations of the selling agent of the Pepperell Manufacturing Company. We should not forget that the use of a selling agent reflected to some extent the old system of mercantile capitalism, in which merchants, staying close to their treasure chests and countinghouses, had appointed agents—subordinates—to carry on functions in distant places. The use of an independent partnership as a selling agent left Pepperell free to concentrate on the manufacturing function, after the manner of industrial capitalism, with its specialization and with its large-scale operations which were made possible by new machine techniques. At this time the selling houses, such as Francis Skinner & Co., offered certain services and advantages the textile companies could not easily provide for themselves. They were aware of the need for financing through outside units, of which the selling agent might be one. Above all, they were conscious of their own shortcomings in the field of marketing, which was becoming highly intricate. They needed advice as to the qualities and quantities of goods to produce.

Now it happened, and the circumstance was not unusual, that Francis Skinner, the senior partner in the house Pepperell chose, had himself risen from the ranks of petty capitalists and not mercantile capitalists, though the spirit and methods of the latter were honored in his life and practice. Indeed, the late 18th and 19th centuries constituted a period during which these petty capitalists had an opportunity to rise to new heights. Long submerged as dependent factors in mercantile capitalism, they were experiencing opportunities for growth and independence. In fact, they were the human material out of which industrial capitalism was usually created. They often became the manufacturing agents, the operators of railroads and steamships, and the sellers of goods on commission, at wholesale and at retail.

Francis Skinner showed a creative capacity in the field of marketing. He was well equipped to build up his small store into a large specialized house. He became one of the notable industrial capitalists of New England and New York in the marketing field. There were many ways in which he demonstrated his affiliation with the new system of industrial capitalism. One of them was his increasing willingness to invest heavily for a long period in the companies for which he sold. In this respect, he differed from many of his predecessors: They invested large sums in the new industries for a short time and then took their capital out to put it into still newer ventures. Skinner also was willing to assist his textile clients in securing working capital, which many of them lacked during their early years of operation. In performing this function, the sales agent was rivaling the commercial bank.

Contrary to the Boston practice of staying at home and directing the efforts of agents elsewhere, Skinner exercised his independence of judgment by opening a New York office. He saw that business could be carried on more profitably by one of his partners on the spot than by a subagent who received the business of many agents. He also proved his ability by concentrating on jobbers near at hand, whose credit rating he could watch personally, rather than on those scattered over the country. Thus, he was strong enough to weather storms, which blew occasionally over the country and toppled the weaker firms. Also, although he did business with important exporters, he did not depend on them entirely for markets; he had alternative goods which could be sold to the domestic market. In addition, he thought of ways of making the cotton goods easy to sell. He adopted and maintained a policy of reliable quality. Particularly was this true of goods which were exported, such as Pepperell drills stamped with the Dragon.

Skinner's prices and terms were fair. In good times, he did not try to bargain too sharply with the buyers but kept prices at about the same levels. He granted the customary periods for credit but with greater certainty of payment than many agents experienced, since most of his customers were close at hand. He shortened the period of credit twice, after the panic of 1857 and during the Civil War, as others did. He seems to have resorted to sale by auction only once between 1850 and 1870, a practice the regular customers probably did not like. They would have been glad, of course, to buy at lower prices; but in periods of poor business, they would have had on hand a large stock of goods bought at higher prices. During the Civil War, Skinner secured government business for the various companies, partly because he made reasonable bids, partly because he knew he could fill the contracts in a short time with the cooperation of the mill agents, and partly because he knew the treasurers could find money with which to tide them over the long period before the government certificates and notes matured.

Skinner, however, could not live forever. For five years after his death in 1865, the partners, inferior in ability or experience, attempted to carry on the business but could not weather the storms of the late 1860's. Their failure in 1870 inflicted losses on the manufacturing companies; but, it is to be remembered, Skinner had assisted in building them up so that in the years to come they could cope with competition from new quarters—first in southern New England and then in the South.

6. AREAS OF FRICTION BETWEEN PLANTER AND COTTON FACTOR[*]

This examination of the factor's role in the cotton industry reveals the high degree of interdependence that can exist between marketing middlemen on the one hand and producers on the other. The range of services performed by factors for their principals was quite broad. This close association, however, demonstrates the mixture of conflict and cooperation which has become so typical of present-day channel relationships. The following selection focuses on the many types of disagreements that could and did arise between these two groups. Both the alleged grievances of each party and the author's judgment as to the justification of their complaints are presented. This is done, however, with full realization that neither party could have dispensed with the other; and all things considered, "the antebellum planter and factor came as near to achieving harmony as did any combination of merchant and agrarian."

AMID THE FINANCIAL CHAOS of the late Jacksonian period, a Mobile cotton factor wrote reflectively: "Commerce must regulate it[s] Self . . . the Planter Should Carefully and Closely attend to his Interest: and the merchant do the Same, thereby a ballancing power would be exerted—and both parties will be equally benefitted." The proposition was sound in theory but difficult in practice. For the factor had touched upon one of the fundamental problems of American economy—how to reconcile the interests of producer and middleman. Historically, this relationship has been marked by strife in varying degree, and the Old South was no exception. That the grievances were not all on one side is equally apparent. This study is not concerned with efforts to solve the mutual problems of factor and planter; rather, it is an analysis of some of the outstanding differences, partly as contemporaries saw them, and partly as they appear in the light of research. Dissension did not outweigh harmony, for the latter was the rule and the former the exception. However, this paper is concerned with the points at which friction did occur.

To say that the cotton factorage system exerted a profound influence

---

[*] Reprinted from Ralph W. Haskins, "Planter and Cotton Factor in the Old South: Some Areas of Friction," *Agricultural History*, Vol. XXIX (January, 1955), pp. 1–14.

on the antebellum South does not necessarily identify one with the "moonlight and magnolia" school. If the factor had comparatively few ties with thousands of rural southerners in the smaller income group, he played a prominent role in urban life; and above all, his was a key position in the plantation system. The commercial practices known collectively as factorage were the products of a slow evolutionary growth which dated back to the work of joint-stock companies, continued through the colonial period, and were characteristic of antebellum times.

Marketing the cotton crop was probably the most important of the factor's varied services. As agent for the planter or interior merchant, he watched the fluctuations of the market, offered timely advice in this connection, and gauged the most favorable opportunity for disposal. His responsibility did not end with the sale; accountable to the shipper for the proceeds, he was indirectly liable to the consumer for the quality of the cotton. Scarcely less significant was the factor's role as supply agent for the plantation. To a certain extent, he took the place of the retail merchant as a provider of goods for the planter, although he did not dominate this field. His buying function was twofold: In addition to his capacity as supply agent, the factor sometimes purchased cotton either independently or for others. Not only did he supply the plantation, but he shouldered much of the burden of financing this enterprise. He held the planter's funds subject to order, extended credit through a system of advances, procured bills of exchange, discounted notes, and remitted specie. Finally, contemporary records show conclusively that he was not only a banker but a personal agent as well—investment counsel, stockbroker, collector, real estate operator, and jack-of-all-trades. In short, he rendered a multitude of services so diverse in nature that he was a veritable "planter's factotum."

Though the community of interest between planter and factor centered around the plantation, the cotton crop, and the system of advances, it was further promoted by common origins, by blood ties, by an overlapping of professions, and by reciprocal services of various kinds. In the main, the relationship was a cordial one. Granted that much sentiment was strictly commercial—in the interests of bigger and better business—plantation and mercantile records nevertheless contain many expressions of friendship and confidence. Perhaps the antebellum planter and factor came as near to achieving harmony as did any combination of merchant and agrarian. But neither in individual cases nor in the wider sphere of group interests were the relations of factor and planter entirely free from discord. Producer and middleman wrangled over the manifold problems connected with marketing, purchasing, banking, and general agency.

Since selling the crop was the factor's most important function, it was but natural that friction should be greatest in the field of marketing—as regards forecasting, quality of cotton, transportation, the selling process itself, and the various assessments levied by the factor.

Even before the crop was on its way to market, many planters came to question the accuracy of crop forecasts and cotton statistics issued periodically by factors. There were obvious defects. Communication prior to the telegraph was slow, a fact amply illustrated by the exchange of market reports. A more pointed though unproven accusation was voiced in 1852 during the course of a movement by cotton planters to obtain more accurate statistics on the growing crop. Spokesmen for this project attributed much of the sudden price fluctuations to the tardiness with which the amount of the American crop was ascertained.

More specific were disputes over the quality of the cotton itself. Much of this controversy centered around "false packing," which took several forms and was sometimes accidental but often deliberate. One method involved the use of thin strips of prime cotton on the two sides of the bale usually sampled. The inside was composed wholly of inferior material. At other times, there were layers of various grades, each of poorer quality as one penetrated toward the center. A widely used technique consisted of labeling inferior varieties as "prime" or some other high grade: low-quality Alabama, billed as Mississippi or Louisiana cotton, was sold on the New Orleans market. Less ingenious shippers placed stones, dirt, trash, or water inside the bale to increase the weight. Georgia petitioners, addressing the legislature in 1823, observed with rare insight that the poor showing of the state's cotton could be attributed to the presence of rocks within the bales.

It was sometimes difficult to fix the responsibility for false packing within the plantation force. Some planters were not overly scrupulous, but a share of the blame lay with others. When overseers or slaves received a percentage from the sale, they were occasionally tempted to "load" the cotton.

Factors, either to enhance their profits or to protect their reputations as dealers in high-grade cotton, occasionally resorted to substituting one quality for another. A curious letter from an upstate Georgia firm to an Augusta commission house sheds further light on usages in the trade: "You must crowd our lots with others that are better, in selling, and make Gus weigh our Cotton, so as to gain, or in other words, not let him take off so much for wet."

Not all such cases could be attributed to dishonesty—a number were due to carelessness in picking, ginning, and packing, to exposure to damp weather, or to damage en route. Under these circumstances, the term "false" or "irregular" packing might also mean less merchantable cotton. Many planters did not closely supervise the raising of their crop and its preparation for market; with essentially unskilled labor involved, it was not surprising that a bale might contain several grades. Not uncommonly, the product defied classification. Extensive damage resulted from exposure to the weather prior to arrival at market. The Indiana farmer Solon Robinson, visiting the South in 1850, declared that the handling of cotton was "one continued waste" all along the line from producer to consumer. Landing and exposure to the elements, the method of sampling, and other practices contributed to reduce the quality.[1] Robinson may have exaggerated, but Southerners were slow to adopt habits of economy in production and marketing.

Losses in weight—the difference between plantation and market figures—elicited much controversy. In the forties an Alabama planter shipped to a New Orleans house 51 bales which she claimed amounted to approximately 24,500 pounds, and received a sales account which credited her with nearly 4,000 pounds less. "Common courtesy tells us to treat your communication   .   .   .   with respect, yet the writer of the same deserves no consideration from us," remarked the factors in rejecting a demand for remuneration; "and [we] are somewhat surprised that after transacting the business of your husband & self for so many years   .   .   .   the writer should insinuate that we had willingly wronged you out of a cent." To assess responsibility for these discrepancies is difficult, if not impossible. In a sense, it is beside the point. No matter whether the fault lay with the planter and his force, the carrier, the factor, the weigher, other intermediaries, or even the elements, it often occasioned bitter dispute, in a cycle which ran the gamut from agency to agency, from destination back to origin.

Moreover, there were numerous quarrels over sales. Aside from the unpredictability of the market, inadequate returns could be traced to various influences operating singly or in combination: ill-luck, poor handling, and the violation of contract or instructions. One such experience might well render the producer wary. It is not difficult to imagine a Louisiana planter's reaction when, after he complained of a meager return, his factor explained the loss as an unwise tactical move. "The lot   .   .   .   was unfortunately sold two days too Soon   .   .   .   .   I requested my partner not to offer   .   .   .   until the following monday   .   .   .   .   instead of waiting   .   .   .   he Sold on Saturday, Thereby not participating

[1] Franklin Robinson to Samuel Pickens, Mobile, April 18, 1831, "Samuel Pickens Papers," Alabama Department of Archives and History, Montgomery; Byrne, Vance & Company to James Sheppard, New Orleans, February [28], 1857, "James Sheppard Papers," Duke University Library, Durham, North Carolina; Richard Nugent & Company to C. D. Hamilton, New Orleans, September 21, 1859, "C. D. Hamilton Papers," Mississippi Department of Archives and History, Jackson. Depositions in a South Carolina court case illustrate the way in which false packing might be accidental. In eight bales of Sea Island cotton, the product was found to be mixed with hair one or two inches in length, in the proportion of a pound or a handful to each bale, or of 100 or 200 hairs to each handful of cotton. Untanned hides had been used as bands for the machine in which the cotton was ginned. (*Carnochan v. Gould*, Bailey, *South Carolina Law Reports*, 1:179–81 [1829]).

at all in The mark[ed] improvement in prices, which Commenced on the following monday." Breaches of contract brought ready complaint. Written or verbal contracts were not fixed custom, but the planter generally gave directions for the disposal of his crop. Parties to verbal contracts or "understandings" found to their sorrow that these agreements were susceptible to varying interpretation.

Still other disagreements stemmed from the terms of sale, particularly when the extension of credit to the purchaser was followed by difficulty in securing payment for the cotton. That this widespread practice led to considerable abuse is suggested by the comment of a Louisiana jurist in 1825. In New Orleans, said John Slidell, it was quite too common to repose confidence in the buyer—confidence to such a degree that the latter obtained control of the merchandise before the price was paid. Speculators, without real means but enjoying an undeserved credit, thus made large-scale operations in the market. Such laxity was a prolific source of fraud and litigation. Perhaps the fact that they received comparatively small consignments from individual planters but often sold in wholesale lots to buyers may have influenced some factors to overextend themselves in dispensing credit to consumers' representatives.

Incidental costs of marketing contributed further to the differences between planter and factor. The situation was scarcely overstated by the southern correspondent of a New York newspaper. "The steamer charges a dollar a bale. The sampler, weigher, drayman, piccory, warehouse and pressmen and brokers, all have a snug per cent. The factor has on an average a dollar a bale for selling . . . and all that comes out of your pocket and mine, and all but the great unshirted." Far from acquiescing in these levies, growers frequently and emphatically registered their disapproval of assessments for drayage, storage, labor, insurance, compression, and sales commissions. There were probably few planters of the Old South who did not at one time or another complain of such exactions.

The significance here does not lie in charges alone; more subtle were the growth of custom and the inertia of routine, through which certain practices gained such wide acceptance that they are almost totally disregarded in contemporary records. One example was the "average account." In 1845, Austill & Marshall of Mobile sold an upstate planter's crop as part of a larger lot, which averaged 13 cents per pound. But the factors paid the planter only 12 cents, the relative value of his cotton. Austill & Marshall maintained that this procedure was according to "usages of trade," but their appeal was denied by the Alabama Supreme Court.

In the same category were tendencies to maintain fees at unnecessarily high levels or to charge for services that had not been rendered. Though they continued in the fifties to assess planters for drayage, storage, and labor at the old rate of $4, certain New Orleans factors obtained the same accommodation for $1, through contracts with local cotton presses. The savings represented were not being passed on to the producer. One innovator proposed to cut these costs by one third: "as it [$1] is all I pay, therefore, it is all I have a right to charge. Whilst Most of the larger houses here actually pay less than this—and Still retain the old charge of 4/. But upon what ground I am unable to learn." A South Carolina planter, examining some sales accounts, discovered that he had been billed twice for insurance he had not required. Considering the fact that many planters were careless in their bookkeeping, it is a moot question whether such charges appeared by accident or by design.

As supply agent for the planter, the factor furnished the necessities for day-to-day existence on the plantation, as well as the luxuries. Less often, he obtained slaves. Upon numerous occasions, he lent credit through the acceptance of drafts or settled the planter's bills rendered by others. Finally, as the planter's personal agent, the factor received and forwarded goods to their destination. The problems connected with plantation supply provided an additional source of friction.

High prices drew their share of criticism. In December, 1834, an Alabama planter complained of an excessive charge for supplies. This was denied by his Mobile factor, who demanded a retraction in order to protect his standing. Controversy often resulted from the leeway allowed the factor in the selection of goods. In filling a Carolinian's order for three sacks of ground salt, a Petersburg house bought from another firm at $2.75, instead of drawing from stock at $2.50. Though the factors explained that superior quality and quantity really made the salt cheaper than their own, the substitution was not acceptable, and the 25 cents in question was refunded.

A notable trend in the period from 1800 to 1860 was the shift from cash to credit sales. Planters who were "under advance" from their factors often found this accommodation a mixed blessing which brought with it the inconvenience of credit prices. For example, a New Orleans factor's "bill of sundries" furnished to a Mississippi planter under date of May 24, 1828, carried the additional statement: "Due in cash on 24th Sept. next. after which I shall charge you at the rate of 10 PCent Interest until this amount is paid."

The most significant feature of commissions and other expenses was the factor's adherence to accepted standards. Southern chambers of commerce regulated such fees in the major ports. Yet there were violations of these "tariffs of charges." Some factors charged more than 2½ percent for purchasing; some assessed commissions at times and at other times omitted them; and a number required no commissions at all. Such proceedings suggest that, depending upon the circumstances, it might at times have been a matter of how far one could go. Whereas factors as a group spoke piously of "tariffs of charges" and "usages of trade," some individual merchants had little hesitation in departing from the "norm." "Custom," or general mercantile practice, might occasionally mean nothing more than the policy of a particular firm.

Factors also bought cotton on a limited scale, either for others or on their own account. This procedure seems to have been customary at the beginning of the 19th century, when the factor was more apt to be a jack-of-all-trades than a specialist and often purchased the planter's entire crop for resale or consignment elsewhere. As the cotton traffic grew increasingly intricate, contemporary opinion became more and more opposed to a factor or commission merchant acting as both buyer and seller of cotton. In this business, where a respectable fortune could conceivably be made by a few timely or lucky maneuvers, factors must have found it hard to withstand the temptation to plunge. Probably most factors were conservative in this respect, and with good reason: Not only were they concerned with their standing in the mercantile community, but news of speculation and other untoward practices eventually reached their customers. Some planters were not above speculation, but they did not condone such tactics in their agents. Nevertheless, some cotton transactions were purely for speculative ends. When a Charleston merchant declared that no factor could sell and at the same time buy cotton because the two functions militated against each other, he was merely voicing the opinion of the majority of producers.

Despite the essential nature of the factor's services as banker and personal agent for the planter, these services frequently caused much bickering. Though dishonesty was occasional on both sides, there were more fundamental differences. With the planter, it was the "vicious cycle" of indebtedness, and the burden of interest and other charges; with the factor, it was the liquidation of old accounts, the misappropriation of loans, and the loss from overadvances.

The character of the cotton trade and the methods of transaction lent themselves to chicanery. The factorage business, with its relatively small initial capital investment, its constantly fluctuating personnel, its keen competition, and its expansion to inland trade areas, gave ample opportunity for unscrupulous individuals. Cotton planters and cotton factors were not always a select group. At times, too, policies followed by some factors demonstrated that there was a very thin line between honesty, expediency, and bad faith. Not a few producers would have accepted at face value the pointed jocularity of a Louisianan newly embarked in the factorage and commission business—"depend on it we are Smart fellows —& very honest—for Merchants."

Nor were planters above reproach. A Charleston concern, furnishing a client with $800 for a trip to the springs, was astonished to find him apparently requesting a duplicate advance. It developed that the forgery had been attempted by a man who had once before swindled the factors.

The system of advances, which had prevailed since colonial times, was a major source of controversy. Long before the Revolution, southern planters had fallen into chronic indebtedness, and the habit continued with the rise of the cotton kingdom. "A disposition to contract debts is one of the vices of the Carolinians," declared an early 19th-century historian. "When crops are anticipated by engagements founded on them before they are made, ruin is often the consequence, and much oftener since the Revolution than before." A half century later, it was charged that factors were advancing money as required during the summer, thus carrying over engagements into the cotton season—an arrangement beneficial to one side only, according to the writer, since it placed planters under obligation to continue their business in the hands of the factors.

From the planter's standpoint, one particularly objectionable feature of the system was its tendency to give the factor a measure of control over the cotton crop. Despite all that has been written about southern credit based on word of honor and little else, the factor was a businessman, and sound business dictated that a liberal credit policy rest on security wherever possible. Many factors were loath to extend loans on the casual basis of a conversation, an "understanding," or even a letter, and imposed conditions of all kinds. Some expected to receive a planter's crop in time to meet his drafts at maturity; others premised the acceptance of any drafts upon the receipt of the crop or the producer's valuation of the cotton to be shipped. A few declined such services during the inactive season of the year. Some refused to advance unless they were allowed to sell at their own discretion; others expected the proceeds of the sale to cover the advance; and a smaller number withheld any accommodations unless the whole crop was shipped to them. Historians have long stressed the heavy burden imposed by the penalty commission, which bound the planter to cultivate so many acres of cotton, and to forfeit a certain sum per bale for each bale by which the crop fell short of the stipulated amount. It is likely, however, that this practice was more prevalent after 1865. If the penalty commission had been employed on an extensive scale, one might expect it to be the subject of litigation in southern supreme courts, as were most of the difficulties between planter and factor.

Equally controversial were the "customary" fees—charges for interest and commission for advancing, negotiating, and carrying over unpaid accounts. It is not enough to say that commissions were fixed by law or standardized by locale at from 2½ to 5 percent. An observer noted with a considerable degree of truth that "he lends the planter money, on which he gets interest you may be sure; sometimes what the law 'allows,' and sometimes 'what money will bring.'" Factors often circumvented legal restriction by written contracts which authorized excessive interest rates and commissions. At times, these fees were highly complex in their ramifications. When factors' accounts were vague as to the use of funds, it was sometimes difficult for customers to grasp financial technicalities. Sometimes, it was a matter of open discrimination.

Much depended upon the alertness of the planter. Few were as vigilant as the Alabamian who checked all accounts and noted characteristically on one, "This Act [account] paid but not rected. To be taken to Mobile when I go." Of a different stamp was the Louisianan who said that he was satisfied with the usual "reservation of errors" and had "no curiosity to look into it, until a final settlement." In quite another category were those who detected discrepancies but failed to register protests. Such failure was generally tantamount to accepting the statement as correct. Considering the laxity of planters in general, it might well be assumed that many travesties committed in the name of "usages of trade" or "clerical errors" went unnoticed or unchallenged. The system had its possibilities for the arbitrary use of funds.

Such devices for control, together with credit prices, tended to mire the planter in a debtor-creditor relationship. With all its exactions, this routine was continued despite the warnings of such reformers as M. W. Philips of Mississippi: "Draw bills! This bill business is the very thing that ruins us. *Keep out of debt and control your cotton.*" Even after 1865, former planters complained of "long years of bondage" in which Charleston factors held Sea Island growers.

It was commonplace to speak of "years of bondage," of "endless shackles of debt," and of "planters harnessed to the factor's plow." But the system of advances did not favor one side exclusively. If many planters found it well-nigh impossible to escape indebtedness, creditors had their own problems. A Mobile factor, in advance to a client, finally sent his clerk upstate to obtain cotton, money, or negotiable paper. And in the midst of financial issues created by the formation of the Confederacy, an old New Orleans factor, who was reputed to have made and lost a fortune, commented cynically: "Extend credit indeed to the Planters; who Knows them better than I do. & who has Suffered more. . . . they would swamp any Government on Earth & themselves along with it." When a planter owed several creditors, the problem was infinitely more complex. Here the factor had to consider prior liens—"debts of superior dignity."

No less irritating were difficulties attending overadvances, the misuse of borrowed funds, and breaches of contract. In large part, the factor's dilemma stemmed from the peculiarities of the southern system, an economy of a colonial type: the presence of a planter class, with its demand for agricultural credit on an extensive basis, and the reliance upon paper rather than specie—upon bills of exchange, notes, orders, receipts, or drafts. Far from being self-sufficient, the factor himself depended almost entirely upon the credit system. His strength often lay not so much in his own means as in his *access* to various sources of capital. The financial state of many houses was somewhat nebulous, with a comparatively small investment in capital, a large backlog of acceptances, and no little stake in optimism. It is surprising how often factors were hard pressed to raise even a small sum of money. The factor had his time of troubles, a critical period in which he was under the necessity of meeting the planter's bills at maturity and frequently lacked the funds or produce to do so. Small wonder that he sometimes despaired of the future.

It was particularly galling to advance money or accept drafts and then fail to receive the expected consignment of produce. Planters solicited loans and later shipped their crops wholly or in part to other merchants. There were numerous instances were the factor financed the planter in anticipation of consignment, only to find that the returns were not sufficient to cover the loan. Seldom were producers as conservative as the Georgian who contracted with his factors to advance 9 cents per pound on the crop prior to sale, but declared that he expected no more than the value of the cotton, *"as he wanted no anteing back on him."* The court records indicate that factors often found it necessary to "ante back" because of overadvances. Literally thousands of these credits were based on a mere "understanding" or conversation. Such mutual confidence was highly laudable but not always prudent; in the absence of a written agreement, it was difficult to prove the existence of a contract—a frequent avenue of escape for delinquent debtors. Though well-nigh indispensable to the plantation, this complex system of agricultural credit had its shortcomings.

Friction between planter and factor revolved chiefly about marketing, supplying, and banking, but other practices provoked mutual distrust. Planters who were themselves careless refused to tolerate these qualities in their factors. Absentee planters were one thing; a factor off the job was something else again. Negligence in forwarding accounts or answering correspondence generally brought strong reaction and might result in a change of factors. Less frequently, it was sheer incompetence. Upon occasion, a few skeptics came to question the ability of factors in general.

The factor had other grounds for dissatisfaction. Writers of the past and present have emphasized the fundamental nature of the services rendered by factor to planter. Yet the assistance of planter to factor was also highly significant. It is well to remember that this relationship involved in many cases a mutual exchange of favors in the form of loans, endorsements or guarantees, negotiable notes, and, in general, a reciprocal use of credit. When a New Orleans factor expressed his appreciation for a token of confidence, he was merely observing that the support of prominent planters might well mean the difference between success and failure. Lack of such support or the withdrawal of credit facilities could bring disaster. Thus the reaction of a factor when a planter relative failed to furnish the blank signatures deemed necessary for the transaction of certain business: "Is it from want of confidence [or] are you afraid to trust such documents in my hands?"

Of course, it was irritating enough for a patron to change factors without explanation. Still more harmful was the effect of "talk" among planters—of facts or rumors regarding incompetency, insolvency, speculation, or dishonesty. The result was to threaten the factor's standing among his planter customers or perhaps to cause a "run on the bank." Likewise, it injured the merchant's reputation in the city and might well affect his credit facilities at home and elsewhere. It is only natural that factors thus victimized went to great lengths to clear away the clouds of suspicion.

Controversies involving individuals were sometimes accompanied by a diversity in viewpoint between planters and factors in general, a difference in outlook which may have reflected something of the historic distrust between producer and middleman. Often, members of the one group tended to "see eye to eye" against the other. In this respect, the planter's irritation from specific grievances may have influenced, and in turn been influenced by, stereotypes. The factor was an outlander, said some, often a veritable bird of passage, who lived in the South only during the cotton season. Was it true that New Englanders had by 1820 monopolized the Charleston factorage business? D. R. Hundley pointed an accusing finger at commission merchants who were outwardly respectable, yet willing to finance the slave trader and thereby enjoy a snug portion of the latter's proceeds without partaking of his social stigma. Or was the factor in reality a conservative businessman, trusted friend and servant, loyal to the planter and southern interests? In the light of these and other descriptions, factors were a highly contradictory group. Indeed, such stereotypes represent departures from strict truth. Yet the changing opinions of contemporaries are sometimes more significant than the actuality.

Contributing to the planter's state of mind was his ignorance of the city. If by chance he held the landed aristocrat's legendary contempt for the "vulgar pursuit of trade," if he was comparatively isolated and knew relatively little about city ways in general and city cotton transactions in particular, if times were bad and cotton prices low, and above all, if his individual relationship with the commission merchant had been an unhappy one, then the planter might listen with a receptive ear to stories about citified factors, sophisticated men of big business. He might readily believe rumors about "syndicates" or "combinations" which threatened the freedom of navigation on the Alabama River. His misgivings about the factor's specialized knowledge of the cotton trade—a field in which some planters had little more than vague notions—might give color to tales of designing middlemen leagued together to defraud the producer by means of drawbacks and other devices. Perhaps personal experience in court cases tried outside his own county or parish led him further to distrust the seaports, where mercantile influence and prestige were greater. In short, even the rural South experienced something of the traditional antipathy between city and country.

At any rate, planters chafed at "systematic oppression." They believed themselves the victims of duplicity: The factor was extending the right hand of friendship while rifling the planter's pocket with the left. In the light of available evidence, one may wonder whether some of these allegations were well founded. There was inaccurate crop information, whether accidental or deliberate. Fraudulent selling was notorious. Some factors were also purchasers of cotton and hence tended toward a double standard of values. Not only was the producer saddled with various forms of open exaction; usury and more subtle practices such as average accounts, clothed in the guise of "custom," were by no means uncommon. Nevertheless, the relationship between factor and planter, considered in its entirety, suggests that these complaints were of comparatively little significance.

Factors as a group were hostile to innovation, particularly when reduced fees were contemplated. In 1855 a New Orleans factor announced the negotiation of a contract with a local cotton press: in the future the cost of drayage, storage, and labor would be only $1 instead of the usual $4. Whether this arrangement was successful is not disclosed. In one sense, it increased the risk to the producer, since the factor tended to become less responsible; seen from the mercantile standpoint, its directness implied the elimination of lucrative middleman's fees. After Georgia planters criticized the $2\frac{1}{2}$ percent sales commission charged by Savannah factors, a correspondent of the *Daily Morning News* pointed out that this increase was due largely to the extension of railroads. And who had benefited most from such developments? The planters of the state. "Then we say why not live and let live?" When a Savannah firm announced its intention of handling cotton at 50 cents, a critic expressed his fear that the success of this experiment might result in forced retirement for the city's cotton sellers, thus deprived of their sole means of support. Such attempts at uniformity in Savannah must have seemed the more incongruous to Georgia and South Carolina growers, when fees in Charleston ranged from $2\frac{1}{2}$ percent to 50 cents or even less on the bale, and at least one Augusta firm advertised at 25 cents. The trade was basically conservative, and such schemes met with sharp disapproval.

On the other hand, factors sometimes attributed to calculated intent certain moves on the part of planters. In general, the antebellum commercial conventions reserved for the factor a place within the southern framework; broadly speaking, they called for the cooperation of planters and factors. Yet, during a convention of the fifties, an orator could speak disparagingly of past meetings "designed to circumvent the commission merchant of New Orleans . . . . Every planter who had a dozen negroes wanted a railroad running by his house and another by his kitchen." Though such sentiments may reflect nothing more than city or regional rivalry, the theme of these gatherings—commercial autonomy of the South, with the elimination of middlemen through direct trade with Europe—suggests that the history of antebellum commercial conventions, with their lack of positive accomplishment, may warrant further investigation.

But producers took even more decided action. In the late thirties, planter resentment against Mobile factors reached so high a pitch that the Alabama legislative session of 1837 was the scene of acrimonious debate following the introduction of a bill to remedy alleged abuses in the sale of cotton. Although the measure, which provided for the establishment of a state marketing agency, was passed after a heated debate, action did not progress beyond the planning stage. In 1858 a Cotton Planter's Association met at Macon, Georgia, and appointed an agent for receiving, selling, and shipping cotton for Savannah and Charleston. The group expressed its desire that "planters shipping their cotton to either of the above markets will prefer their appointed agent." Such experiments in producer control were interrupted by the Civil War.

Without considering its effects on the South at large, the burden of the factorage system fell unevenly upon the planter class. Business policy was influenced by many considerations. In some cases, factors were under obligation to their principals. Through individual arrangements, or for purely personal reasons, they often refrained from charging commissions on unpaid accounts, assessing interest, or collecting other fees. There were additional reasons why growers did not remain in the same state of dependence upon the factor. In contrast to the colonial period, with its predominantly English market, the staple producer of antebellum times lived relatively nearer the shipping point; not infrequently, though location was but one of many considerations, his degree of autonomy varied in proportion to his distance from the seacoast. Planters strategically situated might expect to keep abreast of the market, withhold shipment of their cotton (depending upon transportation costs) for favorable prices, and purchase their own provisions in town. Moreover, larger or more solvent planters, though they were apt to be at the mercy of the carriers, were perhaps less under the control of commission merchants. Some maintained their own transportation, obtained supplies elsewhere if they so desired, traded with several factors simultaneously, and shifted agents almost at will. Whether factors discriminated against the smaller planters is a proposition exceedingly difficult of proof.

Regardless of individual relationships, planters in general chose largely, if by no means exclusively, to patronize the coast factor rather than the home merchant. That the choice was a wise one is open to question. Room for doubt lies not so much in the familiar sense of "shop at home and save," though seaport rates for supplies were not always lower or cotton prices higher. Rather, the crux of the situation seems to have been the planter's greater familiarity with things local. Given the dearth of evidence at hand, one can do no more than speculate that the city factor's gain at the producer's expense came above all in some of the highly technical and less well-known facets of this relationship: in money matters, particularly as regards exchange, with which some planters were familiar but few expert; in certain aspects of the trade with which the producer was not directly connected; and in the vagaries of double-entry bookkeeping, as expressed in "customary" fees, in "clerical errors," or in various hidden charges. That planters would have enjoyed more convenient arrangements with local merchants is problematical; at any rate, they would have been more likely to understand the local merchandising process. In the long run, the returns to the planter himself and to his own community might have been greater if his capital had circulated largely at home.

To say that the information now available on the factorage system comes mainly from plantation records is to imply that the association between planter and factor has been seen primarily from the producer's viewpoint. This is not strictly true. Nevertheless, the balance has favored the producer, and anything resembling a definitive judgment must necessarily await more detailed studies of commission merchants and their operations.

A comparative lack of information does not obviate the broad conclusion that neither side realized a very definite advantage. If, indeed, this was a "contest," it was in the larger sense a contest without a victory. There was something enervating about the antebellum factorage process, bulwarked by tradition and unfriendly to innovation. To say the least, it was expensive for both producer and middleman; its often loose and informal basis of credit made it doubly dangerous; and its colonial foundations rendered all the more difficult a major break in the cake of custom.

Even with its many drawbacks, would a new system or even a major change in the old have been really satisfactory? Suppose direct trade with Europe had been established. Would the producer have found the Liverpool market less mysterious than the transactions in New Orleans? Just how long would a planters' association have continued to depend upon a single agent for Charleston and Savannah? Considering the prevailing attitude toward governmental paternalism, how feasible was a state marketing agency? In the minds of many Southerners, such proposals for control, either through voluntary restriction or by law, had their limitations. Ideas of this kind were too far ahead of their time; they were overridden by a routine of two centuries' standing and by the incentive for individual gain. Intent on the production of a cash crop and basically hostile to regulation of any kind, most planters paid little more than lip service to these suggestions. They were alternately enthusiastic and lukewarm as their personal interests were affected. Their complaints varied with times of prosperity and depression, rising in the wake of the panics of 1837 and 1857. Among them, there was too much individualism and too little unity of effort.

Indeed, a much sounder brief can be made for harmony than for discord between antebellum planter and factor. For all their carping and complaining, for all their differences great and small, it is doubtful whether the one could have dispensed with the other. Perhaps each really hoped, and sincerely tried, to attend carefully and closely to his own interest and in some way exert a balance, to their mutual benefit.

PART II

Marketing in
America, 1790-1860

D. ADVERTISING AND
MARKETING PRACTICES
OF THE PERIOD

1. AN EARLY USE OF BRANDS AND TRADE NAMES*

The tobacco industry was one of the first to utilize brands and trade marks in an attempt by competing manufacturers to differentiate their offerings. The names chosen were no less colorful and flamboyant than those of modern times. The success of certain brands encouraged many trade abuses, including exaggerated claims and even false or deceptive branding. This selection also discusses in some detail the markets in which branded tobacco products from Virginia were consumed and the channels of distribution employed to reach these markets.

BY THE 1850's the more alert manufacturers had learned the effectiveness of distinctive trade labels and had largely freed their product from the often commonplace name of the maker, christening it instead with seductive words, reminiscent of orchard and pantry. Not that the maker's name was entirely outmoded, but the accident of birth no longer automatically determined the brand. For those manufacturers who marketed more than one grade, designation by separate brands was convenient, if not absolutely necessary.

James Thomas, Jr., established a series of brands. Fruity names abounded. In addition to Cherry Ripe, Winesap and Cantaloupe were well-known trademarks. Those of Cosby and Winfree were Rock Candy, Pride of Virginia, Golden Pomegranate, and Palmetto Twists. The favorite product of the Richmond manufacturer C. P. Word was The People's Choice. There were references to historical characters and to attractive sections of the United States. Ellyson Yerby, who operated one of the few smoking-tobacco factories in Richmond, advertised the trademarks Lafayette, Pocahontas, and California. An appreciation of the value of established brands is nowhere more plainly brought out than in the friction over the distribution of marks after Poitiaux Robinson's decease.

The brand was literally branded on the container with a smoking-hot iron or stenciled with commercial branding ink. Early in the century, chewing tobacco was packed into kegs, later into boxes or packages containing as little as 70 pounds or as much as 140 or even more, but

---

* Reprinted from Joseph C. Robert, *The Tobacco Kingdom: Plantation, Market and Factory in Virginia and North Carolina, 1800–1860* (Durham, N.C.: Duke University Press, 1938), pp. 218–26.

averaging slightly over 100 pounds. Oak was considered best for the boxes, though sometimes poplar was used. For the convenience of the consumer, the smoking-tobacco manufacturers put the granulated leaf into small cotton sacks; and for shipping purposes, these were packed into pine boxes, reinforced with iron hoops.

Unscrupulous manufacturers falsely labeled their boxes of plug and twist so that they might be confused with the products of more popular establishments. Richmond manufacturers, more sinned against than those in other cities, bore this in silence until out-of-town knaves began to mark their inferior product "Richmond" and their best grades with some other name. At this gratuitous insult and libel, Richmonders sponsored in the General Assembly of 1834–35 an act fining persons falsely branding their tobacco in respect either to name or to address of maker. After the law was passed, however, it was still possible to omit all reference to the name of manufacturer or place where made, a deficiency in the statute which was not corrected, despite a move in that direction in the House of Delegates of 1845–46. According to a strong protest drawn up in 1857 by representative manufacturers of the Virginia district, many of their rivals in the western states dishonestly used the names of prominent Virginia and North Carolina manufacturers, and of their towns and states. This parade of "an inferior western article" under false colors served to damage the reputation of the Virginia manufacturers, to diminish their sales, and, in part, to supplant their product in the market.

Such formal advertising as appeared in the periodicals of the day was inserted principally by retail establishments. The typical notice was a small display, sometimes merely an item in a series of goods presented for sale. Though they bought little or no space, manufacturers made earnest efforts to gain for their products admission to the editorial or news columns.

In addition to paying fancy prices for their raw materials, manufacturers attempted a less subtle but no less successful approach to the editorial citadel. For example, Gilliam and Matthews presented to P. D. Bernard, proprietor of the *Southern Planter*, a box of Winesap, which Bernard, who claimed thirty years' experience as a chewer, described in his next number as "good—*very good.*" The editor of the *Milton Chronicle*, C. N. B. Evans, obviously a man fond of his quid, was the recipient of sample plugs from the Samuel Watkins factory, largest in Milton. In editorial comment, he acknowledged the gift, "made of splendid leaf and manufactured in the very best style." More generous was he with donations from two Danville manufacturers, for in his columns he promised: "[If] you will all assemble, after we open it, each one of you shall have a 'chaw' but no more." The editor of the *Richmond Daily Dispatch* was grateful for a box of Winfree's Rock Candy brand, "an excellent article, admirably adapted to our taste," and put up in comfortable pocket size. Six weeks later, with becoming impartiality, he reported that he had tested specimens of the finest tobacco manufactured by his old friend Robert J. Christian, and found them superb. With kindly words, he also acknowledged the receipt of a box of the celebrated Huntsman's Choice from his friend E. A. Smith, who had "reason to know our fondness for a good chew." The arrival of this last plug prompted the philosophical meditation that "Good tobacco is just as necessary to the comfort of an old chewer, as good tea is to the happiness of an old lady."

Selling agents were perhaps even more conscious than the manufacturers of the importance of establishing a good tobacco brand and then keeping it on the market. Though he did not always obtain it, each factor preferred a monopoly of the special brands sent to him.

PEDDLER AND NORTHERN AGENT

Although nearly all of the tobacco manufactured in Virginia and North Carolina was consumed within the United States, a significant beginning was made in the penetration of foreign markets. The exports of manufactured tobacco and snuff from the whole United States showed a steady increase. The Virginia district had an appreciable share of this business, though its exact part is unknown. Petersburg manufacturers established English and Australian connections which survived the century. By the middle 1830's, Richmond manufacturers were boasting that their tobacco manufactured for export sold more readily than other tobacco in foreign markets.

The great bulk of the domestically consumed tobacco was distributed through northern factors, but hundreds of wagons loaded with plug and twist were sent by manufacturers of the western Virginia district directly to retailers in the backcountry farther south and west. The trader packed into his two-horse canvas-topped wagon provisions, cooking utensils, and several dozen boxes of tobacco, then left the Dan Valley, going southward through the valleys and foothills. He drove through the Carolinas, Georgia, and Alabama, and sometimes even farther, selling for cash or, if coin was scarce, bartering for portable produce. Not only the professional peddler, but also the small manufacturer and the factory overseer as well, in seasons of slack manufacturing, brought the processed leaf to the land of cotton.

The typical route of the Virginia tobacco on its way from the presses to the chewer was from the Virginia or North Carolina manufacturer to the northern factor (or agent), to the jobber (or wholesale grocer), to the local retailer, and finally to the individual consumer. In making the first leg of the journey, the plug and twist were sent coastwise to New York City, Boston, Philadelphia, or Baltimore. Even New Orleans, despite the fact that it was a great market for all Mississippi Valley produce, including the rival western plug, received shipments of the Virginia varieties. In fact, the Virginians sought customers even within the western tobacco-raising section. With the opening of California in the 1840's, the manufacturers of Virginia made successful efforts to capture that market.

The trade between the Virginia district and New York City was well developed as early as the middle 1830's. By 1850, almost half of all the tobacco manufactured in Virginia and North Carolina was being sent to that one city. Since at that time two thirds of the Virginia and North Carolina crop was being manufactured within the bounds of the two states, it is apparent that almost one third of all the tobacco grown within the Virginia district was sent in a manufactured state to New York City. So thoroughly did New York dominate the distribution of tobacco that many southern merchants bought their Virginia plug and twist from New York factors. Certainly, the New York trade did not diminish from 1850 to 1860, though with the large increase in yield from field and factory the relative proportion sent to New York City might not have been entirely maintained. The businessmen of Virginia recognized the paramount importance of the trade in manufactured tobacco between the Virginia district and the North. The brisk sale of manufactured stocks by northern factors was always reflected in healthy general trade in the tobacco area. Almost all of the exchange on northern cities was furnished by the traffic in manufactured tobacco; and when that was depressed, difficulty was experienced in effecting payments. The Richmond banks alone, by the late 1850's, usually held $1 million of discounted acceptances, almost all of which had been drawn on the selling agents in northern cities.

Several circumstances, some more pertinent than others, persistently affected the general price of the manufactured article in New York and other market centers. Among these were fluctuating demands of the retailers, sometimes varying widely from the expected normal consumption; expansion and contraction of agents' stocks, which served as a reservoir between shipments of the manufacturers and orders from the retailers; and movements in the price of labor, of leaf, and of other raw materials. For example, in October, 1849, a time when quotations were unusually high, an agent for Virginia manufacturers analyzed the sustaining factors in the New York market as follows: an increasing general consumption in the old section and the opening of new markets in California and elsewhere; the small quantity in agents' hands, only one fifth the normal 40,000 packages, a scarcity duplicated in other markets; and the high price of leaf tobacco. The high price of leaf was a result of "short crops, and the scarcity and high value of slave labor in Virginia, caused by emigration to the cotton-growing regions, where they command high wages." Obviously, the expansion of cotton production and the price of plug tobacco were even more intimately associated when the cotton acreage encroached upon the tobacco district. The more usual story was one of overproduction in both field and factory. Manufacturers were accused of making a great display of cutting down on operations in order to strengthen the market, and then privately rushing production to take advantage of the better prices created by their deceptive gestures.

Despite occasional rumblings of discontent, usually the relationship between factor and manufacturer was agreeable enough. Letters from the agent to his principal were, if pessimistic, sympathetically so. There were sorrowful reports of the state of the market and the quality of the tobacco consigned: This was flea-bitten; that had too little moisture; another lot was beginning to mould. One factor, after submitting to an extremely low sale, offered philosophical consolation thus: "This is one of the contingencies of trade that the best of us has sometimes to endure."

For his services the agent customarily levied from 5 to 7½ percent of the sales price, plus sundry minor fees. The factor sold on long credit, usually 8 months, sometimes 10 or even 12; and the manufacturer had to bear this loss of interest. Sometimes the agent succeeded in disposing of the jobber's note, but at a heavy discount. Usually the manufacturer was forced by circumstances to draw on his factor in anticipation of collection, if not sale.

When business was poorest, manufacturers grumbled loudest at the long credit which agencies gave jobbers and wholesale grocers. Citing the fact that other articles were sold to jobbers for cash or seldom over four months' credit, tobacco manufacturers protested against this "useless, absurd and glaringly unjust discrimination." They vowed they paid ready money for their raw materials and produced an article which the grocer usually sold for greater profits than that averaged on his other goods. When appealed to by the manufacturers to aid in curbing the evil, the factors always presented labored arguments for maintaining the custom of extensive credits.

2. THE MARKETING POLICIES OF REED & BARTON*

From 1837 to 1845, the firm of Reed & Barton employed a variety of pricing, credit, and distribution policies to sell its teaware, castor frames, lamps, and other products. The manner in which the company established these policies, and then changed them over time, demonstrates the necessity of adjusting to external conditions. The company's desire to deal exclusively with wholesalers, rather than commission merchants, was severely restricted by the limited number of wholesale houses in existence. Likewise, Reed & Barton's policy of exclusive distribution was hampered by the ineffectiveness of franchise holders. The manner in which this firm's marketing program evolved over the period provides considerable insight into 19th-century marketing.

THE DEVELOPMENT of the Reed & Barton marketing organization paralleled in certain respects the building up of a factory organization. In both fields the company followed a pattern which was characteristic of business growth throughout the nation—the general trend toward specialization. In marketing, the passage of time and the accumulation of experience established an ever-clearer definition of distribution channels. Special agents arose to perform special functions, and a great increase in trade made possible concentration of individual efforts upon one line of goods or one function. The great class of merchant middlemen gradually became divided; and the wholesaler, the retailer, the commission agent, the importer, and a host of other specialists emerged.

WHOLESALERS AND COMMISSION AGENTS

Middlemen specialization had progressed far enough by 1837 to provide Leonard, Reed & Barton with a group of dealers who confined their efforts mainly to the field of household hardware. Certain of these, to be sure, still carried on the multiple functions of importing, wholesaling, and retailing, but the trend toward selectivity was clearly established and promised the britannia company that the efforts of their sales representatives were not to be dissipated over too wide a range of products.

* Reprinted by permission of the publishers from George S. Gibb, *The Whitesmiths of Taunton: A History of Reed & Barton, 1824–1943* (Cambridge: Harvard University Press, 1943), pp. 153–69.

Leonard, Reed & Barton hoped with justifiable optimism that before long the large hardware houses might abandon importing, retailing, and other functions irrelevant to the wholesale distribution of britannia ware. Even the achievement of the ideal goal—an agent devoted exclusively to the interests of the company—was not beyond the realm of possibility.

Leonard, Reed & Barton's wares were placed in the hands of two types of middlemen—the wholesaler and the commission agent. Wholesale houses were considered safe, for they purchased outright; but still vivid in Henry Reed's mind were the credit crisis of 1834 and the long rows of dust-covered teapots on the shelves of southern commission agents. The 1837 partnership would have preferred to have nothing to do with the commission-agent type of dealer, but necessity demanded otherwise. The depression which followed 1837 was a difficult time to persuade dealers to purchase large inventories. Wholesale houses were not numerous. Most of the few market contacts which Leonard, Reed & Barton possessed, moreover, were the customers of the Taunton Britannia Manufacturing Company; and for the most part, these were commission agents. A compromise between the desirable and the necessary was at length negotiated, which eliminated the proven dangers of a large unsold inventory on dealer shelves. Sales were made on a commission basis, but an ironclad restriction guarded against a recurrence of the events of 1834: "It is a rule of our concern not to consign." Agents received a sample line only, from which orders were taken and forwarded to Taunton to be made up at the factory as received.

Leonard, Reed & Barton policy called for distribution of wares through one large wholesale house or commission agent in each of the principal market cities. Formal agreements were drawn up in each case, and the exclusive distribution privilege was extended for a minimum of 12 months. In return for granting this privilege, the company insisted that agents should not "buy or sell wholesale or retail in England or the United States the Tea Ware of any manufacturer or Company but ourselves." The exclusive agency arrangement was stated by the company to apply to sales everywhere. In January, 1839, Elijah Braman of Warren, Rhode Island, was informed that "in consequence of an arrangement with some wholesale Dealers in Britannia we cannot sell any Tea Ware excepting in large Cities say New York, Boston, &c., and cannot therefore fill any orders from you."

Company policy in this repect was flexible, however; and actually, substantial sales were made outside the metropolitan areas. Usually, such sales were made only to wholesale customers who ordered well in advance and in substantial amounts, a wholesaler's rating being assigned any dealer who purchased more than $1,000 of goods a year. Occasionally, these restrictions were relaxed to favor old and well-known customers.

These restrictions on sales had very obvious advantages at the time they were imposed. Slow and uncertain communications continued to make market contacts difficult to maintain. Gustavus Leonard was the only "salesman," yet his time necessarily was divided between shop and road, and he was unable to make calls on large numbers of customers. The company felt, quite rightly, that the promotional efforts of dealers could best be supervised if the number of those dealers was small. Finally, the demand for company wares was more than adequate to crowd production facilities to the utmost, and there was little apparent need for seeking new outlets. Yet, in the end, the confining of sales was destined to prove both unnecessary and undesirable.

TERMS OF SALE

The terms on which the company did business with its agents are quite clearly defined by the correspondence which has survived. One fact stands out with great clarity. A definite plan was in use, which, though frequently inadequate and often changed, did constitute the first attempt by the britannia company to pursue a consistent and reasoned market policy.

In an effort to substitute order for the haphazard bargaining of earlier years, an attempt was made to set up a standardized scale of discounts which would apply with consistency to all dealers. In 1837, Leonard, Reed & Barton was quoting the following terms to wholesalers:

Teaware	25% discount from list price
Nickel-silver castor frames	17% " " " "
Plain frames (britannia)	10% " " " "
Lamps	20% " " " "

Commissions given to agents were not clearly defined, and terms appeared to vary considerably. The commission agent assumed no inventory risks and therefore received a smaller discount than regular wholesalers. Since the usual fee for commission agents dealing in domestic products was from $2\frac{1}{2}$ percent to 5 percent, the Leonard, Reed & Barton representatives seem to have been waxing fat on their agreement; but too little information has survived to make any final appraisal of the rates paid.

Usual practice was for the company to pay shipping expenses to the wharf in New York, Baltimore, or Philadelphia, the customer assuming risk of shipment or paying insurance charges thereon. The matter of shipping terms was a legitimate field for bargaining, however, and all degrees of compromise were arrived at. Great was the relief and clearer the air in Taunton when a penny-wise negotiation over some large shipment was at last concluded!

One of Henry Reed's most cherished desires was for a cash business. In an endeavor to achieve this end, the company offered a liberal discount of 5 percent for cash payment in 10 days. In 1838, working capital needs became acute in Taunton, and an 8 percent discount for cash is quoted. "Necessity compels us to make this offer."

However firmly the company stated its policy of cash business only, the times made this impossible, and credit was frequently extended to tried-and-true customers. Six-month terms were quoted, usually with the stern admonition that future business must be for cash, and customers' notes were taken to the Taunton Bank to be discounted. As in past years, the matter of collecting accounts required delicate negotiations and no small amount of patience. Scarcity of specie and the periodic contraction of banking facilities between 1837 and 1843 added greatly to the difficulties of trade, and the exchange of funds was often expensive. When exchange rates between cities became excessive, prices of wares were raised to cover the difference between the value of money in Taunton and in the southern markets. Gustavus Leonard frequently complained that "As it is with difficulty we make Tea Ware nett the Cost of manufacture [we] cannot save ourselves in selling the article and losing the exchange."

Customers themselves performed valuable services for the company in collecting accounts and furnishing credit information. The usefulness of the New York, Philadelphia, and Baltimore agents, however, went far beyond this. Leonard, Reed & Barton made frequent inquiries of its dealers on the state of local trade and sought advice from those close to the market on matters of styling and pricing. Usual practice in deciding whether to undertake a new line or pattern was first to ask dealers what the market would be willing to pay, then to see if the article could be manufactured to yield a profit at that price.

PRICE POLICY

In general, the pricing practice followed by the company consisted of a rule-of-thumb policy, having reference, on the one hand, to direct costs of manufacture and, on the other, to the bargaining position of the buyer. In certain cases, customers were successful in holding prices down; in other cases the company succeeded in getting either higher prices or lower discounts. In all cases, pricing was a continuous process of bargaining, with both parties pleading poverty. The popularity of Taunton britannia ware gave the company an edge in the dickering and usually made higher prices obtainable in the periodic emergencies created by sharp rises in the cost of metals. In 1841, 1853, and 1857, small upward price revisions were conceded by the market as the cost of metals soared.

The southern agents performed a further vital function in procuring for the company a substantial part of its raw materials. Tin, antimony, copper, wrapping paper, polishing earth, hides, and other articles were purchased by customers and shipped to Taunton, the cost of the purchases being credited to the customers' accounts. In fact, a very substantial barter trade was taking place during the 1837–43 depression and did much to alleviate the difficulties imposed by lack of cash. The company also expressed a willingness to accept scrap metal in payment of outstanding accounts; and as late as 1859, old coffin plates, teaware, and pewter, at predetermined rates per pound, were being used by customers to settle bills or pay for new orders.

Occasionally, dealers wrote and expressed a desire to exchange their stock for newer models. Reed & Barton disclaimed all responsibility for style obsolescence, but at the same time recognized the problem dealers faced. Gustavus Leonard informed Davis, Palmer & Company of Boston, in 1840, that the company did not consider that justice demanded exchange of new stock for old, since "the main advantage of selling over consigning we deem to be the sale being final at time of delivery." Leonard conceded this much to an old customer, however: "We are prepared to fill small orders at same dist. we have formerly allowed on larger ones—so that the loss by change of style or by Interest for goods on hand shall after this come on us." Several years later, company policy relaxed somewhat to allow one customer to return some remnants of unsalable patterns, the sacrifice being made with the expectation that he might thereby revive his flagging promotional efforts.

The one company practice which admitted of no bargaining, and which seems to have operated absolutely without exception, was that which pertained to Reed & Barton's right to regulate prices at which dealers disposed of company wares. Any company representative who underbid "ticket" quotations in selling to retailers stood in imminent danger of losing his agency.

The company stated that wholesale dealers might make a discount of 5 percent to retailers or purchasers of small lots, and 10 percent to other wholesalers, "but maintain the ticket prices when you retail or sell not to sell again." Later, the retailers' margin was increased to between 7 and 10 percent.

Firmness in some respects was matched by leniency in others, and many favors were extended to customers over and above the contractual requirements involved. Misunderstandings between Reed & Barton and its dealers invariably were settled promptly, and usually in favor of the latter. Customarily, the company acquiesced with the dealer's viewpoint on any first complaint, but at the same time made clear the terms under which the same situation would be settled should it arise again.

At all times was Henry Reed willing, and even anxious, to make up special orders to meet special wants. The boast of Leonard, Reed & Barton and later of Reed & Barton was that the company could and would make anything in the line of britannia ware its customers desired.

Such special orders were made up, however, with the understanding that after a certain period of time had elapsed, the articles should be made available to all the trade. Certain dealers resented having designs they sent to Taunton thus released to competitors, but the company agreed in turn to bear the cost of making up the dies and molds and often gave a special discount to the house which originated the pattern. In this way a compromise equitable to both parties was usually effected.

It is most unfortunate that so little information has survived about prices, terms, and trade practices in the britannia industry prior to 1850. There is little basis for a comparison between Reed & Barton and competing firms, but there seem to be no complaints from customers that the Taunton company was undersold. In 1841, Leonard boasted to a New York dealer: "As to prices and terms we shall make the terms better to you than you can do with Dixon—or better than we find others do in the English trade."

CHANGING CHANNELS OF DISTRIBUTION

The relations between Reed & Barton and its agents, though cordial under normal circumstances, were not completely satisfactory. Less than a year after Leonard, Reed & Barton had commenced operations, the commission agency system and exclusive representation began to show signs of inherent weaknesses. Some agents and some exclusive houses proved more satisfactory than others, but the eventual fate of these methods of distribution was to be the same.

Wherever the company had made a happy choice of agents, the granting of exclusive privileges worked out very well. A poor choice of agent, however, meant a great loss in that agent's territory, for there were no other dealers there to augment his efforts. Actually, the practice of appointing one representative in a district began to break down in the southern markets as early as 1839.

The commission agent, when chosen as the sole means of distribution, proved exceptionally unsatisfactory and failed in most cases to provide promotional effort adequate to satisfy the company. Selling from samples, moreover, involved many delays and brought complaints from purchasers who did not wish to wait for their orders to be forwarded to Taunton and made up there. As time went on, Reed & Barton inclined more and more toward the wholesaler; and experience proved that the dealer who purchased a stock of wares outright exhibited far greater vigor in pushing the line than did the commission agents, whose sense of responsibility rested upon ethical rather than monetary grounds.

The practice of granting exclusive agencies resulted in almost constant bickering among agents and invoked the ill will of dealers who were not favored with an agency. In New York the firm of St. John &

Wetherell complained bitterly when, at the expiration of its contract in 1838, Young, Smith & Company was given the agency. Krug & Colladay in Philadelphia reported that its exclusive rights in that city failed to protect it from New York competition, and then was completely alienated when Reed & Barton granted Berkley & Shipman the Philadelphia area.

The appointment of Young, Smith & Company as New York agent soon proved to have been a bad mistake:

Taunton, June 11—1840

Messrs. Young, Smith & Co.
GENT.

We wish to know from you decidedly, and we wish to know immediately what course you are calculating to pursue in giving us orders for this Summer and the coming Autumn. That we cannot content ourselves with New York Sales as they have been under our existing contract with you (Being lately only about one Quarter of those of Boston) You will readily perceive. *Something must be done* and that very soon too—You may tell us if you choose of the general stagnation of Business. You may detail if you wish the dull sales in the City of New York—we have various sources of information which substantiate the fact that a good deal of Brittannia Ware has been retailed and wholesaled in New York the two past Seasons. That it has been but a very small part ours you must admit. We have wated patiently for you to give us orders, but we have wated in vain.

We want a decided and immediate answer as to the inducements you offer for a trade in New York the coming Summer and Autumn. If you are willing to give up the contract we are allowing you the privilege of ordering ware to close up what you have on hand.   .   .   .

Resply yours
LEONARD REED & BARTON

Nevertheless, the contract was renewed for 1841, but the results were even less satisfactory. The company complained that in New York, "sales were limited much more so than was anticipated at the time the contract was made, leaving us a chance to dispose of less quantity of goods . . . than we should do if no such restriction existed." At the same time, it became evident that Young, Smith & Company was selling wares below ticket; and when this fact had been confirmed by cautious investigation, the agency was terminated.

One more attempt was made to sustain a commission agent on an exclusive distribution basis in New York, and Nathaniel Witherell was nominated in place of Young, Smith & Company. In 1843, however, Reed & Barton announced its determination not to have a commission house in Philadelphia, and the same policy appears to have been put into effect in New York. Henceforth, company wares were sold outright, mainly to wholesalers. The number of dealers in the large cities multiplied rapidly, indicating the abandonment, once and for all, of exclusive privileges.

The reviving prosperity of trade after 1843 undoubtedly played an important part in hastening the change from commission agents to wholesalers, and from limited to general distribution of Reed & Barton wares. Better times created means to finance outright purchases, and wholesale dealers regained confidence, at last daring to place stock on their shelves. When general business emerged from its six-year depression, the demand for Reed & Barton wares quickly outstripped the limited provisions for distribution which had been made in less prosperous times. Pressure from within the trade at length became so strong that it smashed through all artificially imposed restrictions on the market.

The story of distribution in Boston during the 1837–43 period is a far brighter one than that in the southern markets. The commission agency gained no foothold in Boston, and the explanation for this fact can be made in terms of miles. With the britannia works only two hours distant by Boston & Providence and Taunton Branch railroads, dealers there were able to keep small stocks on hand, reorder frequently, and receive their orders with practically no transportation delays. With inventory risks virtually eliminated, little incentive existed to sell from samples on the less profitable commission basis.

The choice of representatives in Boston was far more fortunate than it had been in New York or Philadelphia, possibly because the Boston dealers were better known to the Taunton men.

The performance of the Boston dealers between 1837 and 1843 brought the center of company sales back to New England for a brief time; but with the multiplication of New York, Philadelphia, and Baltimore houses after 1843, the southern markets once more began to assume great importance. The results of abandoning the commission-agency type of business caused considerable satisfaction in Taunton.

TRANSPORTATION AND SALES

Success in the 1840's inspired many changes in the Reed & Barton organization, but trade methods and customs savored strongly of the beaver hat era. Communications southward were still slow and uncertain, and the company continued to ship its wares by coasting schooners. The wharves of the Taunton River fleet still echoed to the rumble of wagons from the britannia works, and winter continued to place a chilly interdict on trade.

Both railroad and steamship lines facilitated travel, but rates were too high to allow the shipment of sizable orders for long distances. Direct communication was always an object, and the company preferred to ship by Taunton vessels sailing a through route to New York or Philadelphia. Steamship freighting required unloading at Providence, for these vessels could not negotiate the Taunton River, and the company complained of "the detention almost always attending the latter way of sending." In winter, when the river was closed, or when no through vessel was scheduled to leave Taunton, wares were sent by the recently constructed New Bedford Railroad to that port for reshipment; and in time, New Bedford captured permanently much of the river fleet business.

The ways of trade were still informal, exhibiting only a minor acceleration in tempo from the previous decade. Beyond extending permission to a few houses to represent them, Reed & Barton exerted no great effort to cover the market or systematically canvass for orders. The general sales philosophy, apparently, was to let the mountain come to Mahomet. The regular commercial drummer was an institution of the future, and merchants frequently visited the factory to place their orders for the season.

Few new experiments were attempted by Leonard, Reed & Barton or by Reed & Barton in the line of advertising. In 1842 the New York agent placed small advertisements in certain newspapers; but in general, this medium of promotion seems to have been ignored. The practice of showing company wares at exhibitions of the Massachusetts Charitable Mechanic Association, the American Institute, and the Franklin Institute was continued and resulted in much beneficial publicity and a formidable accumulation of first-award medals.

The 1840's, however, terminated the rough-and-ready period of distribution, and after 1850 the picturesque yielded rapidly to the practical. In time the railroads displaced the river sloops, and the telegraph sliced through the isolation of distances. Change-provoking growth altered the marketing structure of Reed & Barton, and the appointment of George Brabrook as the first full-time company salesman since 1834 heralded great expansion.

Brabrook's career set a splendid precedent for future generations of Reed & Barton salesmen to follow. Up from the ranks through a hand-soiling apprenticeship, Brabrook soon proved his worth on the road, and orders piled up at the factory in ever-increasing volume. New terms were instituted to meet both greater competition and the enlarged scope of Reed & Barton trade. Discounts on teaware were extended from 25 percent to 27½ percent, and occasionally to 30 percent. The "cash in 10 days" policy of 1845 became cash in 30 days, and large customer balances began to be carried on the books. The increasing demand of dealers for credit forced the company into short-term borrowing, and by the late fifties the Taunton Bank began to provide Reed & Barton with working capital.

3. REPORT OF AN EARLY COMMERCIAL TRAVELER*

The marketing influence of local and regional wholesalers declined between 1830 and 1850 as more and more manufacturers used their own sales forces or manufacturers' agents to reach potential customers. Contributing to this development were the increased size and more diversified product lines of certain manufacturers, the growing importance of the large eastern metropolitan centers, and the improvements being made in the nation's transportation and communications systems. As is often true today, early attempts at direct distribution were not undertaken in the belief that eliminating middlemen would increase profits. Rather, manufacturers wished to exercise more control over the selling effort in order to strengthen their relative market position. Also, the information obtainable from shortened distribution channels facilitated product planning and efforts to judge the creditworthiness of customers.

CHANGES IN THE ROLE of the commercial drummer during the 30 years prior to the Civil War are suggested by comparison of reports received from a salesman in the 1850's with similar reports received from a salesman for the same firm in the 1830's. The chief complaint of the salesman in the 1830's was that the merchants of any importance made regular trips to Philadelphia or New York. Such merchants preferred to make all their purchases at one time in order to save trouble and expense in transportation, and they also bought most of their goods from established jobbers to whom they were known and who would extend credit.

Complaint on this score continued in the 1850's; but by that time, such buyers were often directed to the manufacturer's depot in New York. Such complaint was, furthermore, overshadowed by reference to drummers for competing manufacturing concerns who had been through the territory some short time previously and had increased the discounts. At one time, such a salesman, mentioned by name, was said to have been on the "western route" some three or four years and was described as carrying samples "of a good many styles of goods."

In the 20-year interval, there was a significant change in the conduct

AUTHOR'S NOTE: A grant from the Princeton University Committee on Research has been of assistance in the preparation of this article.

* Reprinted from Theodore F. Marburg, "Manufacturer's Drummer—1852," *Bulletin of the Business Historical Society*, Vol. XXII (June, 1948), pp. 106–14.

of the Scovill Manufacturing Company's marketing. There was a decline in the importance of the commission agents who had filled a key role in New York and Philadelphia sales in the 1830's. At the same time, there was an increase in initiative taken by the manufacturer to establish contact with wholesalers and retailers that purchased directly from the firm. The change in this firm's practice conformed to a general shift in marketing at this time.[1]

This decline in the relative importance of commission agents may have resulted in part from a change in the type of products sold, particularly the addition of several new lines. During the 1830's the firm undertook the manufacture of butt hinges and other fabricated items. Subsequently, German silver was rolled and made into spoons and novelties. A new item of some interest in the middle 1830's was silver-plated brass or copper; and in 1839, this was used for the "plates" employed in the new daguerreotype cameras. During the 1840's the concern undertook to manufacture the metal components for cameras and for plastic daguerreotype cases in which pictures were mounted, and later operated a plant producing the cases as well. A Scovill depot was opened in New York in 1846 which stocked a complete line of imported and domestic daguerrean supplies. The depot was visited by dealers in these supplies and by operators of the larger studios who came to New York to make their purchases.

Two additional Scovill partnerships that had been formed in the 1830's and 1840's were brought under one management, together with the original firm in 1850, when the Scovill Manufacturing Company received its corporate charter. The following year the younger Scovill brother, William H. Scovill, went to Cincinnati and the South on a trip which may have combined business with an effort to improve his health. In the summer of the next year, 1852, an intensive sales trip to the Midwest was projected.

The points to be visited included those in the Ohio Valley covered by the earlier salesman in 1832 and the newer cities of Chicago and Cleveland, as well as St. Louis and other cities farther down the Mississippi and scattered through the South. The proposed distance of about 4,500 miles was to be covered mostly by river and lake steamboat and railroad, and only in small part by stage.

The man selected for this journey was Samuel Holmes, the salaried assistant manager of the New York store and a stockholder in the firm. He was accompanied on the first lap of his trip by one Blakeslee, who

---

[1] See, e.g., N. S. B. Gras, *Business and Capitalism* (New York, 1939), pp. 195–200. Documentation for a specific case of such transfer from commission agency to wholesalers by a metal products firm in the year 1843 is given for Reed & Barton in George S. Gibb, *The Whitesmiths of Taunton: A History of Reed & Barton, 1824–1943* (Cambridge: Harvard University Press, 1943), p. 164.

returned from Cincinnati by way of Pittsburgh when Holmes proceeded down the Ohio River to Louisville.

This trip was conceived possibly as a measure necessary for maintaining and expanding sales in the face of competitors' vigorous drumming activities. It was undertaken at a time when general business activity and prices were rising moderately, and when Scovill sales were also increasing at a moderate rate.[2] No quantitative evaluation of the success of this trip has been made; but the fact that it was repeated several times suggests, as in the case of the 1832 trip, that the management considered the results to have positive value. The circuit Holmes completed took him four months; but after he had been on the road only three months, an additional salesman was hired by the New York office for the express purpose of traveling full time.

The buyers of daguerreotype supplies were in the habit of purchasing some of their stock from each of the competing suppliers. Perhaps they believed that in this way they could pit one seller against another for the purpose of getting both the best prices and early delivery of new contrivances. In such cases, Holmes's personal visit was doubly important in order that he size up the importance of a customer after visiting his establishment and after estimating the quantity of goods he purchased from other suppliers.

The increase in direct selling by the manufacturer to wholesalers or retailers, especially the increase in such selling on credit, called also for credit information. The correspondence makes clear that determination of credit standing was an important part of Holmes's contribution, and it leaves one with an awareness that the credit agencies established in the 1840's assumed their important role only slowly.[3]

---

[2] An index of domestic trade shows a rise of only one point, from 93 to 94, in 1852 as compared with 1851; this rose another seven points for 1853. See W. B. Smith and A. H. Cole, *Fluctuations in American Business, 1790–1860* (Cambridge, 1935), p. 104. An index of copper sheathing prices shows a comparable movement, with the greater part of the change in 1852 occurring during the latter part of the year. See A. H. Cole, *Wholesale Commodity Prices in the United States, 1700–1861* (Cambridge, 1938), pp. 325–26. For Philadelphia, monthly prices of nonferrous metals and their products have been tallied. These may suggest the course also of New York prices. Those in Philadelphia rose very moderately during the year except for the last month, when there was a sharp increase. See Anne Bezanson, Robert D. Gray, and Miriam Hussey, *Wholesale Prices in Philadelphia, 1784–1861* (Philadelphia, 1936), p. 380. The Scovill sales of 1851 were $285,000; for 1852, $307,500; and for 1853, $392,000. Quantitative data on sales after 1850 have been furnished the writer by Professor P. W. Bishop of Yale University.

[3] The Mercantile Agency was organized in 1841, and Robert G. Dun joined the firm in 1854. Service in the South and West was offered a few years later. At about the same time, John M. Bradstreet started his agency in St. Louis. See Muriel Hidy, "The Capital Markets, 1789–1860," in Harold F. Williamson (ed.), *The Growth of the American Economy* (New York, 1944), p. 297. At the time of Holmes's visit to Cincinnati, both the Bradstreet concern and B. Douglas & Co. were listed in the city directory as mercantile agencies. See *Williams' Cincinnati Directory* (Cincinnati, 1853), p. 294.

The first comments came from Syracuse and Rochester, which were reached by rail. From Rochester, Holmes wrote of the established trade and of the difficulty in making collections or effecting cash sales on account of the low prices for flour and grain, which he referred to as the "great staple" of the region. In this letter, Holmes started the refrain which runs through all his correspondence by mentioning five competing firms whose salesmen had been through the market within the last month. Two days later, he gave a comparable picture of the metal products trade in Buffalo, writing as follows:

I find here as in Rochester Curtiss & others have all been along here & to every man that spoons it at all, be he large or small, whatever is wanting in that way they have just been getting in from orders given those parties. Curtiss must have done a large trade here—almost everybody buys his plated ware and there are some 30 or more establishments that keep it more or less, but our G.S. [German silver] takes generally the lead . . . .   There are some larger houses here in hardware, crockery, fancy goods & variety store which sell a good many spoons: & I find most of them depend upon giving their orders to agents [salesmen] as they come along—& I see that to do anything in this way we shall be obliged to adopt the same course.

The next week, in a report from Cleveland, Holmes brought out the difficulties of winter transportation for passengers as well as freight. He wrote of the irregularity in departure of lake steamers, which he attributed to the lateness of the season. He added that merchants were unwilling to place orders so late in the season for fear the goods might have to move by land from Buffalo at $9 per hundredweight.[4]

Chicago was reached with travel from Detroit to Michigan City by the Michigan Central Railroad and from that point by a conveyance Holmes described as the "dirt and gravel train." He found that transportation difficulties, owing to an unusual winter freeze, prevented merchants from conducting ordinary business and also prevented his traveling on directly to St. Louis. He was nonetheless enthusiastic about Chicago's prospects as a rising entrepôt, recognizing, perhaps correctly, that the city's growth was to be achieved by expanding her trade and rail transportation facilities.[5] He wrote of this growth, on December 17, as follows:

This is going to be a very important place in trade & we must look to it with care—There is going to be a large wholesale trade done here—& are now sev-

---

[4] This rate amounts to approximately 4½ cents per mile, which is more than double the per mile rate between Buffalo and Niagara Falls four years earlier, quoted in C. E. MacGill *et al., History of Transportation in the United States before 1860* (Washington, 1917), p. 580.

[5] In the rivalry between Chicago and St. Louis, attention must be given the matter of facilities for trade or storing goods, with Chicago's leadership perhaps most marked in the handling of grain. See Wyatt W. Belcher, *The Economic Rivalry between St. Louis and Chicago, 1850–1880* (New York: Columbia University Press, 1947), p. 103 *et passim*.

eral quite large houses here of that character. It is astonishing to see how the place has gone ahead; increasing 33⅓ per Ct. the past year & now numbers between 40 & 50,000 inhabitants. They will have a large back trade, having already four railroads under way to this point—besides a fine communication by water with considerable country about.

After completing his visits in Chicago, Holmes returned to Ohio in order to avail himself of such rail facilities as were available on the route to Cincinnati via Sandusky and Columbus. His original plan of going directly to St. Louis from Chicago was thwarted by the freezing of the Illinois River. The direct route by land would mean doing 350 miles of the distance by stage, he wrote, and would take six to eight days over roads that were not macadamized and in coaches which were, he observed, "in some respects hard to heat." The effects of cold weather upon transportation are further indicated by later letters from Cincinnati. Both mail and freight were held up, with no mail coming through from New York for nine days. Shortly afterward, however, he reported the receipt of one letter from New York that was only six days in transit.

Holmes wrote that merchants in Cincinnati were holding off orders "till navigation opens." He added: "You can hardly form much of an idea of express charges this way." For a small box from New York the charge was $1.90, but this had come before the navigation closed. It is surprising, in view of the obstacles to river travel, and in view of Holmes's enthusiasm for railroads, that he had nothing to say of Cincinnati's plans and hopes in this matter, especially since it was in 1852 that ground had been broken for the construction of the Ohio & Mississippi Railroad.

From Cincinnati, in a letter written on Christmas day, complaint was again made of competitors' drummers and the price discounts they were offering. Holmes justified his having met competitors' price discounts by referring to the jobbing or wholesale business of Cincinnati merchants. He wrote:

In the spoon business as I have written you I found Curtiss was furnishing mostly at 25% & 35%—everybody posted up & have been obliged to name the same terms generally when I named any or else no chance to do anything with them. . . . I know this at first seems hardly just to our N.Y. trade, but they did not generally buy there—but of the manufacturer . . . . I was quite at loss in many cases what to do; one of two things must certainly be, either we offer at same terms they did, or else neither we nor the N.Y. trade get any benefit but Curtiss all. Under these circumstances I think you will think I did right. All the large trade this way buy of the manufacturers and under all circumstances think they should [that jobs] be put on the same footing . . . .

The next point visited was Louisville; and from there, Holmes commented on the established houses that sent buyers to New York in a manner which sounded very much like the practice in the 1830's, except for the fact that buyers were going to make direct contact with the firm's New York office instead of calling on the Philadelphia commission agent. He wrote, in a letter of January 5, 1853: "I find here some very extensive houses in the hardware & fancy goods line—also in the Queens Ware, some of which may order a few goods to fill up, but as most of them are going on soon [New York], will then make their purchases."

A week later, Holmes commented again on the presence of a competitor's salesman, and he also remarked on the importance of Louisville as an entrepôt. He wrote:

I think we can get a good trade from this place. There is a large business done here with the West & South, & the merchants are generally heavy & good. It is considerably in the boat building & furnishing line. . . . I have taken today an order from Mr. Beard (who has bought of Curtiss generally) to last for the present till he will be on in May when he will want in a large way. It is now so late Mr. Colston will not order until he goes on which will be this week as also Mr. Semple. . . . Several others will be on in the hardware & fancy & dry goods line. The latter trade generally are in the Notion Business.

A number of the Louisville concerns had partners in New York who did the purchasing. As to this practice, Holmes added:

Mr. Low is an old & wealthy merchant but posted up—sells a good many spoons, specks, buttons etc.—he will be on soon probably—though one of the partners resides in N.Y. & has an office he thinks with Coe & Wright. . . . Think it would be well to call & see him & ask him round. Mr. Davidge of the other firm has his office at J. & J. Stuart & Co. & does *all* the buying for that house. Wish you would drop in & make his acquaintance & think we can do quite a trade with them in all our Notions. They have kept Curtiss' spoons. They buy on best terms & would offer as well to all these houses as are doing with our *best customers.*

From Louisville, Holmes went to Cairo and then up the Mississippi to St. Louis. At St. Louis, he had been preceded, once again, by the salesmen of competitors. A trip down the Mississippi from St. Louis proved halting and slow because of ice and fog. After a stopover in Memphis, Holmes arrived in New Orleans. From there, he reported on February 18 concerning the establishments at Memphis, as follows: "I found at Memphis three hardware stores, two large Jewelry and fancy good stores, in most of which I think we may be able to do something with them, when they come on in June. They only come on once a yr. and as was then too late for their trade they will defer purchasing till that time— they are all good and doing considerable business."

In New Orleans, Holmes was troubled by the short workday, which, he complained, lasted only from 10:00 in the morning to 3:00 in the afternoon. The buying practices were similar to those of Memphis. He wrote from New Orleans:

The purchases for this market are generally made in June, July & August and they go to market but once a year. I am visiting the trade and showing samples but do not expect much in the way of orders now. Most of the hardware trade have bought English Butts [hinges] direct & Curtiss & Filley & Mead's Spoons—all I can do with them is to talk and drum. . . . Slash Day & S are doing a very large business here, but their eastern purchases are all made by their N.Y. house. There are some other very good hardware, Queensware & other houses which I think we shall do something with. . . .

Holmes next stopped at Mobile, where competitors' salesmen had preceded him in visiting the leading houses. He wrote:

I think we shall do something with all the hardware trade of which there are five good houses & three do a very large business. There are a good many spoons sold in this market, but the trade seems to be divided up pretty well between Curtiss, Parker H. E. & C & Filley & Meeutz house. The latter, have a pretty good hold in the Southern market & their plated goods look very well —Henry & Mott have not yet rec'd their last order—& another house which buy largely have ordered of our goods of Churchill & Wetmon. There are also some Queens Ware houses & Jewelry I think we shall do something with— but at present all are well stocked for this season, unless they should have a good & late trade.

Holmes proceeded to Georgia and South Carolina and returned to New York. He made several more trips west through the same territory. In the late 1850's, when he was promoted to the position of manager of the New York store, he probably delegated such traveling to others. His subsequent recognition and promotion gives one added confidence in the accuracy of the comments he sent home.

These observations from Holmes's trip reveal, either by direct statement or by implication, that drumming by manufacturers' representatives was by this time general practice and that it was considered important to implement direct selling to western buyers who came to New York by such visits from a drummer. Nonetheless, the drummer's main purpose was to get actual orders from these customers when he visited them at their own establishments in the field.

Although the role of wholesalers and jobbers is not altogether clear from the comments, it was evidently undergoing change. New York jobbing houses were still handling some of the products; and for that reason, Holmes feared that he ought not to have lowered the prices he charged western buyers. However, he justified his having met competitors' discounts on the grounds that the western buyers were increasingly taking over the jobbing function and were therefore entitled to the same discounts as New York houses, and also that these buyers were purchasing in increasing measure directly from the manufacturer. The development of specialization among western jobbers, wholesalers, or retailers is also revealed by Holmes's reference to houses specializing in queensware, hardware, dry goods, and fancy goods, even to variety stores and jewelers.[6] At Louisville, however, he observed that the dry goods merchants were generally in the notions business; evidently, there were fewer specialized firms handling such goods in that city. Wholesalers in daguerreotype supplies were noted in a few cities. There is still much to be filled out concerning the changes in distributive organization here only suggested.

The role of manufacturers' direct sales to industrial users is suggested in a small way by the sales of plates to operators of daguerrean studios. In one sense, Holmes's role in this particular connection was as a salesman from the New York depot that jobbed a variety of daguerrean supplies rather than as representative of the Connecticut manufacturer. He does not mention such direct sale of hinges to the Louisville boatbuilders, and the quantity used by such boatbuilders may not have been large enough to warrant direct sales. Some direct selling of sheet metal to Cincinnati fabricators had been started in the 1830's. Characteristically, even as early as the 19th century, the Connecticut rolling mills and metal fabricators sold a significant portion of their output directly to industrial users, who performed a later stage of manufacture, as is the prevailing condition today.[7] Further light on this practice would be useful.

---

[6] The broader lines of development toward specialization in midwest markets are indicated in N. S. B. Gras and H. M. Larson, *Casebook in Business History* (New York, 1939), pp. 385 ff.

[7] See the writer's "Commission Agents in the Button and Brass Trade a Century Ago," *Bulletin of the Business Historical Society*, Vol. XVI, No. 1 (February, 1942), p. 8. In 1929, two thirds of the sales of manufacturers of nonferrous metals and their products were made directly to industrial users. Further historical data on this procedure would make possible a more complete treatment of a practice sometimes summarily handled in marketing texts. On the other hand, see a somewhat more detailed treatment in C. F. Phillips (ed.), *Marketing by Manufacturers* (Chicago, 1947), pp. 34 ff., and particularly pp. 178–86.

4. THE PRODUCTION, PROCESSING, AND TRANSPORTATION OF FOODSTUFFS*

The mid-19th century saw the beginnings of a national market for food products. Limitations of time, distance, and technology were still significant, but the growing railway complex was beginning to have a profound effect. Improved transportation permitted a considerable variety of foodstuffs to be shipped to the larger urban centers, created regional markets for many products, and stimulated wide-scale geographical specialization. In cereals, grains, and meat, the West was already becoming predominant. In the East, seafoods and fisheries became highly developed. Perishability, however, was still a critical factor because of the almost complete lack of refrigerated facilities for transportation and storage and the inadequacy of then existing commercial canning procedures.

FOOD AND THE BUDGET

OF ALL THE COMMODITIES and services which it is the function of the economic order to provide, food is the most important. Studies of family budgets leave no room for doubt on this point. The National Resources Committee has estimated that in the year 1935–36, about a third of all expenditures made by American families were for food; for the two thirds of the families with the lowest incomes, something over two fifths of all expenditures were for food.

There were no such budgetary studies made for the 1850's; but the few estimates that were made (which may or may not be typical) seem to indicate that an even larger proportion of family income was spent for food before the Civil War—as, indeed, one would expect. A budget in the *New York Tribune* for May 27, 1851, indicates the allocation of the weekly expenditures of a Philadelphia family of five; of the $10.37½ total, $4.26½ (41 percent) went for food. Other estimates, not cited by Cummings, would not change the proportions very much. *The New York*

---

* Reprinted from Edgar W. Martin, *The Standard of Living in 1860* (Chicago: University of Chicago Press), pp. 11–35, by permission of the University of Chicago Press.

Times printed a "standard workingman's budget" for New York City, in 1853, supposed to apply to a laborer, his wife, and two children, "living moderately." Of the total annual expenditures of $600, groceries accounted for $273, or 45.5 percent. *Hunt's Merchants' Magazine* estimated in 1857 that a New York businessman with an annual income of $1,500 would spend $415.66 (31.3 percent of the $1,329.91 spent for current consumption) on food and liquor. This last estimate, if it can be regarded as typical of expenditures in that income scale, illustrates the "law" that the proportion spent on food decreases as the income increases. A $1,500 income was distinctly a high income in 1860, and even the first two budgets would have been out of range of the greater part of the population. I have the impression that the ordinary city family would have spent close to 50 percent of its income for food and that the same could be said of farm families if food consumed on the farm be included in income.

Even such statistical evidence cannot indicate the real importance of food. Expenditures for food contain much less of the "conventional" element than do expenditures for even clothing and shelter. That smaller proportions are spent for food as family income increases does not mean that food is less important to the rich than to the poor. What it means is that one can eat only so much food; and while those who can afford it can eat more expensive foods (and waste more), their desires for greater variety and finer quality in foods are less expansive than their other desires. This suggests another reason for giving special attention to food production and consumption: Until the economy produces an ample amount of food, the main effort must be to produce it; beyond that point the increasing proportion of productive resources which can be directed to the production of other goods causes their production (and consumption) to rise faster than income. Former "luxuries" quickly become "necessities."

THE PRODUCTION OF MEAT AND FISH

Every kind of meat now customarily obtainable was obtainable in the fifties—obtainable, that is, in some part of the country and at the proper season. Pork was the staple meat product for the country as a whole, but there were lamb and mutton, veal and beef. There was poultry to be had. Besides these more commonplace meats, to which the destruction of wildlife has very largely limited our own diets, there was then an abundance of game. Fish there were of all kinds, the product of commercial fisheries or of one's own catching.

Meat-packing was confined largely to the local curing and packing of hog products. Most slaughtering was done in winter by farmers who, after satisfying their own demands, sold the remainder of the carcass to a neighboring storekeeper or small packer, who cured it for the market. There were numerous small slaughterhouses in eastern cities; in the South, there were not so many, as the plantations did their own slaughtering and curing. In 1860, as now, meat-packing was essentially a western industry; but in that year the pork-packers of Cincinnati packed only 434,499 hogs, and Chicago had yet to pack more than 185,000 hogs in a single year. Progress had been made, however, in methods of packing; and the packinghouses were beginning to take on the characteristics of large-scale enterprise. Hogs came to Cincinnati by steamboat, by flatboat, by rail (in crates), and on foot; and when they arrived, they were handled quickly and expertly. More attention was being given each year to sanitation and inspection. Summer packing was done as early as 1858, but on a very small scale. Standing in the way of further progress was the absence of stock trains and refrigerator cars, which meant that all meat not locally consumed had to be salted, smoked, or pickled.

The fisheries had been important in American economic life from the earliest times, and by the fifties were important even in the Great Lakes region and the South. The bulk of the $6 million output reported to the census for 1860 was concentrated, however, in the New England and middle states. Most of the oyster fishing was done along the Atlantic coast from Virginia to New York.

THE TRANSPORTATION OF MEAT

The problem in 1860 was not one of production, but one of transportation and refrigeration. Before the coming of the railroad, pork-packing had been less important than beef-packing, because it was easier to drive cattle long distances on the hoof. The railroads brought more and more swine to the packinghouse centers; but I have the impression that the greater number of the livestock was still driven, not carried, to the packinghouse or slaughterhouse. The great western cattle drives of romantic fame were still in the future; but already the leading cattle-raising states were Texas, Missouri, and Iowa rather than those of the East; the yearlings were sent to Illinois, Ohio, and Indiana for fattening before being moved on to the stockyards. In these states the need for driving cattle and hogs to market played a large part in determining land values around the packing towns.

In the East, where distances were short, the cities could draw upon the surrounding territory for live and dressed meats; and the westward extension of the railroads early in the fifties meant that the East could be supplied with cured meats—though not yet with fresh meats—from the western packinghouses. There was some use of refrigeration en route. The express shipment of oysters packed in ice had begun in 1842; and 10 years later, fresh codfish and haddock brought on ice from Boston were selling in Chicago streets a few days after they had been caught. In the summer of 1857, fresh poultry, game, and meats were sent from the Ohio Valley to New York in cars constructed on the "principle of the refrigerator." But in the South, dependence was upon locally slaughtered meat; and in the West, although the railroads had somewhat cheapened the cost of shipping stock, only a few communities were close enough to benefit from it.

THE REFRIGERATION OF MEAT

If consumers were to be able to have fresh meat with convenience and safety, the meat had to be kept refrigerated from the packer to the retailer and at the retailer's place of business; refrigeration at home would presumably be a matter of convenience only. Although there is little satisfactory evidence, it is my impression that butcher shops and meat markets were using ice, but that there was as yet little domestic refrigeration. If this last is correct, it does not mean that refrigerators and ice could not be had, but merely that they were still regarded as luxuries. Refrigerators of some sort had probably come into use around the turn of the century; and there were numerous advertisements for refrigerators, apparently not greatly different from the ice refrigerators still in use, in the city newspapers and illustrated weeklies of the late fifties. Artificial ice had not yet come into use, but in the North the cutting of ice was a considerable business during the coldest months; and apparently, the ice was kept in icehouses in sufficient quantity to be fairly cheap even in summer. The shipment of ice from the North to the South had begun at the turn of the century, and ice had become a normal article of trade, coming both from the Northeast and the Northwest.

THE PRESERVATION OF MEAT

The almost complete absence of household refrigeration meant that the use of fresh meat could not be very economical, and the lack of refrigerated facilities for transportation and storage would have prevented any great use of fresh meat, anyway. During the northern winters, there was some freezing of beef for home consumption. On the whole, however, if meat was not to be eaten soon after being slaughtered, it had to be cured or pickled. Hams and bacon were usually smoked and salted, the rest of the hog pickled in strong brine. Beef, when preserved, was corned, salted (dried), or pickled; but salt beef was notoriously dry and tough. To "jerk" beef was to cut it in strips, dip them in brine, and dry them; frequently, jerked beef was powdered and mixed with other foods or food products. Occasionally, a strong meat broth was mixed with flour to form "meat biscuits." The use of such unpalatable foods was largely confined to the frontier, and especially to travelers across the plains. Fish might be preserved in a number of ways—salted and dried, smoked, potted, baked, pickled, marinated, preserved in oil, or pounded into a dry mass.

The early history of commercial canning is now fairly well documented. The real development of the industry came after 1850, based upon the canning of Baltimore oysters, Maine lobsters, and (possibly) sardines. Oyster canning had been an established business as early as 1850, and by 1860 had benefited from such technical improvements as that of opening the oysters by steam. The development of the canning industry around Chesapeake Bay is particularly interesting. Here, within a small area, were oysters, crabs and fish; peaches, apples, plums, berries, and other fruits. The climate was ideal for tomatoes, and the location was close to a labor supply and to transportation facilities. Here and elsewhere along the coast, canneries began operating on a year-round basis, alternating the canning of oysters, lobsters, crabs, and fish with that of fruits and vegetables. The canning process then used involved cooking after canning, with the result that the product lost bulk and became unappetizing in appearance; not until the seventies was this corrected. The industry was using stamped tin cans with extension edges, and tops and bottoms put on by a "pendulum press"; improvements in canning were made only slowly, and the processes—trade secrets—were purely empirical. Not until the Civil War made it necessary to provide troops with large quantities of provisions which would keep did the output become large enough to have much effect on food consumption.

MEAT MARKETS

Boston's Faneuil Market was 585 feet long and 50 feet wide, on a base of blue Quincy marble; it was divided into numerous stalls for the sale of all sorts of meat, fish, poultry, and vegetables. Of another Boston market, James M. Phillippo wrote: "Quincy Market is a splendid edifice of granite, and is the most clean, commodious, and best supplied of any market in the United States. The abundant supply of wild fowl, together with poultry of all kinds, successively exhibited here, is astonishing to a foreigner." Besides these, there were the Blackstone, Boylston, Franklin, Gerrish, St. Charles, South, Washington, and Williams markets.

But if we may judge conditions in other cities by what we know to be true in New York, visitors were likely to be so impressed by the size of the markets and the variety they offered as to be oblivious to less attractive features.

While the markets might be deficient in sanitation, even by the standards of their own day, they did provide convenient places to purchase a considerable variety of food. Some of these were quite extensive, with stalls for butchers, fish peddlers, hucksters, and dealers in poultry, vegetables, fruit, and dairy products. To these markets came fish wagons from Long Island and other fishing grounds, with clams, mussels, eels, lobsters, and fish of various kinds. Live, dressed, and cured meat came from the countryside and might be shipped in from some little distance.

Other large cities also had their markets. In 1854, Buffalo had a new public market, and $50,000 had been appropriated for the purchase of two more locations. Philadelphia, in the winter and spring of 1859, got rid of the old market sheds in the middle of Market Street and built a new market house at Sixteenth Street. Pittsburgh, in 1852 and 1853, built the Diamond, a new city hall and marketplace. In Cincinnati the markets extended for a mile along the streets, where were to be found beef and pork, eggs, poultry, and other sorts of meat; fish came there from Lake Erie by train, oysters from Baltimore, game from the prairies. St. Louis had 10 market houses. Markets in the South were likely to be rather different from those in the North. Savannah's market, for instance, was merely a roof supported by pillars, with a brick floor and a pump in the middle. Female slaves sold fresh vegetables the year around, and there were fish and shellfish, domestic and wild fowl, tropical and other fruits. People came from miles around to buy and sell. New Orleans' "Old French Market" was famous. In the West the Washington and the Metropolitan were a "creditable" feature of San Francisco, roofed in and clean. The supply of vegetables was great throughout the year; fruit of all kinds was plentiful in summer but, except for apples and oranges, was scarce during the winter months. Game was abundant—venison, rabbits, wild geese, chicks, quail. Altogether, San Francisco had five public markets, of which two had over two dozen stalls each.

EGGS AND DAIRY PRODUCTS

Milk

The growing importance of dairying in New England had long been apparent; it was important also in New York State and was a specialty of the Western Reserve district of Ohio. During the fifties, butter and fluid milk were displacing cheese as a dairy product. But prior to 1860, while much butter and a good deal of cheese were being manufactured, dairying received special attention in but few parts of the country, and much of the product was inferior in quality.

In the cities a large proportion of the milk came from "swill-milk" establishments—enterprises located within the cities, usually in connection with distilleries, which fed their closely confined cows on slops and distillery refuse. In 1852 the swill-milk establishments of New York City had 13,000 cows. Not only was the milk itself of doubtful quality, but it was likely to be adulterated. It was estimated that New York City drank about 330,000 quarts of milk a day in 1852. Of this, 100,000 quarts consisted of country milk brought in and 30,000 quarts of adulterants added to it; 160,000 quarts were swill milk produced in the city, and 40,000 quarts were additions to the swill milk. The milk supply of Chicago and other cities was about as bad. There was practically no regulation. Massachusetts, in 1856, took the lead by prohibiting adulteration of milk and, in 1859, the feeding of distillery waste; and New York State, in 1861, made swill milk illegal.

Milk is even more subject to rapid bacterial action than is meat and consequently requires a still greater degree of refrigeration and rapid transportation. In the years preceding the Civil War, the greater advances had been in transportation. The railroads made it possible for the big cities to draw on larger areas for their supplies of milk. Chicago had obtained its milk "on the hoof" in the early days; but by 1853, it was being shipped in over the Galena Railroad, soon to be called the "Milky Way." During the last six months of 1854, 27,338 gallons of milk were brought to Chicago over that line. There was practically no refrigeration of milk. *Hunt's Merchants' Magazine,* commenting on a table that showed that in 1860 only two fifths of the milk produced was consumed as fluid milk, suggested that this proportion would have been much higher if there had been any way of keeping milk fresh until it got to market. Nor was there much preservation of milk by condensing it. Borden's processes had been patented in the fifties; and by 1860, he was selling unsweetened condensed milk from 40-quart cans on pushcarts and sweetened condensed milk in tins. But the whole output was too small to be of commercial importance.

OTHER DAIRY PRODUCTS

The production of butter in the United States as a whole amounted to 14.62 pounds per capita (21.5 pounds in the middle states, somewhat more than 16 pounds in the New England and southern states, 6–8 pounds per capita in the regions farther west); and allowing for exports, the average per capita consumption would have been 14.35 pounds, as compared with 17.28 pounds during the five-year period 1926–30. In the absence of domestic refrigeration, it was difficult to keep butter fresh. It was frequently kept in the cellar, sometimes in the well shaft.

The production of cheese in the census year 1860 was 3.29 pounds per capita (6.89 in New England, 6.15 in the middle states, less than 3 in other regions), and consumption only 2.84 pounds per capita, as compared with 5.45 pounds in 1929.

In the early part of the century, making ice cream had been a laborious task which involved beating the cream with a spoon and then agitating the container by hand in an ice-and-salt mixture, but by the middle of the century the familiar form of mixer equipped with crank and paddles had appeared. It was reported in 1860 that more than 20,000 freezers of one type had been sold in three years.

EGGS

I have found no estimates of the production or consumption of eggs before the Civil War. That there was some shipment of them to consuming centers is indicated by the fact that Norfolk, in 1852, shipped about 1,800 barrels of 100 dozen eggs each, packed in oats. I think it is probable that most farmers kept a few chickens and so had enough eggs for their own families; the difficulties of shipping and storing them may have kept city consumption at a minimum, especially in the off-season. There were various ways of keeping eggs, most of which involved coating them with some impervious substance to close the pores and packing them in bran, salt, ashes, powdered charcoal, cornmeal, or limewater.

CEREAL FOODSTUFFS

CROP PRODUCTION

The few years preceding the Civil War had been years of rapidly increasing productivity in agriculture. Not only was there new farm machinery, but there was greater use of natural and artificial fertilizers, crop rotation was being practiced, and there was some selection of seed to overcome plant pests and diseases. Meanwhile, the expansion of transportation facilities was making it possible to exploit western lands, where the new equipment and methods were particularly suitable. In the East, in many sections, cereal crops were declining in importance; in the West, rapidly increasing. The five states of Ohio, Indiana, Illinois, Wisconsin, and Iowa, which in 1839 had supplied one fourth of all the wheat and corn produced, by 1859 were supplying one half. The use of the reaping machine and other farm machinery of recent origin was confined almost entirely to the large farms of the West; elsewhere, the old hand implements and methods were still used.

Of the grain crops, corn continued its undisputed lead. The amount exported was highly variable but, during the decade of the fifties, ran well over the 1860 figure except in 1859. Production of wheat was 173,124,904 bushels (5.5 bushels per capita). With deductions for exports, there was an apparent per capita consumption of about 4.99 bushels—little different from the average consumption of about 4.8 bushels for the years 1926–30, although the differences in the form in which it was consumed may have been considerable.

Production of other cereal crops was as follows: rye, 21,101,380 bushels (0.66 bushels per capita); oats, 172,643,185 bushels (5.49 per capita);

barley, 15,802,322 bushels (0.4 per capita); buckwheat, 17,558,253 bushels (0.56 per capita); rice 187,167,032 pounds (5.95 per capita). How much of this was consumed as human food, it is impossible to say. Oatmeal, for instance, was negligible as an article of human consumption.

TRANSPORTATION AND PROCESSING

The decade of the fifties was one of increasing facilities for the transportation of breadstuffs, and of decreasing freight rates. Since grain required neither care nor speed in handling, it was well suited to waterborne transport. By the late fifties, through shipments by lake and canal were a matter of course. Flour was less suited than the whole grain to water transportation, and the interregional shipment of flour was more closely tied to railroad expansion.

Flour-milling processes were in transition; and though substitution of rollers for millstones did not begin until the seventies, all the large mills had taken over the basic ideas of Oliver Evans—a continuous flow of materials, the use of gravity conveyors, and improved power devices. Bolting processes simplified the separation of the white flour from the bran. Agricultural expansion and improvements in transportation were having still greater effects on the milling industry. The flour-milling centers of the East continued to be important; but more and more milling was being done in the West, with St. Louis, Chicago, Milwaukee, and the lake cities of Ohio taking the lead. In 1860 the western states produced more flour and mill products than New England and the middle states combined.

An interesting development of the fifties was that of large-scale bakeries, designed to use machinery for the mixing of the dough through all the baking processes, and using up to 800 barrels of flour a day. But these bakeries failed to revolutionize bread baking; and while there must have been a great deal of baking by the old-fashioned bakeries, business historians have ignored them in their interest in the large-scale baking of biscuits, crackers, and ship bread. By the middle of the fifties the original products of "pilot bread" and hard, "cold-water" crackers had been supplemented by soft or butter crackers, square soda crackers, and round sugar biscuits, all made of fermented dough and containing shortening. Production of macaroni and similar products was unimportant.

VEGETABLE AND FRUIT GROWING

GARDENS AND ORCHARDS

I can think of no other consumption goods in which actuality fell so far short of potentiality as it did in vegetables and fruits. Here I intend only to suggest what the possibilities were.

That there was a great variety of garden vegetables available to those who were wealthy enough to buy them or who were willing to take the trouble to grow them is shown by the garden manuals of the fifties. Not only were these vegetables known and, to some extent, actually grown; there were only a small proportion of the population living in such crowded conditions that they had no garden space. While there was little leisure, it is hard to believe that no member of the family had time enough to do a little gardening.

Much the same thing can be said of fruits. Up to the fifties, there had been little care in the selection of varieties of fruit trees or in the maintaining of them. But by 1860, there were numerous state and national horticultural societies, with annual congresses; and there were several state and national horticultural journals. With the fifties, there came a number of books on horticulture, describing in detail many kinds of fruit and their cultivation. Some enthusiasts were endeavoring, but without success, to spread the cultivation of such fruits as figs and olives. In the West, wild fruits and berries took the place of cultivated fruits; but in such states as Michigan and Illinois, large orchards were beginning to bear.

We can hardly say of these fruits, as we can of vegetables, that they should have been available to everyone. Some of them were not suited to domestic cultivation at all, and many of them were rather exacting as to soil and climatic conditions. Many of them do not begin to bear until years after planting. They were, as a rule, more perishable than vegetables, less easily kept or marketed. Nevertheless, there were a few easily cultivated annuals and various kinds of berries which the working classes might easily have grown for themselves.

Among nuts, chestnuts, English and black walnuts, filberts, hickory nuts, and butternuts were domestically produced; but attempts to introduce the production of almonds had not been successful. What fruits and nuts could not be produced at home could be imported. Even tropical fruits were to be had.

Surrounding all the large cities were truck gardens supplying fruits and vegetables for the city trade. There were hundreds of acres devoted to the production of tomatoes for the New York market and other hundreds of acres in Cape Cod, producing cranberries. Eastern Virginia and Maryland did what seemed an immense business in supplying truck produce for the northern market, though handicapped by the impossibility of refrigerating in transit. During the decade, there was a great development of fruit nurseries and orchards; and each year, millions of new fruit trees were set out. Orchards were being started in the South (Georgia was then trying to grow oranges) and in California, as well as in the states of the Old Northwest; and vineyards were planted along the Ohio, where the Catawba grape was especially popular.

PRESERVATION AND TRANSPORTATION OF FRUITS AND VEGETABLES

For the most part, perishable fruits and vegetables were consumed only in season; at other times of the year, dependence was on those which could be kept without much difficulty. Geographical differences in consumption were due not so much to different growing conditions as to differences in the possibilities of storage: Irish potatoes, which ripened quickly and had to be dug in weather too hot for storage, were used in the North; while in the South, sweet potatoes, maturing in the autumn, were the staple vegetable.

Despite the progress made in commercial canning, most of the preserving was done in the home by methods which had been in common use for many years. Some fruits and vegetables were dried, some packed in syrup or in hermetically sealed jars.

The commercial canning of fruits and vegetables was developing in much the same fashion as that of meats; and packers were canning pickles, catsups, sauces, jellies, jams, and mustard, and a variety of fruit, tomatoes, and corn. Canners were still processing their foods by boiling; and the industry was still a small-scale business, centering in Maryland, but with some firms farther north.

One can find numerous instances of apparently speedy and efficient transportation of vegetables and fruits. In 1852 a Chicago commission merchant imported green peas from New Orleans in May by express; and three years later the *Chicago Press* stated that since the extension of the railroad to the Ohio River, people in southern Illinois enjoyed fresh fruits no sooner than they did. Berries were shipped in ice down the Mississippi to Louisiana; the Illinois Central was putting special fruit cars on its passenger trains to speed the movement of fruit to Chicago; and Oregon apples were sold in California. Other fruits were coming in from abroad—oranges and lemons from Sicily, bananas, pineapples. The most important part of the trade, however, was the shipment from South to North. Georgia and Carolina fruit growers, responding to urban demands, had begun to ship fruit from inland points to the seaports, from which steamboats took them north; there was also some shipment of citrus fruit from Florida.

The New York markets were especially well supplied. On a single night in June, 1847, the Erie's milk train brought in 80,000 baskets of strawberries; and by 1855 the strawberry business of New York City was said to be the largest in the world. Other railroads were bringing in fruit and vegetables from the North and West. One effect of this was to lengthen the seasons during which fruits and vegetables could be purchased in the market. Between 1835 and 1865 the strawberry season was lengthened from one month to four, the grape season from four to six, the peach season from one to six, and the tomato season from four months to the full year. The season for sweet corn was increased from one month to five months, that for string beans from one month to nine months.

Nevertheless, we should be on guard against exaggerating the effect of this. It was only the populous districts of the Northeast which could exert sufficient demand to make such shipments possible; and probably these were the only districts where the transportation was adequate to permit a very large segment of the population to draw on the outside for its supply of fruit and vegetables. Only the beginnings had been made in the transportation of early fruits and vegetables from South to North and the products of the western market gardens and orchards to the East. Transportation was both too slow and too expensive to permit much interchange of foodstuffs, and refrigerator cars were not yet in use. Such fruits as apples could be shipped if properly packed, but even apples were likely to be dried before shipment. Foods which were highly perishable could be consumed only in the immediate region in which they were produced. In the West and South, where the population was scattered, people were dependent upon their home gardens.

Fruit and Vegetable Markets

What has been said of meat markets applies to the produce markets— that they were likely to be impressive in size, in variety of commodities offered for sale, and even in their facilities, but that they were likely also to be deficient in the ordinary sanitary provisions. It is surprising that no hint of this disagreeable feature creeps into the comments of foreigners, usually so quick to point out the Americans' disregard for cleanliness.

Olmsted wrote of the Washington, D.C. markets that they were notable for the trifling quantities of articles brought in for sale—he thought an average stock in trade would consist of a single peck of potatoes, three bunches of carrots, two cabbages, six eggs, and a chicken. In North Carolina the larger towns usually had a public market where country produce was brought for sale. When there was no market, the courthouse yard or the street in front of it served the purpose. Some towns boasted a city hall, the first floor of which sometimes housed the town market. Produce was brought in from distances as long as 200 miles. Stalls came to be operated by townspeople who raised their own produce or bought out the supplies of those who had produced them. Olmsted wrote that the markets of most southern towns seemed mainly to be supplied by poor countrypeople, who brought in all sorts of produce in exchange for such small stores and articles of apparel as they had to obtain from the shops. Sometimes, owing to the great extent of the backcountry, produce was offered in great abundance and variety; at other times, produce was scarce, and prices were high.

New Orleans' markets were then, as they continued to be, very interesting to strangers. Cincinnati's markets were well supplied with the fruits of the region. Even frontier towns had their markets: Denver, in June, 1859, had on sale in its markets locally produced radishes, lettuce, onions, and peas.

5. FINANCING AND MARKETING THE LOUISIANA SUGAR CROP*

Southern sugar planters, located primarily in Louisiana, were faced with heavy demands for capital. Processing cane into raw sugar required a substantial investment in heavy machinery. This, coupled with a seasonal harvest, created a need for both long- and short-term financing. Some credit was supplied by banks and other planters, but factors supplied the bulk of the growers' needs. In his role as agent, the factor insured the crop, stored it if necessary, paid outstanding bills, and provided the planter with market information. The most frequent destination for Louisiana sugar was New Orleans, where the great bulk of the crop was purchased either by western buyers for shipment up the Mississippi River or by representatives of the sugar brokers of the Northeast.

OF ALL PHASES of southern history, upon few has the historian focused more attention than upon the antebellum plantation. In spite of this emphasis, however, it is striking to note the scarcity of material on the commercial aspects of the plantation regime. About the cotton, tobacco, rice, and sugar plantations, we know much; about the financing and marketing of these products, we know relatively little. This amazing paucity of information becomes even more striking when one stops to consider that financing and marketing are of primary importance to commercialized staple-crop agriculture.

Credit, it is generally conceded, is the mainspring of staple-crop agriculture. In no instance was this more clearly demonstrated than in the case of sugar. The antebellum sugar industry, centering in Louisiana, was characterized by several factors that made adequate capital essential. In the first place, sugar culture, unlike the other southern staples, was both agriculture and industry. The cane was crushed and the juice manufactured into raw sugar on the plantation. This process required the use of expensive machinery, in addition to the usual capital outlay for land and slaves. And with improvements occurring in the technique of sugar production from 1845 to 1860, new and more up-to-date equipment was often desirable. Moreover, the rapid expansion of the Louisiana sugar

* Reprinted from J. Carlyle Sitterson, "Financing and Marketing the Sugar Crop of the Old South," *Journal of Southern History,* Vol. X (May, 1944), pp. 188–99.

industry during those years required large amounts of capital and extensive credit.

During the early 19th century the chief source of capital was the Louisiana banks. Until 1837, New Orleans banks readily extended long-term credit to the Louisiana planters. One authority reports that during the early 1830's, with speculative fever high, credit easy, and banking practices loose, the New Orleans banks extended credit up to 50 percent of the estimated value of the planters' property. Such loans, often for periods of 20 years, generally bore from 6 to 8 percent interest; but at times, rates of 10 to 12 percent were charged. After the passage of the Louisiana banking law of 1842, which restricted bank loans to short-term commercial paper not exceeding 90 days, planters' credit was not supplied so readily by the banks.

Of course, there were always cases of planters borrowing directly from other planters. How frequent such direct lending and borrowing was among antebellum planters is uncertain. Though the example just cited involves exceptionally large amounts, it seems likely that smaller loans from planter to planter were fairly frequent. Nor was it unusual for planters to purchase their plantation supplies on credit from wholesale dealers in much the same manner that the southern farmer today buys from the time merchant.

Although the above sources of capital were available, the antebellum sugar planters depended for the greater part of their credit needs upon that noted yet enigmatic southern financier, the factor. It is one of the striking facts in southern history that one who played so important a role in the antebellum economy appears so little in recorded history. The sugar factor performed a variety of services for the antebellum planter. He extended him credit, purchased his supplies, marketed his crop, and acted as his agent in the city. As planter's agent, the factor frequently rendered such services as insuring the planter's crop and sugarhouse, paying his bills, and informing him of general business conditions. On occasions, the factor even visited and advised the planter's children who were at school in the city. It might then be said that he was at once personal friend, planter's banker and financier, purchasing agent, and marketing medium. Relations between Louisiana sugar planters and their commission merchants were in most cases personal and friendly. When in New Orleans, the planter called upon his factor for innumerable business and personal services, and a social visit by the merchant to his planter client in the country was not unusual. Correspondence between planters and factors indicates that there were relatively few disagreements between them, and evidences of antagonism are rare indeed.

Generally, in the winter and spring, the planter would call upon his factor for the extension of credit for the purchase of plantation supplies. Sometimes, the factor was himself a wholesale dealer and would forward the supplies, charging the amount to the planter's debit. More often, however, the factor was merely the agent and financier. He would purchase the needed articles from the appropriate dealers, making his own arrangements with the sellers. The supplies would then be shipped to the planter, and his account would be charged with the amount of the purchase plus the legally prescribed buyer's commission of 2½ percent. When short of capital, the factor often called on the planter for a draft sufficient to cover the amount of the purchases. These planters' drafts or notes were sold by the factor to exchange dealers, money brokers, and bankers. In such instances, it is apparent that the real credit was extended not by the factor but by the money brokers or bankers, and the factor was no more than the planter's agent for the disposal of commercial paper.

When the factor was extending his personal capital as credit, apparently his own business judgment was the only restriction upon the amount extended. The probability is that the practice varied among the factors, and each probably pursued different policies with different planters. Undoubtedly, such matters as the wealth of the planter in land, slaves, and equipment, the annual value of his crop, the intimacy of the personal relationship between planter and factor, and finally the amount of capital the factor had available, all played their part in determining credit policies.

All in all, the problem of financing the antebellum sugar crop appears to have been little different from that of financing one of the staples in the postbellum South. To those planters with agricultural assets, credit was available at rates somewhat higher than general commercial bank rates. How much of a genuine economic burden debit financing was to the southern sugar planter, it is difficult to say. With interest charges of from 8 to 12 percent, however, it is safe to conclude that it was at least as burdensome as debit farming always is to agriculture.

Since Louisiana accounted for more than 90 percent of the cane sugar produced in the antebellum South, it seems justifiable to limit the description of marketing practices to those followed in that state. From 1840 to 1860, an annual average of from 45 to 60 percent of the Louisiana crop was sold on the New Orleans market. The remainder was sold in a variety of ways. It was customary for small producers to sell small quantities of sugar to retail merchants in the surrounding countryside or even to exchange sugar for other products. In cases where plantations were located within easy reach of Mobile, planters often marketed their crops in that city. The prices on the Mobile market approximated those of New Orleans plus freight charges between the two cities. Consequently, plantations readily accessible to Mobile benefited from lower freight costs. Nor was it unusual for a large planter to ship his crop by boat directly to Savannah, Charleston, Baltimore, Philadelphia, or New York, to be marketed there by a factor or commission merchant. The prices for Louisiana sugars in the eastern cities were somewhat above the New Orleans prices, generally enough higher to take care of the cost of shipment. When planters shipped directly to these markets, it was generally because they believed the New Orleans prices to be out of line with the eastern prices. Such differentials naturally tended to correct themselves by diversion of sugar to the higher market. Occasionally, a planter would attempt to benefit from what he thought to be high prices in New York. For example, in April, 1855, Andrew McCollam of Terrebonne Parish sold 104 hogsheads of sugar and 502 barrels of molasses in New York for a gross of $9,903.38. After paying the transportation and marketing costs, however, his net was only $6,830.09. Of the gross amount, 50 percent in the case of molasses and 22 percent in the case of sugar was consumed in freight and marketing costs. Apparently, McCollam was convinced that little was to be gained by shipping directly to New York, since he never sent any more to that city.

Although sugar was sold in the ways mentioned above, the larger portion of the Louisiana crop not marketed in New Orleans was sold to buyers who visited the plantation. The buyers were either brokers who were purchasing for northern refiners or speculators who hoped to resell at higher prices on other markets. Sugar sold "on plantation" generally brought the New Orleans prices less the cost of transportation.

The most important market for the sale of sugar was New Orleans, where about 50 percent of the Louisiana crop was sold. Generally, the sugar was shipped to the city by boat between November and May. Adequate transportation facilities at reasonable costs were of primary importance to the sugar planter, as to the producers of other staples. Plantations located on the Mississippi or Red rivers or other navigable streams had a cost advantage over other plantations. With a scarcity of well-built roads, bad weather sometimes delayed the hauling of sugar. The sugar planters of Louisiana enjoyed the advantages of transportation on the Mississippi and its tributaries. Yet, if we are to believe the complaints of some planters, the very ease of transportation afforded by the waterways discouraged the building of railroads. Occasionally, low water in the tributary streams was a real obstacle to the shipment of produce. Kenneth Clark of Rapides Parish complained bitterly in December, 1854, of the high freight rates resulting from low water in the Red River. He further complained that "from the lethargy of our people, we have no other mode of conveyance to New Orleans."

For plantations located on the outer fringes of the sugar belt, transportation charges were an important cost factor. Freight rates from Rapides Parish occasionally reached the figure of $5 per hogshead, which meant approximately 10 percent of the gross sale. Freight charges were even more of a burden in the shipment of molasses because of the bulk of the product relative to its value. On a shipment of 28 barrels of molasses that sold in New Orleans for $236.98, the freight charges from Rapides Parish were $58.24, or approximately 24 percent. For plantations nearer New Orleans, transportation cost was not a major item. In addition to freight charges, the planter usually carried insurance on the shipment, the cost of which varied from three eighths to three fourths of 1 percent.

The sugar and molasses were usually shipped to the planter's factor or agent in the city, who saw to their sale. Upon reaching the city, the hogsheads were landed on the levee, where transactions in sugar, molasses, cotton, tobacco, and other commodities took place. According to the regulations of the New Orleans Chamber of Commerce, produce landed on the levee had to be sold within 36 hours or moved into storage. This regulation was to prevent the overcrowding of the levee with produce. If moved into storage, sugar had to bear storage charges of 40 cents per hogshead per month. The factor saw to the weighing of the sugar and molasses, and then put them up for sale on the levee to the highest bidder. The factor's commission for selling sugar and molasses was 2½ percent. In addition to this, the planter had to pay small charges for cooperage, weighing, and drayage. These charges plus the cost of transportation came to considerable amounts in many instances. On occasions when the price was low and freight rates high, it was not even profitable to ship molasses. Once the sugar and molasses were sold, the net returns were credited to the planter's account with his factor.

The demand for sugar on the levee came mainly from four sources. Most important quantitatively was the sugar purchased for shipment up the Mississippi for consumption in the West. In the years from 1840 to 1860, approximately 50 percent of the Louisiana crop was purchased by western buyers. Secondly, there were the buyers from the Northeast, either the representatives of sugar refiners or sugar brokers who counted upon reselling in the eastern markets. Generally, from 30 to 35 percent of the Louisiana crop was purchased for export to the eastern cities, especially New York. Thirdly, there were sugar buyers who bought for the local demand. A part of the sugar thus purchased was refined in New Orleans, and the remainder was sold as raw sugar for consumption in Louisiana and adjoining areas. This source accounted for the remaining 15 to 20 percent of the crop. In addition to the above buyers, there was a fourth type of sugar buyer, the speculator, who occupied much the same position that speculators in cotton, tobacco, and other commodities do on southern markets today. He purchased with the hope of reaping profits from the day-to-day fluctuations of the sugar market.

The unloading of sugar and molasses on the levee, where they were subject to the hazards of weather, was criticized by planters and commercial journals alike. In January, 1847, *DeBow's Review* urged the erection of warehouses on the levee and of colonnades for the warehouses to the water's edge in order to prevent injury to produce being unloaded in bad weather. In spite of such complaints, however, as late as 1856 nothing had been done to remedy this situation. In January of that year a planter of Rapides Parish commented on the situation as follows: "I have come home thoroughly impressed with the conviction that New Orleans is the meanest commercial port in the world. The day I landed there was 2400 bales of cotton on the levee in a most miserable condition and great quantities of sugar & molasses—parts of the wharf were breaking in from the weight and produce [was] sacrificed to get it out of the way."

More important than such inadequacies in marketing facilities was the lack of organization of the commercial phases of the sugar interest. There was no special organization of the sugar factors or businessmen in New Orleans which purported to protect and advance the sugar industry. Such important matters as adequate levee facilities, investigation of complaints, consideration of marketing improvements, and regulation of credit practices were all left to agencies having no special interest in the industry as a whole.

Numerous complaints finally brought an attempt at remedy. On January 22–23, 1856, a sugar planters' convention was held in New Orleans. One prominent member of the convention declared that the short time—only 36 hours—sugar and molasses were allowed to remain on the levee before being sold often resulted in sales at unjustifiably low prices. Moreover, he charged that frequently such produce, once sold, was allowed to remain there several days, giving rise "to strong suspicion of partiality for the benefit of speculators." This convention appointed a committee to investigate the marketing facilities. The committee made the investigation and in April made the following report: First, the space on the levee allotted for the receipt and sale of sugar and molasses was considered inadequate; second, it was estimated that at least $150,000 would be required to purchase the necessary ground and build sufficient platforms, sheds, and wharves for the accommodation and protection of the produce; and finally, the committee proposed the formation of an incorporated association of those interested in the Louisiana sugar industry, to be known as the Louisiana Sugar Mart. It was not until the postbellum period, however, that such an organization was formed.

In conclusion, what may be said of the commercial aspects of this important antebellum industry? As is generally true of agricultural products, the facilities for financing and marketing the sugar crop of the Old South developed haphazardly. Persistent criticisms of the inadequacies of the practices brought more concerted attempts to improve conditions. But the absence of any central organization caused many inefficient practices to go uncorrected. Yet, it must be said that the sugar industry was awakened to the need of an agency to promote its interests. This awakening was to bear fruit in the postbellum years.

6. THE FUR TRADE OF THE FAR WEST*

From 1807 to 1843, the period during which the Mississippi River was the nation's western frontier, the fur trade flourished. This article describes the importance of St. Louis as the major market center, the various methods used to procure furs, and the key role played by the Indians in this industry. Of particular interest is the discussion of "value," as it was perceived by the white man and the Indians. In the words of the author, "each gave to the other something that he valued lightly, and received in return something that he valued highly; and each felt a keen contempt for the stupid taste of the other."

THE FUR TRADE of the Missouri Valley began early in the 18th century, but it did not assume large proportions until after the cession of Louisiana to the United States and the exploring expeditions of Lewis and Clark, and Pike. Its career thereafter continued practically unchecked until the tide of western emigration set in about 1843. The true period of the trans-Mississippi fur trade therefore embraces the 37 years from 1807 to 1843.

In this trade the city of St. Louis was the principal, if not the only, emporium. It is true that the headquarters of the American Fur Company and of some other fur-trading concerns were in New York; but even in these cases, the actual base from which all operations in the western country were carried on was the city at the mouth of the Missouri. All parties were organized and all outfits were made up there. The returns of the trade en route to market all passed that way. Most of the traders resided there, and all nonresident firms maintained houses there. Great establishments arose for the convenience of the trade, while the port of St. Louis became a center of commerce almost as widespread as that of New York itself.

In the earlier year, communication with New York and other seaboard towns took place principally by way of the Ohio River or the Great Lakes. In the latter case the route was sometimes by way of the Illinois River to Lake Michigan, thence either by water or across the country to Detroit, thence to Black Rock near Buffalo, and thence overland to New York; at other times, it was by way of the Mississippi, the Fox, and the

* Reprinted from Hiram M. Chittenden, *The American Fur Trade of the Far West* (2 vols.; New York: Francis P. Harper, 1912), pp. 2–8.

Wisconsin rivers to Lake Michigan, and the rest of the way by the route just described. In later years, after the use of steamboats became general, commerce usually passed by way of New Orleans.

The business of the fur trade, as the name implies, was mainly a traffic in furs and peltries. There were the fine furs obtained from the beaver, otter, mink, fox, and other animals, and the coarser products such as buffalo robes and bear- and deerskins, which were not used as furs so much as for lap robes, heavy coats, and the like. Besides the furs and peltries, there were regularly brought to St. Louis cargoes of buffalo tongues, buffalo and bear tallow, and limited quantities of other products. The trade from the Southwest, particularly from Santa Fe, dealt more largely in horses, mules, and specie.

There were several methods of procuring furs. The one most generally resorted to, and which on the whole yielded the largest results, was by traffic with the Indians. The first thought of the trader on going to a tribe of Indians was to supply himself with those articles which he knew had an attraction for the native fancy, to a large extent things of trifling value but of showy appearance. The white man valued the native furs altogether beyond what the Indian was able to comprehend, and the latter was only too happy to find that he could trade them for that gaudy and glittering wealth which had been brought from a great distance to his country. Thus, in the early intercourse of the white man with the Indian, each gave to the other something that he valued lightly, and received in return something that he valued highly; and each felt a keen contempt for the stupid taste of the other. The trade thus began by imposition on the one side and ignorance on the other, and developed upon more thorough acquaintance into a regular system.

All the fur companies regularly employed hunters and trappers who killed buffalo and caught beaver and gathered such other furs as came in their way. These men worked at fixed wages, and the product of their labor belonged to the company. No goods were brought into the country for furs taken in this way, except in payment of the men's wages, which were generally absorbed as fast as earned in new outfits and in liquor or feasting.

A third source from which the products of the country were obtained was the free hunter and trapper. These men worked on their own account, being bound to no company, and generally sold the product of their labor at some regular trading post or rendezvous, although they occasionally went to St. Louis with it themselves. A large portion of the payment for their furs, if sold in the interior, was in the form of articles required for new outfits and for tobacco and liquor. The free trappers worked only in the finer kinds of fur.

It thus appears that from whatever source the trader obtained his furs, he generally paid for them in merchandise carried into the country. This merchandise comprised such articles as were used in traffic with the Indians and for the equipment of trappers and hunters, the more necessary articles of food which could not be obtained from the country, and finally plenty of liquor and tobacco.

A large proportion of the merchandise of certain classes was imported from Europe; for at this early day, American manufactures, in blankets and cloths particularly, were so inferior that the Indians did not want them, having learned through the British traders what a really good article was. It thus happened that while the furs found their principal market in Europe, the merchandise for which they were traded was mostly manufactured there. It would be interesting to trace an invoice of fur-trade merchandise from the manufactories of Europe in those early days to New York, New Orleans, St. Louis, and thence to the remote and obscure trading posts in the heart of the wilderness; and there, where the innocent beaver falls a victim to the wily trapper, to witness the exchange of these goods for his rich coat of fur, and to follow the latter back through St. Louis, New York, and London, to its final destination in the comfortable garments of the aristocracy of Europe. The complete round occupied fully four years. Could we know the price of the merchandise as it left the factory and its equivalent in fur as sold in the completed garment, the increase would be found to be several hundred percent. This did not, of course, all represent profit. The insurance by sea, the losses by river and land, particularly in the Indian country, and the services of the many hands through which both the merchandise and the furs had to pass, account to some extent for the increase; but there was still a heavy increment that represented the profits of the trader. That these profits were enormous is sufficiently attested by the immense fortunes which were made in the fur trade.

In the matter of profits and losses, as well as in that of volume of business, there are numerous early authorities. Nathaniel J. Wyeth, a close observer, though rather too optimistic, has left on record an estimate of what a well-managed hunting expedition, in the best days of the fur trade, might reasonably be expected to accomplish. According to this estimate, the cost of an invoice of merchandise at the Teton Mountains, or in that vicinity, was about 400 percent of its first cost in the eastern market. This increase was taken up by the expenses of interest, insurance, wagons, provisions for food until the buffalo country was reached, horses and mules, pack and riding saddles, blankets, pack covers, halters, bridles, horseshoeing, and other expenses incidental to the transportation of the goods across the plains. If the furs were obtained through hired trappers, the wages were paid in goods at an advance of about 600 percent upon their cost in the mountains. The wages of a hunter being counted at $400 per year and of common men who did the work of camp at $200, a party of 20 hunters and 10 camp keepers, with their necessary horses (which "cost about $4 in goods prime cost in Boston or New York") could be kept in the field for one year for not to exceed $2,000. With average success, each hunter would take 120 beaver skins in this time, the value of which, in Boston or New York, was about $1,000. With due allowance for the cost of the return journey, the outlay of $2,000 would net in the neighborhood of $15,000. "This, as you will perceive, will leave a large profit," is the logical deduction by the author of this simple calculation. Of course, such successful enterprises were of rare occurrence, for there were many sources of loss in these perilous expeditions, but there are nevertheless authenticated instances of very high profits. In 1827 the house of Bernard Pratte and Company joined with General Ashley in equipping an expedition for the mountains. The whole enterprise lasted only about six months and netted the company 70 percent profit on its investment.

In the Santa Fe trade, 40 percent was a high profit, while the average was between 15 and 20 percent.

In regard to the magnitude of the trade, it is difficult to give definite figures; but the following table of statistics, compiled about 1832 by Indian Agent John Dougherty, embracing the 15 years from 1815 to 1830, gives a fair idea, not only of the extent of the trade, but of the wages paid, the prices of furs, and the profits realized, during this period:

EXPENDITURES

20 clerks, 15 years, @ $500 per year	$ 150,000
200 men, 15 years, @ $150 per year	450,000
Merchandise	1,500,000

RETURNS

26,000 buffalo skins per yr. for 15 yrs. @ $3 each	$1,170,000
25,000 beaver skins per yr. for 15 yrs. @ $4 each	1,500,000
4,000 otter skins per yr. for 15 yrs. @ $3 each	180,000
12,000 coon skins per yr. for 15 yrs. @ 25¢ each	45,000
150,000 lbs. deer skins per yr. for 15 yrs. @ 33¢ per lb.	742,500
37,500 muskrat skins per yr. for 15 yrs. @ 20¢ each	112,500
Total	$3,750,000
Total profit	1,650,000
Average annual expenditure	140,000
Average annual returns	250,000
Average annual profit	110,000

At an anniversary celebration of the founding of St. Louis, held on February 15, 1847, it was stated that the annual value of the St. Louis fur trade for the past 40 years had been between $200,000 and $300,000, and this may be taken as a fair estimate for the period covered by our present studies.

The losses incident to the business of the fur trade were, in the very nature of things, large. They arose almost entirely from encounters with hostile Indians, and involved both life and property. The danger of losing horses was an ever-present peril, for even friendly Indians had no compunctions about stealing these animals. Reliable statistics covering the period from 1820 to 1831 give the losses of life from the Indians at 151 and the loss of property at $100,000. It is probable that for the entire period from 1806 to 1843, these figures should be doubled.

7. ADVERTISING AND THE NEWSPAPERS THAT CARRIED IT*

The dramatic changes that occurred in newspaper publishing between 1800 and 1860 were in large part spurred by advances in advertising techniques and policies. At the turn of the century, newspaper publishers thought of themselves as in the "news" business and viewed the cost of the paper as a fee for services rendered. Advertising was generally considered a necessary evil required to "keep the paper going." During the period under review, however, advertising emerged as a major force. It made possible such important newspaper innovations as penny journalism, mass circulation, and comprehensive coverage. Important changes in advertising techniques and presentation also occurred. Small one-column "want ads" gradually evolved into modern, display-type advertisements. This selection also demonstrates the effectiveness of an early marketing strategy. Entrepreneurial innovators successfully cast aside established traditions and forced others to copy the new techniques that had won public acceptance.

CONSIDERING ADVERTISING in its physical form, the first quarter of the 19th century may be called "the legal notice period in display." The reversion from the style set by Dunlap and others in the last quarter of the preceding century was decided and general. The type-size decline had its origin in paper shortage and mechanical necessity for conserving space. An idea that number of advertisements gave prestige to a newspaper also was an influence. The publisher would rather have several short advertisements than one long one. Advertisements were set in the style of the modern notice to John Smith to appear or be divorced by default. Use of large display type, or of white space to set all text, was rare. The old Caslon 12-point gave way to 6-point in both news and advertisements, with only occasional departures.

Mechanical limitations which kept the size of a newspaper to four pages, and other influences, shortened the length of most copy. There was now a fixed price for running advertisements, $30 per year. The preponderance of advertisements inserted on this basis resulted in adver-

* Reprinted from Frank Presbrey, *The History and Development of Advertising* (Garden City, N.Y.: Doubleday, Doran & Co., Inc., 1929), pp. 176–243.

tising columns that had the appearance of a modern want-ad page. The thumbnail cuts of ships, usually the only illustrations, were reduced in many of the papers to quarter-inch squares and, poorly printed, often were recognizable as ships only because the reader knew they must be ships if they appeared in a shipping advertisement. Text was, however, well printed, and uniformity in type gave the papers a neat appearance when there were no badly printed cuts.

But if display suffered, the total volume expanded. The good accomplished for advertising with display methods in the earlier decades showed in the increased number of advertisers. Risk of loss in newspaper publishing had become less. This brought many new papers into the field. With the help of some commercial printing, a circulation of 300 or 400 copies an issue was sufficient to keep a paper on its feet, if it succeeded in collecting 75 percent of its bills, which appears to have been the average. The merchant paid $40 for a subscription and a year's advertising.

The area covered by the printing press spread. Papers had been issued in western Pennsylvania and Ohio since as early as 1786; and at the turn of the century, there were a half-dozen papers west of the Alleghenies. The *Cincinnati Gazette* was established in 1793, when Cincinnati was in "the Northwest" and Ohio was "a wild region." St. Louis got a paper, the *Republican*, in 1808. The printing press had begun to spot the collection of a half-dozen huts which has ever since been sufficient reason for it to settle down and make itself useful. As soon as a county was organized, the official county printing usually was sufficient, with job office work, to keep a plant alive.

Some of these early 19th-century newspapers were, however, kept up by considerations other than advertising. Many sheets were then, as for generations after, mouthpieces for political leaders. In 1788 and 1789, Alexander Hamilton, James Madison, and John Jay had again demonstrated the power of publicity in a national crisis with their famous "Federalist" letters in support of the proposed Constitution of the United States as adopted by the federal convention in 1787.

Great names of the period were linked with journalism. Among the papers established by men whose names have lived to be familiar to every schoolboy more than a century later is the *New York Evening Post*, founded by Alexander Hamilton in 1801, three years before the fatal duel with Aaron Burr.

It was a time of violent disputes over policies to be adopted by the young nation. News from Washington and the state capitals had overshadowing importance, and journalistic enterprise was directed toward obtaining the earliest and most complete reports from these centers of political activity. The papers had no editorial page, and editorializing was done in the news reports, especially in the letters reporting legislative proceedings. These letters, usually signed with a pen name, were the cause of formal duels between rival editors and between editors and men in office, and the cause also of many a gunning expedition when "Pro Bono Publico" got too personal. Where the newspaper reader of 1928 gets his excitement out of an unusual crime story or a big prize fight, the man of 1800 got his from the political quarrels, and it was largely on these that circulation was made. Political agitation gave birth to scores of papers.

By 1810, there were 359 newspapers and periodicals in the United States, a growth of 75 percent in 10 years. They served a white population of 7.5 million, 95 percent of which was on farms or in towns of under 8,000 population. In the support of some of these papers, official advertising from the national and state governments played a not unimportant part. The percentage of politicians in the newspaper business was large. Nearly every editorial beaver had a bee in it.

Engrossment in politics, and particularly in his own political ambitions, made the newspaper publisher a poor businessman, and little or no study was given the advancement of advertising. It "just grew." Dull, monotonous columns of 5- to 20-line advertisements were inserted by the year and seldom changed copy. So long as advertisements were numerous enough just to keep his paper going, the average publisher did not worry about ways and means for improving their visibility or effectiveness. Job work helped keep the wolf from the door. Auctioneers were political appointees, and in the larger cities the editor with most political influence obtained the profitable auction room advertising.

Occasionally, an advertiser would get in a one-column illustration, but the infrequency of this dominating display indicates it was a great concession by the publisher. Where any sustained effort at enterprise was displayed, it was in patent medicine advertising. An excursion on that great novelty, a steamboat, sometimes would splurge with a one-column cut; a stagecoach line might do the same. A hairdresser would get through with a cut of a woman's head. At rare intervals a merchant would attempt to picture a carpet or a bit of beauty in furniture, but such intricate work appears to have been more difficult for the makeup man of the period than it had been in earlier days, and it was experiments with cuts containing more or less detail that caused the publisher of 1800 to 1825 to regard illustrations as disfiguring to his paper.

In 1816, there were seven daily papers in New York City, which then had a population of about 125,000. What these dailies gave advertisers in circulation was estimated some years later by a pressman who had made a little table of figures at the time:

Mercantile Advertiser	2,250
Gazette	1,750
Evening Post	1,600

Commercial Advertiser	1,200
Courier	920
National Advocate	875
Columbian	825
Total	9,420

One explanation of the increase in advertisements in this period of nondisplay is found in the growth of towns and their environs; the merchant could no longer believe that everyone was near enough to his store to know he existed. And then there was increased circulation, which made up for the lack of display. In the larger towns the average circulation in 1810 was three or four times that in 1780, when typographical display for advertisements was relatively common.

It is difficult for the modern businessman to picture results from a five-line merchandise advertisement. But in 1810, there was less to read. In a four-page paper, the invariable size of that day, the attention an advertisement received from an individual reader gave the advertiser more than he got a half century later from larger copy in an 8- or 12-page paper. It was not then so necessary to "hit the reader in the eye." Money was scarce; people were slow in buying, shopped around, and were likely to look through columns of small advertisements and compare offers of the article they wanted. Evidence of this is found in the growing number through those years of short advertisements offering a single article at a bargain price, and in differences in the price asked for the same article.

We can, moreover, afford to forgive that first quarter of the 19th century for its neglect of the physical development of advertising. The contributions those years made to transportation and manufacture were of such great significance to the future of advertising that they constitute one of the most important periods in the early history of the subject.

When the *Clermont* steamed up the Hudson in 1807, there was inaugurated a method of transportation that took the high cost of wagon freight off the price to the consumer and made it possible for more people to buy. That gave new incentive to manufacturing and selling effort. In the same year, President Jefferson issued his famous Embargo against foreign trade. For a time, this looked like a disastrous action. It is estimated that 100,000 men, sailors and others connected with commerce, were out of work for a year. But the Embargo had the effect of at last giving a real start to American manufacture, the prospect for which had been dismal, 15 small cotton mills being the net result of 20 years' effort in textiles, with other industries in a corresponding situation.

In the newspapers the economic change was visible in a steadily growing number of advertisements offering *Amercian-made* goods. Where formerly an advertisement was introduced with the words "Fresh importations," the appeal now was "Just arrived from the factory in Massachusetts," or Connecticut, or New Jersey. The change was especially noticeable in the papers devoted to commercial interests, like the *New York Mercantile Advertiser*, the *Gazette*, the *Commercial Advertiser*, and the *Courier*, several of which later were merged with the *Journal of Commerce*, which in 1928 is still being published as our leading commercial newspaper. The advertising columns of these papers, theretofore used almost exclusively to list arrival of goods from abroad, were now employed to advertise the output of American factories.

Newspaper publishing everywhere in the country kept pace with other developments. Heavy migration westward had raised the population of the western states from 1 million in 1810 to 2 million in 1820. By 1828, there were 852 newspapers and other periodicals in the states and territories; and in 1830, with a population of 12 million whites, the number reached 1,000, or one for each 12,000 white persons. This liberal supply of newspapers had, of course, far-reaching effects on all development.

A NEW KIND OF NEWSPAPER

A contributing influence in 19th-century advertising development was the perfection in 1820 of the Fourdrinier papermaking machine, which presently ended the era of handmade paper. This machine, which turned out newsprint in an endless sheet, led to the cheap newspaper and, with steam-power printing, to large circulations. Its influence became apparent in the United States about 1830. At about the same time, employment of the chlorine bleaching process gave the mills the use of colored rags and of rope and other scraps. Importation of rags from Europe followed, and newsprint output increased fast.

The usual price of a newspaper in 1827 was $10 a year, or 6 cents for a single copy. In that year, newsprint, still made for the most part by hand, was $5 a ream, or about 1 cent per sheet. Five years afterward, improvements in papermaking had been so great that a sheet a quarter larger cost 25 percent less.

This reduction in newsprint cost had not, however, up to this time resulted in a lessened price to the reader. Instead, the publisher gave more for the same money by enlarging the size of his sheet. From four columns the papers widened to six, and the depth also increased. Competition took the form of larger paper size, which was regarded as giving prestige. The practice common with most of the papers of permitting the advertiser to use almost any number of lines daily he desired at a flat rate of $32 a year also was an influence for large-size sheets. In 1828 the newspaper page made a width of 24 inches and a height of 35 inches, or double the dimensions of the papers of a few years earlier. Among the conservative papers, distinguishing them from the popular type of newspaper that came in with the *New York Sun* in 1833, this rivalry in page size continued for more than a generation, until the *Journal of Commerce* became an 11-column paper, 35 inches wide and 58 inches high. That four-page enormity contained about 2,000 square inches of type, compared with 200 in the four-page newspapers of the previous century.

The "blanket sheets," a name given the large-size newspapers by James Gordon Bennett, came to an end when the basis of newsprint price was changed from the ream to the pound and a paper shortage caused the price to soar to 14 cents. But that was not until 1853. In that year the conservative papers, which through 20 years of competition from the popular journals had doggedly adhered to tradition, stopped giving the advertiser unlimited space for $32 a year and fixed a limit of 10 lines at that price, or a cent a line per day. Twenty years earlier, their awkward expanse had suggested an idea which developed into a new type of journalism that was to have a very profound effect upon advertising as well as upon popular education.

James Gordon Bennett began, in 1832, publication of the *New York Globe* in a size 12 by 17 inches, half the standard size of that year. That he depended upon the smaller dimensions to sell the paper is evident from the attention given size in his prospectus. But the greater convenience of the *Globe* was not enough. Mr. Bennett asked $8 a year, which was too close to the $10 price of the old, established papers. The *Globe* lived but a few days.

That low price had the greater importance was proved the following year by Benjamin H. Day. On September 3, 1833, Benjamin H. Day issued from a 12- by 16-foot room at 222 William Street the first number of the *New York Sun*, the first successful 1-cent newspaper. And with the *Sun* came more than small size and price. The character of the *Sun's* news appealed to a wider class of readers. Its prospectus said: "The object of this paper is to lay before the public, at a price within the means of every one, ALL THE NEWS OF THE DAY, and at the same time afford an advantageous medium for advertising."

In that *New York Sun* of nearly a century ago, we have an old example of the tabloid's influence in spreading the newspaper habit among people not previously newspaper readers. For the *Sun*, in its first years, was decidedly a tabloid. Its paper size was 9 by 12 inches, a third the size of the conventional papers in the year it was born. It missed by only an inch being as small as the diminutive *Boston News Letter* of 1704. In news, also, it had what in 1833 amounted to a tabloid appeal.

The *Sun*, from the start, gave special attention to local and especially police and other human-interest news. Such matter, combined with the 1-cent price, created a new class of newspaper readers. To mechanics and others earning a small wage, the 6-cent price of the conservative journals was prohibitive. In them, the mechanics found little of interest, anyway. The *Sun* was interesting, and the *Sun* they could afford to buy.

True, the *Sun's* news in the beginning was not all fresh and of its own gathering. That was because its initial working force consisted of only Mr. Day and a boy. Most of its local news was "lifted" from the 6-cent papers, and its out-of-town items also were scissored. But in his selections, Mr. Day chose matter of interest to his 1-cent clientele, so that they got all the "popular" news and none of the heavy business and political matter and other "ponderosities" of the 6-cent sheets.

Getting three copies out of a sheet of paper from which the standard-size *Courier-Enquirer, Journal of Commerce,* and other papers got only one, the *Sun's* newsprint expense per copy was of course much smaller than theirs. That alone would have enabled Mr. Day to carry on for a time if he had not achieved a quick success. The *Sun* was the first sheet to sell on the streets through newsboys. The paper was sold to newsboys at 67 cents a hundred, a system which provided cash daily, another advantage to the publisher. Route carriers found it easy to collect the small sum of 6 cents a week. The publisher had no unpaid subscriptions. He did not run into debt for paper.

The exertions of America's earliest "ragged newsboys" produced magical effects. They covered every part of New York, not omitting the fashionable residential quarter near the Battery. In two months the *Sun* had 2,000 circulation. In a year, it was selling 10,000 copies daily and had left the conservative papers well behind. In two years, it had 20,000 the largest circulation of any daily newspaper in the world, the *London Times* having but 17,000. Ninety percent of the *Sun's* 20,000 was in New York and Brooklyn. New York had then a population of 270,000.

When it was two years old, the *Sun* perpetrated the famous moon hoax, describing in detail the batlike men and queer animals an astronomer in South Africa, using a powerful telescope, had observed on the lunar planet. The story was a tremendous sensation and made the *Sun* known in Europe as well as in every part of the United States. The moon hoax, which ran serially for some days, added several thousand to the paper's circulation.

Like its 6-cent contemporaries, the *Sun* had an advertising rate of $30 a year, but allowed only a "square" of 10 lines daily at that price, equivalent to a cent a line. Mr. Day himself wrote most of the copy for advertisers and managed to say it in 10 lines or less. That helped keep the *Sun* in tabloid size.

Following the custom of the time with new publications, the advertising in the first few issues was bogus. In the initial number, there were four columns of advertisements taken from other papers and printed to make a showing. Some of these advertisers agreed to stay in and pay for the space. Others were eliminated as fast as payers were found to take their place.

The new journalism set out to create new advertising. The printer-publisher who saw the greater circulation value of local news discerned also the business possibilities of the want-ad column. Possibly the success of London newspaper publishers for more than a quarter of a century in building a big volume of small miscellaneous advertisements was of help to Mr. Day. Petty wants of various kinds, and offers to exchange, were encouraged and gave additional reader interest to the paper. "Help wanted" advertisements especially were solicited on the character of the *Sun's* circulation and were obtained in increasing number. These appeared under a classification of "Wants." Two or three lines in length, and not the kind of advertising for which space could be sold by the year, such advertisements paid a one-time rate of 50 cents.

Amusements was another classification to which the tabloid *Sun* gave constructive attention. Theaters and museums advertised regularly. Presently the theaters were printing their casts. Inexpensive excursions were given prominence on the first page from the first day. Marriage and death notices, which had the typography of advertisements, appear to have been run in the beginning for their news interest. Later, they also provided revenue. There was evidence from the earliest issues of a systematic building up of small advertisements from new fields and of an effort to obtain the kind of advertisements that help make circulation.

For the first two years of its life the *Sun* remained distinctly tabloid. Increase in number of columns from three to four in 1835 brought the size to only a 10-inch width and 14-inch height. But by 1836 the *Sun* was a 12- by 19-inch paper. The reason was growth in advertising to 13 columns a day.

Begining with a hand press capable of only 200 copies an hour, the *Sun* after a year or so acquired a double-cylinder flatbed press which ran off 2,000 an hour. It was taking 10 hours to print 20,000 papers when, in 1835, Mr. Day bought a press capable of 3,000 an hour and introduced steam power in the pressroom. In the following year, he is said to have cleared $20,000 on his paper.

The *Sun* was the second newspaper in the United States to use steam to run its presses. The *Cincinnati Gazette* had employed steam since the year before, the *London Times* since 1814. With the change to steam the *Sun* announced that advertisements handed in by 6:00 p.m. would appear in the next morning's issue.

In the panic year of 1837, when Mr. Day's revenue fell to a point which made him less sure of continued high success, the *Sun* passed to Moses Yale Beach for $40,000. Under Mr. Beach's management the paper became even more enterprising. The line "Circulation 32,000" appeared in the publisher's corner in 1839; the distribution of the leading 6-cent paper was about 5,000. The *Sun's* advertising volume was now 17 columns in a 24-column paper. "Help wanted" and "situation wanted" advertisements alone had been built up to four columns. This was accomplished in the face of competition in the *Sun's* own field, for the path of a new journalism blazed by the *Sun* had quickly become a great lure for others.

QUICK GROWTH OF PENNY JOURNALISM

During the six years 1834 to 1839, 35 penny papers were started in New York alone. Most were short-lived. The notable exception was the *Herald*, which James Gordon Bennett established with $500 capital, beginning publication from 20 Wall Street on May 1, 1835. There were then 11 6-cent and four 1-cent papers in New York. Owing to the accent Mr. Bennett's prospectus gave to the nonpolitical character his paper was to have, the *New York Herald* is regarded as having inaugurated the era of the "independent press," the journalism which broke away from the idea that a newspaper's chief function was that of a political party organ. The *Herald* devoted its energies instead to the collection and presentation of news of every character, including local happenings and items of deep human interest. The real exposition of the possibilities of this idea was not to come until more than a half century later, and compared with the "yellow journalism" of the end of the century the police news and village gossip of the 1830's was insipid stuff. But in its day the early 1-cent newspaper was regarded as quite sensational.

With the penny papers came a new space-selling method. Instead of giving unlimited space for $32 a year, they made the square the unit. This was 10 agate lines in some papers and up to 16 in others. And instead of payment at the pleasure of the advertiser, cash was demanded. The *Herald* made its square of 16 lines and brought rates down to a per day basis.

These rates represented the turning away from the flat rate per advertisement that had prevailed for more than a century and show the first American efforts at a line rate. One little detail has special significance. The *Herald's* reduction for two insertions indicates that results of the first scale had been studied and that two-time insertions were found to need encouragement. The study and change in space-selling methods were another important feature of the birth of the new era in journalism and advertising. Like the *Sun*, the *Herald* started as a tabloid and gradually enlarged as advertising patronage grew. Policy—and paper cost— kept it well under the great paper size of the 6-cent sheets.

But while the two revolutionizing papers were alike in size and for a time in price, they differed in their editorial content. The *Herald* was more sensational. This only added to the circulation of the *Herald*. Mr. Bennett chose to call it a "newspaper war," in which he saw Wall Street allied with his rivals. The *Herald* was the first newspaper to raise the cry of "Wall Street." It was, incidentally, the first to print a review of stock exchange operations, which it severely criticized, causing a great sensation in financial and commercial circles. Habitués of the 6-cent papers who scorned the news that appealed to the mechanic bought the *Herald* to see what it was saying about stock exchange and other operations, in which the editor found so much to denounce.

Supplying a want which obviously had been a long-existing one, penny journalism made a new pattern which newspapers were compelled to use if they were to be more than moderately successful. Hundreds of thousands of newspaper readers were created over the country in a short period. The beneficial social effect of the inexpensive and independent newspaper was clearly seen by the 6-cent *Journal of Commerce*, which, two years after the birth of the *Sun*, made this comment on the new educative force in the community:

> These issues exceed those of the large papers and, for aught we see, they are conducted with as much talent, and in point of moral character we think candidly they are superior to their six-penny contemporaries. By observing the course of these papers we have been led to think them as quite an accession to the moral and intellectual machinery among us. The number of newspaper readers is probably doubled by their influence, and they circulate as pioneers among those classes who have suffered greatly from want of general intelligence. . . . Let all classes of the community but read and they will think, and will become less entirely the dupes of designing individuals. Those who have read them will, as a natural consequence, come more or less to the commission of the execrable offense of forming opinions for themselves.

Even the penny papers esteemed the enterprising and fair and tolerant *Journal of Commerce*, which, in criticizing their methods, never did so in abusive terms. The *Evening Post* also kept its dignity.

Full credit to the *New York Sun* and the *New York Herald* for extending the newspaper habit to a wider circle does not mean that the new idea in journalism found nothing in the 6-cent papers to go on. On the contrary, in both collection of news and development of advertising volume the conventional press had made steady progress since the beginning of the century. In news, the "blankets" devoted their energies to interesting the merchant and manufacturer, and this policy of catering to potential users of space was an aid to advertising. That policy had given advertising a great impetus 50 years earlier in the *Philadelphia Daily Advertiser* and the *New York Daily Advertiser*, and had been operating ever since to develop interest.

With the arrival of the *Journal of Commerce* upon the scene in 1827, news rivalry between the business papers had become intense. For foreign news, the *Journal of Commerce* made a big improvement on the rowboat method of meeting incoming vessels. It employed swift sailing yachts, which met the vessels outside Sandy Hook. In conjunction with these ship-news yachts, it established a system of semaphore signaling from Sandy Hook via Staten Island to Manhattan. This often beat the other papers by a day. Carrier pigeons also were used. From Washington, relays of fast ponies gave the *Journal of Commerce* a service so speedy that papers at Norfolk, Virginia, received their Washington news earlier by ship in copies of the enterprising New York paper than they did direct from the capital.

News from abroad frequently had an important bearing on the business of the New York merchant. Legislative and departmental news from Washington also might be vital. Merchants acquired the habit of dropping in where they knew the news would be received first, at the *Journal of Commerce* office. This led to an interest in advertising. Another help the business papers gave to advertising was the lower subscription rate accorded the advertiser. By the end of the 1840's the *Journal of Commerce* had some 800 advertisers on annual contract.

James Gordon Bennett's sensational enterprise in news collection, which after the middle of the century brought the *Herald* worldwide fame, began as an amplification of methods that were being used by the business papers, and especially the *Journal of Commerce*, when the *Herald* was born. The influence of *Journal of Commerce* initiative on the *Herald* was direct. Gerard Hallock of the former paper proposed to Bennett that they join forces in news gathering and share expense, to which Bennett agreed. This arrangement grew into the New York Associated Press in 1849 for the collection of routine news. That released individual effort for special fields, where the *Herald* soon excelled. For more than 40 years the president of the New York Associated Press, the progenitor of the present vast organization, was first Gerard Hallock and then David M. Stone, both of the *Journal of Commerce*. To that paper, we can trace the beginnings of the benefits that joint effort in systematic and economical news gathering have brought to American journalism and to the dissemination of advertising.

ADVERTISING INNOVATION

Activity in American newspaper development in the 1830's and 1840's was coincident with and contributed to a more general avidity, a greater mental activity, and a spreading of ambition among people of all classes in the United States. American inventiveness and adaptiveness had now begun to show themselves in big things. The machine that solved the world's food problem, the McCormick reaper, was patented in the thirties. Morse announced his telegraph. Howe invented the sewing machine. These three epoch-making inventions, all by Americans, came in one generation. A skeptical attitude toward innovations changed to a ready acceptance. No longer did it take a good European idea the customary 20 years to come into use in America. We became alert to ideas that we could apply to our own uses and, in everyday life, more responsive to suggestions contained in advertisements.

In this accelerated progress, there was one laggard, outstanding to the later student of advertising. In several papers in Boston and Philadelphia, merchants were encouraged to use display type and columnwide illustrations; but in the great majority of papers, typographical display was held back. Solicitation of advertising was active and more methodical, but mechanical limitations kept down the physical development of advertisements. Want-ad style, with a two-line initial or agate-caps first line, was the standard, the only relief being the tiny cuts of ships, houses, hats, and a few other stereotyped illustrations of less than fingernail dimensions which served to identify a particular class of advertisement. The *Herald*, when it came, improved somewhat upon the current display by setting the first three or four words of each advertisement in bold capital letters, but soon there was a reversion from even this.

Until the epoch-making penny papers arrived, the tradition against breaking of column rules had been generally observed. The ban had reason partly in the trouble the sawing of a column rule involved. Column rules did not then come from the foundry in various lengths down to a small fraction of an inch. Sawing them was a bother where the plant had a saw, and impossible where there was no saw in the shop. An advertisement two columns wide, or news matter set in double column, was consequently so rare as to be practically nonexistent.

One day in 1836 the iconoclastic *Herald* appeared with a paid sensation. The advertisement not only was set two columns wide but had a double-column illustration, a fire scene depicting the "Unparalleled Attraction at the American Museum," namely, "Harrington's New Grand Moving Deorance, Showing the Awful and Devastating Conflagration of a Large Part of the City of New York on the inclement night of the 10th of December, 1835, and ensuing days." Thereafter, a limited number of two-column advertisements appeared in the New York papers for a time. A striking one noted in the *New York Evening Post* in 1838 carried a two-column cut of the British royal arms. It advised the use of Cullen's Prophylactic Pills. In the *Herald*, these two-column advertisements would run from 10 to 40 lines in depth; and sometimes three or four of them would appear the same day, always over or under others of the same width, and never scattered in the paper. Pianos, shaving cream, and cooking stoves were among the articles for which double-column width was used in 1840. In the luxury class, the piano and organ are, incidentally, our oldest advertisers.

Probably the largest piece of newspaper advertising copy that appeared in this brief period of display was a machinery advertisement. It measured 12 inches on three columns and was set in 8-point type across the three columns, with a 14-point caption. It doubtless started as a handbill. The subject was Hardy and Roche's Self-Setting Saw Mill Dogs, the manufacturers of which were "confident they need only name the positive advantages which are to be derived from their use to induce every owner of a saw mill to cause a set to be immediately placed in his mill." The advertisement concluded with what a 20th-century advertising man would regard as a naïve suggestion: "Persons receiving this advertisement will please cut it out of the paper and put it up securely in Mills, Stores and their Hotels."

James Boyce, seller of wrought-iron pipe, who advertised in the *Herald* in the 1840's, must have done well while he was permitted to use display. He ran 35 lines, single-column measure, framed in a border that pictured sections of his wares. In the sea of headless, undisplayed agate, his 35 lines in the art border stood out like a mountain peak in the ocean.

But display by a few advertisers making only occasional insertions brought complaints from advertisers who used small space the year round, and caused the *Herald*, in 1847, to put a ban on all display, including cuts, as being unfair to advertisers not using display. That made the daily small-space advertiser happier, but the publisher was still dissatisfied. Regular advertisers ran copy without change month in and month out, and the advertising of one day read like that of any other day. In an effort to reduce this monotony and make the advertising more interesting, Mr. Bennett announced that no copy would be run longer than two weeks. This rule brought fresher copy but did not change the physical appearance of the dull agate page as a whole.

Eleven million advertisements appeared in some 2,000 American newspapers in 1847, according to an estimate made the following year. In England, in 1847, only 2.5 million advertisements were published, although the large London papers individually had twice the amount of the *New York Sun, Herald*, or *Tribune*. By 1854, with the population only 25 percent larger, the estimated number of publications in the United States had grown 100 percent, or to 4,000. These figures present a quick index to the influence of the cheap newspaper on reader growth and to the increasing interest in newspaper advertising which made it possible to maintain so many papers.

Interest in other forms of advertising had also been developing during the second quarter of the century, and for this extension of advertising to other media the failure of newspapers to give display was partly responsible. There were advertisers who wanted to see their copy in large type. Since 1800 or thereabouts, the advertisement painted on a rock or wall—advice to use a certain medicine, or the name and the nature of the business of a merchant—had added its effort to that of the agate lines in the newspaper. Sandwich men appeared in lower

Broadway in the 1820's, and street-parading wagon advertisements were introduced in New York in 1830.

RAPID EXPANSION IN THE 1850's

"How well dressed everybody is—have you no poor people in America?" exclaimed Jenny Lind as she gazed at the holiday crowd of 30,000 that greeted her at the dock in 1850.

Jenny Lind's exclamation epitomized the economic state of the United States. It was the beginning of the golden age. Europe had begun to take really great quantities of our agricultural products, and agriculture was at the billion mark. Manufactures had, for the first time, passed farm products in total value. Farm and factory operation, extensive railroad and telegraph construction, and the building of towns that followed better transportation required so many men that there was a scarcity of labor despite heavy immigration, and none who wanted to work were idle.

Things were being done on a large scale, and the newspapers did not fail to give great undertakings their due. We had found ourselves and begun to be sure we were big. How the newspapers fed this spirit, which was to produce extraordinary enterprise in advertising as well as in other activities, is revealed in an article by Charles A. Dana in the *New York Tribune* in 1851. In comparing European and American newspapers and newspaper writers, he drew a picture of the American journalist which also portrayed the 1850 man in the street for whom the newspaper man wrote:

American journalism . . . is superior in a certain living interest. . . . The American regards nothing with indifference, and even where he does not take sides as a partisan, he carries with him a degree of genuine sympathy in the event and its actors which renders him an excellent observer and reporter. He is no dull analyzer, and sees the thing before he attempts to speculate on its philosophy and consequences. He is the most practical of men, and thus his enthusiasm—of which he has a large stock—concentrates itself upon persons and deeds, and makes him almost a part of the occurrence he describes. His element is action, and his method rapidity; his weakness, if he has one, is a too excitable patriotism, and the habit of forever glorifying his country, its institutions, and its people.

Railroad lines reached the Mississippi in 1853. Less than 3,000 miles in 1840 had 10 years later become 9,000, and by 1859 had grown to 30,000 miles. Greater railroad mileage was later built in the same time, but in no decade since has railroad construction trebled the mileage of the previous decade. Telegraph construction likewise made great strides. Before railroad construction reached 40,000 miles, half the population of the country was living west of the Alleghenies.

Without the earlier growth of newspapers which advertising revenue had made possible, the rapid expansion in all lines which marked the fifties would not have taken place with the same speed. The golden lure of California, spread by several thousand newspapers, in two years sent 200,000 men on a long journey of great hardship and opened up the Far West many years earlier than would have been the case if there had not been the quick and wide dissemination of news a high development of the press made possible. And newspaper support contributed importantly to the swift extension of railroads and to the development of new farms, new towns, and new factories which followed.

Invention of machinery and improvements in methods were due in a large measure to the spread of the newspaper among all classes. Velocity of growth in the number of patents issued at Washington appears to have followed the rate of expansion in number of newspapers and in newspaper circulation in the United States: Three hundred patents were issued during the 10 years 1790–1800; 6,000 between 1840 and 1850; 33,000 between 1850 and 1860.

Newspaper support to the development of communications at once had a beneficial effect on the newspaper business itself. Beginning in the 1840's, the use of the telegraph gave newspapers a new reader interest, the line "By Telegraph" appearing over many of their dispatches. The fact that the matter had come over this marvel alone made it interesting. That the mode of transmission was chosen for the heading in preference to the subject of the dispatch indicates the importance attached to news that came by telegraph and the value of it to the paper, proved by continuance for some 20 years of the practice of strongly featuring the line "By Telegraph." As early as 1851, five New York papers together were spending $100,000 a year on telegraph tolls.

Much of the rise in circulation was due to the new facility of distribution afforded by railroads. In the 1850's, 40 percent of the circulation of metropolitan papers was in the country. The $2-a-year weeklies which New York dailies issued reached a circulation of 100,000 and more, compared with 25,000 for the daily, and probably three quarters of this weekly distribution was carried by the railroads. Reports of the Postmaster General give a quick picture of the expansion which took place: In 1840, mails were carried 3,889,000 miles by railroads and steamboats; in 1859 the figure was 31,838,000 miles.

The influence of newspapers on extension of communications and the influence of better communications for new growth in the press furnish an example of the reciprocal action of advertising and other developmental forces. Newspapers encouraged rail extensions and by this helped all business, obtaining for themselves increased circulation and more advertising; increased demand created by advertising gave birth to new business enterprises, more employment, more money for purchases, and renewed expansion all around the circle of agriculture, trade, manufacture, advertising, and communications.

In the larger cities, circulation was helped by better mechanical facilities. Newspapers that could afford it had quickly taken advantage of Hoe's new invention of the "lightning press," the first rotary machine, which turned out up to 18,000 impressions an hour as against 3,000 by the flatbed. In this new press the type forms were fastened to a revolving cylinder (stereotyping did not arrive until 1861). The rotary press enabled the papers to go to eight pages. It also made it possible to get in the midnight news and still deliver the paper on the doorstep at 5:00 or 6:00 a.m.

Illustrations in advertisements had disappeared almost entirely from the penny papers by 1850, though the 6-cent business papers continued to use ships, houses, and other thumbnail identification cuts. Necessity for wetting the paper to get good type impression, and other conflicts between type-matter requirements and the needs of cuts, made illustrations too troublesome for the paper of large circulation; and then, too, there was the rule of some of the penny papers which required uniformity in typography and no special display by one advertiser to the detriment of another.

Advertisements were short, 30 lines being a long one, and the effort still was to get many small advertisements rather than fewer and larger ones. The penny paper was bought for its advertisements as well as for its news; and numerousness, variety, and freshness in advertisements were desired. The *New York Herald* regarded new copy as so important that it endeavored to get a daily change and, in a top corner of each page, ran a display line, "Advertisements Renewed Every Day," for the reader interest and circulation value it believed newness in advertisements to have.

Volume of advertising grew by leaps and bounds in this "golden age" period. In the *New York Tribune*, which had taken the lead in volume, the amount of advertising more than doubled between October, 1849, and the same month of the following year. In the latter month the *Tribune* was running 22 columns of advertising in the 48-column, 8-page paper. The sole advertiser under the classification "Telegraph" was the owner of a "magnetic medical treatment" who used the interest attached to the new wonder of science to lure readers into his advertisement. This medicine man's trick is an example of the devices advertisers resorted to in their efforts to get attention among the mass of uniform agate.

In the half dozen 6- to 20-line advertisements classified under "Dry Goods" were both wholesale and retail announcements, forcing the retailer to begin his advertisement with the words "At Retail." With rare exceptions, newspapers of the period appear to have made no special effort to develop dry goods advertising. A dozen coal dealers were advertising and were having difficulty convincing people that anthracite coal, which railroad extension in Pennsylvania was now bringing in quantity, would burn. Resort advertising appeared under the heading "Water Cure." Notices of religious meetings were beginning to show volume and were regarded as a promising field. In the *New York Tribune*, they were given place in column 1 of page 1. They were 6 to 10 lines long and were inserted at the flat rate of 25 cents.

Newspaper pages of the early 1850's show occasional signs of effort by advertisers to overcome the handicap of a uniform physical form demanded by publishers. The *New York Herald* was especially insistent upon adherence to rules following its letdown for a time in the previous decade and its decision then that no advertiser should have any advantage over another except what he got from longer, fresher, or better copy. A generation later, under James Gordon Bennett, Jr., the advertising columns of the *Herald* were given distinction with a special advertising type which was made up of small letters that formed larger ones. That outstanding feature of the *Herald*'s physical appearance during the last quarter of the 19th and into the 20th century may have been first suggested by a photographer's advertisement of 1856.

IMPACT OF DISPLAY ADVERTISING

"Agate and no display" was the status of American newspaper display when Robert Bonner enters the history of advertising. In 1851, Bonner bought the *Merchants' Ledger* and gradually turned it from a purely business sheet into a family story paper, changing the name to the *New York Ledger.*

Like other literary publications of the day, the *New York Ledger* took no advertising, and it was not in the *Ledger* that Bonner made advertising history. What Bonner did for advertising in the *Ledger* itself was to give fuller recognition to female interests, which helped develop the reading habit among women for the benefit of future advertisers. His great service to advertising was performed as an advertiser of his publication. As an advertiser, he broke down the newspaper bars against display and demonstrated to publishers of the penny papers that their rules had been a mistake and that there was more revenue for them in permitting a greater latitude. The examples he set in expenditure, and in copy and typography, resulted in a better idea of the uses of newspaper advertising. His own reward was a circulation of 400,000 for the *New York Ledger*, a stupendous figure in those days, and a fortune of several million dollars. The *Ledger* sold at 4 cents a copy. Most of its circulation was through news dealers and brought cash.

In 1856, when the *Ledger* had definitely become a weekly periodical devoted to "choice literature and romance," Bonner paid Fanny Fern, a popular writer of the day, $100 a column for a 10-column fiction story and then spent his last dollar advertising in the newspapers that he had paid this unheard-of price for the coming bit of fiction. Advertising of the $100-a-column romance made the *Ledger* the subject of talk everywhere and caused a big jump in circulation.

In the years that followed came other and bigger sensations: $30,000 to Henry Ward Beecher for his novel *Norwood*, $5,000 to Tennyson for a short poem, and $5,000 to Charles Dickens for a short story. Bonner purchased numberless stories and articles on various subjects from prominent persons of the day—statesmen, clergymen, college presidents, newspaper editors—to all of which added importance was given by the extraordinary prices paid.

Without advertising, these literary productions would have left the *Ledger* comparatively unknown to fame. The high prices were paid not because Bonner thought the manuscripts intrinsically worth the price, but because the sensational price provided advertising material. Barnum with high-priced Jenny Lind, and Bonner with his high-priced authors, supplied an idea that publishers and theatrical managers ever since have been using to good effect.

Bonner's originality rebelled against newspaper rules that limited his advertising activities, and he set his mind at work to get around them. His interest in typography had led him to study many newspapers, including those published in London. In the solid pages of short agate advertisements in the *London Times*, he had noted how the eye was caught by repetition in the auctioneers' advertisements. The auctioneer, instead of making one long advertisement, would split his message into separate announcements and run a series of advertisements of equal length down a column, each starting with the same two-line initial and the same phrase in capital letters, "DANIEL SMITH & SONS WILL SELL AT AUCTION." Repetition of the two-line *D* and the capped phrase some 20 times down a column gave that column an appearance so different from the columns of miscellaneous small advertisements on the same page that the auctioneer's announcements instantly caught the eye. Similarly, two columns of 20-line items, each beginning "PURSU-ANT TO THE DECREE OF THE HIGH COURT IN CHANCERY," would be sure to be the first to come into the eye when the reader opened his paper at the page on which they appeared.

Bonner had attempted to advertise in display type but had been refused space for such advertisements. Recalling the attention value of the repeated phrase in the London papers, he wrote 93 advertisements in the want-ad style required by the penny papers, all alike:

O RION, THE GOLD BEATER is the title of Cobb's
sensation story in the *New York Ledger*

and filled a column with them. Nobody who read the *New York Herald*
that morning missed the *Ledger* advertisement. Bennett protested to
Bonner against his "trick." Bonner asked how he could change his advertising to meet the rules. Bennett declined to make any suggestion except
that the *Ledger* avoid display that was unfair to the many small advertisers in the *Herald.* Whereupon Bonner took a single phrase and repeated it all run in until it filled a column. This pillar of type was even
more prominent in the page than the paragraph repetition had been.
Mr. Bennett threw up his hands and guessed Mr. Bonner had better be
let alone so long as he kept in agate type.

From 93-time repetition of a phrase in a single column, Bonner went
into two columns with iteration and then to a whole page of repetition
of a single thought, involving the iteration some 600 times of a single
message such as "See the *New York Ledger* with Cobb's new story," or
"Don't go home to-night without the *New York Ledger.*" Suggestive of
hysterics was the repetition of lines like "Let the news go forth that the
New York Ledger is out," "Let the news go forth that the *New York
Ledger* is out." Then there would be an acrostic formed by the two-line
initial of each advertisement, the message in the first column taking an *L*,
the second column *E*, and through six columns until the whole formed
L–E–D–G–E–R. The 14-point letter was, however, not large enough to
tie the initials together through a column width of type, and it was necessary to run the line "Acrostic" in agate caps over each column lest the
reader miss the idea.

Bonner was the first big advertiser, the first to run a full page, the
first to expend as high as $27,000 a week for advertising, and the first
outside the patent medicine men to invest $150,000 a year in newspaper
advertising. At times, his friends were greatly concerned about his large
expenditures and their possible effect on his finances. It is related that
on the day that four full pages of *Ledger* advertising appeared in a single
issue of the *New York Herald* the pastor of Bonner's church could
scarcely eat his breakfast, so full of anxiety was he over the recklessness
of his friend. He hurried to Bonner's office and asked the publisher what
the four pages had cost him. When Bonner smilingly replied, "Two thousand dollars," the clergyman wiped his forehead and exclaimed: "Two
thousand dollars! T-w-o t-h-o-u-s-a-n-d d-o-l-l-a-r-s! Mr. Bonner, I have
called upon you as a friend. This is a terrible waste of money. Would
not an ordinary advertisement like that" (*pointing to a 20-line item*)
"have answered your purpose?"

"If I had used that small space, would you have noticed my
advertisement?"

"Why, no; possibly not."

"Of course not. And every other reader of the *Herald* is as astonished as you are and talking about it. That is the secret of advertising. I think you have confirmed my judgment. Those four pages are worth $2,000."

Bonner's expenditures and his display methods had an immediate effect on advertising. The sums he paid made newspaper publishers less sure that ban on display and encouragement of small advertisements was the best policy, especially as retailers and others everywhere were taking up the Bonner iteration style and using larger space. The result was a loosening up of stringent rules.

The success of the iteration style inaugurated by Bonner brought in a long run of that kind of copy in both the United States and England. It lasted for more than a generation and led to a great variety of type tricks. The single-phrase repetition was the parent of the advertising slogan, which developed from efforts to obtain a short, striking sentence for iteration. The "Use Sapolio" suggestion that met the eye everywhere in the late decades of the century is traced to the agate iteration phrase of the earlier period.

BIBLIOGRAPHY

BIBLIOGRAPHY

BOOKS

ALBION, ROBERT G. *The Rise of New York Port*. New York: Charles Scribner's Sons, 1939.

ATHERTON, LEWIS E. *The Southern Country Store 1800–1860*. Baton Rouge, La.: Louisiana State University Press, 1949.

BAILYN, BERNARD. *The New England Merchants of the Seventeenth Century*. Cambridge, Mass.: Harvard University Press, 1955.

BASSETT, JOHN S. "The Relation Between the Virginia Planter and the London Merchant," *American Historical Association Annual Report for 1901* Vol. I.

BAXTER, WILLIAM T. *The House of Hancock—Business in Boston 1724–1775*. Cambridge, Mass.: Harvard University Press, 1945.

BELCHER, WYATT W. *The Economic Rivalry Between St. Louis and Chicago*. New York: Columbia University Press, 1947.

BERRY, THOMAS S. *Western Prices Before 1861*. Cambridge, Mass.: Harvard University Press, 1943.

BIDWELL, PERCY W. AND FALCONER, JOHN I. *History of Agriculture in the Northern United States*. Washington, D. C.: Carnegie Institution, 1925.

BISHOP, JOHN L. *A History of American Manufactures from 1608 to 1860*, 2 vols. Philadelphia: Edward Young and Company, 1864.

BRIDENBAUGH, CARL. *Cities in the Wilderness*. New York: The Ronald Press Company, 1938. (This volume was reprinted in 1955 by Alfred A. Knopf, Inc.).

———. *Cities in Revolt—Urban Life in America 1743–1766*. New York: Alfred A. Knopf, 1955.

BUCK, NORMAN S. *The Development of the Organization of Anglo-American Trade 1800–1850*. New Haven, Conn.: Yale University Press, 1925.

CARSON, GERALD. *The Old Country Store*. New York: Oxford University Press, 1954.

CHITTENDEN, HIRAM M. *The American Fur Trade of the Far West*, 3 vols. New York: Francis P. Harper, 1902.

CLARKE, VICTOR S. *History of Manufacturers in the United States 1607–1860*. Washington, D. C.: Carnegie Institution, 1916. (This book was reprinted in 1929 by the McGraw-Hill Book Company, Inc.)

CLEMEN, RUDOLF A. *The American Livestock and Meat Industry*. New York: The Ronald Press Company, 1923.

COLE, ARTHUR H. *The American Wool Manufacture*. Cambridge, Mass.: Harvard University Press, 1926.

————. *Wholesale Commodity Prices in the United States 1700–1861.* Cambridge, Mass.: Harvard University Press, 1938.

COMAN, KATHERINE. *Economic Beginnings of the Far West,* 2 vols. New York: The Macmillan Company, 1921.

CRITTENDEN, CHARLES C. *The Commerce of North Carolina 1763–1789,* New Haven, Conn.: Yale University Press, 1936.

CUMMINGS, RICHARD O. *The American and His Food.* Chicago: The University of Chicago Press, 1940.

DAVIDSON, ROBERT A. *Isaac Hicks, New York Merchant and Quaker, 1767–1820.* Harvard University Studies in Business History, Cambridge, Mass.: Harvard University Press, 1964.

DEPEW, CHAUNCY (ed.) *One Hundred Years of American Commerce 1795–1895,* 2 vols. New York: D. O. Haynes & Co., 1895.

DEVOE, THOMAS F. *The Market Book, A Historical Account of the Public Market in the City of New York,* New York: 1862, (The second volume, covering public markets in Boston, Philadelphia, and Brooklyn, was never published.

DEVOTO, BERNARD. *Across the Wide Missouri.* Boston: Houghton Mifflin Company, 1947.

DUFFUS, R. L. *The Santa Fe Trail.* New York: Longmans, Green and Co., 1930.

EAST, ROBERT A. *Business Enterprise in the American Revolutionary Era.* New York: Columbia University Press, 1938.

FONER, PHILLIP S. *Business and Slavery: The New York Merchants and the Irrepressible Conflict.* Chapel Hill, N.C.: The University of North Carolina Press, 1941.

FOULKE, ROY A. *The Sinews of American Commerce.* New York: Dun & Bradstreet, Inc., 1941.

GIBB, GEORGE S. *The Whitesmiths of Taunton: A History of Reed S. Barton, 1824–1943.* Cambridge, Mass.: Harvard University Press, 1943.

GIESECKE, ALBERT. *American Commercial Legislation Before 1789.* Philadelphia: University of Pennsylvania, 1910.

GRAS, N.S.B. AND LARSON, HENRIETTA M. *Casebook in American Business History.* New York: F. S. Crofts & Company, 1939.

GRAY, LEWIS C. *History of Agriculture in the Southern United States to 1860.* Washington, D. C.: Carnegie Institution, 1933, Vol. I.

GREENE, ASA. *The Perils of Pearl Street.* New York: Bells & Anstice, and Peter Hill, 1834.

HAFEN, LEROY R. AND RISTER, CARL C. *Western America.* 2d ed. New York: Prentice-Hall, Inc., 1950.

HANNA, CHARLES A. *The Wilderness Trail.* 2 vols. New York: G. P. Putnam's Sons. 1911.

HANNA, MARY A. *Trade of the Delaware District before the Revolution.* Smith College Studies in History, Vol. II No. 4. Northhampton, 1917.

HARRINGTON, VIRGINIA D. *The New York Merchant on the Eve of the Revolution.* New York: Columbia University Press, 1935.

HEDGES, JAMES B. *The Browns of Providence Plantations.* Cambridge, Mass.: Harvard University Press, 1952.

HULBERT, ARTHUR B. *The Paths of Inland Commerce.* New Haven: Yale University Press, 1921. (This publication is Vol. 21 in the Chronicles of America Series.)

JENNINGS, SISTER MARIETTA. *The Pioneer Merchant of St. Louis 1810–1820.* New York: Columbia University Studies in History, Economics and Public Law No. 462, 1939.

JENSEN, ARTHUR L. *The Maritime Commerce of Colonial Philadelphia.* Madison, Wisconsin: The State Historical Society, 1963.

JOHNSON, EMORY R.; VAN METRE, T. W.; HUEBNER, G. G.; AND HANCHETT, D. S. *History of Domestic and Foreign Commerce of the United States.* Washington, D. C.: Carnegie Institution, 1915, Vol. I.

JOHNSON, LAURENCE A. *Over the Counter and on the Shelf: Country Store-Keeping in America, 1620–1920.* Rutland, Vermont: Charles E. Tuttle Company, 1961.

JOHNSON, VICTOR L. *The Administration of the American Commissariat During the Revolutionary War.* Philadelphia, (Unpublished Ph.D. Thesis, University of Pennsylvania) 1941.

JONES, FRED M. *Middlemen in the Domestic Trade of the United States 1800–1860.* Urbana, Ill.: University of Illinois, 1937.

JONES, JOHN B. AND SHORTFIELD, LUKE. *The Western Merchant,* Philadelphia: Grigg, Elliot & Co. 1849.

KIRKLAND, EDWARD C. *A History of American Economic Life,* 3d ed. New York: Appleton-Century Crofts, 1951.

KNOWLTON, EVELYN H. *Pepperell's Progress.* Cambridge, Mass.: Harvard University Press, 1948.

KUHLMANN, CHARLES B. *The Development of the Flour Milling Industry in the United States.* Boston: Houghton Mifflin Company, 1929.

LARSON, HENRIETTA. *The Wheat Market and the Farmer in Minnesota 1858–1900,* (Columbia University Studies Vol. CXXII No. 2, New York 1926).

LIPPINCOTT, ISAAC. *Economic Development of the United States.* New York: D. Appleton and Company, 1921.

LIVINGWOOD, JAMES W. *The Philadelphia-Baltimore Trade Rivalry 1780–1860.* Harrisburg, Pa.: The Pennsylvania Historical and Museum Commission 1947.

McILWAIN, CHARLES H. *Wroxall's Abridgement of the Indian Affairs.* Cambridge, Mass.: Harvard University Press, 1915.

MARTIN, EDGAR W. *The Standard of Living in 1860.* Chicago: The University of Chicago Press, 1942.

MARTIN, MARGARET E. *Merchants and Trade of the Connecticut River Valley, 1750–1820.* Smith College Studies in History, Volume 24, Nos. 1–4. Northampton, Mass: 1939.

MORRISS, MARGARET L. *Colonial Trade of Maryland 1689–1715.* Baltimore: Johns Hopkins University Studies XXXII, 1914.

MYERS, MARGARET G. *The New York Money Market.* New York: Columbia University Press, 1931.

NETTELS, CURTIS P. *The Money Supply of the American Colonies before 1720.* Madison, Wis.: University of Wisconsin, 1934.

NYSTROM, PAUL N. *Economics of Retailing.* 3d ed. New York: The Ronald Press Company, 1930.

PORTER, KENNETH W. *The Jacksons and the Lees: Two Generations of Massachusetts Merchants 1765–1844.* 2 vols. Cambridge, Mass.: Harvard University Press, 1937.

PRESBREY, FRANK. *The History and Development of Advertising.* Garden City, New York: Doubleday, Doran & Company, Inc., 1929.

ROBERT, JOSEPH C. *The Tobacco Kingdom: Plantation, Market and Factory in Virginia and North Carolina 1800–1860.* Durham, N.C.: Duke University Press, 1938.

SCHLESINGER, ARTHUR M. *The Colonial Merchants and the American Revolution.* New York: Columbia University Press, 1918.

SELLERS, LEILA. *Charleston Business on the Eve of the American Revolution.* Chapel Hill: The University of North Carolina Press, 1934.

SITTERSON, CARLYLE J. *Sugar Country.* Lexington, Kentucky: University of Kentucky Press, 1953.

STALSON, OWEN. *Marketing Life Insurance: Its History in America.* Cambridge, Mass.: Harvard University Press, 1942.

TAYLOR, GEORGE R. *The Transportation Revolution 1815–1860.* New York: Rinehart & Company, Inc., 1951.

TOOKER, ELVA. *William Trotter: Philadelphia Merchant 1787–1853.* Cambridge, Mass.: Harvard University Press, 1955.

WADE, RICHARD C. *The Urban Frontier: The Rise of Western Cities 1790–1830.* Cambridge, Mass.: Harvard University Press, 1959.

WENDER, HERBERT. *Southern Commercial Conventions 1837–1859.* Baltimore, Md.: Johns Hopkins University Studies in Historical and Political Science. (Series XLVIII, No. 4) 1930.

WHITE, PHILIP L. *The Beckmans of New York in Politics and Commerce 1647–1877.* New York: The New York Historical Society, 1956.

WOOD, JAMES P. *The Story of Advertising.* New York: The Ronald Press Company, 1958.

WOOD, RICHARD G. *A History of Lumbering in Maine 1820–1861.* Orono, Maine: University of Main Studies Second Series, No. 33, 1935.

WRIGHT, RICHARDSON. *Hawkers & Walkers in Early America.* Philadelphia: J. P. Lippincott & Company, 1927.

ARTICLES

ALBION, ROBERT G. "New York Port and Its Disappointed Rivals, 1815–1860," *Journal of Economic and Business History,* Vol III (August, 1931).

AMES, SUSIE M. "A Typical Virginia Business Man of the Revolutionary Era—Nathanial Littleton Savage and His Account Book," *Journal of Economic & Business History,* Vol. III (May, 1931).

APPLETON, JOHN B. "The Declining Significance of the Mississippi as a Commercial Highway in the Middle of the Nineteenth Century," *The Bulletin of the Geographical Society of Philadelphia,* Vol. XXVIII. (October, 1930).

ATHERTON, LEWIS E. "Auctions as a Threat to American Business in the Eighteen Twenties and Thirties," *Bulletin of the Business Historical Society,* Vol. XI (December, 1937).

―――. "Early Western Mercantile Advertising," *Bulletin of the Business Historical Society,* Vol. XII (September, 1938).

―――. "Itinerant Merchandising in the Ante Bellum-South," *Bulletin of the Business Historical Society,* Vol. XIX (April, 1945).

―――. "The Pioneer Merchant in Mid-America," *The University of Missouri Studies,* Vol. 14 (April, 1939).

―――. "Predecessors of the Commercial Drummer in the Old South," *Bulletin of the Business Historical Society,* Vol. XXI (February, 1947).

―――. "The Problem of Credit Rating in the Ante-Bellum South," *The Journal of Southern History,* Vol. XII (November, 1946).

―――. "The Services of the Frontier Merchant," *Missouri Valley Historical Review* Vol. XIV (September, 1937).

BEAME, EDWARD M. "Rochester's Flour-Milling Industry in Pre-Canal Days," *Business History Review,* Vol. XXI (Summer, 1957).

BERG, HARRY D. "The Organization of Business in Colonial Philadelphia," *Pennsylvania History,* Volume X, No. 3 (July, 1943).

BIDWELL, PERCY W. "Rural Economy in New England at the Beginning of the Nineteenth Century," *Transactions of the Connecticut Academy of Arts and Sciences,* Vol. XX (April, 1960).

BIGELOW, BRUCE M. "Aaron Lopez: Colonial Merchant of Newport," *New England Quarterly,* Vol. IV (1931).

BRIDENBAUGH, CARL. "The High Cost of Living, 1728," *New England Quarterly,* Vol. V (October, 1932).

CARSON, GERALD. "The Great Auction Controversy," *Autograph Collectors' Journal,* Vol. V (Spring, 1953).

COLE, ARTHUR H. "Marketing Non-Consumer Goods Before 1917," *Business History Review,* Vol. XXXIII (Summer, 1959).

―――. "The Tempo of Mercantile Life in Colonial America," *Business History Review,* Vol. XXXIII (Autumn, 1959).

DAVIS, WILLIAM W. "Ante-Bellum Southern Commercial Conventions," *Transactions of the Alabama Historical Society,* Vol. V.

DODGE, WILLIAM E. "A Great Merchant's Recollection of Old New York," in Henry C. Brown (ed.) *Valentine's Manual of Old New York.*

DOWNES, RANDOLPH C. "Trade in Frontier Ohio," *The Mississippi Valley Historical Review,* Vol. XVI (March, 1930) pp. 467–94.

―――. "Dry Goods Trade of 1857," *Bulletin of the Business History Society,* Vol. V (May, 1931).

EAST, ROBERT A. "The Business Entrepreneur in a Changing Colonial Economy 1763–1795," *The Journal of Economic History* Supplement to Vol. VI.

EDELMAN, EDWARD. "Thomas Hancock, Colonial Merchant," *Journal of Economic and Business History,* Vol. I (November, 1928).

ELLIS, DAVID M. "Rivalry Between the New York Central and the Erie Canal," *New York History,* Vol. XXIX (July, 1948).

FRIEDMAN, LEE M. "The First Chamber of Commerce in the United States," *Bulletin of the Business Historical Society,* Vol. XXI (November, 1947).

———. "The Drummer in Early American Merchandise Distribution," *Bulletin of Business Historical Society*, Vol. XXI (April 1947).

FRUER, ERNE RENE. "Retail Merchandising in Chicago, 1833–1848," *Journal of the Illinois Historical Society*, Vol. XXXII, Number 2 (June 1939).

GALPIN, W. F. "The Grain Trade of New Orleans, 1804–1814," *The Mississippi Valley Historical Review*, Vol. XIV (March, 1928).

GIDDENS, PAUL H. "Trade and Industry in Colonial Maryland, 1733–1769," *Journal of Economic and Business History*, Vol. IV, No. 3 (May, 1932).

GLAAB, CHARLES N. "Business Patterns in the Growth of a Midwestern City: the Kansas City Business Community Before the Civil War," *Business History Review*, Vol. XXXIII (Summer, 1959).

GRAS, N. S. B. "An Early Sedentary Merchant in the Middle West," *Bulletin of the Business Historical Society*, Vol. XVIII (February, 1944).

GRAY, L. C. "The Market Surplus Problems of Colonial Tobacco," *Agricultural History*, Vol. II (January, 1928).

GRONERT, THEODORE G. "Trade in the Blue Grass Region," *The Mississippi Valley Historical Review*, Vol. V (December, 1918).

HARPER, LAWRENCE A. "Mercantilism and the American Revolution," *Canadian Historical Review*, Vol. XXIII (March, 1942). (This article is reprinted in Edward N. Saveth, (ed). *Understanding the American Past*. Boston: Little, Brown and Company, 1954).

HASHENS, RALPH W. "Planter and Cotton Factor in the Old South: Some Areas of Friction," *Agricultural History*, Vol. 29 (January, 1955).

HEINLEIN, PAUL C. "Cattle Driving from the Ohio Country, 1800–1850," *Agricultural History*, Vol. 28 (April, 1954).

HIDY, R. W. "Credit Rating Before Dun and Bradstreet," *Bulletin of the Business Historical Society*, Vol. XIII (December, 1939).

HOUSE, ALBERT V., JR. "Two Yankee Traders in New York, Letters on the Financing of Frontier Merchants," *The New England Quarterly*, Vol. XI (September, 1938).

HOWER, RALPH M. "Urban Retailing 100 Years Ago," *Bulletin of the Business Historical Society*, Vol. XII (December, 1938).

———. " 'Wanted' Material on the History of Marketing," *Bulletin of the Business Historical Society*, Vol. IX (October, 1935).

"Jacob Peabody and Company Auctioneers," *Bulletin of the Business Historical Society*, Vol. VIII (May, 1934).

JENNINGS, SISTER MARIETTA. "Notes on Joseph Hertzog, An Early Philadelphia Merchant," *Bulletin of the Business Historical Society*, Vol. XIV (November, 1940).

JONES, FRED M. "Retail Stores in the United States, 1800–1860," *Journal of Marketing*, Vol. I (October, 1936).

KANE, LUCILLE. "Hersey, Staples and Company, 1854–1860: Eastern Managers and Capital in Frontier Business," *Bulletin of the Business Historical Society*, Vol. XXVI (December, 1952).

KEIR, R. MALCOLM. "The Unappreciated Tin-Peddler: His Services to Early Manufacturers," *Annals of the American Academy of Political and Social Science*, Vol. XLVI (March, 1913).

KLINE, P. C. "New Light on the Yankee Peddler," *New England Quarterly,* (1939).

LEDER, LAWRENCE H. AND CAROSSO, VINCENT P. "Robert Livingston (1654–1728): Businessman of Colonial New York," *Business History Review,* Vol. XXX (March, 1956).

LEE, GUY A. "The Historical Significance of the Chicago Grain Elevator System," *Agricultural History,* Vol. II (January, 1937).

LIPPINCOTT, ISAAC. "Internal Trade of the United States 1700–1860," *Washington University Studies—Humanistic Series,* Vol. IV (October, 1916).

LOVETT, ROBERT W. "Squire Rantoul and his Drug Store, 1796–1824," *Bulletin of the Business Historical Society,* Vol. XXV (June, 1951).

LOW, W. A. "Merchant & Planter Relations in Post-Revolutionary Virginia, 1783–1789," *Virginia Magazine of History and Biography,* LXI Vol., (July, 1953).

LYNN, ROBERT A. "Installment Credit Before 1870," *Business History Review,* Vol. XXXI (Winter, 1957).

MARBURG, THEODORE F. "Commission Merchants in the Button and Brass Trade a Century Ago," *Bulletin of the Business Historical Society,* Vol. XVI (February, 1942).

———. "Manufacturer's Drummer 1832," *Bulletin of the Business Historical Society,* Vol. XXII (April, 1948).

———. "Manufacturer's Drummer 1852," *Bulletin of the Business Historical Society,* Vol. XII (June, 1948).

NETTELS, CURTIS P. "British Mercantilism and the Economic Development of the Thirteen Colonies," *Journal of Economic History,* Vol. X (Spring, 1952).

———. "The Economic Relations of Boston, Philadelphia and New York 1680–1715," *Journal of Economic and Business History,* Vol. III (February, 1931).

———. "The Menace of Colonial Manufacturing 1690–1720," *New England Quarterly,* Vol. IX (1931).

NORRIS, JAMES D. "One Price Policy Among Ante-bellum Country Stores," *Business History Review,* Vol. XXXVI No. 4 (Winter, 1962).

"The Persistent Fringe of House to House Selling in American History," *Bulletin of the Business Historical Society,* Vol. IX (March, 1935).

PETERSON, ARTHUR G. "The Alexandria Market Prior to the Civil War," *William and Mary Quarterly,* Vol. XII, Series 2 (April, 1932).

PLUMMER, WILBUR C. *"Consumer Credit in Colonial Philadelphia," The Pennsylvania Magazine of History and Biography,* Vol. LXVII (October, 1942).

ROBERT, JOSEPH C. "Rise of the Tobacco Warehouse Auction System in Virginia, 1800–1860," *Agricultural History,* Vol. VII (October, 1933).

RUSSEL, ROBERT R. "Economic Aspects of Southern Sectionalism, 1840–1861," *University of Illinois Studies in the Social Sciences,* (March, 1923).

SCHMIDT, LOUIS B. "Internal Commerce and the Development of National Economy Before 1860," *Journal of Political Economy,* Vol. XLVII (December, 1939).

Scott, Kenneth. "Price Control in New England During the Revolution," *New England Quarterly,* Vol. VIX (December, 1946).

Shafer, Anita. "The Williams Brothers, Merchants and Shippers, 1825–1850," *Bulletin of the Business Historical Society,* Vol. XXVI (June, 1952).

Shapiro, Stanley J. "Marketing in Massachusetts Bay Colony: 1629–1685," *Economics and Business Bulletin,* Temple University School of Business and Public Administration, Vol. XVI (December, 1963).

Shaw, Steven J. "Colonial Newspaper Advertising: A Step Toward Freedom of the Press," *Business History Review,* Vol. XXXIII, Number 3 (Autumn, 1959).

Sitterson, J. Carlyle. "Financing and Marketing the Sugar Crop of the Old South," *Journal of Southern History,* Vol. X (May, 1944).

Stalson, J. Owen. "The Pioneer in American Life Insurance Marketing," *Bulletin of the Business Historical Society,* Vol. XII (November, 1938).

Stephens, E. F. "Missouri and the Santa Fe Trade—Economic Effects of the Santa Fe Trade on Missouri," *Missouri Historical Review,* Vol. XI (April–July, 1917).

Stephens, George W. "Some Aspects of Intersectional Rivalry for the Commerce of the Upper Mississippi Valley," *Washington University Studies —Humanistic Series,* Vol. X (April, 1923).

Stone, Alfred H. "The Cotton Factorage System of the Southern States," *The American Historical Review,* Vol. XX, No. 3.

Tooker, Elva. "A Kentucky Merchant's Problems in the Early Nineteenth Century," *Bulletin of the Business Historical Society,* Vol. VIII (October, 1934).

———. "A Marketing Problem 100 Years Ago," *Bulletin of the Business Historical Society,* Vol. XII (September, 1938).

Tonning, Wayland A. "The Beginnings of the Money-Back Guarantee and the One-Price Policy in Champaign-Urbana, Illinois, 1833–1880," *Business Review,* Vol. 30 (June, 1956).

Tunell, George E. "The Diversion of the Flour and Grain Trade from the Great Lakes to the Railroads," *Journal of Political Economy,* Vol. 5 (June, 1897).

Wallace, Wesley H. "Property and Trade: Main Themes of Early North Carolina Newspaper Advertising," *The North Carolina Historical Review,* Volume 32 (October, 1955).

Westerfield, Roy B. "Early History of American Auctions—A Chapter in Commercial History," *Transactions of the Connecticut Academy of Arts and Sciences,* Vol. XXIII (May, 1920).

White, John B. "The Missouri Merchant One Hundred Years Ago," *The Missouri Historical Review,* Vol. XIII (January, 1919).

Wooster, Harvey A. "A Forgotten Factor in American Industrial History," *American Economic Review,* Vol. XVI (March, 1926).